The Me

SIR RONALD STORRS

1937

G · P · PUTNAM'S SONS · NEW YORK

PRINTED IN THE UNITED STATES OF AMERICA
BY THE VAN REES PRESS

THE AUTHOR

(*From a drawing by Eric Kennington in "Seven Pillars of Wisdom"*)

A noi venia la creatura bella
Bianco vestita, e nella faccia quale
Par tremolando mattutina stella.

DIAMOND JUBILEE, 1897

Dal primo giorno ch'io vidi il suo viso.

2, vii. 1923

THIS has not been been an easy book to write. My books and papers were destroyed by fire with the rest of my property in 1931, so that of material, consciously prepared or preserved as such, I have none. I had, however, the habit ever since leaving England in 1904 of writing weekly to my mother, and of enclosing briefly minuted items I thought might entertain her. All these documents she kept with my letters, including a few diaries of special missions or journeys during the War. In the longest of these, describing Baghdad in 1917, she inked over my pencil version with the result, as in a palimpsest, that some of the words she could not read then I cannot decipher now. These surviving records I have wherever possible quoted in original with, I hope, a gain in immediacy and actuality by recording not only historic facts, sometimes already known, but also my feelings at the time; with stories and details, trifling in themselves yet constituting atmosphere—the hardest of all things to recapture after many years. There are no corrections but many omissions, especially of personal remarks intended only for home consumption. The retention of many faults of youthful slang and flippancy proceeds not so much from any illusion as to their intrinsic demerits as from a preference for the varied patina of the past over the shiny smoothness of a *Vernis Martin* surface.

The loss of a slowly collected library bearing on the chief interests of a man's life is a handicap, less only than the loss of serious documents. Not total replacement, not even the Socialist ideal of the British Museum Library—access to everything, possession of nothing—can recall the annotations and cross-references of many years.

In a book full of Oriental names it is impossible to avoid the vexed question of transliteration. That is a subject upon which, as indicated, I have strong ideas and even stronger feelings. In 1920 Sir Herbert Samuel made me Chairman of a small Committee appointed for the purpose of transliterating Palestinian Arabic. We worked long and hard, and in due course submitted to His Excellency the neat little brochure which at this moment meets my resentful gaze. By the time it had reached London the Colonial Office had decided to adopt the system of the Royal Geographical Society. Lawrence was pleasant about his spelling; members of our Committee cannot be. My object now is to present the strange sounds and symbols of the East with a minimum of fatigue to the reader. The system is that of English consonants with Italian vowels, and I add accents and quantities. There are one or two irregularities. The name of the founder of Islam is accurately rendered to convey the pronunciation of Mŭhámmăd; even for personages such as Prince Mahomed Alī, in whose reigning house is a tradition of pronunciation *alla Turca*. (By the time the name has reached Cyprus it has become Mehmet.) Nevertheless, with a positive advantage of differentiation, I write the Sharīf and King Husáin ibn Ali of Arabia (correctly according to system) but the Prince and Sultan Hussein of Egypt, with the French spelling that comes close to (his own) Turkish utterance. By holding, though illogically, to accepted spellings of some famous words, I have at least avoided the exasperation of Qur'an and Makkah and of that intolerable clenching of the glottis, the letter ', 'ain.

All passages in close printed type without explanation are taken from letters 1904–23 to my mother; 1923–9 to my father, and occasional others to my uncle the late Henry Cust; and in later chapters from my diaries.

There are no blotches or blurs in my memory. Where the image does not stand out sharply detached there is an utter blank. Thus the startling accident of 1916 described on page 216 had completely gone out of my mind until I came upon my letter this year. Within this limitation and the destruction of my written impressions I stand ready to be corrected. Figures and statistics are available in official publications, generally accurate, and I have added references from *Seven Pillars of Wisdom*.

Such as these Memoirs are, they contain no attacks or recriminations upon the names of persons living or dead, or of peoples once allied, neutral or enemy. I am content to let documents speak, even those that in matter as well as in manner no longer represent me. An Egyptian Nationalist in 1904 was in the eyes of most Englishmen as dangerous as a Turk in the War or a Communist in 1920. Some of us now are glad to be good friends with all three.

In striving that *da fatto il dir non sia diverso* my ambition is to present both sides, especially the less-known, of every question, and so perhaps to add to the material, raw but genuine, awaiting the future historian of the Near and Middle East.

My acknowledgements are due to *The Times*, *The Daily Telegraph*, *The Sunday Times*, *The Observer*, *The Spectator*, *The Near East* and

India, for permission to reproduce matter that has appeared in their columns. Also to The Lawrence Trust, Sir John Murray, Sir George Arthur, Sir Sidney Cockerell, Viscount Astor and V. B. Holland for authority to use letters from T. E. Lawrence, Elizabeth Barrett Browning, Lord Kitchener, Wilfrid Scawen Blunt, the late Viscount Astor and Oscar Wilde; and again to The President, Jacob Epstein, at All Souls, to Eric Kennington and to Beresford Pierce. I owe a deep debt of gratitude to Sir Edward Marsh for the constructive and creative criticism he has shed over all these pages: one more prodigality of his memorable kindness to writers and friends. I owe much to the help of Mrs Henry Cust; most of all, in this also, to my wife.

R. S.

The Porch House   San Michele
   Potterne   Anacapri
      Devizes   Capri

CONTENTS

Contents

of Mark Sykes. Russian nuns singing Wagner. Zaharoff. Audience with the
Pope. And with the King of Italy. Palestine under snow. Nabi Mūsa—The Prophet
Moses. Easter-tide 1920. The first of the Commissions of Inquiry. The Wailing
Wall. Provisional decisions. New Mayor of Jerusalem. Samuel appointed High
Commissioner. Preparations to receive him. The Reception. The last orders of
O.E.T.A.

General British ignorance about Jewry. Irredentism to the *n*th. Announcement
arrival of the Zionist Commission. My attempts to unite Arabs and Jews. Theodor
Herzl. Joseph Chamberlain offers Herzl Uganda. The Balfour Declaration. The
Hebrew language. The Wall. Space for Jewish prayer. Disappointment of Jews.
Ill-informed carpings. Dedication of World Zionism. Arab expectations. Disap-
pointment of Arabs. Putting back the clock. Suspicions and apprehensions. Delays
in promulgation of mandate. President Wilson intervenes. Further reasons. For
Arab disquietude. Interpretations of the National Home. Arabs poorly represented.
Jewish criticisms of O.E.T.A. How far justified. Admitted defects. Anti-"Chinovnik" East European immigrants. Unsubstantial accusations. To what end? "Uses
of adversity." Zionist neglect of Sephardim. Predominance of Russian *Kultur*.
A noble Italian Sephardi. British Jewish officials "Little Ease." No Jewish or
British monopoly of error. Revulsions of the long oppressed. Tendency to attitudinize. Lapidary judgment of Mr Lloyd George. Fallacy of "economic absorptive
capacity." The Legislative Council. Scouted by Westminster. Arguments of Arab
opposition. The Faisal-Lawrence papers. Zionist propaganda. No question of surrender. The Mandate stands. Palliatives. A few unofficial "open" houses. Promotion
of Palestinians. Who conquered Palestine from the Turks? Unfair to put all
blame on Jews. Criticism of method not opposition to principle. A voice out of
Zion. Postscript.

Qualities of Herbert Samuel. Pleasant defiance of Whitehall. Our mutual nepo-
tisms. His practical support of Pro-Jerusalem. Government in Jerusalem. "Distribu-
tion of Duties." Mobilization for religious festivals. The Wall always with us.
Possible solutions. Importance of religious Communities. The Moslems. Rāgheb
Bey Nashāshībi. Latin Catholics. Franciscans and Dominicans. The Orthodox
Church. The Patriarch Damianos. Orthodox Christmas in Bethlehem. The Copts.
Copts and Franciscans. The silver star of Bethlehem. The Anglican Community.
St George's Cathedral. The "American" Colony. The Armenians.

Orthodox Jews. Political Jews. Pinhas Rutenberg. The resurrector of Hebrew. A
daughter of Israel. Her triumph. The Hebrew Press. Zealots. Painters. Music. Grand
Opera. The poet Bialik. Tel Aviv. The Consular Corps. Social and Dramatic.
Hunting, and Fox Films. Decline and fall of Faisal. He is expelled from Syria.
Faisal's reception in Palestine, Egypt, and London. Balfour's in Tel Aviv, Jerusalem,
and Damascus. My second Audience with the Pope. The Cardinal Secretary of
State. Journey for Pro-Jerusalem to the United States. Allenby and Lloyd. The
Big Four of Zionism. The end of Pro-Jerusalem. The wrench of leaving Jerusalem.
If I forget Thee, O Jerusalem.

Contents

MAPS

THE MEMOIRS OF
SIR RONALD STORRS

CHAPTER ONE

1881-1904

Man is the shuttle, to whose winding quest
And passage through these looms
God ordered motion, but ordained no rest.

HENRY VAUGHAN
(1621-1695)

EARLY IN THE 1840's Captain Henry Francis Cust of the 8th Hussars was returning to England on leave from India. He was the eldest son of that increasingly rare combination the "Reverend the Honourable" Canon Cust of St George's, Windsor—the taller though younger of Hoppner's "Cust Brothers" which now hangs at Belton—and of Lady Anna Maria Needham, aunt of the Lord Kilmorey who was fortunate enough to have been twice smuggled out of a Debtors' Prison in a coffin. Henry Francis (who had held his Commission six months before leaving Eton) was a graceful scholar, without claim to erudition, but with Horace, Pope and Byron absorbed into his very being.

Captain Cust broke his home journey in Spain, and elected to pay his first homage to the Alhambra by moonlight. After wandering awhile through the enchantments of the splendour that was Islam, he entered a courtyard and there met an English couple of the name of Streatfield. The lady, a Cookson of Meldon Hall, Northumberland, was tending her invalid husband. "She is charming", Elizabeth Barrett Browning had written of her, "even fascinating; one of the most graceful, elegant crea-tures the age ever looked at, and good and intelligent, and sympathetical besides." [1] Such, indeed, was her charm that there was henceforth no other wife for Henry Cust, who, on the death of Streatfield, married his widow. The marriage was utter content, and there is no doubt that the bride

[1] Be happy, dearest Mrs Cust and go on and love me as much as you can. *I* love *you*, and if wishes of mine were worth anything, you should be very, very happy. I will write to you, be sure. Yes, indeed." (From an unpublished letter of Elizabeth Barrett Browning.)

added elements of life and music to the sterling qualities of the Cust family. Henry Cust now left the Army and became the agent at Ellesmere in Shropshire for the Bridgewater estate of his cousin, Lord Brownlow. He had four daughters and two sons. The eldest daughter, Lucy Anna-Maria, was my mother, and the elder son, born much later, Harry Cust. Under the easy taxation of the 'sixties, 'seventies and 'eighties, my grandfather found it possible to preserve the little family seat of Cockayne Hatley in Bedfordshire as an occasional or summer residence, to exercise a large hospitality at Ellesmere House, to represent the Borough of Grantham, and to maintain 16 Eccleston Square for the Parliamentary season. There Lucy Cust met with increasing frequency a good-looking young man with a charming voice—the Reverend John Storrs, curate of St Peter's, Eaton Square. His father, of Yorkshire parentage, had sold his property in England and taken the living of Cornwallis in Nova Scotia, where (I discovered on a recent journey) his name is still as revered as his appearance is remembered and admired. He wisely decided to send his oldest son to be educated in England, and John gained a mathematical scholarship at Pembroke College, Cambridge.

I do not envy John Storrs his wooing. Not only was Major Cust (though himself a son of the Church) indignant that his favourite daughter should bestow herself upon a clergyman, but the Cust family was large, abnormally united by allusion and shibboleth, and not particularly encouraging; whilst Lucy herself repeatedly postponed the date, first of engagement, then of marriage, because of her passionate devotion to her father, whose household and affairs she had managed since her mother's death when she was sixteen. My grandfather for all his charm was an excitable man, with the habit of taking suddenly to his bed when unduly crossed by his family. On the day the engagement was announced in *The Morning Post* he summoned John Storrs to breakfast with him at the Travellers' Club. There came a moment for the shy and only curate in the coffee room when he felt rather than saw all faces converging upon his table while his prospective father-in-law cried aloud: "I like you very much, my dear young fellow, but I know what will happen: you will die and I shall have Lucy back on my hands with a half-dozen of children"— and burst into a storm of tears. However, the curate was shortly presented to the living of St James's, Bury St Edmunds (one of the most beautiful parish churches in the country) so allayed my grandfather's fears.

After a few years at Bury St Edmunds, where I was born on 19 November 1881, my father was chosen by Mr Gladstone to succeed Canon Wilkinson (on his elevation to the Purple of Truro) as Vicar of St Peter's, Eaton Square, with St John's, Wilton Road, and St Peter's

Chapel, Buckingham Palace Road, on the site of the present Westminster Theatre. (How many Prime Ministers since Mr Gladstone have found time to apply the supreme test of going in person to hear the candidate preach?) We moved into the Vicarage, 2 Grosvenor Gardens, the first home I can remember, and the kindest and happiest that any boy ever had.[2]

Throughout his life my father remained a sportsman in the best sense of that painful word. After supper with three Pembroke colleagues on the eve of the Coxwainless Fours, a pious member of the crew suggested that all should kneel and offer a silent word to the only sure source of victory. "Hang it", said my father, already an ordinand, "we mustn't take an unfair advantage of them." He was before his time in liking and admiring Americans, but he found their concerted college cries comic. At Henley one year supporters of their university shouting:

"Cornell! Cornell! I yell! I yell!"

were surprised to be countered by a silver-haired Prebendary with:

"Trinity Hall! Trinity Hall! I bawl! I bawl!"

He was a sincere and earnest rather than a scholarly preacher, with a beauty of intonation enhanced by absence of manuscript. The most original and successful service at St. Peter's in his time was the Children's Service, which far excelled anything else of that kind I have ever known. He would come down from the chancel steps and walk slowly up and down the aisle, calling the children by name and asking them questions, without making one of them shy or self-conscious. Preaching to children may be easier than preaching to a congregation of intelligent, or (assuming such to exist) of intellectual adults. But complete mastery of the art must be very rare. Even now I am greeted all over the world by grown-up members of the "Three o'clock"; so fixed and far-flung is his influence. At this children's service I sang, carried the Cross, and collected the offertory as leader of the "Purple" or "Gentleman's" choir; the period snob synonym for "Amateur" or (franker) "Unpaid" still preserved in "Gentleman *v.* Players", and recently re-vulgarized (in despair at the universal breaking of contracts) by the "Gentleman's" agreement. My father was practically, but not deeply or widely read: a foolish disappointment later to an undergraduate son, who nevertheless learnt by experience that, for the parish priest (and maybe for his superiors) too many books

[2] The leasehold belonging to Queen Anne's Bounty, on the Westminster Estate, was sold in 1930 for £16,000 in order to endow the position. I could never enter it after my father left. The present Vicarage is at 24 Chester Square. 2 Grosvenor Gardens is now the Offices of the Palestine Hydro Electric Corporation.

spoil the Cloth. On the other hand he was both ahead of the Wagnerian 'eighties and in advance of the Beecham 'thirties in adoring Handel as a supreme musician. He was a mass of sublime prejudices and contradictions. He could see only the moral blanks [3] of Napoleon, (to my mother a glorious incredible dream). Diplomats were loafers. Soldiers were the same so long as they were preparing for war; during war they became automatically, as in Kipling's ballad, national heroes. The Navy could do no wrong. He had indeed prejudices, but nothing of the bigot or the fanatic. He preferred us to read what he called serious books on Sunday (and why not?) and considered some games less suitable to that day, especially before noon or if the player had not been to church.

There is Relativity even in religion. The London Sabbath of the 1888's to 1895's was, compared with the rigour of the North, a mitigated, with the laxity of the Continent, a still drastic ordeal. My father's churchmanship, being without incense or like ritual was considered slow-going and rather behind the times for London, a criticism which did not prevent his stricter cousins in the North from alluding to him as "poor John who has gone over to Rome". There seemed to be an immense number of services at St Peter's, I suppose to suit all categories of worshippers; for besides two or three Celebrations in the early morning, there was the "ten o'clock", a sort of anticipation of Matins; Matins at eleven, followed by a later Celebration: the children's service at three; the "four o'clock", which from their numbers we privately thought must be for the consolation of despairing spinsters, and Evensong with anthem and sermon at seven. Among these, Matins easily predominated. Every seat in the body of the church and in the vast galleries was occupied by a rustling but attentive congregation,[4] each member of which knew and was known by the vicar personally. During his thirty years the East end of St Peter's was re-created in beauty by means of a screen and pulpit of wrought and hammered iron, framing arcaded perspectives of marble, alabaster and golden mosaics. The organ, now of five manuals, became the finest parish church organ in London.

My father worked and took pleasure in life until the end of it, and died at his post as Dean of Rochester in his eighty-third year, younger than any of his five surviving children. From him I learnt at least to cherish

---

[3] Victorian impatience at the defects of qualities, still surviving in hopes for a Hitler without Jew-baiting, a Mussolini without Corfu or Abyssinia, a Cromwell without an Ireland.

[4] The "week-end" habit was beginning to diminish the congregations of the early 1900's. Since the War the whole of Grosvenor Gardens and most of Grosvenor Place have been turned into offices. The consequent difficulties of the Church might still be arrested by an occasional subscription from some of the great houses (that lament them loudest) still left in the parish.

Photo: *Elliott and Fry*

JOHN STORRS, DEAN OF ROCHESTER

the Church of England, to work for it when in authority and to realize something of the cheapness of attacks upon the Anglican priesthood. And I would here record that, though not unwidely travelled, I have never encountered that side-splitting figure the "Punch Curate" outside the pages of *Punch*.

My mother resumed in her person the irregular brilliance and kindliness of her parents. Her life was on a basis of personal likes and dislikes, personal service (a phrase she had put into practice at least forty years before its invention) and personal loyalty to her family, or to any one who had been kind to her, for better or worse until death. She had almost no sense of abstract justice, and, like many women who, as daughters, wives and mothers have always had their own way, was strongly, indeed violently, anti-feminist. She was a born ruler, and it was not only the choir, organist, curates and vicar of the parish who found themselves to their surprise, but never to their regret, performing tasks or partaking in expeditions hitherto undreamt of. I must confess she thought universal State tutelage the end of initiative: "What! Is every little clever boy to go to the University!" Sad and reactionary sentiments; yet the Arab peasants have a proverb: "Ana Bāsha w'ánta Bāsha; mīn yasáwwaq al-humār?"—"I a Pasha and you a Pasha; who's going to drive the donkey?" "Your new doctor sounds a miracle", I wrote from my first school, "I presume he obeys orders and takes your prescriptions quite regularly." In early youth she had loved animals, keeping great deerhounds, and arriving in Bury St Edmunds as the vicar's bride with a small white lamb tucked under her arm. But as a mother with several children, little good china, and few frocks to spoil, her love passed from practice into theory: "Dear little doggie—sweet little doggie: *run away little doggie.*" Her family will will always treasure with peculiar gratitude, as for a precious legacy, her precept and example in values and standards of living. She grudged expenditure on temporary and momentary gratification, scorned taxis and expensive hotels and, dying in her seventieth year, having several times crossed Europe (on her way to Egypt and to Palestine), had never once travelled first class or taken a sleeping berth. But her home, furnished in Queen Anne and Chippendale furniture against a background of clear greens and reds, and pleasantly free from "amusing" Victorian revivals, was beautiful and characteristic. Though she spent almost nothing on dress, she was always distinguished, and certainly the most delightful member of any assembly in which she found herself. The congregation of St Peter's awaited with impatience the latest contribution from the vicar's lady. They were frequently rewarded. She was sitting one Sunday in the second pew, behind an unknown worshipper who, what with dropping and picking up first her Prayer Book and then her purse, adjusting hairpins, setting her hat and looking for her handkerchief, seemed to exhaust every permutation and combination of the fidgets. When my mother could bear it no longer she leaned forward, touched her on the shoulder and whispered clearly: "My dear, this is St Peter's Church, not St Vitus's."

Again, the Parish Magazine published a portrait of my mother which by some error of the printing came out so dark as to be almost unrecognizable. Three days later, the editor, the Rev. J. Fairbanks, was horrified at receiving an official communication from Barnum's Show, offering his Skeleton Dude for a week's exchange with the Black Vicaress. The indignity of the suggestion preyed upon his mind, until he decided that it was his duty to reveal it to the vicar, who received it with evasion and uneasy condonation, divining only too well its real authorship. She had a lively temper, but deflected it as a rule upon inanimate objects. Once, when her few pieces of Spode and Staffordshire porcelain had been washed and set on a gate-legged table to await reshelving, my father came in and wandering round the room caught his foot in one of the gate-legs. The flap fell, and a dozen pieces crashed to the floor. My mother grasped in both hands a gilt ball-room chair, raised it about her shoulders, brought it down and smashed it to matchwood murmuring almost without emotion: "There but for the grace of God goes John Storrs." She was, at moments embarrassingly for the young, indifferent to appearances; and would scandalize shop assistants, to save their trouble and her own time, by carrying off somewhat intimate purchases without having them "done up". Many an impossible Christmas parcel (or unwrapt offering) have my brothers and I borne blushfully by hand down Eaton Square to poor parishioners scattered in the wastes of Pimlico. When later you became conscious of the size of your head it was hard to hear the smiling hatter asked if he had a bowler that would fit the dome of St Paul's. The compensation was her instant response to our distress signals of "Thou didst not leave his soul in Hell" from the *Messiah*, hummed when a visit or interview threatened to continue indefinitely. Finding private school dress requirements silly and common (as well as excessive) she kept us in blue jerseys and sailor trousers until we were full ten years old, exposing us to the laughter of jacketed, collared and, too often, satin-tied manikins of eight. I was ashamed then, and did not realize for twenty years how sure her taste had been. She illustrated her envelopes to us at school with lively pen drawings of schooners and steamers, the address on the mainsail or streaming with the smoke from the funnels. When after *Exeat*

I left my toothbrush at home it arrived at Charterhouse next day with its label enriched by the following quatrain:

A ruddy little Mission Brush
To darkest Africa I rush;
To spread within that gloomy waste
The gospel of Carbolic Paste.

The constant loving-kindness of my parents made any breach in our relations, however slight or short, very bitter for me. There occurred one such when I was about seven years old. The thing has recurred in my life and I called it from the first The Fear. A friend had sent my parents a box of hothouse grapes, a very rare luxury in our house. I had gone to bed, as usual, about their dinner-time and was dozing off when my mother came in and asked me, deeply distressed, who had eaten the grapes. I had not eaten them and said so. But the crime was unhappily so probable that she begged me to confess, as to one that loved me and would understand everything; saying truly enough that the eating of them, though naughty, was a small offence compared with a lying denial to my mother. I could only persist that I had not taken them. She said no more, but went out without kissing me good night, and I lay awake until breakfast. Next day she was distant to me, and it was not until the third day that I felt sure that I had not lost her love. Long afterwards I found that my younger brother had eaten the grapes and, not being charged with the offence, nor knowing that I had been accused, had properly enough kept the matter to himself.

As the eldest of six and somewhat spoilt, I remember with shame displaying a dictatorial selfishness of which the best that can be said is that it is at least less ugly than the egocentric heartlessness of that *Chimaera Bombinans in Vacuo,* the Only Child. For an eldest, however intolerant of the claims or even the rights of his brothers and sisters, cannot but admit their existence and so acquire a certain humanity and loyalty to the family in general. "Now Master Ronald" (in my nurse's appetizing simile), "please to remember that you're not the only hair in the butter."

I think we amused ourselves by ourselves without external expenditure to a degree that would be considered strange to-day. We read with delight all we could get. We held family chess tournaments, my father having taught us this king of games and game of kings, because, as he said, once having acquired the love of chess you will never waste time or money on cards.[5] It was exciting to play cricket and football in Belgrave Square or

[5] In this he was anticipated by the Jewish poet Bedraschi who wrote in thirteenth-century Spain a prose panegyric of "this ingenious and warlike game, especially as a means for the prevention of gambling and card playing", *Noble Families Among the Sephardic Jews.* Ida Costa, Oxford, 1936.

Grosvenor Gardens, to lay out golf courses for tennis balls and the wrong end of walking sticks, and to organize sports with towel horses as hurdles. We liked to hurl pebbles from the Gardens at or into passing horse buses. We found it good sport to drop neat pellets from the earth of our balcony boxes on to the heads of the devout passing beneath on their way to Evensong. Worse still, on one occasion we deranged for months the social adjustments of Belgravia by emptying into our pockets the bowl of visitors' cards which stood in our front hall and redistributing these in pairs, chosen at hazard and without fear or favour, at every mansion in Belgrave and Eaton Squares. Useful or useless, creditable or the reverse, we did things ourselves and neither expected nor required money, assistance or attention for our entertainment. I was thirteen before I saw a play—and I only saw it then because it was *The Sign of the Cross*.

After a chequered year at the Francis Holland School, Graham Street, Pimlico, I was sent to Fretherne House, York Place, Baker Street, almost opposite the legendary apartment of Sherlock Holmes. The pupils were collected daily from their homes by a private bus and returned thereby in the evening. The teaching was good and thorough but there was far too much beating for trivial offences. In 1892 I went to Temple Grove, East Sheen, once the home of Sir William Temple, where Dean Swift is said to have composed *The Tale of a Tub*. Here there was a fine classical tradition. The perfection of Horace, the frightening excitement of the *Oedipus Tyrannus,* even odd lines of Longfellow, such as "Shrilly the skater's iron rings" for rendering into elegiacs, bit hard and sure at that age. Gepp's *Latin Verse* and Dean Bradley's *Latin Prose,* hierophants of these mysteries, still appear to me as miracles of classical understanding. Some of the material discomforts of the school were almost those of the Classical era. The lavatories would have been condemned in a slum tenement, and the gymnasium, to save mattresses, was floored with tan, the atmosphere of which returns to my nostrils every time Macbeth adjures Black Night to "pall thee in the dunnest smoke of hell". There was anyhow the spirit of freedom. Well I remember the astonishment of master and pupils when I asked whether we might talk in his momentary absence: an eloquent commentary upon the spying discipline of Fretherne House. Sir Edward Grey, Monty James, Provost of King's and of Eton, Arthur Benson and my cousin Charles Cust had been pupils of Temple Grove; among my contemporaries were the Grenfell twins who were killed in the War and that graceful writer, Father Martindale.

At Temple Grove I met the second Fear. One of the boys had "cheeked" the music-master who, swept with fury, put him across his knee and gave him six. As in other schools, none but the Headmaster had the right to

flog. Although this was no flogging, the boy, who was popular, complained to his friends, and they summoned a secret meeting of the school
at which it was resolved that they should register their indignation
(comically enough) by maintaining a silence of icy disapproval in the
Headmaster's presence throughout luncheon: further, that if this conduct
were called in question, there should be no ringleaders. I knew nothing
of these events, having at that time been absorbed in a game of chess
with the German master. As I walked into the dining-room with the
others I was told to hold my tongue, but neither explanation nor warning
was added. The moment the meal was over we were summoned to the
big schoolroom, where the Headmaster, a highly-strung scholar, asked in
broken accents the names of those responsible for the dastardly plan of
humiliating him before all his pupils. Fully expecting to be joined at
least by the boy who had instructed me, and surely by some of his companions, I stood up, to find myself the only erect figure in the room.
There was a brief and terrible pause. The Headmaster then looked
mournfully upon me and said with disgust that he had had enough of
such behaviour, that I was a bad influence, that I must pack up and leave
the school that very afternoon. In a word, I was expelled. I walked out
before my comrades in a dreadful silence and the meeting broke up in
mingled discomfiture and awe.

I remember pacing up and down a lonely path, a small bewildered figure. It seemed impossible that I, who was neither high in the school nor
good at games, had suddenly become of tragic importance. And assuredly
I would have left but for the school sergeant who had seen me playing
chess and therefore knew that I had nothing to do with the incident. He
put the matter to the German master and between them they persuaded
the Head of my innocence. This he might perhaps have established more
handsomely than by sending for me and announcing in public that I
would be pardoned this time.

Having missed an Eton Scholarship, I gained one next year at Charterhouse, but afterwards failed to renew it as a Senior Scholar. Charterhouse
was, from the classical point of view, a repetition of Temple Grove. Little
attention was paid to modern languages, save in "C" form where boys
were prepared for the Army; and Science came well after Classics,
Mathematics and even History. Association Football dominated our life,
not only in the football season, but indirectly throughout the summer,
having for Charterhouse, then supreme at the game, a prestige far over-
shadowing cricket. Any member of the football eleven could be seen wearing his colours in mid-July, whereas not even the captain of the cricket
team would have dared to sport his in December. The Headmaster, Dr

Haig-Brown, and his family took a loving interest in every Carthusian and kept it up long after the boy had left, or they themselves retired—indeed into the third generation. I remember giving this second Founder of Charterhouse, when he resigned, the little India paper Oxford Horace, inscribing above his name *"Exegi monumentum aere perennius"*; and being infinitely touched on learning, years afterwards, that he had kept it beside him till he died.

For permanent inspiration in the great humanities there was none to compare with the Sixth Form Master, Thomas Ethelbert Page. As a housemaster, as a schoolmaster, he was compassed about by details and difficulties with which he should never have had to cope. He had none of the technique of coaching or of cramming, but those who sat under him, as I did for three years, had the opportunity of drinking in the quintessence of scholarship. If the object of classical study is to create, not mere grammatical, syntactical or textual erudition but the deepest and broadest education, a love of spiritual greatness increasing through life— Macaulay's scholar reading Plato with his feet on the fender: T. E. Lawrence in the desert with his sole volume, Aristophanes—then it is a tragedy that T. E. Page, one of the few who could inspire as well as teach, was not in the prime of life appointed a University Professor of Latin or of Greek or the Master of some great college. But it is a tragedy of which no sixth-form Charterhouse boy can complain, and for which some of us must always feel and express, though we never can repay, an infinite debt of gratitude. Between the qualities of a good don and a good schoolmaster there is fixed a great gulf which has never been spanned. How often, through life, have I seen these (and other) kindred and complementary talents unsuitably and therefore wastefully employed. Haig-Brown's successor Dr Rendall, a don, had noble qualities as a scholar, a writer and a gentleman; but he knew nothing, and never at Charterhouse learnt anything, about boys. At Pembroke, Cambridge, the Headmaster of a well-known school was appointed, with brief but shattering results, Senior Tutor of the College. Many an admirable Senior Tutor has failed as a Master, just as the best Chief Secretary is not necessarily the best Governor. A high judicial officer, popular in Central Africa, will cut a comparatively poor figure in the currents and complications of the Levant; a Minister of the Crown, master of quotas, drawbacks and adjustments, may give less than his best when promoted to a post where he must deal with men.

More dreaded than any master by the boys of Saunderites—the Headmaster's house—was their Matron, Miss Attfield. Her inflexible resolution was reinforced by her appearance, as of a scorbutic martello-tower.

Whether your head ached (for which ailment proof was required), your hand bled or your ankle was sprained, no reasoning with "the" Attfield until you had absorbed a tumbler of the powerful drench known as House Mixture: ("Otherwise I shall 'ave to speak to the 'Ead Master at our next Teat à Teat conversation.") The only occasion on which I saw her for the moment set back was when a newly arrived Siamese Royal Prince answered that he did not know how many brothers and sisters he had, because he had never counted. The Attfield seemed genuinely appalled by the implications of this artless reply.

Racquets and fives were both cultivated at Charterhouse but racquets more assiduously, as a superior game, rewarded with a maroon cap and the possibility of representing the School at Queen's Club.[6] There were too many "caps" and far too much watching rather than playing of cricket and football. There was not enough of that personal and individual interest in the boys exhibited now for many decades at Eton, where music and other studies off the beaten scholastic or athletic track have been consistently tolerated and sometimes encouraged. Thirty-five years ago at Charterhouse, one did one's music by stealth without the faintest fear of ever having to blush to find it fame. There was no association—as with a Cory or an Arthur Benson—of masters and boys "out of school". We were taught nothing whatever about the surrounding country, and were consequently incapable of amusing ourselves through the holidays unless provided with the best cricket pitches and squash courts together with suitable opponents; so that for years after leaving school anything like a walk or a ride was, compared with such known and universal entertainment, "dull" and avoided. Our standard of school work was low, and every sort of shirking considered correct. We jumped at holidays, legal or otherwise—unlike some boys with whom I was to be afterwards associated. I shall never forget the astonishment of Lord Plumer, that fine flower of the public-school spirit, when he inspected Gaza in Palestine and announced that in honour of his visit the local schools would be given a half holiday—at finding the news greeted by the studious Arab pupils with almost tearful dismay.

It is, however, easy enough to criticize public schools and the public-school tradition, which stand in some ways for sameness, mediocrity and narrowness of outlook. The Schools have been notably humanized in the past thirty-five years, and are, like all things human, susceptible of yet further improvement. If negative and uncreative critics would only travel abroad and make a study of youth in general from Calais to Calcutta and

---

[6] Unlike several other public schools, Charterhouse then played no cricket or football matches at Lord's or on other public grounds.

Khartum, instructed (rather than educated) for the most part without any idea of this spirit, they could hardly fail to realize the positive magnitude of the public-school achievement. Like salt in food, it must be absent to be appreciated. Though I left Charterhouse vaguely unfulfilled and so disappointed, I found myself at the last suddenly forced to pray that the Attfield would not notice the tears in my eyes.

I won a not very high Classical Scholarship at my father's college, Pembroke, Cambridge, and greatly disappointed my tutors by failing the first time over algebra in the Littlego (a defect of mind I have not yet repaired). This noble old Hall of Mary Aymer de Valence had suffered cruelly in the hands of that *architecte démolisseur* who had nearly ruined two ancient foundations at Cambridge and two at Oxford. He had not hesitated to lay low the old college hall, said to be the only one with two storeys at either University, on the ground that the building was in a dangerous condition; to discover when the desecration was irreparable that he had to employ dynamite to get it down. My rooms, in the rather obviously named Red Buildings, were even in summer murk-dark by reason of the trees. Indeed, my sitting-room was only well lighted when the ground outside was covered with snow; some ten days, that is, during my three years' occupation. Unlike several other colleges, we had neither electric light nor bathrooms. Pembroke had then achieved and has since maintained perhaps the highest all-round average of athletic and scholastic eminence of any Cambridge college. The College did well on the river and at cricket, extremely well at football, both Rugby and Association, and well in the schools, winning for example five Firsts in Classics during my last year. It was indeed a continuation of the public-school system at its best. The general level was high and the tone impeccable. A little too impeccable in some respects for a growing mind. There were none of the odd little sets which could be found at Trinity and at King's. Save for one, of my year, who read Chaucer and drank Hippocras, we had no originals; nor would you find in Pembroke, as elsewhere, socialists, aesthetes, atheists, platonists, devil-worshippers: pleasant and harmless phases through which many future pillars of the Church, of the State and even of the Stock Exchange have made their early way. Yet Pembroke was not lacking in dons of great distinction. My tutor, Leonard Whibley, the younger brother of Charles, the writer, was an admirable scholar, as well as a true friend (and a superb judge of hock and Moselle). R. A. Neil was a profound and brilliant classic, who had he lived would almost certainly have ended as Regius Professor of Greek: and E. G. Browne— "Persian" Browne to the public, "Johnnie" to Cambridge—the University

Professor of Arabic, was a teacher, a linguist and an Orientalist second in the world, if indeed he was second, to Vambéry alone. Nevertheless, there was somehow an absence of that *chaleur communicative* which creates University Societies like the Apostles or the Decemviri; and the general effort was directed rather towards athletics. Rowing I shunned after one term of slavery on the river, and devoted myself, sometimes even in winter, to the less exacting and more manageable lawn tennis. I was conscious at the time, and am even more conscious now, that I passed many hours in idleness and dissipation of energy—and of money—upon Sunday "Brunches" with Bridge from eleven to eleven; upon grained briar pipes, perfect "mixtures", and that interesting variant of snobbery, the collection of first editions—the pleasure of knowing the ancient great "at home"; but I did read widely, a habit which although not directly profitable to career, yet helps to keep one independent and critical of worldly success; and I can say that I left Cambridge with a lifelong devotion to the Greek and Latin classics enhanced by deep drinkings of Meredith, Swinburne, Maupassant, Anatole France, Brahms, Wagner, Bach; by a visit to the Bruges Exhibition of 1902 and by attending Conway's Slade Lectures of 1903. These last gave me a permanent and passionate admiration for the Flemish Primitives; so that I began life at least able to "approve the things that are more excellent".

The nearest approach to the Symposium in Pembroke was provided by "Johnnie" Browne's Saturdays, when from about nine until midnight or sometimes later, his friends were privileged to appear, take their seats, fill their glasses, coffee cups and pipes and remain as listeners, talkers or both, as long as they liked. Johnnie's range was illimitable. He discussed art, letters, religion, politics, and university life with a generous and evocative impatience of the professional outlook which almost blinded one to his own marvellous capacity for concentrated labour. Like other great linguists, he was unliterary in his outlook on his own language, and I believe the only book society for which he was personally responsible was a Dolly Dialogues Club.

Within 300 yards in King's College, Oscar Browning, "O.B.", framed in a whole series of the Arundel Society's chromolithographs, would be expounding to an interested but sometimes sceptical audience his theories and history of the world, particularly of the Royal world; whilst over the way Waldstein, his rival in that domain, skimmed centrifugally over the aesthetics of life—an inspiration in classical art, yet never wholeheartedly received by the scholars of Cambridge, because, though an undoubted authority on Greek sculpture, he had no Greek.

As for the King's visit it was a success. Waldstein, in Elysium, darted forward in the Senate House and wrung the Queen's hand; O.B., not having been asked to anything, spent the day in Oxford.[7]

Henry Jackson, perhaps the greatest Cambridge figure of his day, surviving from another age with something of the genius, much of the manner and all the appearance of Socrates, saw me once at David's bookstall in the market-place turning over folios in a drizzle of rain, and recognizing me by a Cust family likeness took me to his rooms in Neville's Court where he surprised me by stepping out of his trousers and hanging them to dry in front of the fire, whilst he recalled the period of which our meeting had reminded him. On a Boat Race day he had been sitting with Arthur Balfour in the Savile Club discussing the Race. A group of members entered pricking reverent ears at this conjunction of intellect, and A. J. B., anxious not to disappoint them, had concluded his prediction with "... and so, Professor, you incline to a gloomy view of the prospects of Ontology in the immediate future". I hear him now summing up Guy de Maupassant's *Bel Ami* as a book written about a cad, by a cad, for cads to read—but devilish good reading all the same.

I can still remember my pride and pleasure in being elected to the Decemviri, a society of ten elected from different colleges, which met every Wednesday night in one of its members' rooms and discussed such topics as "A polished coal is better than a rough diamond", or "That the public school system is rotten", until cut off by the midnight Gate. Leading members of this society were Charles Tennyson, then as now an admirable talker and accomplished versifier in the heroic couplet; J. M. Keynes, an inhuman opponent in debate; and Lytton Stracey who, balanced on the fender, would wind up in a high-piping voice, tearing to absurdity the most plausible arguments of proposer and opposer alike. Stephen Gaselee was already at the age of twenty what he still is to-day, a Cambridge Personality; Gaselee, with almost as many friends as interests, a first-class classical scholar, a bibliophile, a bibliographer, a liturgiologist; Gaselee, who when playing tennis wore his hair in a net; who kept Siamese cats, fed with a revolting portion of cow's lung preserved on a plate above his bookshelf; who had a fire every day in the year because England has a cold climate; who founded the Deipnosophists' dining club, where the members, robed in purple dinner-jackets lined with lilac silk and preluding dashingly on Vodka, would launch forth into an uncharted ocean of good food and even better talk; Gaselee, who read, wrote and spoke Ancient Coptic (which the Copts themselves had not

[7] As explained in the Preface, passages in closer printed type unless otherwise described are quotations from letters to my mother.

done for 300 years); Gaselee, nightly puffing his long churchwarden whilst he expatiated on Petronius, vestments, Shark's Fin and cooking problems; a lay Prince of the Church, Ecclesiastic Militant and Gastronomer Royal. Next to the memory of afternoons spent with him in a canoe on the Backs with immense bags of cherries reading aloud to each other Guy de Maupassant, comes that deepest blue of King's Chapel windows in the grey cool of Evensong; the almost daily visit to David's bookstall; the fun and excitement of Parry's *Birds* of Aristophanes in 1903, when I took the part of Prometheus [8] and, owing to a generous issue by the management of port on the last night chose to return to college in classical costume with my ordinary clothes over my arm; a choice recounted by Charles Tennyson as

> ... how Prometheus, swollen with applause,
> Sandalled and chiton'd fled the scenic doors;
> And how next day men gathered up his things,
> His drawers in Downing and his coat in Kings.

Although averse from cards and gambling I had early been initiated into the refinements of the Sweepstake. At Charterhouse, besides the normal or lay opportunities of this kind, the Hall of our House indulged during Sunday tea in a sixpenny quasi-religious event in which, by drawing the correct opening sentence of Evensong you might find yourself at bedtime the richer by half-a-crown. I partook, during the Papal Election of 1903, my last year at Cambridge, in a Sweepstake on the new Pope. Here the attraction of sixty-four entries with no blanks almost counterbalanced the absence of Place Betting. I drew Rampolla, a most promising starter for whom I refused £10, only to be disappointed by his being disallowed owing to the last exercise of the historic power of veto possessed by the Emperor of Austria.

I worked hard for the last two months before the Tripos and, to the surprise and I hope pleasure of all concerned, was awarded a reasonably good First. Flushed with pride I returned home and plunged with the utmost zest into my first real London season, answering my father when he asked what I proposed doing, that it must be something that involved no more examinations. Chance made Rennell Rodd mention to Harry Cust that Sir Eldon Gorst, Financial Adviser to the Egyptian Government, had started a new system of recruiting for the Egyptian and Sudan

---

[8] "Prometheus is extremely well done by Mr. R. H. A. Storrs of Pembroke. This very part was played by his uncle, Mr. Harry Cust, in 1883, and it was quite right that Mr. Storrs should establish a family tradition by the piece of business in which he took a furtive glance over the umbrella towards Olympus, and then terrified nipped back again like a rabbit into a hole." (*Manchester Guardian*.)

Civil Services (hitherto staffed from the Ministry of Public Instruction in Cairo) and was now in London for that purpose. I was interviewed and chosen, and returned to Cambridge for another year with the other successful candidates; savouring rather than studying Arabic under Browne and Shaikh Hassan Tewfik, my first of many Egyptian friends. In him I observed for the first time that utter ignorance of Comparative Semitics which I was to encounter afterwards in profound Arabists of Egypt, Palestine and Mesopotamia. Etymologically he was a child, really believing that the Americanism "So long" was derived from "Salaam". Living out of Pembroke and nearer to King's, I was able to see more of other colleges and to enlarge my horizon. After passing our examination in Arabic we had arranged to give Browne and Hassan Tewfik a farewell dinner of gratitude. As we stood waiting for the Shaikh we received a message saying that he was indisposed and begging us to begin without him. Before the end of the meal I was summoned to his death-bed; and there were many undergraduates as well as dons quite unconnected with our work yet somehow constrained to follow to his grave this gentle courteous stranger who had died alone in a foreign land.

Shortly before this, we had learnt to our dismay that Sir Eldon Gorst, the author of our Egyptian being, was leaving Egypt.[9]

You must have seen that a great blow has fallen upon us of Egypt—to wit, the promotion of Gorst to the Foreign Office: Johnnie is in despair about it; he says there is only one word in all the languages that he knows that at all meets the case; this word he refused to divulge.

On going down from Cambridge I accepted an offer from the Rodds to travel with them for two months to Sorrento and teach their boy Francis, Latin and Greek, the Old Testament and, apparently, a general conspectus of civilization. This journey gave me my first real experience of foreign cities and the diplomatic life, besides daily intercourse with two interesting and interested personalities. Of Naples I seem to remember nothing but the beauty of the bronzes and the ugliness of nature's most intimate rites performed before a listless public in the open streets. At Siena on my way home I had the good fortune to visit three days running the 1904 Mostra [10] and to make my first acquaintance with the underworld of Art criticism. In Florence I spent the whole of the pay I had earned at Sorrento upon my first Primitive. At the end of September I said good-bye to England, stayed two or three days in Paris with my mother and brothers, and left the happiest home and the most loving and loved of parents, for Marseilles, the P. and O. S/S *Arabia,* and Egypt.

[9] To be prepared (though the world knew it not) to succeed Cromer.
[10] Exhibition (of Sienese Primitives).

CHAPTER TWO

1904–1905

A stranger here
Strange things doth meet, strange glories see;
Strange treasures lodged in this fair world appear,
Strange all, and new to me.

THOMAS TRAHERNE
(1637-1674)

I

THE *Arabia* reached Port Said on 5 October, too late for the afternoon train to Cairo. My companions chosen for the Egyptian service were Norman Macnaghten, of a well-known Eton family, A. C. Nation and H. F. Archer.[1]

In the evening, spurred on by the common tag that Port Said is the wickedest place on earth, we all debarked: never was a more miserable delusion; the place is slightly quieter than Westgate, and contains a few shops selling tinned goods.

Next day the journey, owing to a breakdown of six hours through the heat of the day without food or drink, proved a fiery Ramadan. We drove to the Continental Hotel and took *pension complète* at twelve shillings or sixty piastres a day:

the piastre is a damnable coin: two of them make five pence and five a bob: they are each equal to twopence-halfpenny and ninety-seven and a half go to a pound—could you ask worse?

We interviewed the Financial Adviser, Sir Vincent Corbett, and I found that I had been chosen for the Ministry of Finance, while my three companions were to be sent down to Alexandria to train for the Ministry of the Interior.

The Continental was more than I could afford on a salary of twenty pounds a month so I

---

[1] Afterwards Commandant of the Cairo City Police.

put in at the Pension Tewfik, run by Italians, not at all bad. For nine francs (and one piastre for light), good bedroom, breakfast, lunch and dinner.

The Ministry of Finance itself was a huge and ramshackle edifice. Built chiefly of lath and plaster, it was continually being underpinned at one place or another; and its main subsidiary staircases converted from straight to circular or from circular to straight. The building had been the Harémlik—the Harīm Palace of Ismail the Mufáttish, "Inspector" or Minister of Finance, the evil counsellor of the Khedive Ismail. From those gates the Mufáttish had driven out daily to meet his master and to discuss, without fear of the deaf coachman overhearing, the best means of preventing the further millions about to be squeezed out of the ruined fellahīn from reaching the coffers of the foreign bondholder.

Of the State Departments that of the Post was almost wholly French; the Railway Administration (including the Telegraphs) an appanage of the Copts; and the Ministry of Finance, which wielded identically the same power as does the Treasury in England and in other European countries, the last surviving citadel of Sephardic Salonika, of the Lebanon and of the Levant. The only British officials in the Ministry of Finance besides the Adviser, were the Under-Secretary, the Controller of Taxes and the Director of State Lands, together with a small inspector class; with the result that any measure of accounting that ran against Coptic or Syrian interests bristled with so many impracticabilities as to daunt the most resolute reformer. But already the second generation of Egyptian Moslems, educated under Lord Cromer, were coming into their own, and needing less and less the assistance of the unpopular *Shami*.[2] Office hours at the Ministry of Finance were from eight to one daily, including Sunday but excluding Friday, the Moslem day of rest and prayer. Cups of Egyptian coffee were brought in half a dozen times during the morning— seven-thirty to one-thirty is a long interval between meals—and were also offered whenever one went to do business with a neighbouring Department.

I shall always remember the kindness of my first pilot there, H. N. Bowden Smith, the Financial Adviser's Private Secretary, and my astonishment at his faithful imitation of the speech and handwriting— even of the stylographic pen—of his first Chief, Sir Eldon Gorst. Twenty years later I learnt without surprise (a faculty long since exhausted by service in the Near East) that one of my own subordinates was copying my manner of dealing with Arabs, and of holding myself—nay the very roll of my unfashionable old felt hat.

2 Arabic for "Syrian".

The Under-Secretary, Alfred Mitchell Innes, had not yet returned from leave, and I found myself at the disposal of Nubar Innes Bey, a friendly and indulgent Levantine of Scotch-Armenian extraction, who kept the inefficient clerks of the Secretariat in tremendous order without improving them in the smallest degree. Much of the official correspondence was still conducted in French, and abounded in *virements* and *prélévements*— transfers and previous deductions; *numéraire, frais de déplacement* and *frais de monture,* all sounding, as well as looking, so much more important than bullion, travelling allowance and horse allowance.

Nubar was kind enough, but I was given no regular work. For weeks I sat over mining *dossiers* with the academic detachment of one who knows that he will not be called upon to take any action. The time hung heavily and uselessly. A little forethought on the part of the authorities would have given me a couple of weeks in each department with some sort of examination or questionnaire at its conclusion. My colleagues at Alexandria were put very thoroughly through their paces in the matters of riding, drilling, inspection of horses and police stations. They returned to headquarters after three or four months secure and happy in all the practical experience that I lacked, though a little dashed to find themselves described in a published report as having arrived "alert and respectful".

But the Ministry of Finance occasionally furnished incidents to which I can still look back with pleasure:

last night a rat was trapped in the Adviser's room and before he turned up Bowden brought it in to Wells and self: we sent for a cat, but a white and perfectly useless one was produced. We made the man go again, and this time he brought so fierce a black tom that it chased the rat into the messenger's pants, he calling upon Heaven to preserve him from the Unclean. He was indignant at my suggestion that he feared the teeth more than the defilement.

Another time when I was helping Bowden Smith, he appeared, only a few minutes before the Adviser was expected, without the key of the safe. There was no time to get it from his house, so Mahmūd (the polished orderly who never failed to take his ten piastres off every Egyptian coming to see the Adviser) set out to do something about it. He returned almost immediately with a blind criminal, enlarged but the day before, who being led up to the safe produced a few skewers, on the first thrust of which the ponderous door swung back, saving our bacon and confirming my respect for the immemorial craft of the East.

Egypt has always been the father of improvisation and of its first cousin, bluff. In what other country would a young civil servant, before the end of his first week, be requested by his chief to exhibit the ancient Capital to a high dignitary of the Anglican Church?

I lunched with him at Shepheard's; and, leaving him for half an hour, during which I rushed home and read all up in Baedeker, I drove him to old Cairo, showing him the Nilometer, the place where Moses mewled in the bullrushes (there are none now) and the oldest Coptic Church, Mari Girgis,[3] where the Holy Family are supposed to have rested on their way through Egypt.

Travellers in the Near and Middle East—to themselves visitors, tourists to us—were sometimes our joy, more frequently our misery, and on occasion our positive delirium. A few days later I was dining with a tourist family at Mena House Hotel. Asked by my host whether the frieze round the dining-room represented arabesques or flowers, I explained that it was a text from the Koran, read it aloud and translated it. "The Koran," said my host, stupefied by this virtuosity, "let me see. Yes. The Koran: by Rameses, I suppose?" As I was to remark later in Palestine they seemed to veer between extreme scepticism and extreme credulity. I knew an old lady who took a dragoman up the Nile and would never fail to ask him the meaning of each succeeding frieze of Egyptian hieroglyphics. Hassan, who could not read his native Arabic, let alone English, still less ancient Egyptian, would scan the surface gravely and reply: "That, Miladi, mean 'God very nice' ", with which she was on each occasion perfectly satisfied. One or two young donkey-boys adopted the annual practice of falling upon their knees before isolated tourists crying "Lady, lady, me believe! gibb it blenty Bibil!"[4] when the catechumen would find himself rewarded by a new suit of clothes and a five pound note which carried him pleasantly through the summer until next year's conversion.

Apart from the officials and the Army, Cairo was still mainly French-speaking-thinking-and-living, just as Alexandria was Italian and Greek. The Turf Club (once the British Agency), situated in the Shāria al-Maghrábi next to the self-respecting but architecturally painful Sephardi Synagogue, was the fenced city of refuge of the higher British community, many of whom spent anything between one and five hours daily within its walls. The porter was a Montenegrin of a distinguished melancholy, the head waiter a swift and agile Greek, universally known as Alphonse because in the opinion of Harry Boyle, the Oriental Secretary, his real name, Socrates, was not a possible name for a waiter. The annual subscription was seven pounds; you could get a bedroom for five

[3] St George.
[4] There is no "p" in the Arabic language. One speaks of "Bashas" and "Brinces"; "in for a benny in for a bound".

pounds a month, with all meals for eight pounds extra. Not having frequented a club before I was at first enchanted by the number and variety
of the newspapers and magazines, but soon found them spiritually a diet
of *hors d'œuvres* and so restricted myself to *The Times* and the *Vie
Parisienne*. The Sporting Club at Gezira, on an admirable site presented
in the 'eighties by the Khedive Tewfik and improved since then almost
out of recognition, was the other British headquarters. It was difficult for
foreigners to be elected and not easy for Egyptians even to make use of
either club; as I discovered by the glances cast in my direction when I
came in with one of the few Egyptian members [5] to play tennis.

The chief thing I remember about my first six weeks in Egypt was that
I was very lonely and infinitely homesick. I soon moved from the Pension
Tewfik, with the idea of bettering myself, to the Hotel Metropole, a
stuffy unattractive building which sounded finer than it really was. Few
residents had heard of it; worse still, no cabman could find it. For five
pounds a month I got a bedroom, bath, light and a hearty breakfast every
morning at seven-thirty. In transferring my effects from the Pension to
the Hotel at a cost

from room to room of one and sixpence, three flights down and four up, I
broke a vase of the 12th dynasty. Bought last Sunday, aged 5000 years, and
I have smashed it in four days.

My comrades at Alexandria, though I did not envy their life, were at
least together and worked under a discipline which occupied part of their
minds and all their time. In Cairo, the junior English ranks were attached as inspectors or sub-directors of departments and had their own
friends and acquaintances. I, a newcomer, with none other of my low
status in the Finance, had hardly any, and the beginning of my advance
in this direction was an introduction to Ernest Richmond, son of Sir
William Richmond the painter, and grandson of George Richmond, artist
and friend of William Blake. Not only was he the most charming and
hospitable friend and companion, but he taught me much for which I can
never be grateful enough. Richmond liked and was liked by the Egyptians, and I caught from him the habit of entering into conversation with
all and sundry, talking either sense or nonsense as it came into my head,
and in this way getting to know the Egyptian people and gaining experience in the Arabic language.

He took me to live at the flat he occupied with Howard Carter, Inspector of Antiquities, then based on Saqqāra.[6] It is a curious commentary

---

[5] Afterward Prime Minister of his country.
[6] The cemetery of the earlier Egyptian dynasties, five or six miles from the Pyramids.

on Carter's rumoured sharpness of temper (which I never experienced) that for the first month Richmond feared to acknowledge me as other than a guest, though I was in fact a partner.

One evening Carter came in, unharassed but rather fierce, and told us the following story. As Inspector of Antiquities at Saqqāra, he was in charge of the Serapéum where are four and twenty sarcophagi of the Sacred Bulls. Carter's head guardian there had run up to the office to inform him that a number of French and Belgian lower-grade employees from Cairo had arrived at the Serapéum very much the worse for liquor, and were misbehaving themselves in various ways. Carter went down, remonstrated with them, and was answered with impertinence. To preserve order and safeguard the antiquities for which he was responsible, he was forced to let loose upon them two or three of his Sudanese Ghaffirs [7] who swiftly laid out two or three of the offenders. These at once returned to Cairo and lodged a formal complaint against Carter before M. de la Boulinière, the French Consul-General. Carter was summoned by Lord Cromer for the morrow and was of the opinion (which we shared) that he was For It.

In the event he found "the Lord" [8] less terrifying than he had anticipated. The French Consul-General had no particular sympathy with the complainants, but feared lest reports in the local gutter-press might reach Paris; the Entente Cordiale was hardly a year old, and Lord Cromer must give him some satisfaction. This satisfaction was an apology, which Lord Cromer ordered Carter to tender forthwith. To his amazement Carter refused, saying that he had only done his duty; going indeed so far as to decline even the conditional formula of apologizing "if he had been in the wrong". He therefore had to leave the Egyptian Service, and so to provide a standing example of official ruin leading to a celebrity which could not have been achieved officially. For though his abilities might have carried him far, and though his admirable water-colours of Egyptian frescoes could not have failed to win the admiration of the discerning, both united would never have brought him the world fame achieved by his discovery of Tutankhamen; like Klindor in Corneille's *Illusion*: *"de son bannissement il tire son bonheur."* Richmond and I, not foreseeing this, sympathized with him as a perversely self-ruined hero.

Flat lessees in Cairo thirty years ago got no more for their annual rent than enclosed cubes of space and the primal sanitary needs. Electric light fittings, baths—even bells—were no concern of the proprietor and Rich-

---

[7] Guards in charge of the tombs.
[8] Lord Cromer was generally known as The Lord by British and *al-Lurd* by Egyptian residents. The Agency was *Bait al-Lurd*—the house of the Lord.

mond and I had to pay for these when we took over the topmost flat of No. 2, Shāria al-Sharīf, the property of al-Sayyid Ibrahim Waffa, one of the terms of whose contract was that *"le locataire devra se servir du lieu loué comme un bon père de famille"*. There we lived happily and cheaply, though furnishing was up-hill work.

Furniture buying out here is heartbreaking: no one can conceive the depths of Syro-Italian taste: gilt, light-blue plush, marble-tops, grained wood, in shapes to make one gasp,

and in the end Richmond designed and the local carpenter executed.

I might have remained in the Secretariat indefinitely, rising to unknown heights or sinking to unimaginable depths, but for the kindness and indiscretion of the late Lady Cromer, to whom I had letters of introduction and who sent for me on her return from England. She enquired whether I liked my work and I answered thoughtlessly that I couldn't say because I hadn't any. This confession she passed on to Lord Cromer who, delighted to receive a piece of inside information, rallied the Financial Adviser next morning about his policy of "importing expensive University Honours men" and then giving them nothing to do. This settled a move for me in some direction, and that very morning I was asked by the Adviser whether I would like to be Secretary of the newly formed Department of Mines. I perceived this to be one of those questions which require an affirmative answer; and accepted on the spot. My new chief, Mr J. F. Wells, Inspector or—as he soon had himself called—Inspector-General of Mines, was a man of many admirable qualities which did not, however, include the sympathetic understanding of a technically ignorant but very willing and not uneducated young man.

Of a primitive violent tongue, for which he apologizes afterwards by saying "I forgot that you are not used to an office"; he told me he hadn't had a holiday for eight years, nor read a non-technical book for twelve; he has been right through the mill, and is, I think, rather sick with me because I haven't.

As Secretary of the Mines Department, I accompanied Wells on some of his journeys into Upper Egypt: through Edfu, past the lonely desert temple at Redesía with its pathetic inscriptions in Greek and Latin by prisoners dying of hunger and thirst, and beyond the purple mountain from which the Romans hewed and lifted across land and sea their imperial porphyry. I was sent ahead the first night to pitch my first desert camp. I found the camel men

the most ignorant people in the world: hardly one had ever seen a chair or table: pleasant men though, I encouraged them by telling them how excellent is knowledge and how they might in the end be Beys or Pashas. "And we may perchance be camel men" said one who was carrying a heavy water barrel.

We inspected the Nile Valley Company's gold mines at Allāgi, descending the ancient Egyptian shafts two or three hundred feet and exploring the long drives and galleries. What we found there, or rather what we failed to find, coupled with my compulsory reading in Cairo of reports from experts, convinced me that we were not giving the ancient Egyptian method enough credit, and that the Prospecting Areas and Mining Leases for which the London Market was competing resembled (and would surely strike Wells as resembling) Hilaire Belloc's

> Fair land of Ophir, mined for gold
> By lordly Solomon of old,
> Who, sailing northward to Perim,
> Took all the gold away with him
> And left a lot of holes;
> Vacuities which bring despair
> To those confiding souls
> Who find that they have bought a share
> In marvellous horizons, where
> The desert, terrible and bare,
> Interminably rolls.

—my quotation of which, though in itself accurately descriptive, was perhaps not in the best of taste, especially from a young subordinate to a chief fired with enthusiasm for the development of a Great Industry, still under the shadow of a recent crisis. Egyptian Mines seemed, indeed, to move from disappointment to disappointment. One morning the Department was thrilled to its depths by the news that coal had been discovered at Redesía. A specimen consignment duly arrived at the Ministry and was taken to the Minister's room for a demonstration. We put on our tarbushes, buttoned up our coats and were ushered into the presence of Mazlūm Pasha. We gathered round a crackling fire as Wells carefully emptied upon it a shovelful of chosen lumps; but the flames, far from brightening, immediately died down and out, and with them all hopes of a coal boom for Egypt.

Though my work was uncongenial, life in Cairo had its compensations. You could get a reasonably good back stall at the Khedival Opera House for the equivalent of four shillings. Italian and French companies were subsidized some four or five thousand pounds in alternate years, the Italians giving infinitely better value for opera and the French for drama. The Opera House, almost entirely composed of wood and plaster but said by Coquelin to yield the best acoustics he had ever known, had its

right-side grand tier occupied by the gauze screen of the Harīm boxes
through which you could observe in the entr'acte the flashes of magnificent
jewels and even more magnificent eyes. It was also pleasant to contemplate the Ministerial boxes. The Pashas arrived fairly late and remained in
a twilight sleep until the ballet, when, as if at the word of command, they
awoke and raked the *ballerine* with powerful prismatic binoculars. The
entr'actes, as throughout the Levant and Southern Europe, were intolerably long, and we were never out of the theatre until well after
twelve. I could not afford supper, but was sometimes taken by friends to
the St James's Restaurant—"Jimmy's"—at that time a rendezvous for inex-
pensive revellers. My ignorance of life was so complete that I once whispered to my host: "Is the Comtesse really a Countess?" not realizing that
the lady understood English, and was dumbfounded when, to the delight
of the company, she rose to her feet, and flouncing centrifugally round
afforded me the flashing autopsy of an immense golden coronet embroidered upon the broadest expanses of her lingerie.

Best of all I enjoyed walking by the mosques and through the bazaars,
trying to learn what the people in them really wanted and really thought.

I suppose the three chief bazaars of the Near East are Cairo, Constantinople and Aleppo. Of these the Bezistén of Constantinople was,
until the War, infinitely the finest and most interesting, but the War
wounded, and Ankara killed the Bezistén. Aleppo provided, and still provides, local necessities rather than international *bibelotage*. I loved the
Cairo Bazaars the first time I went into them and, though they are now
less interesting and more sophisticated than in 1904, I love them still. But
even in those days they showed elements of artificiality. Ninety per cent.
of both merchants and their wares came from without Egypt. There were
Syrians, Persians, Jews, Armenians, Greeks, Tripolitans, Georgians and
Circassians; there was scarce one Egyptian. Beyond a little brass and
tinned copper, with an occasional strip of Mehalla silk from the palace of
a Pasha, every object of merit was imported from Constantinople, from
Syria, from Persia, from Tunis or from the Greek islands. Of the junk,
the cheap machine-made embroidery was Bulgarian; the Spanish shawls
were Japanese, as were the ancient Egyptian lacquered pencil- and ciga-
rette-cases. The velvet Zouaves, sequined Harīm fezzes and "Whiff of
Sahara" perfumes, the reconstituted amber and the perennial glass and
celluloid necklaces varied their origin with the fluctuating price of labour,
factory competence and distributing abilities of Paris, Birmingham, and
what is now Czechoslovakia. Customs duties, almost the only method of
taxing foreigners in Egypt, were (and are) high, and even were they not
it is a commonplace that in London, Persian and Anatolian carpets are

cheaper than in Cairo, Greek marbles than in Athens, Botticellis than in Florence. Still it is pleasant for Nordics to buy things in the setting of the *Arabian Nights*; no less pleasant to look back, and recall the lights and the scents of that atmosphere; and I doubt not that once the guileless West has been able to resume mass production of tourists, the six-feet cubes of bazaar space will once again enable their landlords, travelling abroad on profits of several hundred per cent., to see almost nothing of Egypt save in the coolest weather. Egyptian and classical antiquities were for the most part sold in shops within an easy radius of the big hotels. Here again, as at Luxor, the temples and pyramids have encouraged and imposed alike on fellah finder, purchasing agent, merchant vendor and happy visitor (piously computing the number of centuries before Exodus or even Abraham) a level of price far above London, Paris or Berlin. I have seen dealers from Cairo laying in their stock of *Ushabtis* and bronzes at Spink's in St James's, to be released next season upon their (and possibly his) clients in the purlieus of Kasr al-Nil or the Ezbekía.

The Khan al-Khalíli, which was the tourists' alley, and indeed the whole of the great Hamzáwi Bazaar were to me always enchanting—the mutual optimism of the morning, the perfumes, the incense and loud cries of the busy afternoon, the thin smoke of little fires and braziers towards evening, the ink-black depth of shadow against the shafts of the midnight moon striking through the crazy roofings of the narrow ways, the contrasting silence, broken by the snore of the watchman or the distant crash of dice and counters from an invisible *Qáhwa*.[9] Hashāshīn—hashish addicts—known to one another as "pilgrims" (of, indeed, a strange and awful shrine), would call aloud through the darkness: *"Ya hagg Ahmad, fain al-taamíra?"*—"Pilgrim Ahmad, where is the hashish pipe?"—and could generally be comforted by the assurance that it was somewhere round the corner. (I once asked an Egyptian friend what was the particular gratification he derived from the drug. He told me that, amongst other merits, if under its influence you took a cab and drove towards the mosque of Sultan Hassan along the Sharia Muhammed Ali,[10] each arch would appear to be about a quarter of a mile in span. And when I enquired if that made them look less hideous, he treated me as a profane, unworthy of his mystery.) [11]

In the holy month of Ramadan would be tethered outside shops and

---

[9] Small coffee house.

[10] A base imitation of the Rue de Rivoli in Paris.

[11] Hashāshīn (who have given their name to "assassins") play with time as well as space. "One will answer a question after a lapse of many minutes, without realizing that there has been the slightest pause in the conversation. He may also feel aggrieved because he imagines his companions have ignored a remark of his completely and finally, whereas he has actually not allowed them time for a reply." (*The Last Plague of Egypt*, p. 81.)

houses a sheep with henna'd tail, feeding against the Feast of Bairam. *"Ramadán Karím"*—"Ramadan is generous"—you called to its fasting owner, who replied (sometimes, I used to think, not without an effort) *"Walláhu ákram"*—"And God is most generous." In bargaining, the decencies of delay were still observed (not least where "Bree Figs," pathetically interjected, drew your attention to the notice of *Prix Fixe* on the wall). The object you were unwise enough to prefer too early or obviously was offered according to convention as a free gift; you refused and, at the price then quoted, you cried aloud: *"A'úzu billáh min al-Shaitán al-Ragím"*—"I take refuge with God from Satan, worthy to be stoned"; nor was it until after the merchant had replied (not because it made sense but because it rhymed) *"Bismilláhi al-Rahmāni al-Rahīm"*—"In the name of God the Compassionate, the Merciful"—that the negotiations could take their destined course and the Bukhara rug, Yaldúzli gilt tureen, Naxos ikon or Red Sea peridot, for which twenty-two pounds had been required and two "finally" offered, change hands for a reasonable and self-respecting five-pound note.

I should think no young civil servant abroad has ever ached for his leave more, or deserved it less after so brief and ineffective service in a civilized and hardly even sub-tropical country, than the new Secretary of the Department of Mines. Although no longer lonely, I was still intensely homesick, and as a son, a brother, a Londoner, a Belgravian, and a Pimlican, I longed for home. The regulations, which properly forbade first leave until at least two winters had been passed in Egypt, were somehow stretched (though my pay was cut);

I only receive pay for the first fifteen days away: £11 for two months should keep me pretty firmly in the narrow way, anyhow,

and on May 6th I stood on the deck of the Austrian Lloyd *Semiramis* bound for Brindisi, Venice, and home.

Before we started I was to my great joy introduced to Lord Milner, returning melancholy but unembittered from so much glory, so much unhappiness in Africa; through the Egypt which had known him as a brilliant Under-Secretary for Finance, to an England which seemed for the moment disinclined to know him at all. Milner was the first example I had met of the comforting truth that the greatest are also the most humble and the most kind, not only to their few equals but also—and even more, to their innumerable inferiors. He walked me up and down the deck after luncheon and dinner, talking with illumination on any and every subject, from the books that he preferred to the best methods of employing Secret Service Agents. When we reached Venice, I managed, as youngest and swiftest of the debarking passengers, to reach Danieli's, the only hotel I knew of, before the rest. I asked for a room; the reception clerk offered me the last left. Knowing that Milner was also bound for Danieli's, I asked if a room had been kept for him, and learnt that it had not. Thinking it a dreadful thing that so great a man should be inconvenienced by so stupid a vexation, I told them to book the room in his name. I must have looked pensive as I left Danieli's, for I was hailed by Sir Hubert Miller, another of the passengers, asking me whether I had lost sixpence; and was immediately invited to his charming apartment as his guest for a week: the only instance in my life when a good deed has met with immediate reward. I dined with Milner, visited churches with him, and admired his ever youthful and receptive interest in everything—not least his sympathy with the whimsical expression of the dragon in Saint George of the Slavs.

II

I drank in my first Home leave with an almost aching intensity, partly because it was my first, but even more as the beginning of a momentous admiration.

I spoke on my first page of the romantic parentage of my uncle, Henry John Cockayne Cust. He was a generation senior to me, but he had so deeply impressed all who knew or even met him in his youth as well as afterwards that I am emboldened to recall from their memories something of that golden emergent individuality as it was before I myself passed under his spell. He stands forth, as Captain of the Oppidans at Eton, with the profile of a Greek coin, presenting the sword of honour to Roberts, victor of Kandahar, "the most remarkable performance," wrote Henry Broadbent, "of my Eton experience." Whatever he did there, in School or Field, he did with an incomparable ease and grace; with dazzling promise of great achievement. Arthur Benson told me at Cambridge towards the end of his life that another Eton master who had under him in succession Rosebery, Curzon and Cust, had of the three chosen Cust as the future Prime Minister. At Cambridge I found him still remembered as an "Apostle," as Prometheus in *The Birds,* as Teucer in the *Ajax,* as the most brilliant undergraduate. As a Scholar of Trinity and a barrister-at-law he presented himself in Paris for the *Baccalauréat en Droit* and with three French candidates attained the final select for *viva voce* questioning. *"Messieurs,"* demanded the Examiner, *"qu'est-ce que c'est qu'une théorie?"* His compatriots stared at him and at each other (as well they might) but answered never a word.

Harry, his head throbbing with legal jargon and fresh from a generous luncheon of port and fierce black coffee, replied at once as if enouncing a standard definition: *"Une théorie, Monsieur le Juge, c'est une généralisation centralisatrice."* The Examiner, bracing himself and looking intently upon the *insulaire*, requested him to oblige once more. Harry did so, and passed out at the head of the list. He was never able to discover whether his improvisation had been sublime or bathetic, and years later I heard Lord Haldane, after deep thought, pronounce himself unable to decide.

Harry was a member not only of the dazzling and much discussed company of the Souls ("the most brilliant of us all" was their leader's considered judgment) but also of the small and exclusive Club, named after Crabbet Park. At this beautiful and hospitable seat Curzon, Wyndham,[12] Lord Crewe, Esmé Howard, George Leveson Gower and a few others joined their host, Wilfrid Blunt, for a week annually to contend in games, in talk, and in verse competition, the prize for which, voted at dinner, was a Georgian silver goblet, inscribed: "Crabbed age and youth cannot live together." Harry was awarded it one year for a poem in the metre of Myers's *St Paul*, unblushingly Aristophanic but to him so unworthy that he had torn it in two and thrown it away. It was picked up and unanimously acclaimed as the best. They talked through that night and bathed at dawn; after which Harry and the future Viceroy defeated the future Secretary for Ireland and their poet host at lawn-tennis, all four stark naked, until breakfast.

He was Conservative Member for the Stamford Division of Lincolnshire when in 1892 he met William Waldorf Astor at a dinner party. Astor listened to his conversation and, as soon as the ladies had retired, crossed over and offered him the editorship of *The Pall Mall Gazette,* just bought by him from its Liberal owner. Harry accepted, and entered journalism on the spot. In a few weeks he had gathered around him a galaxy of talent and had raised *The Pall Mall Gazette* to a height of renown which (I believe Fleet Street would admit) has been attained by no other evening paper in England, before or since. Henley was his early mentor; Rudyard Kipling, H. G. Wells, George Steevens, afterwards the most famous war correspondent of his time, Charles Whibley, his assistant editor Iwan Muller, George Street, and Mrs Meynell were on the staff or his constant contributors. He printed several poems by Stevenson including *Blows the wind to-day and the sun and rain are flying*. I find inscribed on the flyleaf of *Mr Britling Sees It Through:*

---

[12] He defined the Club as meeting "to play lawn-tennis, the piano, the fool and other instruments of gaiety". Shane Leslie.

"To the Perfect Editor"; on that of *What is Coming?*: "To God's own Editor"; and on *The World Set Free:*

> To the Honorable
> H. C. Cust.
> Noblest and Best of
> Editors,
> Inventor of Authors,
> Friend of Letters,
> from his affectionate contributor
> H. G. WELLS.

The praise is not too high. From his own leading articles, often composed as he was dressing for dinner, from the *Wares of Autolycus,* with Alice Meynell's delicate reflective essays, from the young poetry he always encouraged, could be gathered a presentment of much that was best and most lasting in the political, social and literary life and thought of the early 'nineties. *The Pall Mall Gazette* was I believe the first journal to start literary competitions—"for the most pathetic line in literature" and so on; the first to include one poem at least in every issue. It was in this series that there appeared unsigned in January 1895 *Non Nobis,* which Quiller-Couch found worthy to be included with the great anonymous in the *Oxford Book of English Verse,* discovering the name Henry Cust for the second edition. Payment for poems was arbitrary, according as the editor liked the verse, so that the poet never had any idea what he was going to receive. Posters were witty, not to say flippant: on the rumoured disgrace of the Grand Old Man of China *The Pall Mall Gazette* placard ran: "LI CHANG? HUNG?"

The Crabbet Club pretended to be shocked by the spectacle of Harry beating Fleet Street at its own game:

Nov. 25th, 1892.

My Dear Cust,

I feel it incumbent upon me as President of the C.C. to write to you a few words of warning in regard to the dangerous form of public life on which you are about to embark.... We have as examples before us Stead and Morley, who have made use of *The Pall Mall* as a stepping stone to their positions of dull respectability.... You have been put forward at this critical moment of England's social history to do battle against the Non-Conformist Conscience. ... The Club has its eye on you.

Yours ever presidentially,
WILFRID SCAWEN BLUNT,
President C.C.

An incorrect attribution of Robert Hichens's *Green Carnation,* which had continued what *Punch* and *Patience* had begun for the aesthetic movement, drew a characteristic reproof from Oscar Wilde:

To the Editor of *The Pall Mall Gazette.*
Sir,
Kindly allow me to contradict, in the most emphatic manner, the suggestion, made in your issue of Thursday last, and since then copied into many newspapers, that I am the author of *The Green Carnation.* I invented that magnificent flower. But with the middle-class and mediocre book that usurps its strangely beautiful name I have, I need hardly say, nothing to do. The Flower is a work of art. The book is not.

I remain, Sir,
Your obedient servant,
OSCAR WILDE.

Worthing.

In comparison with these W. G. Grace, evading a review of Daft's book on Cricket, or pressed hard for his Memoirs, strikes a plaintive, almost a pathetic note. Even between the wickets the Doctor was not safe from *The Pall Mall Gazette.*

21a Berners Street,
June 13th, 1895.

Dear Mr Cust,
The article will do, but I do not consider it one of my best. I have corrected all the mistakes I can find but please let me look over it again as I am very tired. Someone came to me this afternoon at Lords and wanted the Proof, but as I had never read it, I could not let him have it. If you had mentioned in your letter that you wanted it for this afternoon, I would have gone without luncheon and got it ready for you. You paper gentlemen think I have nothing else to do on the cricket field but to look after your interests. Never mind, you have got the article and I am glad to oblige you.

Yours truly,
W. G. GRACE.

And he writes from Kennington Oval: "... In case you cannot find all you want in the Biog. I could do something for you in a fortnight's time, but not now as I am very tired." A sterner voice is wafted from "The Pines," Putney:

May 7th, 1893.

Dear Sir,
I am sorry that I did not make my meaning as clear as I certainly thought I must have made it to your emissary, when accosted by him without any sort of introduction and solicited for some sort of contribution to *The Pall Mall Gazette.* A courteous refusal may be none the less a decisive refusal: and such a refusal I supposed myself—wrongly it would seem—to have ex-

pressed as unmistakably as it could possibly have been conveyed in the bluntest and most brusque form of expression. But as the civility with which your proposal was declined would appear to have misled you as to the decision with which it was rejected, I am compelled to point out one very sufficient reason why it is obviously impossible for me to entertain it. I need only refer you to the third page of your issue of April 6th. You will there find a long anonymous letter in large type headed—

Mr Theodore Watts—Critic? . . .

I am, Sir,

Your obedient servant,

A. C. SWINBURNE.

(This is clearly before T. W. enlarged his name, to receive immediately a post-card with no other matter but the address: "Theodore! What's Dunton?" and the signature "J. M. Whistler.")

The Pall Mall Gazette bull-dog, Lobengula (commemorated by a sonnet in his master's Poems), became a London figure:

The Central News Limited,

5 New Bridge Street,

London, E.C.

Dec. 27th, 1893.

Dear Mann,

You mentioned on Saturday that the dog sold to Mr Cust was to be kept at *The Pall Mall* Office and that there are already a number of dogs of various breeds quartered at that office. Mr Moore is interested in the matter and would be glad if you could jot down a few notes of what you saw at *The Pall Mall* Office, that is about the dogs, about Cust's personal appearance, whether he is a judge of dogs, etc. and what sort of a place his editorial sanctum is. Also could you supply a photo of the pup's mother or father or both. If you could jot down these points tonight or tomorrow and send them along to the office we shall be much obliged.

Yours sincerely,

JOHN JENNINGS.

R. J. S. Mann, Esq.,

House of Commons, S.W.

P.S. We particularly want a complete pedigree of the dog sold to Cust.

Early in the day there had been warnings, sometimes whimsical in character, that the relations between proprietor and editor might become delicate:

Lansdowne House,

Berkeley Square,

W.

Dec. 16th, 1893.

Dear Mr Cust,

I have decided to adopt your good suggestion that I should call "any morning at 7.30" at the Gazette office, and see the busy morning's work commenced at that early hour. I intend to arrive there at 7.45 and shall wait ten minutes to see whoever is in charge. If no one of the staff of the paper can be found at 7.55 I shall leave this note. You always get the better of me on so many points that it makes me merry to be able to score now and then.

Wishing you a pleasant Xmas holiday, believe me,

Sincerely yours,

W. W. ASTOR.

The note was, clearly, "left."

When Harry Cust went from *The Pall Mall,* the entire staff, including the compositors, printer's devils, and the doorkeeper, offered to resign with him. The *Pall Mall poster,* his last, read *Qui Cust-odit caveat;* the family motto, which he had in early life adopted for his bookplate, elevated from a precept to a menace. A bound and illuminated address signed by the father and the clerk of the compositors' and readers' chapel, records that: "We feel that you have been in touch with us in a way that no other editor has been," and expresses "our heartfelt regret at your departure from us." And indeed, with the disappearance from Fleet Street of that swift, human intellect, planing over varied fields of thought and action, the journalism of the time lost a much-needed and unreplaced enhancement.[18]

But his success as an editor had conflicted with his parliamentary career. In the Election of 1895 he did not stand, and he was out of Parliament until his return in 1901 for Bermondsey, whence he was swept, with most of his Party, by the overwhelming Liberal victory of 1906.

In the spring of 1910 he visited Egypt with his wife. From thence we made the pilgrimage to Jerusalem together, absorbing even in those few days the austere distinction of the landscape and the brooding poignancy of the atmosphere. As we stood on the Mount of Olives watching the sun set beyond the City, he repeated musingly the stanzas from *In Memoriam* beginning:

> When Lazarus left his charnel cave,

and as he reached the lines

> A solemn radiance even crowned
> The purple brows of Olivet

I remember the last rays wrapped the whole mountain in glory.

Wherever Henry Cust went, in England, on the Continent or in the

---

[18] "The progressives . . . attracted not a few Conservatives. . . . The brilliant Harry Cust, for instance, who from 1892 to 1896 edited *The Pall Mall Gazette* as a Conservative paper, gave consistent support to the progressive cause." R. C. K. Ensor, *England, 1870-1914. Hinc,* in part, *illae lacrimae.*

East, his wide knowledge and deep appreciation of the humanities awoke in others an interest which survived his departure, and an affection and admiration for himself which have not even yet passed away. He could throw an atmosphere of friendliness round him like sunshine. Although his visit to Egypt and Palestine was as remote as 1910 and he spent but a few weeks between them, yet, when I revisited Palestine in 1931 and Egypt in 1934, I came across Englishmen, Frenchmen, Egyptians and Armenians whose memories of him were as fresh as if he had been with them but the year before.

He never stood for Parliament after 1906. Throughout his life Fate had given, taken away, and given again, with an almost rhythmical irony. He was conscious of this himself. In one of his many copies of Goethe I find pencilled at some crisis in his thirties the words: "Crooked eclipses 'gainst his glory fight." After long frustration came, with the War, an opportunity of serving his country. As Chairman of the Central Committee for National Patriotic Organizations (which anticipated by two years Crewe House and the activities of Lord Northcliffe) he won a public tribute from the Prime Minister, when Mr Asquith referred to him in the House of Commons as "Mr Henry Cust, to whom the country owes a great debt of gratitude for unremitting services throughout the War". To the satisfaction of public duty had been added deep happiness in a beautiful and romantic home. But the rhythm of his destiny was inexorable. The straining toil had weakened the resistance of a heart never strong and, struck down suddenly by pneumonia, on 2 March 1917, Harry Cust died.

Δάφνις ἔβα ῥόον

Hard it is to re-create for others the image of sheer brilliancy without the material framing of demonstrable achievement in public life—political, administrative, diplomatic, or artistic. As I look on my lines they seem, compared with what he was, the mere *grisaille* cartoon of some heroic Venetian radiance.

Harry never pretended an interest in children or boys, even when closely related to him, and I had seen hardly anything of him until my latter Cambridge vacations. But then his kindness grew until he treated me almost as a son. From the first I was fascinated by the swiftness and concision of his comments upon his panorama of the world, and exalted, as youth is, by the suddenly extended intellectual horizons he opened. Round his table in St James's Lodge, Delahay Street (house and street now engulfed by the Board of Education), you encountered, magically assimilated to the surroundings, a variety of social experience ranging

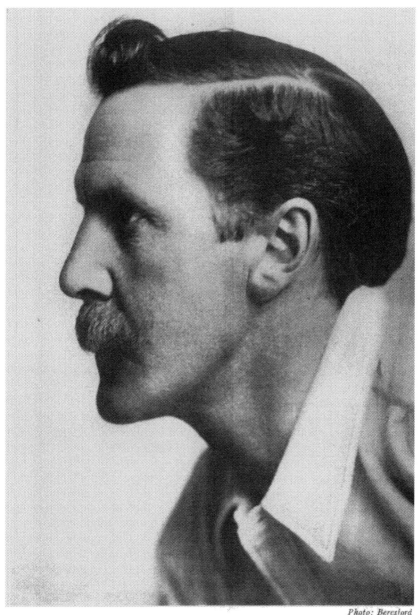

HENRY JOHN COCKAYNE CUST

from the presence together of Ras Makonnen of Abyssinia and the Archbishop of Armagh, to a combination during the heat of some political controversy of Mr Asquith, Prime Minister, and Mr Balfour, Leader of the Opposition. H. G. Wells has in *The New Machiavelli* described one of these parties at which a fire broke out in the drawing-room above. The water from the hoses dripped through the ceiling and the butler draped bath-towels round the shoulders of the guests; while the talk went triumphantly on until after midnight.

As a conversational *agent provocateur* Harry was supreme; not only witty himself, but the cause of wit in other men. The company became under his wand an orchestra, from each instrument of which he could draw with a distinguished but unstudied virtuosity the appropriate tone, colour and dissonance. He waged a standing and successful warfare against the holder forth, the anecdotist, the retailer of sporting or social insignificances.

His intellectual presence of mind never failed with the immediate, the unrehearsed *parola rivelatrice*. Questioned as to what he proposed doing when the Chamberlain Protectionist controversy first broke upon the Conservative Party, he replied instantly that he had nailed his colours to the fence. Suddenly asked to describe a too good-looking young man, he provided his immediate pedigree: "By Truefitt, out of Madame Tussaud." Shortly before the War, I brought Lord Kitchener to luncheon with him at his house. The eye of the collector soon lit upon a small but valuable Chien Lung tea-pot. Moved by fear from audacity to recklessness, Harry began to say how greatly the family were looking forward to the honour of his guest's visit to Ashridge: "one of the finest collections of china in England, Field-Marshal—and no inventory." I felt that another joke of this calibre might well lose me my place, but to my relief the victim received it laughingly in good part. His resourcefulness was no less immediate in action. Mr Winston Churchill has recorded [14] in a paragraph on rowdy election meetings that:

In Great Britain they very rarely try to hurt you. If they do, well then it becomes a simple proposition of self-defence. Harry Cust, at a Meeting in his fight for South Lambeth [Bermondsey], suddenly noticed an enormous man advancing on him in a pugilistic attitude. He took off his coat and squared up to him, whispering to his friends behind him: "Hold me back! hold me back!"

Again, Wilfrid Blunt tells how

Harry was at Lynn with Asquith and Herbert Gladstone, and the suffragettes striking Asquith in the face with their fists, Harry intervened as

[14] *Thoughts and Adventures,* pp. 203-4.

Secretary of the Golf Club (of which he was not a member), telling the
women that whatever their dispute with the Prime Minister might be, it was
impossible that they should be allowed to walk on the grass, as it was against
the regulations of the Club. This impressed them and they desisted from
their assaults.[15]

Harry combined in his personality a variety of accomplishments and
interests rare even in the days of Crabbet, now hardly ever found together. Like most commodities of life they are now distributed amongst
a larger number of persons: the gold is beaten thinner. The physical and
the intellectual sides of life—sport and letters—have been divorced.
Bloomsbury and Chelsea are steeped in thought—the only horses they
have ever seen are the bronze horses of St Mark, while Newmarket and
Melton could (in Macaulay's phrase) as soon decipher a Babylonian
brick as a *Cantica* of Dante. Harry read the *Georgics* driving in his
dog-cart to the Meet. Like Charles James Fox he would cap quotations
from Horace while walking down St James's Street after a dance at
three in the morning. His kindness and the trouble he would take for
a neighbour (in the Samaritan sense) were unbounded and he would
give a no less concentrated and eager attention to a humble stranger or
obscure kinsman than to a wit or a statesman. Never could he be at less
than concert pitch. Twice only have I felt myself close to the springs of
life: when under the "deep questionings that probe to endless dole" of
T. E. Lawrence, and when I drank at that fountain of joy—Henry Cust.
    A recumbent marble effigy covers his ashes in the little church at
Belton, near the ancestral home he did not live to inherit. The monument is inscribed above "Of all sorts enchantingly beloved" and below—
the grandeur of Longinus:

$$ὕψος \ μεγαλοφροσύνης \ ἀπήχημα.$$
Sublimity, the echo of a great soul.

The sculptor was his wife. It is such a piece of work as may well make
those who come after us pause awhile and wonder about one who apparently did so little, yet was so much. His lyric also, *Non Nobis*—even
more, perhaps, her poems (wrought in the intervals of sculpture) dedicated *Dilectissimo*—may keep his spirit living in the minds of men:

A Thanksgiving

I who the watcher of your ways have been,
I who the radiance of your days have seen,
                Thank God.

[15] Diaries.

I who the fire of your mind have known,
I who in flame of your soul have grown,
> Thank God.

I who to you owe each least thought,
I who by you am less than naught,
> Thank God.

I who in you found all life's stay,
I who for you lived all life's day,
> Thank God.

I who from you draw all life's light,
I who for you live through life's night,
> Thank God, thank God.

The thought, humbly and in degree, is mine also, for my debt to him is incalculable—the hint, the flash of shining treasure unrevealed; "the glimpse of an immortal weather". To be with him was delight. His place in my life cannot be filled. I think that even now, a score of years after his death, there are still some who, remembering him, sigh in Shakespeare's tremendous homage: "Would I were with him, wheresomever he is."

CHAPTER THREE

1905–1907

Quant au douanier c'est notre affaire,
Tout comme un autre il aime à plaire.
                                    CARMEN.

I

FROM surroundings and atmosphere such as these I returned to Egypt in July 1905 with a homesickness approaching despair. My journey across Europe to catch the Austrian Lloyd at Trieste was enlivened but retarded by meeting in the train an Italian patriot so patient of my crudities and my ignorance of his language, literature and politics, so appreciative of the Barolo (*tipo classico*) in which we continued to pledge one another that, when he got out at Verona, I fell into a dreamless sleep, missing the Mestre connection and waking only with a start in a midnight and trainless Venice. My bewilderment was so obvious that a lady in the compartment, foreign but speaking fair English, questioned me, ordered her gondolier on the platform to embark my luggage, and took me to a palace on a Rio out of the Grand Canal. She gave me supper, questioned me about Egypt, and returned me to the station for the one-thirty train to Trieste. I have never been able to identify her, and, be she alive or dead, can only thank her again now. When I reached the platform I found that this train would not, in fact, start until seven-thirty, nor reach Trieste until noon; the *Semiramis* weighing anchor at twelve-thirty. I got into a carriage, disposed my things under and about me, and went to sleep. We started punctually, but soon after Mestre had so bad a breakdown that we clearly could not reach Trieste until well after one: despair for an unsuccessful junior not yet confirmed in his appointment and arriving five days late from his first, premature and ill-deserved holiday. I lost control, and getting down at half a dozen alternate stations despatched to the Captain telegrams in English, French, German, and Italian from

40

Mr Robinson, the *famille* Duval, Ritter von Finckelstein and Commendatore Caracciolo, begging him to accord each but one hour's grace. I then, as the Arabs say, committed my affair to Allah. We reached the town station at one-thirty. It was nearly two o'clock before my cab had trailed me along the blinding white Molo San Carlo and I saw, with mingled relief and terror, the Blue Peter and the Austrian Lloyd house-flag floating over a still moored *Semiramis*. I clambered up the gangway, ticket and passport in hand, and presented them to an officer standing in front of a small group, feeling that it was vital for me not to look at the sheaf of papers he was grasping. "Where are the rest of the party?" he said. I could only answer that I was travelling alone, had seen no others, was glad to be in time myself; and achieving my cabin with as slow a haste as I dared, locked myself in until, after waiting a further ten minutes, the Captain abandoned "the rest" and put to sea, with an extra revolution or two to make up for lost time. Pride I think forbade him to ask me point-blank whether I had sent the telegrams, nor, I suppose, could he make enquiries, still less act upon suspicion; but the four days' voyage to Alexandria proved too short for me to re-establish my position with him, his officers, or even my fellow-passengers.

In those days the Egyptian Ministers and Under-Secretaries, with their skeleton Secretariats, descended for the summer to Ramleh, once the garden suburb of Alexandria and even now far more a garden than that solid concrete block, the Garden City of Cairo. Suites of rooms were taken for offices in the Casino Hotel, San Stefano. Most of us did what work there was to do on balconies facing towards the sea under high glass roofs. Below there was the perpetual din of dining and dancing at night, children playing and screaming in the forenoon, *consommations* in the afternoon, and marble-topped tables being cleared, cleaned, and rapped to call up a corps of European and Berberin waiters; whose toils —*labor actus in orbem*—seemed to pause but never to cease, even in the small hours of the morning. I knew no one in the hotel (where I had a stuffy little room over the entrance, away from the sea, for thirteen shillings a day full pension), and at that time no one in Alexandria; so I went for long walks alone by the canals or along the eastern shores without meeting a soul; sometimes bathing, sometimes riding, once combining both in an experimental gallop naked to see what it was like, and proving it to be better adapted for bronze or marble than for human contours. I renewed my Cairo friendship with Harry de la Rose Farnall, C.B., C.M.G., of the Foreign Office, British Commissioner of the Caisse de la Dette, at that time one of the few sinecures surviving outside the Russian Empire. Farnall combined, with the features and expression of a Praying Mantis and the clothes of a Regency Beau, a heart of gold and an outlook encyclopaedic in range but capable of transmuting even Shelley into factual, statistical prose. All three aspects come back to me as I see him stopping after a two-miles exposition of the Berne Postal Convention, to exclaim with surprise that he had his left and right buttoned boots on the wrong feet. (Who else could have put them on thus, or walked in them for ten yards along the sands?) Having no buttonhook with him, he must return to the hotel and I must dine with him in compensation for the loss of my walk.[1] Without personal influence on my life he nevertheless put into my hands the small poorly printed volume that led me into communion, how remote and unworthy soever, with Dante.

The guilty couples dining in the Casino seemed to fit each other not so very much better than Farnall's boots, and I often thought they would be at least as happy with their respective *légitimes*. If, as Balzac tells us, *"Les grands amours commencent dans le champagne et finissent dans la tisane"*, these silent pairs, plunged they never so deep in Bollinger, were spiritually well advanced in the *tisane* stage.

In the autumn I returned to that Cairo which Dean Butcher used to describe as The Death of the Soul—as indeed to those without work or interest it often proved to be.

On New Year's Day I went to the Early Service and was surprised to find myself the whole congregation. The priest peered round the vestry door in his lay clothes, hoping against hope for an early breakfast, but I fixed him with an earnest beady eye and in two minutes he came up to the scratch and went through the service for me, altering the Rubric and the person of the verbs as was seeming.

The lavish modernity of Wells's filing and reduplicating apparatus was my first glimpse of the extent to which people will let themselves go over stationery when they do not have to pay for it themselves, and was in comic contrast with the primitive and pleasant haphazardry of the Secretariat.

To the office at 5.30 to get a *dossier* for Mitchell Innes. The orderly, who keeps the key, had not turned up, and I was reduced to breaking open the doors by running at them with my clenched fists.

My relations with Wells went from bad to worse. That the Secretary of his new Department should be an amateur, however eager, was hard

---

[1] "Farnall took the solar eclipse with delightful earnestness and sat for 20 minutes (until Totality) with a towel over his head, so that his eyes might be properly receptive." In order to study views and pictures for colour and design rather than subject he had formed the arresting habit of standing astride with his back to them and gazing upon them from between his legs.

on him, and not altogether easy for me. This was my first personal
experience of the evils of unintelligent posting, none the less miserable—
like others which I was to encounter intermittently throughout my
career—because it was not altogether the fault of the posting authorities.
The reasoning seemed so simple and obvious. There was no work for
me in the Secretariat. There was no Secretary to the Department of
Mines. Why bring in fresh blood when you could use the man on the
spot and, incidentally, break in a raw Cambridge cub? Fortunately
(though I thought not so at the time), there fell vacant an Inspectorship
of the Customs Administration, and Chitty Bey, the Director-General,
applied to the Finance for an "educated man". The Adviser grasped
occasion by the skirt. He decided to relieve Wells of me—and me of
Wells—and, by a happy discard from weakness, to crown Chitty's ambition. The proposal, for so it was tactfully disguised, was treble agony to
me; as reflecting on my work, as exiling me from the Cabinet-atmosphere
and the Capital, and (in my snobbish apprehension worst of all) as
relegating me to the search of passengers' baggage for lace, spirits and
cigars. On the other hand I was enjoying my work in the Egyptian mines
about as much as the Athenians did theirs in the quarries of Syracuse.
Besides, young men should accept what they were offered, and be thankful. I therefore accepted, ἑκων ἀέκοντί γε θύμῳ, before the proposal
should become an order.

Three days before leaving,

Lady Cromer handed me a Latin invitation which the Lord had received
from the University of Aberdeen (quadringentenary celebration) and bade me
answer it in the same tongue. I, not aware that a Judge and another man had
evaded the offer, on the plea of having neither Lexicon nor Latin books,
undertook to do it most cheerfully: I had no books of any kind, but furbished
up a good Roman roll, which I gave her when she came to tea. She hadn't
been gone an hour when I got a note, asking me to luncheon and telling me
the Lord had called it "devilish" good. I found the old man very much
pleased about it: he said he felt an infernal hypocrite signing it, and was
quite sure he'd be found out, etc. Gave me a copy of his translation from the
Greek Anthology, and hoped that the 'Varsities would retain Greek.

This was music at the close, and I left for Alexandria (where a scholar
or autograph hunter stole my Anthology within three hours) in relatively good heart. Before leaving I gave my cigarette-case to a friend.
I smoked my pipe continuously for the three hours' journey and, five
minutes before arrival, flung it, together with pouch and tobacco, out of
the window, to enter for some years into This Freedom of a non-smoker.

Chitty Bey, now Sir Arthur Chitty, K.C.B., who had, and deserved, the reputation of being the Sir Robert Hart of Egypt, welcomed, as afterwards he always treated me not only kindly but sensibly.

He was very decent: said he thought I should dislike my work but hoped I would take to it. Sensible opinions.

Many a Chief who had made his name over Customs Administration would have told me that Customs was my chance in life, and how lucky I was to have ascended into the Customs. The consequence of his enlightened gambit was that I soon found myself, though never technically *douanier d'âme,* thrilled with interest in and admiration of the mighty machine which was Chitty Bey's creation. Chitty gave his genius for the details of administration, waking and (most of us believed) sleeping, to the prosperity of the Customs and to the happiness of the Egyptians serving therein; with the natural result that in the country of all others where people really know whether they are liked or not, this shy, silent, unsociable man was then, and for generations is likely to be remembered as "Chitty Bey—*Wallāhī Rāgil Tāyib:* By God, a good man". Now for the first (I have since thought for the last) time I contemplated, from within, a little world where all was, really and demonstrably, for the best. Vast sums of money—two odd millions of it merely from a stream of tobacco pouring through a narrow wicket to re-issue therefrom shortly as Egyptian cigarettes—were collected over the two miles of Customs area, to say nothing of Port Said, Suez and Damietta; and it was largely owing to the Director-General's ruthless but simple system of routine checkings and incalculable counter-checkings that the immense majority of these riches flowed, humanly speaking undiverted, into the Public Fisc. Things had not always been so, for there was still shown a splendid villa erected by an official who had been in control of the valuation of cotton piece goods, and which was called in the Customs "Manchester House". Chitty, with Gorst, had made the Direct Taxes Department, and here also it was manifest—and acknowledged—that everything was going automatically right: *et tout ce qu'il contrôe est fort bien contrôlé.* The Egyptian Customs was a microcosm of Alexandria: polyglot, Levantine if you will, but friendly, interesting, entertaining and generally delightful. Officially, as well as commercially, Alexandria was nearer to Europe than Cairo; and, remarkably for those old Islamic days, the *repos hebdomadaire* was kept, both in the city and on the quays, not as elsewhere on Friday, but on the Christian Sunday. Besides the half-dozen British *douaniers* there were Moslems of good family; Gheriāni, a Customs as well as a religious fanatic, and Rāsem Bey, a skilled amateur photographer; amusing Copts,

like Negiīb Bey on the Khedivíeh Quay ("the overwork, dear Sir, from
these pimps of Pilgrims!"); Maatum Bey, whose admiration for *Edouard
Sept, ce parfait gentleman,* had not saved him from financial *embête-
ments,* both in the Customs and *en Ville;* the tender and cultivated
Barker, ex-Private Secretary to the Empress Elizabeth of Austria, who
had been with H.I.M. when the Hapsburg raven pecked the nectarine
out of her hand and who (even more exciting for me) could add up
simultaneously three columns of figures. Finally, there was the *Directeur
Local des Douanes d'Alexandrie,* Khalīl Pasha Hamdi Hamāda, a
capable, despotic and, I found, most agreeable Damascene.[2]

The promotion of one of the two *Sous-Directeurs,* an Englishman,
which had indirectly caused my vacancy, provided me with an example
of the flouting of patient merit which at the time almost overset my
belief in the Immanent Justice. For years this official had come early
to his work and had stayed at it long after office hours. He had kept an
official diary in Arabic and had never failed to button up his jacket
before entering the Pasha's presence. As a reward for his conscientious
deference, he was criticized, blamed, kept waiting, interrupted, and
treated as though he were a *stagiaira,* a probationary clerk, who had no
hope of being confirmed in his appointment. His successor, the breezy
young Morice Bey (his father had been made a Pasha) [3]—Duggie—
dressed with the dash of his great prototype on the last page of our
illustrated weeklies; arriving hours after time and throwing in his hand
to his colleague Gammāl Bey long before the office shut; fluent enough
in a sulphurous brand of local Alexandrian, but quite incapable of keeping a diary in Arabic (as of bothering to keep one in any language), was
from the first a complete success with his Chief, his colleagues, and the
staff in general. As he strolled into the *Direction,* you heard: *"Y'Ahmad,
hāt itnain 'áhwa mazbūta"*—"Bring two exact (or accurate) coffees"—
one of which Duggie would be good enough to sip, leaning against the
Pasha's desk and óffering him a cigarette from a jewelled case. Duggie
was from the first very kind to me, taking me with him into these and
other like informalities, where I learnt that in an official dispute both
sides were prepared to admit *en principe* suggestions which, presented
first through the clerks, or in a departmental note, they would have
indignantly scouted.

As an Inspector of the *Direction Générale,* it was my duty to make
routine and surprise verifications of my Sections (unmistakably defined

2 After the Young Turk Revolution he was appointed Minister of Evkaf in Constantinople
where he promised me, should I ever desire it, a free railway pass to Medina.
3 Sons of Pashas enjoy the courtesy title of Bey.

by Chitty) of the Customs Area, and it was everything to have started on good terms with the Local Director. I had to be in the office by eight, and to begin soon after wandering about Treasury, departments, sheds, and quays, note-book in hand, applying a variety of tests which were cheerfully accepted by the hard-worked officers, and rarely revealed the slightest irregularities, and which I recorded in a diary perused by Chitty at unstated and unpredictable intervals. Or one might have to preside at the Menufîh. Egyptian Customs Duties were at that time 8 per cent. *ad valorem*. If an importer could not or would not pay, the duty was taken in kind in the proportion of eight tooth-brushes, sewing machines, bottles of port, from each hundred of the same. But the Egyptian Government could not pay its officials, still less the Debt coupon, in these commodities, and therefore held a bi-weekly auction of them in a room called the Menufîh. The auctioneer (whose possible collusion with bidders I was there to prevent) was Mîshmish, a little old man gifted with a Periclean eloquence which I have only heard equalled by the boosters proclaiming the illicit pleasures of "Paris Streets" in the World's Fair at Chicago. No printed advertisement could impart one-tenth of his passionate belief in the hygienic value and social prestige of a Balkan depilatory, and I am still under my first surprise that his climax *Alle une, alle due,* and, with a bestial howl, *alle tre,* could meet with so languid a response from the local ring.

Estimation *ad valorem* was especially trying to the Administration in the realm of Art; I wrote from Cairo:

I get my journey paid by the Customs, as six pictures, invoiced at £15, were estimated by our specialist at £160: the owner naturally threatened an action, and I was sent up to re-estimate. They are utter trash, copies of bad copies, and I reduced the value to £30.

The glare, the dust and the rattle of the mule carts and the long paved quays, were equally hard on eyes, ears and feet, and the four night inspections a month, for three hours controlling the Police posts—sometimes in torrential rain—were a new but on the whole agreeable experience. Hashish smugglers introduced their drug in chair-legs, piano pedals, false calves, olives, as well as in unbelievable fastnesses of the human frame. Hashish was forbidden under severe penalties and was said to be worth anything between three and five thousand pounds per ton—about five pounds a kilo. Yet it was always procurable and (in proving your thesis with visitors) you had only to tell your servant to bring you a few piastres' worth for him to return in a couple of minutes with a reeking specimen in his hand. If only hashish eating and smoking had been the climax of Egyptian misfortune! Its successful extirpation by the universally praised but officially unrecognized energies of Russell Pasha prepared the way for the more easily manufactured and smuggled, and less visibly obtrusive heroin; whose subsequent elimination, again by the Pasha, has now induced the continuous sipping of stewed black powdered tea. The craving for some sort of dope, stronger than tobacco, seems endemic in the East. *Et vetabitur semper et retinebitur.*

Illicit traffic was by no means confined to drugs: one day

I was watching the Inspection of Luggage from a French boat from the Lebanon: a Syrian woman, veiled right up (you couldn't see her forehead or eyes) and wearing green silk gloves and stockings with a Tartan check, stooped to get some money from her pocket, and I, who was meditatively thinking how much better black silk hose would have suited her, observed a fairly thick piece of metal pointing down her leg. Having no competence to investigate the affair myself, I called one of the Female Searchers (kind Mrs. Brown), and she, grasping the lady's hand and leading her aside, soon returned with a revolver loaded in all six chambers and three very efficient knives which she had plucked from the patient's garters. It was no criminal business, but merely that the husband wished to avoid paying Duty.

Immense quantities of arms and ammunition were continually being confiscated together with books, postcards and pictures *contre les mœurs publiques;* and from time to time Duggie and I would take a Customs launch freighted with this equivocal and exciting cargo out beyond the harbour and there consign to the deep Mausers and Brownings; belt after belt, gross after gross of cartridges; polyglot incitements to anarchy; prurient postcards, and gilt-framed miniatures attesting at once the delicate artistry and the perverse decadence of *Mittel Europa.* Once we bathed on our way back. I dived from the boat and came up face to face with a staring marine monster; my blood ran too cold for speech but I must have indicated apprehension, for the boatman called, "Fear not, O Bey; *dhōl ashābna*—those are our friends", and the dolphin, who had not been exposed to this sort of thing since Arion, swerved and vanished.

About this time occurred the now forgotten but then absorbing Aqaba incident, a clumsy and pointless try-on by the Sultan Abd al-Hamīd to drive the Turco-Egyptian frontier westward from the Aqaba-Rafa line (the present southern border of Palestine) into the Sinai, toward the Suez Canal. Boundary pillars had been overthrown by Turkish agents. Pan-Islam was canvassed to rally to the Khalífa and on the Wall of Egypt there was darkly discerned the writing of 1914. England was trebly committed to calling this bluff. She could not yield to threats, she could not hand over the territory of an Egypt she had undertaken to protect, and she could not forget that, from the fifteenth century before Christ, history had shown that the Power, whether from East or West, holding the Sinai held Egypt also. A ten days' ultimatum was issued to the Sultan ... and accepted about one hour before the expiry.

The *Lewa,* the most hostile newspaper in Cairo, says that "England having done all that the Sultan commanded, he, in justice and mercy, has acceded to the English requests. Turkey has gained immensely by this: and *all* the other newspapers in the World have been deceived". The Editor, Mustapha Kāmel, was made a Pasha by the Sultan: and is subsidized by Germany. The keenest regretters of the peace are the unhappy Turkish soldiers at Tabah who have, up till now, been fed entirely by the British gun-boats, the neighbouring Beduin being too poor to be worth plundering.

Alexandria is not an obvious city; she requires, before revealing herself, time, study and love. I liked her well, from the Shāria Sharīf Pasha, which has something of the brilliant narrowness of Bond Street, to the sinister rowdiness of the Anastássi, the Gúmruk Quarter and the Attarín Caracol. Under the spell of this Egyptian atmosphere I began to confess myself *anima naturaliter Levantina*—of the Levant of Pharaoh, Solomon, Homer, Alexander, Virgil, St Paul, Dante and Dandolo, *Antony and Cleopatra* and *The Merchant of Venice;* a world that may look back, rather than forward like the Great Continents, but which between Homer and the Sermon on the Mount—the "clear fountain of eternal day"—has given us that whereby we live, move and have our being.

My life was physically hard and unsparing. I had leased for three pounds a month the coastguard cottage on the eastern promontory of Stanley Bay in Ramleh, half surrounded by the sea and never silent from the roaring of the waves, and had there a few books and a small piano; but I was seldom in it. I had become (for the sake of the free stall) operatic critic to *The Egyptian Gazette* and thus absorbed by nightly draughts at the gracious little Zizinia Theatre the unexacting modes and measures of *La Bohême, Tosca, Thäis* and *Lohengrin,* the severest form of Wagner then acceptable south of Naples, though *La Valkiria* and *I Maestri Cantori di Norimberga* were soon to follow. It was something of an effort after ten minutes' walk to the tram into Alexandria, twenty-five minutes' journey and then twenty minutes' walk to the Customs, to return home after duty, change and attend the Opera, write the critique on some marble-topped table, post it, catch the 1.30 a.m. tram—the last—from Alexandria, and catch it again outwards after some four hours' sleep, for next day's work.

In 1906 I took my leave through Greece, staying for an unforgettable week at the British School and living on the Acropolis. The boat from

Patras landed me at Brindisi before 7 a.m. and I went straight to Cook's to enquire for the next train to Milan. The clerk said it went at two. "Heavens!" I cried, "Have I got to stay in this hole seven hours?" I can still, with a flush of shame, see and hear him answer: "I've stayed here for seven years." I found my conduct in this matter so dreadful that I returned a few minutes before the office closed and took the clerk out to luncheon. During that holiday I was through the kindness of Murray Guthrie offered a position in the National Discount Company, but considered my gift for technical finance too slender to justify my acceptance.

At the end of the year Chitty Bey left the Customs to become Adviser to the Ministry of the Interior.

Chitty left on Friday amid universal mourning: I managed to see him and let him have some written suggestions (by request) as to *"Expédition par chemins de fer des marchandises dédouanées"*. That evening Morice and I gave a little dinner at the club for Hamāda Pasha and the other high Customs officials. Having heard from Chitty's private secretary that he was leaving by the 11.30 we all turned up to see him off, but he had misinformed his secretary purposely, and left at 6 a.m. without a soul there. Typically.

He was not to get away so easily when after two years of uncertainties and difficulties, which included the assassination of Būtros Pasha, he finally retired from the Service, and the road from Shepheard's Hotel to the station was for two hours completely blocked by the stream of Pashas, Omdas, Shaikhs and countless Government officials, drawn by grateful affection from the remotest ends of Egypt to press the Bey's hand for the last time.

Two particular debts I owe to my time in the Customs. The first is that dull, negative, precautionary viritue, rare in men, unknown to women: a Customs conscience. Far from considering Customs evasion an indifferent, almost a meritorious action, the thought of any cash deflected from that till, and the resulting disappointment to the Heads of Sections, the Accounts Branch, even the Statistical Department, to say nothing of the Director-General, still eats into my flesh. The second is the happiness of walking round and about the quays of ports and harbours at any hour of the day or night; of watching the leverage of the great cranes; the delicate aerial ways of the coal-shoots (waiting to be etched by Muirhead Bone) and the long ramparts of moored ships where

I see the cabin window bright,
I hear the bell struck in the night.

Chitty Bey was succeeded but never replaced, and I had had my fill of the Customs when a telegram arrived appointing me assistant Private Secretary to Sir Vincent Corbett, the Financial Adviser.

Last Wednesday Lewis sent for me, and said he was sorry to say that the Finance had stolen me away. He was good enough to add that he was very pleased with my work, and that he had recommended me for an increase of screw, i.e. to thirty pounds a month. However, I fear my transfer will do away with any idea of that—not that I care particularly.

II

I found the Ministry of Finance very much as I had left it. In the Financial Adviser's office Etherington Smith had succeeded Bowden Smith (Amurath to Amurath), and there was emphatically not enough work for two.

Here am I, hard on twenty-six, with a working knowledge of English, French, Italian and Arabic; of Customs, Mines, Secretariat and F.A.'s Office; of pleasing manners and a desire to labour, and Nothing To Do!

Every morning the Financial Adviser visited the Lord (of whom he was in effect Prime Minister) for his daily interview, and Etherington and I learnt to draw from his expression deductions which sometimes proved surprisingly accurate. For the Lord was no respecter of persons, and the weight of his prestige could on occasion impart a dread momentum to his impact. The power of Lord Cromer's name was tremendous,[4] and the status of the Agency,[5] in official precedence ranking with the other Consulates General, wholly without the splendours of a Viceroy, an Indian or Colonial Governor or an Ambassador, amounted in Egypt, for foreigners as well as Egyptians, to that of 10 Downing Street multiplied by Buckingham Palace. The Egyptian Princess Nazli Fazïl told me that she was sitting once with her cousin the Khedive Tewfik when a shout was heard far down the street. "Listen", he muttered, and turned pale. "I recognize the cries of the Sais before the carriage of Baring. Who knows what he is coming to say to me?" On a day of high political tension Cairo had been reassured by the mere sight of that well-known figure driving across the bridge to play tennis Gezira. Recommendations for employment issuing from the quarter where the will became the fact were in effect orders; so much so that it was not until a number had been received by comparatively minor officials that they were discovered to have emanated from one of the Agency Cavasses,

---

[4] ". . . There is a great deal of friction between the Civilians and the Military. There would be more if the Civil were not represented by Lord Cromer, who don't allow anyone else, military or divine, to have much of a show. It works well enough." Spring Rice, 1901.

[5] His Britannic Majesty's Diplomatic Agency and Consulate General; during the Protectorate and until the Anglo-Egyptian Treaty of 1936, The Residency; now The British Embassy.

who was selling official note-paper at five pounds a sheet—the prospective candidate supplying his own requirements in a script as near as he could get to the notorious illegibility of the Lord. Of his influence on the home front I saw later many proofs. Lord Salisbury had been Prime Minister as well as Foreign Secretary; redoubtable as either, omnipotent as both. I found a telegram addressed to him by the British Consul-General thanking him for instructions but informing him that the previous Cairo telegram had been intended to announce, not what he proposed doing, but what he had already done. Only once was his authoritative impatience of ceremony rumoured to have sustained a reverse. Arriving in London on leave from Egypt he applied for an audience with the King. It was granted—for three days later. Lord Cromer intimated to the Private Secretary that he had hoped to be received that very afternoon, in order that he might catch the night train for his holiday in Scotland. "He seems to take me for the Khedive", answered King Edward.

His reading was wide and deep, as can be seen in his privately-printed Common-place Books. He must be one of the few Hellenists whose approach to ancient has been through modern Greek. His modesty in the two fields of letters and scholarship bordered upon humility, which, however, stopped short of tolerating literary decadence. He went once to the sitting-room of a brilliant young writer who was staying at the Agency. The occupant was out, but the illustrated French volumes he had left on the table were such that the Lord gathered them up, pitched them into the fire, and had poked them well behind the bars before the owner, contemplating from the doorway this Gothic work, waved a Byzantine forefinger, wailing reproachfully, "Savage! Savage!"

The second Lady Cromer was as noble in spirit as in appearance. She cared little for diplomatic and social life, and was far more interested in Egypt, ancient, Saracenic and modern. "Dear Mr Storrs, it will be very kind if you will come with me to-morrow by the 3 o'clock tram to the Pyramids. Yours sincerely, Katherine Cromer." The friendliness, and royal command manner and the simplicity of the object and method of the expedition are equally characteristic.

It is difficult after some thirty years to realize, still more to describe, the shock felt in Egypt on Lord Cromer's retirement; by most, of regret, almost of consternation; by some, of exultation at the simultaneous removal of the driving power, the fly-wheel and particularly the brake from the machine that had for so many years guided and controlled their progress. The effect was heightened by the admirable manner in which the Foreign Office and the Agency had kept the secret until its appearance in Reuter's telegram.

12. iv. 07. I said there would be news this year, and last night at seven an event was announced which will have far more importance than the death of an average reigning sovereign. The Lord has been rather bad for the last three months—living entirely on Benger's Food—and is now simply worn out. As he has worked now for forty-nine years from morn till dewy eve without stopping for meals, and as he does business right through his leave, and has perpetual responsibility combined with eternal heckling and conspiracy, the wonder is that he is alive at all. An old Turk, the Governor of Alexandria, said to me: "God is indeed most knowing, but this is a bad day for Egypt." On Monday I had a talk with Lady C. and the Lord came in, looking terribly old and shaken, and walking very slowly. When I remember trying to make him play tennis at Ashridge in August, the change is shocking. He is too weak to accept a public banquet; so will receive instead a public address in the Opera House. Corbett's making arrangements, which means that all other work is suspended. The Egyptians, acting under fear of and threats from the Khedive, are having nothing to do with it; and quite half the Arabic Press is cursing the Lord.

Three or four clear memories stand out for me from that great gathering. Of all the Egyptian Princes (then, before King Fuad's effective weeding, far more numerous than to-day) only Prince Hussein (who became Sultan during the War) and Prince Said Halīm [6] had the good will or the courage to attend. The International Committee had, with no less tact than taste, delegated to the unofficial head of the French community, Comte de Sérionne, the expression of their sentiments, and I can still see his courteous inclination from the stage toward *Celle,* the gracious associate of the Proconsul, erect in her stage box. Cromer's reply was clear, direct and militant; containing a fateful tribute from the latest of the foreign to the first of the national dictators of Egypt:

"Unless I am much mistaken, a career of great public usefulness lies before the present Minister of Education, Saad Zaghlūl Pasha. He possesses all the qualities necessary to serve his country. He is honest; he is capable; he has the courage of his convictions; he has been abused by many of the less worthy of his own countrymen. These are high qualifications. He should go far." He did.

Lord Cromer was happy in his comparison between Anglo-French relations on his arrival in 1883, when "the two nations looked at each other askance *comme deux chiens de faience",* and when he was rarely mentioned in the local French Press save as *l'infâme Baring,* or, later as *le brutal Cromer* and "recently, when I have been on more than one occasion termed *cet illustre viellard;* which clearly denotes a change of tone".

Both Lord and Lady Cromer gave me books.

[6] Dummy Grand Vizier of Turkey by the beginning of the War: afterwards murdered in Europe.

Treasure the enclosed in the family archives: it shows the extraordinary kindliness of the Lord that he should think of such a thing at such a time. "British Agency, Cairo, 22nd April 1907. Dear Mr. Storrs, I cannot go without asking you to accept a small personal souvenir from myself. I am, therefore, sending you Ricardo's works. If not the father, he was very nearly the father of modern political economy, and maintained his rule until that science was banished by Mr. Gladstone to the planet of Saturn. Very sincerely yours, Cromer."

Although there had been, ever since Gorst had left Egypt, a hint of the weary Titan in his administrative powers, his power remained. His departure was something more significant than the conclusion of the Cromerian Epoch. It was the real end of pre-War Egypt.

III

About this time Philip Graves, Cairo correspondent of *The Egyptian Gazette* (published in Alexandria) and I, for some months joint occupants of a two-roomed flat, were searching for better accommodation.

If I had one decent small room with a cupboard and bookshelf, I believe things would go easy; it is the mingling of Dante with sock suspenders, coin-cleaning powder with evening shirts, etc. that unmans one. But I shall not live more expensively till my screw is raised, and am simplifying everything that does not tend to edification; smoking I have long abolished. Water, bread and oranges for breakfast, no alcohol for the last six weeks (a six months' trial and devilish trying): entire avoidance of cabs—make a showing for one's stipend that very few men can produce. Bed whenever possible at ten; very early morning hours more difficult now with cold and dark. You will gather from this that wings are hesitating at my shoulder blades? They are.

Even when we were "suited", it was with a misfit.

A calamity has fallen upon us, in the shape of a large and rowdy café, the property of some Berberin, that has just been opened exactly opposite. Their landlord is Manzlūm Pasha, our Minister. These unclean dogs make such a noise from 8 p.m. to 3 a.m. that life on the ground floor is intolerable. However, I am moving in the matter. After ascertaining that Mazlūm and Shawarbi Pasha, our landlord, are on good terms, I visited the other *locataires*. including a Greek grocer, who lives opposite, and egged them on to sign a petition to Shawarbi that the nuisance may be abated, and a *quartier fort respectable* cleared of these *saletés*. If Shawarbi will do nothing I shall go direct to Mazlūm, and tell him that the value of his Real Estate is decreasing hourly: and if he fails, I shall call upon the POLICE to close the place, *à cause de Tapage Nocturne,* a valuable plea under our Law. The Law failing us, we shall quit the flat, and look elsewhere for lodging.

The Law did fail us (as it must one side), so we did quit, staying in odd places until I found an attractive apartment in the Midān Kasr at-Nil (cheap enough even for us because, I learnt later, the bankrupt owner had no interest in the rent). I had just signed a year's lease when Graves was appointed *Times* correspondent in Constantinople. This was a set-back which I thought I had countered by finding a substitute.

Devonshire, the lawyer came in last night: I hope the thing will be a success, but he wants hot water to shave with, tea, eggs, butter, etc. with which I have long dispensed. However, he will save Filippo from paying rent, and maybe keep me civilized and unsubmerged.

Poor Devonshire was unable to face my music (even though a little tuned up towards his scale) for long, and I was alone again. I missed Philip Graves. Besides being an admirable companion and a master of his absorbing and entertaining craft—his esteem for me would have risen to affection if I had been capable of developing from a friend into a news fact—he was, apart always from T. E. Lawrence, the only man I have known well who had, in one respect, a lower standard of living than my own. This respect was clothes. Graves never knew the exact extent of his wardrobe, but it always proved to be, in emergency, smaller than he had hoped. Bidden to dine at the Agency, he would discover at seven that he was "out" of dress shirts and despatch Ahmad with a handful of silver to bring him one, quick, before the shops shut.

His work kept him up later than mine did me, so that, leaving for the Finance about 7.40 a.m. I was frequently privileged to observe the pleasant and unusual manner of his levée. Delicately raising the mosquito curtain, Ahmad would insert a cigarette between the lips of his sleeping master and hold to it a lighted match until one or two puffs had awakened him. As he left his couch it could be seen that he had omitted to don or had shed during the night one of the halves of his pyjamas. On his way to the prepared hot bath, he would pick up an uncut copy of the *Nibelungen Lied* or of some entomological journal, and read it edgeways, absorbed, until he found himself—and the bath—uncomfortably cold. A year later he could (and would) repeat to you word for word the strangely-assimilated information.

Sir Vincent Corbett was succeeded as Adviser in 1907 by Sir Paul Harvey and I found that under him there was even less for me to do. By this time (and none too soon) it had been decided to establish an Audit Department in the Egyptian Government, responsible to the Adviser only. Once more, as for the Mines, the time the place and the bored one found themselves all together: and I was remobilized, puzzled rather than unwilling, under the orders of Mr Arthur H. Middleton Middleton, a retired Anglo-Indian from the Egyptian Railways, who had (he was unable to deny) saved that Administration scores of thousands of pounds annually. My colleagues were: Leland Buxton, now a Stock Exchange magnate; Alexander Pallis, a very able Greek, of Eton and Balliol; and two Copts, Nákhla Effendi Tadros Nákhla (to whom when work slackened I used to give boxing lessons), and Sādiq Bey Hanain, after the War Zaghlūl's Minister of Finance, and Egyptian Minister at the Quirinal. We all liked each other and enjoyed the happiest of relations. I

began work with Middleton, the Arch Auditor: we enter every office in the Government, and the head clerk turns a ghastly livid green as his frail mortality is laid bare under our trained scalpel. Some of the verification is dull, but on the whole (though one's screw remains unchanged) I have the satisfaction of learning, and doing something which matters: for on our reports the Government will base its whole further system of Accounts and Expenditure. "Our" comes well from one who has never managed to show one quarter's personal budget; but the same has happened with Kings of Finance.

Although it was my privilege to accompany Middleton round the Departments, I never learnt much more of the elements of official auditing than suffice to implant in me for life a sincere and equal sympathy with auditors and with their victims. I was surprised and pained to find how little our revelations were appreciated by the interested parties. Even the friendship, basic in my life, of Richmond cooled for a few weeks after our second morning of "costing out" the nineteen official houses he had recently erected in the Zamalek quarter. Inspecting the Public Works Department at Giza:

It is very pleasant to hear the clerk adding up the columns of figures, singing the while in a loud voice praising God; but it does not make for easy verification. And I can*not* count large sums of money, especially when they include broken George IV's which have to be weighed, Napoleons and Egyptian Bank Notes. So I make Nákhla Effendi Nákhla, my colleague, do this; and he being fresh and vigorous (about forty-five years of age) does it with alacrity.

These audit inspections brought me into touch with all classes of Egyptians, from Alexandria to Aswān, and I found then, as I find now, that in the ordinary give and take of life there is in the world no more agreeable, courteous or entertaining race. Their credulity was almost frightening, and is still a deadly weapon in the hands of agitators.

The opinion of the masses here about Messina is that there has been no earthquake or disturbance of any kind, and that the reports have been spread by ingenious Cabinet Ministers anxious to bring a little money into Italy. You will remember that the Aswān Dam was supposed by the same class to be built for the purpose of carrying Nile water to England.

Mediaeval Damietta, my next inspection, continued, both in appearance and in sentiment to live in the past. In the once famous harbour floated a few sailing feluccas: the Milner safe in the Markaz-office had been delivered twenty-five years before and still remained upside down. When I asked why, *"Dumyāt"*, replied Tewfik al-Bash-Katib, the Chief Clerk, sad with long exile from Cairo, *"balad gāmid áwwi"*—"Damietta is a country exceedingly tough"—implying by the epithet the countless lapses from civilization to which he had been subjected. As an ex-douanier I was free of the Customs Rest Room, and I lunched next day with an old colleague,

Abāni Bey, the Director: an Egyptian who hungers for Turkey and deplores the corruption of his nation. He told me that the best Mudir (Governor) he'd ever known was an old Turk that could neither read nor write; but habitually kept his sword drawn on his desk, using flat or edge as the occasion seemed to warrant. There was not one murder in the province during his tenure of office (about three years): to-day there are eight a week in Behéra. Damietta is indeed a dead city, killed by Port Said. Forty years ago it had 150,000 dwellers; now about 40,000. It has been reduced from a Governorate to a Markaz, which is like turning a Lord Mayor into a Borough Councillor. The Governor keeps an admirable discipline to make up for his waning glory: the guards present arms with an appalling crash, and, as he strolls up the corridor, Chief Clerks appear at the open doors of their offices, with hands crossed and heads bowed, the while H.E., looking in every direction but theirs, presents me with a button-hole of violets.

Yet this sunken Damietta typified for Dante, who mentions neither Alexandria nor even Cairo, the direction of the East. For Hannibal's Carthage the final degradation is extremer still—her entry in the Telephone Directory of Tunis, reading:

Carthage,
(Région de Tunis)
Bureau, 3me Catégorie.

Verily, *Deleta est Carthago.*

Dumyāt has at least kept the sound of *Damiata* when other famous names have fallen to a mockery of their former selves: Heraclea becomes Eregli; Nicaea, of the Creed, Isnik; Ragusa which names the argosies, Dubrovnik; and Spalato, the Palace of Diocletian, Split.

The Ministry of Finance was fortunate in possessing at least one occasional poet in the person of George Burnett Stuart. When the Minister nominated, to investigate complaints about the Inspectors' *Frais de monture,* two elderly lawyers and a learned but unequestrian currency expert, Stuart was moved to write as follows:

> Hishmet Pasha turned in his chair,
> "This horse allowance", he said, "is not fair.
> I'll appoint a Commission to make it fairer,
> Hayter, Roussin, and Roccaserra."
>
> At eleven o'clock the very next morning,
> The Commission assembled blinking and yawning.
> They usually came up very much later,
> Did Roccaserra, Roussin and Hayter.
>
> They soon decided the obvious course
> Was to answer the question What is a horse?
> For a horse is rather an *avis rara*
> To Hayter, Roussin and Roccasera.
>
> The next thing to find out, Roussin said,
> Is the food upon which a horse is fed.
> "Can either of you supply any data?"
> "None", said Roccaserra and Hayter.
>
> Hayter here interposed a word,
> "Your question", he said, "to me is absurd,
> I'm purely a lawyer, what is the use in
> My knowing about anything?" "None", said Roussin.

He likewise recorded the advancement in Honours of an official reputed to frequent the Agency for that purpose:

> For ever with the Lord!
> Amen so let it be,
> That is the way to add a K
> To my well earned C.M.G.

That achieved, the hymnologist continued

> Most gracious Lord, who gav'st to me
> My hardly earned K.C.M.G.,
> Sustain me in my devious course
> With visions of a Knight Grand Cross.

The two Moslem and therefore Official holidays of the year were *Id al-Kabīr,* the Great Festival, in Turkish *Kourban Bairam;* and *Id al-Fitr,* the breaking of the Ramadan Fast, the Turkish *Bairam;* whose respective four or five days could with the intervention of Friday be expanded into the better part of a week. During one of these I visited the monastery of St Anthony on Mount Colzim travelling with the Director-General of the Coast Guard. Sailing from Suez we landed below the Gulf on the western shore and turned inland with a caravan of the best riding camels in the world.

We made out the Monastery about four miles from our evening halt. The wind blew down North and the cold was damnable. In the morning we rode over, and found that, besides giving me letters of recommendation, the Patriarch (112th from St Mark, and Pope of Alexandria) had sent out a man from the Nile to prepare the Abbot: the entrance was decked with palms, and the brethren gave us a Hosanna or so as we came in at the Great Gate only used on Occasions; the usual admittance being per cord and basket forty feet from the ground. The place is genuine enough—third century, just before Julian the Apostate. The garden, of which a great deal might be made, is fed by a crystal stream, perennial from the mountain: no work appears to be done, and they refused to show us the ancient books they are said to possess, resolutely denying their existence. The rest of the party declining, Mrs. H—— and I toiled up the sheer rock to St A's original cave, hard work but worth it, to track the fakir to earth.

The sharpness of desert air was the breath of life. After camp was pitched one could walk on the hard clean sand until the sun dropped, like a golden-scaled fish, over the edge into Oceanus. Underfoot the smooth pebbles clinked and tinkled like metal, with echoes like the voices of children playing just out of sight.

A year or so later I was invited by Arthur Weigall, Inspector-General of Antiquities in Upper Egypt, to accompany him in the Government Dahabia *Dendera* for his inspection of the ancient Egyptian temples between Aswān and the Sudan frontier at Wadi Halfa. ("Don't ask me to tea now, Sir", said the engine-man, "dirty my 'ands are—dirty as my feet.") Day after day we glided on past rolling sands, yellower than cats' eyes and more golden than Pactolus, with pillars and pylons jutting forward into the river every ten miles and culminating in the tremendous fane of Abu Simbel. When we tied up at night we could hear from the shore the antique refrain of some love-lorn peasant woman:

Ya habíbi, ya Muhám
Taalýni fil manám.

Oh my loved one, oh Muham
Come and see me in my dream.

The temple of Philae, "Pharaoh's jewel box", we found flooded to the roof owing to the recent increase in the height of the Aswān dam. We reached the long sunken colonnade just before sunset and could not resist throwing off our clothes, diving into the Nile and coming up underneath the lintels into the dim painted shrines. The sun refracted from the green water struck up against the gods and goddesses moving along the frieze and "quivering in the waves' intenser day". The animals turned this way and that, and the merry little god Bez danced once more for joy in the birth he personified.

By this time I began to know a good many people in, and something about Cairo.

On Friday morning I got up at about five, took the tram out to Old Cairo, to attend a Mass which is held once a year in the Crypt of Abu Sarga, on the supposed date of the Holy Family resting on that spot. An interesting, and fairly impressive show. There are not many rituals with an unbroken tradition of fifteen hundred years—that are chanted in Ancient Pharaonic, Greek and Arabic. I've not met anyone out here who has turned up to the service. I was given the front chair (there were only two) the rest of the congregation sat on the stone flags (no doubt contracting all manner of trouble). A priest and two acolytes (in high antique mitres) chanted throughout with neither music nor book, but with dreadful penetrating clarity. A baptism was going on noisily in the South Aisle and the vault was lighted with four tapers only, and densely clouded with incense. Two hours of it proved my master, and I fled up to the level of the church, where another service was going on—the only music being a small pair of brass hand-cymbals.

Trinity. I went to the Circus at the Abbas Theatre, an exhilaration I've denied myself these twelve years and more. The clowns bad but acrobats good, the whole concluding with a Stag Hunt "all 'Inglese"; men with side whiskers, loud check coats and pith helmets, cantering after a tame deer, assisted by a bull dog and a small pomeranian. All pleasant enough.

Opera in Cairo was not much worse than Opera in many other places: that is more Opera than Music.

The Opera opened last night with *Africana,* a piece which made yawn our grandsires. My only satisfaction was to stand in the wings and watch the panting supers rock the Doomed Vessel up and down and then (still dripping with their toil) nip round with *papier maché* clubs and bludgeon the shipwrecked adventurers.

Graves and I patronized *Cavalleria,* at the little Abbas Theatre: the Prima Donna having omitted to tip her *claque* in the gallery, the claque booed and hissed her, nor was it until she had resorted to floods of tears that public opinion veered round.

To Nubar's stall for Massenet's *Hérodiade:* Salomé is unsuccessfully wooed by our old friend the Tetrarch: all the time she is in love with John the Baptist, who does not return it till a duet in a dungeon in Act IV. Observing the *Précurseur* violently gesticulating in this piece, I asked my neighbour what the trouble was: he said, "he is angry because they have forgotten the lime-light". *C'est ignoble.*

We have here the worst Opera, *Anna Karénina,* I ever saw. The last Act takes place on a railway line, between a culvert and a tunnel, and moving indeed is the plate-layer's long solo: so moving that many, including our party, would have left the house, had we not been buoyed up by the hope (inspired by the programme) that Anna was going to commit suicide by throwing herself under a train. Even here, however, we were deceived; she rushed past the plate-layer (who had somehow become a signalman) into a tunnel, and the matter was adjusted by the trombas and instruments of percussion.

I have been four or five times to see Grassi the Sicilian actor and his troupe: to-morrow night with the Gorsts and Maxwells. Realism *in extremis.* The first night an excited husband cut a gentleman's throat: the second he bit it in two; what could be more agreeable or better value for money?

Marmaduke Pickthall, author of the sublime *Said the Fisherman,* chose for one of his collections the title "Oriental Encounters", in itself a happy suggestion for an infinite variety of unlikeliness, of improbable blends of things, words and deeds. In twentieth-century Egypt *Credit Foncier* lotteries and the price of cotton were still described in an Arabic which might well be found in the Old Testament. There might be better Rolls-Royces in Bond Street, better camels in Turkestan—in Cairo camels and Rolls-Royces moved together, shoulder by radiator past the Savoy Hotel (as they now halt together on the red light, and resume on the green). The guards and porters on the station-platforms cried *"Oáh ríglak"*—"Ware feet" when the train came in or went out, as if it were still a camel. The navigator of the elaborate and luxurious steam Dahabiahs on the Nile shouted down to the engine room *"Tawákkil 'al Allah"*—"Put your trust in God", the accepted (and necessary) equivalent of "Full steam ahead".

Popular reactions to casual incidents were no less unexpected. A friend was driving me down a side street in his dog-cart when we had the misfortune to knock a man over. We naturally jumped down to help him, when several passers-by collected and warned us to drive swiftly away "lest the Police come upon you".

Sometime in 1906 I was walking in the heat of the day through the Bazaars. As I passed an Arab Café an idle wit, in no hostility to my straw hat but desiring to shine before his friends, called out in Arabic, "God curse your father, O Englishman". I was young then and quicker tempered, and foolishly could not refrain from answering in his own language that I would also curse his father if he were in a position to inform me which of his mother's two and ninety admirers his father had been. I heard footsteps behind me and slightly picked up the pace, angry with myself for committing the sin Lord Cromer would not pardon—a row with Egyptians. In a few seconds I felt a hand on each arm. "My brother", said the original humorist, "return, I pray you, and drink with us coffee and smoke. [In Arabic one speaks of "drinking" smoke.] I did not think that Your Worship knew Arabic, still less the correct Arabic abuse, and we would fain benefit further by your important thoughts."

CHAPTER FOUR

1907–1908

L'occasion est belle, il vous la faut chérir.
CORNEILLE *Horace*

I

HAVING tasted Italy and Greece I took my third holiday through Turkey. The Luxury Voyage (so revealingly named) of to-day has supplanted by dint of ease, expense and standardization those old amusing journeys by the Khedivial Mail which showed you so much life of all kinds at so little cost. At Smyrna I

went ashore in the British Post boat: (every nation has its own P.O. here, in order to save the Turks the worry and inconvenience of opening all European letters). Walked up Mount Págas with the most infernally loquacious Greek there ever can have been. Saw, with intense satisfaction, the tomb of Saint Polycarp: the Turks opened it about four hundred years ago and put a holy Shaikh in too, so now there is a cross one end and a turban the other.

At Haidar Pasha Station over against Constantinople we missed by five seconds a ferry, which might easily have waited for us. My host, Dick Graves,

rebuked an official on the Quay, who appeared surprised at our disappointment, saying: "In an hour there will be another boat." On our continuing the debate, he pathos'd us by the information that he was only a policeman, and had received no pay for four months. No one ever is paid anything.

It was my good fortune to see, from the Diplomatic terrace at Yíldiz Kíosk, almost the last Selamlik (the Friday State visit to the Mosque) of a still Imperial Abd al-Hamíd. I had to exchange my Embassy nomination for an official pass, and appear in frock-coat and top-hat (which I managed to borrow) on the terrace overlooking the drive from the

Palace to the Mosque, about an hour before the Friday Noon Call to Prayer. Close behind every guest stood a Court Functionary whose terrified suspicion even of diplomatically guaranteed persons I was, as the procession drew nigh, soon to experience. I moved my hand towards my pocket and, in a trice, felt both elbows gripped and pinned hard against my ribs, not to be relaxed until I had shown my quest to be neither revolver nor bomb, but the black leather case of a pair of pince-nez. By this time the Sultan Caliph was at hand. Seated alone in a low open phaeton he drove, at a slow trot, two magnificent Arab horses. His beard was dyed with henna to a bright rust; he was rouged and lacquered up to the eyes; but such was the natural kingliness of his poise and regard that even the spectacle of the Ministers and Chamberlains gripping the dashboard and scrambling beside him and behind, failed to detract from his personal dignity.

When at home I was offered through the kindness of Arthur Richmond, who worked under the commanding oracle of George Morant, an Inspectorship under the Board of Education; but passionately as I loved and shall always love London, I felt that I should be wasting knowledge and experience if I accepted—the bitterest of all wastes, as I was to find toward the end of my career.

By next year a better prospect appeared. The Princess Nazli had given me a letter of introduction to Kiamil Pasha, the Grand Vizier, on the chance of his finding me work in the Turkish Government. I therefore returned to Egypt by Constantinople. An audience was arranged at the Sublime Porte, and I spent the two days before it in attending another Selamlik and in conversations with Turkish politicians and journalists. This time it was a very different Selamlik I was called to witness. Turkey had exchanged tyrannies; young Turkey ruled, and what we now saw was no more than *Magni Nominis Umbra.*

Graves and I drove to the Embassy at eleven, where Ryan,[1] the 2nd Dragoman, put himself at the head of a rapidly swelling tail of cabs—we picked up some of the Navy on the way—and drove to Yildiz. As most of the shops were shut, a considerable throng gazed stupidly upon us. Last year there was no such crowd: last year three squadrons of cavalry had to be propitiated by the sight of a Permit before ever one reached the Palace gates. Now all difficulties are at an end, it is even rumoured that he who cares may bring a Kodak—and use it. The old terrace, with its seedy Court official to every guest is done away with: now you sweat with the mob or swagger with the ambassadors. As far as I could make out, the extreme Western wing of the Palace forms the diplomatic room and stand. Beneath us stood the Syrian, Hejaz and Albanian troops, now reduced to a total of 5000. Occasionally a tall eunuch, in an im-

[1] Sir Andrew Ryan, K.C.M.G., now H.M.'s Minister in Albania.

mensely long frock-coat, and spurs, lurched down the hill. At five minutes to twelve, a double line of Field-Marshals, about ten yards apart, sullenly self-conscious and swinging bellies like the Tun of Heidelberg, tramped slowly past at the goose step. Then a bugle blew and, in a flash every sword was out and every rifle up. An indifferent band blared out the National Anthem (composed by a younger brother of Donizetti's and sounding so). The Imperial Carriage trundled down at a fair pace, the Old Fellow on the back seat talking to the Grand Vizier on the front, and saluting guardedly. As he knew there was no one on the terrace of greater importance than a Balkan Minister, he refrained from looking up at it. After prayer he returned in the same carriage, his own pair of ponies being led up by four Sudanese (swearing audibly in Arabic) behind him. He disappeared; and some Greeks, with laurel wreaths round their bowlers drew up under us. Suddenly there was a click in the wall behind, a window opened and there he stood, dignified enough, ten feet off, saluting with an easy grace. The blind went down, but the frantic applause of the Achaeans brought it up again, and once more his gloved hand went up, and his lips conjured up a rictus. It would have been child's play to shoot him; however, the blind descended again, and the Old Man knew that, humanly speaking, he might live another week.

The Bulgarian menace brooded over Constantinople.

We talked with Behá ed Dīn, and came to the conclusion that this Bulgarian business is getting on the nerves of the Young Turks. And well it may, for if Bulgaria demands its Independence, Turkey cannot initiate a new regime by giving way: and if they refuse, Bulgaria will proclaim her own, leaving Turkey the *onus bellum dicendi*. And Turkey will get its head knocked off, tho' courage and endurance abound—for so do they in Bulgaria, plus training. Behá ed Dīn persisted that the powers would never allow Bulgaria to begin: which hope, tho' something of an admission in itself, we all piously echoed.

My audience with Kiamil Pasha translated these rumours and prophecies into fact. His Highness the Grand Vizier was some five feet in stature, kept his face in profile and seemed to munch with his chin. He spake perfect English, said he would like to employ me, but had no vacancy; and expressed an admiring affection for Princess Nazli. Nothing escaped him in talk, and he seemed strong and able, but too old for the stress in which he stood. As I went out the Chäush announced Monsieur Gueshoff,[2] come (I knew it not, but the Grand Vizier must have known it) to announce to the Suzerain Power the final Independence of Bulgaria.

On my return to Cairo I wrote:

The Rumanian boat is swift and driven by petrol, with which also the passengers' food is seasoned. I landed at Smyrna and lunched with Heathcote Smith the Vice Consul: bought one or two Alexanders [3] rather dear from the

[2] The Bulgarian Minister.
[3] Silver tetradrachm of Alexander the Great: see p. 107.

Dutch Consul Van Lennep (a dealer) and visited the Railway, which was controlled because of the Strike by soldiers with loaded rifles. A man had been shot the day before and nearly all the engines lopped of their reins and colons. For the few that remained the Manager and Directors had no drivers and were in a great despair. I suggested begging from the Egyptian Government; drafted them a letter, for which they were pathetically grateful; interviewed the General Manager here, and had just procured them three drivers, six firemen, three fitters and three boiler makers, when we got a wire saying the Strike was ended, and I resigned my post of *Deus ex Machina* with some regret: I might have had a Season ticket from Smyrna to Ephesus for life.

II

Lord Cromer and succeeding Consuls General were assisted in their high tasks by Diplomatists from the Foreign Office endowed with varying degrees of zeal and ability; but these were wandering stars, at any moment liable to shoot or be shot from the Egyptian firmament. Tradition within the Agency—that is of documents and archives—was (and is) preserved by the archivist; tradition without—political, diplomatic and social—by the Oriental Secretary, who must anyhow be the eyes, ears, interpretation and Intelligence (in the military sense) of the British Agent, and might become much more. His influence extended with that of his Chief, and in the zenith of British power in Egypt—that is from 1890 until the War—the post, usually filled from the Levant Consular Service, was one of the minor key positions in the Near East. The first name I heard at the Turf Club was that of Harry Boyle. He had been Oriental Secretary for a good many years, and was frequented and admired by a few senior Englishmen. In the French Press the changes were rung on the *éminence grise* and *âme damnée de l'Agence*. By the juniors I met he was inevitably cited as "knowing the East very well—a bit too well, if you ask me; what you want's a plain straightforward Englishman who'll put these fellows in their places, and keep 'em there". I remember thinking at the time that it was lucky for England he could not, anyhow, much resemble those who discussed him. Boyle went out but little, and for months my only visible proof of his importance was the sight of the brougham and pair of Fát-hi Pasha Zaghlúl, Under-Secretary of State for Justice, waiting every day outside the little house that stood opposite to what is now the Cercle Mahomet Ali. At last I was sent round to the Agency with a confidential message from the Finance. I was ushered into the Oriental Secretary's office. On a deal table a typewriter clacked. Above it there loomed a vast drooping moustache surmounted by a hooked nose and melancholy kind dark eyes. I stood at the side and understood that the Oriental Secretary was taking his luncheon. Before the typewriter was a plate of buttered eggs, on the right a small conical carafe of water, on the left one of brandy, from all three of which he helped himself severally and impartially. Against the plate was balanced the current issue of *al-Mokattam* (then the paramount of Arabic dailies) the leading article of which, as he ate, he read, translated in his head, and transmuted directly through the machine into mellow Johnsonian prose.

Boyle's name was not found in the lists of official banquets (even at the Agency); he went not with the Lord to Abdin Palace; but his service to his master was as invaluable as his devotion was unlimited. Though he was criticized towards the end for viewing Egypt through Syrian rather than through Egyptian glasses, his knowledge of what was going on, and likely to be going on, beneath as well as above the inscrutable surface of the political Nile, was unrivalled, and might be said, without exaggeration, to extend to the waters of the Jordan, the Orontes and the Golden Horn. His detailed memories of the causes and manners of the deaths of the Khedives were only surpassed by his curious knowledge of the irregularities and aberrations of living Pashas and Beys. In addition to his proper Oriental work Boyle found time for the tedious mechanical labour of enciphering and deciphering many Secret telegrams. He typed his signature as well as the body of his letters, of which I found the other day two specimens. "Dear Man, The Lord said send a reply to this saying we can do nothing, but it seems civiller to be able to say that we've made some sort of enquiry. H.B." and (for the list of Church dignitaries for the Farewell ceremony): "Dear Corbett, As regards the True Church, the Lord thinks you are the best judge. Only he would remind you of his friends Père.... Yours H.B." He was extremely well read, especially in English and French eighteenth-century literature, an exquisite precisian in language and a perennially amusing conversationalist. On most afternoons he walked abroad, dressed with a distinguishing improbability. His coat was old, his trousers bagged at the knee and sagged at the waist, his boots were almost mediaeval in their turn up. On his head a battered straw hat; rather beyond heel a mongrel but *sympathique* cur: the whole enclosing a man of genius. This very appearance was the occasion of a triumph of resource. He was taking his tea one day on the terrace of Shepheard's Hotel when he heard himself accosted by a total stranger: "Sir, are you the Hotel Pimp?" "I am, Sir", Boyle replied without hesitation or emotion, "but the management, as you may observe, are good enough to allow me the hour of five to six as a tea interval. If, however, you are pressed perhaps you will address yourself to that gentleman", and he indicated Sir Thomas Lipton, "who is taking my duty; you will find him most willing to accommodate you in any little commissions of a confidential character which you may see fit to entrust to him." Boyle then paid his bill, and stepped into a cab unobtrusively, but not too quickly to hear the sound of a fracas, the impact of a fist and the thud of a ponderous body on the marble floor.

Great contemporaries sometimes fail in their appreciation of one another. Gorst had never liked or approved of Boyle, and on succeeding Lord Cromer he reduced his work, his position and his influence to nil. I saw more of him after his decline, and had occasion to admire more than ever the profundity of his knowledge and the elegance of his mind and his diction. One night Graves returned to the flat and, binding me to mortal secrecy, informed me that Boyle would be going in the autumn, and that I was to be offered his place. The news of that hope (which I concealed even from my mother) surrounded the Turf Club, the Ministry of Finance, the Audit—even the verification of Public Health Imprests—with the prismatic radiance of the solar spectrum. I trod on air. When the formal offer was made I accepted, being seconded for one year from the Egyptian Service (whose five per cent. for Pension had been from the first deducted from my salary) and, though pretty certain that from the Pension aspect I was ruining my old age, considered myself the luckiest man in the world. Although my financial apprehensions have been more than realized, I have never regretted the decision. I hurried to England, calculating elaborately for two extra days by taking a Thursday boat, when, with the official Friday you could date your leave from the following Saturday, but the *Ernest Simon* was late, a loss of two days' leave to me.

It speaks much for a Sound Anglican Grounding that, on the receipt of this news, I was able to refrain from abuse, and answer, chanting a well-known hymn:

> "If I take my ticket by er,
> Is she *sure* to go?
> Captain, Porters, Stewards, Tourists
> Answer No."

I cut short my leave that year to return through Syria in order to learn in Damascus some Arabic other than Egyptian before taking up a post which I imagined must be assailed by suitors of all dialects. On the way out in the Orient Express,

I shared a through carriage with a German woman (with a pension she will lose on remarriage), and an Inventor of machine and automatic guns and rifles. He was smuggling some through to show the Servian Government, well

knowing the Austrians would arrest him at once if they found out. . . . He lost
his head crossing Vienna and I had to rescue his luggage and put him into the
right train. Sure as the guns he concealed, when we reached the Servian
frontier, he was seized and frog-marched violently out into space, so that I
saw him no more.[4]

Philip Graves, once more at his post, helped me in Constantinople; and
I travelled through Beirut up the Lebanon to the summer resort of 'Ain
Sófar, hoping to sample its splendour, but finding *The Grand* (*à cause
de le crise*—even in 1909)

officially closed but unofficially let out by the caretaker (very reasonably) to
as many as care to lodge there. A Syrian sitting next to me told how the place
last year had been full of *"grosses légumes de Damas, un Paradis*—you couldn't
hear yourself speak for the crashing of dice and dominoes, the crack of champagne corks, and the whirring and whining of gramophones". Left for Damascus at 10.40, breaking with seven packages and a second class ticket into a full
first class compartment. An artillery general, a Pasha, and a Qadi protested
each according to the commination of his Faith; but when I defeated the last
on father's chess-board, and abused the Cretans to the first, they combined in
my favour against the ticket collector. Their system with the two or three short
tunnels was to call upon the Creator's name, and then bury their faces in a
cloth, or the filthy carriage curtain. By imitating the groans of one abhorring
a stench, I deluded the Qadi into covering his head long after we had emerged
from the dark; and this was considered a very exquisite humour by the rest
of the company.

Damascus may be the oldest continuously inhabited city in the Near
East, and it is memorable to dip in Abana and Pharpar. But the wretched
horse-trams seemed to follow you everywhere, and the Bazaars, recently
burnt down, had been roofed again with corrugated iron. Street cries were
my compensation though I have long forgotten all save *"Bālak Asnānak!"*
—"Beware for your teeth" from the vendor of ice-cold drinks, and *"Sāleh
hamātak!"*—"Propitiate your mother-in-law" from the flower-seller.

I had hardly arrived when I found I should have to shorten my Syrian
sojourn, as Boyle had put forward his departure a whole month; and
there was only time to acquire a little Arabic by wandering about rather
than by book-work and to contract a sharp attack of fever, from which
I was cured by Anatole France's *Ile des Pingouins*. But before leaving

I asked Devey the Consul if he'd care to climb Mount Hermon. I hired
a horse and, rising at four on Saturday, left Damascus with Neville of the
Ottoman Bank and Devey, escorted by two *Zaptiehs* with rifles across
their saddles. After about two hours' riding, Devey elected to descend and
have some food (we had ours before starting), and An Event occurred. I gave

[4] But he wrote to me in Jerusalem in 1918 reminding me of his misadventure.

my horse to a *Zaptieh* to hold, which he omitting to do, the brute went for the other horses and ran amok. It kicked D. and knocked him down (he said afterwards that he flung himself down, preferring to be trampled rather than kicked) frightening the beasts (and me) out of our senses: and at last charged down on me. I tried to catch the bridle and he jumped and bit my right thumb, so that the others called out "Shoot, shoot" to the *Zaptiehs*, and D. who had now completely lost his head began hurling great boulders at the animal. I, foreseeing a series of heavy payments for the hirer, adjured him to do no such thing and, after twenty minutes excitement, I sucking my thumb and beating the creature over the head with father's stick—it broke at last— we caught him and I decided to sit heavy on him for the rest of the journey.

Late in the evening we reached Ernai, a Druse village high up in the hills. A score of tall Druses in white robes and white turbans advanced to meet us and rapidly debunked my carefully prepared Arabic speech by exclaiming in rich Broadway: "We're sure glad to see you strangers; sit right down": almost every one of them having passed years in the States in order to earn a livelihood denied him by his native land.

They gave us eggs and honey and wonderful water from the runnels which abound in that place. D. knowing no Arabic and looking very bedraggled, they would not be persuaded but that I was the Consul, rendering me almost divine honours. We tried to sleep—useless because of dogs and insects—till 1.30 a.m. when we began the climb on local beasts. The morn made the crags and rocks look even sharper than they were, and we had to dismount every other minute and drag the animals up. There was an extraordinary yellow star to which I whistled the Ninth Symphony till it went out and the Eastern Desert began to glow. Five hours of the hardest grind I have ever had brought us to the summit, 9050 ft.—and a bitter gale blowing. The sight is sublime; Lebanon and Anti-Lebanon, with Coelo-Syria between them; to the North the sources of the Jordan; to the Southwest Tiberias, and far away under the cloud-wrack the Dead Sea—Bahr al-Lut, Lot's Sea, the Arabs call it. Hermon is *Jabal Shaikh,* the Mountain of the Old Man, and the summit *Kasr Antar*— Antar's Castle. There are the ruins of a High Place and a cave Temple. Once we had a bear alarm and here again I entreated all to hold their fire, as the *Zaptiehs* were sure to miss, and our revolvers were just powerful enough to irritate an otherwise very good-natured beast. We started down by a sharper descent, riding from seven to ten and from ten-thirty to three-thirty along a very hot valley to Kátănă. We left Devey to dine with the Qaimakam and ourselves rode from four-thirty to seven-thirty into the Western gate of Damascus. We had ridden seventy miles and had been up Hermon and back in thirty-eight hours, but the glory of this was somewhat diminished by a conspicious inability to Sit Down. I am profoundly thankful to have two thumbs left: the offender is practically healed now. The white horse (truly as Virgil said *Color deterrimus albis*—the white ones have the worst colour) gave trouble all the way and at the end I rode him nearly off his legs racing a Bedu into Damascus.

As a general result of my travels, I note that

by far the best educated and the best-informed men I'd met in my wanderings were Commercial Travellers, and of these Scots, Germans, Armenians are the best. The English are too gentlemanly to know much.

We left Beirut under the searchlights of the Austrian Battleships at 11 p.m. and arrived at Haifa (Mount Carmel) next morning. I went ashore with a Scottish engineer, bought a few coins and drove over to Acre—St Jean d'Acre —about one and a half hours along the sand; my companion shooting at eagles with his revolver as we drove but hitting none. Acre a most interesting place, taken and re-taken by Richard Cœur de Lion. It has the exact appearance of the ancient Phoenician city it originally was. We visited Abbas Effendi, the head of the Bāb religion, Johnny Browne's name being a *passe partout* with Persians. He had been exiled and imprisoned there about forty-two years, but seemed cheerful enough.

I took over from Boyle on 15 September. He had decided—rightly, I think—to pass on to me neither his methods nor the names of his agents, and from the applications that I received from such I derived the impression that he depended as little as I upon paid sources of information.[5] His office, which faced due south into a courtyard, was, save in mid-winter, so oppressively hot that the Chancery were good enough to let me sit with them, thus adding a fourth to the existing three tables and chairs, all served by one wall telephone. The Councillor was Ronald Graham,[6] the magnitude of whose official tolerance and unofficial kindness grows upon me in proportion as I reflect upon my general rawness and abysmal ignorance of diplomatic procedure. He had, in Oriental rugs especially, a cultivated knowledge some of which, on our expeditions to the Bazaars, he was good enough to reveal to me. Graham had succeeded Charles de Mansfeld Findlay,[7] remembered in Egypt chiefly for his misfortune in having acted for Lord Cromer throughout the Denishwai incident of 1906; when some British officers, misled by a treacherous or incompetent dragoman had shot a number of village pigeons, had been murderously assaulted by the villagers, and one officer had died. The sentences inflicted by the special court were excessive and mediaeval, and although few with knowledge of Egypt or of our officers will accept George Bernard Shaw's doctrinaire and anti-British account of the affair

[5] In 1932 my wife and I visited him at his Lake home of Ambleside. His old conversational fire was undimmed, but there was now pathos as well as pleasure in noting his eagerness to know the latest from Palestine and Egypt. In the spring of 1934 Boyle's five succeeding Oriental Secretaries found themselves by an odd chance all together in Cairo. We sent him a cable of enquiry after his health, describing ourselves under our names as *"Khulafá. Talamídh"*—"Successors. Pupils"; and were happy to learn that he had been touched by our homage. He died in April 1937.

[6] Afterwards Ambassador in Rome.

[7] Afterwards Minister in Norway.

in the preface to the otherwise delightful *John Bull's Other Island,* some
of us had felt that a mistake had been committed.

The Head of the Chancery was Robert Clive, whose languid ease of
manner and draft Despatches, the delight of Gorst, early prepared those
who knew him for his success in Munich and his Embassy in Japan. Under
Clive's able rule, the Chancery coped easily with the duties of a pre-War
Agency. The most important event of the Cairo year was the appearance
simultaneously in London, and in Cairo in English, French and Arabic,
of the British Representative's *Annual Report.* Months before publication,
the Reports of the Ministries and Departments were submitted in remorse-
less detail and distributed amongst us by Clive for the tedious process of
"boiling". It is, I fear, an index of our nineteenth-century training that,
after Public Health, Education was dreaded as at once the dullest and
least reducible of all the "slushes". Sir Eldon Gorst was critical of stereotyped effects, so that (for instance) the White Slave Traffic had to appear
in alternate years as "this abominable commerce" and as "this detestable
traffic".

At the table next to mine sat Robert Vansittart. He had already written,
and produced in Paris, two French plays; and the aureole of his poetry
from Persia seemed to surround his marked and unusual personality.
Most afternoons and some mornings he would beat out upon a Chancery
typewriter the text of his first novel *John Stuart.* There is little in that
clever complication to presage the mastery of *The Singing Caravan,* but
the certainty of his future greatness was borne in upon me when Sir
Ernest Cassel visited Egypt and, in due course, dined at the Agency.
After dinner a bridge four was arranged, consisting of Gorst, Cassel,
Vansittart and another, whom I can only define with certainty as having
been other than myself. Robert Vansittart, in early and even in later
life, had, like other distinguished members of his Service, exhibited
neither aversion from nor lack of skill in games of hazard. He cut in
with Sir Ernest, and, the points having been decided, presumed the
addition of five pounds on the rubber. His opponents accepted; his
millionaire partner, whether on principle or as a gesture of deprecation,
declined, when the Second Secretary, to the general stupefaction, announced that he would "carry" him and, justifying his courteous insolence, duly won his double reward throughout the evening. We used to
share experiences, and infused into current Chancery work a *joie de vivre*
that once or twice came near to costing me dear. It was the custom of
Porphyrios II, Archbishop of the Autocephalous Church of Mount Sinai,
who wintered in Cairo (where I once met him at a Shepheard's Hotel
Fancy Dress Ball disguised as himself), to present annually to the

British Agent a basket of pears, of a consistency far beyond the digestion
or teeth of the most bigoted fruitarian. My duty was to draft, in French,
a letter of thanks to His Beatitude, and to hand the pears, *à toutes fins
utiles*, to our Egyptian orderlies. I communicated my irritation at this
annual farce to Vansittart, only wishing we could write what we felt. In
a moment he had typed out in a faultless blend of classic *argot* an alternative draft (strangely prophetic of Max Beerbohm's *Thanks for a Wedding
Present*) of which there remains in my memory the picturesque "... *qui
ont fichu à tout le monde une dysentérie tonitruante*". He had scarcely
finished when the bell rang. I gathered up my papers, took them in and
submitted them one by one to my Chief. Suddenly he turned round and
stared at me, his face sharp with amazement. I looked down, found I had
substituted for my own the Palace of Truth version and could only mum-
ble something about the wrong draft. It was characteristic of Gorst
that he was immediately appeased by the production of the right draft
and insisted upon retaining the ribald text, feeling perhaps, like the old
commentator, that *"arridet mihi lectio obscenior"*. Vansittart's artistry
in verse, prose and the conduct of life, stopped short of the visual arts.
On his return from a trip to Damascus he informed Graham and myself
that he had bought one or two rugs which he would like us to inspect. It
was a hot day when we visited his flat. After one glace at the pride
of Ispahan, Graham asked for a glass of water into which he dipped his
handkerchief and kneeling down and applying it briskly to the surface
of the most brilliant of the exhibits, waved before his rueful host a
miniature but faithful rendering of Joseph's Coat of Many Colours.

III

Notre personnalité sociale est une création de la pensée des autres.

The appointment of Sir Eldon Gorst had long been foreseen and caused
no surprise, though some resentment and personal apprehension with men
whose careers he had outshot and with whose capacities he was acquainted
at closer range than was his great predecessor.

John Eldon Gorst—Jack Gorst to his friends, Sir Eldon Gorst on
knighthood to distinguish him from his father Sir John Gorst, the legal
brain of the Fourth Party—had joined Lord Cromer's staff as a Third
Secretary, and had made a brilliant career in the Egyptian Civil Service.
He had shown his efficiency in the details of Finance by reforming the
Direct Taxation Department; his sympathy with Egyptian Administration
as Adviser to the Ministry of the Interior; his diplomatic and political
ability as Financial Adviser, the *de facto* Prime Minister of the Cromerian

Veiled Protectorate. Alone of higher British officials he had succeeded in winning the confidence of the Khedive, hitherto assumed irreconcilable with that of Lord Cromer. He was fiercely capable, and achingly ambitious. He could not bear fools gladly: he could hardly bear them at all. No less unsparing of his own body and brain, he knew not the meaning of repose. In his life were no intervals. He would gallop his race-horses before breakfast, work with swift concentration until luncheon, "relax" his mind in some abstruse scientific work until it was time to play three sets of tennis, straining for every stroke with companions twenty years younger than himself. He would submerge himself in interviews until 7.15, when he would pedal out sonatas upon his pianola. By eight he would have plunged into the maelstrom of an official dinner, no single detail of whose arrangement had escaped his critical (though not unappreciative) observation. If he played bridge, he could repeat the tricks, in their order, at the end of the game. When he bathed, he swam till he was tired—no splashing or floating—and then got out, to plunge immediately into some other exertion. Not for nothing had he been described as "a locomotive on the point of starting, with steam up".[8] During his last year as Financial Adviser he had been largely responsible for the successful issue of the Egyptian (and most delicate) side of the negotiations in the Entente Cordiale. As Assistant Under-Secretary of State for Foreign Affairs he was always the first to leave Downing Street, having completed his own work and never managing to collect enough from others to last him through the afternoon. Here, if ever, was

> A fiery soul which, working out its way,
> Fretted the pigmy body to decay,
> And o'er informed the tenement of clay.

For he lacked stature, and he lacked the personality which sometimes outweighs that disadvantage.[9] Nor was this his only handicap. The British Government had decided to use the occasion of the great change of persons to introduce an equally great change of method, and had given strong if not very precise instructions in this sense. The Liberal Cabinet entrusted Gorst with a policy of steadily increasing Egyptian self-government; essential if Great Britain was ever to redeem her promise of ultimate Evacuation and (in the opinion of some of us) no less essential even if we were to remain in Egypt for ever.

Lord C. created Egypt: his successor has to produce good Egyptians.

[8] Spring-Rice, 1902.
[9] I was to observe later that Kitchener and Allenby, both well over six feet tall, could make a cynical remark without it sounding cynical. Gorst could not.

But it was a policy which, however necessary, could obviously not be proclaimed from the housetops, or there would have been no end to the immediate, impracticable and unrealizable exactions of the extremist agitator in London as well as in Cairo, where indeed the spirit, had such instructions been divulged, would have been the *Tutti Conti, Tutti Principi* of a Verdi finale. This policy, not formally explained as emanating from His Majesty's Government, was ascribed to the "weakness" of Gorst, not only by the British officials, most of whom believed it hopeless and many of whose personal situations it might have affected, but also by that considerable body of Egyptians, apprehensive no less of Khedivial than of Nationalist absolutism, who had banked upon the indefinite maintenance, and even extension, of the British power. The *epitheton constans* for Gorst and his policy, originally applied by the Turf Club, adopted by the Press and still automatically released by such of the British public as take an interest in pre-War Egyptian affairs, is "Weak". Gorst was as Strong a man as I have ever served or met. Having first-hand knowledge of his (and others') utter fearlessnes and extreme inflexibility of purpose, I have often wondered what my friends really meant or wanted when they adjured in succession Gorst, Kitchener or Allenby to show "strength", and have found no cause to modify my 1911 definition of their "Strong Man" as "one who will do what the critic wants him to do, against all other reasons (and often against reason itself) at the moment of criticizing". Gorst was anyhow strong enough to pass a long needed law controlling the scurrility of the Press, nor can I recall one instance of his yielding against his reason to public clamour or hidden pressure.

Last night at six Gorst gave a *résumé* of his policy to about two hundred of the British officials here; it was plain and, though of necessity containing nothing that was very new, instructive.[10]

Like President Theodore Roosevelt's warmly British *pronunciamento* two years later, advising England in Egypt to "get on or get out", this statement was at first well received and accepted as the frank *exposé* of an inconvenient necessity, and with equal inconsistency picked to pieces within twenty-four hours by the many who saw clearly enough the inconvenience but wholly failed to perceive or allow the necessity.[11]

With such instructions in his pocket Gorst had arrived in Cairo, to

[10] And curiously resembling the 26 Principles which T. E. Lawrence laid down for his British assistants.

[11] That speech was equally resented by the Egyptian Nationalist Party which held an indignation meeting to protest against the President's condemnation of those who had extenuated the murder of Bûtros.

find the lawful ruler of the country smarting under a few real and many imagined slights and therefore united with the Nationalists—though their aspirations were directly opposed to his interests—in an unnatural but solid phalanx of hostility to Great Britain. Though better aware than most of the Khedive's defects, he had early adopted and always maintained the practice of ascertaining irregularities in advance, before they had been committed (or the sovereign committed to them), and of then hinting or laughing them out of existence as improbable rumours disseminated by His Highness' enemies. Friendly advice thus privately tendered could be and frequently was accepted by a sensitive and intelligent Oriental whose chief dread and implacable resentment were aroused by open rebuff and public humiliation. The system obviously depended upon that close and continual contact between the Palace and the Agency which had, unfortunately, not always subsisted. On the other hand anything like overt consultation or collaboration could not have failed to lower the Khedive's prestige in the eyes of the Egyptians, and probably that of the British Agent before his own people. Gorst was quick to show the Khedive courtesies and allow him occasional minor latitudes, especially in the disposition of the family finances and the distribution of Pashaliks, Beyliks and the Ottoman Orders of the Osmanieh and the Mejidieh. The Nationalists became suspicious. They attacked the Khedive in their Press as having sold himself to the British, and angered him into striking back by means and methods of which he was a master. Within six months the Agency had become the arbiter of their mutual, instead of the object of their united, hostilities. In his advances towards self-government, such as the creation of the Provincial Councils, Gorst was confronted with another difficulty. Most Egyptians, many foreigners and some British, endowing our policy as always with more head than heart, deemed it impossible and incredible that we could be questioning the validity of the Cromerian achievement. They therefore concluded that these premature reforms were being ridden for a fall: the administrative incompetence of the new authorities would by a series of demonstrative crashes prove to British Liberals, the British public and the world that the experiment had failed; and Great Britain would, cynically as always, but to the general relief (in a country where many loans and other contracts were terminable on Evacuation by the British) resume and tighten her grasp. Reforms thus estimated could hardly be expected to go with a swing.

Even if they had so gone, they were for many British officials an unsatisfactory and an uncomfortable business. At the beginning of the British occupation the theory of government, well enounced in Milner's *England in Egypt* (and not then considered slighting), had been "British heads and Egyptian hands". The Egyptian Minister had his British Adviser; the Egyptian Provincial Governor, State Engineer and Irrigator, their British Inspector, sometimes Inspector-General.[12] This thesis worked admirably so long as these Advisers and Inspectors were, like the poems of Sappho, "few indeed, but roses". But by 1910 there were too many of the first, and far too many of the second.[13] Those of the 'eighties and 'nineties had left a fine tradition of technical and social standards, of tactful dealing and happy relationships. The development—so logical, so reasonable—of the system bore within itself the seeds of its ruin.

In Cairo the disadvantages had been less apparent than in the Provinces. The Financial and some of the other Advisers were men of the world. The Ministers had large salaries, little work beyond an occasional signature, scarcely any responsibility and no constituents. Until the appointment of Saad Pasha Zaghlūl to the Ministry of Education (an impact from which it has hardly yet recovered) all was quiet on the Ministerial front. But in the Provinces the powers and the numbers of the Inspectors, Assistant Inspectors and Sub-Inspectors had grown with the scope and activities of Government. Worse still, from the Mudīr's point of view, their influence and prestige began to approach, to equal and soon to surpass his own. The slighted subordinate, the oppressed widow, the waterless irrigator addressed their petition not to the Egyptian Mudīr or Engineer but to the British Inspector, who reported direct and unchecked to his Adviser. The Adviser had only to walk into the office of the Minister (from whom the Mudīr or Engineer took their orders) for his advice—in the disturbing form of a reprimand, enquiry or counter-order—to become fact. There is no doubt that many and sometimes grave injustices and scandals were thus obviated. Some of the Inspectors proved themselves and were accepted as the good friends of the Mudīr as well as of the countryside. They did admirable work and their final departure is still deplored by many Egyptians.

Even if the British Inspectorate had been infallible and gifted with the tact of men and of angels, this general situation inherited by Gorst, as tending to weaken rather than to strengthen Egyptian initiative and responsibility, was increasingly false. In default of Crown Colony Government (*"fard al-mústahil"* as the Arabs would say—"Imagination of the Impossible") the policy now settled in Downing Street, confidentially promulgated to British officials and put into effect by Gorst, was in

---

[12] A sad bewilderment and vexation to my Auditing Chief from India (where apparently Engineers were great and Inspectors small men).

[13] By 1920 their gross and unwarranted inflation was to become one of the juster causes of the Egyptian outbreak.

theory unassailable. So it might have been in practice also if all his senior British lieutenants and the Egyptians with whom they had to deal had possessed at once his faith, his sensitiveness and his adaptability. The trouble was that the sceptical manœuvred for a minimum of change; while the methods of the earnest who took the problem seriously were apt to be extreme and not always considerate to their British subordinates. Thus a British Inspector, arriving at the Ministry on his monthly visit from Alexandria or the Provinces, might now be kept waiting in the Adviser's ante-chamber for a couple of hours whilst junior Egyptian officials were ushered in to audience before him; and it is to the honour of the natural good manners of an Egyptian gentleman that, with but few exceptions, Mudīrs refrained from taking a leaf out of the Adviser's book. It was discouraging also for the Inspector to find his advice less and less regarded, and no action taken upon his reports of injustice and abuse. Hitherto the mere mention to the Mudīr of a complaint had often procured its remedy. Such information was now received rather than accepted, with a polite but detached objectivity. In the eyes of his Egyptian friends he read disquietude, whilst the horn of enmity and malpractice was exalted. True that the position might, and probably would in the end adjust itself, at a cost of much he held high and dear. But meanwhile the transitional stage was of a delicacy, a difficulty, that seemed intolerable for all concerned. It is no disparagement of Lord Cromer—the greatest Proconsul in the nineteenth century—to remember that the absorption and extension of authority, with its demonstrable achievement of construction and production, demands hardly more exceptional gifts of brain and character than does its magnanimous yet gradual retrocession.[14]

Sir Eldon Gorst's political and administrative discomfort followed him into the fulfilment, with which he took infinite pains, of his social duties. In this he was not alone amongst our representatives abroad, diplomatic or colonial. Wherever a considerable British community is found, there also will be qualities of honesty, enterprise, public spirit, of sportsmanship and hospitality on every side, which need not fear comparison with any other nation in the world. You will also come across a generous proportion of individuals kindly, charitable and appreciative of the difficulties of the situation—even of the efforts made by the British Representative to grapple with those difficulties. But in the mass, and especially in clubs or drawing-rooms, this individual reasonableness and charity tends to suffer the sea change so convincingly described in

---

[14] Mothers have had for centuries to face this situation with their daughters: "I find it so infinitely easier to do things myself." The Government of India has to face it now, amplified beyond example in history.

Gustave Lebon's *Psychologie des Foules,* summarized centuries before by Lord Halifax: "There is an accumulative Cruelty in a number of men, though none in particular are ill-natured." How many times did I pass, to and from leave, through Constantinople, the Balkan and the Central European capitals, without discovering one exception to this attitude towards the British Representative: great expectations, sharp disappointment, sharper criticism, and possibly long after departure, canonization. *Extinctus amabitur idem.* He might be well liked by the local inhabitants and on good terms with the foreign colonies; but whether he were either, or neither, he was endured rather than praised by his own people.

Cairo was far indeed from being an exception to this rule, and Gorst still farther. Granted that he was, personally as well as politically, a more controversial figure than his great predecessor, it was nevertheless astonishing and depressing to observe how pettily and how unfairly, for all his good will, he was treated by his own people. Lord Cromer during his last years in Egypt had, after the death of his first wife, and under the weight of his labours and his age, no longer entertained on a large scale; and though the invitations that did issue from him conferred such distinction as to be retained on the mantelpiece long after the entertainment, the complaints of the far more numerous uninvited were as deep as they felt and as loud as they dared. Sir Eldon Gorst, aware of this, assisted by a young and charming wife, with the means and the desire to show a large hospitality, was at great pains to give pleasure by taking the utmost trouble with the numbers, the frequency, and the arrangement of his luncheon and dinner parties, which indeed could not have been improved either materially, or in the choice and placing of the guests. As a reward for this solicitude the same critics pronounced that it was really no compliment to be asked to the Agency now: you seemed to meet everybody there. And his endeavours to stem the rising flood of insularity by a judicious mingling of elements served but to evoke the classic dialogue "Were you at the Agency last night?" "No; but then you see I'm not a foreigner; I'm only British." [15] Clouds were not long in gathering round his head. By refusing an unneeded and unwanted loan [16] of two millions "to steady the market" he incurred the resentment of high finance at home, thenceforth hostile in the local and the European Press. *Alarmer les intérêts, c'est conspirer.* His general impa-

---

[15] The legend is still occasionally reproduced. "His civilities were reserved for Egyptians and for such foreigners as he deemed it diplomatic to placate." *A Lifetime in Egypt,* Miss N. Caillard. A just and true appreciation may be found in Sir W. Willcocks's *Sixty years in the East,* pp. 268-9.

[16] "At the Gorsts on Tuesday I met Cassel and Murray Guthrie, who are, I am informed, trying to force our Government to borrow money from them. We don't want any—but they say we can have it *so* cheap, Mobbs can't think."

tience of ceremony, his practice (then considered undignified) of sometimes driving his car himself and of galloping his race-horses, were
multiplied up by local rumour and refracted through returning tourists,
until a saga of discredit, still accepted by persons interested enough to
remember, was on the lips and in the ears of Whitehall and, particularly, of Mayfair. Opening the mail one evening I came upon an article
in an English weekly in which Sir Eldon was charged with a whole
series of offences, culminating in that of having gone to meet a British
Royal Prince at the Cairo Railway Station, riding a motor bicycle and
wearing a cloth cap. The article (emanating I afterwards learnt from the
disappointed jealousy of an unbalanced woman), was a tissue of demonstrable exaggerations and downright lies. Realizing this, and unaware then of the bitterness of irrefutable calumny, I took it in to him
almost jauntily, as worthy of his laughter rather than of his indignation.
He turned pale with chagrin and immediately telegraphed to the Foreign
Office for permission to bring a libel action with damages of £10,000.
Permission was naturally refused; the calumny went unchecked, and
the grotesque and ruinous legend (which I pray my testimony may help
to destroy) was established for a generation.

On the retirement in 1908 of Mustafa Pasha Fehmi, the Prime Minister whom Lord Cromer had termed "one of the most thorough gentlemen I have ever met in my life", Sir Eldon took his courage in both
hands and advised the Khedive to appoint "the versatile intellect" of
Bútros Ghāli Pasha, a Copt, to take his place. There was indeed precedent for this: the famous Nubar Pasha had been a Christian. Nevertheless

I spend my few merry moments easily—bantering my Moslem friends who are
as sick as the devil at the appointment of a Copt as Prime Minister. I point out
to them that this gives them their chance of showing how baseless are the
current opinions that Islam is bigoted and fanatical: but even Nazli is rather
shook up. As for Judge Arfan Bey, that reverend man raising his hands to
heaven (opposite the Splendid Bar), openly cursed the day of his birth. You
must remember that with them religion entirely takes the place of nationality.[17]

There might conceivably be a chance for any other Copt of outstanding
genius to become Prime Minister of an Independent Egypt, but Bútros,
an Egyptian no less loyal than gifted, had nevertheless signed the Con-
dominium Treaty of the Anglo-Egyptian Sudan, and was always subject
to the taunt that he was the nominee of a Christian Occupation.

About this time the Suez Canal Company, whose hundred years'
Concession was due to lapse in 1969, applied to the Egyptian Govern-

---

[17] The death-blow to this demoded theory was dealt by Ghazi Mustafa Kemal.

ment for its renewal for another term of sixty years, offering as premium four million pounds. The Government Reserve had been seriously diminished and the immediate windfall would at the moment have been welcome. There were other strong arguments for the project, and some against it. The maintenance of a tried and skilled control would have been assured, together with something of an international status for one of the world's principal waterways. On the other hand a proposal to alienate for a further half century a unique and increasingly prosperous enterprise, created by the blood and bones of ten thousand Egyptians yet producing never one piastre of direct profit to Egypt, aroused in the hearts of the Nationalists, in spite of its obvious advantages, a not altogether factious or unreasonable opposition. Gorst showed that this was his opinion by leaving this national issue to the decision of the General Assembly. The arguments for extension were being sustained by Bútros with extraordinary skill and supported with convinced and unquestioning loyalty by Zaghlūl; but were fated not to prevail.

On 21 February 1910 Gorst had been kind enough to arrange an excursion to Badrashain and Saqqāra for my uncle Harry Cust (whom he had known at Eton) and his wife.

We were returning from Saqqāra when the local station-master, very white, suddenly appeared speeding over the plain, a telegram in his hand. Sir Eldon, who was luckily riding an Arab pony (the rest on donkeys) galloped to the station, where a special train whirled him to Cairo.

Nobody knew what had happened. In his agitation he had not even paused to give us the grim news of the murder of Bútros Pasha.

Whenever Gorst received an anonymous threat he would hand it to me, praising God for one letter which required no answer. Bútros used to crumple them in the palm of his hand and thrust them into his pocket, murmuring "they will not dare". Wardāni did dare. Once more the fatal heroism of Harmodius and Aristogeiton, of Brutus and Cassius, was aped not by but against greatness; and Bútros, like Sir Henry Wilson, like the King of Yugo-Slavia, fell by the folly of a deluded idiot. Bútros bore the agony of an operation with fortitude, gasping to the Khedive with his last breath: *"Dieu m'est témoin que je n'ai fait que du bien à mon pays."* Egypt at heart agreed, and the venerable Shaikh al-Azhar proclaimed in a speech over the grave: "Few Moslems have done for their country the good this Christian did." But the public temperature rose to boiling point, the extremists openly exulting and the British and foreign communities calling almost derisively for "strong action", which Gorst was strong enough to decline. For this crime there

was to be no Denishwai Tribunal but the constituted Courts of Justice.
The trial was lengthy but normal, and Wardāni was, greatly to the
honour of the two Egyptian members of the Bench, sentenced to death.
By this time he had become something like a national hero, especially
with the student class.[18] Bands of these patrolled the streets singing

> *Wardāni! Wardāni!*
> *Illi 'atal al-Nusrāni.*
> That slew the Nazarene.

Older men had bound themselves by solemn oath that he should not
die and opinion was almost universal that, somehow, he would escape.
But Gorst's instructions were sharp as well as cool, and on the day
and at the place announced Wardāni was executed.[19] His revolver was
mortal not only to Bútros but also to the hopes of Gorst. Civil commotion, whatever its real cause, is ascribed to the policy or personality
of the ruler: "things would have been different if it had been anybody
else." The minds of Egyptians and Europeans were alike unsettled, and
in England no less than in Egypt Gorst, although he was honoured by
the almost unanimous approval of the House of Commons, was generally felt to have sustained at least a set-back if not a reverse.[20]

The Home Press is fantastic: the British Flag has *not* been insulted, ladies
are as safe as Pantechnicons and the Provinces safer than Piccadilly Circus.

Aqaba and Denishwai, the going of Cromer and the murder of Bútros,
were the four major events of the Egypt I knew during the ten years
before the War.
It was during this time of unsettlement that Graves and I walked one
evening up the Shāria al-Dawawīn, the street of the Divans—the Ministries—to find a vast crowd about a house on the left and from within
the shrieking of the hired mourners.

As you saw in *The Times* Mustafa Kāmel [21]—Caramel Pasha, the French
called him—died this week, and was accorded a slap-up funeral. Though he
was a charlatan of the first order, discreditable in his private life and *bak-*

---

[18] Before the news of Bútros' death had reached the Government School of Engineering
the students had decided to send a telegram to his family expressing their regret that the
shots had not proved fatal. Pupils chalked on the blackboard and carved on their desks:
"Long live the murderer!"
[19] "Ernest had bet me 5 to 1 against, and it was only because people here imagine that the
Agency must know everything in advance, that I did not take him in fivers."
[20] "Belloc ... tells me that Gorst is now looked upon at the Foreign Office as a complete
failure, and that he himself admits that the whole of his policy has broken down." Wilfrid
Scawen Blunt, *My Diaries,* Part II, p. 285. Only, it was not "his policy".
[21] First leader of the Egyptian Nationalists.

shished up to the eyes by all parties, it was evident that he had a great hold over the town effendis. The Khedive too sent his Master of the Ceremonies, so as to identify himself with the Nationalist movement. It is a game of double bluff—each firmly believing that the moment the Occupation ceases, he will boot the other out.

Tiresomely enough,

the Italians of Alexandria have chosen this juncture for proposing that the Municipality should erect a large statue to Dante, which plan, seeing that Dante placed Muhammad and Ali in hell with the other Schismatics, cleft from chin to tank with their insides hanging out, is meeting with frantic opposition from united Islam.[22]

I was beginning to find that the position of an Oriental Secretary was so ill-defined that it became in fact very much what he chose to make it.

The Bandmann troop have been here a week, and I obtained permission to make them withdraw *An Englishman's Home* (representing the conquest of England by Germany) which they had announced, as being unfit for Levantine consumption.

We are in the thick of King Edward's Memorial Service, local representation at which, though the Ministries are responsible, has devolved upon me. I envy all of you whose meat it was to attend in ease a magnificent spectacle, rather than to make many life-long enemies in arranging accommodation for local notabilities.

...a verbatim report of my interviews with Grand Rabbis, Patriarchs, Princes, Pashas, grandees, magnificos and mandarins—in a word the great unemployed—would go far to sap your faith in Potentates. We had the hottest day of the year and several soldiers fainted. The massed bands were moderate only, lacking in Bass, and they contrived to lower the quality even of Chopin's *March,* which one would have thought just suited to their taste and skill. *Saul* we expected to be massacred, nor were we disappointed. However, you will see from the General's letter that he for one is apparently satisfied.

In the summer the Agency moved down to Allendale, a large villa with a beautiful garden in Ramleh outside Alexandria. Clive and I lived with the Gorsts, and as all members of the staff played chess, I found conditions almost perfect.

We have had the ex-Sultan of Morocco on our hands: which gives rise to such edifying questions as who calls first, and what does he call him when he gets there. We decided on Majesty, which costs no more than lucky Jim, and gives so much more pleasure. I was sent down to meet him and present him to Russell, his bear-leader. We tactfully let the French Vice-Consul on board first

[22] As original *Seminator di scandalo e di scismo.* Dante had nothing against their followers, and places Saladin in the limbo which holds his master Virgil, with Homer and the other great unbaptized.

—to his eternal gratitude. I then drove H.M. in Sir Eldon's car to his hotel, where he nearly lost his reason in the lift. "God is greatest! We remark the floor to heave beneath our feet." I said Providence would continue to push it up till we reached the Imperial Apartments. Afterwards he tried to explain his fear away, saying he had heard of the System, but "For a long time it had escaped Us". I must say he seemed a very decent fellow and I trust, as indeed is not impossible, he will resume his Throne in the West at no distant date. He brought no Harem with him, at which Russell was, ignorantly and prematurely (I thought), relieved: I venture to prophesy he will live to regret the omission.

About midsummer, The Fear came upon me for the third time making me realize something of what Henley meant by "the fell clutch of circumstance". Some of the staff being on leave and there being comparatively little entertainment at Ramleh, I had taken on such work as this entailed in addition to my own. Sir Eldon made up a dinner party and handed me the list. I dispatched the invitations at once, and stood by for the acceptances, which came in at about the usual rate. Two mornings later the bell rang, and I went in, to find Gorst's face somehow different. He enquired how the dinner was going: I thought all right. He asked me if I had sent out all the invitations. I had. Whether I had done them myself: I was surprised at the question, but I had. Was I quite certain that I had written both the cards and the envelopes all myself? I was still more surprised, but again assured him that I had. "Then what", he asked me very quietly, "is this?" And he put into my hand an envelope bearing the name of one of our guests scrawled and misspelt in the crazy writing of a drunkard or a lunatic. "Is that your handwriting?" he asked. I said "No", but I would find out whose it was. Gorst said nothing, but looked at me, and I left the room with indignation and despair. With the envelope was a letter from the guest, an old friend of Gorst's, drawing attention to its unofficial and generally disreputable appearance. I walked out hardly knowing where I was going, stunned by the thought that he could have disbelieved me, and not seeing how I was ever to put myself right. I found myself near Stanley Bay, and seeing the house of the addressee was drawn to walk past it. The Berberin Bawwāb, whom I knew well, greeted me from his porter's chair. I asked him whether there had come within the last two or three days a letter from the Agency. He first said there had not, and then asked me why I wanted to know. Something made me threaten him that unless he told me instantly who had tampered with the envelope I would put the police on him. He promptly confessed that, as his master was considered eligible for an Under-Secretaryship, he had attempted to open what he had thought to be the Agency intimation without being discovered, in order to obtain from him a *Bashāra* or reward for the bringer of good news. Unfortunately he had (in every sense of the word) torn it, and in his despair had obtained from one of our Cavasses a British official envelope, upon which he had rewritten the address, not dreaming that anybody would bother about the envelope of an invitation. I took back the torn pieces of my own envelope, handed them to Gorst, and told him the story. He got up, put his hand on my shoulder, and asked whether I had reported the Bawwāb to his master. I said "No", and asked if he wanted further proof. He answered, memorably: "Be more generous to me than I was to you."

These three and later experiences have given me a life sympathy with the accused, perhaps caught and unable to explain or defend himself in the dreadful web of unassailable evidence. What would he or I do if at such a moment our honour were in charge of someone neither loving, loyal nor friendly, when he might even find that deadly action had been taken upon the unproved, perhaps unchallenged accusation? I determined from that moment that in charges depending upon unsupported statement, I would hardly condemn save on the explicit confession of the accused: in some charges, not even then.

> None of the sorrows of your youth
> None of the passions of your youth,
> Concern me much. But tell me here—
> What was your fear?

Meanwhile, the gravity of the political situation which had preyed upon Sir Eldon's mind lightened, and it seemed that the worst was over when he was attacked without realizing it by a fatal malady.

I am sorry to say Sir E. has been rather bad this last week: a touch of the sun, it is thought. I play the piano to him of an afternoon and read a little— Browning or Gibbon.

He was able to take no more exercise and I thought it best to travel with him when he went on leave. No specialist seemed able to help him, and though he returned to Egypt he grew slowly but surely worse throughout the winter. He held to his work as he had held to a losing set of tennis, fighting inch by inch his last deadly single against pain. Still he wrote his dispatches and his Annual Report, the sweat of agony pouring down his face. On 1 April 1911 I entered to receive for ciphering his last telegram to Sir Edward Grey, stating that his neuralgia was getting steadily worse and was incapacitating him for work, and asking to go on leave at once for treatment. But neither Acqui, his first attempt, nor any

treatment on earth could help him now, and the final operation served
only to show there was no hope. He was driven down to his home at
Castle Combe in Wiltshire for the close of his brief brilliant life. As he
lay there one afternoon, the servant informed his sister that there was a
gentleman waiting in a cab at the back door, the front drive being barred
for privacy. There she found the Khedive of Egypt, who had travelled
from Paris and driven in a fly the twenty-three miles from Swindon to
say good-bye to his friend. She told her brother, who could just understand her words, and brought His Highness to the bedside. The Khedive
took his hand and said: "God has not of late been very good to you; but
I think He is going to be very good to you now." The dying man raised
himself, touched his forehead and fell back; never to speak or perceive
again. Orientals (and not only orientals) are said to be sparing in their
worship of the setting sun; but the manner of this tribute was such that,
whatever his faults, I have never since been able to think unkindly of
Abbas Hilmi.[23]

On the day of King George's Coronation, we in Cairo had read in
Reuter's telegram that Sir Eldon had been wheeled to the window in
order to watch the fêtes over which he could not preside; and the rancour
of his enemies was exemplified by an Under-Secretary who remarked to
me in the street: "Advertising I see to the end." He was awarded the
G.C.M.G. long after he had ceased to be conscious, and a few days later
he died.

Gorst's social and administrative theories were of a piece, identical;
and the more I consider how well he was establishing both when he was
checked by the death of Bútros, how near he was to achieving them when
he was himself struck down,[24] the more deeply do I realize how irreparable was the loss of this experienced and sympathetic interpreter of
England to Egypt and of Egypt to England, and its reaction upon the
Anglo-Egyptian misunderstandings.

Two of the Ministers spoke to me to-day with tears in their eyes, as of men
losing a personal friend; and the prominent note of the vernacular Press is
the same.

I have lacked both the time and the talent to be an historian, but how
often have I wished that those who employed both for revaluations and
rehabilitations of Tiberius or of Lucrezia Borgia could have devoted them

---

[23] "The Khedive was greatly concerned at his death; and it is a touching fact, much
appreciated by our family, that he never fails to go every year to Castle Combe, where my
brother is buried, to lay a wreath upon his grave." Harold E. Gorst.

[24] "Before he died he told me that he thought it very hard that he should be removed
from the scene before the result had vindicated his policy." *Ibid*.

to the vindication of an unappreciated and calumniated Servant of the British Crown.

> When all its work is done, the lie shall rot,
> The truth is great, and shall prevail—
> When none cares whether it prevail or not.

A few days after Gorst's death Lord Haldane announced at dinner with Lady Horner that Kitchener had been appointed to Egypt. He was jubilant. For months the Press had been enquiring why the War Office had been unwilling or unable to utilize the services of the first soldier in the Empire; now the responsibility was assumed for a period of years by the Foreign Office.[25]

---

[25] The transfer incidentally released some twelve hundred pounds per annum, the emoluments of a Field-Marshal, it being contrary to the law of the land to draw simultaneously military and civil pay.

CHAPTER FIVE

1909–1914

The Egyptians whom ye have seen, ye shall see them again no more for ever.
EXODUS xiv. 13

I

FOR Cairo Society the golden epoch must have been the later 'eighties and the 'nineties. The genius of Lord Cromer had established peace, progress, and prosperity. British influence dominated, but had not yet learned to domineer. The social standards and conventions were continental, on the French model with a faint tinge of the Levant; not yet cosmopolitan. Cards were exchanged with Moslem, Coptic, Armenian, and Syrian, as well as with European notables, even by the British Agency. English society was relatively small, and still not too formal to indulge in picnics, reading and musical parties—even in donkey rides. The Sirdar himself thought it no shame to be seen riding daily from his house to his office on a white Asyūt donkey. In the early 1900's these stood, tall as ponies, well fed, closely clipped and glossy, with their forefeet on the pavement, brushing away the flies with independent motion of their enormous ears; the muscles of their necks 6 inches thick, the end of their tails bright with henna; the *hagab*—a triangular silver charm containing a verse from the Koran—hanging below their throats, and somewhere about them (as on all the cab-horses) a blue bead to keep off the evil eye. Those for hire bore a number plate in English and Arabic, "Donkey No. 172", on their saddle pummel. The creatures greatly enjoyed cigarette smoke being blown up their nostrils, and would lay their heads back and half close their eyes in a voluptuous ecstasy. (Long before my arrival donkeys had been relegated to the use of tourists—and not the best tourists —and had been given, like the camels at the Pyramids, the names of Derby winners or American Presidents, such as "Izinglaz" or "Lankun"—according to the nationality of the hirer.)

87

Entertainment took place in private houses rather than in clubs or restaurants, and English visitors who "wintered" in Cairo often returned there annually and were adopted as members of Cairene society. Of this social phase 1904 may be said to have marked the decline, 1914 the fall. The final application of the Entente Cordiale, abolishing the French appeal by pin-prick, "unveiled" the Protectorate, registered for Egypt an almost Crown Colony status, and relegated the effective control or criticism of Foreign Office policy to the spasmodic and not always informed interest of His Majesty's Opposition. Officially, and for a time, the change was entirely for the good. Flagrant abuses and "protections" vanished and a score of harmless necessary reforms were made possible for the Egyptian Government. The British Agent was no longer compelled to bargain, hat in hand, with his colleagues, offering some *quid pro quo* concession for the appeasement of disappointed place-hunters.[1] But with the decline of foreign political influence and so of foreign social prestige with the increasing numbers of minor British officials and the extension of the club and sport system; with the multiplication of the hotels, and the mass production of the peach-fed standardized tourist "doing" the whole country in ten days and demanding indiscriminate hotel dances, there came less mixing with and understanding of Egyptians and foreigners, and a general diminution of social caste, *cachet,* and character. Easy communications corrupt good manners, and I remember blushing to hear it said, as praise of a distinguished visitor: *"Il a même eu l'amabilité de rendre ma carte."* The classic process of colonization had begun. Everybody and everything was becoming cleaner, richer, easier and more proper, but somehow (and I have seen the symptoms elsewhere) there was less fun. Once more we had multiplied the harvest but not increased the joy.

The British official in Cairo and Alexandria (upon which two cities the provincial inspectorates were now increasingly based) was a hard and honourable worker, punctual and punctilious in his Department or Ministry from early morning until well after noon. He would then drive or bicycle to the Turf Club or his flat for luncheon, play tennis or golf until dark at the Sporting Club, return to the Turf Club to discuss the affairs of the day and dine there or at his flat. All, therefore, that the Egyptian official, high or low, saw of the average British official was a daily face gazing at him across an office desk from 8 a.m. to 1 p.m., Fridays excepted. The unofficial Egyptian saw not even that. Exchanges of visits were now almost unknown and the hundred contacts and hu-

---

[1] Such as minor Powers, holding up some necessary reform until another of their nationals had received a judgeship on the Mixed Tribunals.

manities that come from knowing people "at home"—from little Ahmad's teething or Mustafa's progress in English or in football—were hopelessly excluded. Nor was there, save for one or two notable exceptions, the faintest effort on the part of the official's wife to make the acquaintance, still less cultivate the friendship, of the wives or daughters of her husband's colleagues or subordinates; and it was with an air of virtuous resignation that she steeled herself to sacrifice an afternoon for a call upon an Egyptian or Turkish lady, as likely as not better born, better bred, better read, better looking and better dressed than herself.

It would be unfair to ascribe these neglects and abstentions entirely to condescension or indifference. Between persons of different race, climate, language and religion the conversational going is not always easy, largely because of the lack of common ground; and this was especially so before the spread of European education. If in Cairo you had to exclude on the one side all knowledge of tennis, golf, social information and the latest English novel, and on the other of Egyptian politics (and grievances), French literature and the cotton crop, the attainment of the statutory hour on family and symptom talk was sometimes hard labour. There were of course—and even now are heard—the familiar arguments to the effect that "Egyptians and foreigners don't appreciate visits and really prefer our keeping ourselves to ourselves"—a disingenuous depreciation of a most sociable, generous and hospitable race. I found those who saw them least most able to dogmatize about their likes and dislikes. The grave omission was only discovered, and by the sincere admitted, after the War, too late for remedy; nor is its importance as an agent in the general and apparently sudden disintegration of 1922 even yet appreciated. The awakening of Asia by Japan, the exactions and hardships of uncontrolled Labour conscription during the War, the war-weariness of England, and not least the Spirit of the Age, were in their consecutive degrees all responsible for the great Evacuation. But the process would have been more gradual and less bitter for both sides had it been prepared and softened by a reasonable measure of human intercourse between the governing and the governed of two peoples whose interests had always been, were then, and are now, absolutely identical.

In Palestine there subsisted during the early years of the Mandate a much better spirit; in Cyprus it was even worse; but I think that anybody with close and practical experience of all three countries will be disposed to allow that while the social estrangement in Cyprus and ultimately in Palestine was the result, in Egypt it was a contributing cause, of political exasperation.

I cannot pretend that the perception of these deficiencies (any more than of my own) caused me any personal affliction. Everything interested or amused, especially as the duties of an Oriental Secretary were—and should be—almost inextricably interwoven with his pleasure.

In 1909 Bowden Smith and I took a flat, whose previous successive occupants had been Sir William Garstin and Lord Edward Gleichen, immediately over the residence of its owner, Ibrahim Bey Helbawi, and less than two hundred yards from the British Agency. Helbawi Bey was an able and distinguished lawyer, a home of lost (but not unremunerative) *causes célèbres,* the advocate of the assailants of Denishwai. In order to ensure the profitable cultivation of his estates he had sent his attractive son Hassan to study agriculture in England; a routine existence which Hassan had found so tedious that, eager for more immediate and spectacular results, he had apprenticed himself instead to Messrs Maskelyne and Devant, without, however, disquieting his father by informing him of this transfer of his energies. He had recently returned, one of the most refined conjurers I have met, without offensive patter or back-chat; an inimitable producer of apples and oranges from curtains, waistcoats and even nostrils—from almost anywhere, indeed, save from the paternal acres. Delightful as Hassan proved himself at some of my lighter entertainments, I could not help sympathizing with the Bey's disappointment, audible sometimes even through the flooring.

The flat being too large and expensive for our unaided resources Bowden Smith and I co-opted my old comrade in Audit, Alexander Anastasius Pallis. His distinguished father had represented and led in Greece a movement of a necessity not obvious save to persons acquainted with literatures and countries under the domination of a Book. His ambition was so to remould the archaic Byzantine Greek, obligatory in all official or polite writing (but never spoken and often not understood), that Greeks should speak what they write and write what they speak. His experiments with Homer, amongst a people concerned less with the works of the poet than with his glory, passed relatively unnoticed; but his Revised Version of the New Testament, affecting the same sort of vested interests as had the early English versions, provoked such rioting in the streets of Athens that he had to fly for his life. An exponent of his theories was known as μαλλιαρος, "hairy", and "hairiness", μαλλιαρισμος, was their generic term. His Eton and Balliol son was naturally and properly μαλλιαρώτατος, and he indoctrinated us so early in the morning as breakfast with such earnestness, that he half converted me and drove Bowden Smith almost off his head. There is substance in the contention, not only in modern Greek. The noble Arabic language is still dominated by the Koran. You must still write *"Faras"* for "horse" though for centuries you have said *"Hosān"*: as if only "steeds" or "destriers" were worthy to appear in English black and white. It is not for foreigners to quarrel with peoples zealous and jealous to preserve the glories of their language. But speech, expressing live thought, is a living thing, growing naturally from a dialect into a language, dying and suffering by its rich decay rebirth into another language. When and how does a dialect cease to be a dialect? Not I think through committees and propaganda, not even through the most logical and scientific of translations, but after fusion by the white heat of creative genius into *Canterbury Tales* or *Divine Comedy*. Whatever the process, until, by his way or by mine, the dream of Pallis comes true, no great work of poetry or prose can be hoped from the Arab or Greek-speaking countries.

When Bowden Smith was removed by marriage, Pallis and I were joined by John Young, a sensitive artist and so reactionary to the vulgarization of the East he adored as not only, like me, to compel his Egyptian servant to wear a turban rather than the popular tarbush, but to declare in all sincerity that he would be happy to meet his death leading a forlorn hope of turbans against a tarbushed enemy.[2]

We kept three Egyptian servants, preferring their appearance and Arabic speech to that of those slaves by nature—Aristotle's φύσει δοῦλοι—the Berberin and, though it was none of our business to "look after" them domestically, we found them honest and hard-working, with the Egyptian capacity for rising to the unexpected occasion. The cook was a major solicitude: if Abd al-Azīz served an entrée below even our standard he would be summoned, thanked and requested to serve it again, with identical ingredients, that day two years.

From 1908 to 1917 I slept, with infinite pleasure, in a camp-bed on the north balcony, a tarpaulin stretched across the mosquito-curtain poles against the rare Egyptian rain.

I have never regretted that duty as well as inclination kept me from absorption into any one clique in the infinite variety of Cairo. There were in 1910 still surviving personages of the pre-Occupation period, with full memories of the Arābi Rebellion [3] in 1883; such as Riaz Pasha, an ex-Prime Minister, politically "impossible" but a most courteous old gentleman. Turkish survived, like Norman in our twelfth century, as the language of the Reigning Family, of the aristocracy, and of the Harīms. Princess Nazli's Arabic was far from pure or even correct. She addressed her sisters, nephews and nieces, and summoned her retainers, exclusively

[2] See pp. 102-3.
[3] Two of my Egyptian friends would urge me to resign when losing at chess with the expression *"Sállim Siláhak, Ya 'Arābi"*—"Yield up your arms, 'Arābi", as his troops had cried at the battle of Tel al-Kebir.

in Turkish. Indeed, I heard more than once on the lips of her ministerial visitors the expression (anomalous in the greatest Arab-speaking country) of *Pis Arabler,* "Dirty Arabs". I heard it even from her nephew, the stout good-natured Prince Haidar Fāzil, who divided his devotion between the mystical Order of the Bektashi in a cave under the Mokattam Hills and an *étude approfondi* of the works of *"mon maître révéré Gustave Flaubert".*

This is not to say that there survived, with the Turkish language, much enthusiasm for the Sublime Porte or the Ottoman Turks, either among those who knew of their deeds (rather than works) in Egypt or those who had occasion to compare, on the Golden Horn, Turkish dilapidation with the ever-increasing Egyptian prosperity. Nevertheless, Egyptians still respected Turks as a ruling class, for their air of authority (the *"grande autorità nel lor sembiante"*), as men who, in the delicate Turkish speech, spoke seldom, and softly. Still more, they sympathized with Turkey as the one great independent Moslem Power, the abode of the Vicar of God, the Guardian of the Holy Places, Mecca, Medina and Jerusalem. These sentiments were exploited, when convenient, by those same Nationalists whose creed had been inspired, fostered and made possible by the Occupation they so bitterly arraigned. That Occupation had therefore to reckon with pan-Islam until it was disproved by the War, beaten to its knees largely because of the Revolt in the Desert, and forced to suicide by Mustafa Pasha Kemal. As a factor in British policy, the doctrine of the Califate—of pan-Islamic Theocracy [4]—was mainly the creation of the India Office. The supposed indignation of "His Majesty's sixty million loyal Indian subjects", who appeared alternatively under the journalese disguise of "Moslem Susceptibilities", delayed many reforms in the Near and Middle East, kept several million Orthodox Christians as *"Rayahs"* [5] under Ottoman domination, and helped to paralyse intervention in the torture and massacre of countless innocent Armenians. Nevertheless, there was until the War a foundation of truth in the scare of pan-Islam, as Lord Cromer, after the Aqaba [6] incident, took occasion to remind his Government and public by quoting in the White Paper the following letter from an unknown Moslem:

In the name of God, etc.

To Lord Cromer, His Britannic Majesty's Agent,
The Reformer of Egypt.

Translation.

It is well known to you that the telegrams and newspapers appear each day, bringing nearer to us, as it seems, the likelihood of grave differences between

[4] As Signor Nallino has shown in his masterly monograph on the *Califato.*
[5] Oppressed Ottoman subjects.
[6] See p. 47.

England and the Ottoman Empire on matters relating to our land of Egypt. But as the hopes of men for things desired are often disappointed, so also— for God is merciful to his creatures—do their fears of evil come to nought. We pray the Almighty that it may be so now. I who write these lines in the name of "All the People of Egypt", am not a statesman or a man of great name; my person and my dwelling are alike unknown to you; but I feel constrained, inasmuch as I see many foolish acts committed, and hear many foolish words spoken, to stand on my feet and say the truth, as I think God has put it into my heart.

It is often said by fools, or by those who think thereby to make favour with the great: "The curse of God upon the Christian"; "May hell consume the unbeliever, his household and his possessions." These are unbecoming words, for curses pollute the lips of the curser, and the camel lies in wait for the driver who smites him unjustly. At the head of this letter I call you by the name of "The Reformer of Egypt", and by this name you are known between the seas and the deserts; also many, but not all, of the English who serve under you have followed in your footsteps as wise children carry on the traditions of their father. He must be blind who sees not what the English have wrought in Egypt: the gates of justice stand open to the poor; the streams flow through the land and are not stopped at the order of the strong; the poor man is lifted up and the rich man pulled down; the hand of the oppressor and the briber is struck when outstretched to do evil. Our eyes see these things, and we know from whom they come. You will say: "Be thankful, Oh men of Egypt! and bless those who benefit you"; and very many of us—those who preserve a free mind are not ruled by flattery and guile—are thankful. But thanks lie on the surface of the heart, and beneath is a deep well. While peace is in the land the spirit of Islām sleeps. We hear the Imām cry out in the mosque against the unbelievers, but his words pass by like wind and are lost. Children hear them for the first time and do not understand them; old men have heard them from childhood and pay no heed. But it is said: "There is war between England and Abdal-Hamīd Khan." If that be so, a change must come. The words of the Imām are echoed in every heart, and every Moslem hears only the cry of the Faith. As men we do not love the sons of Osmān; the children at the breast know their works, and that they have trodden down the Egyptians like dry reeds. But as Moslems they are our brethren; the Khalīf holds the sacred places and the noble relics. Though the Khalīf were hapless as Bayazīd, cruel as Murād, or mad as Ibrahīm, he is the shadow of God, and every Moslem must leap up at his call as the willing servant to his master, though the wolf may devour his child while he does his master's work. The call of the Sultan is the call of the Faith; it carries with it the command of the Prophet (blessings upon him). I and many more trust that all may yet be peace; but, if it be war, be sure that he who has a sword will draw it, he who has a club will strike with it. The women will cry from the house-tops, "God give victory to Islām!" You will say: "The Egyptian is more ungrateful than a dog, which remembers the hand that fed him. He is foolish as the madman who pulls down the roof-tree of his house upon himself." It may be so to worldly eyes, but in the time of danger to Islām, the Moslem turns away from the things of this world, and

thirsts only for the service of his Faith, even though he looks in the face of
death. May God (His Name be glorified) avert the evil!
  Signed by one, in the name of the people of Egypt.
Cairo, May 10, 1906.

Though these sentiments are now as dead as mutton, as Palestinian
extremists have found to their disappointment, yet any proved Christian
or Jewish encroachment upon the Precincts of the Haram al-Sharīf in
Jerusalem would still kindle a fire which might blaze from Alexandria to
Aswān. But for practical purposes Theocracy has been displaced as in
Europe by Ethnocracy: pan-Islam by National Independence, so that it
is no longer true to repeat, *"Lā wataniya fil Islām"*—"There is no nationality in Islām." Girgis Bey Hanain, the Coptic sub-Controller of Direct
Taxes, could remember how during the Arābi Rebellion he and other
Christians in the Provinces had been compelled to climb the Minarets of
Mosques, and, by reciting the Moslem call to Prayer, proclaim their be-
lief in the Apostolate of Muhammad. By 1922 Copts were being cordially
invited—and consenting—to preach Egyptian Independence in that
stronghold of Islam, the University of al-Azhar.
  Some of the characters and characteristics of the Cairo I first knew
deeply impressed my imagination. The Prime Minister, Būtros Pasha
Ghāli seemed a reincarnation of the Pharaonic Grand Vizier. In appearance he strikingly resembled the Fourth Dynasty wooden statue in the
Cairo Museum known as the "Shaikh al-Balad", the burgomaster. He
had been born in his ancestral village of Kemān in Upper Egypt (the
birthplace of St Anthony); had been educated in the Coptic College
founded by the Patriarch Cyril IV (1854-61, who according to tradition
was poisoned for attempting to bring about a reunion of the Coptic and
Greek Orthodox Churches); and had attained steadily and by undenied
merit to the highest positions in the State. Unlike other Egyptian Christians
who have succeeded in politics he manifested a deep interest in the welfare of his own community. He was (again as few Copts of his time) a
profound Arabic scholar; a lover of Arabic poetry who used constantly
to recite verses while dressing for dinner. He had begun to learn English
at the age of forty, and spoke it fluently. His French prose was clear, con-
cise and elegant. Asked in private audience by Pope Leo XIII whether he
knew Coptic, he was so vexed at having to confess his ignorance that, on
his return to Cairo, he surrounded himself with Coptic grammars and
lexicons until he had thoroughly absorbed the elements of his own
ancient language.
  Bútros was humorously proud of the financial instinct of the Copts,
some of whose greater fortunes have issued from unusual origins. Futan

Effendi Majhūl was travelling southward from Cairo in the days before corridor trains. He alighted for a minute at a wayside station near Minia, and before he was able to rejoin it the train moved on, leaving him stranded. Two of his countrymen, eyeing him with disfavour, asked him what brought him there; Futan Effendi, racially averse from a direct answer and somewhat shy of his *contretemps,* replied that it was chance and no particular business. Nothing in Egypt is less probable than the simple truth, and the two retired for a few minutes. When they returned it was to offer him £100 if he would go away. What European would not have taken the money, praising Heaven? Futan Effendi thanked them with unhesitating dignity but found the amount hopelessly inadequate and, when it had been raised to £500, protested that he was no petty clerk, that his time was precious and that he had not come there to be insulted; nor was his honour appeased until he had received from them in bank-notes £8800, with which he returned to Cairo. There he learnt that his benefactors had arrived on secret information of a land sale (quite unknown to him), ultimately profitable to the tune of some fifty thousand and that they had suspected him of being there with the same object. From this beginning a very few years of scientific lendings and foreclosings were required, to found one of the most prosperous families in Asyūt.

At the beginning of the century the great Armenian families of Nubar Pasha, the Prime Minister, and of Tigran Pasha still maintained some influence and much prestige. Of Nubar's knowledge of life it was quoted that, hearing a junior had spread vile rumours about him he had replied: *"Et pourtant je ne me rappelle pas lui avoir conféré aucun bienfait."* [7]

All too frequently an imposing Renault (in the early days of cars) would sweep up to the Agency, disembarking *Saheb al-Saada w'al Irshad al-Sayyid*—"His Excellency the Very Reverend and Venerable" Abd al-Rahīm Mustafa al-Demerdash Pasha. The Cavasses rushed forward to welcome the best Egyptian-dressed man in Egypt and to assist (quite unnecessarily) up the steps his exquisite striped silk *quftan,* the floating peach-rose *abaya,* the perfume of Yasmin or Narkis, the cabochon emerald, and, alas, the elastic-sided boots. The Sayyid's property had been rescued by British protection from a miscarriage of justice in the Religious Courts and he would impress upon his countrymen with more zeal than tact that, but for the Occupation, he and they too would be going not so much *Lābis mulūki*—royally clad—as "like the Turks", in rags and tat-

[7] "Les hommes ne sont pas seulement sujets à perde le souvenir des bienfaits et des injures; ils haïssent même ceux qui les ont obligés, et cessent de haïr ceux qui leur ont fait des outrages." (La Rochefoucauld.)

ters. These expressions caused him to be cited in the Arab comic papers as "Mister Demerdash".

In sharp and pathetic contrast were the visits of the great Zubair Pasha, calling almost weekly to claim an outstanding matter of some two million sterling which, so far as I was able to ascertain, was really owing to him, but the reimbursement of which no living soul would have been prepared to discuss. Gordon had evicted him from his vast domains and exiled him as a slave-dealer: and his son had been shot dead. In the stress of the Khalīfa's Rebellion he had offered to return and lend the weight of his name and forces to Gordon's garrison. Gordon had pressed the British Government to accede, but they had refused; bowing, it was said, to Exeter Hall. Now the discrowned King of the Sudan lived on into another epoch, with a small pension, in the suburb of Helwān, marrying an occasional wife (the cause of his gentle importunities) and leaving with me the memory of his courteous patience, his rough silver turquoise ring and the deadly cold of his hands.

The aged Contessa della Sala resembled Zubair Pasha only as being also in method and manner a pre-Occupation survival. She was Russian, a natural daughter of Prince Gagarin, and had been married to an elderly Comte Beketoff who brought his young wife to visit Egypt. She had exaggerated the merit of an attractive Italian adventurer, the Conte della Sala. At a shooting party near the Pyramids somebody's bullet found its billet in Beketoff, and the rich widow married and paid the debts of della Sala on condition that he gave up gambling; which he duly abandoned for horse coping. The Contessa had resumed her widowhood long before I came to Cairo. She was intimate with the Cromers, with Princess Nazli and with the leaders of the foreign colonies. As the phrase went, *elle courait les harems,* in which no less than elsewhere she had built up an unassailable position, based not only upon her swift and exact repartees but upon her rare and invaluable talent of providing without hesitation a formula which, as occasion demanded, marked or liquidated the situation. On the entry into a drawing-room of a newly accredited diplomat's wife with her hair towering behind like that of an El Greco seraph, a far-pitched voice was heard to remark: *"Ophélie, sortant des eaux."* The departure from the railway station of a high British official, with crowds, bouquets and red baize, was cruelly but correctly registered as *"enterrement de première classe."* *"Il a trouvé sa planche de sauvetage",* was the comment on the engagement of a penniless young man to a particularly slender heiress. One of the Pashas, *très snob,* lavishly entertained visiting celebrities, but as they seldom returned his hospitality when in Europe he was driven by his *snobisme* to entertain them there again. *"Le pauvre",*

she would say, *"il rend à Paris les dîners qu'il donne au Caire."* On the
other hand she could bless as well as bruise. The *Salome* [8] of Strauss had
enjoyed in some capitals not only a musical success, but also a *succès
de scandale,* and the delicate question of whether *jeunes filles* should be
permitted to attend in Cairo was referred to the Contessa. *"La musique
couvre tout",* was her verdict; and it did. An Indian conjurer at an At
Home stripped himself, to show that there was no deception, absolutely
and finally nude, but the *sauve qui peut* was easily averted when we were
calmly enjoined: *"Ne vous inquiétez pas: ce ne sont que des bronzes."*
In spite of these public services, it must be recorded that the Contessa's
head was better than her heart. When the Russians for whom, in their
absence, she had for forty years proclaimed her admiration and devotion,
arrived in Egypt by thousands as refugees, and even the anti-Slav by temperament succoured them to the verge of the possible, the Contessa della
Sala's contribution was two dozen toothbrushes.

I have already mentioned the Princess Nazli Fāzil.

Last week I went with Graves to tea with the Princess Nazli, the only
emancipated female member of the Blood. She came in at three, and talked
till 4.15 without our getting in so much as a word: good English, tempered
with Arabic.

This once beautiful and still brilliant sexagenarian, keeping, and using,
fiercely interesting eyes, was a niece of the Khedive Ismail and implacably
resentful of his grandson the Khedive Abbas. She had married young and
lived for many years in Constantinople, where our Ambassador, Sir
Henry Layard, had cherished her with the kindness of a second father,
showing her the best side of European freedom and giving her full access
to the life of the day. She maintained with some scores of servants and
old family slaves great state in a large palace immediately behind the Abdīn. Nazli had known Queen Victoria, King Edward, the Sultan Abd al-
Hamīd and most of the famous statesmen and other personalities of her
day. On the death or divorce—I never could remember which—of her husband, she had returned to Cairo, marrying, for general convenience, an
agreeable Tunisian, Bu Hāgeb Bey, Mayor of La Marse (who continued
to reside in Tunis), and receiving and entertaining, with the gracious
manner of the House of Muhammad Ali, chosen members of Egyptian
and European Society. Saad Zaghlūl was her lawyer and it was at her
advice or command—they were not always easy to distinguish—that the

---

[8] This, my first Richard Strauss, was an event for me, and I attended all the rehearsals.
Twice the conductor (and my good friend) Signor Bracale, flung down the score and rushed
from the house, his fingers writhing in his hair. "5. ii. 1911. Tues. and Wed. undress
rehearsals of *Salome:* I regret to say that this lady, completely losing her temper, so far
forgot herself as to throw the charger and head at J. the B., who was talking in the wings."

Azhar student had learnt French and generally rendered himself first *ministrable* and in the end *papabile*.

You walked in past the two eunuchs, named according to custom after flowers or precious stones, lounging outside the Bawwāb's Lodge, across a crunching gravel courtyard where a club of friendly cats dozed round a cluster of palms; you stood before the inner door and cried, *"Ya Sātir"*— "O Discoverer"—(one of the ninety-nine epithets of God) the conventional warning to ladies that a man is about, and that they must veil. There was a scramble, and one or two slaves, giggling with tactfully magnified excitement, ran up the stairs to warn "al-Brincessa"; whilst you followed, took your seat in the drawing-room and waited. Whether you were early, punctual or late, you always waited—if only for a minute.) The room, regarded aesthetically was, by any standard, of comic horror. But it was infinitely more interesting and expressive of its owner than the most doggedly consistent Period that sudden wealth aided by the best hired advice could have achieved. The electric light hung in (yet was not of) immense gilded gasoliers. The chairs and sofas were debased *Modo Luigi Khamastāshir* (the local Louis Quinze), in magenta plush surrounded by hard shiny gilding and of an extreme discomfort. Every table was loaded with photographs glazed but not framed, and so was the old concert grand complete with pianola attachment. There must have been near a thousand photographs in the room; as well as richly framed pictures of the British Royal Family, the Sultan Abd al-Hamīd, Lord Kitchener, Lord Grenfell and Lord Cromer. Not only the numerous gilt screens, but every inch of the four walls of the vast apartment, were covered with pasted pages of the illustrated papers, enabling you when bored with your neighbour to con the history of the past twenty years over his shoulder.

The Princess was strongly, sometimes embarrassingly, pro-British of the Get-on or Get-out school, and, like Afrikaner ladies I have known, strangely distrustful and intolerant of her own people, or of any attempt to reason with or convince the "other side". When J. M. Robertson, The Liberal M.P., known to be in sympathy with Egyptian "aspirations", paid his last visit to Cairo, Nazli wrote to him twice inviting him to call, and on his regretting his inability to find time finished him off as follows: "Sir, After having received yesterday your second excuse of not being able to come to see me I fully believe now that my friends were right in telling me that your Egyptian friends would never allow you to have a talk with me. I would not believe them as I never thought an English could be greatly influenced by an Egyptian but I see now clearly that your affection for the Egyptians is stronger even than mine for the English. I should have been most interested to meet you in order to have a long discussion with you about my country and yours without being afraid of anybody nor taking a *parti pris*. I hope before leaving Egypt you will have studied both parties well and will at least have given credit to your own country for having brought justice and great prosperity to Egypt. Believe me, most faithfully yours, Nazli." A document of which I shall be pleased to furnish a free copy to all self-constituted investigators of British incompetence or tyranny throughout the Near or Middle East.

We dined with Nazli on Thursday: though still Anglophil, she is anti-Gorst and becoming pro-Khedive. Kitchener wrote her a long letter this week. After eating I played chess with Rushdi Pasha, Director-General of the Wakf, or Department of Religious Endowments, and, partly owing to his skill, but more owing to the din of N. playing Tric Trac (backgammon) with Raouf Pasha (the Turkish High Commissioner), and calling upon Baal Peor, or whatever their Gods are, in Turkish, I lost.

Hussein Rushdi Pasha Topuzzáde,[9] who afterwards deserved, and received, well of England as Prime Minister of Egypt throughout the War, was an agreeable mixture of ability, integrity, and *Quartier Latin Gaminerie*. When the game went well he exulted aloud. In adversity he would endeavour to "put me off" by a continuous ribald commentary. *"Faites, jeune homme, faites: c'est votre droit: personne ne peut le vous contester." "Vous trouvez que cela est intelligent de votre part? Eh bien! je m'en fous, refous et contrefous."*

There also I often met Shaikh Ali Yusuf, editor of the *Moayyad*, the Palace "organ", who richly, though by careful negative inference, repaid an hour's conversation; while Saad Pasha Zaghlūl, always honest, then balanced and unspoilt, thundered against his ruler, and supported Lord Cromer with all his strength. His brother, Fát-hi Pasha Zaghlul, a frail disembodied intelligence, for all his services (including an excellent Arabic rendering of Gustave Lebon's *A quoi tient la supériorité de la race Anglo-Saxonne?*) never became a Minister and died a disappointed man.

Princess Nazli was a fervent Moslem:

Graves and I lunched with Nazli; she was in excellent form, furious against Dante—"the Italians, a horrible wretched low kind of a people"—and about to remove the offending page [10] when I suggested that she should merely excise the two names, and insert small slips bearing that of the person she hated most *pro tem*. Plan greeted with rapture. She told us she was once staying at a large house in Bavaria, and left it at five minutes' notice because a "horrible disgust-

[9] Of which, as I had the pleasure of informing him, the exact English rendering is "Son of a Gun".
[10] See p. 82.

ing man told her he was writing a book about the vices of the Prophet"; and we quite believed her.

Nazli's kindness extended to the arrangement of pleasant and unusual expeditions:

We lunched on Monday at the Bektashi-Tekia, the monastery of a Shiite [11] Muhammadan order, under the Mokattam hills. The Prior, or chief Baba, called Muhammad Ali Dada Baba is a charmingly benignant and distinguished looking old fellow. He had asked Nazli's Prince Haidor to meet us, and a sheep had been roasted whole in our honour. The truth is that such dishes are never quite hot or quite cold, which spoils the taste a good deal. Also, their courses are far too numerous, and you must not pass dishes. We had to climb the hill to work away that meal. We visited their cemetery, tunnelled far into the rock: all the time you must mutter *"al-Salāmu alaikum, ya ahli l'ḳubūr"*—"the peace upon you, O people of the tombs", and then, answering yourself for them: *"al-Salāmu alaikum, ya ahli l'dínia"*—"the peace upon you, O people of the world." If you forget or omit this formula, your only son dies within three months, your house is destroyed by fire, and your name forgotten as it had never been. We were naturally at some pains to comply with the regulations.

Nazli's set-piece luncheons and dinners for Egyptian Ministers and couples from the *Corps Diplomatique* conferred the relative glory of entertainments recorded in *The Morning Post*. Chance meals, like my chess evenings, when you telephoned that you were coming, and took what you found, discovered the spirit of the place. *Sitt Tawasíla,* a poor dependent, had a pretty touch on that tinny rather pointless huge mandoline *al 'Ud,* whose beautiful name of Lute has become the high romance of psalmody. Or a vast Abyssinian slave would ascend the pianola stool and pedal out a suite of Variations on *Home Sweet Home,* to which the exquisite little Tunisian Fattūma in shimmering azure whatnots, her loose hair braided in sequins, would gravely revolve and undulate through the oldest dance in the world. On some nights, which were accounted the greatest (and were perhaps the most interesting), Shaikh Yūsuf, the Caruso of the Near East, would consent to sing. The Shaikh, no less modest than charming, was past exhilaration at applause from his own people but puzzled by Western insensibility to his art. There were no verses nor any preordained beginning or ending to his song. Holding the palm of his right hand to his ear, and swaying slowly from side to side he would pass from phrase to phrase, cadenza to cadenza, pausing at the end of each for breath; the expression varying (though the theme never) from an indication of unfulfilment and resulting distress to a shrill sexual shriek.

[11] See footnote 8 on page 167.

At each pause the audience vented their appreciation in voluptuous groans, calls upon Allah: "God upon you, O Shaikh"; "Have mercy"; "Refrain from us"; with hissing intakes of the breath as if suffering an intolerable delight. I love these sounds now with my memory, as *Evocacions* of Albeniz, for what they recall, but they are to me as "melodies unheard, sweeter", and I place them in the world of music below the bagpipes though well above the chatter-compelling strains of the West End restaurant. I cannot believe in music without harmony or counterpoint expressed or implied, and I see no greater superiority to our scale in an octave divided into quarter and even smaller tones, than in the two hundred and fifty squares of Halma over the chess-board. Further, from the almost comic ecstasy of these otherwise very intelligent hearers and the serious, not to say deleterious impact of the noise upon their emotions, I incline to believe that Plato, in banishing "Music" from his Republic, was legislating for very much the same sort of stuff; that the names (beautiful as a dream) of the Dorian, the Hypo-Lydian and Mixo-Phrygian Modes represent not much more than the modern *Daur* [12] of *Kurod* and of *Nahavand;* and that even the simplest forms of music tolerable to us are a comparatively late Western development. I heard sometimes snatches of truer music during my late returns home: the sweet huskiness of that flute which so sounds its name, (as olives look their taste) the *Nai,* heard from a Mevlevi Dervish—or the rhythmic thudding of a *Tabla* or *Darabūḳa* within some latticed casement over a high narrow gateway.

31. xii. 1913. I was called to the telephone last Sunday morning and told that a message had been received from the Palace that Princess Nazli had died at 4 a.m. Only the day before I had telephoned to enquire after her health, and had been informed by one of the slave girls that she was much better. I went round at once to ask whether I could be of any use, and found Prince Hussein,[13] Zaghlul Pasha and others sitting in the big room downstairs. Prince Hussein told me that he had been with her until half-past seven the night before when she had appeared in fair health though in poor spirits, and was convinced that she would not survive the month of December in which both her parents had died. Her death which was painless was the result of cardiac paralysis. Just before drawing her last breath she closed her eyes with her own hand. Her death leaves Prince Hussein the eldest surviving member of his family. He seemed very much concerned at her death, and kept repeating rather incongruously: "*c'était un type, c'était un type.*" I, remembering her as a very kind and intimate friend of about seven years, felt her loss. Only five days before her death I had gone in to see her fairly late at night, and sat talking and laughing with her for an hour: she was in excellent spirits and made some jokes fairly broad in nature,—having reference to the hour and place.

12 Scale or Mode.
13 Afterwards Sultan of Egypt.

Of others of the Khedivial House I remember Prince Fuad, afterwards Sultan and King, energetic, enlightened, European in tastes if not always in methods, fond of poker and the supper-parties of Kasr al-Dubara; Prince Yusuf Kamāl who collected with discrimination the brilliantly enamelled glass mosque-lamps of thirteenth-century Egypt; shot big game all over the world and gave me a day's hunting after jackal with English huntsmen and hounds, through the sugar-canes of Nag Hamādi; and Prince Muhammad, afterwards Regent, with his great "lucky" emerald ring, the revived Oriental splendours of his *Manial* Palace, his courtly bearing and graceful entertainment; his fine devotion to his mother. More than one member of that House has inherited the Royal manner of their founder Muhammad Ali. One of them was showing a visiting couple round his garden. The husband, walking behind, suddenly beheld a cactus of such surpassing rarity that he involuntarily stooped to detach it from the soil. Even as he stooped the Prince turned. Crimson, the unhappy man fumbled as though adjusting a shoe-lace. The Prince made no allusion to the incident; but when, after coffee and compliments, the pair drove away, they found in their car the identical cactus, neatly packed in a petrol tin.

During the first decade of the twentieth century the faint hope—battle it cannot be called for none was fought—for preserving the Egyptian national costume, furniture and architecture was irretrievably lost. All over the world the nations were fighting, with instinctive homage to Goethe to preserve or acquire identity: *Höchstes Glück der Erdenkinder ist nur die Persönlichkeit*. With most the issue was simple and obvious nationalism: sometimes merely linguistic, as with the Flemish; generally political, as with the people of Iraq; occasionally both, as in Hungary. Those, especially outside Europe, who could not for the moment obtain all they demanded in these directions were inclined to adopt the outward characteristics of a superior material civilization, imitating physically where they could not politically. They abandoned the beauty (with the economic freedom) of what they had made themselves, and clutched at whatever commonness the mass production of the West was prepared to sell them. The extreme hopeless protest against this slavery of universal sameness was to be Mahatma Gandhi's spinning wheel.

In Egypt some of us before, during and even after the War believed that it was still possible for Egypt to retain Egyptian interest and tradition without sacrifice of modern necessity. Only a few rich Egyptians—mostly of the Provinces—realized this possibility. Demerdash in his *quftan* was the best-dressed man in Egypt. Prince Muhammad Ali set the example with his magnificent Oriental palace, and one or two Pashas have followed him. But the vast majority regarded such practices as eccentric, affected, or at best *de luxe,* nor did the Syrian and the Italian furniture factories in the Mousky, the ivory fly-whisks of the al-Hāmi Wakf establishment in the Kasr al-Nil, nor even the art-leather bags fostered by the Ministry of Education, do much to encourage the young Egyptian who aspired to live, as well as to vote or demonstrate, nationally.

Yet there was so much that Egypt could and did produce, but which Egyptians would not use: so many things national, as well as useful and beautiful, which were crowded out by foreign production. By my time no Government official, from the Minister to the probationary clerk, was to be seen in the dress of his country. There was no local pride, as in the Scottish kilt or the Bavarian *lederhosen,* in the *'ámma* [14] the *galabía* [15] or the *quftan;* [16] which on the contrary were derided as *baladi* (rustic) and precluding the wearer alike from Government employment and European consideration.

I firmly, John Young fiercely,[17] compelled our respective servants to appear before us in *ámmas* and *galabías;* but they hated them and always went to and from their homes in tarbushes; fearing, as Ismain admitted, to be taken for Azhar students from the provinces. I do not believe that the just triumph in 1936 of an honourable nationalism will extend to the revival of a national costume which, though suitable to a hot country, is yet pocketless and ill adapted for rapid motion.

The fast of Ramadan, extending from dawn to sunset and excluding even water and tobacco, severely tried the poorer classes who still strictly observed it; the servants in particular scamping their tasks in sullen exhaustion. The upper and official classes revolted increasingly against an ordinance which wrecked one twelfth of the working year. Drinking of wine was now public as well as frequent:

On Monday night the Prime Minister gave a river dinner to the Cheethams, Bells (Americane Minister), R. Graham, the Ministers of Justice and of Education and the Oriental Secretary, who found himself seated between the Minister of Education and the Prime Minister—both Moslems. The former tanked up very liberally with the champagne, and rebuked me for not keeping him company. [I was for some years a teetotaller.] I remarked that it must be the first time in the history of Islam that a Moslem over his own brimming beaker had cursed an unbeliever for abstemiousness. "By God", replied His Excellency, "I am a Copt! The Coptic newspapers say that we are converts from their stock; let us share their principles." Continuing to converse in Arabic, the Minister said to me: "The proportions, O my soul, of this party are adverse." I asked: "The reason, my paternal uncle?" He replied: "When I prepare a

---

14 Small turban wound round soft fez.
15 Long-sleeved close garment reaching to the ground.
16 Outer long-sleeved close garment opening in front and often of silk.
17 "A man who found good in many things, but little good in things now being made." *Seven Pillars.*

feast for thee, O my Sir, we will have not eight men and two ladies, but two men and of ladies at least a score."

Beer began to invade even the bazaars. Observing a friend there one day enjoying a glass of Lager I asked what sort of Moslem was this. *"Ana mush Muslim"*, he answered merrily. "I am not a Moslem: *ana wáhid 'libre benseur'.*"

Among Europeanisms adopted, the visiting card played an important part. These generally afforded a good deal more information than they do in England. They were as a rule lithographed very cheaply by Armenians in Arabic and French, and nearly always gave full details of the profession or official function of the owner. That of His Beatitude the Coptic Patriarch was the only card, to my knowledge, printed in ancient Coptic. Those of leading Freemasons were enriched with gavels, compasses, all-seeing eyes and various Euclidean abbreviations. The rough-edged card of my good friend the Archbishop of Mount Sinai, resident in Cairo throughout the season (after which he went to Carlsbad), bore, together with his Cambridge Honorary Degree, a miniature presentment of the Holy Mountain, with a small Cross emerging from the summit. A European employee of the Railway Administration was about to be married, *moyennant un dot raisonnable,* to the sister of the Lady Companion of a Princely Personage. Unhappily the sum required was not forthcoming, and the romantic alliance had to be broken off: but not before the suitor had printed and begun to circulate his new style (of which I long preserved my copy), as *"Beau-frère morganatique de Son Altesse".*

II

My love of mediaeval Cairo was in time rewarded by the honour, of which I am still proud, of being appointed a Member of the *Comité pour la Conservation des Monuments Arabes,* a small mixed Egyptian and European committee meeting monthly, in charge of the ancient monuments of Cairo. This made it a duty, as it had been a pleasure, to explore the noble and unique series of Mosques—the splendid Sultān Hassan; Qalaün, sumptuous as a casket of the Ptolemies; the mystery of al-Ghūri; Ibn Tūlūn, like a great Assyrian palace; Ibrahim Ágha, the tiled Blue Mosque; and the Citadel Mosque of Muhammad Ali, architecturally indifferent yet, by pride of place, the crown of the city. There is in these fluted domes and tiered minarets of the Mameluke sovereigns a jaunty, a temperamental quality which I have observed in no other architecture. The dinning cries and crashes of the narrow streets seemed to float upward, muted and transmuted into an immemorial harmony and rhythm. I think I climbed every climbable minaret in Cairo; and I would begin again to-morrow if ever I returned.

The *Comité,* being advisory to the Director of Wakfs (Moslem Pious Foundations), was not much concerned with Coptic remains, of which indeed the interest and importance were only just beginning to be generally known. Christianity had once been the State religion of Egypt (without its "E" the same word as Copt): the Copt, unmingled with the blood of the Arab invader, descends directly from the people of the Pharaohs. The vast majority of Copts, however, took about as much interest in pre- or early-Christian as Moslems did in pre-Moslem Egypt— or as most Englishmen do now in Roman or semi-Saxon Britain. Ancient Egypt had been "pagan" for Copts, for Moslems the *Jāhilia,* or Period of Religious Ignorance. The Churches of the Coptic minority had been since the Moslem conquest humble and retired compared with the public magnificence of the great mosques; and had thus been overlooked even by the European zeal which had in the first instance been responsible for the intelligent preservation of Saracenic architecture. Yet here was a unique survival in design, in ornament and in liturgical language, of Ancient Egypt. These, with remote traditions and decorative motives from Greece and Asia, had been moulded into a distinct personality by the all-absorbing plasma of the Nile; and were found in the form of exquisite wool and linen weaving of the early Christian Era; church vessels of copper, bronze and silver; manuscripts, ecclesiastical vestments and wood carving of an unusual depth; scattered or buried throughout the length and breadth of Egypt.[18] Maspéro, the first archaeologist to devote attention to Coptic antiquities, gave them a special but inadequate section in the Egyptian Museum. The first person to perceive that as the majority of the Coptic churches and convents were outside the scope of the *Comité,* so there remained many categories of objects unsuitable to the Egyptian Museum, was Morcos (Mark) Simaika Pasha, a high official in the Railway Administration and (still more to the purpose), Vice-President of the *Maglis Milli,* the Coptic Community Council. Simaika Pasha began, none too soon, to catalogue all objects of interest that had survived the apathy of the abbots and the centenarian Patriarch, and the enterprise of the dealers; and he had begun to house ikons and bibles in a room adjoining one of the churches of Old Cairo. He was good enough to associate me with him in the fascinating conception of a Coptic Museum in which as many as possible—the vast majority—of the

---

[18] The period has been well realized in Dean Butcher's *Story of the Church of Egypt.* 2 vols. 1897.

exhibits should be not only exhibits but integral portions of the structure, within and without.

I have taken advantage of a happy dearness in the price of timber to arrange for a Dome over the corner of the Museum. The art is traditional here, and there are hundreds of little unknown men that can neither read nor write, who can execute (wholly without paper plan) an excellent mud-brick dome which will last 1000 years. We are also using every ancient pillar, capital, drum, or marble slab (at present wasting floor or shelf room) in the structure itself: a practice followed by Byzantine and other builders all over the Near East, and leading to very picturesque effects.

We began erecting our buildings in the part of Fustāt known as Babylon, in the precincts of the beautiful tenth-century Muallaqa church and (appropriately enough) in the Christian fortress of Qasr al-Sham which capitulated to the Arabs in 641. We gave them the form of a sixteenth-nineteenth-century Coptic house, adorned with (and constructed of) ancient marble columns, lattice *mushrabia* windows, panelled doors and walls, carved beams and ceilings, and curiously inlaid fountains; and the cumulative effect (much of it dating from long after my departure from Egypt), of the gentle glowing colours of the Museum, churches, fortress and gardens is not to be forgotten.

I lifted from Yassa Bishara in Luxor about a dozen very ancient Coptic crosses and bronzes, which have enriched our little Museum. He got a good puff for his generosity in the Coptic Press, partly as a reward and partly to stimulate others; with the result that the Coptic Archbishop of Alexandria appeared this morning and handed me a manuscript New Testament about four hundred years old. There is plenty of money in this country for all kinds of projects, if only people are approached in the right way.

Such has been the subsequent growth of this little enterprise that it was in 1931 granted by Royal Decree the status (but I trust has not yet acquired the character) of a Government Museum. This was my first taste, twenty-five years ago, of creative foundation—a taste which I was enabled to gratify on a larger scale in Jerusalem and Cyprus; nor have I ever discovered any feature in politics, diplomacy or routine administration which confers a more abiding satisfaction.

I think I must have begun that interest in the physical presentment of a lost world, which some call "collecting", from the moment I left school. At Cambridge it was a Queen Anne bureau, a few folios and some mild excursions in pewter. All that side of life—books, pictures, porcelain and furniture—is precluded in Egypt; so that he who would adorn his house individually and from within the country must make use of what can be found there, to wit: statuary, rugs, Near Eastern *faïence,* cottons and silks, brass and copper jugs and bowls, Persian paintings and Byzantine ikons. I never in my life bought an *antika* because it was antique, or unless it possessed some use or beauty, being temperamentally unable to appreciate archaeological fragments, ruins or ground plans, until they have been assimilated into history. Nor was I ever led away by the desire to possess objects in series. From this rule I excepted Greek coins. Wherever Alexander the Great advanced his victorious standards he minted his own issue, striking on the obverse his own ideal portrait as Heracles helmed in a lion's head, and on the reverse the throned Zeus with sceptre and eagle, having in the field or beneath his feet the crest or token of the territory conquered. From time to time the life savings of his veterans would be found beneath the soil of Egypt, buried in earthen amphorae; so that you can travel with his armies from the Ram's head of Ammon in the West through the Rhodian Rose and the Phoenician inscriptions of Tyre and Sidon, up to Babylon and the gates of India, tracing his name with his fame from the first Alexandria to its easternmost presentment as Kandahar. For some years I followed this fascinating trail, amassing some six hundred varieties of his Drachmas and his Tetradrachmas until, what with the complications of the cabinet and its trays, and the look of sick despair on the faces of friends to whom I attempted to show them, I abandoned the pursuit (together with that of minute objects in general), and did not set eyes on the collection for ten years. My marbles and ikons were invested by well-wishers with a local renown to which their intrinsic value (and certainly the prices I was able to pay) hardly entitled them. Much of the pleasure of the acquisitions was in the acquiring; for frequent expeditions to shops and bazaars alone or with a friend brought one into further contact with an intelligent, amusing and very human array of Syrians, Armenians, Copts, Persians, Jews, and such characteristic Egyptian Moslems as the Shaikh al-Gabri of Giza and Haj Muhammad Muhassib, the Arch Venerable of Luxor. I can say of the collection, if so it must be called, as of the by-product of a more celebrated leisure, that there was sport in its making.

There were but few concerts in Cairo before the War and no permanent public orchestra. If you were of those to whom music is not a luxury but a necessity you had, with gramophones still scratchy and no wireless, to play it or to organize it yourself. I will make bold, as I contributed none of the talent, to look back upon my Wednesday afternoons with mingled pleasure and pride. Like the Russian in the *Bois Sacré* who, though deprecating presents of all kinds, was yet prepared to accept *"une émeraude, un automobile"*, I had received with a grateful absence of protest a small Blüthner Grand which a friend in Europe had announced was on its way to me, and which was duly carried up the staircase on the back of one Egyptian porter. The guests, never more than twelve, were asked for half-past four and, whether they came punctually or not, the entire tea service was removed at five-fifteen when the music began. Arrivals during a song or sonata waited until its conclusion the wrong side of the front door; strikers of matches were softly conducted to an inner room; by an arrangement with the local policeman barking dogs were chased out of hearing and all traffic down our by-road diverted, as for an *accouchement,* into another street. The only lighting was an orchestra lamp for the piano and a tall Fourth Dynasty cylinder of alabaster, glowing through the dusk like an amber tiger. Many musicians passing through Cairo were kind enough to help us, but the brunt for the eight months of the Egyptian year was borne by a French, an Austrian and an Italian lady. I hope there are still left some who remember with happiness the delicate silver flute of Madame Sabatier-Chevally's Weckerlin and Debussy; the Wolf and Strauss chanted by Frau Amster's noble organ; and, most of all, the willing and inexhaustible youth and fire of *Chromatic Fantasy* or Duparc accompaniment, shed for our delight by Lucia Adamoli de Cramer. These Wednesdays, the joy of my week, I was able to keep musical, and not social; though, as they became known, not without strong hints and even demands that I should enlarge my list. One of the pretences more or less abolished by the War is that the intelligent woman must "love" music. In those days the lack was almost equivalent to an admission of a hearty appetite, even of snoring. The standard neighbour at dinner had—*ex officio*—"played" as a girl, been discouraged by her husband's lack of appreciation and had so gradually (but not without a struggle) "given it up"—and then there was so little really good music in Cairo—of course you couldn't count restaurants. Once, and even twice, I was young enough to take these laments at face value and to send the plaintiff notices a month, and again three days, before a concert by some eminent instrumentalist; only to scan the hall in vain for her or the other starved souls, and to learn next day their desolation at having been compelled to sacrifice their higher instincts upon the altar of a Bridge Tea.

As a real bazaar—and an assumed mosque—expert, I must have conducted hundreds of visitors, often with satisfaction, sometimes with positive pleasure, never without learning something I knew not before, round the steadily diminishing Egyptian Cairo. The strain was frequently considerable, especially if it was a question of "matching" colours or materials. Some ladies wanted a different stuff they had seen last year in

Algiers with the same name; others, apparently the same sort of stuff which however could not be right because it had a different name. Preference was general for whatever was not there. Similar criticism was passed on the bazaars themselves: either they were exactly like what visitors had seen in a dozen other countries or—they were not at all what they had expected. I tried to cater for all tastes, drawing the line only, but very firmly, at bead necklaces. Women knew best how a given object would "go" with themselves or their surroundings, and it was soon easy to prophesy with exactitude what their choice must be. Men knew what was intrinsically genuine or good of its kind. I rarely met a woman knowledgeable about or interested in Oriental rugs.

Some tourists, in their fear of being overcharged, cut the vendor down to the bone, until he cried in bewilderment: "But hwere is my brofit from the burchase?" The same sort of tourist would invite one to dine at Mena House and, exclaiming that the desert air was as good as champagne, proceed to order a sound *vin de table*. Some cared so little for the things wherein Egypt differed from the standard European winter resort that I used to wonder why they had bothered to make the journey. Showing a party of seven to the best of my ability round one of the many chambered tombs of Saqqāra, I suddenly found we had dwindled to three and hastening anxiously back found the remainder enjoying a quiet rubber of bridge on a Fifth Dynasty sarcophagus.

The so-called Ladies' Eastern Fishing Fleet took us annually between Malta and India, and again, if unsuccessful, between India and Malta; casting their nets chiefly over the Army of Occupation and somewhat ostentatiously narrowing their meshes for the Civil Service. Not all catches so made were permanent or satisfactory, for each party saw the other under artificial lighting. An ordinary young man fluent in Arabic, no less at home in the desert than in the bazaars is already half a hero to an unknown goddess descending fresh from the cool of Europe in the latest Paris fashion. *Omne ignotum pro magnifico;* and if they settle down in England his accomplishments are at a discount and her elegance by no means unique, so that either and sometimes both are liable to rancorous devaluation. The hotel ballrooms, where most of these "romances" were crystallized, if remote from the spirit of an eighteenth-century salon, were not unhappy in their distribution of nicknames. My friend Richard Graves, as stately as he is unpretentious, was from the first greeted as *Graves Supérieur*. Two swanlike but large-scale sisters were hailed from afar as *The Powerful* and *The Terrible* when they steamed into action; and another pair of an unusual all-round development as "The Drums of the Fore and Aft".

The converse of a tourist in everything save zest was Dame Ethel Smyth, who visited Egypt in 1913 to complete her latest Opera *The Bosun's Mate*. Whether at a tennis party slipping behind a box-hedge to remove an undergarment and hiding (and forgetting) them in a flower-pot, or extemporizing to my piano, with the orchestral parts hummed, a fugal chorus, "You are putting back the clock twenty years", from her Oratorio based on Lord Cromer's anti-Suffragette speeches, she brought to my friends and myself perpetual stimulus and delight. She had made for the Suffrage great sacrifices, which her vehemence sometimes caused us to share. Some found her venturous inquiring spirit too powerful a tonic. I could not, and still cannot have enough. She seemed to bring her atmosphere of the hunting-field, Johannes Brahms, John Sargent and our friends in Paris with her every time she came into the house—and it was life.

During a summer holiday I met for the first time Princess Edmond de Polignac. This lady, daughter of the Singer who I suppose has eased the life of the seamstress and the housewife more than any other public benefactor, maintained a cottage in Surrey, a house in Chelsea, an *hôtel* in Paris, a palace in Venice; and, using her wealth with a wise and appreciative artistry, led (and continues to lead) a life resembling in many ways that of a great Renaissance princess. She painted pictures that were later sold, without her knowledge, as undoubted Manets; she played on her studio organ the Fugues of Bach; she took one of the pianos in a double concerto with Arthur Rubinstein. You could say that musically she "fed on the advancing hour", for she was the liberal and evocative patroness alike of Gabriel Fauré and of Igor Stravinsky. She circled the globe in her yacht and she drove a long and straight ball at golf. If her concerts were the best in Paris you would hear no less, hard upon your welcome to her house in Venice, an admirable Schumann Trio or Quartet, in which she might well be taking a part. Jean Cocteau has recorded the finality of her aesthetic verdicts in her Paris *salon: "elle broya des jugements irrévocables."* I was reminded of Jove "as he pronounces lastly on each deed". Prince Edmond, who had died long before I knew her, had been the close friend of Wagner and the co-founder with him of the *Cercle de l'Union Artistique*. I treasure some of his chance pearls preserved by her from oblivion. The depth of humiliation, he conceived, would be *"pleurer comme un veau dans le gilet d'un inconnu"*. *"Si on me coupait en deux"*, he observed of our universal habit of detraction, *"une moitié dirait du mal de l'autre; mais si on me recollait, je ne m'en voudrais pais."* When they talked of chiaroscuro in music he said: *"Pour rendre le silence dans la musique, il me faut trois orchestres militaires."* He was once the principal guest at a large country house party, where he underwent without flinching all the resources of the *cuisine,* the cellar, the *chasse-à-cour* and the local magnates. Years after his death the Princess found this comment, written across those four days of his diary: *"Décidément, je n'aime pas les autres."*

Madame de Polignac gave me in 1913 a little yellow volume of poems entitled *Les Vivants et les Morts,* and at her house I met next year the divinely, the almost frighteningly gifted poet, Anna de Noailles. Anna was little and slight in every dimension but that of the soul. She had fine-streaming dark hair, and tiny, delicate, expressive hands: great mournful eyes that could be now flashing topaz, now smouldering coal; a nose prow-like, as it might have been the Egyptian God Horus. We had arguments about this feature to which she attached importance; she wrote: *"J'ai vu un jeune poète anglais ici hier, qui m'a dit qu'il avait appris le français à cause de mes livres. Cela m'a touchée, car les plaisirs de l'orgueil sont immédiatement bons pour la santé. Mais il avait un nez sans dignité; le mien, que vous trouvez accusé, ressemble, m'a dit Clémenceau, à Bonaparte en Italie."* Her mouth was lapped in curves of unmistakable power. She could immediately and finally dominate any gathering that had the sense to listen—indeed she accorded them, like Victor Hugo *dans un de ces monologues qu'il appelle une conversation,* little option. Edmond Rostand, Maurice Barrès, Colette herself could provoke (praise enough!), but not parry, still less return, her dazzling attacks, and this in spite of the continued physical fatigue that seemed to be her life. I never failed, passing through Paris, of my pilgrimage to the conventional casket of such rarity in the hideous rue Scheffer. Anna lay back, facing the Athéné of the Acropolis, very pale, her dark hair spread over the pillow, robed in brilliant scarlet and green, her jewelled hands on the crimson coverlet, and the whole room—bed, tables, drawers and wardrobes, packed, stacked, straining, dropping and cascading with books. *"Pourquoi vous voit-on, Anna, si rarement verticale?"* *"Ne me le reprochez pas, mon pauvre petit, car"* (she would answer during some standard Anglo-French crisis) *"vous vous trouvez en présence de la dernière française qui puisse supporter un insulaire."* She shrank increasingly from effort, save of the spirit, and often passed weeks without leaving her room. Nevertheless, we went to Jean Cocteau's version of the *Antigone,* rejoicing to find the chorus reduced to a megaphone in the pediment over the proscenium; danced once at *Le Bœuf sur le Toit,* and she sped me to Jerusalem in a swirl of white, wonderfully improbable on the platform of the Gare de Lyons.

Nothing was pleasanter than to provoke from Anna an outburst of what I may term her sharp Gallic indulgence for the natives of this island. "I am happy to have news of you, Dear *Insulaire*" (she wrote), "... I should like to know why you are called *Insulaires, puisque* your country and your people are on all the world and sea, under every sun and star—I explained it very well in my poetry to Kipling—*j'espère que vous l'avez lue! ... Cher ami, à quoi pense-t-on quand on fait, comme vous à ce moment, du contrepoint? A rien? Je crois que les Anglais, même les plus magnifiques, aiment à travailler, à avoir raison, a rire, à exprimer ce qu'ils veulent dans le moment où ils le veulent—et à ne penser à rien. Les Latins ... pensent tout le temps à quelque chose, et souvent à la même chose....*" Anna finished that letter with the only sporting metaphor I ever heard her use: "*C'est vous le plus occupé de nous deux; moi je possède l'univers en rêvant, mais vous il faut que vous le repreniez dans vos mains comme au Rugby.*"

She spoke often of death, and liked to hear (however barbarously rendered) the μὴ φῦναι τον ἄπαντα νικᾷ λόγον [19] of Sophocles, with the Bible alternative "To go thence, whence we came". But who could think of death on those lips more living than fire? Nor was there, in the end, known reason why she should die, and she murmured continually: "*Je meurs de moi-même.*"

It is not easy now to imagine Venice before the War, before the Crisis, before the Italian Adventure, in the fulness of its social splendour. Viewed from the Palazzo Polignac in the autumns of 1911, 1912 and 1913, the Grand Canal, the Lagoons, the Piazza and Piazzetta seemed to glitter against my annual gloom at leaving Europe like the signs of the Zodiac. Mrs Eden reigned in her gracious unlikely garden; Lady Helen Vincent in the Giustiniani Palace; and in the *Rio Marin*, Madame de Pourtalès. The essence of Venice was distilled in the memories (as preserved in the pages) of Horatio Brown. But as a travelling companion in study, for walks and talks about Venice I never met any that excelled Mr Asquith (in 1913 on his first visit) then staying with his family as guests at the Catecumini Palace of Lady Cunard. Baedeker in hand, the Prime Minister would question us in the gondola as to who had painted what saint, in which church that we had examined within the last half hour; and it was humiliating, how few good marks he was able to award. But not always; for when we returned from San Giorgio Maggiore Harry Cust had no doubt whatever that the saint of the choir

---

[19] "Never to have lived is best, ancient writers say;

*   *   *   *   *   *   *

The second best's a gay goodnight and quickly turn away." (w. b. yeats.)

stalls was Tryphonius, and that his animal was a Basilisk; illustrating his conviction with:

> Tryphonius had a Basilisk
> Who with his tail was wont to whisk
> The fleas from off Tryphonius;
> But they, returned with holy greed
> Upon that sacred flesh to feed,
> Cried "Whisk no more! It's on'y us".

Yours ever
Philip *Manners-Jons*.

Could a Basilisk possibly look like this?

CHAPTER SIX

1911–1914

χειρὶ καὶ βουλαῖς ἄριστος. πολλά νιν πολλοὶ λιτάνευον 'ιδεῖν.
ἀβοατὶ γὰρ ἡεώων ἄωτοι περιναιεταόντων
ἤθελον κείνου γε πείθεσθ ' ἀναξίαις ἐκόντες.

Foremost in might and in counsel. Many a time did many a man pray that
they might behold him; for the flower of the heroes that dwelt around him
longed with gladness to submit to his rule of their own free will.

PINDAR, Nem. 8, 8-10

I

SHORTLY before seven-thirty in the evening of Thursday, September 28th, 1911, the arrival platform of the Cairo Railway Station was crowded by the representatives of the Powers—official, religious and financial as well as diplomatic, who then constituted one of the most varied and interesting societies in the world. In the twenty-five years that have elapsed many of those figures, then so well known, have passed away. Others have become Governors, Ambassadors, Cabinet Ministers. One only, Said Zulfikar Pasha, the Grand Chamberlain of the Khedive Abbas Hilmy, still stands, where he stood; still, continuing his courtly functions into the fourth reign, welcomes the coming and speeds the parting Minister and High Commissioner and, after a quarter-century which included the recasting of the Egyptian Dynasty and the War, still holds his unrivalled experience at the disposal of the cousin and third successor of his first master.

As the special train slowed in, watches were pulled out of pockets and it was observed as natural that Lord Kitchener had arrived one minute before his time. From the coach there stepped that figure famous everywhere, in Egypt a household word, erect and martial but conspicuously civilian in the classic grey frock-coat and top hat traditionally reserved for the representative of Great Britain. He appeared in high good humour, which was increased by his advantage, nowhere so valuable as in the Near East, of knowing personally a large proportion of those assembled to greet him. He paced down the red baize, through the great central doors opened only for personages of the highest distinction; inspected the Guards of Honour mounted by the British Army of Occupation and the Egyptian Army; and, accompanied by the loud and demonstrative hand-clappings of the Egyptian crowd (generally impassive and on this occasion expected even to be hostile owing to the extremist Press campaign against the appointment of the "Butcher of Khartum"), proceeded to Kasr al-Dubara. Some of those present contrasted these acclamations with the departure of Lord Cromer, the greatest foreign benefactor that any Oriental nation has known, as he drove to the station in that same carriage through streets lined by troops armed with ball cartridge, amid a silence chillier than ice.

Having outstripped my new Chief by a swifter if more devious car, I arranged my papers and sat in the Chancery awaiting the summons of the bell. Though stimulated by the emotion and pageantry of the arrival, I had small cause for personal enthusiasm. I owed my original appointment to the recommendation of Sir Eldon Gorst, with whom Lord Kitchener had for years been on terms of cordial and reciprocated antipathy. My first meeting with him was in 1910, when he lunched at the Agency on his way home as retiring Commander-in-Chief in India. I then thought him aloof and hostile, and the atmosphere generally had been bad. The second was at an heroic dinner party in Arlington Street, where he was to meet Curzon for the first time since they had parted in India. (When, a few days later, Harry Cust asked Curzon what was their present relationship, he answered: "We meet without embarrassment on my side; I do not however seek his company.") This was the third.

There had come a Pharaoh who knew not Joseph and, worse still, disliked his official origin. I had, indeed, been given to understand that I was on approval and liable to be returned at any moment; and I suspected that my number was up. The bell rang, and I stepped into that dark headmasterly room in which such momentous decisions had been taken, so many Egyptian careers made or marred. I carried with me a tray, heavy and overflowing with telegrams of congratulation. They were written in English, French, German, Italian, Greek, Turkish, and, above all, in Arabic; and they bore the signatures of Princes, Pashas, Prelates; Bankers and Shaikhs; Mudīrs and Generals; with a liberal sprinkling of those scallywags, bad hats and other *illustres inconnus,* whose wont it is to squeeze from occasion their quota of publicity or profit.

The Field-Marshal, gazing fixedly over his desk, enquired what these papers were. I explained; and, asked what I proposed to do about them, replied that in my opinion greetings from the Reigning Family, Ministers and ex-Ministers should be acknowledged in the first or third person, according as the senders were or were not personal acquaintances; that lesser, but respected or known individuals should be thanked by the Oriental Secretary; and that the rest should be—silence. I was surprised—and dismayed—to receive the curt order that all should be granted the equal honour of an identical appreciation. Field-Marshals are, as a class, accustomed to swift unquestioning obedience—Lord Kitchener perhaps more than most; and in the circumstances I decided that any comment that could be taken for backchat, particularly civilian backchat, appeared on the whole to be contra-indicated. But I was anxious, so long as I occupied the post, to deserve the pay and, pulling myself together near the door into the Chancery, registered compliance; adding that after all we could afford to discount the consequences. As in a trance I seemed to feel rather than to hear the impact: "What consequences?" and replied, hopelessly, that the first category would be insulted by receiving no more consideration than the second; that the second would henceforth demand parity of treatment with the first, and that the third would use His Excellency's name to extort cash from the ignorant and illiterate provincial. A dreadful pause ensued; spent by me in a lightning calculation whether if dismissed on the spot I could afford to travel home first class, anyhow by sea; until at the end of a minute's aeon, I dreamt that a voice snapped: "You can do what you damned well like", and awoke to find myself the other side of the door getting the answers out of the house before my master should have time to change his mind. From that first day's encounter followed three years of such happiness, interest and responsibility as no gratitude could repay. Many Chiefs, but by no means all, approve and reward their juniors when successful; not so many have the greatness of soul to remember positive achievements in the face of error or unsuccess. Above all, where he trusted, he trusted absolutely.

During Kitchener's first week in Cairo I was informed on good authority that a number of British officials might be tendering their resignations; some from old dislike of him, others in order to forestall compulsory retirement. When (without mentioning individuals) I warned him of this tendency he significantly tapped a drawer in his desk and said: "You'd better go down to the Club and let it be generally known that I've always kept printed acceptance forms for resignations, only requiring the name to be added to become effective." I duly circulated this news and need hardly say that, for whatever reason, not one single resignation was submitted. Next day, curious to see how the forms ran, I opened the drawer, and found it to contain a box of cigars.

Three years of close daily contact with Kitchener afforded ample occasion for comparing reputation with reality, and of proving how much richer and more various was the truth than the stereotyped halfpenny Press image of the roaring 'nineties—the strong silent Empire-builder who hated women, had no interests outside his work, and rarely opened his mouth save to order an execution. There was his feminine sensitiveness to atmosphere (and to physical appearance—"I don't care about that man: he looks like a pin", he said of a thin bullet-headed Under-Secretary); and his ultra-feminine *flair* for the workings of his opponent's mind. He would never hesitate to try a course and to go into open reverse if it proved unfavourable. This was illustrated shortly after his arrival as British Representative. On the eve of the Khedive's Levée, Lord Kitchener sought and obtained a private audience in the country Palace of Kubbeh. Next morning his staff were instructed that he did not propose to attend the Levée, but that two of them, whom he indicated, should do so. His choice lit upon Robert Greg [1] and myself who, though modestly conscious of such merits as we hoped we possessed, could not help doubting how far these were likely to prove acceptable substitutes for greatness in the eyes of the critical and suspicious representatives of the other Powers. Our apprehensions were but too painfully realized. It was immediately assumed that this "arrogation of a special position" was a *coup d'état* heralding a change in the status of Great Britain in Egypt. The general atmosphere of our reception at the Palace by the Diplomatic Corps was as though we personally had been proved guilty of some major misdemeanour. Whole groups dissolved at our approach, and colleagues whom we had met only the night before upon excellent terms, fell into an abstraction or seemed to study over or through us, with an interest which could only have a disjunctive and political significance, the large-scale and richly uniformed portraits of the House of Muhammad Ali. Cipher cables of immense length were dispatched through the Eastern Telegraph Company (the impartial beneficiary of every crisis), to the Foreign Offices and greater journals of Europe. And at the next Levée Lord Kitchener presented himself without any loss of prestige, and to the universal relief, in his official precedence as the last appointed, and junior, of the Agents and Consuls-General.

[1] Sir Robert Greg, K.C.M.G., afterwards British Commissioner on the *Caisse de la Dette,* Cairo.

He was quick at disposing of unpalatable issues, as we had the pleasure of noting one day when the most variously betitled servant of the Egyptian Government—al-Ferīk General Baron Sir Rudolph von Slatin Pasha —arrived for luncheon. He had come primed to discuss his pension, and it was immediately clear that he was leading up to something. "Well, Lord Kitchener, I am afraid I've not made a great financial success of my life." "No one who knew you, my dear Slatin, ever thought you would." An unpromising and, for an appellant less distinguished and pertinacious, even daunting reception. "Here was I, for twelve years prisoner of the Mahdi, naked, often in chains, captured on active service— and yet not one piastre of pay throughout." "Well, Slatin, you can't say your out-of-pocket expenses over the period amounted to much", and the party suddenly found itself discussing aviation and the cotton crop. Yet any who may have thought him unfeeling should have seen the look on his face as he stood beside the open grave of Captain McMurdo, almost his oldest friend, who had saved his life in a skirmish near Suakin in 1888.

In May 1913

a Russian ex-editor of a Liberal St Petersburg newspaper came in a great fright to tell me he had been summoned to appear before his Consul, and had grave doubts whether he would be set free again after the interview. His house had just been rifled by secret agents, and he assured me that on more than one occasion incriminating documents and even bombs had been placed among his effects by their secret police. Of course we cannot interfere with the Russian Government in this country, but when I told K. he remarked with characteristic cynicism that all I need do was to tell the fellow to let me know directly he got out of the Consulate. "And if I don't hear from him?" I said. "Then you will know he is still inside", was all the assistance I got in solving the problem. What he really meant, as often in such cases, was that he was too busy to be bothered with the thing, and I might do what I thought best: so I told the suspect either to refuse to appear and so force his enemies to show the Egyptian Government proofs of his guilt, or else if he feared such proofs really existed or was averse from the risk of contempt of court, that he should take with him a legal adviser, and hold on to his hand as long as they would let him.

He could be decisive in phrase, and also humorously courteous. On one occasion when it suited the Khedive to take a decision as Sovereign and to excuse himself for it on the ground that he was but the vassal of a Suzerain Sultan, Lord Kitchener said: "My own position here is anomalous enough; we really can't have two Incomprehensibles." Again, at a ball which Kitchener gave for the Crown Prince and Princess of Germany, Count Hermann von Hatzfeldt, the German Consul-General, wooed and won Fraülein von Stumm, the Princess's charming Lady in attendance. He received from Kitchener next morning a cordial note of congratulation, together with the embroidered cushion upon which he had sat whilst making his proposal.

When the aged Cypriot, Kiamil Pasha, four times Grand Vizier of the Ottoman Empire, tried and convicted defender of the traditional friendship between Turkey and Great Britain, arrived in Egypt after his virtual deportation from Constantinople by the young Turks, he received no recognition from the Egyptian Government but was immediately visited by Lord Kitchener at the Semiramis Hotel. Kiamil Pasha reminded him in perfect English that they had met before when he was British Consul in Anatolia and Kiamil Vali of the Province. "Yes", replied the Field-Marshal and ex-Commander-in-Chief of India, "but Your Highness achieved higher and swifter promotion. I was a Consul then, and it has taken me thirty years to become a Consul-General." Kiamil Pasha was nearly ninety years old and had frequently conversed with Muhammad Ali, founder of the Egyptian Royal Dynasty, who was born in the same year as Napoleon.[2] It was good to see the faces and to hear the talk of these two illustrious K's, both by temperament and by association life members of that great club, the friendly and unmandated Near East— that intimate atmosphere of manner, of feeling and of policy which can only be comprehended by those who have been steeped in it by many years of work, travel and affection. It was during this visit that King George V and Queen Mary passed through the Suez Canal on their way to the Delhi Durbar. Kiamil Pasha was invited on board the *Medina*, and a photographic group was taken in which the Khedive, his brother Prince Muhammad Ali, Lord Kitchener and the Sirdar stood in the back row. With them stood King George immediately behind the venerable Grand Vizier, to whom he had insisted upon giving up his chair beside the Queen. Age is still respected in the East, and this kingly gesture evoked an almost tearful admiration throughout Egypt and the Sudan.

On Kiamil Pasha's second arrival in Egypt

I met him again, and was amused to note the difference in his reception this year, when he may at any moment become Grand Vizier.[3] The Royal waiting-room had been opened and a red carpet laid down: the Governor, Prince Haidar and the Ottoman High Commissioner all pawing the platform. . . .

Kitchener was free of the uglier blemishes, grave or comic: he had no rancour, and no snobbishness, but he could be petulant. One morning he tossed me a note just received from the ex-Premier Mustafa Pasha Fehmy

---

[2] 1769, which also included the births of Wellington, his conqueror, and of his gaoler, Hudson Lowe.

[3] He never was again.

requesting for his son-in-law Zaghlūl Pasha the position, recently vacated,[4] of Controller of Egyptian students in France. Zaghlūl, though zealous and honest, had proved a difficult administrator. When Minister of Education he had frequently received discontented or actually expelled students over the heads of their schoolmasters, even of his own Under-Secretary. He had fallen out first with his colleagues, finally with the Khedive; and was now out of employment, restless and dissatisfied. Lord Kitchener invited opinion. I could not deny these defects, but considered that the sympathy which they indicated for youth should not disqualify the Pasha from the care of his young compatriots abroad. "He's more trouble than he's worth", said Lord Kitchener, "and we must find something better." He may have been right, yet the history of modern Egypt might have been strangely different if Saad Pasha Zaghlūl had spent the next few years of his life in Paris and not in Cairo.

Sir Eldon Gorst, loyal to his instructions, had restricted his intervention in the affairs of Egypt to matters directly affecting British interests. This involved a more or less blind eye to much that was irregular, and a deaf ear to petitions against Palace or Pasha—as often as not from the fatherless, the widow and the oppressed. The abstention was, save with a few highly placed personages, universally unpopular; from the Princes and Princesses complaining (rightly or wrongly) of interference with their property by the Head of their House, to anti-British Nationalists fleeing from injustice to the focus of their bitterest denunciations. The discouraged petitioner, Royal or other, had therefore taken his grievance elsewhere, to places and atmospheres not necessarily more helpful, but certainly more "interested", though naturally at a price which included political adherence.[5] It is no disparagement of Gorst's imposed neutrality nor, necessarily, praise of its reversal by Kitchener, to record that the change was immediately and immensely welcome. People of all ranks and classes felt that they had once more direct access to supreme authority, and left the Agency happier with an entire rejection of their demand by *Kuchnir,* or *al-Lurd,* than they would have been with an eighty per cent. concession by a minor official. A formidable spate of callers—Omdas, Notables, Beys, Ministers and old Egyptian officers who had served under him in the Sudan, to say nothing of senior British officials, the Diplomatic Corps and the Army of Occupation, swept through the Agency; which became forthwith, in the local journalese "the Mecca of an Egyptian social, political, commercial, industrial, and agricultural Renaissance".

---

[4] By the death of the distinguished Armenian scholar Yacub Artin Pasha.

[5] Absalom canvassed Israel on this grievance: "See, thy matters are good and right; but there is no man deputed of the king to hear thee." II Sam. xv. 3.

In a moment the hours, the difficulty and the importance of the Oriental Secretary's work were trebled. The time available for interviews was wholly unequal to their number and, although Kitchener recognized no social bar, there had to be a limit of unworthiness for the *entrée,* to deal adequately with which he must be early and exactly informed.

The simplicity of his manner seemed hardly to accord with such an overwhelming personality. Many who came prepared to be awed went away charmed; but the surprise could be the other way, as the Beduin Shaikh Lamlūn Bey al-Saadi very soon found. Kitchener had arrived shortly after Italy had declared war upon Turkey and invaded Egypt's Western neighbour, Tripoli. This invasion of a Moslem-Arab territory aroused very strong feeling in Egypt and, though the country maintained neutrality, the people showed their warm sympathy by organizing and contributing liberally to a Red Crescent Society (to which Kitchener's donation of £100 was very well received), as well as by a general subscription to aid Turkey in her need. There are no means of neutralizing hearts. The Egyptian no less than the British Government did all in its power to prevent the smuggling of arms and ammunition into Tripoli through Egypt; but the frontier was long, ill-defined, and in desert country almost impossible to patrol effectively.[6] I had ascertained, and informed Lord Kitchener, that the night before Lamlūn al-Saadi was to visit him, he and other leading Beduin had arranged at a secret meeting to run through on camels a large consignment of rifles and cartridges from the neighbourhood of Mínia. The Shaikh entered and took the upright armchair offered him. He embarked upon an obviously set piece of congratulation and of delight at the coming of the *Mareshál:* all Egyptians were enchanted, the Beduin in ecstasy. Kitchener let him go on awhile and then asked him sharply what he was doing last night. The Shaikh paled and crumpled as if the blood had been expelled and the spine extracted from his body. "Nothing of consequence", he gasped, "I was with my family." "If", Kitchener continued, "the Beduin have in truth a yearning for war, I can easily cancel their exemption from military service." The threat of abolishing a privilege the Beduin had been granted by Muhammad Ali—the dread of the hated conscription—was enough, and Lamlūn, his family, his clan, his tribe and the neighbouring tribes canalized their sympathies henceforward into iodine and lint.

Unlike Cromer, Kitchener was neither a scholar nor a writer, nor even a serious reader. Though never contemptuous of the arts that did not appeal to himself he was, in dispatches, content to remain "under" his

---

6 "The Turks have just run through a heavy lot of rifles, so forcing us to sterner measures, with a resulting decline in our popularity both here and in Stambūl."

circumstances, and at no pains to re-splice infinitives however widely gaping for first aid. Shortly before a journey, he would send Colonel FitzGerald to bring back from the bookshop next to Shepheard's any half dozen of novels.[7] The only game except cribbage that he ever mentioned as if he had played it was chess, which he liked for train and sea journeys, and at which it may be said that his heart was better than his head. He lacked Gorst's taste for music and science, and Allenby's for sport and poetry. But in his love and pursuit of the fine arts, more especially the decorative and the antique, he surpassed all who had gone before or have come after him. I can remember—but not repeat—his subsequent remarks when informed by Sir Gaston Maspéro, the distinguished Director of Antiquities, that the Great Temples of Nubia, after their recent restoration, looked "as your Lordship would say, like a new 'peen'"; and his expletives when he learnt that the superb and unique portrait group of the builder of the Third Pyramid, Men Kau Ra (the Mycerinus of Herodotus) and his Queen, a national monument of Egypt recently discovered by Dr Reisner, had been allowed to go to the Boston Museum.

The Cavasses at the Agency doors abandoned their chocolate and yellow liveries (dreadfully matching the front hall carpet) for scarlet and gold worn with the disengaged Turkish sleeves. The hideous drawing-room became a gallery for his collections of china and Byzantine ikons; the unfurnished ballroom, a state reception room, with dull white cornices gilded and mournful wall spaces enlivened by Chippendale mirrors and panels of brocade; and a new ballroom was built. He would imagine and execute his improvements at the most unexpected moment; as when he was discovered about noon changing the place of a heavy console with the panting assistance of Muhammad Said Pasha, the Prime Minister, who had called to discuss a Cabinet crisis. Twice a week at least he visited the bazaars and antika shops where he had been well known for a quarter of a century, and it was pleasant to see and to share his happiness. The years fell from his shoulders, his expression concentrated with the intentness of an eager and prehensive child. On his return to the Agency, he almost ran up the steps to undo his parcel and to ring for one or more of the staff to approve the purchases.

The climax of the Agency week was the arrival of the P. and O. mail, which conveyed the Foreign Office bag. When Kitchener's letters were brought to him, he would add them to the perennial confusion of

[7] Just before his last holiday. "I am making him read *With Edged Tools:* quoted him the plot of *From One Generation to Another* in which a man, under the influence of a pre-natal hatred, murders another. He said it reminded him of Laban's peeling the wands before the ewes, a theory refuted by modern Science."

his writing table, and then dive his finger into the heap, scattering to right and left dispatches from the Secretary of State, the War Office and the Departments, to fish up a long narrow envelope containing his agent's progress report upon the latest developments of Broome Park, which appeared to be undergoing a total reconstruction. Ceilings were being lowered, floors raised and gutter-pipes dismounted and concealed within the old brick walls. "I am sorry to have to inform your Lordship that Perkins hasn't finished the garden railings, and that the range has been giving trouble again, I always did say...." Having read this carefully through twice, he would turn with a sigh to the Malta Naval Conference, the Capitulations, or the incident of the Mariut Railway.

Lord Kitchener was often approximate, rather than textually or phonetically accurate in his nomenclature, and it was a point of sport and of pleasure (as well as of honour) to keep up with his train of thought and to carry out instructions without fatiguing him by unnecessary questions. If, for example, he asked after Bruce, he clearly meant Birch, the elusive third Secretary; nor, when he spoke of writing to Minto for some more china was there any difficulty in getting into touch with South Audley Street. A desire to see Smyrna and Cettinge this afternoon was not an order to book passages with Cook and Son, but to convene Monsieur Alexis Smirnow and Count Louis Szechenyi, the respective Consuls-General of Russia and of Austria-Hungary. But you had to be a little quicker, and well up-to-date with the Visitors' Book when, being informed that it was about time we had Walsingham to luncheon, you telephoned to the late H. W. Massingham, editor of the *Nation*, at that time camping with John Galsworthy near the Pyramids.[8]

His Arabic was intelligible rather than idiomatic, and, as might have been expected, stronger in military than in civil practice. For ordinary linguistic purposes he needed no help save for the visits of such elegant precisians as the Qadi, Mufti or Shaikh al-Azhar. His French, inclusive of accent, was fluent and good; and he could follow any conversation. He loved France; not only the stereotyped Lafayette projection of France, but actual France and living Frenchmen: on one occasion he took the unusual step of writing to Monsieur Cambon, French Ambassador in London, on behalf of the French representative in Cairo, who, he feared, might be prejudicially affected by a local intrigue. In general he liked and was liked by the Diplomatic Corps; and was particularly diverted

[8] This inability to remember names and titles (never contemptuous in the great) is a not unlovable weakness. Byron writes of his own local banker "Corgialegno (is that the name?)" and, in the same letter, "Corgialegno (I think is the name)". In the next letter he appears as "Messrs Kornologni (or Corialegno)". *Letters*, 1901 ed., vol. vi, pp. 254-6. Lord Balfour was sometimes a sufferer, see pp. 274-5.

by one of the Consuls-General who after an hour's detailed exposition would exclaim: *"Maintenant, Monsieur le Maréchal, je vais vous dire la vérité."*

His English expression was as clear and strong as his handwriting so long as he wrote down what came into his mind; but he had a weakness (loyally resisted by Robert Greg, as Head of the Chancery) for introducing and even forcing into a sentence tiresome words like "albeit" and *"entente"*. On one occasion he was with difficulty restrained from employing *"détente"* as the equivalent of "disagreement". ("Why not? *entente*—you agree: *détente*—you don't. I can't see it.") Unlike his two predecessors he had never learnt to dictate, though you might sometimes find yourself sitting with a pencil at his desk whilst he strode about the room pulling at his cigar and throwing off ideas and phrases.

In dealing with an outstanding problem or a crisis (and in those days in Egypt when there was not one it was because there were both) Lord Kitchener had two habits at first disconcerting to a subordinate. He would invite opinion as to the course to be taken, deride it with merciless wit and not infrequently bring forward next day a solution of his own indistinguishably similar. Or he would gravely propound fantastic improbable choices of action, solely for the purpose (and sometimes for the malicious pleasure) of observing whether—and how—they were countered.

While it is true that he conversed as a rule more easily with men, he could in the society of women he had known long and well relax into the readiest company in the world, as was seen at the Agency during the visits of old and intimate friends, such as Lady Layard and much later Lady Salisbury and Lady Desborough with their families, when he was visibly confident and happy in being led on rather than, as too often by the casual and compulsory tourist, drawn out. But for a junior nothing could exceed the fearful joy of luncheon or tea in his company with the Princess Nazli Fāzil. The Princess had known the Field-Marshal when he was a junior captain and was affectionately indisposed to let him forget it. Seated with her back to the light, a half bottle of sweet champagne on an inlaid Arab table beside her, she would smoke continuously half-way through innumerable Russian cigarettes, crushing them with a small wicked hand into ashtrays which Fattūma or Aziza,[9] standing with a dozen other slaves just outside the room, would on the cry of *"Kim var orada"*—"Who's there?" rush in and remove. Against the combined volume and velocity of her

---

[9] Who greeted me as if no time had elapsed twenty-three years later, when my wife and I called on Bu Hāgeb Bey, Nazli's widower, in Tunis.

conversation in English, French, Arabic and Turkish, the protests of the Field-Marshal rang surprisingly mild. "You think, I suppose, that the Egyptians are afraid of you, Lord Kitchener, sitting in Kasr al-Dubara? They laugh. And how should they not laugh when you allow to be made Minister a dirty, filthy kind of a man like. . . ." "Really, Princess Nazli! I don't think. . . ." "You don't, and if you had . . .", and the next victim would come up for dissection.

Nazli is back, full of holy joy at K.'s appointment. The Khedive, who has neglected her for nineteen years, sent a Palace eunuch to meet her, and paid her ticket up to Cairo, at which she continues to be highly amused. I heard her combing down two of the Ministers, whom she assured that the anger of Providence, if they misbehaved, would be slower in effect than that of K. One of them, Hishmet, winked at me during her peroration.

Lord Kitchener declined to receive lady petitioners of whatever race, status or age, even with a witness, from a vague fear of their making a scene, fainting, or spreading rumours he could not control. His sole departure from his rule was not altogether happy. He had sent me one morning with some message to the Prime Minister. On my return I was surprised to learn from the Cavass that "al-Lurd" had been seeing a "Brincessa". He had made this exception under the impression that the lady was a kinswoman of Princess Nazli Fāzil, and was dismayed to learn afterwards that she was, in fact, a European known in the cynical Cairo world as *La Princesse Ali Facile*.

The envelopes of the innumerable petitions I had to read and analyse bore when in English such addresses as "For you Kuchner Basha", "His Majesty Mr Kitchener" (mine ranged from "Mr Staurus Esq." to "Mr Storiss, the profissor of the British hotel in Cairo") and their contents, even when from England, were sometimes no less fresh and artless. "Sir, may I remind you of a meeting in 1874, which may not be as deeply impressed upon your memory as upon mine." "If a matron is required for the Soldiers' Home at Khartum, my daughter is in every way suitable, being an authoress, musician and artist besides being in direct descent from Alfred the Great and of Royal descent from Alfred to Llewellyn the Great and last Prince of Wales." There was ingenuousness in some of the telegrams as well as comedy and pathos. "Lord Kichner, Cairo. Please demand me I am at the door A. Yusef"; and "To-day mother four brothers about to turn Mohammadans please prevent Milad Hanna"; and again: "I cry to your justice to kindly interfere into my case between me and my wife. . . ."

For my preliminary interview with these visitors there was then no waiting-room other than the front hall, a deficiency which did not always suit those desirous of invoking the assistance of the Agency but of denying to their friends that they had or ever would set foot in the place. The Oriental Secretary had no assistant, clerk, stenographer or typist. His office was the curtained but doorless recess (of which he could touch the opposite walls simultaneously) on the right of the hall door, the present receptacle of men's coats and hats at smaller dinner parties.

Like many other public servants (and indeed most reasonable men) Lord Kitchener, though quite prepared to be left to himself for much of the day, refused to eat his meals or spend his evenings alone. Apart, therefore, from formal invitations, there were increasingly frequent suggestions (which were naturally taken as summonses) to dine with him, in the abscence of FitzGerald the Military or Lord Colum Crichton Stuart, the Private Secretary. These dinners for two showed Kitchener at his best, since with the slightest encouragement he would launch into a sequence of admirably told reminiscences. There was the "French unseen" at the entrance examination into Woolwich, when the description of a bull-fight by Mérimée came up for translation. The candidate seated next to him whispered hoarsely: "What's Caramba?" and Kitchener replied in the same strain: "Spanish." When the two met outside in the interval the questioner said: "I put down 'Spanish' for Caramba, but it didn't seem to make much sense." "I said to myself", Kitchener concluded, "I shan't see *you* at the Shop next term—and I didn't." The staff derived a pious satisfaction (and we thought he did himself) from the knowledge that the identification of several Bible place-names in the Holy Land had been decided by him when working with Conder for the Palestine Exploration Society. The two young officers were occasionally surprised by reverently enquiring missionaries whilst they were hard at cribbage, which they marked (although not gambling) with half-sovereigns, to the scandal of their visitors.

It was always clear that the two heroes of his life were Lord Salisbury, his first great supporter, and, even more, General Gordon; though he admitted that as a Governor-General at the end of a telegraph line several hundred miles long Gordon was liable to lapse into inconsequence. He had a habit of tapping out with his own hand his telegraphic instructions to remote and assumably corrupt Mudīrs, and would begin: "It is I, Gordon Pasha. I see along the wire. I am watching you. Do not demand that bribe. Let that man go." And such was the force of his personality that the officer taking down the telegram would sometimes drop his pencil, struggle to his feet, salute—and obey. There was the incident occasioned by his cable from Khartum to the Egyptian Government proposing that a certain Bey should be promoted to the rank of Pasha. The reputation of this Bey was such as to stagger even the Cairo War Office, at that time not over-censorious in such nominations; and they refused. Gordon replied threatening immediate resignation unless the Bey became a Pasha, upon which Cairo, painfully aware that there was no second Gordon, and that Pashas had not always been ex-officio Galahads, telegraphed a reluctant consent. They had hardly done so when they received a third telegram from Khartum requesting the cancellation of the two previous recommendations as "I have had occasion to hang the man".

He told me that he had an hour's talk with King Edward VII on the Thursday before his death. The King was in admirable form, and presented K. with his Field Marshal's bâton—which he unfortunately left upon the table when he went out of the Palace. He then spent a feverish ten minutes telephoning to Stamfordham, who managed to recover the gewgaw before H.M. had found out what would have been to him an insupportable sacrilege.

In 1912:

Lord K. in excellent humour. He remembered that on the decease of the Mikado, Admiral Nogi's death by harakiri was announced at dinner at Balmoral. King George said: "Would you do as much if you saw my body carried out?" K. replied: "Would you wish me to, Sir?"—tolerably well for camp diplomacy.

And in April 1914:

Last night I dined alone with K. He told me, rather to my surprise, that Buller was a man of great ability, force, push, personality and power of organization: failing only as a general in the field because (*a*) of listening far too much to the advice of other generals, and (*b*) "doing" himself and his men grotesquely too well. He did everything in his power to avoid leaving Aldershot for South Africa at all: knew perfectly well his weak points from start to finish, and was, when K. met him at Pretoria, a mere wreck of his former Sudan self. K. said the crux of his own career as a general was at the Atbăra, when all his advisers were against his giving battle, and he gave it and won it in their teeth. The thought of taking an army out to fight 40 miles in the desert had completely destroyed his night's rest and he had determined, if defeated, never to return himself.

Dined alone with Lord K. As he stood last year in Buckingham Palace talking to the Kaiser's daughter, William advanced upon him and said: "Well, Lord Kitchener, have you any communication to make to me about my daughter?" He subsequently explained with every detail the new arrangement of his kitchen at Broome, and how you can't have your scullery on the remote side (however much you may dislike noise and smell) because the cook objects to the plates being marched and countermarched through the kitchen. By this I had dropt into a sort of coma, from which I awoke with a start and said: "Yes, but how about the garage?" an incoherence from which it was not easy to emerge with self-respect. His object is to save servants at all hazards, by numerous lavatories, bathrooms, telephones, electric lift and gate-openers, and I think he will succeed. The reason it takes him so long is that he is building out of income, with not more than a dozen men at work.

II

Kitchener did not confine his contacts to Agency callers but made a practice of returning provincial calls *en masse* and in the grand manner, by visiting the Provinces and so seeing for himself the condition of the Fellahin. These semi-Royal visits in special trains [10] (in which the *Wagons-Lits* provided luncheon on a heroic scale) were, like his accessibility in Cairo, most popular all over the countryside though regarded without enthusiasm by the Khedive.[11] An immense marquee would be pitched, on the dais of which sat Kitchener, the Mudir of the Province, the local judge, the *Hakemdar*—Commandant of Police—the two or three leading notables, FitzGerald or Crichton Stuart and myself. Over us there would tower a huge coloured enlargement of the illustrious visitor, under the legend in English and Arabic: "Welcome to Lord Kitchener, the Friend of the Fellah." The British and Khedivial Anthems were rendered approximately by the band of the Trades' School. Addresses would be submitted, rather tedious classical poems intoned by advanced pupils, and agriculture projects freely ventilated. His reforms were simple and for the most part practical; the *Halaqas,* where a peasant could have his cotton officially weighed and stored; the cleaning and draining of the horrible village ponds; the training of *Dayas*—midwives—for the villages; roads, railways, land reclamation and irrigation schemes; the Five Feddan Law, whereby five acres and agricultural implements were exempt from seizure by creditors; and Post Office Savings Banks. Not all of these were equally successful. It was said that exemption from seizure, by abolishing the lender's security, made necessary loans almost impossible. It was suspected but impossible to prove, that some progressive

---

[10] During one tour: "From Sohag to Girga FitzGerald and I had ourselves roped to the bogey in front of the engine, a glorious method of travel unless you chance to run into a camel or buffalo and receive the three stomachs of the one or the 100-foot colon of the other full in the face. We were informed, rather to our surprise, that we were the first, official or other, that ever burst into that noisy seat. (On my return I found that the astonished inhabitants were convinced that we had ridden thus by order of Lord K. so as to be able to detect logs, iron girders and dynamite placed for his benefit upon the permanent way.)"

[11] At any rate they cost the neighbourhood less than the Khedivial descents, after one of which the caterers presented a bill of £1000, charging £3 a head for a temperance and non-smoking luncheon. Amongst other amenities a local notable provided a mechanical chair which, on His Highness sitting down, played the Khedivial National Anthem. The Palace "entourage" were as a rule the chief beneficiaries, by methods which revealed their ripe knowledge of the world.

Mudīrs forced their poor to borrow, at heavy rates of interest, sums of money which were placed in the Savings Banks before Lord Kitchener's inspections to swell the total of accounts, and withdrawn on the morrow of his departure. The peaks of the graphs certainly coincided with his visits. These, however, and other defects, were generally and rightly discounted as spots on the sun of his evident interest and goodwill.

Kitchener's heart had indeed always been in Egypt, and his return in glory to the scene of his early struggles and dawning celebrity proved the serene and golden autumn of his career. He was considered the real friend of the Fellah, and none that saw will ever forget his gazing from his railway coach in deep contentment upon the green illimitable wealth of the Delta. He actively liked meeting, talking and laughing with Egyptians, who in spite of the habitual sternness of his expression never said of him, as of some of his compatriots, that the Englishman's face is *mubawwiz*—sullen or overcast. He had a personal and life-long knowledge of places and of families, and always cherished an affection and admiration for Moslems, without, however, finding it necessary to make superficial and unfair comparisons to the disadvantage of his own Faith. I must, however, record one utter failure. In his eagerness to increase the vote available for agricultural and technical education Kitchener hit upon the expedient of Death Duties; and since no fresh taxation could be imposed without the consent of the Legislative Council, he summoned to the Agency some twenty members who were also large landowners. For nearly two hours we sat round the table in that long gloomy dining-room while the Field-Marshal explained (and I translated) the supreme and unique advantages of a tax which not one of those present would ever have to pay. The project had about as much chance of success as Sir William Harcourt would have achieved had he attempted to obtain adoption of his celebrated measure from a Round Table Conference with the Dukes of the United Kingdom and Ireland. Several of the notables convened were millionaires. Two or three of these lived at the rate of three or four hundred a year: all admired Lord Kitchener and approved his zeal, but the expression on their faces was identical; it was that of their forefathers who in the reign of Ismail had died under the Kurbash sooner than reveal their hidden savings to the tax-gatherer of the *Mufattish*. The Death Duties Bill was never introduced or indeed mentioned again, and we ate our luncheon that day in silence.

The only other occasion on which Kitchener was definitely at a loss arose over one of those *crises ministérielles* that are only less popular in the Egyptian than in the Athenian Press. By March 1914 Muhammad Pasha Said, the Prime Minister who succeeded Bútros Pasha, had incurred the disfavour of the Palace to a degree that had made his position untenable. There were reasons which made it difficult for Kitchener to insist upon his retention by a master whose confidence he had forfeited, and he agreed somewhat reluctantly to his dismissal, assuming in the absence of any other obvious candidate that Mustafa Pasha Fehmi, the retired Premier of the Cromerian epoch, would be willing to take his place. Unfortunately he was not willing. In the words of the Syro-French Press: *"Le noble vieillard n'a pas voulu abdiquer sa liberté de con-science...."* To add to the difficulty of the situation Mustafa Pasha was at Luxor, not then telephonically connected with Cairo. I was therefore secretly despatched to interview the Pasha, and to induce him to re-consider his refusal. An hour's respectful wrestling in his stifling hotel bedroom brought him round to the point of accepting conditionally upon his being permitted to change two unstated members of the Cabinet; with which conditional solution I was fain to return. In Cairo, I found my secret mission had become common knowledge, and although Mustafa Pasha, the soul of honour, had divulged nothing, it was generally inferred that pressure was being put upon him to become Prime Minister. At the subsequent interview with Lord Kitchener he firmly declined office, probably incited by his son-in-law Zaghlūl, unless he were allowed to remove two of the most capable and energetic Ministers. Neither side yielding, the Pasha retired. Lord Kitchener accepted my suggestion of Rushdi Pasha, whose position was now strong enough for him to exact the dismissal of the better of Mustafa Pasha's discards. The incident was soon terminated, but it left upon me an indelible impression of the indignity of greatness such as Kitchener's being driven to hawk the Premiership, almost hat in hand, round the criticisms, conditions and objections of unwilling candidates; a memory that was to serve me in good stead on two subsequent occasions.

It must not be forgotten, in close reference to this "crisis", that a con-stant preoccupation of the three British Representatives in Cairo from 1892 until 1914 was the attitude of Abbas II, seventh ruler in descent from Muhammad Ali and third and last Khedive of Egypt. Abbas Hilmy was unfortunate in several ways; in none so conspicuously as in the choice of his entourage. Their gross corruption was inevitably attributed to their master; their influence incited him to courses which are most mildly described as ill advised, such as the granting of an option to the Dresden Bank for the purchase of his railway line from Alexandria to the West, provoking the intervention of Lord Kitchener and a grave warning from His Majesty's Government. Titles of Bey and of Pasha, Orders of the Mejidíeh and the Osmaníeh were said to be hawked round the

Provinces, or even to be auctioned by unscrupulous courtiers (without profit to their master) in the *Sphynx* and *Splendid* Bars. Some of these honorifics might be handed to editors of newspapers who by selling them would be recouped, without cost to the Palace, for Palace propaganda.

His latest move has been to bespeak a French journalist, who daily insults Lord K. and the Ministers. The effect on the public, who do not understand in their leaders the principle of turning the other cheek, is bad; and if the journalist had been an Egyptian, his paper would have been suppressed long ago. As it is, owing to the grotesque régime of the Capitulations, we are not able to shut up his printing-press; but,

> "Though his bark may not be lost
> Yet it shall be tempest-tost":

we can seize every copy that appears in the streets and prevent any from being sent through the post or the Railways.

And a little later:

The Annual Report, of which I send a copy to the Very Rev., is an even duller document than usual. K. agrees in this opinion, remarking plaintively that the smallest admixture of undiluted truth would wash H.H. off his throne.

This perennial antagonism was peculiarly embarrassing to the Egyptian Ministers, whose position at the Palace varied in inverse ratio with whatever it might be at the Agency. Nevertheless, I do not believe that full justice has ever been done to the difficulties of the Khedive. The hand of Cromer had been strong, and not light. The presence of a younger and more sympathetic figure in Kasr al-Dubara on the accession of an untried, wayward Prince might have entirely altered the situation. With Kitchener, though now well disposed, Abbas had in the past had more than one serious and humiliating encounter. Few Egyptians conceived it their business to enlarge in the Palace upon the good intentions of the British Agent: what British advocate had the Khedive at the Agency? He was well aware that matters affecting his personal honour were being constantly discussed behind his back and to his detriment by foreigners with Egyptians, and was often goaded by artfully exaggerated rumours into retaliations ill according with the dignity of so courteous a Prince. What proportion of hard, basic truth does even a constitutional European monarch hear? How infinitesimal is the quota likely to percolate to an Oriental sovereign under an alien occupation! "For our Kynges live neither by meate nor by drinke, but by havinge great lyes tolde them." Deprived of what he considered the power and prestige of the lawful Ruler of Egypt, Abbas attempted to substitute for it an influence gained by playing off against each other the British, Egyptians and Turks—Young and Old. The policy ended by losing him the confidence of all four, brought about an attempt on his life in the middle of 1914, and before the end of the year had cost him his throne.

About this time occurred an episode which, with a Chief evilly disposed, might well have enshrouded me for the fourth time under the Fear. As we walked in to luncheon Lord Kitchener asked me: "what I had done with the three hundred pounds." I failed to understand him, and said so. He laughed and related this story.

Abd al-Rahīm al-Kenáwi bought four *feddans* of land at Mex near Alexandria which he had to surrender, the Court of Appeals deciding that it belonged to Government. His friend Khalīl al-Sáyyid, a Cairo broker, bade him never lose heart, as he knew "someone" at the Agency who could influence Lord Kitchener to reverse any decision: with the Oriental Secretary, however, time was money—and some of the money had to be passed on higher. Abd al-Rahīm forthwith produced one hundred pounds, which he soon had to double and treble, without, however, obtaining any practical result. Becoming suspicious he demanded to meet Mr Storrs himself, which Khalīl found to be the most natural of desires, and the easiest to gratify. Mr Storrs would call personally upon Abd al-Rahīm in Mex to arrange terms. A fair-haired individual duly arrived, wearing dark glasses and speaking Arabic with an English accent. The dinner was a complete success and Mr Storrs was pleased to accept from his host, in addition to a roll of notes "not for himself" (which he thrust without counting them into his pocket), two Persian rugs and a gazelle. Within four months the arch-crook Mustafa Kāmel Effendi had touched Abd al-Rahīm to the tune of £660. Still nothing happened. Khalīl now invited him to see Mr Storrs at the Agency. Whilst he was waiting in the porch with one of the Cavasses,[12] also in the plot, "Mr Storrs" arrived in a large car and once more Abd al-Rahīm was reassured. Finally losing patience as well as being mocked by his friends for his folly he informed the Police, who arrested all four conspirators in a café as they were planning further developments. Lord Kitchener was particularly pleased by the "English accent" of the Oriental Secretary's Arabic as well as by the sinister features and expression of my successful impersonator. The incident was finally disposed of by *The Egyptian Gazette*: "The curious adventures of the pseudo Mr Storrs, who impersonated the Oriental Secretary of the British Agency, have aroused great interest. Oriental Secretaries seldom come before the eye of the public except in

---

[12] "The latest acquisition, an ex-Dragoman against whose appointment I had, too feebly alas! protested at the time."

their social capacity. The last occasion on which an Oriental Secretary figured in the Press was in 1906 when Captain Jorge Nelken Y. Waldberg, the Roumanian Jew, with a commission in the Argentine Army, an American citizen with a Swedish name, belonging to the Orthodox Church, who edited a French newspaper in Cairo, attacked Lord Cromer's Oriental Secretary, Mr Boyle, now the British Consul-General at Berlin, and accused him of having received a backsheesh of £10,000 from the Princess Sāliha, Maître Carton de Wiart also being accused of having benefited to the same extent from that lady. The slander aroused considerable interest at the time, for as Keats's famous lines go 'the trees that whisper round a temple become soon dear as the temple's self'; so the world in Egypt always takes an interest in Oriental Secretaries."

After the Entente Cordiale in 1903, no Power was represented with more charm and distinction than Germany, whether by Count Bernstorff, Prince Hermann Hatzfeldt or, immediately before the War, the scholarly and cultivated Herr von Miquel. But their courtesies were social rather than political. As early as 1905 Ghazi Mukhtar Pasha, the gallant old Turkish High Commissioner, had declared that "with twelve Army Corps in Syria, and the Germans at our back it should not be difficult to turn the English out of Egypt". The same year Philip Graves had noted the semi-official activities of Meissner Pasha and his German assistants in the survey and completion of the Hejaz Railway as far as Medina. In 1905 Baron Oppenheim, known to us all as "the Kaiser's Spy", organized a large reception for the Nationalist leader Mustafa Pasha Kāmel in Berlin. He was also in close touch with Mukhtar Pasha, and was known to lose no opportunity of reminding the Extremist Press of the syllogism that Islam was threatened with extinction by Europe, that England and France were at the head of the anti-Islamic movement, that the Sultan was the last hope of the Faithful and that Germany was the friend of the Sultan and therefore the only Moslem-minded European Power. It is true that "the Kaiser's Spy", who was attached as Oriental Secretary to the German Agency but described as "unofficial" though enjoying diplomatic privileges, was not, save as a genial host and an enterprising rather than a profound archaeologist, taken very seriously by the British or indeed by the Germans either. When Gorst succeeded Cromer, a German diplomat in Berlin stated that Baron Oppenheim was not at all happy, as he seemed no longer to be given by the British the importance which he had previously enjoyed. In former days, whenever he had an interview with Mustafa Pasha Kāmel, Lord Cromer used to get "much excited", post men to watch his house,[18] etc.; whereas now Sir Eldon Gorst simply laughed at him. In 1907 two Germans had obtained permission to travel in the Sinai by a route indicated in their Representative's application. They had not followed this route but that of Saladin against the Crusaders and, as it proved later, of 1914. In 1909 a German mechanic, obviously a man of straw, bought up *Misr al-Fatāt,* the most scurrilous Anglophobe rag of the vernacular Press. *Misr al-Fatāt* thus passed under the aegis of the Capitulations. To suppress it German consent was necessary. If Germany refused and force were employed the Egyptian Government would be involved in an Anglo-German incident. In Berlin again, Baron Schön had assured Sir Edward Goschen that Germany was anxious to oblige over the abolition of the Capitulations and persuade the other Powers to agree. The same morning he had answered the Italian Ambassador that the "Great Powers should hold fast to what they'd got".

But a climax was reached over the appointment of a successor to Dr Moritz, the Director of the Khedivial Library. This Directorship was in principle reserved for a German, as was that of the Antiquities for a French scientist, by an understanding included in the negotiations preceding the Entente Cordiale. On the retirement of Dr Moritz the Egyptian Government was informed by the German Agent that Dr Kurt Prüfer had been chosen to fill the post. The manner of announcement was curious, for it imposed upon the Egyptian Government not only, as agreed, a German librarian, but a particular German, without choice or alternative. Even if this method had been acceptable the actual selection was yet more curious, for Dr Prüfer was none other than the official Oriental Secretary of the German Agency; in the modern phrase, my "opposite number". I knew and liked Dr Prüfer, but the more I learnt of his talents and activities the less suitable a candidate did he seem for a position which would maintain him, *ex officio,* in close and daily contact with the Intelligentsia of Young Egypt. So gravely perturbed was Rushdi Pasha by this nomination that he immediately consulted Lord Kitchener. They decided it to be inadmissible, and there ensued a series of offers from the Egyptian Government of higher and better paid German posts in the Antiquities and Quarantine Departments with an ultimate decoration for Dr Prüfer, all of which were rejected by the German Agency on the only too comprehensible ground of their not being an equivalent for the Khedivial Library. They declared that Dr Prüfer was interested not in politics but only in scholarship and Oriental literature; yet it

[18] Here the Baron flattered himself.

seemed that the united Universities of Germany could produce no efficient substitute. In the end the place was given to Lutfi Bey al-Sayyid, an Egyptian Moslem. For the Turco-German attack the following year upon the Suez Canal, the Director of Political Intelligence and Secret Service, with headquarters in Jerusalem, was Dr Kurt Prüfer.

In April 1914 occurred a visit to Cairo the ultimate impact of which upon the War and the destinies of the Near and Middle East is not even yet fully calculable. The Amir Abdallah, second son of the Grand Sharīf of Mecca, arrived from Constantinople as the guest of the Khedive and was received by Lord Kitchener. He appeared to have something to say but somehow did not reach the point of saying it. Meanwhile we were advised from Constantinople that such audiences were displeasing to the Sublime Porte, always suspicious of Arab intrigue in the Hejaz and in Syria. Lord Kitchener therefore received Abdallah no more, but before long Abdallah asked me to call.[14] I visited him in the Abdīn Palace and sat for two hours under the spell of a charm which subsequent close association has only enhanced and which long absences have failed to diminish. I was astonished and delighted at the range of his literary memory. He intoned for me brilliant episodes of the Seven Suspended Odes of Pre-Islamic Poetry, the Glories and the Lament of Ántar ibn Shaddād, during which we must have accounted for whole quarts of the rich Khedivial coffee. Travelling by a series of delicately inclined planes, from a warrior past I found myself in the defenceless Arab present, being asked categorically whether Great Britain would present the Grand Sharīf with a dozen, or even a half-dozen machine guns. When I enquired what could possibly be their purpose he replied (like all re-armers) for defence; and, pressed further, added that the defence would be against attack from the Turks.[15] I needed no special instructions to inform him that we could never entertain the idea of supplying arms to be used against a Friendly Power. Abdallah can have expected no other reply, and we parted on the best terms.

14

Lord Kitchener to Sir W. Tyrrell
(private letter).
British Agency, Cairo, 26 April 1914

Grey MSS., vol. ix.

"... Sharīf Abdullah.... He sent for Storrs who under my instructions told him the Arabs of the Hejaz could expect no encouragement from us and that our only interest in Arabia was the safety and comfort of Indian pilgrims.... The Sharīf seemed to be disappointed with the result of his visit to Constantinople and with the determination of the Turkish Government to push the railway on to Mecca which he saw would mean the economic death of the camel-owning population of Arabia.

It will be interesting to see developments as the Arabs seem to be much excited."

15 There were constant rumours of friction between the Sharīf of Mecca and the Turkish Vali of the Hejaz; and the Arabs were continually closing the road from Jeddah to Mecca.

Kitchener left Egypt for his last holiday on 18 June 1914. On 7 June I had written:

The heat wave I mentioned last week continued, and proved to be the worst known in the country for twenty years. 117° in the shade all day for two or three days. The iron of the Kasr al-Nil Bridge expanded so much that it refused to open. Coming out of the Agency on Monday Greg and I found two of those grey hooded crows under a tree. One was lying on its back fluttering feebly, its eyes already going blue; the other was standing, unable to move when we came up to it, gasping thickly and heavily. We got some water and sprinkled them; the first was too far gone but the second absorbed just enough energy to fly out into the sun (you cannot help a B.F.) where we had to head it into a bush. On recounting the story to K. and Fitz we were greeted less with the respect due to humane ornithologists than with a salvo of imprecations. It appears that these birds are, from the gardener's point of view, a pest: and that Fitz spent his evenings frightening them away with an air-gun on one side of the house, and was disgusted to find G. and me applying artificial respiration on the other. The same day I observed a water-cart driver look this way and that and, thinking he saw no man, remove first his clothes and then the lid of his tank (the cart's), into the depths of which he presently disappeared for the space of about five minutes. It is better now, though still bad: K. childishly counts the days to his leave, as I did at Temple Grove.

On the Austrian Lloyd S.S. *Helouan* he showed me, after unusual hesitations, a cipher telegram from the Prime Minister proposing to submit his name to the King for the dignity of an earldom. He said he had decided to call himself the Earl of Broome, after Broome Park, his Kent property, and asked me what I thought. I thought there was already a peer, Lord Brougham, whose title was pronounced exactly the same; and even if there were not, the disappearance of the name of Kitchener of Khartum would be the loss of an Imperial asset. He answered, that was nonsense, and persisted in the project; which I afterwards heard was overruled with more or less the same arguments far more forcibly applied by Highest Authority.

Later he welcomed me to Broome and throughout a summer afternoon concealed from me no aesthetic, economic or sanitary improvement. He was still in the agent's house and I believe never lived to sleep one night in the place which for so long had been his interest, his pleasure and his pride. Unless summoned I calculated rather carefully the times of my visits to his London headquarters, Pandeli Ralli's house, 17 Belgrave Square, for there was always the risk of being landed with a mass of correspondence (much of which might be outside my province) with a general order to "take it away and let me hear no more of it". One of his defects was to ignore the certain resentment of neglected seniors.

In July a curious attempt was made upon the life of the Khedive. Shaikh Abd al-Aziz Shawish induced a neurotic young Egyptian called Mazhar, ex-instructor in Arabic at Oxford, Egyptian nationalist and tool of the Young Turks, to shoot the Khedive, as Wardāni had shot Bútros, guaranteeing him immunity. The murder was to take place in Constantinople. As soon as Mazhar had consented, Shawish informed the Committee of Union and Progress, warning them to order their agents to wait until the murder had been committed and then to dispatch the murderer. Shawish left for the interior. Four days later the Khedive drove by appointment to visit the Grand Vizier. As the carriage slowed down opposite the Sublime Porte Mazhar approached within three yards and fired at His Highness the bullets of two Browning automatics, wounding him slightly in the cheek and tongue. Hilmy Pasha, an A.D.C. of the Court, detailed to accompany the Khedive, crouched back in the carriage and made no attempt whatever to protect him, whilst the coachman, instead of whipping up the horses, pulled them to a standstill. Mazhar was allowed to empty both Brownings before being cut down. After three days' "investigation" the only Report issued by the Constantinople Police was that Mazhar had become unbalanced owing to his hopeless passion for a young Jewess. The object of the outrage was never established, but it was thought to be the removal of the Khedive as possible head of an anti-Turkish Arab Confederation. I remember drafting for Lord Kitchener in Belgrave Square his telegram of congratulation to His Highness upon his escape.

I met Lord Kitchener constantly, for business or pleasure, throughout the glittering season of 1914. Twice he attended that vast club of nightly resort, the Russian Ballet at Covent Garden. The slaves were lashed across the stage in the *Joseph* Ballet by the composer who in his *Electra* had lashed the very drums of his orchestra. The cruel impossible ecstasies of Thamar and Sheherezādé were keying the world up to yet more monstrous gratifications. For the summer holidays (I was joining Mrs Leeds's yachting party on the *Lysistrata* at Cowes, and afterwards going for a motor tour in Sicily) man was proposing and God disposing. Lord Kitchener visited Ashridge in July and knew at breakfast on the day of his departure that dreadful quickening of the European *tempo*, the murder of the Archduke. He said: "This will be a war." [16] After the Austrian ultimatum to Serbia the volume of calamity seemed to acquire the geometrical progression of momentum of the great Zambesi heading for the brink of the Victoria Falls. Kitchener, anxious to avoid strange political adven-

[16] "July 27. K. fears our being dragged into War."

ture and to serve where he knew himself master of the situation, hastened his plans for return to Egypt. By the middle of the last week in July, he had ordered me from Broome to be ready to sail on Monday, August 3rd. On July 31st FitzGerald telegraphed: "We do not start will wire later." Aware of the demand for accommodation I cancelled my berth on the P. and O. before joining my family in the Deanery at Rochester: immensely relieved, and still hoping against hope for peace. At ten o'clock on Monday morning I was playing clock-golf with my father when another telegram arrived: "Cancel former telegram we leave as first arranged by 1 o'clock boat but enquire whether it is running to-day from Dover to Folkestone." This detail none that I could discover knew. Trains were useless and on Bank Holiday it was difficult to find a car. We hired one nevertheless, tried Dover first and at 11.55 found the boat there and Kitchener striding alone up and down the deck. "Tell the Captain to start", he kept saying. I reminded him of the boat-train, but he fretted, dreading to be held back at the last moment in an advisory capacity, with functions unspecified. After fifteen difficult minutes the boat-train came in bearing FitzGerald with a message from the Prime Minister instructing Kitchener to remain. He returned, his dread with him, to 17 Belgrave Square. I remember the blessed peace of the Kentish scene as I drove back, my mother's exultation at this second reprieve, and her wild ambition that I should continue to serve with Kitchener.

Who can forget *Dies Irae?* The fears and reproaches of the French, both justified; our pardonable revulsion—what had *we* done to be involved in these sickening follies?—the unreality, the impossibility, and the clock ticking steadily towards 10 p.m. About six I went to say good-bye to the German Embassy, realizing that next day might be too late. From the Ambassador and Princess Lichnowsky I had known nothing but kindness. She had sat more than once in the long library of my uncle's house reading aloud *Madame Bovary* far into the afternoon. Her habit of inviting one alternately to official dinners and to early morning breakfast was as unconventional as her tennis. They were sitting in a little room close to the door of the Embassy, his life-work broken, their hands in their laps, with nothing further to be done. In the eyes of both were tears. I thanked them and wished them God-speed. He said: "In Berlin—I don't know—I don't know." To Harry Cust, calling later for the same purpose, he kept repeating: *"Sie sind verrückt in Berlin, sie sind verrückt."*

It was not until the afternoon of the first day of the War that Kitchener was summoned to the Cabinet. He went, determined to refuse anything less or other than the full position and powers of Secretary of State for War. In the front room of No. 17 were gathered those of us most in contact with him: Sir Reginald Wingate, Sirdar; Lord Edward Cecil, Financial Adviser; his host, Pandeli Ralli; FitzGerald and Sir George Arthur: straining for the verdict. The telephone rang, and we were put out of our suspense by the news of unconditional offer and acceptance. Next morning I was instructed to be by ten at No. 17. I started so early that I found myself with nearly an hour on my hands, and looked into a few shops to see how the War was affecting them. I was affected myself by the agonized but lapidary summing up of Mr Bloch, the antique dealer: "Everything's worth nothing, and nothing's worth anything."

Lord Kitchener informed me that he had decided to make me his Private Secretary in the War Office, put into my hands two enormous baskets of papers and told me that he would like the indefinite loan of a house in Carlton House Terrace, and of a Rolls Royce, before luncheon. I asked him if he had arranged for me with the Foreign Office and he told me not to bother him with details but to go and do it myself. It was useless to insist (upon what was equally clear to him) that I knew nothing about war, but something about Egypt, and that the Foreign Office might object: so, having procured the house and car, and finding it impossible to break through the crowds of recruits and sight-seers to rejoin him in the War Office, I crossed with some misgiving into Downing Street. The first man I interviewed in the Foreign Office replied that the whole thing was absurd, that I belonged to Egypt, that I must see that now (his expression said "at last") I had a chance of showing my worth. I could deny nothing of this, but only repeat that I was acting under the orders of my Chief, and that if, as now appeared, I was indis-pensable, perhaps they would acquaint the Field-Marshal. The suggestion seemed unpalatable, and after a pause I was ushered into the presence of Sir Arthur Nicolson, the Permanent Under-Secretary of State. This frail, bent figure, apart from his office, had in him that which men call authority. He listened awhile, cut me short and instructed me to tell Lord Kitchener that I must return to my duty to-morrow. I went back to Belgrave Square with a heavy heart and found him, stript to the waist, washing before dinner. Behind him on four cane-bottomed chairs sat three French Generals, and Mr Walter Long. He came out with me into the passage; said that he had heard from the Foreign Office; that they were right and he was wrong; that it was a pity but that I knew what he wanted in Egypt; shook hands, called "Good luck" over the banisters and went back into his room. I never saw him again.

Those who can be content with history as it occurred may study his life in the Biography of Sir George Arthur. For others, snappy paragraphs,[17] smart chapters, and not unreadable volumes have been written, explaining the failures (and explaining away the successes) of the Sirdar who made the Egyptian Army; of the General who planned and won the battle of Omdurman—the greatest General, according to the German General Staff History, of the Boer War; of the Governor-General who founded the Sudan Administration and made the British public build Gordon College at Khartum; of the Commander-in-Chief who reorganized the Indian Army; of the Diplomat still revered by Afrikander statesmen for his large unniggling spirit, by the Egyptian people for his sympathy and kindness; of the War Minister whose name and face called into being the greatest volunteer army ever known; of the world figure whose passing was felt as a portent of nature. By any who had the good fortune to enjoy in close association his confidence, his ready and humorous adoption of constructive suggestions and the free hand he accorded, with entire absence of fussing over detail, for their carrying out, his loyal and constant support in face of that detraction which in the East is the natural pastime of undirected leisure—by any, still left, that knew these, he will also be gratefully remembered as the Perfect Chief.

> The sea became his resting-place
> The Ocean wave his tomb;
> But for his fame, on Sea or Land,
> Was not sufficient room.

[17] As late as the spring of 1937 there was an edifying correspondence in *The Times* about Lord Balfour's description of Kitchener as "a stupid man"; at the same time we were reminded that other British Generals had foreseen a three years' duration of the War. Anyhow, they never foretold it publicly. This is the comment of a German Major-General who met Kitchener in India, in 1908-9:

"I was deeply impressed by the clearness of his outlook regarding the future of Europe. He spoke with the greatest firmness of conviction in telling me that in his opinion war between England and Germany had become inevitable—not because of any vital antagonism between the two nations, but because of the weakness and indecision of leading statesmen on both sides—that an Anglo-German war, whoever else participated, would last at least three years, and finally that there would be no victory at all, both countries being bound to lose most of their influence in world affairs, especially in the Pacific area, the only possible winners being the U.S.A. and Japan." *The Times*, 5 January 1937.

CHAPTER SEVEN

1914–1916

A great country can have no such thing as a little war.
DUKE OF WELLINGTON

I

THE spirit and appearance of England, even of London, during the first few days of the War were bustling rather than bellicose; partly I suppose because we were not then (any more than we are now) a Military Power, and partly because of a notable change in the technique of warfare. During the South African campaign in 1899, troops of all arms had marched with bands through the streets escorted (and frequently "treated") by weeping relations and cheering strangers. Their bearing and numbers, titles and units, with any other information (such as their names, weights and ages) of possible use to an enemy were printed and pictured in the Public Press, and were therefore in the hands of the Boer generals long before the gallant originals had taken the field. In August 1914 the majority were across the Channel and marching to the Front before their wives and sisters were aware they had left their barracks. Nevertheless, there was not much visible evidence of *dernier bouton* preparedness; on the contrary there prevailed a pleasantly deceptive absence of obvious purpose or plan. I remember very well feeling that we were carrying this *insouciance* rather far when on the second day of the War Lord Kitchener wanted General French on the telephone, and I was informed that the line was out of order.

On Friday the 7th I was to return to Egypt. I bought a Browning pistol and a hundred cartridges, thinking how foolish it would feel to be held up, unarmed, by some enemy agent in a back street of Cairo. Harry and Nina Cust said good-bye to me from their door—he for the last time. My father, mother and brother Francis waved from the quay at Tilbury,

141

and the P. and O. *Mooltan*—later to carry me on a grimmer voyage—bore me away from England for three incredible years.

Ship ludicrously crammed. Seventy officers above total accommodation with 1st class tickets, sleeping like sardines in a sort of cockpit under blinding arc flares . . . dinner took 2½ hours to serve . . . eight men standing outside every bath this morning. We have a cruiser escort to Gibraltar, *Monmouth*, and hope to find the *Goeben* so much slag.

(Long before we reached Egypt came the news of the fateful break through to the Bosphorus.) We stopped tantalizingly for several hours at Plymouth, which looked alternately the hardest and the easiest place in the world for capture by any foreign Navy—always granted that it could live to get within range. The *Mooltan* had been virtually commandeered for Egyptian officials. She carried General Wingate, the Governor-General of the Sudan, with a future Governor-General in the person of his Private Secretary, Captain Symes; also an unassuming Captain Clayton, soon to become one of the best known figures in the Near East. There was Prince George, the present King of Greece, returning from his first London season; and his uncle Prince Christopher, a member of our countermanded yachting party, with an agreeable touch on the piano.

Gibraltar at 10.0 p.m. proved the most beautiful sight: as we came in at sunset six torpedo boats ran out like black beetles across the bay, and submarines played round us like dolphins. Now, utter calm; all the stars out; lights of Ceuta across the water, and 56 large ships—including 17 prizes—anchored outside the boom, winking and twinkling at each other. Great splashes and flashes of silver sweeping the sea, showing up the smallest skiff like diamonds and pearls. Behind, the fixed lights climbing the side of the rock. The whole inconceivably effective.

At Port Said the real nationality of the *Mikado* and *Au Nippon* Stores was revealed when from them and every *baccal* [1] and fruitseller and the surrounding streets there poured and swarmed twelve thousand Greek Royalists, greeting the Heir to the Throne.

Cheetham, the Councillor to the Agency, acting for Lord Kitchener, and known to be doing well in the crisis, had hastened back from summer quarters at Alexandria, and we found ourselves in Cairo very busy indeed.

Very few Anglo-Egyptian women (D.G.) are expected just yet. B. struggles piteously to avert his newly wedded wife: on the ground that she will be so dull in the mornings.

In order to be upon our work at a time when the telephone never ceased

[1] Grocer.

ringing, we lived in the Agency, sleeping on the great balcony overlooking the Nile.

You may see any night the beds of myself, Colum, Stuart, Cheetham, Greg, Keeling, John Cecil and Craig out under the shining stars. The one defect of the arrangement is our extreme proximity to the river, which exhales every night such a damp that one's clothes are wringing wet in the early morning.

I computed that the catering, managed by two of our party, was about as economical as if we were staying in Jubilee time at Claridge's, paying corkage upon champagne brought round by special messenger from the Ritz. It was an important part of my duty to know what Egyptians and foreigners were saying, thinking and feeling—reactions which within a year were being estimated and tabulated by a variety of (sometimes conflicting) civil and military departments.

In the evening I receive those persons whose notoriety makes it undesirable that they should be seen entering this Agency, or indeed any other building, by the light of day. They bring in every sort of information, from the real tracking of a Turco-German plot to a warning against an individual unnamed of furtive and suspicious appearance. On enquiry these usually prove to be blameless members of the body politic or, at the worst, of the Secret Police.

I am putting a number of articles, as well as *Times* and other cuttings, into the Arab Press: in the evening I send forth emissaries who mouch about the Bazaars and hear the comments of the people upon my lucubrations. These are usually signed 'Independent Moslem', 'Patriot', or 'Dweller by Nile' (corresponding to our Indignant Ratepayer, Oldest Inhabitant or Mother of 19), and evoke a good deal of comment. The last, which held up to ridicule those who were too clever to believe the plain facts of our glories, etc., was at first ascribed to an Englishman, until it was pointed out that the writer compared K. to the righteous Khalif Abu Bakr—'and how should a Nazarene have imagined this?'

In this Press side of my work I had occasion to realize the damping and blanketing effect of remoteness, whether of time or place. The Agency was, for example, immediately informed of the Maritz Rebellion in South Africa, and warned to keep it entirely secret; so that when at length it did begin to leak through, the news was relatively stale and had been robbed of its terror. The horrors of Louvain and other atrocities certainly lost nothing in Allied accounts but, though brutal facts, they meant less to us than the more immediate fear of Turkey joining the Central Powers. Time-space is a natural statute of limitations, and news must be sensational indeed to survive transmission over a month or from the Antipodes.

The disposal of enemy subjects was no less delicate than difficult.

Aug. 24. ... You will hardly believe that the Austrian Minister and German Chargé d'Affaires are still in Egypt, actively intriguing against us.

Many Germans and some Austrians were predestined internees; but there were individuals, especially Austrians, of Constantinople and Smyrna, whose parents or grandparents had only adopted Austrian nationality for the protection it afforded, some of whom had been educated in England and were profoundly loyal to the Allied cause. It seemed impolitic and uneconomic as well as unjust to apply detention by rule of thumb, and I was able to intervene in some cases—not one of which did I have subsequent cause to regret. I find a letter from the Postmaster-General thanking me for saving from internment Goldstein, an invaluable and irreplacable member of his Administration:

Goldstein has returned here with Russian protection and I am extremely obliged to you for your kind offices in the matter. It now merely remains to call him Ivan Ivanovitch and get him back into his job. For the latter item I am writing to the Ministry to-day and if there is any difficulty I will trouble you again.

All enemy subjects lost their Government positions, shops, and other businesses, an inevitable measure which ruined most of them. But British financial and commercial interests were not nearly so swift as was represented by enemies and neutrals in taking advantage of these displacements.

I am stirring up Philip Graves to write a trumpet-call in *The Times* and various trade journals to galvanize our comatose merchants into some form of life. Austro-German enterprise had proved too much for them up till now even in fields where I had thought we were supreme; and it was a more or less admitted principle in Cairo that under a virtual British Protectorate the tailoring, haberdashery, grocery, photography, book and tea-shops should be in German hands; though an outsider might have imagined that for the sale of English books and for the management of an essentially English habit of 5 o'clock tea English brains would have sufficed. Now all this competition is removed: Diemer is shut and the German tea-shops and photographers are tabooed, yet not the smallest attempt has been made to step into their shoes and pick up the money which is only waiting to be spent. Many Egyptians have complained to me that they cannot get an English cup of tea in an English tea-shop, and I myself have been ashamed at the necessity of having to sell our various White Books and pamphlets on the War through French, Greek or Italian agents; also when I am informed by Government officials that large tenders for clothing or machinery very seldom fall to British firms.

Diemer, the bookshop already mentioned, near Shepheard's Hotel, provided a good example of this sluggishness. The shop was in a key position and might have controlled a propagandist agency, besides being a most profitable investment; yet none of the Departments or individuals in Egypt or in England whom (supported by *The Times* letter) I canvassed could be induced to take any interest in it, though stock and goodwill could have been bought for under two thousand pounds. Even Lord Northcliffe, while commending my zeal, was sorry he "could not undertake the suggestions about The Times Book Club in Cairo"; and the shop passed into the Greek hands of Mr Livadas.

Some of my Egyptian and foreign friends had reason to regret having succumbed to German financial blandishments.

Demerdash was caught cashless at Marseilles: and, as much of his balance was in the German Bank, (against which I have warned him for years) he thought he would on his return have to sell some land at ruinous loss in order to carry on. His wife, however, drawing with difficulty a heavy sack from beneath the flooring, asked if he imagined that whenever she had asked for money she had also needed it. "And have you lied to me in this also, Shameless One?" he replied, as he seized the bag, and with trembling hands counted out £600.

I have said that our major preoccupation was the threat of Turkey on the Canal; less for its military effect than for the repercussion upon a Moslem Egypt. All the signs of intercepted information, of Turkish preliminary Press *barrage*, pointed to war. *Al Adl* (Justice), the only Arabic paper published in Constantinople, printed as early as August 10th an article commiserating "Dear Egypt, the land of the Pharaohs, the seat of al-Azīz (the Beloved, the Khedive) who is the hope of the Arabs and the Persians. . . . See how the cruel world has wronged the benefactress of mankind, now that she is weak! . . ." "Others have dealt despotically with Egypt, but the Turks have dealt gently with her. If there had been no rebellion of Arābi—may God make hell his abode—Egypt would never have been occupied. The Egyptians are indebted to the Turks for good taste and noble sentiments. It was from the Turks that they know how to eat, dress and live. The Egyptians are indebted to them for tidiness, propriety, good management and noble aspirations. In truth the Egyptians have great hopes in the Turks. . . ." The Turks had indeed at that time great hopes in the Egyptians, not one of which was ever realized.

Have lunched with Rushdi and Adli and find them very friendly, but desirous of knowing more exactly how this country stands. I feel they desire us to discharge them from their loyalty to Turkey, and I wish we could cut the knot in some way that would not savour of making profit out of the War.

In the notes for the first of my situation-reports, submitted on 31 August, I find that news from the Provinces was slow to arrive.

From that of the towns a heavy discount must be made for alarmist Syrian, Christian, Coptic, Jewish and Armenian witnesses. At the beginning of the War there appears to have been in certain circles a wave of anti-English and German-ophil feeling so marked as to amaze Europeans and to puzzle even Egyptian observers. Strong anti-British sentiments were to be expected from the extreme Nationalists, and an Anglo-Russian Alliance was traditionally distasteful alike to Moslems and to the powerful Austro-Jewish families of Alexandria. The highest classes—always excepting the Khedivial family, about which there is temerity in the vaguest conjecture—and the lowest, are, the former by instinct and the latter by conviction, strongly in favour of Great Britain. Pious Mos-lems shake their heads and say, "We wish the Turks all success—from afar", the last portion of the benison receiving the emphasis; and the wealthier and better informed understand that, even if the legends of German brutality and colonial repression are exaggerated, their advent would signify at best the substitution of an unknown for a known evil. The most striking feature of the opposing faction is the apparent vigour and thoroughness with which the local middle-class Turks, Circassians, lawyers, students, and extremist journalists have absorbed, and continue to impart to others, the doctrine of affectionate and even passionate interest in and expectation of German successes. Germany is represented as the one great Power that has befriended Islam without acquiring one acre of Moslem territory, and the Kaiser's Syrian journey, and his noble generosity in providing, as from the clouds, two "battleships" [2] in place of those maliciously and at the last moment withheld by the English when most needed,[3] are cited and magnified with a unanimity which most clearly indicates a propaganda sedulously maintained up to and at the present moment. (This can hardly be checked until the removal of all Austro-German officials and non-officials.) It is circulated (and believed) that, in the event of the Allies winning, Russia would immediately occupy Stambul; that English and French telegrams are one mass of *suppressio veri* and *inventio falsi*, that half the British Navy has been sunk [4] and that the Germans have invested Paris; and finally, that after the culminating German victory the English will be expelled from Egypt, which will be handed back to the Turks. These will be faced with the alternatives of governing the country in the old fashion by Pasha and favourites, or else admitting it to the Constantinople Parliament, where the numbers of Egyptian deputies would (it is not explained how) out-vote and consequently control the remaining Vilayets of the Ottoman Empire. Certain well-disposed Egyptians of the upper classes who have relations with Constantinople, have heard that assurances have been given by His Majesty's Government to the Porte, to the effect that the present political situation will not be changed so long as Turkey remains calm. As it has been almost uni-versally assumed that annexation or at least the Protectorate will be proclaimed in the immediate future, these assurances have occasioned some surprise and a little uneasiness. Unmistakable hints have been received that a formal change

[2] The *Goeben* and the *Breslau*.

[3] On order for the Ottoman Government and retained, according to contract, when the War broke out, though Turkey had not yet come in.

[4] "Many Egyptians who I meet them in these days have in their pockets postcards contain the figures of the British fleets in an agitated ocean and above them the sky a 'Zebbelin' throwing the bullets of dynamite upon them; we find in the end of these postcards German writing containing bad explanations to the British fleets." Local Agent's report.

of regime, leaving the position of the Occupation unimpaired without wounding Egyptian *amour-propre* and "sense of nationality", would be far from unwelcome. It is pointed out that a transference of the temporal suzerainty from the Sultan to His Majesty the King, accompanied by guaranteed "autonomy" (for England must not show herself less generous than the Turks) or "independence" with subsequent abolition of Capitulations, would go far towards disembarrassing the conscientious from the incubus of Ottoman loyalty; localizing aspirations and diminishing almost to a vanishing point the attraction and influence of pan-Islam. Desire that the responsibility for acquiescence in this transfer should be borne by somebody else largely accounts for the Ministers' anxiety at the Khedive's continued absence.[5]

A reign of always increasing terror was reported from Syria. "Ever since I dropped my last message to you in the British Post Office", writes a trembling correspondent from Beirut, "Moslems (misled by Constantinople to believe in Allied aggression) have been fleeing from Beirut into the interior." A rain of warnings about suspicious characters, whom I appeared to be meeting daily unaware, descended upon me. To the miserable uncertainties induced by this unhappy spirit one could but apply the knowledge acquired by ten years' close and wide contacts[6] which (to the best of my belief), did not betray me.

There has been a tendency, in my opinion both unfair and dangerous, to suspect Egyptian officers and officials of treachery: and I have spent much time and tissue in persuading my betters that they must love all in all or not at all; in other words trust or sack.

Under the damp heat of early autumn these occupations and preoccupations were something of a strain.

I intend a descent upon Alexandria before long, for I am not certain how long it is physically possible to interview in four languages from 9-1.30 every morning and through the afternoons, seven in the week, and also a good deal in the evening, with no assistant or assistance.

Meanwhile it became daily clearer to us that Germany's Islamic and Turkish campaign was about to succeed, even to the extent of inducing

---

[5] My first information was largely derived from townsmen, subject to daily propaganda and with a relatively small stake in the country and so awaiting the "hour of deliverance". In August 1914 the provinces were pro-British, not so much from love as from the economic certainty of being able to dispose of their cotton. The contrast at the end of the War was the more tragic.

[6] I like to hope these were not useless: "*M. R. Storrs, secrétaire oriental de l'Agence diplomatique d'Angleterre, se trouvait mercredi au Khan-Khalili lorsque, reconnu par les nombreux négociants il fut entouré et assailli de questions pleines d'anxiété sur la durée de la stagnation actuelle des affaires, de la misère qui étreint le commerce, etc., M. Storrs rassura tout le monde affirmant que le gouvernement britannique avait pris toutes les mesures nécessaires pour que l'Égypte ne manquât de rien pendant la durée de la guerre européenne.*" (Local Press.)

the Ottoman Government at any moment to declare war on the Allies, including England—for half a century her constant and best friend.

Turkey continues to pinprick us by massing large quantities of troops just far enough away from our Sinai frontier to be able to disclaim any aggressive intention. Military authorities are agreed that invasion by land is a hopeless business; and many Syrians, Arabs and progressives in general are openly expressing their hope that the attempt will be made and the consequent final dissolution of the Ottoman Empire begun. Money for the Prince of Wales's Fund has begun to trickle in by steady driblets, but this only took place after about three weeks of encouraging news, for although the Egyptians have no reason to like Germany, and detest the Turks, they are yet so easily impressed and deceived by appeals to Muhammad William, Hajji Gilliōm (under which names the Kaiser is now by order prayed for weekly in Syrian mosques), that they might have shown a good deal less *bonne volonté* if things had not gone so well for us. The Indian troops were marched through the streets about ten days ago and though in the opinion of those who have seen both they were not so smart as the Turcos, they seemed to me a formidable body of men. The people were unanimously of opinion that the Gurkhas were really Japanese in British uniforms, a rumour which I made not the smallest endeavour to contradict, seeing that the Egyptians have something like a veneration for the Japanese, considering as they do that their war against Russia was the beginning of the general renaissance of the Orient.[7]

When, at the end of October, Turkey threw off the mask, the snapping of the tension came almost as a relief.

The night before last we were informed that two thousand armed Beduin had advanced over the Sinai frontier and occupied wells twenty miles within it. Last night a telegram from London stated that Turkish torpedo boats had sunk a Russian cruiser in the harbour of Odessa. It is nothing short of a miracle if there is not war to-morrow; for it seems impossible that the Turks can stop at the eleventh hour the German Naval and Military Mission upon whom they have so much depended and from whom they have taken so much. The news of the Turco-Russian hostilities is generally known now owing to an extraordinary piece of carelessness on the part of the Censorship, which passed a Reuter telegram at Port Said though they remembered to stop it in Cairo and Alexandria. As a result I am bombarded with anxious questions as to the state of this country. Those with Turkish blood in their veins are in a very difficult and delicate position.[8] The participation of Egypt in an Anglo-Turkish

[7] The arrival of the other and unmistakably Indian regiments was peculiarly welcome; Egyptian Nationalists having hitherto proclaimed that the British "rode" Indians like asses, and that these would never fight. I found Indians, on the other hand, inclined to despise Egyptians, as lacking in tradition.

[8] Proclamations by the Commander of the Fourth Turkish Army were being secretly circulated in Egypt. They included "Fatwas" or decisions on religious problems submitted to the Grand Mufti of Constantinople. "Is it or is it not categorically and legally forbidden the Moslems of the Governments which are at war with the Moslem Government to fight against the troops of this latter, even if menaced by death, they and their families? Do they or do they not deserve the fires of Jehannum as murderers if they should? Give us a Fatwa, may God reward you! Answer: Yes, they deserve that Khairi ben Auni al-Arkāni."

war comes to them as a shock against a tradition which has spread right into their blood. This morning for instance Gaafar Bey Wāli (a Circassian), the Under-Secretary of State for the Interior, came round to see me. He told me frankly that the news has upset him so much that he had come for comfort. As there were at that moment 120 Beduin from all parts of the country waiting to be harangued by General Maxwell (for whom I translate), his visit though flattering was hardly opportune. Last night I gave a dinner to the Prime Minister and the Minister of Foreign Affairs—Rushdi and Adli. They were both exceedingly nervous, and threatened to resign unless we are able to offer them some concession in the line of autonomy or self-government with which they can go to the country in the event of our proclaiming a Protectorate. I prophesied this demand a week after my return from leave, and I am glad to say sent it home in a note describing the situation in Egypt. However, for two months nothing has been done, and now confronted with a crisis we have again to face the music, for although it would perhaps be possible to find other Ministers and Prime Ministers (Hishmat is only too ready to dash into the fray) yet it is by no means certain that they would command the respect or confidence of the country.

Egypt was not the only Moslem country to feel the embarrassment.

I dined on Thursday with a Tunisian friend. He told me that at the beginning of the War, the German Consul-Gen. was requested to leave, and refused to do so without a written order from the Bey. Upon this the French Resident waited upon the Bey, and instructed him to declare war upon Germany. The unhappy monarch, all of a tremble, ventured upon a feeble protest, but was informed that it was an "order from Paris", upon which he seized his pen and dashed off his declaration: *"après quoi, mon cher ami, il e eu la diarrhée pendant vingt jours."*

Martial Law was proclaimed on 2 November:

Outlying residents are foolishly nervous of the Turks, and it is related that two of the Matrons of Maadi, by no means in the first flush of youth, have arranged to shoot each other upon the arrival of the Bashi Bazuks.

His Majesty's Government had now to be prepared with a counter-stroke in Egypt, and the two emergent questions were, what was to be her international status and who her immediate ruler.

The Khedive, whatever may have been his previous rights and wrongs (to neither of which is the writer unsympathetic) had not proved himself before the gathering of the clouds even a fair-weather friend: and agreement between Egyptian as well as British authorities was unanimous that his return in such a crisis was out of the question; the Ministers in Cairo showing particular eagerness that he should be deposed. Neither Turkey nor the rest of the World could imagine that the Occupying Power, if attacked by the Suzerain, would any longer tolerate a suzarainty that had been but a figure of speech for the past half century. The only question was, what form of Government should replace the forfeited suzerainty. The uncertainty of Occupation, with its remote hopes and hypothetical fears, must obviously be abolished. There could be no doubt as to the choice of the new Sovereign. Prince Hussein Kāmel was known and respected by Egyptians as a practical agriculturist; by foreigners and the *Corps Diplomatique* as a *grand seigneur* brought up in the stately court of the Tuileries; by both as the brother of the late sovereign, Tewfik, and the son of the great Khedive Ismail. He was ambitious, and in principle not averse to the throne: but was not unnaturally apprehensive of his position in the Moslem world, as successor (imposed by a Christian Occupation or Protectorate) of dethroned legitimacy. When sounded at the beginning of November, he twice refused the throne. Meanwhile, time pressed and the British Government, bored by the delay, proposed to cut the knot and annex Egypt.

There was a strong party in London, provided with convincing arguments (admirably marshalled in Lord Lloyd's *Egypt*) for Annexation: so much so that by 13 November the Agency was specifically informed that the decision for Annexation had been taken, the Order in Council drafted and the date for its promulgation fixed. To the men on the spot these instructions came as a sharp shock. Cromer had insisted, Gorst had proclaimed, Kitchener had allowed, that the Occupation was a temporary measure, designed to prepare the Egyptians for eventual independent self-government. This had been for forty years the declared policy of successive British Cabinets. We were still making heavy and successful, and wholly justified, play with the doctrine of the Scrap of Paper. To go back now on all these assurances by stripping from another small country the last appearance of an individual identity seemed to us the end of our accepted word, anyhow throughout the Near and Middle East. The Egyptian Ministers had accepted the grave responsibility of Administration and secured the support of the religious party with a view to a possible Protectorate. Had Britain annexed Egypt they must have resigned to a man, with consequences none could foresee. Cheetham therefore despatched an eleventh-hour protest, begging that the death sentence of Annexation should be commuted to Protection; thereby merely transferring suzerainty, registering and legalizing the Occupation as *de jure* as well as *de facto,* and preserving intact the throne of the House of Muhammad Ali, with the Constitution and international status that Egypt had enjoyed before as well as after the Occupation.

By the time you get this, it is possible the political status of Egypt will have been decided and announced. I am anti-Annexation and pro-Protectorate. It is too late, in the twentieth century to denationalize or attempt to absorb races; and even if it were practicable elsewhere, the Nile Mud, which has absorbed Hebrews, Persians, Greeks, Romans and Turks so completely as to efface every trace of them, is not a suitable medium for any such experiment.

To our enchanted relief the alternative was accepted by His Majesty's Government on 19 November. But before proclaiming the good news it was necessary to provide the throne with an occupant. Prince Hussein procrastinated in the hope of better terms. The fact of the negotiations was known, and strong family and general pressure was secretly exerted upon him through emissaries from Constantinople to drag on discussions until mid-January—by which time the Turks would be ready to attack Egypt—and then to break them off. I do not think the Prince was appreciably influenced by this sort of thing, though Harīms in those days were almost exclusively Turkish, and domestic pressure, like the Mills of God, though it grind slowly yet grinds exceedingly small. He considered, and I agreed, that he was conferring as well as receiving a favour and that, in the matter of status, his wishes should be met. The Prince was strongly of opinion that Egypt should be transformed into a Kingdom under an Egyptian King. As it was impossible that a vassal prince should bear the same style as his suzerain, I ventured to suggest the alternative of Sultan, an Arab name signifying "the bearer of ruling power" which had been first adopted in Egypt by Saladin, and which was incidentally the title of the ex-Suzerain ruler of the Ottoman Empire. My proposal was accepted by both sides. Majesty being impossible for the same reason as King, *Hautesse,* the ancient and dignified double of *Altesse,* was suggested in order to distinguish the sovereign from the spate of obscure and sometimes ignoble collaterals all claiming the title of Highness. Meanwhile, nothing was settled, neither side was committed to anything, and a sharp Allied reverse on any front might plunge us into the dreaded inferiority of hawking round an ever less desirable crown and continually having to offer higher inducement for its acceptance. I had spoken frequently but, as a junior, unofficially, with Prince Hussein, having fresh in my memory the perplexities and humiliations of the Mustafa Fehmy crisis. Negotiations dragged on for about a month. At last the question was narrowed down to the offer by the Government of the throne of Egypt to Prince Hussein with the title of Sultan and— nothing more. The Prince behaved with great dignity, but pointed out that the document contained no mention of heredity in his family or indeed among the descendants of Muhammad Ali; that he was allowed no voice in the choice of a flag nor was even sure he would have one at all; and that he was not informed whether Egyptians would be British subjects or retain their own entity and nationality under a British Protectorate. I considered him entirely justified on these three points, but we had our instructions, and it seemed impossible to persuade him to accept. The alternative was the proclamation of a Protectorate without any Egyptian Sovereign at all.

The imposition of the Union Jack, containing as it does the cross in three forms, would have had a bad effect in Egypt and a worse throughout Arabia; and the Khedivial Turkish party, which though dormant still existed, would have been immensely strengthened when it became known that we had not been able to make the rival claimant an offer which his dignity could accept. The Ministers told us frankly that they would not continue in office under a throneless Protectorate. We had given up all hope, and a telegram embodying the Prince's refusal, drafted and typed, lay ready for ciphering on Cheetham's table. As a last resort I primed Shaarāwi Pasha, a rich landowner who had been intimate with the Prince all his life, and Ambroise Sinadino, a Greek, in more or less intimate contact with the Agency for the past thirty-five years. They went round independently and as if with no knowledge of the circumstances (I had in fact told them very little) pointed out to Prince Hussein how nervous the country was getting at the prolonged delay in the production of the proclamation, and hoped that the responsibility did not lie on his side, as that might force the English to do things repugnant to them and disastrous to the country.

On Sunday evening I received a note from Sinadino. "*Mon cher Storrs, J'ai fait de la bonne besogne pendant une heure et demie. Son Altesse aimerait beaucoup avec l'autorisation de Monsieur Cheetham que vous alliez le voir demain lundi avant midi à sa Daira;* [9] *il pourra ainsi vous parler à cœur ouvert. Je vous serre la main; bien à vous. Ambroise.*" I persuaded Cheetham to postpone his final telegram and telephoned to the Prince asking him to see me that evening instead of the next day. He received me very kindly in his Palace at Heliopolis and kept me from 10 till 12. A laconic brevity and a direct coming to the point are not the virtues of Prince Hussein, and he began by quoting a number of instances of his friendliness and loyalty to Great Britain from the very beginning. My soul fainted within me when he described with a wealth of horticultural detail how he had rooted up trees from his own garden at Giza and presented them to the first Lady Cromer and I longed to say: "*Monseigneur! passons au Déluge.*" However, he eventually attacked the subject and speaking without any reserve at all told me that he wanted to accept the Sultanate, but as offered by H.M.G. could not face it. I begged him for his own sake and that of the country to trust the British Government,

[9] Estate Office.

which had recalled him from exile and which had never yet betrayed him; still he would not accept. At about half-past eleven I said I feared I was intruding upon his leisure, and he asked me whether I would leave with an impression of an obstinate man: I said No, but with a distinct impression of a Prince who had no confidence in Lord K. or the British Government. He appeared a little staggered at this and said: "I cannot let you go away under this impression; what do you think I had better do?" I recommended him to allow us to put in a strong appeal for the heredity, and to leave the question of the flag and the nationality to the wisdom of the British High Commissioner who was coming out. I pointed out that a Sultan on the throne was in a much better position for bargaining than a claimant however illustrious, and that the Foreign Office, confronted with this notable proof of his *bonne volonté* would be likely to allow him a larger share of confidence and consequently a freer hand in the future. He thought awhile and said: "If you will guarantee that the High Commissioner will decide the other two points in my favour and procure for me the heredity, I accept." I told him that this was not an acceptance at all, but only a post-dating of his demands, that I regretted so small a thing should keep him from doing all the good I knew he would be able to do, but that there was nothing for it now but to dispatch the telegram embodying his refusal. He took leave of me very cordially, and said he very much appreciated my anxiety that the Sultanate should not pass into less worthy hands. I left him at midnight, impressed by his dignity and the real justice of his cause, and informed Cheetham of his offer. Early next morning Prince Hussein sent for the Ministers and, after informing them of what had happened, telephoned to me that he was prepared to accept my suggestion of the night before. He visited Cheetham (who was not a little pleased), withdrew his former refusal and made the new proposal which we have now embodied in a telegram and sent home.[10]

I have ventured to record thus at length the last inner workings of that rumbling and irregular but beneficent old machine, then about to be thrown on the scrap-heap—the British "Occupation" of Egypt.

The transfer from Moslem to Christian Suzerainty was, like other Allied successes, better received in the Provinces than in the towns. *Ghaffirs* and *fellahin* in Menūfīa told my friend John Young [11] that they were pleased to hear about Hussein because he was "a good man and understands us and the country". In the Cairo Mosques the prayer for the Moslem *Khalīfa* was repeated three times in succession and each time response was general and loud, whereas that to the prayers for the Sultan of Egypt was feeble or inaudible. The students of the Law School appeared wearing black ties and lugubrious expressions; many girls in the Government Secondary Schools sported black rosettes. When in his inaugural drive to the Palace the Sultan passed the grandstand of the

[10] From my account written next day.
[11] Sleeping in the Menūf Rest House over the lock-up he was kept awake by a *Hashāsh* assuring the Police that he was now an *Ingliz* and should be treated with respect.

Omdehs and Notables in the Abdīn Square they clapped half-heartedly, each one looking sideways to see what his neighbour was doing. The truth was that many were unable to believe that the Germans could be defeated, and were still expecting a victorious Turkish advance upon Egypt.

Prince Hussein deserved well of his country, of his dynasty and of Great Britain, by thus providing a transition period, free from bloodshed or repression, from which better statesmanship on one side and more goodwill on the other might have evolved a happier relationship.

I send you amongst other enclosures the leading article of the *Bourse Égyptienne*, the best European paper here, upon the Protectorate and the Sultanate. You may recognize some familiar touches in this majestic prose. Both events have passed off excellently well, as you will have seen from Philip's telegram in *The Times*. On Saturday morning I drove with Cheetham in the state carriage—*Daumont* as it should apparently be called—to offer the throne to the new Sultan. He was very nervous and profoundly impressed by the magnitude of the occasion (after all the thing does not happen every day to any of us) but exceedingly agreeable: and he has by far the best royal manner I have yet seen. At half-past two I went by instruction to visit the Aga Khan, who has just arrived with the idea of convincing the dubious Moslems of the possibilities and advantages for Islam under British protection. I liked the Prince himself; but he is accompanied by an Indian Moslem called Baig, member of the Council of the Secretary of State for India. Both will be received by the Sultan to-day, and afterwards come to tea with me to meet the Prime Minister and Adli Pasha Yeghen whom I will subsequently leave alone with them. Yesterday morning Cheetham and the staff drove (again in a *Daumont*) with a military escort, behind the Sultan to the Palace through the streets lined with troops; and were received by him before anyone else. We came in, I am glad to say, for a certain amount of the acclamation on the way; but I will confess to a certain relief when the thing was over, for I had discovered only the night before a band of five Turks who had bought Browning pistols early in the week and had been practising with them ever since with the idea of plugging the authorities in general. The streets were decorated by day and illuminated by night very effectively, with the odd result that Cairo looked gayer than it ever had in the period of its most brilliant prosperity. The Private Secretary was so affected by the entry of his Royal master into the Palace of his Fathers that he broke down and wept, as the French say, like a veal; and had to be removed into an antechamber and restored with cognac. At six in the evening our visit was returned; Cheetham made me responsible for all the arrangements as it was assumed (I am unable to find out why) that I have an intimate acquaintance with the procedure for receiving Sultans on the day of their Accession. It was too dark for the Guard of Honour to be very much seen, but I had them placed round the door, and turned on all the electric lights in the house to show them up. I likewise borrowed from the Bazaars jewelled coffee cups worth a King's Ransom, thus I trust conveying to His Highness the impression of habitual splendour in His Majesty's Agency.

If we estimated for ourselves a twenty or thirty per cent. chance of being bombed or shot during the formal drive to Abdīn Palace, how high, we wondered, did the Sultan compute the odds against himself? Two serious attempts were made later against his life,[12] and I remember being throughout the War astonished that there were only two, and that so little resort was had behind the universal front to political assassination of foreign sovereigns and statesmen. The horrors of Belgium and Armenia have shown that this abstention was not due to high-mindedness on the part of belligerents, but rather to the extreme difficulty of finding assassins prepared not so much to risk as to fling away their lives, unpleasantly perhaps, in cold blood. On my return from the Palace

I warned Ismain (my Egyptian servant) that upon the first attempt of him, or of his colleagues, to cut my throat (or even Cheetham's), their wages will be reduced by half: dismissal to follow upon the second offence. Of course the servant class is very strongly with us, and is cynically disillusioned as to the prestige or utility of the Turks.

II

Hussein Kāmel, first Sultan of modern Egypt, was a younger son of the Khedive Ismail and brother of the Khedive Tewfik, that eldest born for whose succession by primogeniture Ismail had paid so many scores of thousands to the Sublime Porte. Hussein succeeded his nephew, the Khedive Abbas Hilmi. He was in turn succeeded by his younger brother —Sultan, afterwards King—Fuad, father of the present Sovereign.

The Sultan Hussein was of medium height, the effect of which was increased by the royal dignity of his carriage, whether seated or standing. There was romance in the fine sad eyes, *crânarie* in the great Turkish moustache and the high tarbush worn rakishly to the right side. By instinct and by original training he was in all matters of finance, government, and attitude towards Egyptians and foreigners, pre-eminently the son of his father Ismail, as was shown in his reckless generosity, his ultra-Edwardian desire that things should be done well, his complete freedom from fanaticism and anti-European feeling. Himself of great

---

[12] I find my description of the second attempt: "He was driving out in his carriage when the youth stepped forward with his revolver wreathed in roses and discharged it almost point blank. If His Highness had been sitting upright he would almost certainly have been killed; as it was, the drive being of a private nature and he a little tired, he was leaning back; so the bullet passed within three inches of the front of his body. I heard the news quite early, crammed on my frock coat and was at the Palace just before he returned from his drive. Smirnow the Russian Minister and Doyen of the Diplomatic Corps appeared in a suit of snuff-coloured dittos, presumably with the idea of bringing off an Essex-Elizabeth *coup*, which was not however received with any great favour."

personal charm it was essentially to personal influence and consideration that he was amenable; so much so that it was possible, given adequate care and preparation, to present almost any proposal to him in a palatable and finally acceptable form. His educational and cultural sympathies were, as might be expected from one who had spent so much of his youth at the Court of the Third Empire, decidedly French; but this had not in any way affected his pro-English views, often maintained at some personal risk during the Occupation, and now at once rewarded and consolidated by the Protectorate.

Of his first Cabinet, he was said to appreciate Rushdi Pasha the Prime Minister, but to repose his private and personal confidence in Adli Pasha—a friend of many years' standing. Sirri Pasha he accepted without any great enthusiasm as a permanent institution. Of Sarwat he professed to admire the intelligence; of Fat-hi the character; for neither Wahba nor Hilmy had he any enthusiasm. His memory registered verbal and other details with a curious and meticulous accuracy.

I saw him constantly throughout the first year of his reign and invariably found him kind, gracious and on family matters most entertaining. Having despatched the business for which he had summoned me: "*Storrs, mon ami*", he would continue, "*J'ai roulé ma bosse un peu partout, mais jamais je n'ai rencontré un méli-mélo pareil.*" I could respectfully sympathize, aware that His Highness had hardly mounted his throne before he was assailed by a throng of princely relations, some well disposed but needy, all smarting under years of real or imagined grievances and each clamouring for immediate preferential treatment. "*Mon pauvre Storrs, vous êtes jeune, mais vous êtes intelligent: et je vous demande—qu'est ce qu'on peut faire pour contenter une famille pareille? Vous avez le Prince Azīz Hassan, qui a mangé la fortune entière de sa femme, et en conséquence l'a rendue malheureuse....Le Prince Mehmet se pocharde regulièrement chaque soir, et Dieu sait ce que fait sa femme!*" Some were importuning him for money, which he disliked, others for leave to return from exile, which he hated and dreaded. "*Enfin, mon cher Storrs, pour satisfaire tout ce monde il me faudrait. . . .*" He had the contempt of the Turk for nomad, even for settled Arabs: "*Qu'est ce que le Senoussi? Un Marabout,*[18] *mon cher.*"

The Sultan's disposition was to change later, under the shadow of

[18] "In some respects this was the most successful strategical move made by our enemies of the whole War, for these odd thousand rather verminous Arabs tied up on the Western Frontier for over a year some 30,000 troops badly required elsewhere and caused us to expend on desert railways, desert cars, transport, etc., sufficient to add 2d. to the income tax for the lifetime of the present generation." C. S. Jarvis, *Three Deserts.* (John Murray.)

mortal sickness. Of the intercourse I was privileged to hold with him in those early days, I have none but the happiest memory.

Considerable play has been made by European as well as Egyptian writers with the supposed disgust and sense of degradation felt by the people at the use of the word *Himaya* حمايه , the Arabic equivalent of Protectorate. As one whose duty it was to acquaint himself with all grievances general as well as particular (and who performed, and enjoyed, this duty), I affirm that this was a grievance I never heard at the time, even at second-hand. I discussed the translations of Protectorate and High Commissioner—Himaya and Mandūb al-Sāmi—with the Prime Minister. He asked for time to verify them and telephoned to me later in the day confirming both. It was not the name, but the fact (which under any other name would have smelt no sweeter) of nations they considered unbreeched barbarians in the Hejaz and elsewhere being granted the complete independence denied to Egypt, which later in the War exasperated Egyptians beyond endurance.

About this time I made a manful, perhaps tactless, certainly hopeless effort to suggest some ordered system for the transaction of the Residency business. The Residency was in fact not, save incidentally, an Embassy or Legation, still less a Consulate-General. It was the *de facto* equivalent of the Secretariat and Government House of a Crown Colony, issuing to the Ministries and Departments financial and administrative "instructions". Yet beyond the proper diplomatic convention that all work must pass through the bottle neck of the Head of the Chancery, there was no sort of allocation of the work to *A, B,* or *C,* whereby each might in a few months have acquired some real knowledge of persons and of problems. This was sometimes trying for the Residency; for the Administrations it was maddening. The Director of Public Health, who had submitted some scheme of reform, took the High Commissioner's opinion upon it through one of the Secretaries, who might have been consulted likewise upon postal, agricultural or educational proposals. When the Director telephoned next morning to ask a question or suggest a modification, *A* was out, or engaged on something else, but *B,* who had not seen the original memorandum or heard the arguments, was blandly prepared to have the whole matter explained to him again from the beginning. The tedium, irritation and waste of time involved by these explanations and re-explanations unseated the reason of the most patient British and Egyptian officials, paralysing them by the lack of continuity which is essential to administration. Their groans were redoubled upon the Oriental Secretary, the relatively permanent member of the staff, himself a sufferer frequently called in to redress the latest haphazardry. My brief note proposed that the work should be so divided that each officer should know for what branches of the Service he was responsible to the Head of the Chancery (as he to the Councillor or High Commissioner), and that the list of work so divided should be circulated to Heads of Departments. No attention was paid to this presumption, which I rescued, after enquiry, weeks later from a dusty basket and preserved as a curiosity until it was destroyed with my other papers in 1931: but the state of affairs it disclosed was in part the occasion of the Cabinet Committee of 1917, to be described later.

The Egyptian Provinces began to feel the War towards its end. Cairo and Alexandria may be said not to have felt it at all, save pleasurably, until well after it was over; but bitterly then.

From the London newspapers it is clear that Cairo is imagined to be in a state of tense and bellicose anxiety; but in Cairo, with the exception of the British Agency and two or three high officials, hardly a soul knows any more of what is going on than do the arm-chair critics of Pall Mall. Yesterday there was a race meeting numerously attended; the tennis courts are overcrowded; you cannot get a table at the Club; bazaars are open and doing a certain amount of business. This is not to say that in the lower strata of students, politicians and journalists, palpitating rumours are not being manufactured and propagated from hour to hour, but the manufacturers and propagators even as they speak look this way and that; for the arrests of turbulents and ne'er-do-wells have shown that, though it may be a long way to Tipperary, Malta can be reached with surprising celerity. Ismailia—the Headquarters of the Suez Canal—is now also the home of the British Army Staff: the hotels there are over full, and shopkeepers can remember no parallel to the present prosperity since the year 1869 when the Canal was opened and the town built. To anyone who knows the Sinai desert it seems impossible that an adequate force with guns and provisions can ever be sent across it; and now that our aeroplanes have arrived the last fear of a surprise is at an end. On the West we are all right, for the Senoussi's assurances coincide very much with his interest, which is, not to bring us down upon his head by the side of Italy.[14] Italian journalists, "Interventionists" as they call themselves, are starring about Cairo, proclaiming their disinterested affection for England and complaining of the rigour of the censorship, the latter certainly a genuine, almost a justified emotion: but the example of Roumania during the Balkan War has up till now hypnotized neutral States, who think that they have only got to wait with their jaws well apart for cities, provinces and whole countries to drop in.

As for my private manner of life, you may take it thus: Rise 6.30. Homer and Haydon's Autobiography till 8. Agency 9. Letters and dictate till 10. Interviews till 1.30: work again 3.0 to 8.15, whence from a dull dinner to a tired stale bed betwixt sleep and waking. This seven days a week from August 18. Curiously disagreeable weather, and I with an exceptional cold. Philip Graves down at the lines on the Canal and much impressed by efficacy of arrangements.

[14] Not yet in the War.

14. xii. 14. During the last fortnight the general appearance of Cairo has changed, very much for the better. The streets are full of troops, the largest number of whom are Australians. These are at once feared and admired by the Egyptians, and are certainly well equal to any Territorials or Yeomanry we have yet seen. They are reported to be very lax in their discipline, and I have seen certainly one tram-load returning campwards at about 7.30 a.m. chanting with unimpaired freshness "We won't go home till morning". They are also inclined at the smallest provocation to discharge *feux-de-joie* with their revolvers (or rifles if at hand) in any restaurants or similar establishments which meet with their special approval; and being provided with nothing but English silver are involved in frequent and violent altercations with the hucksters, by whom they are in the end unmercifully fleeced. The Ceylon contingent, composed of more or less wealthy planters, has also made a very good impression, and altogether it is very fortunate that we are able to see them and they us.

21. xii. 14. The Australians and New Zealanders are spending between three and four thousand pounds a day in Cairo, out of their pockets that is, and quite apart from the immense military expenditure involved by the presence of the troops here: they are terrifying but popular. Three days ago a friend of mine observed three of them walking along, when an omnibus, drawn by three mules, of the type known as *Suares* (that being the name of its originator) drove past them. Anxious for a lift they hailed it, but the driver whipped up his beasts and the occupants lifted up their voices and mocked the soldiers; whereupon one of these, running in front held up the three mules with such violence as to drive the whole conveyance back three or four yards, and the other two approaching it on one side, upset the whole thing sideways and decanted the fares on to the hard road, after which they quietly resumed their walk and disappeared over the horizon.

I keep a very clear memory of Sir John Maxwell, the General Officer Commanding the Troops. During the previous decade he had been employed in administrative rather than on active service, but for those initiatory transitional days he proved exactly what was required; knowing and liking, known and liked by, Egyptians for the past thirty years. Sitting tunicless in his office he would see every applicant and read most petitions personally, dealing out a summary justice which expressed itself by speech or by a stub of blue pencil in a brief convincing expletive. It was no good bluffing, for "Conkey" had your life-history—whether you were a Pasha or a dragoman, a Sephardi Banker or a Greek cotton broker, a British official or a Syrian Consul-General for a Baltic State; but this patriarchal militarism provided a satisfaction, a finality, very seldom afforded by the Mixed Court of Appeal.[15]

In default of a journal I must rely once more upon letters to present some of the aspects of Egypt during the War.

---

[15] "The recall of Maxwell evoked one of the most spontaneous outbursts of general regret that I have seen during twelve years' residence here." 21 March 1916.

I ate my Christmas luncheon with Aubrey Herbert, ex-interpreter Irish Guards, wounded at Mons, and now attached to G.O.C.'s staff. He gave a graphic, terrible and at the same time highly humorous account of the retreat, in which, as he is nearly stone blind, it is hard to see how he avoided death. On Tuesday the Sultan invited for his first luncheon party the Aga Khan, and to meet him Prince Fuad, Rushdi, Cheetham and myself, with the usual Grand Chamberlains, Proto-Vestiaries and Magnificos. As the latter consider it improper to converse in their Master's presence, and as his habitual vehicle of conversation is a rather melodramatic aside, the meal was not hilarious. The Aga Khan has considerable charm. There is alas another dinner at the Palace to-morrow night for the Generals here present (14). None of them, save Maxwell, will know any French, and the Sultan has but three words of English: "*Je vous donne un vrai* SHAKEHAND *de* GENTLEMAN, *et non pas de* NATIVE."

The official dinner given us by the Sultan passed off without incident, save that the Band was two minutes slow with each of the Royal Toasts. I begin to regret the installation of the private telephone wire which links my desk to the Palace. I originally agreed to it with the idea of saving myself from perpetual summons; but now W. X. has been appointed H.H.'s Private Sec. "in whose hands the thing became a Trumpet, whence he blows" soul-devastating strains, alas. . . . The Sultanate is popular, but, until the Turks have had it really put across them, popular with acquiescence rather than enthusiasm. Continuous moral and political disinfection and inoculation are required to keep what public opinion exists here in a satisfactory condition. Of course the provinces are healthier than the towns.

This morning I spent in the bazaars with the Maharaja of Bikanir, a very fine gentleman, speaking English with idiomatic inaccuracy; intellectually honest, and agreeable. We visited three of his Camel Corps wounded, in the Citadel hospital. One had had his neck almost severed by two sword cuts, but had, nevertheless (apparently holding his head on to his body with both hands), walked back next day twenty-four miles across the desert into camp: and is now near recovery. News from the Canal continues most encouraging, and Anatolian Turks are beginning to desert us. This has slightly increased the popularity of the Sultan and diminished, if not altogether stopped, the undercurrent of extreme hostility to ourselves, which continues to rumour that the Turks have taken Suez and that the French Military Mission has arrived to correct Maxwell's "gross mistakes".

Ismain continues to nourish a poor opinion of the Ottoman Empire, and laughs cynically when accused by me of blasphemy for deriding the Khalīf, whom he now regards with pity and contempt. He assures me that my landlady (a Circassian) never ceased to weary the Bey with her hopes and fears of speedy invasion. The *harīms*, composed largely of Turkesses, are on the whole against us and imagine Enver as a pan-Islamic Superman in shining armour, ready and waiting to take away their reproach.

Student and journalistic circles are still highly disaffected to us and venomously anti-Sultanic; and true it is that they would not—as the Book says—be convinced though one came from the dead, such is the *mauvaise volonté* with which they pervert their adolescent brains. Does the official account announce the capture of prisoners? Then it is assumed that we lost far more of our own; and besides, where are these prisoners? Do we produce them? Then they are nothing more than Indians disguised as captured Turks; and, if they are ragged and barefoot, then we have torn their clothes and taken away their shoes to bring contempt upon the true believers' army. If we go down for three days to Alexandria, it is in order to be close to the harbour and ready for a flying start out to sea. There is indeed no end to their foolishness. I continue to collect such rumours and to ridicule them once a week in the Arab Press; but the effect is short-lived and, as we said of Messalina's friends: "Soon as one fails, another takes his place." However, in the absence of Khedive, Turk and German, much of the variety and most of the salt has gone never to return (though to be replaced perhaps by reform and administration) in the work of

Yr loving
R.

CHAPTER EIGHT

September 1914

Romance: strangeness with beauty.

WALTER PATER

IF, as now seemed [1] certain, Turkey yielded to the long insistence of Germany and joined the Central Powers, Egypt must look to her Eastern frontier; for though our enemies could hardly hope to succeed in invading Egypt (thereby severing the jugular vein of the British Empire) they might at least contain there many thousands of troops which would otherwise be facing them upon the Western Front. Strategically speaking Egypt was until nearly the end of the War an Island, surrounded by seas of water and far less navigable oceans of waterless sand. British political and military thinkers could, in those days, leave the Sea out of their apprehensions: the Air was still a minor, comparatively untried and undeveloped arm. One form of vessel only could cross the parching waste of the Sinai Peninsula, The Ship of the Desert.[2] We were aware that camels were the indispensable and only effective transport for invaders, and that the Arabs of the Hejaz could marshal them by fleets of myriads, and so were in a position either to speed the Turkish attack, to weaken it by abstention, or seriously to threaten its left flank. I could not forget how the Sharīf Abdallah had unlocked his heart during his visit to Cairo that same spring. I therefore submitted a short note, suggesting that by timely consultation with Mecca we might secure not only the neutrality but the alliance of Arabia in the event of Ottoman aggression. But the Agency was more than occupied with the negotiations for the Throne; strategy

---

[1] The secret treaty of Turco-German Alliance was in fact signed on August 2. Simultaneously the Dardanelles were mined.

[2] I remember Persian Browne's just criticism that this simile was artificial and could never have been applied by the Arab owner (for we compare unknown things to known, not known to unknown); if ever a Bedu saw a ship he might perhaps be tempted to call it the Camel of the Ocean.

was the soldiers' business; I was a civilian, and anyhow Stambul had not yet declared war; so that for one reason and another days passed into weeks without my proposal being even discussed. I had recourse (like so many of my betters after me) to the calm, friendly wisdom of Captain G. H. Clayton, the "Bertie" of Khartum, of Cairo, of Palestine and Mesopotamia. His balanced advice could no more be hustled by a crisis than could his beautiful deliberate handwriting: his character as an officer and a man was, when he left Jerusalem, to be well summed up by Sir Herbert Samuel in the last watchword of Marcus Aurelius, *Aequanimitas*. He was in 1914 Agent in Cairo of the Sudan Government (whose Sirdar controlled the Sinai Peninsula and its Palestine frontier) as well as Director of Intelligence in the Egyptian Army; the time and the place and the keys of the necessary knowledge adding to his natural abilities that element of fortune without which none can achieve. Bertie approved my thesis. Further, he actively condoned my proposed irregularity of urging it upon Lord Kitchener in a private letter; which I accordingly dispatched. After all, he was still my Chief, for he had not yet been succeeded in Egypt, or even resigned his appointment there. I waited. I had not waited a week before the telegram came:

Sept. 24, 1914. To H.M.'s Representative in Cairo. Following from Lord Kitchener. Tell Storrs to send secret and carefully chosen messenger from me to Sharīf Abdallah to ascertain whether "should present armed German influence in Constantinople coerce Sultan against his will, and Sublime Porte, to acts of aggression and war against Great Britain, he and his father and Arabs of the Hejaz would be with us or against us".[8]

This direct mandate from the Secretary of State for War was a double contentment, accepting as it did *in toto* the conception of the Revolt in the Desert, and choosing me to follow it up. In truth the Turco-German danger was much greater and more insidious than ever became generally known in England. It was not confined to the certainty of having to meet military operations directed against the Canal and Egypt. There was the further and less-known project to be countered—a project in the execution of which the Germans and Turks went far—of establishing German submarine bases and wireless stations in Turkish territory flanking the whole length of the Red Sea.

The Germans placed a Major Freiherr Othmar von Stotzingen at the head of a party of wireless experts, with orders to "establish an information post in the neighbourhood of Hodeida, for the purpose of opening communications with the German troops in German East Africa. All Turkish military and civil authorities are enjoined to afford

[8] Draft telegram in Kitchener's own hand. W.O. paper.

Major von Stotzingen, and his staff, every assistance. The wireless apparatus, brought by Major von Stotzingen will be utilized for the purpose of forwarding orders and information from the Turkish G.H.Q." The wireless was also to be used for propaganda in the Sudan, Somaliland and Abyssinia.

But the chief menace lay in the influence which Turkish hostilities with Great Britain might have upon the Moslem population of British India, Egypt and Sudan. Enormous importance was attached by the Germans to this possibility and to the influence they hoped the Turkish Caliph would exert.

I prepared a letter for Abdallah and a suitable gift, and chose for secret messenger X, the father-in-law of my little Persian agent Rūhi, who accompanied him as far as Suez. In due course X returned to Cairo with a long and favourable reply from Abdallah and recounted to me his adventures which I translated for the stenographer present into this rendering:

SHARĪF OF MECCA
Verbal Report of X. 30. x. 14

Messenger X left Suez on 5 October and reached Jeddah in three days. He informed me that the search of the Customs was most perfunctory, and that by the expenditure of one or at most two piastres quite large packages might be introduced. He hired a donkey for two pounds and left Jeddah at six o'clock, reaching Mecca at nine next morning, having journeyed all night (a mule takes two days and a camel three). He found no hotels but had to pay eight pounds for a room, during the period of his pilgrimage, in the Bab al-Salām or "Entrance to the Sacred Enclosure". He performed the necessary rites of the pilgrimage which he considered very ridiculous but, from the physical point of view *"Wahid gymnastic kwayis"* ("a good gymnastic"). Everything exceedingly filthy. He ate half a dollar's worth of meat and drank a cup of tea in a Turkish Café, and on the morrow rose strengthened and restored, and his understanding returned to him. The Grand Sharīf Husain with his entire family was absent at Tayif, but X managed to get into communication with the Sharīf's *Wakil*—Deputy—by name Sharīf Sháraf. This representative exercises all the functions which ought to be performed by the Turkish Wali to whom it appears nobody goes for any kind of case, civil or criminal. X was struck by the fact that every man he met, even if he possessed an insufficiency of clothes, was armed to the teeth and bristling with weapons—cabman, donkey-boy or mule-driver. The *Wakil* held a kind of court, very numerously attended, in which he dealt out a kind of rough and ready justice. In the event of a quarrel in which knives were used, an official measurer of wounds is called in who estimates by the depth and length of the wounds the amount of the fine payable: the total of the smaller wound having been deducted from that of the larger, the inflicter of the larger has to pay the difference. X insinuated himself into the graces of the *Wakil* and was invited to his house that night, joining the other Sharīfs at prayer. After prayer a political discussion took place in which X found to his dismay that the political ideas of the *Wakīl* were those of the Egyptians.[4] He continued to visit the house nightly for three nights. After this, not having yet recovered from the effects of his donkey-ride, he hired a camel-driver for two pounds to take a letter from himself to the Sharīf Abdallah at Tayif. Messenger went at great speed and returned in three days, requesting X to wait two days and informing him that the Sharīf was aware "whence he came". He therefore remained, continuing to visit the local Sharīf every night. On Sharīf Husain's arrival at Mecca he telephoned about X to the *Wakīl,* so that X obtained permission to be among the first to visit him and kiss the hem of his garment. Some of the devotees had gone out as much as half a day's journey to meet him. The *Wakīl* retired to his house and the Sharīf to his Palace, which is one of considerable size and four stories high, "in form as a mountain". Finally the Sharīf Abdallah took X into a small room and asked him for the letter, which he gave. Sharīf Abdallah then said that in his opinion Mr Storrs was a Moslem, to which X tactfully agreed. He was convinced of that by reason of Mr S.'s numerous quotations from the Koran, and alluded to him as his brother. He was then taken into a very large and magnificent room in which he ate with the Sharīf and his four sons. This from the morning until two in the afternoon. Shortly after this the Sharīf Abdallah bade him take his ease, refresh himself, and with many compliments said he would give him a letter to take to Mr S. In a few minutes he found himself alone; upon which a servant came and took him to a much finer room on the very top of the house in which he found seated by himself the Grand Sharīf of Mecca. The Sharīf then said to him: "My son, though I am as one uninvited in this matter I will yet speak." (Message had been sent through his son Abdallah). He spoke walking up and down the room and insisted that his auditor should remain seated. He said: "The Ottoman Empire has rights over us and we have rights upon her. She has made war upon our rights, and I am not responsible before God if she has made war upon our rights; nor am I responsible before God if we have therefore made war upon hers." He gesticulated with his arms as he spoke, and threw back the long sleeve of his garments, saying: "my heart is open to S. even as this", and, with a gesture, "Stretch forth to us a helping hand and we shall never at all help these oppressors. On the contrary we shall help those who do good. This is the Commandment of God upon us: Do good to Islam and Moslems—Nor do we fear nor respect any save God. Give him my greeting, fitting to him and to his country." X answered: "To hear is to obey, O my Lord." The *Wakīl* of the Sharīf when he saw the magnificent treatment accorded to X apologized to him subsequently for his pro-German sentiments, although he can have had no possible idea of the reason of his visit. On X's return the sons of the Sharīf journeyed with him and 150 pilgrims with arms and music, ostensibly to escort them into Jeddah but really to repair the road, "a thing of which man had not dreamed". Half-way between Mecca and Jeddah at a place called Bahra they slept, and there the Sharīf Abdallah said: "I have given the instructions to my brother Faisal." Faisal gave the agent, Sulaiman Qābel,[5] at Jeddah the letter (unaddressed) inside another envelope which was addressed

---

[4] To be described in Chapter IX.
[5] Sharifial agent there. When I arrived he was Mayor of Jeddah.

to the Sharīf's agent in Cairo. The letter was finally handed to X by the agent on board a Japanese boat which was delayed two days in the harbour at Jeddah because the Municipality commandeered most of the ship's coal to work the condenser which provides the town with water. X's opinion is that the leaders of the Arabs in addition to their natural predilection for England are of opinion that it is not possible that Germany can ever conquer her. To them Egypt is an ideal Government; just as the country is an earthly paradise. Many Turkish officers but only about 300 troops in Mecca. Nobody there of opinion that the Turks would declare war upon England or the Allies. But they have been informed that shots had been exchanged between the English and Egyptian troops in Egypt. A certain *Agence* published many false reports which X was able to belie and ridicule. He observed that the Arabs of Mecca neglect their womenfolk and spend their entire days and nights in cafés.[6]

On 31 October Lord Kitchener cabled his

Salāams to Sharīf Abdallah. Germany has now bought the Turkish Government with gold, notwithstanding that England, France and Russia guaranteed integrity of Ottoman Empire if Turkey remained neutral in the War. Turkish Government have against will of Sultan committed acts of aggression by invading the frontiers of Egypt with bands of Turkish soldiers. If Arab nation assist England in this war England will guarantee that no intervention takes place in Arabia and will give Arabs every assistance against external foreign aggression.

On 10 December X returned from his second journey to Mecca. The Sharīf was friendly but unable to break with the Turks immediately though awaiting a reasonable pretext to do so.

I do not propose to follow in detail the characteristically protracted negotiations which ensued. In April 1915 the Governor-General of the Sudan was authorized to let it be known that H.M.G. would make it an essential condition in the peace terms that the Arabian Peninsula and its Muhammadan Holy Places should remain in the hands of an independent sovereign state. It was impossible to define at the moment how much territory should be included in this state. The first definite proposals from the Sharīf reached Sir Henry MacMahon in July 1915 (with a personal letter from Abdallah to myself, unsigned and undated), when he solicited the support of His Majesty's Government for the cause of Arab independence, and proposed certain boundaries for the independent Arab area. As I struggled through his difficult writing and even more difficult Arabic, I found myself murmuring

---

[6] This account, possibly because it was one of the first he read, pleased Lawrence, for he says in a letter written the year before his death: "I've often said to you that the best bit of your writing I ever read was your dictated account of the report of an agent's interview, pre-revolt, with the Sharīf of Mecca on his palace roof at night." 13. ix. 34. As it was a mere translation any merit was X's.

> In matters of commerce the fault of the Dutch
> Is in giving too little and asking too much,

for he demanded, with the exception of Aden, the whole of Arabic-speaking South-West Asia. The High Commissioner rightly refused to commit the Government to precise areas, particularly in Western Syria and Lower Mesopotamia, and as time went on (for our communications were slow and risky) boundary questions became less, and the Hejaz revolt more, immediate.

It was at the time and still is my opinion that the Sharīf opened his mouth and the British Government their purse a good deal too wide.[7] It seemed to me that having been little more than a sort of Erastian Administrator for the Turks, the Sharīf and his people would be well treated and amply rewarded if they were gratuitously enabled to defeat and evict their traditional enemy, and were guaranteed immunity from external aggression in their permanent possession of the two Holy Cities, together with the independent sovereignty of their country of origin, the Hejaz. If to this a sufficient majority of Moslems chose to add the Khilāfat, that was their business, and not ours; though, as uniting the strongest religious with the weakest material power, it would be greatly to our interest. But Husain, who had indeed through Faisal been in touch with the Syrian revolutionaries, claimed to wield a general mandate as King of the Arabs for a Spiritual Pan-Araby, to which he knew better than we that he could lay no kind of genuine claim. Of the great Arab peoples of North Africa some must repudiate his Sunni[8] claims to the Caliphate: others, like Egypt and the Sudan, vastly preferred their own superior civilization. The Christians of the Lebanon could never acknowledge him, Mesopotamia was mainly Shia, regarding his Islam about as benevolently as Alva did the Protestantism of the Low Countries; to the South the Imam Yahya[9] recognized him as nothing at all, whilst with Ibn

---

[7] By October 1916 Lawrence had written: "The coast towns are glutted with Gold and the Rupee is only 10-12 to the sovereign." Yet the gold dispatched was less than 10 per cent. of the total cost to the British taxpayer of the Revolt in the Desert, which amounted to £11,000,000. In addition to the initial sums I took, Husain received from 8 August 1916, £125,000 a month: in all less than one million sterling. The remaining ten millions represent military operations and supplies from Great Britain.

[8] Sunni: "One of the Path"; a traditionist recognizing the succession of Caliphs, or successors to the Prophet Muhammad down to the twentieth century. Shia: "Followers of Ali", first cousin of Muhammad and husband of his daughter Fātimah, holding him the first legitimate Caliph, and therefore rejecting as usurpers, Abu Bakr, 'Umar and 'Uthmān, the first three Sunni Caliphs. Sunni and Shia are the two main divisions of Islam, the first representing the great majority, spread over India, Egypt, Syria and the Hejaz, and the second, the minority, to be found chiefly in Persia, Iraq and Morocco. Theologically Shia is analogous to Roman Catholicism, Sunni to Protestantism, and its extreme form, Wahhābism, practised by the Arabs of Saudi-Arabia, to extreme Puritanism.

[9] Ruler of the Yaman.

Sa'ud on his immediate East (feeling for him as an Ebenezer Chapel might for Rome) he had long been on the terms which were to lead to his final ruin and exile. There was in a word not even as much prospect of Arab Union then as there is now. When in addition we reflected that 90 per cent. of the Moslem World must call Husain a renegade and traitor to the Vicar of God we could not conceal from ourselves (and with difficulty from him) that his pretensions bordered upon the tragi-comic. Nevertheless, this partial sacrifice of his name before Islam, vital to our cause though also greatly to his interest, imposed upon us the real obligation of raising and maintaining his prestige to the limit of the possible, so that for this and other reasons we were in the end committed far more deeply in bullion, in munitions of war and in promises very hard to fulfil, than most of us had dreamed of in September 1914.

Much play has been made by Arab and other critics with ambiguities, mutually incompatible undertakings, and "betrayals"; without entire justification but not without cause. Our Arabic correspondence with Mecca was prepared by Ruhi, a fair though not a profound Arabist (and a better agent than scholar); and checked, often under high pressure, by myself. I had no Deputy, Staff or office, so that during my absence on mission the work was carried on (better perhaps) by others, but the continuity was lost.[10] Husain's letters on the other hand were written in an obscure and tortuous prose in which the purity of the Hejaz Arabic was overlaid and tainted with Turkish idioms and syntax. Until Mark Sykes appeared in Cairo in 1916 we had but the slightest and vaguest information about the Sykes-Picot negotiations for the tripartite division of non-Turkish Turkey between France, Russia and England, later nullified (and divulged) by the fall of Russia; and there was far too little realization of Indian operations in Iraq and of Indian encouragement of Ibn Sa'ud. So far as we were concerned it seemed to be nobody's business to harmonize the various views and policies of the Foreign Office, the India Office, the Admiralty, the War Office, the Government of India and the Residency in Egypt. The Revolt, when it began, entailed the co-operation of at least three Military Commanders: the G.O.C.'s of Egypt, Iraq and Aden. After the withdrawal from Gallipoli the Mediterranean Expeditionary Force, merged with the Egyptian, became the Egyptian Expeditionary Force under which, gathering up these threads with those of the

---

[10] I never saw the correspondence again after leaving for Baghdad in April 1917. It was needed in my absence and I cabled to Cairo: "All Sharīf originals ever had are in my files consult index if you pick lock please seal up afterwards."

Naval G.O.C. and the Sudan Government, was constituted the Arab Bureau, directed by D. G. Hogarth, of which T. E. Lawrence was a member.[11]

It will be seen that the complications were very great; and the difficulty of reconciling some of these conflicting claims and interests was at the Peace Conference to become extreme.[12]

The exchange of argument and counter argument, of reference to England (as probably reference from Mecca to Constantinople), of instructions and re-draftings, seemed interminable, but anyhow ensured that Arabs and Arab transport, if not yet on our side, were meanwhile not at the disposal of the Turkish Army. At last Husain, alarmed by Turkish activities and the Stotzingen Mission, took the plunge. On 23 May 1916 a message was telegraphed to Sir Henry MacMahon from Port Sudan: "Sharīf's son Abdallah urgently requires Storrs to come to Arabian coast to meet him. Movement will begin as soon as Faisal arrives at Mecca."

The diary of that voyage has gone; but I have discovered in the Foreign Office the Report I extracted for the High Commissioner, some of which, giving the first published account of the inception of an enterprise important in itself besides being immortalized by the genius of Lawrence, I venture to reproduce.

In accordance with His Excellency the High Commissioner's instructions, I left Cairo at 6.15 p.m. on the 28 May, accompanied by Lieut.-Commander D. G. Hogarth, R.N.V.R. and Captain K. Cornwallis, and taking with me £10,000 in gold in the charge, as far as Suez, of an escort of two N.C.O.'s. The Syrian interpreter who serves *Dufferin* [18] failing to appear, we did not start from Suez until 10.15 next morning.

On the 30th we were not yet in wireless touch with *Fox* or Port Sudan, but received from *Hardinge* enquiries as to our destination. Later we heard from that ship that the Grand Sharīf had given orders that all Turkish troops were to leave Mecca.

[11] "Do you know
The Arab Bureau?"
Asked Hogarth; and answered:
"Clayton stability,
Symes versatility,
Cornwallis is practical,
Dawnay syntactical,
Mackintosh havers,
And Fielding palavers,
Macindoe easy,
And Wordie not breezy:
Lawrence licentiate to dream and to dare
And Yours Very Faithfully, *bon à tout faire.*"

[12] *Vide* chap. xv, pp. 375 ff.
[18] Of H.M. Indian Navy.

On the 31st we stood down West and passed the fine African range up to the Sangarib Light, 15 miles north of Port Sudan, where we met H.M.S. *Fox* [14] [of the Red Sea Patrol] at 12.30. My agent Rūhi came on board at once and explained, more to our dismay than to our surprise, that we had to go north 230 miles to Ras Makhlūk (or Ras Arab), there to meet with Oraifan,[15] who would then hasten into Mecca, returning with Abdallah in four or five days to some other point on the coast. Oraifan offered for £1 to bring us the heads of the seven Germans murdered last week. I promised him instead £5 if he would procure for us all the papers found on their persons.[16]

We left Port Sudan that evening, and on 1 June at midday, having steered through the formidable reef, cast anchor at Qaddīma, where were one or two dhows, with canoes that paddled up to exchange fish for loaves and rice. Oraifan did not arrive until about 3.30 with practically no news, save that the Turks from Mecca in Jeddah numbered not 500 but 200. His figures are, however, so notoriously hopeless that we received his estimate of 10,000 Turks from Iraq at Medina with little more emotion than that of the 60,000 armed friendlies whom he guaranteed from his own neighbourhood. Oraifan's first rendezvous for me with Abdallah at Sarom, close to Samima by Jeddah, was for the following Thursday; an intolerable delay.

I sent a pencil note to Abdallah (reading out a revised time-table to Oraifan to keep him up to time), hinting but not actually naming the "interesting" things that awaited him, and forwarding last month's *Mokattams* [17] besides a few copies of the German-anti-Islamic circular. I also sent a wireless to the High Commissioner posting him to date. About 9 on the 2nd I received a wireless: "Foreign Office has approved payment of £10,000 to Abdallah and £50,000 to Sharīf of Mecca. But this latter payment only in return for definite action and if a reliable rising takes place."

We left Qaddīma about 8 and steamed north past Rābugh where were three dhows neither beached, as according to blockade instructions [18] they should be, nor dismasted.

On the 3rd we made Hassani Island, which lies against the reef of Um Laj town and harbour, about 11 a.m. and, crossing the bar, took a good look at the town. There is a garrison of 20 Turks who run back into the little hills whenever a cruiser comes along. This since *Fox* bombarded the place at half-mile range, destroying the fort but leaving the Mosque intact. Hassani Island is said to be the summer resort of Um Laj, but the Season this year must have been a disappointment, and the bookings so poor that the place contained not one single inhabitant.

Back at 7 to find an Arab, by name Dakhilallah Hamdān, on board, who had seen a number of German men and women going to Yanbo in a *Sambuk*.[19] I proposed to the Captain to take the man and his canoe to Sharm Yanbo, dropping him there at night for news, and picking him up on our way north from Sarom.

[14] A 23-year-old cruiser; the oldest of her class in the British Navy, but young enough to account for anything on the shores or the waters of the Red Sea.
[15] The Sharīf's agent.
[16] He never did.
[17] Then the leading daily of the Arab-speaking world.
[18] The British Red Sea Fleet was blockading all enemy coasts.
[19] Light Arab sailing vessel.

On the 4th at about 10 a.m. I received the following message from the High Commissioner: "India asks whether situation necessitates stoppage of the Haj [20] from India. India is unwilling to offend Moslem feeling by notification of stoppage. Please discuss this with Abdallah."

At Sharm Yanbo, 1.30 p.m. we put off the Arab, Hamdān, in his leaky canoe and steamed slowly past Yanbo town quite close; arid but not badly built and shut in from the north by the splendid mass of Mount Radwan.

We were off Jeddah the next day, the 5th, about 2 p.m. A fine town with four and even five-storeyed houses and one minaret nearly as much out of the perpendicular as the leaning tower of Pisa. Oraifan arrived from *Fox* with a letter from Grand Sharif signed in full "Husain, Amir of Noble Mecca" (but, save for the signature, in the handwriting of Abdallah) addressed to myself. "Honourable and respected. I deeply regret my inability to send Abdallah for an urgent reason which bearer will explain: but his brother will represent him with one of his cousins, Sharif Shākir, Amir of the Ataibah, of the same degree as himself"; with it, an unsigned slip: "Please order by wireless immediately 500 rifles of same pattern as those already sent us. Details of consignment from our sons Zaid and Shākir and also 4 machine guns, both with ammunition"; also, a letter signed Abdallah ibn Husain: "To the most honoured and respected Mr Storrs. I deeply regret I am unable to meet you personally, but an urgent need has called me and taken me, so my brother will come to you with all news. My own request of you is to start operations in Syria to the best of your ability. God is our guide. Later will be our real meeting."

Oraifan had left Rueis on Saturday the 3rd, at sunset, reached Mecca by camel at sunrise on Sunday morning, and met the Grand Sharif Husain at noon. The Grand Sharif had told him that it was not possible to send Abdallah, who was just leaving for Tayif to besiege the Wali, now there; it having been decided that the rising was to take place on Saturday 10 June instead of Friday the 16th as originally intended. Abdallah was present; and at the conclusion of the interview retired with his father, and returning gave Oraifan the above letters with instructions to deliver them at once, as Zaid under the pretext of escorting Abdallah was already leaving the City. The meeting place arranged was Samima (6 miles S.W. of Jeddah) for Tuesday the 6th at dawn. Oraifan had left Mecca by night, reaching Rueis early in the morning, Monday the 5th. He said the movement would be initiated simultaneously at Medina by Faisal and Ali; at Mecca by the Grand Sharif: at Tayif by Abdallah, and at Jedda by Sharif Moshin, Amir of the Harb tribe. Telegraph communications between Jeddah and Mecca in hands of the Sharif: from Medina cut. The railway was also cut. The murdered Germans above mentioned were from Java. Boyle,[21] Senior Naval Officer of the Red Sea, came aboard from *Fox* chiefly anxious to know whether he should, if responsibly requested, make a demonstration at Jeddah on Saturday. I sent wireless to the High Commissioner, posting him to date on this and other matters.

On the evening of the 5th we lay outside Samima and, leaving *Dufferin* at 5.30 next morning at about 2 miles distance from shore, proceeded in the gig with cutter, in tow by steam-launch to the outer reef, into which our cutter

---

[20] Pilgrimage to Mecca.
[21] Now Admiral the Earl of Cork and Orrery.

soon crashed fairly hard, breaking her rudder. With me were Hogarth, Cornwallis, Oraifan, Agent Rūhi, £10,000 and two sacks of *al-Haqīqa* [22] besides light refreshments for the party we expected ashore. Soon a canoe shot towards us directed by Shaikh Ali, who takes consignment of our munitions embarked from Port Sudan. He guided us through the reef to a dhow half-full of sacks of dura—maize—where, there being no sign of Zaid upon the beach, we tied up and sat for over an hour whilst the mariners hauled across a sail as an awning and spread their shawls over the sacks, making us fairly comfortable.

At length a bunch of ten camels appeared on the horizon and descended to the shore where Oraifan, who had meanwhile prepared a tent of honour, awaited them. He soon came off in his canoe, announcing that Zaid wished me to land and see him alone.[23] We had been prepared for this, but I had decided either that Zaid should send for Hogarth and Cornwallis, or better (as they preferred), to bring him and Shākir on board *Dufferin*. I set off, taking Rūhi in the cutter to within about 80 yards of the shore, where I stepped into Oraifan's canoe, the bottom of which was so full of water that I elected for obvious reasons to stand up in it. The last ten yards I was carried to the beach by two slaves, who contrived in that short distance to soak me well above the knee. Without looking up I saw Zaid and Shākir slowly advancing upon me. I continued to arrange my clothes so as to bring the two down in front of their guard to welcome on their threshold one who was, after all, representing the High Commissioner. This they did, and shook me warmly by the hand welcoming me in the name of the Grand Sharīf and Abdallah. I walked with them to the tent, giving them greetings, messages and encouragements from His Excellency. On our right as we entered the tent were drawn up the guard, simply but exceedingly well dressed in Bedwai costume and armed with swords and rifles. There were in the tent two small divans, each covered with two new and poor Shirwan rugs, and beneath our feet two Kīllim carpets. Zaid sat me by himself and Shākir opposite. I told Rūhi in English to remain standing until Zaid bade him to be seated, which in about two minutes he did, next to Shākir. The guard dispersed themselves about us on the Kīllims until Zaid, rather unceremoniously, ordered them to leave the tent, upon which they retired outside to the camel furniture, *makhlūfas*,[24] *khurgs*,[25] etc., all of which were exceedingly good and in good condition.

Zaid, the youngest son of the Sharīf by his second wife, a Circassian of good family, is and looks about 20 years of age. I tested him later in Turkish and found he spoke it well and fluently. He is about five feet five in height, fair in complexion, with fine eyes and the round face and Greek profile characteristic of Circassians. He is evidently attempting to encourage the growth of a some-

[22] *The Truth,* our Arab propaganda newspaper.
[23] "From O.'s attitude and report, it was clear that some difficulty would be made about anyone, besides Storrs, meeting Zaid. Danger ashore was pleaded, and we were told Zaid himself was to come down very secretly "like a robber"; but a desire not to be responsible for more Christians landing in Hejaz than could be helped, and also fear that Zaid would be confronted in council with disproportionate numbers doubtless weighed with the Sharīf." (Hogarth's account.)
[24] Camel saddles.
[25] Camel bags.

what backward beard. Generally an indoor type. At first he seemed a little shy, and perhaps a trifle suspicious, for after delivering more than one cordial message from Abdallah, he asked why, when Abdallah had called for one person, three had been sent. However, he soon put aside his timidity, asking and answering questions with equal frankness and looking me in the face. Shākir [26] is two inches taller and perhaps ten years older. He would also be good-looking if his face were not badly pitted by small-pox. His hair is plaited in seven or eight long thin tails. I remembered seeing him with Abdallah at Abdīn Palace in the Spring of 1914, and think he was pleased at not being forgotten. Both were well, freshly and effectively dressed in *quftans* of rich Egyptian silk; Zaid in a black cloak and embroidered yellow *kuffiya*,[27] Shākir in a brown camel-hair cloak and small check *kuffiya*: both wearing sandals of Mecca and large brilliant gold *aqāls*,[28] and generally so faultless that I am convinced they had halted and changed just before arriving.

As the cutter containing Hogarth and Cornwallis was awaiting outside in the sun, by now (8 a.m.) quite strong, I asked Zaid if I might have the honour of presenting my friends, and on his objecting to their landing proposed rather firmly that he and Shākir should accept for an hour or so the hospitality of the British Navy. He glanced once or twice at Shākir and hesitated, so I assumed his consent, thanked him and changed the subject. I had been obliged to consult my (gold) bracelet watch to see how we stood for time and on turning again to face him, found him looking at it with such interest and admiration that, as I had brought him no gift (the cash being destined for his brother), and with the object of maintaining his good humour, I drew it off, explained to him how to wind it; set it (by a swift and probably inaccurate calculation) to Arab time, and fastened it with, I trust, a fairly good grace on his wrist. I resolved to take them aboard as soon as the coffee, which I clearly heard being prepared behind the tent, had been drunk.

Zaid then confirmed Oraifan's report of the rising being fixed for Saturday next. He gave me a message to myself from Abdallah (which Oraifan had also transmitted on the dhow) that I should remain on *Fox* off Jeddah to observe results. I said I must get back to Cairo, but that if subsequently I could be of any service and was not at the moment required in Egypt, it was possible the High Commissioner might send me; but that I must have a definite time and place on the next occasion as I could not go steaming up and down the Red Sea again. He agreed, and said he hoped anyhow I would come, as Abdallah had many things to say that he, Zaid, was not in a position to speak about and that it was only the advance in the date of the rising that had kept him away. He then handed me a short note of greeting, regret and introduction from Abdallah with a long and execrably written letter from his father describing their plans for Medina. I asked him to tell me exactly what they proposed doing at the various centres of revolt. He said: "We will summon the Turks to surrender and shoot them if they refuse. If they surrender we will imprison them until the end of the war. We intend to destroy the Hejaz railways as far north as Medáin Sálih, which will be our advance

[26] See his portrait, p. 208, in *Seven Pillars*.
[27] Shawl-turbans.
[28] Cords encircling the head shawl.

post." Glancing hurriedly down the list of *talabs* (or requests) in the first of the documents handed to me, I observed the mention of £50,000 with an additional £20,000 making a total of £70,000, and explained to Zaid our position in this matter, saying that the first sum would be forthcoming so soon as we had certain news that the rising had begun and was in progress. He said: "I am then happy to be able to announce to you that it began yesterday at Medina." I asked what news he had of results and he explained that by "begun" he had meant "was timed to begin" or "doubtless began", etc., but that owing to the distance it was impossible to receive details so soon. I then asked whether, if he had a partner whom he was (at that partner's request) assisting financially in a common cause, he would not after a time need a little encouragement in the nature of some practical result of his assistance, before he continued it indefinitely. He agreed that he himself, and still more his father, most certainly would require some such encouragement. I went on further to add that, the movement once demonstrably on foot, they would find His Majesty's Government very far from niggardly in its dealings with its Allies. Was he not aware that we were advancing already some millions per diem to those who had declared and proved themselves our friends? Zaid and Shākir appeared to find this reasonable and said the proofs were now very near at hand. Zaid next took the question of our effecting a diversion in Syria. Assuming the revolt went off as we hoped, was it not certain that the Turks, who had 80,000 men with guns in Syria, would descend upon them and wreak a terrible vengeance? His father felt very strongly on this point. I explained to him the existence and working of the Allies' Supreme War Council which was bound to regard simultaneously all theatres of War, and which would, I feared, find it exceedingly difficult to derange their elaborately matured plans. I contested his numbers in Syria and pointed out that with Iraq, Caucasus and Sinai vigorously beset, it was very far from certain that the Turks would have the will, or the power, to begin upon a fourth venture. If they did, and removed any troops from the Sinai, there was little doubt that this would enable us to fall upon their rear. Zaid said, if we could promise that, it would set their minds at rest. I replied that I was not a military man, nor empowered to promise anything at all save our definite help with money, munitions and supplies once the revolt was started: but I thought the above theory a strong probability. With regard to the extra munitions, the machine and mountain guns, I would at once submit his requests by wireless and they would doubtless receive our careful consideration. But the time he gave us was very short and he must not think that these things were to be plucked like dates from palm trees.

To the question as to the Indian pilgrimage [29] he replied, that as the block-

[29] Difficult to combine with the Red Sea Blockade. I find a reinforcing argument sent home with this object: "It is to our interest and ultimate economy to allow his first independent season to open as brilliantly as possible; any row, scandal, or epidemic, would react swiftly and discreditably upon the management and discourage or even annihilate subsequent bookings. From this point of view the Turkish administration, though bad, was better than no administration at all; hence it is my present preoccupation to create temporary cable, postal, quarantine, and other services sufficient to tide us over this next three months. The military situation (if only we can effectively pull up and twist some 50 kilometres, in two places, of the Hejaz Railway), though by no means free from anxiety, is not in my opinion dangerous; a diversion from the North, for the present impossible, would render us and the Arabs absolutely secure." It was not long before Some One was dealing with the Hejaz Railway.

ade would naturally be raised upon the successful issue of the rising, pilgrims should certainly be allowed to come. In taking note of this I informed him that his father would shortly receive a letter from His Highness the Sultan, asking for instructions as to the disposal of the Mahmal.[30] Zaid then requested that Farūki, a Syrian officer then in the employment of the Sudan Government, should be sent with whatever other Syrian officers might be chosen by the High Commissioner so as to be off Jeddah on Saturday, 10 June. Amongst other things he enquired with deep interest whether Verdun was still resisting. Very much to my relief, he made no reference to the Syrian question nor to the Caliphate, though Ali alludes most emphatically to the first in his letter to the Grand Sharīf. Zaid was in process of informing me that the new flag of Arab Independence would be crimson and without device when coffee was served in large cups (though in quantities hardly visible to the naked eye) by a slave admirably dressed in white and silver. As soon as decently possible after this, I rose, took his arm and told him it was time to be getting to the ship where he would honour us by breakfasting with us and receiving from me that which the High Commissioner had sent for Abdallah. Leaving our own refreshments for the guard, we were carried with much splashing to the boat where I presented Hogarth and Cornwallis (whom I had previously described as high officials with a profound knowledge of the Arabian peninsula). We reached *Dufferin* about 9.15 and I explained and resumed to Hogarth and Cornwallis the points already discussed.

Cornwallis gave Zaid the correct number (as known to us) of troops in Syria as 30,000, but Zaid utterly refused to accept this figure. We then left them, after many friendly protests and adjurations to sit down with them, to breakfast with Oraifan and Rūhi and descending to the Saloon began drafting a telegram. I had then shown and explained the wireless, which appeared to fascinate them, the guns, the Captain's bathroom and other wonders of the deep. Chairs and a carpet had meanwhile been prepared on the afterbridge where we sat going over previous points and eliciting by questions from Hogarth and Cornwallis further information, until Boyle arrived from *Fox*. I asked him if he could provide any Maxims and how soon he could undertake to bring the Syrian officers off Jeddah. He promised one Maxim and the officers to be on the spot next Tuesday, 13 June. On Boyle offering co-operation, Zaid rather doubtfully accepted it, provided it should have been previously requested in writing. We explained to him at some length the impossibility of providing trained gunners at a moment's notice, as also the obvious difficulty of producing off ships guns suitable for field work. Privately we thought it just conceivable that Egypt, or (if things at Darfur were a little quieter) the Sudan, might provide some of the other weapons and possibly some gunners.

---

[30] Shagaret al-Durr (chaplet of pearls) a beautiful Turkish slave who became the favourite wife of the Sultan Nagm al-Din (Star of the Faith) caused herself to be acknowledged Queen of Egypt and performed the pilgrimage in a magnificent litter borne by a camel. For successive years her empty litter was sent yearly to Mecca as an emblem of state. After her death, a similar litter was sent each year with the caravan of pilgrims from Cairo and Damascus, and was called Mahmal after the girths—*namal* to carry—supporting the litter. It is a square skeleton frame of wood with a pyramidal top, and has a covering of black brocade richly worked with inscriptions and ornamental embroidery in gold, in some parts upon a ground of green or red silk. A special department of the Egyptian Government exists for the manufacture and despatch of the Mahmal.

At the urgent instance of the Ship's Doctor we stood and sat for a photographic group of which I promised to send Zaid and Shākir copies; after which they wrote a couple of letters (and I acknowledged those of the Grand Sharīf and Abdallah), filled casks for their water-skins, and left about 12.30 by the steam-launch, Cornwallis and I escorting them as far as the dhow. Here they took leave of us with very cordial farewells, carrying with them, rather to our alarm, the £10,000 and the two bundles of *al-Haqīqa;* [31] I sending after them from the ship 1000 cigarettes for Faisal and Ali, the only smokers in the family, at Medina.

Zaid [32] is obviously the Benjamin of the family; soft in his ways and vague in his ideas. He appears, however, so far as one can judge, frank and truthful and quite capable of understanding and conveying to or from his father any instructions or explanations with which he may be entrusted. Shākir seemed listless and ill-informed and apparently taking in more than he gave out. Although their confidence in immediate and universal success is doubtless much exaggerated and hard to justify by facts, the conception, plan and intended execution of the rising have every appearance of genuineness. After they had left us, Oraifan quoted to me a remark of Shākir: "Do the English not see that if the Sharīf is not able to redeem his money promises to the Arabs, he will be a liar and lose his honour before them? Then where will be success?"

We at once dispatched through Port Sudan a telegraphic account of the above which owing to bad atmospherics did not arrive until late the next day (7 June).

Two other memories emerge from that journey. A graceful gazelle strolled about the deck of *Dufferin,* pronging playfully at strangers and eating cigarettes off the mess table. On 4 June I received through Captain Warren a wireless congratulation upon (and first intimation that I had been awarded) my C.M.G. Hogarth who preferred flat tones thought I had better make certain the congratulations were not addressed to, rather than through, Warren; sobering me for a full half-hour. Later I wrote home:

What gratifies and thrills one is that, after the last twenty months incessant pressing of the authorities, and their turning the smooth cheek to the ill-informed criticism of Simla (upon whose heart I feel sure is graved the mystic and blessed expression Moslem Susceptibilities), with prickings on and heartenings up of friends in Mecca, the Arabs have, as Reuter will announce to-day, definitely thrown off the stupid oppressions and discomforts they have endured all these years, and incidentally struck what should be a fatal blow at the religious prestige of the Turk: and as in this part of the world the division of spiritual and temporal power, the conception of Church and State, throne and altar are to the pious inconceivable (for the strong Sultan puts his throne upon the altar before sitting on it), the loss of the two Holy Places

---

[31] Our Arabic Allied-propaganda newspaper.

[32] The youthful softness and vagueness were physical but not moral or spiritual, and my admiration for Prince Zaid's character has grown every year that I have known him.

they have so long exploited should prove in the end mortal to the Jews [33] now reigning on the Bosphorus.

We returned to Egypt in jubilation, reaching Suez in time for the early morning train. I bought *La Bourse Egyptienne* the pro-British, and *Le Journal du Caire* the anti-British, (but then Ally) organ, glanced at the headlines: *"Les alliés honorent Lord Kitchener,"* and assuming these to represent the Speeches of one more City Banquet, fell asleep. When I awoke in Cairo station I found awaiting me a score of Egyptian friends, grief-stricken—some with tears in their eyes. They had come they said "to present their duty of condolence". I asked upon what misfortune. All protested it was impossible that I of all men should not know—"We are his friends as well as yours; hide not your sorrow, for the news has been printed by Reuter." Then and thus I learnt that the strong hand which had set our endeavours in the path of the possible, the great heart to which I owed so much, the loyalty which in no crisis could fail, were gone forever; and I felt, as I suppose millions of us were then feeling, that now at least we had met disaster. *"Al-Lurd, al-Lurd māt"*—"The Lord is dead", a shaikh kept saying, *"Allah yirhámu!"*—"May God be merciful to him." Ten days later the slow war-mail brought me a letter in the well-known handwriting—his congratulations. Years later I was told by Sir George Arthur that in the last drive to King's Cross Kitchener had reminded him "not to forget about Storrs's C.M.G." I wrote to Henry Cust:

The loss of my dear old chief, to whom you (more than most) know how much I owe, has greatly shaken me. Three years without one disagreeable word or even look from a man with so many preoccupations, who came moreover with a strong prejudice in my disfavour, remain for me an honour and a memory I shall never lose. The effect of the news here was one of simple consternation, and I was touched and sadly pleased to receive as many telegrams of personal condolence as if I had been a near relation; not the least moving tribute was the instant closing (at their own suggestion) for the whole day of the bazaars he had so often and so pleasantly scoured.

II

The result of the final agreement was immediate. Mecca surrendered on 13 June. On the 16th the Turkish garrison of Jeddah, attacked by land and bombarded by H.M.S. *Fox* at sea, surrendered. Tayif fell later, but Medina under the gallant Fakhri Pasha held out to the end of the year, its troops contained by the Arabs without loss of life on either side. These

[33] The Committee of Union and Progress was largely under Dönmé, Crypto-Jew, influence.

successes caused consternation among the Turks and Germans. The *Köl-nische Zeitung* of 23 June stated: "The whole report must be taken as an attempt to damage the spiritual prestige of the Sultan ... as spiritual head of the Shiah. Success is likely to be small." Berlin Official Wireless announced on 27 June: "We are in a position to deny absolutely that there has been any rebellion in the Hejaz at all"; and on 2 July: "A rapid end has been made of local disturbances in the Turkish Province of the Hejaz. ...Order in the Province has been restored. The small number of participants in the rebellion proves how insignificant the affair (so puffed in the English and French Press) has really been."

The news of the Hejaz revolt at first produced among Egyptian intellectuals a feeling of stupefaction mingled with uneasiness. They proclaimed that the news was false and that the English were attempting to bluff the populace in order to discredit the Turks. The local Islamic press warned its readers to await official confirmation of Reuter's telegrams. A popular theory was that the Sharīf was playing with the English "as the Senussi did last year", and that he had already extracted from them some three million pounds. Others, while accepting the rising as a fact, attempted to minimize its importance by describing it as a mere phase in the chronic state of revolution in the Arabian Peninsula: the Arabs were too far divided to be able to oppose a united resistance to the Turkish armies, and even if they achieved a momentary success, their fate would be decided on the battlefields of Europe, as the Turks would easily recover all they had lost after Germany had won the War.

A certain number of the servant, artisan and fellah class including a sprinkling of the al-Azhar University, expressed pleasure that their Arab brethren should once more enjoy an unrestricted food supply. The Anglophobes, including nationalists, Khedivists, Turcophils, and Germanophils, threw discredit upon the Sharīf by representing him as a rebel against the Khalīfa and the servile instrument of the English.

After the publication, some days later, of detailed descriptions of the operations and their results the number of doubters gradually dwindled to nothing. A rumour was, however, circulated, and believed by many, that the revolt was a fiction contrived in agreement with Turkey for the purpose of reopening communications by sea between Hejaz and Turkey in General. The great mass of the populace waited.

If the Sharīf is successful he can count upon a large number of friends in Egypt; if not, he will be condemned for his temerity and disobedience to the Khalīfa, and no contumely will be too strong for him and his supporters.

The Porte proceeded on 16 July to appoint the Sharīf Ali Haidar as

Sharīf of Mecca with the title of Vizier. He issued in August a proclamation, sealed with the seal of the Emirate of Mecca (to which, however, he never got nearer than Medina), pointing out that the revolt had been engineered "under Christian orders".[34] Two immediate results of the Revolt were, to prevent an almost indefinite extension south-east of the Allied Oriental front, by sea and by land; and to convert the British Force on the Canal from a shield into a spear-point that was to pierce the Ottoman Empire to the heart.[35]

Before long incidents at Jeddah gave cause for apprehension. The situation there, whether the revolt failed or succeeded, could no longer remain what it had been. Apart from the preservation of internal order (municipality, police, etc.), it was imperative to set up some form of supervision over the bodies charged with the exterior and international business of the town, such as the Port and Quarantine Authorities. For the moment there must be an Englishman in charge. The appointment of a titular Governor might arouse Arab and possibly Allied suspicions, while that of a Consul could hardly fail to bring about the arrival of Allied and even neutral colleagues. The situation was met by the early appointment as British Representative of Colonel Wilson, of the Sudan Service,[36] who speedily won the confidence of the Grand Sharīf. He was equipped with a competent staff, including Husain Rūhi, my code word for whom was "the Persian Mystic". "I have told Rūhi", I wrote to Wilson, "that he is delivered over to you body and soul. He is to consider himself not only your eyes and ears, but also if necessary your hands and feet. He may even, should an especially unsavoury occasion present itself, be called upon to represent your nose."

The Mystic was already based on the Hejaz, and rendering valuable services to Arabs and British alike. His letters, half English and half Arabic were a perpetual pleasure: "I am right in the town spending the night. I have been to the house of Muhammad Nasif. He told me that Farūki and Jamīl were exerting their zeal to let the people here hate the English. Some other one has been telling me that Rashīd Rida [editor of the Moslem journal *al-Manar*] is coming to Hejaz and that he will do his best to make the people ignore the English. Please take strict measures to keep him in Egypt or deport him altogether to Malta. The majority

---

[34] I visited the Sharīf Haidar, a gentleman of great charm, in 1923 at Beirut. One of his two sons is a distinguished violinist, with a large American public. The other called upon me later in Cyprus as the Representative of General Motor Cars, Ltd.

[35] "(June 1916.) Sir A. Murray was now directed by the C.I.G.S. to consider seriously that advance to al-Arish which had previously been merely a vague possibility." *Official History of the Campaign in Egypt and Palestine.*

[36] Portrait in *Seven Pillars*, p. 64.

idea here is friendly to the English, especially the greater part of the ruling committee. . . . I wish one could get hold of Farūki's bags and take a copy of his cipher book so that we may know all that is going on between him and his chief. He puts his cipher book in his small yellow bag which can be easily taken to a locksmith to be opened in F's absence.[37] I think he is a rascal."

I was still uneasy about Jeddah.

Though it is, as I trust you realize, infinitely more than half the battle to have lit this candle, the wick is as yet far from burning with that hard gem-like flame I could have desired. The Arabs, as you are doubtless aware, are naked, unarmed, and more esurient than the Greek himself; further they have not one *bobbo* to their name. We are therefore at present under the obligation to them, and the necessity for ourselves, of pouring into the yawning mouth of Jeddah a ceaseless stream of corn, cash and cartridges, for the use of a people highly sensitive to any action (even for the maintenance of public health or security), which can be interpreted before the Arab world as an impingement upon their independence. If I could get face to face with the Sharīf, which I expect I shall have to end by doing, I believe I could explain the situation to him and get from him every conceivable facility and guarantee over two cups of coffee. I am not sure that it may not even be worth the journey to Jeddah to talk with him awhile over the Jeddah-Mecca telephone, for the Syrian and Arab intermediaries cannot transmit a message without causing it to undergo a sea-change.

The chance came in September, when I was detailed to accompany Admiral Wemyss whose flagship *Euryalus* was escorting the Holy Carpet to Jeddah. Of this voyage the diary survives, and I quote briefly:

22. ix. 16. Left Sidi Gāber 4.10 travelling in the carriage next to Madame Rushdi Pasha, who sent me her little 7-year old Ghālib to work off some of my Turkish. At Benha observed in our train several Ulama [38] travelling to the Hejaz at the pious expense of our Sultan. Forebore from talking to them partly because I did not wish my journey to be known and discussed among them, and more from dread of the throat effort of high Arab converse against the din of the train. Aboard *Euryalus* at Suez by 10, to find Admiral, Nevill, Burmester, and Secretary playing Bridge in shirt-sleeves.

24. ix. 16. After luncheon chess with Admiral, of whom it may be said that he plays better than dear K., but no more. Whilst we were playing, the fall of Tayif, with 1800 Turks, was announced by wireless. As I had predicted the 24th, my reputation as a prophet is established. The thing is an immense relief, and should mean our seeing Abdallah on his way to meet Faisal, and possibly bringing back with us Ghālib Pasha, Turkish Governor of Hejaz. By the way, very stimulating to have one's morning bath to the accompaniment of the band, four yards away.

[37] Some of Rūhi's disconcerting suggestions.
[38] Moslem religious professors.

25. ix. 16. Admiral beat me at chess (his grey parrot ejaculating the while, in a pronounced Oxford accent, "Damn the Kaisah", "Damn the Kaisah").

26. ix. 16. Passed through the dangerous but well buoyed Jeddah reef about 3.30 to find *Hardinge* dressed and flying Egyptian flag at peak with green three crescented ensign [39] at head to denote she was carrying Mahmal, which indeed was plainly visible on deck. The town under the strong afternoon sun looked as if it were carved in ivory. Wilson came aboard with Boyle from *Fox*, in every way more cheerful than he was in Egypt. He now no longer believes in a Turkish advance south of Medina, and even speaks of reported withdrawals. If this means that it will no longer be necessary to send an English Brigade or French Batteries to Rābugh, it is a very deep relief to me. We decided to go ashore Wed., receive Sharīf Mohsin in afternoon, speed off Mahmal Thurs. morning, leaving immediately after in *Hardinge* for Rābugh —7 hours to N. There it is my hope to take H.M.'s Sloop *Espiègle* 30th or 1st and run for Suez, or I shall be intolerably overdue. Col. Brémond, of French Mission, tall, strong and very *sympathique,* came aboard about 4.30 with Rūhi (in Bedawi clothes) and a Syrian in trousers and turban. Rūhi has I am glad to say arranged to go to Mecca where, if only he can refrain from empty boastings, he should be very useful. The Syrian, who struck me as oily, calls himself Director of Public Security in Jeddah. They were accompanied by a *sbire* of appalling ferocity. Cannot help wishing that our speed might have exceeded 8½ knots (which I now find it to have been) so that we might have had more time here. Weather very hot, damp, windless, and oppressive. More chess with Admiral with whom I subsequently drafted telegrams to Murray and Admiralty. Bed about 11, half-boiled.

27. ix. 16. See my dictated account. But it loses in psychological correctness anything it may gain in *correction officielle.* Done for the Admiral's benefit (and now severely abbreviated):

Leaving *Euryalus* at 9.30 a.m. we steamed towards the town of Jeddah, and drew up at a little jetty to a salute of 18 guns fired from antique mortars. We were received by the local notables, and by Wilson.

Before long Rūhi arrived with a telephone message from the Grand Sharīf inviting the Admiral to a public banquet in Jeddah to-morrow night. This he was fortunately able to decline with the sufficiently valid excuse of proceeding at once to Rābugh upon the Grand Sharīf's own business. I thought it better to reply for the Admiral myself, and going down to the telephone, rang up No. 1 Mecca. After a short pause, I distinguished what I rightly took to be the tones of the Grand Sharīf himself, bidding me a warm and affectionate welcome to Jeddah, and anxiously asking me whether the Admiral would accept his hospitality. At this moment three or four other voices became audible on the wire, and I remarked to the Sharīf that in my opinion we were being tapped. He said it was quite impossible that this should be so at Mecca. I replied that I did not know from which end the sounds proceeded, but that I certainly heard them, and asked him whether he did not also. He said he did, and I immediately had the satisfaction of hearing him call through to the Central in stronger language than I had expected from so holy a man, ordering them to cut off everybody's instrument in the Hejaz excepting his own and

[39] The flag chosen by the Sultan Husain to supersede the Ottoman-Egyptian red flag with single crescent and star.

mine for the next half-hour. This was instantly done, and we conversed hence-forth in a silence of death.[40]

Having enquired after His Highness's health and congratulating him upon the fall of Tayif, I explained to him the reasons which made it impossible for the Admiral to be his guest to-morrow night. I impressed upon him the great pleasure it had been to the Admiral to have the honour of conveying the Holy Carpet to the Holy Land. He seemed to appreciate this, and added that a nation that observed its own religion so well as the British could hardly fail to respect those of others.

He appeared to be genuinely disappointed at being unable to come down to Jeddah to receive the Admiral in person, and explained that at this of all seasons, his own presence in Mecca was imperative. At the conclusion, how-ever, of the ceremonies attending the pilgrimage, it was his firm intention either to send his son Abdallah to Cairo, in order to get into touch with the authorities there, or else to come down to Jeddah himself, in which latter case he hoped to be able to repair his present omission. He spoke much more hope-fully than his recent letters had led one to expect about the situation in the Hejaz, so much so, that at one moment he threw out a feeler deprecating the assistance of the French Government. Declining to comprehend this allusion, I answered that God would doubtless give the victory to the forces of the true believers. After about twenty minutes most friendly, interesting and animated conversation I said I was sure his lunch time had arrived, and so gave him the opportunity of ringing off, promising to bid him farewell before leaving Jeddah.

After luncheon with Young and Cochrane (who appeared to me to be sadly overworked) I walked down through the town past the Municipality to the jetty in order to meet and take on board *Euryalus* the Sharīf Mohsin and his friends. They insisted on my going with them in the Municipal launch as far as *Fox*, where we transhipped to the Admiral's barge, reaching *Euryalus* about 4 p.m. Here not only the Sharīf and his party, but also their numerous and most disreputable looking guard were shown over the more easily under-stood features of *Euryalus*. The big guns struck them so much that they could not at first believe them to be guns at all. The signalling and the loading drill impressed them no less, and the size, comfort and cleanliness of the Admiral's cabin came in for admiring comment. But it was the guns in the end which produced the greatest effect, and the party, after partaking of tea and perform-ing their evening prayers upon the stern walk, left the ship in a state of mind divided between awe and an intense satisfaction at having demonstrably es-poused the winning cause. I was pleased to note that the greatest impression seemed to be produced upon the Sharīf Mohsin and Sulaiman Qābel, the most considerable and most intelligent members of the party. The first remarked: "What we have seen is a representation, in little, of the great British Empire itself", and the second informed me that he had not up till that moment real-ized that so large a ship could float upon the surface of the waters.

As an immediate and tangible result of the afternoon's proceedings, the Admiral was officially invited to ride at the head of the procession through

[40] At my first audience in 1919, I told King George V this story. His Majesty said: "I couldn't do that in London".

Jeddah of the Holy Carpet itself, an honour which we prudently, if reluctantly, thought fit to decline.[41]

As soon as the barge came back from *Fox* the Admiral went on board *Hardinge* to return the official morning visit of Fát-hi Pasha, Amir al-Hajj, the General in Command of the Egyptian Mahmal and Pilgrimage. The General was, as he had been in the early morning, still attired in his pilgrim's bath-towel costume and sandals, completed by an officer's belt, and the salute was played by a military band with conductor all similarly apparelled.

I made for the Admiral a French telegram congratulating the Sultan Hussein in Cairo upon the safe arrival of the Carpet. Jeddah most interesting, if a little fatiguing. Almost entire absence of women in streets. Was informed that Hashish and drink quarter was outside the town. No open selling of alcohol, but Greeks let it down for sale out of windows. Sharíf is putting a stop to this traffic. Town on the whole clean; and, without great pretensions to originality. Most attractive, especially on account of the abnormal quantity of salient woodwork that relieves the surface of the houses. This, though inferior to good Egyptian work, is perhaps more effective in the distance, and at the height of a 3rd or 4th storey. The profusion of wood is the more remarkable in that every stick of it has to be brought from Singapore, Arabia producing none. A certain number of the usual Turkish dogs—practically the only feature I would like to see abolished: for the absence of effendis, tarbushes, cheap ready-made European suits, *opéra bouffe* canvas uniforms, elastic-sided boots, made-up ties, Austrian silver-mounted *cannes de luxe,* local newspapers, Levantine cocottes, sherry-cobbler Club heroes and overfed overprotected disloyal Beys and Pashas, gives one an idea of what the unplumbed salt estranging East might be if left to itself. People friendly but *abruti.* On the whole ugly. Much African blood. The house of a Persian contained a beautifully proportioned little Selamlik or Ka'a, divided by a massy Gothic arch, and surrounded by stone-based divans against the wall. Carpets poor. Decorative Chinese matting on walls. Son spoke English very fairly. N's house was huge and hideous, and he a gross rich worthy ass. Only merit the long low-pitched staircases, reminding me of those in the walls of the great temple of Edfu. On returning to ship dictated for Admiral "extract" from diary for day. My servant Ismain having gone ashore in the course of the day, I saw him no more.

28. ix. 16. Rose 5.30 and left ship with Admiral and staff at 6.30, reaching town just after 7, there to find that for about the fifth time, the hour for the Mahmal procession had been changed and that it would not start till 9. The Admiral, whose life has been passed in the cultivation of exactitude, abandoned himself upon this to a mournful indignation, mingled with a wrathful surprise at my lack of astonishment. We decided to watch the landing from the roof at the Quarantine Office; and what was my gratification, when the Mahmal staggered into sight, at perceiving in the midst of the Hamla,[42] black with fury and as if struggling for his life with the enthusiasm of the crowd, howling obscenities and his eyes starting from his head, my ultra-civilized, *fin de siècle* and cynical Ismain. Back direct to *Hardinge, bateau de luxe* which,

---

[41] For like reasons and with infinitely sharper regret, I had to refuse the Grand Sharíf's subsequent personal invitation that I should visit him in Mecca.

[42] Procession.

as more than one sense reminded one, had conveyed the Mahmal horses, camels *and* pilgrims from Suez to Jeddah. Admiral had very kindly arranged for me to go N. from Rābugh in *Espiègle,* an elderly sloop of under 1000 tons. At luncheon I sat next a man who had served (most suitably) on a Dummy Dreadnought in the N'. Sea. 4.30 Rābugh. In the evening we heard, through *Dufferin* interpreter, that Sharīf Ali had sent a message absolutely forbidding us to land. Admiral upset. We sent Rūhi ashore with a letter saying that we had come at Sharīf's request to help him; and that unless horses, etc. were on shore next morning, as promised, we should possibly withdraw all ships and leave him to his fate. Simultaneously sent a wireless through *Euryalus* at Jeddah for Young to telephone to Sharīf, explaining our point of view. Lost two games of chess to Admiral with such skill that his opinion of my game sunk very low. But he is almost as difficult as Lord K. to force into victory. As Muhammad said: "Verily God shall cause men to smile when they see persons being hauled to Paradise in chains."

29. ix. 16. Rose 6: packed and arranged for my effects to be sent on board *Espiègle.* Found from Rūhi that Sharīf Ali had never uttered the message imputed to him: that, on the contrary, not only were horses, but also *kuffiyas* against the sun, waiting for us. The Sharīf Ali came aboard about 7.30; slight, gentle, handsome and distinguished: under middle height: I divine a weak chin under his small Charles I beard. With him Nūri Bey of Baghdad, military adviser; one of the Arab prisoners we have released from India, in khaki uniform and *kuffiya.* But Sharīf Ali in black *aba* cloak, silk *kuffiya* and golden *aqal:* his very small and shapely feet enclosed alas in Stambul court elastic-siders, complete with rudimentary spurs. We gave him coffee on the Bridge, in the course of which Rūhi announced rather than introduced me to him. He greeted me with affection and made me sit next him. Just before 8 we went ashore, put on the red *kuffiyas* over our helmets—the Admiral's appearance being particularly remarkable; mounted our beasts—mine a gigantic Waler; and set off to inspect the lines of defence, by land and sea, against a Turkish force attempting to break through to Mecca or Jeddah from Medina by Rābugh, the only practicable way. (It had by the way been from the first very clear that the *kuffiyas* were less a protection against the sun than to shield Ali himself from hostile Arab criticism at the bringing of helmeted Christians into the interior of the Hejaz.) I left the Admiral to Sharīf Ali as much as possible; but that was not much, for, as soon as I dropt back, Ali would look about, turn round and say in Arabic: "Why do you ride behind, O Mister?" and I would have to canter back to his side. We crossed a plain stretch of sand, setting our faces toward Jebel Subh and making for the right wing of the Arab position: thence swung round the centre and returned by their left flank, the ride lasting from 8.15 to 11.50. The line is roughly astride of the Sultāni-road from Medina to Rāburgh; and the ship's guns, at 7000 yards range, could certainly cover the flanks—by day. And I suppose the Turks could scarcely venture on attempting to slip through the palm groves (about 4560 yards range) by night. Good aerodrome ground about 3000 yards inshore; but water uncertain as yet. I was astonished to find that Ali had not yet heard of the death of Lord K., in spite of the elaborate letter we sent to his father: he observed with truth that he had been in the desert more than three months, and had seen no papers. I will have these sent him; and began

on the spot with 50 of my Arabic Raemakers,[43] as also 500 Egyptian cigarettes I had brought. The Sharīf seems to smoke almost continually. I explained to him our reluctance at sending British troops even to the coast of the Hejaz, and soon convinced him that it would be, from his own point of view, a heavy blunder. He said three batteries of Q.F., one for defence and two for an advance, would suffice them. Unlike Nūri, who is fair at French and picked up in India a smattering of English, Ali knows nothing but Arabic. On the whole I give him more charm than strength of character, and still consider Abdallah, with Faisal, the ruling spirits of the clan. We passed the Red Standard of Mecca, flying Fridays, and dismounted at the shore. "Flags" took a group of Admiral and Ali (obviously for Balfour and Buckingham Palace), and after much display of affection we parted, and the Admiral shot me at noon into *Espiègle*.

Train: Suez to Alexandria.

Three days all but six hours in *Espiègle* should serve as a warning against the excessive zeal of such as hasten back to their work. *Espiègle* is far smaller than the classic Channel boats, and without any of even their few amenities. The commander thrice informed me that the ship's bottom was 2 inches deep in barnacles, that the engines could never remotely approach their indicated maximum of 13.5 knots, that the tide at once took off one knot, that in the Gulf of Suez it was all he could do to keep her under way—finally that he was very short of coal. If we "got it stiff" in the Gulf, we should be lucky in arriving at Suez on Monday at all. After a less than frugal luncheon (no ice aboard) I made an attempt to read the *Egoist* (a tattered copy of which lay on the desk) but gave it up and lay, practically for the rest of the voyage a high-heaved and higher-heaving log of uncomplaining misery. The natural filth of the vessel, which was great, was constantly increased by the dense pitiless descent of greasy black smuts vomited up by the bad coal. At every (perpetual) larger wave the ship struck her nose into it with a hammer-like blow, while of course the screw and the engines raced in jangling discord. In more conscious moments contrived almost to finish the unique *Egoist* (last read at Cambridge): near the end it approaches a high tragic Vaudeville, and Craye's wit does not wear well; but how direct and simple the whole effect, and how much easier and more compelling than Henry James. Should be included with Chess in Everyman's Education.

III

I had hardly returned to Alexandria when we received a telegram from the Sharīf Abdallah begging me to run back to Arabia and have a few words with him. I suppose I should have been delighted at this importunity,[44] but there was no cruiser at Suez for the moment; the only Khedivial mail boat had been requisitioned by the Admiralty, and I had

---

[43] See p. 212.

[44] From time to time henceforth I would receive a cable from Mecca, through Jeddah and Suakin; "Please come as soon as possible and bring with you the same amount as you brought for me the first time"; expensive invitations, in which my *beaux yeux* were possibly not in the front plane of intention.

some difficulty in withstanding my chief's suggestion that I should travel round by land through the Sudan, or enjoy yet another voyage on a problematical collier; so I wished that Abdallah could have said his say while I was in his country. There was another crisis at Rābugh, where a descent of Turks flushed with victory over the besiegers of Medina was anxiously anticipated.

In October I made my third descent to the Hejaz. The additional justification for my attempt, by reproducing so much of my third 1916 journal, to give the background and atmosphere of this particular voyage, is partly (as elsewhere in my book) to recall the immediate sensations; but far more because it was through—and quickly after—this voyage, that Lawrence of Carchemish, of Cairo—of any place for a little while—became permanently Lawrence of Arabia.[45] His enduring world-fame makes it difficult to replace him now in his original perspective, and I must confess, almost with shame, that my sentiments in applying for him were mainly gratitude for his assistance in the Hejaz stamp issue and in other matters, the high value I attached to his judgment on any question, and his admirable company. Extracts from the journal of October 1916 containing his name, occur with what must now seem a ludicrous infrequency and inadequacy.

12. x. 16. On the train from Cairo little Lawrence my supercerebral companion.

13. x. 16. By 2.0 aboard the *Lama*, a converted B.I. of 2000 tons. Agreeable neat Commander. I was given the doctor's very adequate cabin; two young vets. going to Jeddah to buy, as a first consignment £10,000 worth of camels. Lawrence shared a cabin with one of the vets. Gramophone, "a gift of the Ladies of Bombay", dominant. We were announced as arriving at Jeddah possibly on Sunday evening. Monday morning at any rate. Ten minutes after the Commander had remarked upon the ill omen of a departure on Friday 13, the bursting of two boiler tubes, making Sunday evening impracticable, was broken to us by the Chief Engineer. I foresee great difficulty in getting back from Jeddah, but shall fight hard for Suez under ten days, unless anything of unusual urgency keeps me: for I begin to have enough of these voyages. Talked twenty minutes with two Egyptian officers who seemed a little out of the picture, and to bed, after fifty or sixty pages of *Mr Britling*.

14. x. 16. Rose 7.15 and seem to have spent day writing, going on with Henry James's *Ambassadors*, finishing *Britling*, but most of all sleeping: for the heat begins again, and with it my *abrutissement*. I find we are loaded with coal, ammunition, etc., over two feet above safety line; a pleasant conceit that would mean in peace a fine of some £500. Mastered from Lawrence the theory and practice of the Playfair Cipher: continue to wonder whether for all his amazing knowledge, his sum total of pleasure is, given of course cir-

cumstances favourable to each, any greater than mine. Though he probably meets with fewer *déceptions*. My servant Said seasick again, and ill-consoled when I tell him that it is thrice fortunate to die, even from excessive vomiting, so near the Blessed Hejaz. Bed 10.15.

15. x. 16. On with *Ambassadors* and some of Jane Harrison's *Ancient Art and Ritual:* which makes me fear I shall never rise to the rarer heights of folklore and anthropology. Prepared an informatory and propagandist list for distribution from Jeddah of new Hejaz stamp issue. Revolver practice on deck at bottles after lunch, in which I was too sleepy to take part, tore my ears and effectually ruined my siesta: a climax provided by the discharge of a few black powder rounds from a Turkish rifle, a detonation about equal to that of an 18-pounder cannon. Conceived the idea, for my return, of holding up any northbound vessel, and boarding her. Captain Scott, to my surprise, seemed to find the suggestion quite reasonable. At night spoke K.M.S. pilgrim boat *Mansura* making Suez.

Written on *Bellview* [*sic*]

16. x. 16. Jeddah harbour 7 a.m. Young came aboard to take us off and we reached Consulate about 9.30. Found Wilson in a rather defiant mood: uncertain whom he represented and from whom he was to take orders— uninformed on details, as well as on what he called General Policy. I told him that, outside Germany, the latter had never existed anywhere, save perhaps in America and Greece in the sense of taking the cash and letting the credit go. Sharīf Abdallah having arrived and encamped early in the morning about four miles to the N.E. of the town, Wilson and I rode out through the north gate, passing on our right the Turkish barracks which had been half demolished by our naval gunfire of June, now repaired and occupied by Egyptian Artillery under Said Ali Pasha; and a little farther on, within a plain white-walled enclosure, the Tomb of Mother Hawa [46] (whom we name Eve), a pleasant green dome over a sort of sparse isolated suburb of ten or twelve houses, belonging to a wealthy Indian; to Abdallah's camp, which consisted of six tents, four of Damascus work, and two of Indian from Muir Mills. Abdallah [47] came out into the open, and greeted us very warmly: I introduced Wilson to him. He was quite unchanged since Kitchener and Abdin days two and a half years ago in Cairo, and pleased at my recognizing one of his bodyguard who had been with him then. Wearing yellow silk *ķuffīya*, heavy camel's hair *aba*, white silk shirt, etc. and—patent leather boots. Wilson and I, having no wonderfully agreeable news to impart, nor gifts to convey, had decided on a forty minute call, reserving business for A.'s return visit to the consulate in the afternoon. I have never seen a habitation at once more suitable and beautiful than that double tent of Damascus. Of its eight sides one formed the entrance, and one the door into the sleeping tent. The walls were adorned with *appliqué*, like that of the Egyptian *Khiyamiya*,[48] but lighter and freer, of birds, conventional flowers and still more conventional texts, prescribing virtue and deprecating tyranny. A little square trellis grille let in the fresh

---

[46] Subsequently destroyed by King Ibn Sa'ud.
[47] For Lawrence's estimate of Abdallah (with which I do not agree) see *Seven Pillars*, p. 67.
[48] Tent bazaar in Cairo.

air of the north breeze. Deplorable yellow bent-wood chairs. Abdallah informed us that, having been warned by Dr. Maalūf that there was fever in Jeddah, he proposed camping outside: and that it was for this reason the telephone was being run out to him. He expressed deep regret at the death of Lord Kitchener: and showed distinct signs of sympathy with the ex-Khedive, a sentiment, seeing how often he had been his guest, very much to his honour. Hoped we would Do Something For him. Confessed also to a genuine admiration for the Germans as Men—*Rijāl,* as also, in that sense, for the Turks. After about three-quarters of an hour we attempted to move, but he held us, and presently began to insist upon our remaining to luncheon. This he did with such vehemence that we ended by yielding, and were in the end very glad to have done so, for we found in the Indian tent a regular European meal of stupendous dimensions that had obviously been prepared for us. The author of this benefaction was the head of the Municipality, Sulaiman Qābel, but when I, as a compliment to the food, asked Abdallah for a subordinate municipal post, he emphasized their civic purity by repeated assurances that the money came from Sulaiman's Private Pocket. (Monthly municipal budget of Jeddah £1450; excess of out over in-goings about £400, paid by Sharīf.) Wilson sat opposite Abdallah; I on his right, having opposite me the Sharīf Tasha Mahanna, a bottle-nosed bandit with a smile of dazzling sweetness. On Wilson's right Qābel, and over against him a white-bearded ineffective Ancient Mariner who, I was told, had recently accepted the Finance Portfolio in the Sharifial Cabinet, and on his left a Shaikh from Hadramūt whom I should have taken for a Chinaman. At the end of the table remote from me K.'s old Sudāni officer. Almost at once a burning *Simūm* sprang up and blew past us through the tent. Abdallah suddenly read aloud "Muir Mills", printed opposite him on the tent, and explained to me that he knew the Frankish alphabet, though not one single word in any of its tongues. Half-way through the meal the old Sudāni, blinking as though overcome by honourable emotion, excused himself on the score of military duties, and withdrew; nor did I understand until about five minutes later that the pepper, blown out of the open pots hard into his face, was the real reason of his departure. The incident was considered an excellent joke by the company in general. Bitter, good but thirst-raising coffee in the Damascene tent: I asked for water, which was produced in a large plain one-handled silver bowl which, when I had drained it, Abdallah insisted upon my keeping. I subsequently found it was the Grand Sharīf's own drinking cup, accidentally packed by Abdallah's servants. He showed me Ghālib Pasha's sword, surrendered to him upon the fall of Tayif: ordinary tailor's production.[49] At about two we rode back, this time through the imposing Mecca Gate (recently whitewashed by Municipal zeal) through which in these 1300 years many millions more must have passed out than in. (Mother Hawa again left on the right.) On returning to the Consulate I found that Thomson had succeeded in making arrangements for my returning next day in the French Pilgrim ship *Orénoque:* so wired for Quarantine facilities. .

I was not particularly looking forward to Abdallah's return business call, for I found to my astonishment that Wilson had only just been informed by Sirdar of H.M.G.'s final decision to send no British troops to Hejaz. Col-

[49] *Seven Pillars,* p. 73.

lectively therefore it was our privilege to announce to A. that the Brigade, more than once promised by H.M.G., would not be sent; and that the flight of aeroplanes, promised and dispatched to Rābugh was being withdrawn on the very day that the appearance of Turkish planes had been announced. Individually I had the honour of being instructed that I was to express no opinion at all on military affairs; that in any political request or reply I should not be supported. I was, furthermore, not provided with the £10,000 for which A. had made me a personal appeal. I felt myself therefore somewhat poorly equipped for the rôle of a *Deus ex Machina,* and wrote off mentally heavy drafts upon my friendship with Abdallah and consequent utility in Arab affairs. We met him on his arrival at the front door. Wilson then read aloud to him in English, whilst I translated into Arabic, the substance of the Sirdar's telegram. The moment when we had to explain that the withdrawal of our promise for the Brigade included the aeroplanes also was not pleasant, and I do not wish to have to show H.M.G. to an Arab a second time in this light. Abdallah took the position like a fine gentleman, and asked to be allowed to state his case.

He began at once addressing me. I interposed and said I had neither knowledge, qualifications nor authority of any kind in military affairs: but he replied: "Pardon me: it was your letter and your messages that began this thing with us, and you know it from the beginning, and from before the beginning." He gave a fairly accurate historical summary of the negotiations, quoting several times H.M.G.'s promise that we would do everything possible to help the Arabs, and citing textually a phrase in a letter from Maxwell, placing at their absolute disposal, so far as I could gather, very considerable portions of the British Army. This document was at Mecca, but he could produce it for us in ten hours. He said we were becoming colder to the Arabs and trusting them less: and he asked us, civilly but fairly directly, who was responsible for the actual conduct of operations. My military disclaimers and dissociations were not much helped by the fact that Wilson could follow about half only of A.'s beautiful high Arabic, which I was thus frequently called upon to translate. Lawrence understood much better. The discussion wandered on with no great result: and it was agreed we should resume it with Azīz Ali Bey al-Masri, Chief of the Hejaz Staff, and Said Ali Pasha, Minister of War, at ten next morning. Abdallah then had the agreeable task of communicating our announcements by telephone to his August Parent. I greeted him also, and could hear quite clearly during our brief conversation the strains of a band playing outside his palace in Mecca. He took the whole thing wonderfully well, and said he had entire confidence in our intentions and projects: but implored Wilson and me to send a telegram urging reconsideration of H.M.G.'s last decision, with a pathetic belief in our power to affect the decisions of the War Council. Abdallah left the Consulate about 7.15 (Jeddah time nearly an hour ahead of Egyptian) leaving us all in a state of admiration for him and disgust with ourselves.

Neither Abdallah nor Wilson would hear of my leaving next morning by the *Orénoque,* so I gave up the idea and determined to trust to luck for getting back to Suez before the 26th. At 7.30 I dined with Col. Brémond and the French Mission, at their Consulate. I on B.'s right: opposite, Capt. K. the interpreter, and Ben Ghabrit, Chief of the French Western Moslem Mission, just returned from the Pilgrimage. B. G. had been Grand Chamberlain to Mulai Hafīd [50] and at the same time a spy to the French: now a political adviser at the *Quai D'Orsay*. Fine appearance in his country's costume: clever agreeable utterly false face, with twinkling pertinacious shifty enquiring eyes. A Believer *pour rire:* as his admirable series of Mecca anecdotes clearly showed. He commented upon the behaviour of Rashīd Rida, and expressed some surprise at our having allowed him to go to Mecca at all: and I was careful to reply, for the benefit of the Moslem West, that we could never venture to come between a man and his religious duties. Ben Ghabrit spoke highly of the journal *al-Qibla,* which he said we should do our utmost to circulate: the editor Fuad Khatīb (whom I know for a Francophil) was also a Good Man. Very favourably impressed with Grand Sharīf, who is both feared and venerated: receives and gives coffee to some 3000, of all classes, *per diem.* Luxuries in Mecca grotesquely dear, but necessities, save only house rent, not unreasonable. Slaves still for sale: one of his staff invested in a *jeune négresse: une négresse c'est une Circassienne; seulement on les appelle négresses:* a curious convention. When stoning the statues at Muna,[51] he wasted all his ammunition upon the two less damnable of the three, and was forced to obtain a covert refill of stones for the Grand Slam—(I forget its name). He explained his carelessness to the Sharīf by saying that he had gone on mechanically with the first two, imagining them to be Enver and Talaat: and the Sharīf had volunteered him all the stones of the Hejaz to so admirable an end.

When the champagne came, Brémond charged his glass and told us with simple dignity that he had just heard that his only male relation up till now not killed or wounded, had been seriously injured: it was thus his duty and his pride to drink to the Alliance, and to say how much pleasure it gave him to be associated with Englishmen. The un-French absence of *panache* in his delivery was very striking. I drank to his cousin's recovery and the prosperity of the French Mission.

Our walk back to the Quarantine Jetty reminded me strangely of zigzagging home from the Piazza in Venice lit by the moon. Curiously effective. As we drew near the shore, streets and road covered with people asleep in the stifling damp; some delay in getting the launch: and aboard, after grounding on a reef once only, by about 11.30: rather exhausted.

17. x. 16. Left *Lama* 9 a.m. and had time, before the arrival of Abdallah at Consulate, for a talk with Said Ali Pasha, whom I like very much. Wilson had given me to understand that Said Ali and the officers under him had demanded to be sent back to the Sudan: but I found this was far from being so. He says the Arabs are a cowardly and undisciplined rabble: and fears (not, it must be admitted, without reason) lest they should scamper off one day, leaving the gunners to suffer death, after nameless mutilations, at the hands of the Turks. He complains moreover that their habit of occasionally discharging their pieces over the camp at night: and says that many, having received their rifles and ammunition from the Sharīf, disappeared into the desert, to be no more seen. He adds that Abdallah is well aware of these little deficiencies,

[50] The Sultan of Morocco.

[51] On the tenth day of Dhu l'Hijja, which is the climax and conclusion of the Mecca pilgrimage, the pilgrimage visit (for the second time) the valley of Muna, and cast seven stones at each of three pillars in memory of Abraham's having treated the devil in the same way.

but that the Sharīf is not, and that he will listen to no criticism of the Arab forces. The Syrian officers talk a great deal too much. As for the Turks, if they had not believed there were 30,000 trained Egyptian troops against them, they could and would easily have routed their opponents at Jeddah, Mecca, and Tayif. At Tayif they wantonly burnt the Sharīf's historic collection of ancient Arab books. Said Ali was allowed to take over Ghālib Pasha and the Turkish prisoners: on his departure G. P. thanked him warmly and said he knew the Arabs would have cut their throats to a man. In conclusion he desired no better than to fight for us (even on the Somme), but missed here a nucleus at least of trained and disciplined troops upon whom he might depend. I said that if Lord Kitchener and other British officers had acted on those lines twenty years ago, neither the Egyptian Army nor the Batteries nor Said Ali himself would exist at the present moment.

Abdallah arrived about 10, and we went over yesterday's ground with the additional assistance of Said Ali Pasha and Azīz Ali Bey al-Masri. Abdallah began by reading out to us a telegram from Faisal to the effect that two Turkish aeroplanes had begun to operate, to the dismay bordering upon panic of the Arabs. He said that unless these were driven off or in some way checked, the Arabs would disperse. Said Ali corroborated this prophecy. Impossible to get the machines destroyed by bribery as the Turks employed no Arabs for that section of the camel-transport (which were, in consequence, without exception martyrs to the mange). Azīz Ali was of opinion that Brigade was unnecessary, but could not say so before Abdallah: who finally wrote out an appeal which he begged us to enclose and support in our own telegram. At about twelve the Sharīf began ringing us up, and continued pitilessly without intermission to dominate and interrupt us until 1.30. He repeated himself to me ten or eleven times, appealing for the Brigade and the Planes, till I had to remind him that we had not, unfortunately, got the British Army drawn up in the Consulate back garden. Here again I found my military disclaimers perfectly useless. I made them, however, very clear to Wilson, and refused to have myself quoted for any opinion in the telegram he dispatched. Before going Abdallah expressed a wish to see me alone in the afternoon. After luncheon took a few photographs in the town: and was everywhere assisted by friendly advice from passers-by. One aged man assured me that it was not possible to get so large a building into so small a Kodak: and my view-finder soon showed me that the veteran was right. I found the town cleaner, less smelly and more dignified in every way than the bazaar parts of Cairo.

Rode out again from the north gate, only to meet Abdallah about a mile from the town. I had mistaken the Arab time, and he had to keep an appointment with Brémond. Accompanied him almost (but, so as not to spoil his arrival not quite) up to the French Consulate, having arranged to stay in for him after five. Gathered from inquiries about Mecca from various sources that 20,000 people had attended the Pilgrimage, which was an unqualified success. The Sharīf himself never expected anything like that number. The state of Mecca itself highly satisfactory, and the Jeddah-Mecca-Tayif road as safe as any in Egypt. Egyptian and Indian pilgrims very well treated and highly pleased thereat. Two Indians, Mustafa Ghulam Rasūl and Abdal-Nabi Kashmiri, were talking against the Sharīf, and had even stuck up insulting posters on to his palace. (I believe the matter has been reported to the Indian Government.) The French Mission was popular, but not much liked by the Sharīf, who appears not to want the French to know "more than is necessary" of his country. Sharīf's prestige is very great, and Abdallah the only member of his family not afraid of him, although he handles him with more diplomacy than the blunt and outspoken Faisal. The Egyptian Army was admired and much praised. Living not expensive: excellent fruit and vegetables from Tayif. (I certainly found the grapes admirable.) Money current Turkish, Egyptian and Indian silver. English gold. Loss on exchange, except of Indian money. Shops all small, in hands of Meccans, Indians, Yamanis or Javanese. Practically no interest in War or any exterior topic.

To maintain his reputation for piety, Rūhi had drunk large quantities of holy Zamzam water, with such shattering effect that he has been locked in misery ever since.

Abdallah arrived about six, and I at once took him up to the top north balcony, overlooking the city wall and the desert. He began by saying that the situation at Rābugh was such that, for the moment, it dwarfed all other questions. He was deeply disappointed that I had been unable to bring the £10,000 requested in his telegram. Now that other help expected was no longer forthcoming, this was more than ever necessary and urgent. I explained to him without any *ménagement* that we had considered that the not illiberal subsidy we were supplying to his father should suffice for the operations of the sons also. He replied that his father was doing all he could: and that he himself had spent over £3000 of his private fortune in the reduction of Tayif. He was in real need of every piastre we could send him, and begged me to convey to the High Commissioner a strong personal appeal that the money might be forwarded without delay. I promised to urge this, and most earnestly trust it will be done. After discussing the Caliphate he shifted his ground to the title at Jalāla—Majesty and Malek—King of the "Arab Nation". It seemed hard that Montenegro should assume this style, and the Sharīf of Mecca not. (Oddly enough I had this same argument from Sultan Hussein, during the forty-nine days' discussion that preceded his accession to the throne of Egypt.) I reminded him that when Nicolas proclaimed himself he had at least the whole of his Black Mountain in possession: with these Rābugh and Medina alarms, could the Sharīf say as much? And was there any advantage in providing yet further food for the suspicions, and possible hostility, of the Imam, Idrisi, Ibn Sa'ud and others? At least let them hold the country, before beginning to alter its status. He seemed to agree to these arguments, and said he would use them, when he returned, upon his father. He promised to send me an advance copy of the first Hejab Budget, which, if it ever appears, should furnish remarkable and entertaining reading. Spoke bitterly of Ibn Rāshīd,[52] as a traitor: well of Ibn Sa'ud, but asked how far he would fight to please us; wondered what good we had got, or were ever going to get, out of the Idrisi and quoted, of the Imam: "His harming harms us not, any more than his help helps." I recommended him to do all in his power to expedite the business of our camel-buyers; as also to alter his cipher, which apparently can be read by the Turks. Here Wilson appeared, and after a longish wait for Said Ali Pasha and Azīz Ali Bey (again Arab time) we went in to dinner.

[52] Ruler of Hayil, N.E. of Najd, subsequently conquered by Ibn Sa'ud.

As a compliment to Abdallah we had borrowed from Said Ali the Turkish band and instruments taken at Tayif: with very remarkable results. After a while Azīz Ali said there was a piece called *The Echo* they could render with great skill, and shouted down from the window an order to that effect. The result was two notes of an ineffable *tristesse* on the trombone, followed by a pause in which we consumed more than half a course. Then a few more disjointed and incoherent notes from the rest of the orchestra, and so on *da capo*. Even the Egyptians—indeed all but Abdallah—were stricken with the horror of the melody, and the effort to contain myself reduced me to a very dreadful state of prostration. After a while Said Ali Pasha asked: "Is not this the music that is played for the dead?"—an ill omen I had to explain to Abdallah as being for the death of his enemies. A little later Azīz Ali shook his head and said: "It seems to me that each man is playing according to his own *kaif* or inclination." Grey, the cipherer, a weak musician, thought it might be the "Death of Nelson"—which one could well believe. Such as it was, however, it had its success, for when we got up we found that the Grand Sharīf, having rung up for something, had heard it down the telephone, and had ordered all the windows of the Consulate to be opened whilst he sat afar with the receiver to his ear.[53] Abdallah told me there were only European instruments in Mecca, which is sad hearing. He shares my admiration for the 1001 *Nights* which, however, he finds a little "open"—*maftūh:* though "less so than Zola!"

Brémond, a confirmed pessimist, had suggested that the Sharīf was considering peace terms from the Turks: so I took occasion to ask Abdallah quietly whether any feelers had been put out. He said that several unofficial and disavowable tentatives had been made, but that his father had always replied that the Arabs were now allies of Great Britain and could make no peace apart from her. He left, refusing to say good-bye until the morrow, about 9.30, and I reached the *Lama* well before 11.

18. x. 16. Galloped out to say good-bye to Abdallah at about ten, and took one or two photographs of him. Also bade farewell to his father, who called me My Son on the telephone. Ben Ghabrit, Sharīf Mohsin and Qābel hanging about. B. G. is certainly trying to carry out the instructions of the French Government, and sweating blood to make himself agreeable. Very cordial farewells to Abdallah. I am confirmed in my previous impression of him. He has intelligence, energy and charm, requiring only firm but not too heavy or respectful guidance to prove a valuable asset in future Arabian politics. He gives the not disagreeable impression of being faintly spoilt at home,[54] and, properly to hold him, the process must be, in some measure, repeated abroad. At present genuinely preoccupied by the Turkish threat on Rābugh.

Took some snapshots of Mecca gate on my way back, from Wilson's most tiresome and fidgety pony: and reached *Lama*, only half an hour late at 11.30 a.m. There learnt I could catch "merchant" steamer *Bellview* leaving Rābugh for Suez 11 the morrow, and resolved to chance it. Lay down, exhausted, all afternoon. In the evening had a conversation with, made a study of, and conceived a great liking for Azīz Ali Bey al-Masri, who achieved fame in the spring of 1914 by being rescued, chiefly by Kitchener and *The Times* and

[53] This meal is described, I should think from late memory, in the fine prose of *Seven Pillars*, on p. 75.

[54] I afterwards learned that he was his father's successor-designate.

wholly against the wishes of our Constantinople Embassy, from the deadly effects of Enver's jealousy. His ancestor was one Salīm Arafāt, a merchant of Hasra, who used to trade annually in the Caucasus by the Black Sea. His "Correspondent" in these parts was a Circassian, Hassan Bey, who finally bestowed upon Arafāt the hand of his sister, at the same time formally adopting him into the tribe. All this in the reign of the Sultan Mahmud. The third generation of this alliance migrated to Constantinople and thence, realizing by the sale of their slaves, settled down in Egypt, having by this time become more Circassian than Arab, though still aware of and maintaining their Basra connection: besides enjoying, on account of it, the friendship of Arabs, especially those west of Egypt. Azīz has been engaged (I gather to a European— German?—lady) for eight years, and desires nothing more than to marry her, retire and settle down in Switzerland. It is from her that he draws the very creditable elements of *Kultur* I find him to possess. He is passionately fond of music, aspiring so high as the Pastoral Symphony and the *Liebestod* of Isolde. Knows some of the smaller lyrics of Goethe and has a generous admiration for Corneille: but as for "Zola-Mola" [55]—he shrugged his shoulders. Disappointed with Homer, whom he had read in Bustani's absurd translation: I shall send him Leconte de Lisle's.[56] A lonely man, and a profoundly religious. His views on the Arab races are worth recording. He says the people of Baghdad are the most intelligent and really advanced of all: some of their women assisted and advised unveiled at anti-Committee of Union and Progress meetings in Stambul. Syrians have more education and polish but less real brain and character. Closely following these come the Tripolitans, of whom he thinks a great deal might, but certainly will not, be made. He spoke with a certain pathos and resignation of the shattered ideal, for which he had fought in Tripoli, of an Island-of-Arabs revival. After the Tripolitans, he places the people of al-Yaman, whom he finds greatly superior to that of the Hejaz, generations of a better diet being the probable reason.

Azīz Bey was optimistic about Medina, and critical, though less so than Said Ali Pasha, of the Sharīf's methods (the singular is not applicable here) though devoted to his person. He considers his appointment as Chief of the Staff, *Kalām Fāregh* or so much Rot. He is certain that, if Medina falls, the Sharifial brothers will, after tackling the treacherous Ibn Rāshīd, advance upon Syria: and asked me point blank whether England wanted this or not. I was unable to say. He continued that though he wishes to see the Arabs through their Hejaz crisis, he had no desire whatever to embark with them upon a campaign which, if Great Britain were against it, might involve them all in very disagreeable complications. It was therefore his intention to withdraw, if warned in time; and he begged me to let him know, by whatever means I thought best before 5 November at Rābugh. If he did not hear by then (which I warned him was more than probable), let us not be surprised, but excuse him, if he were carried on in the general current. If he does retire, I trust he will be used in Egypt after the War: he would make an excellent Mudīr.

Bed 10.30, nearing end of the wonderful *Ambassadors*.

19. x. 16. Reached Rābugh 7.30, trans-shipping from *Lama* to *Bellview* (sic), not a merchant greyhound built 1915, but an ordinary battered Tramp

[55] A Turkish trick of repeating names, with letter 'M.'
[56] In 1936 Ali Bey reminded me, in London, that I had done this.

of some twenty-one years' service. Accepted Turton's invitation to breakfast on the R.I.M. *Northbrook*, a floating Ritz which ground in the contrast. Spotless napery, etc., etc., and neat-handed (male Goanese) Phyllises and the classical Breakfast of the English Gentleman in a luxuriously carpeted enclosure on the upper deck. In the middle of this repast the Sharīf Ali came on board for three days' recess: what will his (all too) mobile Arab force do? He brought bad news from Faisal: considerable Turkish reinforcements arriving from Maan to Medina. This damped Azīz Bey's previous optimism, and made us all more anxious than ever for the three Batteries of Q. F. Mountain Guns. Left them to catch my Tramp, by no means consoled by Turton telling me that if *Lama* had applied direct to him he would have kept back for me the liner *Georgian*, that had sailed with the flying men the day before. *Bellview's* maximum speed is nine knots, which she can only attain when loaded 15 feet deeper than she now is. War insured £80,000, but a Tramp of Tramps. Capt. Churchill, a very decent man, turned out of his cabin for me: but I preserved his comfort and my own by asking for a camp bed on the Bridge. Two flying men and some planes aboard. Capt. C. helps every one out of a tin pannikin: and tried me severely at breakfast by "a length of tripe for you, Mr. Storrs?" Somehow a length is a queasy unit of measure. No ice machine, electric light or wireless. Butter a topaz marsh. Late dinner 5 p.m. As soon as we finish each meal, crew, including Said, sit down in our places and do for the rest. Bathing and other arrangements so contiguous that you have to put your left leg in the bath at times when you have little thought of taking one. With that, a northerly gale which has made us more than a whole day later even than their nine knot schedule. No letters, papers, Reuters or news of any kind since Friday the 13th. But having had time to write up this with a letter or so, to finish the amazing *Ambassadors*, as well as *Embarrassments* (I and III especially good) the unusual *Other House* and a volume of Leslie Stephen (a little diffuse), and eaten very little, with never a threat of nausea, I have suffered from nothing beyond irritation at the abnormal delay, with faint boredom at the meals. On the whole, more Devil and Deep Blue Sea than Bread upon the Waters in the experience. Gale very fierce, and noise of wind, especially at night, almost deafening. 19 may be said to include 20, 21 and 22, on the morning of which last we should have reached Suez. One day telleth another and one night certifieth another with peculiar exactitude. Read also five Sonnets every morning.

Reached Suez finally Sunday midnight,[57] and caught not without difficulty 6.45 a.m. train to Cairo: peculiarly disappointed to find that my mails had been sent at random down the Red Sea, and that there was consequently not one single letter for me. Had looked forward most intensely to the great pleasure of reading them in the train.

Cairo 2.15: car having failed us I sponged upon that of the Y.M.C.A. and lunched, having swallowed nothing since 3 p.m. the day before, with considerable interest at the Residency.

[57] The unfortunate Captain wrote to me in 1936: "We arrived at Suez in the middle of the night, and you insisted on my putting a boat out and putting you on shore, which I did. Next morning I was in awful trouble with the Naval Authorities. An R.N.R. Lieut. called Jones, in charge of a Naval picket-boat, bothered me several days until it all suddenly dropped, no doubt you managed that."

I did not meet the Grand Sharīf face to face, nor the Amir Faisal, until my fourth Hejaz descent near the end of 1916, when I wrote home:

H.M.S. *Dufferin*,
10. xii. 16.

I have just descried in the remote East the dark mass of Mt. Radwan (40 miles off), which lies to the North of Yanbo, 200 miles North of Jeddah. I am being run thither because MacMahon [58] at the last moment decided to yield to the yearning cries of Wilson and the Grand Sharīf, and sent me down. *Dufferin* was already 30 miles down the Gulf when she was recalled for the purpose: and is now under instructions to convey. A Good Man at full speed to Jeddah and thence, at his Good Pleasure, to *Lama* at Yanbo, for Suez, making Cairo (with a little more luck than last voyage) by Friday 2 p.m. It seems a lot of machinery to be set in motion for *Cet Humble Individu*, and will I hope justify itself. There is of course far greater heat here than in Cairo— even than at Aswān, but nothing compared to my first Sharifal voyage last June. (Upstairs we have just had "O Come, all ye Faithful" on the gramophone, followed by "And He shall feed His Flock" rather jerkily rendered on the pianola.) After dinner I oblige them with a little Wagner and Puccini, and dreadfully defeat the Paymaster at Chess. In the morning a little *Inferno*. James's *Washington Square* (his first, American manner) and Turgeneff's *Fumée;* but Russian books are always a slight effort to me, I suppose by reason of the leakage of style in translation.

I make bold once more to attach my depersonalized official extract from another lost diary, of this, my last visit, written on my return journey on the *Lama*.

13. xii. 16. On arrival at Jeddah at midday on Monday the 11th. I immediately went ashore and visited Colonel Wilson at the Consulate. There I learnt that the Grand Sharīf had ridden from Mecca on muleback, had entered the town on Sunday the 10th and was lodged in the house of Muhammad Nasif. The same evening he had received in a protracted interview Colonel Wilson, Captain G. Lloyd,[59] M.P., Colonel Brémond of the French, and Colonel Barnabi of the Italian Consulate. The general situation, with special reference to that of Rābugh, had been discussed at length, and the Sharīf had decided to request H.M.G. to send British troops to hold the Rābugh line, a decision upon which he had gone back next morning.

Early in the afternoon, the Grand Sharīf [60] sent his personal A.D.C., an Arab officer of Baghdad origin, to welcome me, and at 6 p.m. I rode, according to arrangement, with Colonel Wilson to the house of Muhammad Nasif, in front of which were two lofty and not very secure scaffoldings bearing a

---

[58] "I hate leaving the MacMahons during their last week. H. E. said: 'It's infernally inconvenient but the larger issue must prevail.'" Characteristic of Sir Henry MacMahon.

[59] Afterwards Lord Lloyd of Dolobran.

[60] His full name was Husain ibn 'Ali, of the ancestry of 'Aun. His official style, carrying the rank of Highness, was Amir and Sharīf. He was the reigning head of the Sharifal family and *ex officio* Chief of the Prophet's tribe, the *Quraish*, and Hereditary Keeper of the Holy Places. The Arabs alluded to him as *Amir* and addressed him as *Sayyidna*, our Lord.

THE AUTHOR WITH KING HUSAIN AT JEDDAH 12. XII. 1916

somewhat crude scheme of illumination and surrounded by a dense and vociferous crowd.

The Grand Sharīf had favourably impressed Colonel Wilson and Captain Lloyd, and I also found him a most convincing personality. After a brief but very cordial greeting, he led us into a small room furnished with comfortable leather chairs of the Club type, and lighted by an acetylene lamp of several hundred candle power, and sat us down on either side of himself. He is, or looks, taller than I had been led to expect, and dresses with an elegant, not to say studied, simplicity in a plain black "evening" cloth *guftan* over a *galabiá* of embroidered Persian silk, without girdle. His head-dress was the usual Meccan *taqia*,[61] under a plain white turban (the end of which hung out a little to the left after the manner of the *bani Abdilla*, the ruling house of Mecca), and over a close-fitting skull-cap; on his feet, so far as I could see, a sort of dull brown Bluchers, with golosh attachment to throw off for prayer. His complexion is fair, and his features regular and fine: large and expressive brown eyes gazing very directly from beneath strongly marked eyebrows, under an ample forehead: a short and delicately curved nose over a slightly elongated upper lip. The mouth full, but for an Oriental far from large; the lower lip prominent and exposed: teeth well formed and well preserved. The beard thick and not long: grey almost to whiteness. Hands long and strong, with square-tipped musician-like fingers. He informed me, unasked, that he was sixty-three years of age (but according to Rūhi sometimes admits up to sixty-six).

The dominating characteristic of the Grand Sharīf is a captivating sincerity of utterance, enhanced by a benignant, a noble simplicity of demeanour. I cannot but remember that he has passed a great portion of his life in Constantinople (in a burst of pleasure he thanked me once in Turkish and hastily corrected himself), where the natural Ottoman gravity, adopting and possibly improving upon the style and carriage of ancient Byzantium, has evolved a tradition of unparalleled dignity of deportment. It was the entire absence of this, far more than any specific delinquencies of their regime, that seemed to open the eyes of Europe to the enormities of the Committee of Union and Progress. In the present instance, just though his cause be and ideal his convictions, few have a greater right to say of themselves, *"Grandi dans le Sérail, j'en connais les détours"*, than this gracious and venerable patriarch.[62]

I began, after the usual salutations, by conveying to him the farewell messages of the High Commissioner, together with all wishes for the final triumph of the Arab cause. The Sharīf in reply expressed himself as deeply touched by these sentiments, and said that in what part soever of the Empire Sir Henry MacMahon might be, he would always think of him with feelings of the sincerest friendship. "The High Commissioner", he pursued, "is the justification of my action, and wherever I meet him I will grasp him (gripping both lapels of my coat) like this, claiming him as my witness."

Continuing in the same affectionate strain, and addressing me alternately as *Ya ibni* (My son) and *Ya azizi* (My dear) he embarked upon a somewhat ample *exposé* of the general position: the ground of which having to my certain knowledge been already well and truly gone over I contented myself with

---

61 Close-plaited coloured straw tarbush worn by Sharīfs under the narrow Meccan turban.
62 "The Grand Sharīf undoubtedly The Only Man: he would knock out London society, from Cantuar to Cunard." (14. xii. 16.)

listening, intervening only from time to time, less to controvert than not to let pass unchallenged such citations (from letters purporting to have come from the Residency) as H.M.G.'s "formal promise to undertake responsibility for the destruction of the Hejaz Railway". It has been my good or bad fortune on three separate voyages to Jeddah, to happen each time upon a Rābugh crisis; and though the present occasion was doubtless graver than others, the chief interest was to see whether, in the place of the usual demands for brigades and batteries, anything in the nature of concerted Arab action would be proposed. No such scheme was forthcoming, but the request for 1500 Moslem troops (to hold Rābugh) was explained, justified, and repeated, although they were "now almost certainly too late to prevent the Turkish advance". Wilson had recounted to me his experiences over the question of Azīz Ali's services, warning me that the matter was delicate and should be approached with caution, and only upon a favourable opportunity. I had begun to despair of this, when after about two and a half hours of criticism and suggestion the Sharīf hinted his disappointment at our not having designated some able Moslem General to the conduct of his military operations. I replied that we had never dreamed of so marked and direct an interference in his internal affairs, but that since he brought up the point, I should beg him to excuse a filial frankness in drawing his attention to the position of Azīz Ali al-Masri Bey.

It had been remarked, I said, that although H.M.G. had supplied close upon 60,000 rifles, with munitions and supplies corresponding, to the Hejaz, no sort of army appeared to be forthcoming or even in the process of creation. The example of the Supreme War Council in Europe showed that all the Allies had now a certain vaguely defined but not ineffective survey of each other's preparations; which enabled one to ask whether it would not be possible to profit by the enthusiasm and experience of this distinguished Arab officer by allowing him an independent command with a moderate budget so that he might train and equip a nucleus which, even if unable to advance direct upon Medina, would at least close the Southern Roads to any Turkish forces that might set out against them. The Sharifial Family would naturally retain supreme control of all operations and if, as was just conceivable, they laboured under any fear that Azīz Bey had not changed his Committee spots and might set himself up as an Enver (or even betray them to the Turks), let them remember that so long as they held the purse, they could by shutting it render him powerless whenever they pleased. The Sharīf enquired if Azīz Bey carried the recommendation of H.M.G. I referred him to the Sirdar's last telegram on the subject, and he was silent for a moment; then he said with a certain air of decision: "Do not think that we have anything but admiration for Azīz Bey; I declare to you that I hereby appoint him Minister of War with an independent budget for his requirements." I said that I trusted that this appointment would not mean removal from the front, the only place where Azīz could be of use. The Sharīf admitted this, and offered to allow him to remain at the front, choosing a representative who should act for him in the matter of transport, supply, etc., at Mecca; the salary of the said representative to be paid by the Sharīf. We considered this decision as most favourable both in itself and as a sign of the Sharīf's reasonableness and good intentions. He undertook to send off the necessary telegram of appointment next morning, and will, I feel sure, do his best to abide loyally by the arrangement. It being by this time past nine o'clock and our interview having lasted just over three hours, we withdrew, promising to meet him again next morning. The conversation though satisfactory was something of a strain, partly on account of the continual uproar outside the house, and still more because of the incredible severity of the acetylene lamp. Returning later by moonlight through the bazaars to the ship, I was amused to notice the unusual and officious energy of the night watchmen who, doubtless because of the presence in the town of their master, passed us on throughout the walk from post to post with a series of mysterious whistles and counter whistles.

I called upon the Grand Sharīf alone next morning and spent another two hours in his company. Having just received encouraging letters from his three sons, he viewed the situation in general under a much more rosy light than on the previous evening. He sent for his private secretary, dictated then and there the telegram of appointment to Azīz Bey, and, strong in this proof of his *bonne volonté*, embarked upon a variety of rather petty grievances, coupled with harmless if impracticable suggestions. He is, for example, far from satisfied with the person of Farūki as his Cairo representative and wishes to appoint another, whom we are at liberty to choose, in his place. He was anxious moreover, as had been Abdallah at our last interview, to establish a private cipher directly between himself and the Residency. I am convinced that both these requests were made from what he considers a sense of fitness and reciprocity, and not in the least from any lack of confidence in, or appreciation of, Colonel Wilson, with whom his relations are obviously of a most cordial nature.

Before leaving Jeddah after my previous visit I had taken occasion to repeat by telephone to Mecca my observations to Abdallah on the proposed assumption of the style of King. I warned him that such a step, the various objections to which he already knew, taken without consulting his principal Ally, must embarrass all concerned, reasoned with him and at last persuaded him to postpone the matter until His Majesty's Government should have had time to appreciate its full implications. Pleased with my success, I had telegraphed it to Cairo and taken the next boat North, to be greeted at Suez with the interesting news that the Sharīf had three days previously proclaimed himself King. Considering the frankness and intimacy of our relations from the beginning of things, I was incensed by this treatment, and on this next visit to Jeddah, told His Majesty so, without mincing words. He laid his hand on my shoulder and replied by a rhyming Arab proverb:

> *Darb al-habīb*
> *ka-akl al-zabīb*
> *wa hajáratu rummán—*

"The blows of a friend are as the eating of almonds, and stones flung by him as pomegranates", which he proffered, and I was fain to accept, as a full and perfect liquidation of the irregularity.[63]

He added that as he had already been officially addressed by the Residency as Khalīfa (a title to which he did not aspire) he had considered that, the greater including the less, it was superfluous to apprise us of his resolution. I remarked that though all the Residency correspondence with himself had passed through my hands, I had never yet seen the document he quoted; but being well aware, from previous experience with Abdallah, that he would at once offer to produce it from Mecca, a challenge that politeness would prevent me from accepting, I pursued the theme no farther (although I noted the strategical advantages of a system of state archives alike remote and inaccessible to infidel enquiry). Before leaving I arranged to return on my way down to the ship and bid him good-bye. This I did at 2.30, taking with me the Staff Surgeon of H.M.S. *Dufferin,* who is an expert photographer, in the hope of securing a portrait. The Sharīf refused at first to pose and desired me instead to make various enquiries as to the nature of a small scar (which he was unable to show) upon his left knee. When I offered to leave the room to ensure his greater privacy he gave me something approaching a wink and said: "I only ask from civility." As he had remarked that he was of course unable to prevent people snapshotting him I directed the Staff Surgeon to take a couple straight off as he sat; and the involuntary sitter underwent the ordeal with remarkable *sang-froid.* On my departure he handed me a letter for the High Commissioner, embraced me twice and escorted me to the staircase; at the same time sending with me his A.D.C. and his private secretary to accompany me on board *Dufferin.* I was very much touched on reaching the quay to find a small guard of honour drawn up to see me off, and learnt with interest the variety of its composition, which included soldiers from Jaffa, Somak, Bukhara, Jerusalem, Baghdad and Abyssinia. I took leave here of Shaikh Sulaiman Qābel, with some other Notables, and returning direct to the ship, left for Yanbo at 4.30.

We reached Yanbo at 8 a.m. on the thirteenth, and I at once transhipped to H.M.S. *Lama,* at the same time advising Sharīf Faisal that I proposed visiting him at about 9. I gathered meanwhile that the state of things in and about Yanbo was far from satisfactory. Two days since, the Turks were within 15 miles of the town, and might have attacked that very night. Monitor *M. 31* (of whose arrival Colonel Wilson had not been advised) was standing close in to bombard them in case of necessity. The aircraft vessel *Raven* was at Yanbo and the seaplanes had been quite recently bombing the Turks. I found that the single trench, though technically an indifferent achievement, yet

---

[63] King Husain's letters may have been obscure but they seldom failed of the picturesque. "Regarding my sons, Abdallah is at Tayif still surrounding the Turks there. He preferred this to bloodshed while the Turks are like a lizard whose back is broken." Nor was Abdallah at all behind him. "I thank you, My Dear, for remembering me while I am at Wadi Ais and very few remember me. Your pleasure towards me for my success is in harmony with what the poet said:

'The eye of content is closed to every defect
While the eye of discontent will fasten upon all failure'.

May you live long and prosper. You are the origin of all the help given to the Arabs in their rise and the recovery of their nobility. I can say no more."

covered the plain across which the Turks must advance. By the 12th there had been a regular panic ashore, and many notables including Faisal had boarded H.M.S. *Hardinge*. The Turks moreover were reported closer still, some said within six miles, and in greater numbers than hitherto suspected. The Arabs had absolutely declined to hold the trench and were hoping that the ship's guns would command the plain.

I visited Sharīf Faisal about 9.15. The notice I had given him had apparently enabled him to crowd on every inch of silk in Yanbo, and I was immensely struck with his personal appearance which in fact realizes that of the legendary noble Arab. He was slightly thinner than I had been led to suppose, and I am informed that the anxieties of the last two months have really worn him down considerably. His youngest brother Zaid Bey was with him, and upon my pushing up his sleeve to see if he still wore the gold bracelet watch I gave him last June, confessed that a "stronger than he had forcibly taken it from him". (I learn from Rūhi that this stronger one is Abdallah, who has recently married a second wife.) After coffee and interchange of compliments Sharīf Faisal, whose mien generally is that of one chastened by failure, reiterated, but always in a minor key, the complaints he had made as to our delay in supplying the Artillery requested four months ago. He admitted that nothing was to be now gained by enlarging upon this grievance, and I took the opportunity of pointing out to him that, after the recent retreats, the courage of his Arab tribesmen stood in some need of vindication in the eyes of the world; even if they were for the moment unable to face their foes in the open field, their intimate knowledge of their own mountainous country should surely render them redoubtable enemies in guerilla warfare. Sharīf Faisal's first and last request, to which he several times reverted, was that the British should guarantee him the possession of Rābugh and Yanbo; with these two as bases upon which to fall back he would not hesitate to advance again upon the Turks and to take Wajh; it was the dread of being cut off that paralysed his strength. Before leaving I informed him of his father's decision with regard to Azīz Ali, and adjured him very earnestly to put his entire confidence in this officer, whose one object was the success of the Arab cause and with it the triumph of the Sharīfial Family. He promised with every appearance of sincerity to work loyally with Azīz, and I left him, strong in these protestations at about 10.15; rejoining H.M.S. *Lama*, which sailed for Suez at 11.30 a.m. and reached it at noon on Friday 15th.

The incoherent and spasmodic nature of Arab organization and operations is an additional proof, if such were needed, of the necessity of one supreme and independent control of the campaign; and as there appears to be no other Moslem who unites the various qualifications of Azīz Ali Bey, it is to be hoped that the Sharīf will have the courage and self-restraint to make his appointment a reality.

None of us realized then that a greater than Azīz was already taking charge.

IV

*Courage! build great works—'tis urging thee—it is ever nearest the favourites
of God—the fool knows little of it. Thou wouldst be joyous, wouldst thou?
then be a fool. What great work was ever the result of joy, the puny one?
Who have been the wise ones, the mighty ones, the conquering ones of this
earth? the joyous? I believe it not.*

GEORGE BORROW, *Lavengro*, chap. xviii.

Into friendship with T. E. Lawrence I know not how I entered; not at
first anyhow by direct official contact. I had never heard of him until the
winter of 1914, when he became a member of the Intelligence Branch of
the Egypt Defence Force and then suddenly it seemed I must have known
him for many years. Lawrence was of lesser medium stature and, though
slight, strongly built. His forehead was high; his face upright and, in
proportion to the back of the head, long. His yellow hair was naturally-
growing pre-War hair; that is parted and brushed sideways; not worn
immensely long and plastered backwards under a pall of grease. He had
a straight nose, piercing gentian-blue eyes, a firm and very full mouth, a
strong square chin and fine, careful, and accomplished hands. His Sam-
Brown belt was as often as not buckled loose over his unbuttoned shoulder strap, or he would forget to put it on at all. Once at least I had to
send my servant Ismain running with it after him into the street. Augustus John's first drawing is perfect of his Arab period; Kennington's
bronze in the crypt of St Paul's Cathedral gives the plastic and Homeric
simplicity of his lines and rhythm, and Howard Coster's photograph,
published in *The Illustrated London News* after his death, besides being
a good likeness hints somehow at the unhappiness latent behind the eyes.

Save for official purposes he hated fixed times and seasons. I would
come upon him in my flat, reading always Latin or Greek, with corresponding gaps in my shelves. But he put back in their proper places the
books he did not take away; of those he took he left a list, and never
failed to return them reasonably soon, in perfect condition. We had no
literary differences, except that he preferred Homer to Dante and disliked
my preference for Theocritus before Aristophanes. He loved music, harmony rather than counterpoint, and sat back against the cushions with
his eyes half-closed, enduring even that meandering stream of musical
consciousness which I dignified by the name of improvisation. Ismain
told me that Lawrence used to ask at the door if I was alone, and go
away if I was not, fearing (he told me when I complained) that he might
be let in for the smart "or" the boring—he meant "and", for the terms
with him were synonymous. He angered me once by failing (without

T. E. LAWRENCE

(From an unpublished drawing by Eric Kennington in All Souls' College, Oxford, reproduced by kind permission of the artist)

excuse) to appear at a dinner of four I had arranged for him; and only told me long afterwards that I had more than "got back on him" by explaining that I shouldn't have minded if he had only warned me in time to get somebody else.

He must, it seemed, gulp down all I could shed for him of Arabic knowledge, then bounded for him by the western bank of the Suez Canal; yet never by the "pumping" of crude cross-examination. I told him things sometimes for the mere interest of his commentary. He was eager and unfatigued in bazaar-walking and mosque-hunting. I found him from the beginning an arresting and an intentionally provocative talker, liking nonsense to be treated as nonsense, and not civilly or dully accepted or dismissed. He could flame into sudden anger at a story of pettiness, particularly official pettiness or injustice. Of all men then alive I think he trusted and confided most in D. G. Hogarth who, by making possible his Travelling Scholarship, had given him his first chance in life.

Shortly after the Arab Revolution we found that its success was being denied or blanketed by the enemy Press (which was of course quoted by neutrals), and we decided that the best proof that it had taken place would be provided by an issue of Hejaz postage stamps, which would carry the Arab propaganda, self-paying and incontrovertible, to the four corners of the earth. Sir Henry MacMahon was quick to approve; and the Foreign Office approved him. I had corresponded with King Husain on the project, and he sent me by return of mail a design purporting to typify Islamic architecture, but to the layman indistinguishable from the Eddystone Lighthouse. I felt this would never do, and wandered with Lawrence round the Arab Museum in Cairo collecting suitable motifs in order that the

design in wording, spirit and ornament, might be as far as possible representative and reminiscent of a purely Arab source of inspiration. Pictures and views were avoided, for these never formed part of Arab decoration, and are foreign to its art: so also was European lettering.

It was quickly apparent that Lawrence already possessed or had immediately assimilated a complete working technique of philatelic and three-colour reproduction, so that he was able to supervise the issue from start to finish. And it seemed only a few weeks before this Hittite archaeologist was on the most intimate terms with machine-guns, with tulip bombs, even with the jealously forbidden subtleties of a Rolls-Royce engine.[64]

These stamp designs (admirably carried out by the Survey Department of the Egyptian Government) drew him still more closely within the Arabian orbit and into meetings with some of my Egyptian friends, and

[64] There still exists the last motor-cycle he had built, never ridden, never delivered, carrying ten improvements, all invented by himself.

I noticed that he grew more and more eager for first-hand knowledge. I sent Rūhi to his office to pass on all he had discovered about the Hejaz; the tribes, routes, wells, and distances. At last he asked me point blank to take him down on my next voyage to Jeddah. Nothing from any point of view could have pleased me more, and permission from his military superiors was (as he has explained) granted almost with relief. He has recorded [65] our mutual hope as we proceeded through the streets of Jeddah, that the other had not perceived that the back of his jacket was dyed bright scarlet from the leather backs of the Gun-room chairs. When Abdallah quoted Faisal's telegram saying that unless the two Turkish aeroplanes were driven off the Arabs would disperse: "Lawrence remarked that very few Turkish aeroplanes last more than four or five days. . . ." [66] "Abdallah was impressed with his extraordinarily detailed knowledge of enemy dispositions" which, being temporary Sub-Lieutenant in charge of "distribution of the Turkish Army and preparation of maps", he was able to use with masterly effect. As Syrian, Circassian, Anatolian, Mesopotamian names came up, Lawrence at once stated exactly which unit was in each position, until Abdallah turned to me in amazement: "Is this man God, to know everything?" My journal records that "I reminded Abdallah of the permission I had that morning extracted, in his hearing, from the Grand Sharīf, for Lawrence to go up to Bir Abbas; and urged him to give L. letters of introduction to Ali and Faisal". Abdallah was now so firmly gripped by Lawrence's personality that he forthwith caused his father to write this eagerly desired letter of introduction to Faisal, [67] the letter that made his dream come true; and I can still see Lawrence three days later on the shore at Rābugh waving grateful hands as we left him there to return ourselves to Egypt. Long before we met again he had already begun to write his page, brilliant as a Persian miniature, in the History of England.

[65] On p. 66 of *Seven Pillars.*
[66] His telegram to the Arab Bureau, besides admirably resuming the discussion, foreshadows unambiguously his own plan, and future position:
"17th. For Clayton:
Meeting to-day: Wilson, Storrs, Sharīf Abdallah, Azīz al-Masri, myself.
Nobody knew real situation Rābugh so much time wasted. Azīz al-Masri going Rābugh with me tomorrow.
Sharīf Abdallah apparently wanted foreign force at Rābugh as rallying point if combined attack on Medina ended badly. Azīz al-Masri hopes to prevent any decisive risk now and thinks English Brigade neither necessary nor prudent. He says only way to bring sense and continuity into operation is to have English staff at Rābugh dealing direct with Sharīf Ali and Sharīf Faisal without referring detail to Sharīf of Mecca of whom they are all respectfully afraid. Unfortunately withdrawal of aeroplanes coincided with appearance of Turkish machines but Azīz al-Masri attaches little weight to them personally. He is cheerful and speaks well of Sharīf's troops."

[67] *Seven Pillars,* pp. 70 and 71. ". . . Storrs then came in and supported me with all his might. . . ."

CHAPTER NINE

1914–1917

Ah, yes, we're all brothers now—all Cains and Abels.

D. JERROLD

OUR first intimation that His Majesty's Government had adopted Kitchener's estimate of a minimum of three years for the War was the appointment in December 1914 of Sir Henry MacMahon as High Commissioner. I wrote to Lord Kitchener thanking him for all he had done for me, and received from him a characteristic "omnibus" acknowledgement.

"14 December 1914.
Dear Storrs,
    Thanks for your letter. I still look forward to the time when I shall be with you all again in Egypt. I am glad the attack on the Canal has been so well met—and dealt with. I am wiring Maxwell to send back some selected deserters to tell the others of what a splendid time they can have in Egypt if they come in. I hope you will give my best salaams to the Sultan and his Ministers and to all friends. I am too busy here to write letters so please ask all to excuse me. Fitz wrote to you about sending off some more things, the stone capital on the verandah, the statue in stable yard, I want for the garden at Broome.
    The war moves slowly but time is all in our favour. Yours very truly, Kitchener."

I can still see Sir Henry alighting from the train, still hear a leading Copt behind me repeating "His eye is kindly".

Sir H. M. the new High Commissioner arrived on Sat. and produced upon Egyptian and English alike an excellent impression. He lunched with me to-day in the flat. He is slight, fair, very young for 52, quiet, friendly, agreeable, considerate and cautious.

Many besides myself will remember the generous and charming hospitality of Lady MacMahon. Their task was indeed difficult, for although

the High Commissioner had already behind him a distinguished career
in India, where his Lady had shown herself an accomplished hostess, they
found themselves confronted with an unforeseen and unique situation set
in an atmosphere and tradition entirely strange to their experience.
Arabic and not their familiar Hindustani was the language of the Egyptians, whilst the numerous foreigners spoke, and thought, in French. In
place of the stately printed protocols and precedents of Calcutta or of
Simla, they had to grapple, officially and socially, with the haphazard
hand-to-mouth methods of a rule which had been until a few weeks since
almost ostentatiously provisional and which had committed hardly anything to paper, having governed in the beginning by interview and towards the end by telephone. The British system in Egypt had been a
mean between the *Hukum Hai*[1] of direct Indian administration and the
almost Byzantine technique which European Governments found necessary to maintain their prestige and privileges, their contracts and concessions, at the Sublime Porte. We deprecated the Imperative, preferring
the Subjunctive, even the wistful Optative mood. We "advised" Egyptian
Ministers. We "inspected" Egyptian Departments. It was to preserve this
system, understood and capable of infinite gradation in either direction,
that the British Agency had fought for the Protectorate as against Annexation. Nor was it in political matters, which the Protectorate left very
much where they had been for the last thirty years, nor in matters which
English people consider important, but in loss of social "face" that the
change of status was in those days principally felt. Who should call first
on whom, and if he did would his card be returned, were questions
which exasperated the hostile and unsettled the well-affected among
Egyptians and foreigners alike. Among English-speaking peoples the
leaving, even the returning of cards, is regarded (like hat-raising between
men) as a more or less comic survival of the ceremonious past. The practice is honoured by other civilized communities as being the accepted and
only obvious manner of initiating, extending, or reciprocating the social
courtesies. I am neither attacking nor defending when I record that few
of our measures adopted from 1915 onwards occasioned more deep and
universal dissatisfaction than the cessation of card returning to persons
leaving theirs or writing their names in the Residency Visitors' Book.
Nor shall I forget the expression of some of the Khedivial Princes when I
had to inform them that they were expected to pay the first call. *"Elchi
zarar yok"*—"No blame to the ambassador"—they may have said to me,
and meant it; but their lips trembled with indignation.

[1] "It's an order."

Sir Henry MacMahon had to face no more delicate, immediate, yet ultimately far-reaching problem than that of the Arab negotiations which had now entered upon their long and weary course. The *terrain* there was as foreign to him as the general Egyptian atmosphere; neither had he from Alexandria to Aswān one single officer of his own Service. Yet all who were privileged to work under him were struck with admiration for his faculty of making up his mind on great matters, of courageously taking decisions and of no less tenaciously maintaining them; and I noted that he never once obtruded Indian repercussions or other irrelevancies into major Near-Eastern issues. It had been well if some of those in England responsible for our policy up to and during the final Turkish settlement at Lausanne had proved equally impenetrable by this well-worn and discredited pan-Islamic bluff.[2]

Considering it anomalous that the Oriental Secretary should be not only non-pensionable and unpromotable but also junior to each new junior attaché from Scoones', Sir Henry MacMahon was good enough to move the Foreign Office to give me local diplomatic rank. They conferred upon me the dignity of a Second Secretary.[3]

It means of course nothing beyond *status* and *locus standi*, and I was a little bashful of announcing it, most Egyptians imagining me to be more than that. However, Cheetham published it in the Press Bureau, and drew to my dismay a cloud of blessings, couched for the most part in disappointed and anticipatory style from the Public.

The Residency made no further Royal Progresses of provincial inspection, being fully occupied by War duties towards our own people. The one week's holiday Sir Henry took was marred by ceremony.

Our Luxor visit was a change but not a rest, and may indeed be taken as a standard or model of how *not* to see such a place. We went about preceded by mounted police, flanked by Cavasses in red, and heavily bolstered by local officials in frock coats. Legrain—"the ghastly priest" of Karnak—poured upon us a mechanical stream of very second rate Baedeker, in which all objects are dated not so much A.D or B.C. as from the year in which he (Legrain) first scraped, altered or filled them up with pink-fleshing cement. Luxor is essentially a romantic and life-enhancing place, and I confess this treatment of it filled my soul with misery. The only bright spot was the entire absence of tourists. The shattering Winter Palace Hotel was shut, and we stayed at the Luxor.

The event of this week has been the arrival of the Prince of Wales. No one at all had been told by H.E. until last Saturday—and then only the Sultan—

---

[2] Incidentally Sir Henry MacMahon's successors (and his country) owe to his vision the purchase in 1916 of the Bacos property adjoining the Residency, which added the present commodious chancery and almost doubled the size of the garden.

[3] The Oriental Secretary now enjoys the local rank of First Secretary.

owing to stringent orders of secrecy. By Monday, however, Villiers, the new (and very *sympathique*) Attaché and I had worked the truth out by united deduction from the following data. 1. Cipher telegrams three weeks ago which H.E. (sweating blood) deciphered and enciphered himself. 2. Rumbling and hammering in bedroom over my head, followed by a punitive expedition upstairs in which I remarked a large (new or hired) *vitrine* of imitation Ming china installed in the small sitting-room. 3. Mysterious dispatch on Monday of Jimmy Watson to Alexandria, no explanation being given. 4. Murray's Military Secretary asking Villiers when "the young man" was arriving, and being asked what young man, replying that he meant a General from Salonika.

Before we knew where we were, we found ourselves under the fascination of that quick, human directness acclaimed later by the Empire and the world. It was my honourable duty to show His Royal Highness something of the bazaars and of Egyptian Cairo, and never have I piloted any person who entered more swiftly into the spirit of the place.

Yesterday morning I took him up the minaret of Sultan Hassan afterwards on foot from the Moayyad mosque through the Moroccan and scent bazaars up to the final altitude of Jack Cohen, incognito throughout and consequently obtaining a maximum of incidents and general *jouissance*. He enjoyed the bazaars vastly.

I had suggested to the Prince that at his first visit he should offer Jack about one-tenth of the price quoted for any object produced. When a fifty-pound Qubba rug elicited no more than a tentative four pounds then Jack let himself go; it was all very well for Mr Storrs to criticize the stock, but if every subaltern in the British Army—then really—; the Prince listening spell-bound by the invective.

But the Bazaars cannot be visited twice incognito by a Prince of Wales, and at our second descent we were followed, until I let loose a zealous Shawish,[4] by a crowd of 200 scalliwags.

Jack realized the horror of his situation; yet, when I hinted that he would not have talked as he had if he had known to whom he was talking, he replied glibly that he had known all the time, but had felt it his duty to respect His Royal Highness's desire to remain unknown.

At the Palace he scored a great and genuine success, from H.H. himself to the lowest chamberlain.

Having occasion some six weeks later to return to Cohen's I was surprised to find facing me on the top of a high pile of carpets a parcel, addressed in large block lettering to

4 Police Sergeant.

HER MAJESTY QUEEN MARY,
BUCKINGHAM PALACE,
LONDON, S.W. I.

I rebuked Jack for this unconscionable delay: he had promised to dispatch the Prince's presents by the next post. "I did", he shouted in friendly defiance, "Of course I did"; and then, dropping his voice as not quite so sure of himself: "This is a dummy—for the advertisement."

Returning later from my first Red-Sea voyage, I was privileged to join His Royal Highness at the Atbara and to travel on his Dahabia from Wadi Halfa to Luxor. Like the members of his suite, I was amazed by the amount of exercise he took on a minimum diet. We reached Abu Simbel on a burning forenoon, and, having visited the stupendous temple, considered that we had earned our repose, when the Prince declared he must have a run. He refused to let any of us accompany him, and set out in khaki shirt and shorts escorted by four tall Sudanese Guards, born to heat and bred to hardship, speeding into the Libyan Desert in the direction of Morocco. After an interval of some two hours I watched from the deck the return of the expedition. Four black figures, gasping and sweating, staggered across the sand after a fair leader who looked precisely the same as he had when he started, and who hesitated before accepting as a pick-me-up a split soda and fruit juice.

Turco-German airmen little knew what they were missing when the Canal yacht *Aigrette* sailed northwards from Ismailia carrying the Commander-in-Chief of "Egypt Force", the Commander-in-Chief of the Mediterranean, the High Commissioner for Egypt, the Viceroy Designate of India, and the Heir to the Throne. But some apprehension must have struck the Military Authorities, for later "he left for Italy preceded by a destroyer on the sea and a plane in the air, bombs having been dropped in Port Said the previous week". It was with more than a regret for departing Royalty that we bade farewell to the Prince in *Weymouth* at Port Said. In a varied experience of Cairo vistors I have met none with equal vitality or with more appreciation of Eastern life. When I returned to the flat: *"Báyyin aláih ibn Málek"*, said Ismain—"it is clear upon him that he is the son of a King. He remembered that my name was *Ismain,* and", looking at Said, "caused *me* to hold his overcoat."

I was sent to Aden in 1915; partly at the request of Admiral Wemyss, who had obtained permission for me to accompany him down the Red Sea as Political Officer, and partly to give me a chance of learning a little of the Arab situation 1300 miles away, and to see some of the places and people about whom we were perpetually drafting notes and dispatches. Every cabin in *Euryalus* was over-bespoke and I slept for the first (and I trust the last) time in an unlighted and unventilated casemate. There was a certain amount of work after which I played chess with the Admiral or with the Chief Engineer. (Throughout my journeys by steamer, it was always the Captain, the Chief, and the Chief Medical Officer that had the courage of their high brows.) At Aden there had been a regrettable incident. Our garrison was confronted by the Turks at Saikh Said, by other enemies and by a number of doubtfuls; we had one friend, the Sultan of Lahaj, whom I had met in Cairo. During the alarum of a Turkish attack, our troops had been sent to defend Lahaj, and a mettlesome (but unknown) warrior, observing a suspicious character on the Palace balcony, shot the Sultan dead. We had plenty to do in the way of interviews, conferences and their recording, quite apart from this inadjustable affair.

Easiest yet most practical of Chairmen, Admiral Wemyss kept rigidly to the point the General Officer Commanding Aden, the Senior Naval Officer of the Red Sea Patrol, the Political Resident, and one or two others, while we discussed Safety of traffic in the Red Sea, Destruction of enemy guns, Prevention of enemy agents crossing the Red Sea, Co-operation between Naval and Military Forces, Political Officers for ships and (what I have tried to advance wherever I have served) Interchange of Political Officers. I have no doubt whatever that if the officers behind the Arab Campaign in the Hejaz had been allowed to exchange awhile with, or even to meet their colleagues from the Persian Gulf, well before instead of long after the Arab Revolution, they could have effected an intense concentration of purpose and a sure economy of many thousands of pounds. Even had there been no other object of interest at Aden, it would have been negatively instructive to examine and analyse the effects upon a small and poor strip of land of being administered collectively and severally, by the War Office, the Colonial Office and the Bombay Government.

No Senior Officer, British or foreign, I met produced so favourable an impression upon society in Cairo, from Abdīn Palace to Mahomet Ali Club, as Admiral Wemyss. This effect was due not only to the charm of his manner, the brilliance of his monocle, his perfect command of French in the drawing-rooms of Kasr al-Dubara, not only to his tact (often a function of hard head rather than of soft heart), but also to an unstudied natural delicacy of disposition.

Several other men of outstanding personality passed through Cairo during the War. Like Lawrence they were not necessarily of the highest

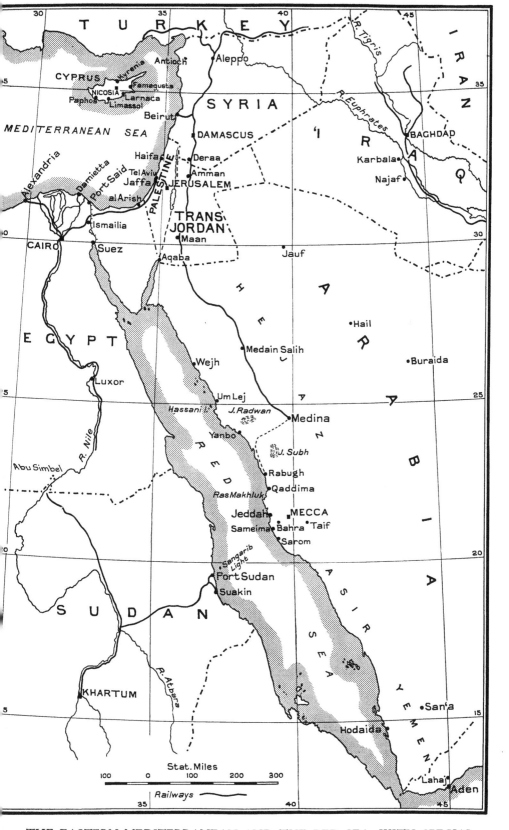

1. THE EASTERN MEDITERRANEAN AND THE RED SEA, WITH SPECIAL
REFERENCE TO CHAPTER IX

civil or military rank. Two, long since gone, still inspire me with affectionate regret. Mark Sykes could have made a reputation in at least half a dozen careers. He was one of those few for whom the House of Commons fills, and he could hardly have failed to become an Under-Secretary, perhaps a Secretary of State. As a caricaturist and political cartoonist he could have imposed his own terms upon the evening Press; as may be seen from "Foreign Office Attitudes" and other specimens reproduced in his Biography by Shane Leslie. These were struck off instantaneously, at white heat, upon the nearest scrap of paper, with rich gurgling at each evocation. The same vein of artistry would transform him into a first-class music-hall comedian; holding a chance gathering spell-bound by swift and complete changes of character, or speaking into my dictaphone a twenty-minutes' Parliamentary Debate (for which I supplied the interruptions), with the matter as well as the manner of such different speakers as Lloyd George, F. E. Smith, John Redmond or Sir Edward Carson rendered with startling accuracy: "I speak on behalf of the God-fearing, Bible-reading, bearded men of the North of Ireland, whose only and least demand is to obtain without further delay the full measure of their requirements..." the noble tones would peal. Mark also dictated for the same instrument a three-act Drury Lane Melodrama, I providing the incidental music and he every other detail, including the trotting of horses, cracking of whips, crash of railway accidents and discharge of revolvers. He could have become a good high comedy or tragic actor and he was an excellent and entertaining writer.

Mark has left for Aden. It did me good to hear this seasoned soldier and politician cry to his retainer: "Sergt Wilson! Will you bring me my Shakespeare?" to remind me of an agreeable conceit in the drunken scene from *Antony and Cleopatra*.

Aubrey Herbert, with something indefinable of Shelley in his crystal, unearthly goodness, resembled Mark in the sympathy and interest he felt and aroused among Orientals, and also in running him hard for being, after Lawrence, the untidiest officer in Egypt. He was tender for unlikely objects of affection, such as Albanians, Laz's and Kurds. Kurds, he was at pains to explain to a sceptical audience, abounded in unknown merits —were indeed almost an ideal race. "Yes, Aubrey", answered FitMaurice of Constantinople, who had been in contact with these paragons for some thirty years, "Yes; a remarkable race. I don't know of any race I'd sooner have to help me—in a surprise attack on unarmed peasants."

As one of the minor features of Cairo still remembered by many, how can I omit the Palladian façade of Jones, butler to the MacMahons at the

Residency? He had come with lofty ideals (like most ideals, not always maintained) from the Embassy at Constantinople; a training which had given him not only confidence but initiative in the interpretation of his duties. He disapproved the consumption of liquor by unmarried women, making exceptions neither for family nor guests; and I used to watch for their expressions when, having been offered champagne, claret, hock or whisky, and having chosen champagne, they found their glasses firmly filled with barley-water. We were leaving one night for a dinner at the Palace when Jones stepped forward and "ventured to suggest to her Ladyship 'a *leetle* less powder for the left nostril' ".

In the Spring of 1916:

> I realized that unless someone took the necessary steps, the tercentenary of Shakespeare would probably pass quite unnoticed in this country; I therefore began an elaborate campaign which has, I rejoice to say, been not altogether unsuccessful. I telephoned to the Bishop, C. MacInnes, suggesting he should work the thing into his Easter Sermon. Similar injunctions through the Coptic Patriarchate obtained an honourable mention (as they say in Horse Shows) from every Coptic pulpit in the realm; I next binged up the Minister of Education to the tune of a memorial lecture in every school, and finally telephoned to the English, French, Italian, Greek, Arabic and Armenian press; provoking a flow of leading articles, prize poems, and enthusiastic correspondence, the back-wash of which continues even now to clog my leisure. These are, at least, better than no notice at all, and I will I hope give to an undiscerning world the impression that an interest in such things exists in Egypt.

The Science of War propaganda dates, I suppose, from no earlier than 1914. We therefore had no sort of text-book upon which to base our methods. All we knew was that careful and progressive handling of public opinion was no less difficult than necessary among peoples of alien race, language and religion. Articles, diagrams and caricatures effective in Europe often produce a negative, sometimes even a contrary, result in the East. Some of the most repulsive excited admiration rather than horror. The best way seemed to be to try them on acquaintances. I found Raemakers' cartoons hardly ever failed, and had recourse to the assistance of the *Mokattam,* in whose illustrated edition—*al-Látaif al-Musáwwara*—an effective series soon appeared.[5]

I had not much previous experience of the Army, and found All Ranks enchanting.

> I continue to get great amusement from listening to conversations between Tommies, especially Australians and Egyptians. They "get on", with a sort of ferocious badinage, exceedingly well. I heard a slightly inebriated corporal

---

[5] See p. 185, chap. VII and p. 224, chap. X.

reply to a well-meaning Bey who showed him his gold ring, "Yes, Very good. Now in England, you know, a gold ring like that would be turned out of a brass foundry", etc., etc., to the delight of a mixed assembly of Dagos and Sudanese, that hardly understood a word, but showed a rich appreciation. "*Wallâhi M'akâr*"—"By God, a prudent man".

1915 and 1916 brought home to the British in Egypt the high hopes and cumulative anguish of Gallipoli. After the first naval assault we had so advertised our military intention as to convince some of my neutral friends (but alas none of the enemy) that we must be feinting for Alexandretta.

One of the most impressive scenes I have ever witnessed in this country took place at Alexandria last Monday, when in the presence of about 15,000 French troops, colours were given to two Regiments. Ian Hamilton, who represents extraordinarily well, was in chief command; with General d'Amade on his left tactfully alluding to him before the troops as *Mon Chef*. The soldiers marched admirably in their brilliant if suicidal uniforms, and I felt as if I was looking at a coloured print of about 1820. The *Chasseurs d'Afrique* in light blue tunics about the length of Eton jackets and crimson riding breeches were exceptionally magnificent; and though individually each soldier looked smaller than the British Tommy, they were certainly no less imposing in the mass. The inhabitants of Ramleh and other suburbs of Alexandria doubtless remarked the reverse of the medal when they arose in the morning to find their gardens as bare as the backs of their hands: a comparison which was noted in favour of our Tommies who had committed no such depredations.

The review would have been even more appropriate and impressive if the gallant forces had been returning in triumph from the assault and fall of Constantinople. Stories even more irritating than tragic added to the Saga of the *gâchis de Gallipoli*.

A Colonel fresh from Mudros told me that the last two things he observed there, were a case of 40 new bicycles left in the open, their lamps stolen, fast congealing into a solid mass of rust, for which no one was responsible; and a vessel which had brought a thousand tons of drinking-water from Liverpool and had been ordered to get rid of it, and forbidden by the Admiralty to pump it into one of the other ships which needed it, pouring it overboard into the Mediterranean.

Nevertheless, so confident were we of taking Constantinople that I was instructed to order myself a khaki uniform, largely as a result of a note which I had submitted for "Civil action after the entry of the troops", complete with suggestions for Staff, badges, passes, and liaison arrangements with the Allied Forces—now pathetic reading.

In my eagerness I wrote to Colonel FitzGerald:

Ronald Graham has spoken to H.E. with a view to his sending me on this mission, which may not take place for some time yet, and might I suppose last a fortnight or three weeks. I have been six times to Constantinople, and in close touch with the Embassy and other persons there for the last six years, and have besides a certain knowledge of Turkish.

There would have been no reason why I should not have been absent for two or three weeks, for

with the absence of the Khedive, Turkish High Commissariat and German Agency, with no General Assembly, no politics and a press muzzled by military censorship, there is comparatively little urgent work for an Oriental Secretary for the moment. We are in a period of stagnation, save for the legal authorities who are finding with delight new problems every day.

Alexandria had to witness, not a victorious return, but steady relays of Hospital Liners freighted with hopeless heroism; with glory, save of the spirit, unachieved. The schools and great hotels became an infinite series of sick bays round which we walked with books, newspapers and cigarettes, amid a cloud of suffering fortitude, and strange terribly true stories. The best Egyptian cigarettes (that is, the best cigarettes in the world) were accepted with pathetic gratitude, but "I suppose you've not such a thing as a Woodbine, sir?"—the War thus marking the great reversal of the smoking tradition of my youth, when you apologized for offering a "straighter" or a "gasper" to a presumably fastidious palate. (During my leave in 1907 I had acted as Secretary to the Selection Board of Egypt and Sudan Civil Service. There were more than a hundred candidates for some half-dozen vacancies, and the attractions of the Service were still so strong that, after seeding out all those who were neither Firsts, Blues, nor Perfect Characters, there still remained over a score to be yet further reduced. The ingenuity of the Under-Secretary for Finance devised and we applied (what was then considered) a social test. As the applicant advanced, one of the Assessors, clapping his hand unsuccessfully to his breast pocket, would ask him for a cigarette. His fate hung upon his taste, for if he offered a Virginia he was ploughed. The memory, trifling in itself, is yet illustrative of a change in fashion which must have deflected from Near-Eastern into Far-Western pockets many millions of pounds.)

We descended for the summers of the War upon the large, ornate and convenient Villa Zervudaki in Ramleh:

Alexandria is half camp and half hospital. The harbour fuller than I ever remember to have seen it; but of Transports and Hospital ships. Muslims four years old stand upon heaps of coal and vociferate Tipperary with perfect accuracy of time and accent, for half piastres flung them by departing warriors. The Jews are playing up admirably all round the wicket, as are the Greeks and Syrians. And there is need, for the beach is dotted with wounded, in large Gainsborough hats and white linen drawers.

Nor were the wounded the only bathers. Alexandria had never known such a season, and there was hardly standing room at Stanley Bay and Glymenopoulo—⁶ a necessary glitter of merriment against the increasingly grim silhouette of Gallipoli. The Higher Command that year thought otherwise.

.Some feeling here because G.H.Q. has stopped dancing and racing. No loss to me, since I have attended none of the first since the beginning of the War, and the last Never. But I think hard on youths up for two days after two months in the Sinai: and possibly impelling them to worse.

I have brought back with me from Cairo a large bundle of English and French novels. The unhappy French officers complain bitterly that they are restricted to such diet as *Sans Famille* and *Les Petits Enfants de Meg*, and that their recovery is thereby retarded. I am supplying them with a very different diet—who knows with what effect?

For my own War reading I found, as the popularity of *The Times Broadsheets* proved, that the essential was, remoteness from actuality. Henry James, by his sublime irrelevance to the general agony, provided escape, civilization—almost intelligence.

My greatest acquisition is some realization of his extraordinary greatness. Since Desdemona dropped her handkerchief, no one has managed to extract such thrills out of the apparently unimportant. My other refuge is William Blake—the first or the second childhood (it does not matter which) of William Shakespeare.

Difficulty was found in directing or rather deflecting the energies of high official and military wives from the Capital. They were indeed willing enough, but

Alexandria society is torn by Red Cross rivalries and jealousies: the so-called "intrusion" and "interference" of Cairo ladies is resented; so much so that they complain they are allowed to do nothing, though there is an admitted shortage of nurses. These squabbles over pain and maiming are pitiful: but I hope in a fair way to be composed.

Arabia continued in the forefront of our thoughts.

1. vii. 16. Ramadan. On Wed. I went up to Cairo for the day with Sir H. for a conference on the Arabian question at G.H.Q. Though we travelled both ways by special, without stopping, in just over 2½ hours, the experience is exhausting, and should not be repeated too frequently. Now comes a request

⁶ Then the two best known bathing places.

from the General that I should lecture on Arabia to the troops: and, two days later, a wire from F. O. suggesting that I should write a life of Lord K. in Arabic.

I complied with the first only.

Meanwhile Port Said is swamped by Armenian refugees, dumped upon us from Cilicia by French battleships. They are fighting the Turks very bravely. Which reminds me, disabuse your pen of the phrase, Good Old Turks, etc. If the massacres of Urfa and Adana were not enough, let the present horrors suffice to erase from our political vocabulary the false and foolish legend of the "First Gentleman in Europe."

Few of us realized then that these unfortunate refugees, who gave an infinity of trouble [7] to the British responsible for their camps to their local compatriots and to each other, were the heroes of one of the major exploits of the War, The Forty Days of Musa Dagh.[8]

In Alexandria I nearly lost my life by what I suppose may be termed a collateral War risk.

Enclosed sub-comic cutting (repeated throughout English and Arab press) relates a real incident. I was returning from a blameless musical evening in Alexandria, by a one-horse (in the fullest sense of the term) cab, when an open taxi, travelling towards us at 40–50 miles an hour, tried to pass a rival, miscalculated the distance and took us fair on the near front wheel. Though I saw the thing advancing upon me, I never doubted it would miss us, and it was to my astonishment, more than any other sensation, that the lamps swelled up to suns in my eyes, that I heard and felt a crash, and found myself sitting in the road, surrounded apparently by 20,000 boxes of matches and curiously observing the driver, who was carrying out a series of complicated evolutions resembling handsprings and cartwheels into the adjoining ditch. There remained of the cab practically nothing, save the shafts and the horse, to indicate its original use. The chauffeur, a Greek, came up white and shaky, and seemed almost relieved to hear my frank *exposé* of his, his nation's and his ancestresses' shortcomings. The car had lost all four wheels, screen broken and engine wrecked. Within, two Syrians, a little blurred, and two Perfect Ladies, were urging the driver to proceed, At Once, unaware, until I informed them, that their axles were on the ground. All trams having ceased, and no cabs being in view, I was addressing myself gloomily to slog the three miles on my flats, when a huge car rolled in from the distance. I stopped it and found to my delight my friend Omar Pasha Sultan (the original of Barudi in *Bella Donna*) homeward bound after a few hours' Missionary Lotto at the Club: and in five

---

[7] I noted of these, as later of some of their compatriots and some of the Jews, in Palestine, that a people can be at once bitterly wronged and yet withal so maddeningly tiresome as sometimes to annihilate surprise, though never regret, for their sufferings. The Armenian community of Cyprus was constantly rent by intestine disturbances, occasioned chiefly by an obscure agitator with the distinction, perhaps unique, of having been expelled from the Club of which he was not only President, but Founder.

[8] I am amazed that Werfel's epic novel, thus entitled, and admirably translated from the German, is not better known in England.

minutes was within the Residency Garden. The Sultan sent his Grand Chamberlain on Tuesday to enquire, but I was in Cairo for the day and missed him.

The War was a chance to take advantage of the virtual cessation of imports into Egypt, and there was held in Alexandria an Exhibition of Egyptian Industries. Building, furniture and the decorative arts were naturally included and I was permitted to suggest the preparation and furniture of a *Mandara* (an Egyptian reception room) which was to be, as I explained in Arabic, English and French pamphlets, "so far as possible, and consistent with a modern standard of comfort, Egyptian in idea, Egyptian in manufacture, and Egyptian in material".

The Exhibition attracted considerable attention, largely I fear because of the absence of counter-attraction. Its merits and defects were so characteristic of this sort of venture throughout the Near and Middle East that I am tempted to quote one paragraph from the review I wrote at the time for *The Egyptian Gazette:*

Although the foreign and European industries merit a most careful inspection, it is naturally to the Egyptian art and crafts that we devoted most of our attention. The *Filatures Égyptiennes* present a brilliant exhibition of their dyed cottons, whose beauty is largely enhanced by the fact that the firms are (mercifully) unable to procure German aniline dyes. For a general negative example we would like to take Class 18, Embroidery and Lace, which appears to present in a space of about 5 metres almost every conceivable artistic heresy. Why for instance was nobody by to warn Khālid Abd al-Hamīd of Alexandria that he should, to begin with, have nothing to do with pink satin; that if that were the last piece of material in the world he should not embroider upon it; and that if he were forced on threat of instant death to do this, he should not have adopted for his design an ancient Egyptian lady with a lotus flanked by two figs with birds' heads growing out of her chin?

So far as I have been able to ascertain, the cumulative effects of this attempt, as of others, to preserve Egyptian art and industry may be estimated at precisely Nil.

After the evacuation of Gallipoli, still said by many to have been effected just when the enemy despaired, Egypt became once more the focus of attraction; and what with the Egyptian Army, the Army of Occupation, the Canal Defence Force, the Egyptian Expeditionary Force, the Depôts and Training Centres, the Arab Bureau (controlling the Hejaz Campaign), the known and the unknown Intelligence Bureaux, and the great Hospital Units, local accommodation began to be tried to the uttermost. Yet, apart from the frictions and pin-pricks resulting from divided and sometimes ill-defined authority, affecting after all but few persons, the only comparative hardship endured by the civil population was the delays and difficulties of travelling in the Canal Zone owing to its control by passes to prevent espionage. There was no shortage of food, though there were occasional petrol famines, and coal went to £8 a ton; sport, racing, and dances for civilians continued, as described at the beginning of the War, until its end. I clung to my Wednesday Musics, so long as I remained in Cairo, reinforced often by varied accessions of War talent; and had once, after a Brahms evening, to prefer the room to the company of two visitors who objected to the use of the German language. (On the other hand Saad Pasha Zaghlūl, the future dictator, began so serious a study of German that I would greet him at the Residency in Arabic as *"Herr Bārūn"*.)

At the end of 1916 Sir Henry MacMahon was somewhat brusquely succeeded—*e il modo ancor m'offende*—by Sir Reginald Wingate, himself to receive similar treatment in a few years. Sir Reginald had long and intimate knowledge of Egypt; he also had an able Secretary of his own, and I, remembering Gorst's relations with the Oriental Secretary he had inherited from Cromer, felt, though a trifle *désorienté,* no sort of surprise or grudge at the immediate diminution of my own duties and position. Nevertheless, when it was decided that a Political Officer should be appointed from Egypt to represent the Egyptian Expeditionary Force in Mesopotamia, and the post was offered to me, I am prepared to admit that it came not altogether unwelcome.

In the midwinter of 1916-17 my father, now over seventy, made the voyage out to Egypt and thence to Cyprus as Messenger of the Archbishop of Canterbury, and I had the privilege of seeing more of him than had been possible since my earliest youth. The end of his visit had been for both of us clouded by the telegram on a night in March announcing the sudden death of Harry Cust.

CHAPTER TEN

Baghdad

April 15th-July 16th 1917

Many a sheeny summer-morn
Adown the Tigris I was borne
By Bagdats shrines of fretted gold,
High-walled gardens green and old.

TENNYSON

MILITARY G.H.Q. in Mesopotamia, which included Political G.H.Q., had been established in Baghdad ever since its capture from the Turks in March, 1917. My journey from Cairo to Baghdad, now a short day's flight, took me by the swiftest way then available one month; there being nothing more direct than Suez, Aden, Bombay, Karachi, the Persian Gulf, the Tigris and Basra; or four thousand miles instead of the eight hundred, had I been a crow.

Throughout my three months' absence from Egypt I received, owing to the mismanagement of my mails, not one single letter. The changes and chances of the journey, to me the opening of a new world, were recorded in the longest of my War Diaries, which, having been written mainly as a record for my mother in England, has escaped destruction. The fresh imprint of the Middle East immediately after our capture of Baghdad; of close association with Sir Percy Zachariah Cox—"Cokkus"— for a decade the outstanding Englishman of the Gulf; of the charm, knowledge and enthusiasm of Gertrude Bell; of what might have been a great adventure—broken by the Sun—will I hope prove my sufficient excuse for continuing the practice of direct though severely pruned quotation of original documents.

15 APRIL 1917. P. and O. *Nankin,* built 1888, Indian Ocean. I left Cairo 6.15, last Sunday 8th, and was seen off from Ismailia by Admiral Wemyss, who put me under the protection of Captain Dugmore, on his way to com-

mand the Mesopotamia Gunboats; with whom and Knox, besides Snagg, S.N.O. Suez, I finished the dreary midnight journey to Suez. Slept Mt. Sinai Hotel, and telephoning next day to Residency learnt that I should receive no home mails, thus losing all touch with Europe for five weeks. We left Suez at 1 p.m. Monday, and did not reach Aden until 11 a.m. Saturday, all lights being covered the last two nights as a precaution against the Raider.[1] At Aden Venning, A.D.C. to General Stewart, came aboard with launch to take me up to stay at the Residency. Went ashore with him and General Tighe and talked with Jacob.[2] Said, who although faring sumptuously hates the sea, keeps telling me how much better it would be to take the train direct from Aden. Across to R.N.O. in hope of quicker cut to Basra, and rejected his alternatives of (*a*) Admiralty oil steamer leaving in five days, and taking eight, (*b*) small military paddle leaving at once and, at six knots, doing the trip in fourteen. Said overcome by sight of camels drawing carts and generally contemptuous of everything not Egyptian or English. Lunched at Residency with Gen. Stewart, a cordial man. Jacobs says we could and should clear out the Turks [3] at once, being numerically superior to them and almost equal in guns; their shells being old and inferior. (This view was not allowed at the Residency.) He was instructive and amusing upon the anger and dismay at Simla, June 1916, when the news of the Arab revolt came through; their closetings in Vice-Regal Lodge, and their predictions of risings all over India.

19 APRIL 1917. P. and O. *Nankin*. Yesterday a boat drill in belts (more belts than boats, which were not even loosed on the davits). Said terrified, but mustered a pale grin.

I instruct some of the sparks of the Flying Corps in chess—son of Rector of Maidstone, a Canadian from Saskatchewan, Captain Larkin of H.M.S. *Doris* and others. Impressed by one Odell, a chartered accountant of Birmingham: a good skull and well hung on the vertebrae. Incredible knowledge of London pubs and tea-shops.

22 APRIL 1917. On the evening of the 19th I went to bed, where observed a steamer showing full lights that watched, stood by, and finally followed us for about an hour, causing many distinct pringles. *Ex hypothesi* there was nothing to say she was not the Raider save her innocuousness, and this we had to take on trust until she disappeared. Late breakfast with one *X*, pessimistic for the War, though for everything concerning himself optimist· *convaincu*. Had been sunk in the *Arabia*, the experience of which was as nothing to that of two days on the exposed deck of a trawler foodless in the rain and cold. On arrival at Bombay I very much regretted having no passport nor telegrams of recommendation, the latter crucially necessary for India. On landing drove with Captains Knox, Larkin and Dugmore to R.N.O. Offices in the Docks. Paymaster Hughes, in charge, failing to appear, I took one of the myriad Goanese clerks that pullulate in that rabbit-warren, and drove to the Secretariat (mid-Victorian Gothic, but a good lift) where I find Jukes (President of the Pembroke Debating Society) a Dana Gibson type of head, in charge. He received me friendly, and gave me notes to the Secretary of the Yacht

[1] Probably the *Wolf*, a German armed merchantman, which got from Germany to New Zealand and back, accounting for thirteen Allied vessels.
[2] Political Officer. Foremost living authority on Aden.
[3] Turkish garrison across the bay at Shaikh Othmān.

Club (for room) and Director of Embarkations. Wrote out passport-form and returned to R.N.O. where Hughes had now appeared and let drop in the course of conversation that the British India *Linga* was just starting. Stung by the urgency of my look he rang up the Company. Stopped boat, arranged for my passage and bespoke me a swift launch, to which, it being now past three, we ran in the heat, I falling heavily over a rope very nearly off the quay. The launch proved a gigantic and abnormally slow tug: however, I recovered my luggage from the Customs, and went the tour of the harbour to find *Linga*, turbine 980 tons, casting loose. Boarded her with some difficulty, hot, dirty, shaken from my fall and put out; not at all certain I had done the most intelligent thing in this forced and literal interpretation of my speed instructions, and rather regretting to have seen nothing of Bombay, until I observed the name of the largest hospital ship we passed, and found it to be *Syria,* which I took for an omen of right, δέξιος ὄρνις. Two women passengers who never came up, a supercilious and uncommunicative Staff Major who silenced me with the sword Simla, and a good-natured Australian B.I. Captain, the only others at Captain's table. To my surprise we went with all our lights blazing. Distance to Karachi 500 miles at 14½ knots. Began with a swell that developed into an early monsoon, which played cup and ball with the ship and, finally, my interior. Endured, but regretted having endured, luncheon. Said completely vanquished: agreed that the excess of meat with which I daily reproached him on the *Nankin* had "got him back in the eye". During the second night an Arab recommended him onion as an anti-nauseac. He ate of it, and "vomited till the morning as it had been *Zift* (Pitch)". Reached Karachi 10 a.m. Sunday 22nd, convoyed into the channel: where observed with dismay the smallness and generally superior wretchedness of the hulk destined to take us up the Persian Gulf.

23 APRIL 1917. At Karachi the tide began to turn for a while in my favour. Whilst moodily surveying my luggage, and debating whether to leave it aboard and return for the night, or descend at the *Carlton* Hotel (yes), I was accosted by a brisk and agreeable Eurasian (I heard an officer, a little confused with official instructions that these are to be styled Anglo-Indians, call one a Uric-Indian) with a message from the Commissioner, inviting me to stay at Government House. Stepped into a car with him, Said and my luggage, and was driven four miles to the pleasant old-fashioned colonnaded Residency, which bears outside a marble tablet to the effect that Sir Charles Napier, Conqueror and Governor of Seind, lived here. Changed and bathed in an old marble bath and joined Lawrence, the Resident, and his wife, at tiffin. He a descendant of the great L.'s: pleasant, quiet. She of the Napier family: tall, fair, has written a number of novels and sings soprano. Both all hospitality, leaving me till five to myself. The decorative livery of the servants with their great turbans, though obviously far cheaper, is infinitely superior to the tarbushed vulgarity of the smart Egyptian *suffragi* [4]—so much so that even Said offered to wear one in Egypt if I gave it him. Their beards moreover give them a virility of appearance which I do not think is borne out by fact: and I should say the Egyptian is physically the stronger being. Lawrence drove me round very slowly in his Fiat. At once impressed by the number, size and quality of the roads, and understand Kitchener's

[4] Butler.

insistence upon their extension in Egypt. Public and private buildings of good unstuccoed brown sandstone, and a happy absence of the dreadful *château, style Arabe* and *art nouveau,* which combine to make modern Cairo and Alexandria two of the ugliest cities on the earth. On the other hand a provinciality, a Khartum atmosphere, a lack of the feeling of a capital. Efficient but excruciating motor-trams: every time a gear is changed a sound as of machinery in process of violent evisceration. Several Indian cricket games in process: Lawrence says the Parsees are exceedingly good: Egyptians have never taken to this and I for one applaud their abstention. A rather rudimentary Moslem football match. Most agreeable sacred cows and bulls loafing upon the charity of the pious. One cow charged our car and only the accelerator saved the radiator from a sharp goring. Hospitals and churches numerous. Motors and one-horse cabs; a few rather pretentious landaus. Wonderful diversity from different castes, and in lower classes practically no harem-veils, a silly slavery I was glad to miss. Lawrence showed me the club and the Gymkhana women's club where I saw for the first time elaborately marked Badminton courts on matting, with electric light enabling enthusiasts to indulge in this passionate sport All Through The Night. Large numbers of side-cars. I find Indian hours difficult at first. Breakfast 10.30, and then nothing at all till five. But I think the arrangement which gives one the best hours of the day for play, instead of, as in Egypt, for work, is probably better. Slept, not very well, under punkah to whose whirring and plunging I am not yet accustomed. Early next morning a note to the effect that the *Dwarka,* for Basra, had two more cases of plague and would be delayed a week. I learnt, by the help of an I.C.S. Coventon, that the Horse Transport *Ula* would leave at dawn next day, and proceed at a maximum of 10 knots by every small port on the Persian Coast. Wired to S.N.O. Bombay in faint hope of some brilliant alternative, and out in car to a small novel-y bookshop, whence to an old wandering Molla who had a little brass and china of no particular merit. To Docks to choose cabin on *Ula,* which I found regorging with cows and calves, and the consequent black columns of flies. At 6.45 in car with Lawrence to desert, where their dog-cart awaited them and took us to a rocky point from which we saw the sun go down in a grape-foam of bubbling frothy clouds. I ran ahead with the three great bull-terriers. At dinner a fatigued refined judge, and a Bengali couple. He army doctor, she in golden national costume, a good type of dusky beauty, especially in profile. Attractive, and forthcoming in a pretty voice.

25 APRIL 1917. Aboard *Ula* by 7.15 and left Karachi punctually at eight, putting back our clocks one hour. Deriving much pleasure from Mr Smith, a delightful little successful military tailor and cutter, whose anecdotes of the Court of India, and the scale and quality upon which these Potentates order their uniforms and underlinen, are beyond praise. Spied a great whale playing and spouting on port bow. Food a little difficult, and bathroom not much more *appétissant*: but ship quite endurable, apart from flies and ever-increasing tedium of the voyage. Cairo-Baghdad is under 1000 miles: I have already journeyed nearly 4000, and am still at least ten days from my destination.

26 APRIL 1917. At 6 a.m. reached Chahbar, the most eastern port of Persia, to find the Telegraph Superintendent and two subalterns aboard. Ashore with them at 9.30 and called upon the one Persian, a seedy individual know-

ing a little English, whom I caused to stand in front of the scales with which he defrauds both Government and public, and there immortalized, I hope, by my new Kodak. Most of the inhabitants Baluchis,[5] with a fair proportion—and blood a mixture—of negro slaves. *Quae caret ora cruore nigro?* is forced upon one at every stage of life. Round the village *en bande* until suddenly a little boy, eleven years old, ran forward and offered me his hand, which on principle I shook, and was at once glad I had done so, for he proved to be the son of a great and friendly chief, who had just succeeded (for the moment only) in taking refuge under our protection. Had him out and snapped him in the midst of his ferocious and unattractive adherents. I thought Husain Khan a nice little boy, told him so and trusted the Lord would give him the victory over his enemies. Over sandy and desert country to the inevitable Shaikh's tomb, past a rudimentary mango and vegetable garden and so, in blazing heat, through trenches and much barbed wire to the Telegraph Station and Fort, defended by 80 S. Indian troops and our two subs. I take off my hat to those youths. Both under 30, pale and thin, but in good health. They are cut off from the outer world, and receive mails once a month. No friends and no neighbours. No sport within forty miles. They keep their men occupied with drill, and are organizing them for a Section Challenge Hockey Cup. Serene, unbored, alone; with two machine-guns, one of which "generally jams", between them and the Continent of Asia. Almost thou persuadest me to be a Kiplingite. Mr Hughes, the Supt., a cheerful man, has been there four years, and hopes for a promotion or perhaps a transfer to Jask at the end of the War. They wanted us to stay for luncheon, but I naturally brought them, when we had exhausted the possibilities of the Fort, tennis-court, etc., out to the comparative change of the *Ula*. Though Chahbar resembles Ispahan as Port Said Luxor, I am glad to have set foot in Persia.

Said informed me that his new brown shoes, for which he had paid 35 piastres before leaving Cairo, had been stolen from his side as he slept. I told him that many had been slain in their sleep, and that he was lucky to have escaped so cheap. But he continued to bemoan his fate until I spoke to the steward ("Staurid", Said calls him) who—rather suspiciously—recovered the goods by eventide.

27 APRIL 1917. After sleeping pleasantly in a cot on the Captain's bridge I awoke at Muscat, than which it is impossible to conceive anything more Byronically picturesque. A fine bay almost encircled by sheer jagged peaks, surmounted by castles and fortalices with antique cannon pointing through the crenellations. On the Western rocks, painted in huge white letters, the names of the ships, mostly British, that have visited the place these many years. Right at the back of the little white town, apparently a few houses but those large: our Consulate, hospital and the Sultan's Palace. I sent off a note to the Consul-and-Political Agent, who sent back his launch with a civil note. Went ashore, taking with me the other passengers. Rowed by a Baulchi, one Arab and two Zanzibaris. By Heaven's grace a pleasant N. breeze chanced to blow, in the absence of which the place is reputed one of the hottest in the world. Left my companions and called upon Major L. Haworth, an agreeable and intelligent Indian Political. The Residency is well and solidly built. Good drawing-room with a new Collard and Collard, and two large China rice

---

[5] Baluchis, etc., hate Persians and utterly renounce their authority.

vases. At my request Haworth sent to the Sultan to ask for an audience. His name is Sayyid Taimur ibn Faisal ibn Turki: one of the Ibadhi [6] persuasion, and he has a son of seven years.

Preceded by the superb Consular Cavass in a long scarlet coat reaching to the feet and a large turban, we walked through very narrow streets, of which the only good feature is the splendidly carved doors of the houses (relic of Portuguese Renaissance tradition?) to the Palace, a plain well-built quadrangle with an inner court. The Sultan with his brother met us, attended by his guard (no uniforms but heavily ornamented antique and modern weapons), outside the front door, and (physically) forced us to ascend the staircase in front of himself. We were shown into a fair-sized chamber of audience. Bad and pretentious Persian rugs, and a little lamentable Austrian furniture (pointless "corner pieces", etc.). Sofa and armchairs well covered with "Club" khaiki. On the walls, plain plaster, the same three-quarter of His Majesty George V in crown as graces the dining-room at Aden. Large signed photograph of President Taft, and some large views of the Cairo Citadel, Sultan Hassan Mosque, and Nile. The Sultan is of middle height and dresses like the Sharīfs of Mecca, even to the brown camel *aba;* but wears a large red and blue turban without wicker support. Brown complexion, eyes and beard, evidently faint negro blood but not the African mouth. His manners are simple, gentle and charming, but he does not convey the impression of strength. We understood each other's Arabic well, and he clutched at the occasion, Haworth, though an excellent Persian and Hindustani scholar, having none. By a very curious chance I quoted to him two lines of al-Mutanabbi which Mark Sykes had cited two years before, sitting in the self-same chair. He professes entire satisfaction (though Haworth informed me that his subjects emphatically do not) with the Sharifal movement; and told me his family had known that of Aun [7] for several generations: I gave him two copies of the Arabic Raemakers.[8] Knew nothing of Egyptian Ruling House nor of the Ministers (who imagine that their sound is gone out into all lands). After a while he presented to me the Commander-in-Chief, his brother, Sayyid Nādir bin Faisal, a merry and friendly blackamoor, effusively pleased at meeting an Arabist Englishman, and forthcoming, though not illuminating, upon a variety of subjects. As Haworth had explained, weakness is the fault of the amiable and even saintly Sayyid of Muscat. Himself a non-smoker, he has forbidden the cultivation of tobacco, as also (perhaps because of a perpetual overdraft) the exaction of interest on loans. Though nominally lord of 1500 miles of coast, it is coast only, the interior being these four years in open revolt under an Imam elected, according to Ibadhi tenets, *ad hoc.* Haworth laments this, the more so as there stands only 60 miles inland a mountain over 9000 feet high, blossoming with walnuts, peaches and violets. Also very considerable towns relatively unexplored. Haworth's remedy is the loosest and easiest imaginable Protectorate (I always think of "Compose yourself, Madame, for to such a situation you must come" for these wretched states), chiefly to keep away possible enemies to ourselves, and partly to bring

---

[6] A Moslem sect founded by Abdallah ibn Ibādh, who said that if a man commit a *kubira,* or great sin, he is an infidel and not a believer.

[7] Founder of the Sharifal House in Mecca.

[8] Chap. IX, p. 212.

Taimur to reason: but giving him a completely free hand, and possibly increasing his subsidy of £13,000 per annum—which he chronically outruns—so much so that certain despairing Bombay tradesmen, established some years in Muscat, are about to shake its dust from their feet. At about 12.30 we withdrew, H.H. exacting my card, and accompanying us to the front door, where we parted almost tearfully. He at once sent me round his photograph in an immense frame. Luncheon with Haworths: he knew, had worked with, and likes MacMahon. Afterwards tested their Collard, and Haworth sang an English ballad. The Sultan had sent me round a guard, with whom I clambered up the rock-cut steps to the fort, built by the Portuguese in 1508, and still containing one of their pieces. Looking into a kind of pit on the way up I descried a dozen prisoners half-naked and chained one to another by the neck and legs. Tried to snap them and one poor devil cried out in mortal terror: *"La tidrab"* [9]—"Don't shoot, don't shoot." Reassured upon this point, he joined the others in clamouring for bakshish, which I promised on condition of their posing for me in the sun. In a mad clank and jingle they were there, and the Foreign Office and Cairo G.H.Q. Propaganda Committee will learn with pardonable elation that, even as I pressed the button, three were unable to relax for one moment their perusal of *al-Haquqāt*.[10] Said shocked and scandalized at the gyves. For two rupees I left the Donjon the most popular character in Muscat: and so to the *Ula* by 3.45.

28 APRIL 1917. Jask by 6 a.m. Hearing that except for its Telegraph Station, Jask was in all respects a similar but inferior and less interesting Chahbar, I remained aboard. At 10.30 p.m. we were held up by H.M.S. *Lawrence,* who removed their mails and a bucket of milk. Our Captain tells me he is under strict orders to notice no signals whatever, and was therefore technically in the wrong. If *Lawrence* had been the Raider we should not have had a chance. But there seems no way out of this dilemma. Strong breeze and weather agreeable so far from Karachi. Green's *History,* Macaulay, Ruskin, *Oxford Book* and Horace every day.

29 APRIL 1917. Hanjam Island about six: large cable station, and, we heard, a cricket match in process: there is no doubt that in these waste leisures and solitudes it saves our people from the mentality of Farrère's *Civilisés.* Away by eight and all day along a glassy sea, mostly within sight of the mountains of S. Persia, like a fainter remoter rose range on the Upper Nile. Read with great interest Dostoieffsky's *House of the Dead.*

30 APRIL 1917. *Truditur dies die.* The clock daily put back but growing heat. Well before 6.0 p.m. as telegraphed to the authorities yesterday morning, we were in the Admiralty anchorage off Bushire, and the Captain was justly indignant to find, as at Jask, no sign of the officers and men who should have been waiting for us. They arrived about seven and took forty minutes to tranship their stuff. Cause of the delay, I discover, bad organization of Brigade Major. There is a Regt. of Punjabis, a squadron of cavalry (15th Lancers) and 3000 camel corps, who protect the cable station, wireless, etc. as also the town from looting. Wassmuss, the former German Consul-General, was busy in the mountains forty miles away, stirring up local talent against us with no

---

[9] I learnt later that their fear may have been due to the occasional practice of the younger Princes of Muscat of throwing coconuts at the prisoners' heads.

[10] Our Arabic Allied-propaganda newspaper.

little success. Signal Officer, boy from Punjabis; also an R.E. Captain on his way to Ahwaz: "Bushire hell, Basra as bad and Baghdad worst of all: why, the Turks have taken even the women [11] with them."

MAY DAY, 1917. About as much significance here as Bairam in Piccadilly. After great heat yesterday a strong wind sprang up at 1 a.m., growing by about four to a gale, which almost blew me off the bridge, and actually went near making me cold. I feared the worst, and sure enough this morning the Captain said it was a Shamāl, the hard N. wind, and that it would almost certainly make us late for the Bar of the Shatt al-Arab, owing of course to the Bushire delay. The custom is for the pilots to await ingoing ships on the little red lightship, and we wasted the best part of an hour getting away and recovering our heavy lifeboat; by which time it was indeed too late, high tide being at 8.22, so we anchored and lay to till three. By now I am broke to, as well as by, delays and misfortunes, and took the extra night with scarce an inward oath. The ebb rushes out pale *café au lait* against the blue main Channel. Our misery was mitigated by seeing the *Jeddah* which had been easily first in picking up a pilot, dash madly for the entrance and ground hard and fast—"Hard and fast" our Captain kept repeating—on the bar. By this time the Shamāl had changed to an Egyptian Khamsīn, hot, sandy, and obscuring sun and sea alike. Shortly after three we began to take the tide, high at five, and thought for about an hour we should never plough through the mud, silt, sand or whatever it is. But the Persian pilot (Sunni, knowing Arabic) [12] pulled us through, and by 5.30 we were steaming up the great river between the Turkish West and Persian East bank. Both far greener than Nile, and West fairly dense with palm groves. Dropped mails at Fao Telegraph Station and anchored for the night five miles farther up. Captain tells me Persians are such good stevedores that it pays to bring them up and return them to Bushire, sooner than employ the Arab [18] (whose women, however, make good coolies).

No news from England since 2 April, nor much hope of any for another ten days.

2 MAY 1917. On at 4 a.m. and at Muhammara 9, anchoring opposite Karūn river. Strong North wind with sand still blowing. Extraordinary density of palm groves both sides, but especially the West. Frequent little canals winding off on either bank give an interest lacking to the Nile, and there is much green grass. At Basra all the navigation and circumstance of a great port: motor-launches especially indicating an immense petrol consumption. Town of Basra inland: on the shores in sight ignoble sheds, etc., but a few fine houses, showing how suitable Venetian palace style might be for riverain use and effect. I lunched aboard, captured a Navy steam-launch belonging to one of the gunboats, landed at the Army Commandant's pier and telephoned to Wilson, Deputy Chief Political officer, the Elect of Cox—good-looking, able and intelligent, and intensely ambitious. We drove in a small black Block car to his office, in which he also lives. With *rem, facias rem, recte si possis si non quocunque modo, rem,* as his motto, stuck over his desk. The house is small. Wilson's office in apparent confusion and rich in the dust of daily

---

[11] I was informed later that this was untrue.
[12] Bi-lingual, as most Persians are at this end of the Gulf.
[18] Arabs, on the other hand, were best for discharging coal.

sandstorms. Persian orderlies with immense brown felt head-dresses, very becoming. Found telegram from Cairo which had been waiting since the 19th asking for keys of my private file for reference to originals of Sharīf letters; from which, knowing how many I never received, I shall not be surprised if someone insinuates that I have lost them and am therefore incapable of being put in charge of official documents. Apart from this I welcome the incident as yet one more proof of the need for some kind of work-plan for the Residency, as outlined by me in March 1915.

Wilson tells me the Mesopotamians as a whole are adaptable, progressive and appreciative.[14] They realize their own weakness and backwardness, genuinely detest and dread the Turk, and welcome innovation with a spirit of surprising toleration. What they expect from us is just government, great material improvement and prosperity, and gradual association of their leading men with power. Their ideal is that Iraq may become another Egypt.

Wilson says there is much excellent material for Politicals in the officers now in Mesopotamia. Four recently chosen had been killed in the capture of Baghdad. But Cox wisely wishes to bring in new blood parallel in all ranks, and not confine it to the top or bottom. They were about to apply to Egypt when Clayton's [15] news came. Though they do not want Indian Civilians or Politicals, they have a just admiration for the mechanism of that great service. At 4.15 we visited Dugmore on *Proserpine*, where I learnt that I was to go up to Baghdad in the river-cruiser *Gnat* on the morning of the 4th. We went aboard for the Commodore, an agreeable hearty old salt: and it was Wilson's pleasant task to ask him how he would like to receive the C.I.E. to which the Indian Government had gazetted him. As he already had the C.B. Wilson was naturally indignant at this inadequacy. Finally, we learnt that the Commodore had absolutely refused to look at it. Told me that Ibn Sa'ud, when aboard *Juno*, having overslept himself for his own prayers, had insisted upon attending the ship's Sunday matins and was overwhelmed with admiration of the Commodore as Warrior-Priest, Admiral and Imam. Wilson then took me for a drive through the Bazaars, well and pleasantly roofed with wood and pitch; at one place with Persian dome and vaulting, and I left a card on Lady Cox.[16]

Venning of Aden had given me a note to Mrs Borrie, wife of Civil Surgeon, with whom, Wilson having an engagement, I dined. Basra by night is like Venice, and the long slim bālăms glide up and down the canal like cruder gondolas. Pedestrians carry lamps and lanterns. Mrs Borrie was all that Venning's enthusiasm led me to imagine: pretty, good-natured, prosperous: Borrie efficient Arabist. Also dining Lieut.-Col. C. whom I afterwards learned (and should have guessed) is an ex-editor of *The Tatler*. I preached after dinner upon the fallacy of the Clean-Fighting Turk, and learnt with disgust the Arab brutalities upon our privates taken at Kut: struck in the face with butt-ends of rifles and, when offered water by their mounted gaolers, kicked in the mouth as they strove to drink. Wilson subsequently related to me numerous instances of the blackest treachery towards our officers. To bed

---

[14] *Vide* Azīz al-Maeri's appreciation, p. 194.
[15] Refusing the post of Deputy Chief Political Officer which had been offered to him with Wilson's hearty concurrence.
[16] Who had not yet left for Baghdad.

about 11 in an *angarīb*—rope-pallet—on the roof, in a chill almost of an Egyptian March night, which reminded me that Basra is about the same latitude as Suez, and Baghdad as Damascus, though the immense surrounding deserts make Mesopotamia infinitely harder to endure. Borrie told me that these regions have a heat-stroke zone, not yet investigated or proved, but bearing grim fruits in immense casualty lists.

Wilson deserves the greatest credit for his admirable economy of Government paper, for which I need only quote his turning of German addressed envelopes inside out (by convicts); and his division, for ordinary local service, of the envelope face into four quarters, enabling the same to be used four times. Suggestion would be ridiculed by Cairo.

3 MAY 1917. *Ruppemi l' alto sonno nella testa un grave* reek proceeding from the stoking up of local Hammam furnaces, for whose consumption no combustible is apparently too vile. At about 11 started in car with Lieut.-Col. S. G. Knox, C.I.E., Senior Judicial Officer in Iraq, for a drive out to the distant village of Zubair, to visit the Shaikh of Zubair and Abd al-Wahhāb Pasha Mandīl. Just out of Bazaars when a bad puncture gave us the occasion to return and walk round them: remarking the prevalence of Manchester goods. Large majority of shops kept by Baghdad Jews: names in English and Arabic. No old brass or copper, of which the new shapes resemble but are inferior to those of Egypt. Carpets not worth inspection. Went some 15 miles across what they call Desert, because there is nothing growing on it now, but which with proper extension of water would blossom like the rose: and again broke down about 1½ miles outside the little town of Zubair, so walked the remainder in great heat to the Shaikh's house, guided thereto by a small boy who offered in the right Arabic spirit of democracy to lead us to "Bait 'brahīm". An Egyptian would have said "To H.E. the Shaikh's house" and an Englishman "To Lord Abraham's". The town is clean: contains several mosques but not a scrap of green. The Arabs are unwilling to sleep in what they consider the corruption of Basra, though their scruples permit them to make money out of it. Shaikh Ibramīm met us at the door of his stone-porched house and led us across a large open courtyard to his *mandara,* a pleasing structure whose roof is supported by three Gothic arches: whitewashed within. Bad carpets and abominable cheap nickel lamps. Tea served in cups of European design made in Japan. Ibramīm is a smaller, equally charming and equally ineffective Sultan of Muscat. He has, however, more control over his sectaries; and when the War reached these parts and the Turkish Army was close upon him, unable to avow his sentiments he yet saved our situation by issuing a pious proclamation, in which he enjoined all, in the name of God and his prophet, to help the Faithful with all their resources: so much so that they must give everything, and not soil their consciences by selling. The natural result of this edict was that they gave for about half a day, then began to say "Hwere is my Brofit?", and finally buried their supplies in remote and inaccessible hiding places. We next visited Abd al-Latīf Pasha Mandīl, the Wakīl, Deputy, of Ibn Sa'ud (known here as Abd al-Azīz). He lives in a larger and finer house and he is a higher or at any rate more *fin-de-siècle* type of Arab than I have yet seen in these parts. Tall and thin almost to emaciation. Like Ibrahīm, in full Badawi head-dress, but robed in a long close-fitting white embroidered silk Persian *quftan*. He smoked

a narghileh and gave us excellent black coffee. His son and several relations are at the American College, Beirut, and he has heard nothing of them since the War began. I offered to inquire (and shall do so in Cairo through Knabenshue [17] in his capacity of Swiss Minister). We started back well after two and passing over the Shaiba battlefield again had a puncture in a date-grove about a mile out of the town, into which we therefore walked. Knox is the son of an Indian High Court Judge. He is apprehensive of Egyptian Law being thrust upon Iraq, but I think I calmed his fears. For a walk through the town. Arab lower class women unveiled, and up to the present make better labourers than the men. Practically only Jews in tarbushes. Some Japanese: but I saw none of the Chinese Labour Corps, who have brought with them their own theatre. A few Egyptians. One or two Armenians. General inchoate appearance: a drier, dustier Port Said. Wilson who is the son of the ex-headmaster of Clifton and has lost two brothers in the War, told me his autobiography which does him infinite credit: gave me full details of the Anglo-Russo-Turco-Persian Frontier Commission which brought him his C.M.G.[18] He has had the good fortune to serve and preserve one excellent chief (Sir Percy Cox) for some twelve years, as also to be a regular member of a recognized and recognizing service: but his abilities, concentration and perseverance would win him success anywhere. Thinks our Teheran Legation should come under India: but I feared Russia would reply by placing theirs under their Colonel or even Home Office. Hates, as do I, the idea of Persia disappearing, and sees no necessity for it, if only the Rusks would play fair. But will they, or can they? Wilson impresses upon me that, once West of Baluchistan, all fauna and flora without exception assume a European character: from this he draws inference favourable to the Persians, whom he regards as akin to Europeans in some respects, including their sense of humour. Left him at 10.30 and board *Gnat,* in a hired bălăm, where to bed on deck under a single sheet in bitter cold about 11.30, tired after my first walk in nearly a month. (The waves lapping the prow of the bălăm, the space and the lights on the water brought me back Venice, with a strong nostalgia.)

4 MAY 1917. We left Basra at 8 against a N. breeze so cool as to be almost cold. I find the surgeon to be Devereux Marshall, the Moorfields oculist whom I last saw on *Euryalus,* where I borrowed his watch. He told me with surprising restraint that it reached him after several months with the jewelling broken in three places. *Gnat* is a local flagship of the *Fly* class; burns oil. *Moth, Caddis Fly, Hover Fly, Gad Fly, Fire Fly,* etc., with *Fly Catcher* as patrol boat. Built to run up the Danube after we had taken Constantinople: draws 4 ft. 8 in., can do 10½ knots, two boilers and two funnels abreast, two 6 in. guns and a variety of maxims, etc. Not uncomfortable, but chicken-ladder companions quite vertical, down which Said cascades with unfailing regularity. Said disliked sleeping between the 6-in. guns and a neat row of

---

[17] American Chargé d'Affaires.
[18] Wilson started in the British Army, thence to the Indian Army, and thus to the Indian Political. Two years surveying in Persia for railways led to his appointment to the Turco-Persian Frontier Commission, which he finished romantically on the slopes of Ararat, two days before Turkey declared War. I subsequently discovered that he had received the D.S.O. for gallantry in the field on the Euphrates with the 12th Division, a few months before. He is now Sir Arnold Wilson, M.P.

shells: "for one of those Bombas may burst in the night, and cause my flesh to fly away in the air, as it were so many hawks." I told him I hoped not, but that before my departure an old woman had prophesied to me that I should lose a servant, name unspecified, by an explosion, and heard him repeat several times with deep uneasy disapproval, "A bad old woman; a bad old woman!"

We passed Kurna in the morning, and the tomb of Ezra in the afternoon. That entertaining writer's mausoleum is in my opinion a seventeenth-century structure: an effective blue-green tiled dome rests upon unambitious brick drum cylinder. My companion calling for his tiresome drinks at all hours of the day. I see I shall have to struggle more and more against developing into a Prig: but the whole paraphernalia of whiskies and sodas, the plugging and wadding up of great briar pipes, the bubbling and sucking, the pointless gusty sigh of relief (from what?), the halting oracular utterance of commonplaces! If it were claret or sack with a little vitality!

> "Come down and redeem us from Virtue,
>   Our Lady of Pain."

Yet he has seen two submarines captured without extracting the Value. The Parable of the Talents; the *Ring and the Book* once more.

The paymaster was on *Edward VII* when she was torpedoed. Informs me (*a*) that our Destroyers got right among the German Fleet after Jutland and might or should have put them all down, (*b*) that a submarine E. 16, lying under the minefield we laid in their path, heard 17 distinct and separate detonations overhead. But why has (*b*) never been published? Bed about 10.30.

5 MAY 1917. *Gnat* contains *le tub* but no bathroom or "toilet", minor obligations being discharged, with an easy grace, over the side. The convolutions of the Tigris are beyond belief, it is no rarity to see dhows and steamers going to and fro parallel and quite close across the land on our main stream. At about 12 we made Amāra, tied up, took in oil and remained there the rest of the day. Almost next to us an old County Council Paddle Steamer that had sailed direct from Greenwich.

After luncheon I took Said across the Bridge of Boats (not much less solid than Galata) and walked through the Bazaars, about one-sixth of which was shut—*sabbata Judaeorum*. They are, like the rest of the town, about 60 years old; excellently built with high Gothic spans. Chiefly Manchester goods: the carpets absurd and the brass negligible. Good variety of types: turbaned Arabs, tarbushed Jews and black tiara'd Persians from Pusht-i-Kuh. Women heavily veiled but in bright broad-striped Baghdad silk, a refreshment after the universal black of Egypt. The façade of the houses on the E. bank is good, and might well be studied: but building indifferent, though not rubble. Inside each a little courtyard with rough first-floor gallery. I called on Philby, I.C.S. (Westminster and Trinity Cambridge), the political of Amāra, of whom W. had said he was clever. He had just been appointed to Baghdad newspaper and propaganda, of which I envied him the interest and opportunity. He was to play hockey (and his pleasant wife tennis) at 5.15, but kindly took us round the Bazaar, town and along the Musharra Canal. Finally, to see the silver work of the Sabians. This sect, whom Philby estimates at a maximum of 20,000, are found chiefly at Amāra, though a few at Baghdad and else-where: none out of Mesopotamia. They are followers of John the Baptist,[19] whose policy of immersion they pursue to the *n*th degree. Thus we were shown a little flight of wooden steps into the canal from which couples were baptized, their immersion forming the marriage service, which Philby had seen. He thinks that a certain degree of Zoroastrianism and Sun Worship enters into their cult, but I could not follow his chiefly linguistic proofs. They dress like Arabs, speak Arabic, and are of fine and dignified appearance. Women unveiled, with pretty features; choose their own husbands and I gather cherish them. I talked for half an hour witH Zahrūn, their chief Mandarin, and ended up photographing him with his sister-in-the-Baptist and two children, while there was prepared for us the first drinkable coffee I have tasted since leaving Cairo: no grounds, no sugar, and strong as capsicum brandy. Their silver-work consists in drawings graven into the metal and subsequently blackened in by means of a paste of antimony, lead and sulphur, of which they have the secret. As far as I am concerned, "they may 'ave it". The work fills me with sick loathing. It is entirely a tourist product, and more so even than Asyūt pottery and shawls: foolish little pictures, generally from photographs, of camels, dhows, date-palms, and approved views *flanquéd* on to cigarette boxes and cases, parasol handles and even shoe-buckles. In spite of a rigorous questioning and search, I could find no single object they were producing or had ever produced *khatr ahāli*—for their own people. I asked Zahrūn, as a friendly tourist who could do him no harm, to whisper his real scale of profit, and he showed me a cigarette box made, as were all his things, to order, for £12, and costing him R.'s 77 (£5). I was astonished at his moderation: which Cairo might envy and imitate.

On to a hockey match in which Indian troops were playing, barefooted, with our officers, a sight that rejoiced me, and made me wish for far more of it in Egypt. Back in Philby's launch to the Club, from the balcony of which a beautiful Venetian *tramonto* rose red on the houses across the river: and so to *Gnat* where a hearty dinner, prolonged by entries from regiments and boats until 11.30. Feeling cold again, and notice temperature has dropped to 73°. (A gunner told me that comforts for troops are now being overdone: all that can be got up by transport at Government's disposal, Government gets up. Private generosity would be better devoted to disabled and widows.)

6 MAY 1917. Left Amāra 5.30 a.m. tying up for oil about sunset at Shaikh Saad, merrily named Sodom and Gomorra by Military (who have also Apple Street, and Temptation Square, Adam's Lane and Serpent Alley).

Captain S. took matins at 11: his uncertainty how to begin should have prepared me for his reading off all the opening sentences, one after the other. Half an hour's walk before dinner towards Sodom, where I heard, from a large Camp (with a good air and bass but no middle parts), "O God our help in ages past", noble on the evening. Another cool night (75°) in which I dropped off, lulled to slumber by the retchings and eructations of Chittagongi oilers on the adjacent barge. There is no doubt that our local oil supply saves the situation as far as Transport goes, and Transport is everything.

[19] As a reincarnation of Seth: consider Moses and Christ to be false teachers. They place Paradise in the Pole Star. Syriac rite. Uncircumcised. Not monogamous. Mentioned in Job as Sabaeans. Real name Mandaeans. Language Mandaitic-Semite.

7 MAY 1917. Cleared Cities of the Plain by 6 a.m. and about midday passed the tragic village of Kut al-Amāra, now a ruin, though only perceptibly more ruinous than most Oriental towns by the absence of inhabitants. Immense holes in the riverside houses from shell-fire, and the top of the only minaret knocked away. Kut should apparently be added to the War's Might-have-Beens, and swells the list already loaded with Coronel, Jutland, E. Africa and the Dardanelles. But all united do not compare with the Boche Might-have-Been of Calais. In the plain N. of Kut, looking close over the river, stands the Turkish monument, put up by the Germans in honour of the three Turkish Generals who fell there. It is a blank obelisk of marble or cement, I could not see which, mounted upon a brick pedestal reposing on a plinth of stone: and, not having been unveiled before the Turkish evacuation this year, still wears its canvas sheeting, flapping furious but forlorn in the wind.

About 7 we went aground, in apparently deep water, for the first time, but were easily off in five minutes. Shoals and channels are constantly changing, and it is the narrows that are the safest, because they are also the deepest. A wonderful European sunset, again striking rose, in a way I have not seen elsewhere. Billowy violet clouds, but no Egyptian afterglow in the high heaven. After dark a great fire, of brushwood, flared up for miles across the marshy plain, intensely incandescent near the ground, and with its pillar of smoke describing, I know not why, a mighty horizontal angle. Finished *Rose and Ring* (how satisfying) and turned over the *Assemblies* of *al-Hariri*, which confirms my old opinion that there is but one book in Arabic, and that the *Arabian Nights*. The Admiralty Handbook of Mesopotamia a compilation of the first order, and invaluable to me. Bed 10, and again cold (72°).

8 MAY 1917. *Multas per gentes et multa per aequora vectus advenio.* We left Azizié about 6 and swirled along an uneventful day past gradually rising banks, and leaving the Diala Canal on our right just before tea. Soon afterwards the arch of Ctesiphon hove in sight, not very impressive in the distance. Though we had wasted the best part of an hour in pulling a Political's pinnace off a shoal we were well up to time, and had the amazing good fortune to be gliding into Baghdad about the setting of the sun. The river broadens out and enhances the dignity and nobility of the entry. To the E. a broken discontinuous façade of Stambūli houses with crooked verandas and deep recesses: the red light splashed about like blood on the uneven glass. An effect of repose on the W. bank, where for some distance there are lush fields and no buildings at all. Everywhere God's plenty of palm trees. Gradually as we rounded the last corner the larger houses, greater minarets and gleaming domes shone out against the powdered gold sky: and amid a mass of shipping, next to *Tarantula* and *Grey Fly*, opposite paddle-boats and heavy barges, hard by an ancient Babylonian wicker guffa, exactly one month since the train took me out of Cairo Station, I came to rest and found myself at my goal. Very soon Lieut.-Col. The Hon. Sir Percy Zachariah Cox, K.C.S.I., K.C.I.E. (once for all) Chief Political Officer and future High Commissioner, stood by with Gertrude Bell, very welcoming, and took me off in a launch to his house, ex-Deutsche Orient Bank, whose middle balcony, with an ultra-Venetian sensation, projects far over the flood. Cox is a longer Duke of Wellington, *bella testa* and friendly of aspect. He pumped me for an hour on the balcony, and G. B. repeated the process at dinner; after which we walked her home to

her Persian garden with a room in each corner, and returned amid the baying of 1000 dogs. I am profoundly impressed with the possibilities of this great prize, and only trust we shall profit by the many negative ensamples of Cairo. Now is the accepted time.

9 MAY 1917. Late up and exercises over the Tigris. Cox being called away to the Army Commander (as they call the G.O.C. here) I had a rewarding talk with Gertrude Bell, who tells me that Cox is almost *au bout de ses forces* with him. After breakfast showed my papers to Cox, who suddenly threw off all externals and told me his position as High Commissioner Elect, with all officials to be, high and low, imposed upon him by H.M.G., with the manner of his future rule severely laid down, and with an omnipotent and unworkable General, would be impossible; and that it would be better for himself, as well as for the Country, to resign now and let Clayton [20] begin with a clean sheet. He was tired; had meant to leave before the War; had only one life and owed a little amusement and civilization to his wife, who had endured with him Somaliland and the Gulf for a score of years. I told him that the premature withdrawal of his knowledge and prestige would gravely handicap any successor; that he would get four and his wife six months p.a. in England; that once High Commissioner, the Foreign Office would treat him with far more deference; that tiresomenesses could always be altered; and generally, that the position was one of the great ones of the world. (I find the stimulus of living, reading and writing over a great river incalculable.)

Work with Cox and Gertrude Bell, whose *maîtrise* of Arab tribe details is amazing, all the morning: and shortly after two with her in car to the Marjanía Mosque, the most notable features of which are the inscriptions, in Kufic, and flowing, cut into stone and brick. The Boches stole 60 tiles from the Mosque, which we shall try to restore. Up to a little room on the lower roof, and conversed with the Shaikh Alūsi, a *sympathique* and cultivated Arab of the old school, who with his companions sat kneeling back, like figures in a Persian miniature, throughout the interview. Cox tells me he aspires to the position of Shaikh al-Islam, which I think he could very well occupy. The mosque dirty and in very bad repair, stucco swelling off from damp and great structural fissures across the walls, domes and vaults. People very friendly, and no bakshish or doffing of shoes demanded. The Imam even carried civility so far as to whisper to an elderly worshipper to hurry up with his prayers and get out of the light. Walking across the road we came upon and into one of the most noble and convincing buildings I have ever seen, the Khan Ortma, also of the fourteenth century. It resembles the inverted hull of a ship, with giant brown brick ribs meeting in a great Gothic span of unusual width. Never have I had more pleasure from structure visibly working as such, and my regret is that Gilbert Scott cannot borrow from it for the Cairo Cathedral.[21] Thence in and round the bazaars, of infinite length, all vaulted according to a still living tradition. The vaulting is varied by an occasional wooden pitched roof as in Basra. Shops and atmosphere more or less as in Cairo, but less sophisticated save only in the matter of prices, where

---

[20] Already applied for, nominally as his Deputy.
[21] Then under consideration: on a large piece of land presented by the Egyptian Government.

they have little to learn. But only one request for bakshish, which died away on the speaker's lips when he saw my expression. After a while we branched out and paid a visit to Mahmud Shukri Alūsi, a learned and pious celebrity who, though indisposed, "up he rose and donned his clothes and opened wide the door". A few other worthies there of the Standard Buffer type, their conversation largely interjectional. Alūsi cultivated and agreeable: like every intelligent man I meet swears by the *Mokattam*. These people are I suppose as were the Egyptians in 1882: Turkish disgusts and annoyances fresh before their eyes, and mightily relieved by *Pax* and *Progressus Britannicae*. I seriously recommend that now, before anything is altered, an accurate illustrated description of the place be published in English, French, and Arabic so that they may not forget the pit from whence they were digged; so that future tarbushed elastic-sided-booted patriots may not claim for themselves before all the world the exclusive credit for cleanliness, health, water, electricity and a hundredfold budget. Let the motto of Mesopotamia be *Non Nobis, Domine*, or Lest We Forget. Back to bazaars and finally called upon the Armenian Madame S. to whom H. of Cairo had given me a letter. This lady lives with her daughter in a pretty but pestiferous little house adorned with a number of very tolerable carpets. (In spite of war and massacres I noticed the February Lingerie number of *Vogue* on their table.) A Turkish officer who had been degraded warned them on no account to leave Baghdad, where indeed, owing to the overwhelming majority of the Jew, Arab, Christian, element, very little harm was done beyond a little looting and bomb-throwing in the bazaars just before the final exit. I saw a few walls, arches and vaults blown in by this wanton petulance. Said says the people genuinely hate the Turks, and curse everything about them except their religion. Walked back; G. B. I fear a shade tired, for I forget everything when I am interested, and we were not in till nearly 7. I remark that Cox uses up old Deutsche Orientbank paper in official dossiers. Dined with C. alone: he tells me they are going to issue Turkish stamps surcharged.

Streaks of white mist steal up the Tigris after sunset, enhancing the wealth of palms as in Hiroshige's *Tokaido*. As for the dogs, their din, indescribably ferocious even from across the river, made sustained conversation almost impossible. I have now been five weeks without a single letter of any kind whatsoever, a deprivation which has a depressing effect upon one's export.

10 MAY 1917. With Gertrude Bell just before 10 for a formal call upon Abd al-Rahman Eff, *Naqīb al-Ashraf*, and Chief (Sunni) Muslim dignitary of the Basra Vilayet. His house on the river has been requisitioned, but his inland mansion with typical ruinous courtyard is far from unpleasant. The *Naqīb* is about 70, of middle height, with an agreeable expression and a nose almost as prehensile as that of a Turkish or Armenian dignitary. He wore fez and *'emma*, white camel's-hair *aba* and brown *markub*.[22] Well known for his anti-Turkish feelings long before the War, and most friendly to me. Said that, though he seldom paid visits, he had done so to Maude, whom he considered the "Wakīl of George". Turks had attempted to combine "Dansa by night with War by day", an unnatural and impossible conjunction. His ambition after the War is to visit Mecca, Medina, Jerusalem and the Azhar. The Naqīb with a sympathetic listener is a voluble and formidable talker, and countered

[22] Slippers.

my remarks in high Arabic with an overwhelming display of technique. As Gertrude Bell had warned me that he had comparatively little use for the Sharīf, I made no allusion to him whatever: nor did he. His genuineness rather impressed me: especially when he openly said that he regretted the blood uselessly shed on both sides. Returning I received a deputation of the local Gregorian (according to Cox's Roman Catholic clerk "Schismatic") Armenians. Vartabed Paron, the Patriarchal Vicar, is a small priest, overrun by his council. He has no French whereas they are at any rate fluent in it. One had escaped from Ras al-Ain, a Circassian town, and promised to give me his experiences in writing. He talked so loud that I was fain to ask for his merciful alternative. He also noted the comparative clemency of the Arabs. The Baghdad community have hardly suffered at all, but nevertheless wish to advertise their miseries in Europe in the hope of tapping Paris and London Committees. Cox wisely discourages this, which is as unfair to us as it is to the real martyrs, whose necessities are primal and bitter. They tell me rugs are rare and dear. Here as everywhere our arrival sends prices bounding up, to the personal benefit of every other race. After luncheon alone in the car out to the little suburb of Muadhdham, through the N. Gate (Bab al-Shamāl) just inside of which is a brilliantly tiled Minaret with a small cupola resembling a single turquoise, near to which, on a ruinous old house, a great stork sat regarding the traffic with superb indifference. The road is both dusty and bumpy, but through luxuriant palm-groves with fruit and vegetable gardens. At length in the distance emerges the shining green and blue-china dome and minaret of the tomb mosque and shrine of Abu Hanīfa, founder of the Hanafi rite,[23] who died about 150 years ago. As I got out of the car a group of reverend men in turbans advanced, and invited me into a large house opposite the Mosque. I accepted, as always, and found myself seated in a large courtyard and drinking, as with the *Naqīb* and every one else, tea as well as coffee. I conversed with those sages, including the *Kiliddar,* keyholder or guardian of the shrine and chief of the Municipality, for twenty minutes and then, escorted by a large group, examined the wheat market and the exterior of the shrine, leaving them with many salutations and a pleasant remembrance of the gleaming mosque, quiet garden and silent *madrassa*. Back soon after four and made arrangements with Capt. Wm. Marshall,[24] A.P.O., to visit Qādhimain next day. Again round the bazaars where bought a little square of old rose Persian velvet, with a round cotton-print table-cloth. My compulsory young Hebrew guide (who tried to pass himself off as an Arab until I tore from him his true name of Salman, but Salman is also an Arab name) though a bore is worth the 20 per cent he afterwards extorts from the merchants. Walking back up the long Khalīl Pasha Street I greatly admired, and addressed individually the Egyptian policemen. They wear puttees, shorts, Indian shirts and brown worsted Kalpaks and look smart and soldierly. Quite happy on good extra pay: and delighted to hear their own dialect. I told all, including the mounted officer Muhammad Izzat, that Egypt expected that every man would do his duty and prove how far more noble was the Nīl than the Digla (Tigris). They all agree that the people of Baghdad are peaceful and orderly, neither drinking nor smoking hashish. Gertrude Bell tells me these policemen are in-

[23] One of the four major rites of Sunni Islam.
[24] Afterwards murdered at Nájaf.

clined to be rough with the *popolo,* but all unite in speaking well of them. To dinner Bullard ex-Levant Consular, quiet and efficient, and Garbett of my year and class in the Cambs. Tripos, and in charge of such seemingly different problems as education and currency.

11 MAY 1917. In bed early morning a cipher from Mark to say that I need not tie myself down to (my original) ten days. A great relief, but I fear meaning that we are held up on the Gaza front. Started in car for Qādhimain, as arranged, at 9.45, only to find the bridge of boats open. The river has fallen so rapidly that the point of contact has become impracticably steep, and the R.E. have to clear masonry to smooth the road. I could not cross till 12.20. Round the Suq, where I found Salman, who took me to an ineffective and ruinous Armenian. No rugs, some very expensive Greek coins and a few Babylonian bricks and cylinders—the local industry: a Turk, arrested about a year ago for being in possession of antiquities, cleared himself by proving that they were his own manufacture. After the Galatesque bridge the road becomes pure Turk, that is cup and ball, and I am surprised the car endured it. Even Said thought the bumping must "break the cawchic".[25] Slightly better when we joined the dilapidated tram-line (which roused his pity and mirth). Qādhimain appears quite suddenly in the midst of the palm-groves. Marshall gave me ration lunch. He is of the Dogra Reget. (Punjab Rajputs): steady men, he says, who never dazzle you and never let you down. All through this campaign since December: Assistant Provost-Marshal the day of our entrance into Baghdad, where such was the enthusiasm that the crowd cheered every provision (including all the Death Penalty Causes) of the detailed proclamation when shrieked aloud by the Town Crier. He rode right round the town at 11 that night and found a total of two persons out in the streets, to wit, a blind man being led home by a boy. In Cairo, Pashas would have been round to complain that Gen. Maude had not *rendu* their *cartes.* M. also saw the White-Flag Trick played by Germans and Turks with a hidden maxim upon a company of Hampshires. I received Shaikh Hāmid the *Kiliddar;* fanatical; he had raised 1500 *Mujtāhidīn* [26] against us last year; Sayyid Ja'afr, chief of the Municipality; and a cheerful intelligent buffoon with a face like Socrates, Husain al-Sarrāf. Qādhimain district population 25,000, town 15,000. Persians? Yes, but they are really Arabs who took that nationality to avoid conscription. *Kiliddar* enlarged upon universal adoration for England, at which I said I was glad to find the rumour I had heard in Egypt of *Mujtāhidīn* was a calumny. He replied without flinching that those few misguided men changed their minds so soon as they perceived the real horror of the German policy. Upon this I gave him an Arab Raemaker which he received with apparent rapture and feigned interest. They remembered fat Prince Haidar Fāzil's pilgrimage some seven years ago. I then went with them *en bande* through the narrow and surprisingly clean streets to the house of a notable, from which we were able to gaze upon the famous golden domes and minarets of the two Imams of Qādhimain. Their loveliness with shame and surprise froze indeed my swift speech. They recall and more than amply justify Ruskin's Lamp of Sacrifice: and the rich noble surfaces of pure gold take the sun with an indescribable radiance. I went round with the friendly crowd to every porch (a thought

[25] Cairene Arabic for Caoutchouc—india-rubber tyres.
[26] Wagers of Jehād, the sacred war against infidels.

too rosily and floridly tiled) and, stepping within, took four films—I fear ineffective—of the unique colouring and gracious line. Thence to the house of Sayyid Mahdi Sayyid-Haidar (they write it thus instead of *ibn* Haidar) one of the leading Shia *Mujtáhids,* up a steep tortuous staircase into a little plain wood-panelled room overlooking a small courtyard. On to Sayyid Hassan Sayyid Hadi, where, *même décor,* a fine old fellow with a long white beard of the centrifugal type who, as soon as he found I understood, sluiced me with a flood of eloquence, beginning with the five Advantages of Travel. After such *maximes de cahier* I was hardened to anything, but he went on to a politic and intelligent discourse; knew Egyptian papers and personalities quite well and received my last Raemaker with a discerning gratitude. I gave him over twenty minutes, and carried complaisance so far as to ask for a second cup of coffee. Marshall says he is the most influential man in Qādhimain, and that all this expense of spirit in a waste of verbiage is not without use and value. Back to Baghdad by 5. Said recounted the atrocities of the Turks and the Shia's loathing of them on every ground. Then to the charming house and courtyard of M. K. Gudenian. Squares and diamonds of looking-glass, in the Turkish taste, let into walls and ceilings as ornaments, are not so offensive as you might imagine. Cox and I dined 7.30 with Gen. Maude. As we came in he was strumming on the piano. He complained with reason of the Russian commander at Khanikin, who, after coffee-housing with him three weeks, made no attempt to push forward at a time when Maude was engaging practically all the Turks; and finally, when these were more or less disengaged, wired to Maude one evening saying he was going to attack next morning, and requesting immediate help. Cox abases himself with a noble sense of discipline. Left 9.10 and good talk with Cox till 10.30.

12 MAY 1917. A planless day, of increasingly oppressive heat. I sent a message to the *Naqīb* asking if he could send me round the Gīlāni Mosque. He replied that he would be delighted, but that a military pass was necessary. So to Col. Hawker, Military Governor. He was in Sudan, Turkish Gendarmerie, and Political Officer Red Sea at beginning of War; charming and best of men. Says there are many complaints against my admired Egyptian policemen, who are rough and inclined to knock people about with pointless violence: is going to return them at the earliest opportunity. I am amazed at the varied activities forced upon comparative amateurs, as also at the success with which they evolve for every difficulty adequate makeshifts. The Latin spirit would recoil before so many opportunisms, irregularities and illogicalities —and do nothing at all. Hawker applied to the Garrison for a pass to admit me to the Mosques and received the intelligent reply that: "If Mr. Storrs is a Mohammedan he can enter, but if he is an Englishman, C. of E., he cannot." This sent me to G.H.Q. where Brig.-Gen. Ready (ex-Egyptian Army) had one typed out for me in no time. I asked him whether the Indian sentry would read English and he solved this fairly obvious apprehension by an Urdu translation. High in praise of the Egyptian Labour Corps, one man of whom performs the daily labour of three Indians. They have raised the standard all along the line. At 5.30 to tea with the ancient Jew Menahem Daniel, in a fine house over the river. Apparently he has others at Kifl and Hilla of which, like the town clerk, I hope to take advantage. The patriarch in an apparent abstraction swallowed several liqueur glasses of cherry brandy. Told me that in

his youth, there being no other school in Baghdad, he was sent to study at the Mosque. Has built a large Hebrew school since. Explains away his own ignorance of Jewish local history by the irrefragable excuse that the records were destroyed by Hūlagū. Showed me his correspondence, Arabic written in Hebrew characters, as the Armenians often write Turkish. To dinner Hawker and Gen. Beach of the Intelligence, pleasant and with a saving admiration of my little genius T. E. Lawrence. Talked with Cox, now much relieved by F.O.'s last telegram which has accepted all his views. I deeply thrilled by his approval and acceptance of my offer [27] to return to Egypt via Ibn Sa'ud across Arabia; as well as, yes, a little nervous, and regretful I have not learnt to survey and take bearings. But I fear my guns may be spiked by Cairo.

13 MAY 1917. Drove to see the mosque shrine of Abdul Qādir al-Gilāni. The *Naqīb* received me pleasantly enough and at once sent for the Indian sentry. There were seated on the floor three Indian Sepoys, with their officer, unable to communicate with the Holy Sage, but doubtless Getting the Benefit. The sentry, a sergeant in whom stupidity and fanaticism maintain a brisk and equal struggle, refused point-blank to accept the documents, pointing to his orders, which he said contained no mention of passes. But if the *Naqīb* ordered him, etc. The *Naqīb* very properly said he wanted me to go in but had no power to order British troops. After forty minutes of this wearisome wrangling, I took the sentry, put him on the box of the cab, drove out a mile in the desert to his camp, confronted him with his British officer who apologized to me and gave the necessary instructions; and returned, incandescent but *triumphans*. The shrine to tell the truth is no great wonder, but after my hours of sweat and swearing, I would not have missed it for the world. Mosque entrance very ordinary: at the shrine entrance I took off my shoes. Large and interested but far from hostile crowd of idlers and hangers-on. My guide said I might enter if I liked, but as one can see everything from the inner doors I preferred the credit of gentlemanly restraint. The grave of the saint is enclosed in a rich, ugly silver grille, adorned without by modern silver candlesticks 4 ft. in height and very solid. In a side-chapel two magnificent brass *shamadans* [28] of the approved Egyptian shape, inscribed with the *tughra* [29] of a seventeenth-century Sultan. Even Said saw how much better they were than the silver, and said they would "do well in the house". Some fine old carpets, including a brilliant Herāt with the border cut off to make fit. In the great courtyard a kind of lighthouse clock-tower built by the *Naqīb* himself. Lunch with Garbett in the old Sorai. Again staggered by the multiplicity of crucial strings in his hands. Under the cloak of Revenue Officer he has dossiers on agriculture, irrigation, education and law. I gave him my views on the third of these, and find they are already up against the question of instruction in the Arabic language. Here again it is the better class Arab that clamours for English, and we who attempt to dissuade them and impose Arabic. How long will it be before we are accused of exterminating Arabism? I warned Garbett against any *badinage* with Law. But he replies with reason that however he may hold his hand people will continue to be born, marry, divorce

[27] Preoccupied by the constant strife between Ibn Sa'ud ruler of Nejd and King Husain of the Hejaz, I had offered to return across Arabia, to visit them both, and to attempt to reconcile them.

[28] Candlesticks.

[29] Cipher.

and die, testate or intestate, have debts and evade them, and that something must be done. Incidentally that unless we can push the Turks a little farther back N.W. and dam a canal, we risk a water famine over nearly 1,000,000 good acres. He showed me the Government School, a fine building, wantonly and utterly destroyed by them before evacuation. Also the two primitive public gallows upon which they hanged alleged spies. (Universal complaints from Christians that we are too lenient in this respect.) At the Serai, haystacks of Turkish archives, with ruined furniture that deeply stirred the heart of Said. I ventured to suggest the importance of profiting by all our mistakes in Egypt and speedily securing river frontage for a mile each side for offices and official residences, in order to have some control over the appearance of the city. I want to prevent outrages like the Garden City, the flats in front of the Residency, the Cold Storage Chimney and Perry's Bulac Bridge. Hawker has found the German plans for laying out a new town on the W. bank, and hopes to use them later. After tea looked at Beach's War photographs, and removed some of his maps and hand-books. Turks have nearly 20,000 men against us, with many guns, good and well handled. Russians no help at all. Dined alone with Cox; whom I admire more every day, for his kindness, simplicity, dignity, knowledge, and intelligence; and to bed about 11.

14 MAY 1917. Early before 9, Cox showed me the cable he is sending about my journey. At breakfast he asked me if I was physically up to it. I could only hope so and quote my former trips, not very exacting, and in tremendous luxury, with the Hunters. I then interviewed personages from 9.30 to 12.30. With G. B. saw the entertaining *Libre Benseur* Jamil al-Zaháwi, ex-deputy and famous writer. He had had it at first hand that the Sharif had been prayed for as Khalifa in the mosque at Khanikin. Jamil is an admirer of Herbert Spencer, and wears, instead of a shirt, a pyjama jacket under his white coat. Intimate acquaintance with English journalism. Some ten years ago he wrote an eloquent *Qasida* [30] in praise of England, and was forced, to his lively regret, to produce four very stiff ones against us during the War. Next I saw alone the Syrian Catholic Bishop. His Patriarch, directly under Rome, used to live at Mardin; now at Beirut. Bishop's diocese stretches from Baghdad to the Gulf, and numbers some 3000 souls, of which 2000 are in Baghdad. He made rather heavy weather about recent sufferings of his flock, but could cite nothing definite. An agreeable and I should say able prelate; told me incidentally that many Christian exiles were allowed to return after the arrival of von der Golz. Then Abd al-Latif Thanayān, a pleasant type of Muslim, with wonderfully ossified teeth. He is of an independent turn, and criticizes. Strongly in favour of *Moḳattam,* etc. And I notice generally that there is, on the part of local Islam, no sort of anti-Syrian prejudice: because, I suppose, they have not yet seen the best posts in the Government entrusted to that intelligent but prehensile and nepotist community. Here every one wants to learn English: and is astonished when I say it is far more important for the English to know Arabic. Thanayān voices Iraq indifference to the Sharif by declaring that a Chinese or Japanese ruler would be equally acceptable. Next Chauriz, reverend sire, came footing slow. He is a Chaldaean priest, *Vicaire de Sa Beatitude le Patriarche de Babylon.* The Chaldaeans form the largest Christian community in Iraq. They were converted by

[30] Lyric poem.

SS. Thaddeus and Thomas. Later embraced the Nestorian heresy. Chauriz and his companion astonished me by raising their hats in salutation like Europeans. I liked them both. They know their own history and were moved to hear that I had visited Kharga, Nestorius's place of exile in the Libyan Desert. Promised to supply me with historical and other details. (And never did.) There have been wholesale massacres by Turks of hill Nestorians, and it is not known if the Patriarch Mar Shimun is still alive. Monseigneur Nerces (Narcissus) Sayghirian, Armenian Catholic, a tall refined figure, then presented himself. They are proud of their superior "illumination" as Catholic Armenians, and spoke of the time when they were *"sous le joug orthodoxe"*. About 500 of them in Baghdad. Two or three holy but not humble men of heart from Qādhimain called to return, and ask for a repetition of, my visit. After them the French Carmelite *père supérieur* and *frère* for some twenty minutes. He wishes to make English the medium of instruction, Arabic *obligatoire*, and French *facultatif*. I agree with the first for Higher Education, but would never admit it for Elementary; which must be Arabic. Pleasant and enlightened men, I think a little obsessed with the debt of gratitude owed to France by Eastern Christians. Mr Hurmuz, Armenian, desiring my presence any day at any meal, and anxious to show me the *orphélinat* of Turkish refugees (Armenian) and discards, concluded the series.

Sent Said out for Bakūba oranges, and ate five for lunch, or, as I then discovered, exactly one rupee's worth. He nervous of the proposed desert journey, dreading camels, and the possibility of attacks by lions, *utt al nimri*—tiger cats —and other savage creatures. About three with Gertrude Bell to see the Abbāsid remains in the citadel. These are few and small but of great interest and beauty. They consist of very fine geometrical designs traced and moulded by hand on a wet plaster surface. Like but more living than anything I have seen in Cairo. The skill of this period of brick vaulting is wonderful: they often achieve the horizontal, with the effect and reality of complete solidity. Two very fine sixteenth-century cannons, covered with designs and inscriptions: about 10-in. bore. The Turks had everywhere attempted to melt metal down for bullets, but evidently were caught for time. As it is, they destroyed the beautiful octagonal gate tower of Baghdad [31] by blowing up the ammunition therein, and left an infinity of bomb and dynamite traps for our troops in the dark and unsuspected corners. We saw the little arms museum, containing a variety of bombs, shells, etc. (unemptied) and a large German flag. Before leaving the precincts of the citadel I removed from my socks three large fleas, and subsequently one from the back of my neck. Gertrude Bell found one in each shoe. Reason I suppose that quoted in *Henry IV*, Eastcheap or Gadshill? At sunset corrected Arabic Reuters for Gertrude Bell and had a brisk amusing discussion with Père Anastase, the savant and Orientalist, ἀντιμαλλιαρὸς,[32] who does not agree that the spoken must also be the written word: Egyptian, Syrian, Moroccan, etc. are for him "dialects". Dined with Gen. *X* in his immense Hebrew palace and was frankly bored. He never hears what one says the first time, nor understands the second. Says inhabitants are making enormous profits out of us, and we should recoup ourselves a little

---

[31] As, a few months later, the Ophthalmic Hospital of the Order of St John, in Jerusalem.
[32] See page 90.

by raising licensing fees. At present not even the Hotel Maude pays more than a £1 a month, which is derisory.

15 MAY 1917. Mark and Leachman [33] leave Cairo to-day for Jeddah, I do hope not before receiving the proposal of my journey. About eight days necessary and an immediate start out of the question. Wrote and read Persian Gulf Gazetteer, a unique and monumental compilation, and a political history of the Middle East beyond compare. About 5.30 took the launch with Gertrude Bell and walked with her, at a pace attainable by few women, out to the tomb of the Lady Zubaida,[34] a construction in the Gunter Buzzard hymeneal manner, reputed of the ninth but really of the fourteenth century. The sausage-shaped dome, mammillated like Diana of the Ephesians is hideous in itself and bears no sort of relation to the clumsy and obviously restored octagon which supports it. The door was closed, so we missed the less ridiculous interior, and walked back past the tiled dome and minaret of Shaikh Maarūf in a brown fog of dust.

Recommended for Education Hum. Bowman,[35] and gave his address.

At dinner Cox related to me some of the grosser gaffes of the Intelligence, as shown forth in their *Iraq Personalities,* where allusion is made to the Engineer of the Hindyia *Garage;* [36] and under the letter I: Issimo—General: Commander-in-Chief of the Turkish forces.

16 MAY 1917. Had in an Arab barber who shore my hair down to the quick, especially over the temples. Notable his combination of the ancient brass shaving bowl (with a place cut away for the neck), with the latest pattern of nickel hair-clipper. I received the Grand Rabbi Eleazer. He tells me there are neither Sephardim, Ashkenazim, Karaim, nor Sadducees in Baghdad: only the right Nabuchodonosor brand, *Kōshar min al-Kōshār.* Over 55,000 and numerous schools. Persecutions here took the milder but (considering the martyrs) more agonizing form of insistence upon gold in exchange for miserably depreciated Ottoman paper. Two British officers and fifteen natives surprised and killed by Arabs whilst surveying on the Baghdad-Samarra reach, where I was to have gone this week. Sir Percy Cox having decided to send me next day to visit the leading Imams and *Mujtáhids* of the Holy Shia Cities Kárbala, Nájaf and Kūfa, took car to Garbett to prepare him. He is to make all plans, providing two camp beds and a portable thunder box. Eight veiled women were sitting on the floor of his office, with two Shaikhs on the sofa, all waiting for their pensions. It remained to raise cars for our expedition, a Ford and two lorries, which I did by a visit to Major Hoskins, Q division; a pleasant Persian scholar aching to accompany me. Cox showed me the reply from Cairo stating Mark delighted with the idea of my opening up Central Arabia, and Wingate placing me unreservedly at Cox's disposal. So for better or worse. With Hurmuz to the *orphélinat armenien,* a small smelly house crowded with women and girls in nightgowns, all rescued from Worse-Than Death with the Turks. But only one child is the result of it all. The admirable Goldsmith [37] is going to put me wise on the prismatic compass and lend me

[33] My "opposite number" representing the "Mespot-force" in Egypt.
[34] Queen of Harūn al-Rashīd.
[35] Humphrey Bowman, C.M.G., C.B.E. He obtained the post, and I subsequently had the satisfaction of recommending him, successfully, for Jerusalem.
[36] Famous irrigation Barrage.
[37] Political Officer from the Indian Army. A charming man: he died a year later of T.B.

his uniquely swift and smooth camel. Gertrude Bell to dinner. It is like Kitchener times again for me to hear and debate important causes, first hand, and before the event; instead of hearing of them long afterwards, generally by accident, and when they have already been the round of the Ministries. Cox the Saint has lent me his camera and 4½ dozen films. Bed 11.30. Scorpio, Corvus and Leo visible from balcony.

17 MAY 1917. Away by 6.30 with a train of eight Ford motors, some of them lorries. Our having to carry a Gurkha escort and petrol for 150 miles reduces the available room by about half. Started with Goldsmith and the *Nawab* [88] (in charge of a great box containing 29,000 rupees). Picked up Garbett with a most elaborate canteen, bedding, etc., which it was the devil to fit in. Over the Bridge we had to pick up the two Shaikhs representing the tribes through whom we pass, for a fortnight ago travellers were being held up by brigands. The unfortunate military drivers had been 100 miles yesterday, and had not returned till seven, when they learnt their fate for the morrow. Very old tyres, and no spare parts. Road along the dyke made a little over five times longer owing to the floods caused by Arabs, who broke through a bund to water their lands. Three or four long breakdowns from various members of our octave, during which I learned a little of the management of the latest prismatic compass, lent me by Gertrude Bell; an operation simpler and less esoteric than I had supposed. The heat grew intense, and punctures and engine "trouble" more and more frequent, the road hardly ever appearing through the hillocks, ditches and ploughed fields. Yet I was glad to have pushed on, sure that, even without reaching Kárbala, we gain a day. Throughout my journey there is a tendency for all to say "Take your time—why rush it?" etc. as if one were on a honeymoon. It is only by going a little faster than everybody wants that I succeed in moving at all. Two miles away from Khan Iskándaría a gigantic yellow curtain began to pace us and draw nearer to us. It reached some 400 feet high, and discovered brown and black chasms. We began to hope to outstrip it, and might possibly have done so, if we had not heard the (hundredth) sharp bleat of a lorry in distress. With a wealth of expletive we turned, and almost at once were caught. It grew quite dark. For about half an hour the thing roared past us, far too loud for any word or talk, then with a few hard raindrops gradually cleared, allowing us to rattle in to Khan Iskándaría, where luncheon was served by Garbett's Indian servant, with the assistance of a Badawi local policeman with four long and beautifully braided pigtails. Thence on a fair road into Musáyib and on to the Euphrates, more picturesque than the Tigris, by 3.30. Musáyib is small and ruinous, but of importance as a granary. Received the head of the tribe responsible for us from Kárbala to Nájaf, also Muhammad Ali Kamúna who is to be my Kárbala host, hoping his house would prove cleaner than himself.

18 MAY 1917. A cold wind came up with the dawn, chilling me through my single sheet: started 10. Said had to sit outside a lorry, on the luggage, and complained of the sun, wind, bumping, etc., till I stole for him an Indian's umbrella, under which he lurched the remainder of the journey in grotesque contentment. By the little blue tiled dome of Aun our half-way halt, we had done 10 miles in nearly two hours, a rate I have lived to think very respectable. At Aun a local Arab notable insisted on giving us tea and wonderfully

[88] Attached Assistant Political Officer Khan Sahib Muhammad Husain Khan.

good and strong coffee in a Damascene tent, whilst some forty of his hangers-on watched each drop anxiously down our throats. After about an hour the
immense palms of Kárbala grew in sight, and outside the town we found the
notables drawn up to escort us in. We alighted to salute these; and then on,
followed and preceded by them in carriages and on horses (one elder galloping
very martially under an old umbrella), and with an escort of some forty
prancing Arabs. Later the two groups amalgamated; and surrounded by an
appalling dust which almost hid from us the green gardens the palms the vines
and the oleanders; with bystanders cheering women thrilling and trilling some
of the procession drawing their swords others their umbrellas; all shouting
like the King's champion loud defiances to non-existent foes; the first motor
in history, gravely punctured in its near hind Stepney, struggled rattling into
Kárbala. Then we went through a wooden door in the wall, down a few steps,
into what I have not seen since August three years ago—green upon green
under green. A Persian garden with long vine trellises and pergolas, and
narrow paths,

> "Annihilating all that's made
> To a green thought in a green shade."

We followed the brother of our host, Muhammad Ali Kamūna, through alleys
of oleanders, palms, roses, apricots and greengages, to a little pavilion—a cottage in a garden of cucumbers—for our private use, with a larger one a short
distance away for Receptions. I walked round and saw how

> "The nectarine and curious peach
> Into my hand themselves did reach",

and under the trellised grapes was complete shelter from the sun. In Europe,
after Ashridge or Ellesmere less perhaps than nothing—for hardly a flower;
but in Chaldaea after the long waste of the East, those voyages, and the bang
and crash of the kettly Fords, generally on first speed, the contrast was astonishing. At about 1.30 we were called for luncheon, which was spread, all the
dishes at once, on a table in the garden. Several sorts of Turkish dishes, including Bámia which I ate with pleasure for the first time—a sort of salt
rhubarb. About a melon each besides *mishmish* [39] and *barquq*.[40] But an excess
of their black coffee gave me a feeling of weakness for the rest of the day. We
were served by a Persian servant of great dignity and charm, who subsequently
smoked a cigarette in a great amber mouthpiece like those that are sold in
Cairo as umbrella handles. A merchant brought us round unbelievably poor
carpets, brass, rubies, turquoise and emeralds, and it is my belief that the place
has been scientifically gutted by German Baghdad. The entire staff having
vanished to the Hammām we were left to our own resources till 4.30 when the
Nāwwāb, returning in a lilac and white silk *aba*, conducted us round the
bazaars and general sights of the town. Arab policemen with slung rifles
and canes in their hands preceded us, and went through the form of technically thrashing the boys out of the way. Tall, narrow and well-roofed bazaars; but Kárbala produces nothing of its own, so of little interest. At a

[39] Apricot.
[40] Plum.

photographer's I found, and had removed, conspicuously hung chromolithographs of Franz Josef, Wilhelm, Ferdinand and Muhammad V; the *geste* richly approved by the throng. The *Nāwwāb* has but little idea of planning our time, being chiefly occupied in cultivating Garbett and so consolidating his own position. He has made no sort of arrangement for getting us even a distant view of the golden shrines, and it was not until we had seen the Municipality that I had to insist upon a roof climb, for which the house of Yázdi was selected. The tread of the stairs, almost 16 inches, is drastic, but the golden dome, golden minarets and golden clock-tower with great storks walking slowly round their summits, and the brilliantly tiled courtyard whose walls are like gardens, is an addition to visual experience; not but what the tiles are in themselves poor in design and colour suffused with that pink which is the sure and fatal sign of contact with the West. The people thronging our path greeted us with an indifferent friendliness; their faces bore an expression, if so it may be called, of dull depravity. We returned about 7, and received the notables, civil and pleasant but a little bullish and less intelligent than those of Qādhimain. I gather from many conversations that the Sharifial revolt is welcome to the Shia world as being anyhow anti-Turk and tending to exalt the Arab-born. Distributed some Raemakers, wishing to the Devil I had brought more from Egypt. Conversed chiefly with the *Kiliddar*,[41] a huge man of the Simon-the-Cellarer type. Our host Kamūna is hated in Kárbala, and the two greatest *Mujtahidīn*[42] will not visit us in his house. Walked and sat in the garden till dinner, chiefly of chocolate and melon, and to bed in the little loggia about 9.30. Exhausted.

19 MAY 1917. Aetat 35½. Up at 6 and after breakfast to a round of visits. The first of these to Husain Mazandarāni, easily the most important *Mujtáhid* of Kárbala. An old man of charming manners (up stairs of appalling severity), sitting in a small library of I should say 400 books, chiefly manuscripts, which fit easily into the arcade of shallow recessed arches, a feature in all these houses. H. M. is a rare example of the vanishing sage. Equally, and, for the visitor, bafflingly at home in Arabic, Persian and Hindustani, he is (alas) prepared upon the lightest pretext to reopen the question of the comparative merits of Plato and Aristotle. Seeing my interest in his books he sent for the key of another library of about the same size and showed it to me with pride. I asked if we might photograph him and he said "after your fortunate return from Nájaf", rightly interpreting which as an evasion, and using the privilege of the Arab Guest, I called to the servants in a terrible voice, "Go, some of you and bring the picture of our master", and in about ten minutes one returned with an admirable portrait which H. M. sealed for me himself. Neither in his house nor in any other, did I see a chair, and in all the sons in a row knelt inclining backwards against the wall. The other *Mujtahidīn* were equally interested in and approving of the Sharifial movement. These visits were repaid us, even by Mazandarāni (who cried Allah some eight times before he faced the stairs), in the house of the *Nāwwāb's* cousin, where there went up a *parfum impérissable,* which only could not be the drains themselves, because there are none; and in spite of the charm of the storks flying slowly round and round high over the courtyard, I left the house only just

---

[41] "Key-keeper" or Guardian of the Sacred Mosque.
[42] Shia, Learned Man, equivalent to Sunni Ālem (plural Ulama).

not fainting. We visited the Persian school, a model of ideal and decorative pedagogy. The plan is roughly Shakespeare's Theatre. The pupils are the groundlings, and the professors sit on Juliet's balcony or pace Crookback's Tower roof. A gallery runs round this first floor, and gives into a score of little rooms, each with its round arched door. Decorative system, tiles on the floor, alcoves with returned white plaster arches. A few Persian maps hung against these; no other implements of science visible. The pupils "ran" from 4 to 10 years. Several wore the green turban of the Sayyid; many, great silver-bossed belts, and only one poor devil a ready-made European suit, complete with black Kalpak and huge black boots. I implored and persuaded the Head-master to make Persian costume obligatory down to the smallest detail. Heard a rather pathetic song, in unison, commemorating the glories of Irán. Photo-graphed the entire establishment and back to luncheon in the garden, after which we left Kárbala with lively regret soon after one. Outside to the West appear three or four perfect glowing turquoises, which are the blue-tiled domes of the saints; among them Hurr. The road to Nájaf is fairly easy, divided into four by three *Khans,* which we made on an average in about an hour apiece. Far away on the western bank of the Euphrates, Birs Nimrūd, the Tower of Babel, is visible for many miles round. Good going on the whole, though we had to get out and shove through the heavy sand several times, in great heat. Soon after half-way a diamond point of light became a glittering topaz, deepened to an inverted golden bowl and finally revealed the dome of the shrine of Our Master the Martyr Ali. Sand-grouse in small coveys walked or fluttered within 20 yards of us and many curious creatures that we imagined were armadillos galloped about still closer and disappeared into their burrows. We reached the walled town of Nájaf before 5.30, which, un-like Kárbala in its cup of land, stands up to view; thousands coming to greet us, and the bazaars being (tiresomely) closed in honour of our advent, which happens to coincide with the feast of the Prophet Muhammad's Mab'ath (Elec-tion, Calling or Mission). Walked through the tall narrow well-roofed ba-zaars; the end of one of which, as by a hanging of gorgeous silk, is barred by the great tiled gate of the Holy Precinct. An enormous crowd was waiting for us at the house of the *Kiliddar,* a triple edifice with kitchen and harem of three stories, including, as everywhere in Mesopotamia, immense *Sardabs,* built deep in the ground of solid vaulted masonry (supported on short fat Norman columns) which keep a temperature of at least 10 degrees lower than any other room in the building. Tea was given us in a long grey-green oddly Venetian room, with ceiling-panels of glass so bad as to be almost successful; on to the central court is a continuous row of small arched windows, and below a number of rather attractive children, some with short hair and tur-bans, others bareheaded with flowing locks, hung about, got in the way, were furiously cursed and, as throughout the East, moved away each time a few feet to return after five minutes, when *da capo.* The din was infernal; we were spent with the banging car, and heartily relieved when invited to visit the great flat roof which gives, within 50 yards, on to the golden dome, minarets and clock-tower, of Sayyidna Ali. There I photographed in the setting sun, and then sat watching the gleam fail until the sun went down, and the clock chimed 12,[48] with all four quarters, taking me back to Cambridge or Big

---

[48] Sunset, the end of the Moslem day.

Ben, a better man than the lot of them. There is not a foot of green in all Nájaf, and as we supped on the still, gloomy roof with our agreeable but eructating host, we sharply regretted not being able to plan another evening in the garden of Kárabala. And so to bed about 9.30, weary after my reception between 7 and 8 o'clock of the heads of the Municipality and leading Shaikhs, whom I harangued on Garbett's behalf on the Key to Egypt's Millions, and the only way of acquiring such, and getting rich, i.e. *Paying Taxes.*

20 MAY 1917. Rose about 6, intending to visit Kúfa at 8, but having seen various persons first, waited till after 10. G. told me I made a speech in Arabic in my sleep. He snores. I called for carpet and silk merchants, and sent for the astrologer most in repute. My shaving was watched throughout by one of the children very much in the attitude of a Sistine cherub, and my bath compassed about with a cloud of witnesses, to the *pudeur* of Garbett, whose home is not, like mine, broke these six years to the Nude.

My horoscope was then cast by the astrologer, without, however, any reference to my own dates or to the Celestial Bodies. The henna-bearded sage, who is also a schoolmaster, after scratching a number of Morse dots and dashes on the writing paper, told me to ask any questions I might wish resolved, as he had no remarks to offer himself. By this I perceived him to be no true Mage, and contented myself with the information that I should return to my country but after a long time, and by sea. This, if it comes true, is certainly worth ten rupees. I then spoke for ten minutes with Shaikh Hādi of Jaaro (7 hours S. of Nájaf), quoting the large current of food going from him to Ibn Rashīd.[44] He replied that food was going, but not from his Arabs, that we overestimated his influence and that his land needed water. I feared this would never flow in his direction until Ibn Rashīd's supplies had ceased utterly, and maintained the same language to other Shaikhs. On our way through the bazaar we saw a young gazelle sitting quietly in a shop, and immediately, by command of Hajji Atia, the creature was transferred to our party. He also urged us to take the little two-horse tram across the desert, offering instantly to turn off the passengers within and without, about 40 in number, for our greater ease and convenience. As our two cars ploughed through the heavy sand we began to regret having refused this civility, but the track improved and we accomplished the seven miles to Kúfa in less than an hour. There we walked into the house of Alwān, Chief of the Bani Hassan tribe, who rules the roost and (what is more important for us) the road, from Nájaf to Musáyib. There we sat on a sort of loggia overlooking the Euphrates, and from 11.15 till 12.15 I harangued Alwān and his principal supporters. Hard work, in their dialect, until I pointed out to them that unless they showed some sign of understanding me or not, beyond saying "Bali", "yes", to my statements, warnings and questions, I might as well be addressing so many portraits. (If I had known them better I would have said Bulls.) Once they perceived my difficulty, which I attributed to their eloquent and my indifferent Arabic, they spoke and reasoned as men galvanized. Finally, I charged them to go over and possess the 10,000 camels of Ibn Rashīd, which they swore to do. In suggesting this simple scheme, I feared I was skirting the obvious until I found that neither Garbett nor the *Nāwwāb* had considered it, and even when I had proposed it to Garbett the *Nāwwāb* thought the Shaikh

---

[44] Then in league with the Turks.

would have to be paid, as if people required bribing to make them accept (at least) £50,000. An excellent luncheon (which we passed on to the drivers who ate a chicken each) consisting for me almost exclusively of stuffed tomatoes. I am indeed the worst possible of explorers, mistrusting and disliking all new and unknown foods, without ever having acquired a taste for even the best Oriental cookery. We left Kūfa, which is little more than a village, stopping to see and photograph the shrine (again under a turquoise dome), commemorating the spot where Ali was slain. I had read somewhere that it contained an ancient granite pillar, with the curious property of deciding whether or no a person was legitimate, by allowing or not allowing his arms to encircle it; and asked if this were so. The Sayyid Abbās and all present replied with enthusiasm that it was, but that we could not see it as it was within the hallowed precinct. I was disappointed, but agreed nevertheless that this discriminating and potentially tactless column is far better left in Kūfa, where it is. We were back in Nájaf by 2.40. On returning we found the gazelle walking about the house, and fed it awhile with green clover; rested a little in the cool of the Sardab and after 5 with Garbett to visit the Shaikh Muhammad Qādhem al-Yázdi, whose word goes through Iraq to Ispahan. His feelings towards us were not considered certain, and he had already refused a gift of £200. Garbett had now been asked to approach him with £1000, and begged me, though he knew it to be a forlorn hope, to attempt it for him. I accepted the mission with reserve, crammed the packet of notes into my pocket, and walking round with Garbett to the Sayyid's house, waited for some five minutes outside his room door, while another Shaikh called upon him very reverently to emerge. He came out, a very old man in white *guftan* and turban, his beard and his finger-nails dyed brilliant red with henna; saluted us distantly, and sat us down beside himself on the mat outside the wall of his chamber. I can well understand his influence and renown. There is a strength in his straight features and tired grey eyes, and an authority in his weary presence and faint utterance that I have not seen elsewhere in Islam. After compliments I began by asking him if there was anything we could do for him. He repeated: "Maintain the Holy Thresholds"—"*Atabāt al-Sharīfa, Atabāt al-Sharīfa.*" By this I took him to mean both the shrines themselves and the body of *Mujtahidīn*. He was urgent that we should employ none but Shia in the Shia Cities. Also that we should release, for political effect, Dr Muzaffar Bey and Jamàl Baba, two Shias now imprisoned in Baghdad: and appoint Mirza Muhammad Kaimakam of Nájaf. By this time he appeared to have thawed very considerably, and favoured me with some very flattering remarks, adding in Persian (I afterwards learnt) to the Ālem present, that if the Turks had behaved thus, they would never have lost the Arabs. I said I would transmit his lofty advice to Cox, and liking my task less and less, requested three minutes' privacy with him, reminded him of the countless poor that looked to him (and that we were naturally unable to relieve) and begged him to help us in this matter; but he pushed away the packet with a gentle but very definite firmness, saying that the time was not yet, and that he must beg to be excused. I thought it undignified to press him overmuch, and talked of the Sharīf, of whom he is an admirer and a supporter. We stayed just short of an hour, and before bidding him farewell I made another appeal, which he again most courteously rejected, consenting only to accept my miserable

Raemakers. I am convinced it is not a question of money with him, but rather an unbought and unbuyable pride: he will yield gracefully when the motive can no longer be imputed—an atmosphere remote indeed from Egypt and the Hejaz. Back and photographed all the children, with the gazelle, which I found strolling up and down on the roof. I begged Sayyid Abbās to join us at dinner, thus making of it I trust a reasonable and lively sacrifice to politeness and policy. The perfect host afterwards assisted in waiting upon our drivers, at the same table. A sullen airless night, in which I had occasion to remark the strange utter dogless silence of Nájaf between 2 and 4, and before the dawn.

21 MAY 1917. Rose soon after five, to be confronted with a complete and universal delay in overnight's plans, which were, that the cars should be ready and waiting to take us at 5.45. After distributing about 150 rupees in tips, or rather cascading the silver into the hand of the chief servant, we left the house by 6.15, only to find the cars unloaded, not ready, and still in the Khan at 6.30. The drivers' excuses were (*a*) that they had no watch, (*b*) that "they had been kept waiting for their tea". The gazelle lay with the luggage in one of the lorries. G. began ferociously damning them, but I stopped him, and pointed out to them that we had throughout tried to do our best "by" them, and regretted that our attempt to treat them as gentlemen had ended in failure. Lent them Said's watch. And so, with terrific farewells, at 7.55 out of Nájaf, returning by Kárbala and past the cemeteries where men pay £60 for a burial-place, into a powerful Shamāl, with sand in our faces almost intolerable, which continued, whenever we left the half-cultivation, throughout the morning. I was glad to leave the oppression of those crowded houses with their pullulating 50,000, wedged and locked within the narrow walls, wherein is no blade of green, and the air listless and second-hand. We pushed across the plain with three or four soft sand and one mud digression, saw the golden dome of Husain at 10.45, entered Kárbala through the gracious approach of palms and lakes, and were in Muhammad Ali Kamūna's garden again at 11.20. Here we found that Fahd Bey had arrived, so decided not to press on to Hilla that night but to content ourselves with reaching Musáyib. Soon after luncheon Fahd Bey was brought in to us, and Garbett handed him over to me for Treatment. A short slight Shaikh, very brown in the face, with weak eyes, and great dignity of manner. Very old (but the *Nāwwāb* says still actively, if optimistically, philo-progenitive). After compliments I gave him Cox's message and hoped he was coming in to Baghdad. I paused for a reply, but he said: "You finish what you've got to say, and then I'll tell you what I've got to say"; so I explained to him about the 10,000 camels removable from Nájaf, and hoped he approved. Finally, that we had heard that his men were looting on the Kárbala-Musáyib road—surely a basely false rumour. Fahd, whom I begin to admire as a man of business, replied: that he was already coming in to Cox, had a letter for him, and would like a car from Musáyib: that Alwān and friends were welcome to the Nájaf camels, but that they had better look sharp about it: finally, that the looting rumours were lies: expressed an almost compromising affection for Gertrude Bell, underwent, with his son, my camera, and was off. Saw the *Kiliddar* of Nájaf and a few more people, besides some execrable carpets, and away through the delightful gardens, groves and thickets, past the sapphire dome of Aun a little after 4, and to

Musáyib by 6.45, seeing as we entered the town a flock of sea-gulls. At Gold-smith's house the gazelle walked over the gallery parapet, fell 18 feet into the brick-flagged court below, and suffered nothing more than a slight limp in its near hind. Garbett proposed that we should sail down the Euphrates to Hilla by bălăm in a sure three hours instead of the motors' dubious four, and I agreed. Clambering up the narrow staircase to bed at 10, I fell with the lamp and broke it.

22 MAY 1917. Again we were about half an hour after time, and did not get off in the two bălăms until 6.45. I made a mental resolve to make all plans for the future myself. They had made for us a sort of reed hood, under which, in always increasing heat and swarms of biting flies, we had breakfast. At the Hindyia Barrage, though the regulators were open, the drawbridge was not, and we had to walk nearly a mile each way to get the key—another 45 min-utes lost. The Turks had smashed up all the houses, and the Arabs had looted them: but when it came to the Turks attempting to dynamite the Dam, and so ruin the country, the Arabs resolutely refused to allow it. Immediately below the fall-race were a score of round guffas [45] bobbing about, and hauling in fish by the dozen. The Euphrates banks are wonderfully picturesque, and almost as varied and beautiful as an English river: palms, pomegranates, apri-cots and un-Egyptian grass. But the hours dragged on, and we did not reach Hilla until 2.30, or 7¾ hours' journey. The town is pretty, and will be of great importance when it has recovered from the late Turkish visitation, in which many of the people were shot, every single notable, to the number of 170, hanged, and many of the women abducted.[46] Goldsmith at present in Mena-hem's clean and pleasant house: he tells me that the Venerable offered to provide him also with a lady companion. Business till three when I suggested a visit to Babylon. Every one estimated its distance differently, varying between 2 and 4 hours: also, the road being considered unsafe, we had to wait till four for mounted police. Walking at nearly five miles an hour, the time from Menahem Daniel's house to the temple of Mardak is 1½ hours, and very hard work at that. This most famous city of remoter antiquity is still impressive in the melancholy vastness and abandon of its mounds. The excavation, though immense, cannot represent one-thousandth of the real area. All brick, save for the colossal stone lion that tramples on a headless man. The animals in relief beautifully executed, and equal, in my opinion, to the best Egyptian work. We could not spend much more than an hour there, and passed on to the German Archaeological Mission's house, in a palm-grove, well and solidly built. The keeper, a villainous looking ruffian, was in great terror of us, and I am sure has been far more guiltily engaged even than in bombing boats, which he is known to have done to extract toll. We warned him to be terribly careful what he did, and went over the house, which has not been visibly pillaged. I will confess to a lively sympathy with those Boches, whose work remains stacked, packed, numbered, ticketed and cata-logued in the best German tradition of conscientious meticulousness. But Oh, to find in the library, as first specimen, *der Telemak von Fénelon*: yet they

---

[45] Deep round hide coracles.
[46] "Said thinks the Euphrates is a continuation of the Nile, and resolutely refuses to be impressed by anything except the Turkish atrocities. . . . It is a good thing for Egyptians to see such things with their own eyes."

say the English take their pleasures sadly. Much Scott, in English, and of course Science. In the study one or two picture postcards of Female Loveliness struck a lighter but not more agreeable note. We rode back on police horses of which I requisitioned one for Said, as the renowned Ālem of Egypt, a title which his turban carries off better than his sheepish grin. Nearly halfway back we met the motors, which had been sent in some anxiety to scour for us. At dinner an able Young,[47] doing local purchase, wore a silk Nájaf *aba*. Amused to find that Garbett, ex-rowing coach, and in face and figure akin to Eugene Sandow, tires and needs water with far greater frequency than myself.

23 MAY 1917. Rose soon after 5, and away by car to Birs Nimrūd, the Tower of Babel. Our four-seater being under repair, I was driven in a lorry by a Blackpool dentist from Burton-on-Trent, who told me the story of his life. Road across the plains very bad, so much so that we had to get to work several times with the spade, and on one occasion lift the car over a difficult chasm. This famous mound is visible far across the plain, and is surmounted by a square brick tower, riven right through by lightning. Everywhere traces of an ancient conflagration. We reached it at 9.40 and stayed till 10. All around, remains in beautiful dull red brick, and about a quarter of a mile away the Tomb of Abraham, or rather Maqām, a little dome over a square mud-brick wall. I asked our armed police: "What is this place called?" "*Qasr* or *Birs Nimrūd*." "And who was Nimrūd?" "*Málik-y-Dúnya*"—"King of the World." Our four drivers delighted, "honoured", to stand on the Tower of Babel—which after all has as good a title to authenticity as most very ancient monuments; for what could be more natural than that indented labour collected by kingly ambition from widely diverse countries, none understanding the other, should lead to rows? Or that the all-dreaded thunderstone should be ascribed by strikers' union-leaders to the Wrath of Heaven? Back at Hilla received Muhammad al-Kaswīni, (Notable chiefly because unhung, or because of his teeth? I know not which): but did not waste even a Raemakers on him. We returned his visit in the midday heat, and afterwards saw in the bazaar the exquisite tile-fronted Maqām, where the last Mahdi [48] Imam was last seen—or once seen—it is difficult to say which, as there is another *Maqām* at Samarra. Domed, of course, and the interior octagon pendentives finely utilized for decorative script. Blue- and yellow-tiled floors and wall wainscoting. The stairs of the Municipality of Hilla are built almost exclusively of inscribed Babylonian bricks, and I urged Garbett to have them replaced and deciphered. The whole town is constructed out of ancient Babylon, though of course not all inscribed cuneiform. We left at 12.40 and reached Baghdad with little mishap at 6.15, beyond our wildest hopes. The second bridge having disappeared we took oars, and reached our houses, deeply caked in sand, about 6.30. Long talks with Cox and Gertrude Bell.

24 MAY 1917. Up at 7, glad of the additional rest. Made out a list of necessities for the Arabian journey, which Gertrude Bell considerably amplified. Lunched with staff mess, and played to them 40 minutes on their fair Schiedmayer. Gertrude Bell very full of a plan, put forward by Père Anatase, who

---

[47] Afterwards Sir Hubert Young, K.C.M.G., my successor as Governor of Northern Rhodesia, 1934.

[48] Lit. "The Directed One," Muhammad Abu 'l Qāsem, the twelfth Imam, the ruler who, according to the Shia, shall in the last days reappear upon earth.

says certain Shia Notables desire to form a deputation and visit the Sharīf. If one could get big enough and holy enough men, there might be enough in it to countervail the certain sneer from Egypt that England worked up the *geste*. I saw Anastase, who has yet no great Alem or *Mujtáhid* to propose. He thought Abd al-Husain Tabātabái might come, but I am certain he would demand at least equality with the propounder of the project, Shahistāni, who, by the way, consistently preached the Jihad against us at the beginning of the War. The other six are *écrivains célèbres*, and I wished I had ever heard their names before. Each would require first-class return Mecca via Jedda: the six minor £100 and the two major £150 for their families during their absence. Cheap, if the men were first class themselves. Anastase was at Kaisaría until last July, and told me frightful and filthy horrors practised by the Turks upon innocent Armenians. He had written down full details of names, numbers, etc., which would have been invaluable to a post-bellum *corps de vengeance*; unfortunately, his brother destroyed all 300 pages, considering they were a death-warrant if found upon Anastase. With Gertrude Bell dined with Col. Dickson. I sat between Gen. MacMunn, who is taking me to Basra on Monday, and Col. Willcox, chief consulting physician to the forces, who analysed Crippen's *tutti frutti* and had him hung over them. He gave me some advice on resistance to the sun, always my fear. (Gen. MacMunn in favour of soldiers marrying in war time: "on the naval principle of never omitting to lay down a new keel".)

25 MAY 1917. Up at 7. Most of the day reading Doughty and trying with Gertrude Bell to settle route after Buraida.[49] I suggested getting MacCallan [50] from Egypt to advise on eyes. In the morning Cox read out and dispatched his telegram to the India Office, suggesting that he should accept the H.C.-ship: or else be replaced, as unable to carry out the policy of H.M.G. A fine message, after being brought to bed of which he cheers visibly. Dined with him. Apparently the cipher Chancery gave me has been compromised in Persia (do they know?) these two years. Continued to glean for a Najd glossary from Doughty's Index till nearly midnight.

26 MAY 1917. I completed my Najd glossary which, so far as I can see, amounts to little more than a few imprecations, and the names of the fouler diseases. With G. B. marked out Doughty's route S. of Anaizah to Ri 'Sail and Taif. It is very vague, and I suspect the map: still I trust sufficiently exact to enable the Sharīf Abdallah to meet me. Interviewed Shaikh Shahistāni, begetter of the Shia deputation, and told him fairly that, unless the other seven names were up to his celebrity (and if possible a little holier), I feared it would be neither to our, the Sharīf's, nor his own interest to dispatch them. At 8 Beach took me across to dine with Gen. Cobbe, a fine type of practical soldier, and looking the part. In command of the Samarra Corps, where, since an accident to one of his two engines, he is never more than two days rations in hand. Enlarged on unique importance of adequate gunning to protect infantry against machine-guns. Turks fighting fairly straight, but one or two white-flag tricks and dum-dum bullets. A sand-gale blowing into my eyes detracted from the pleasure of the repast. Beach tells me that Turks are better 'planed than we, having a wonderful German Schulz who has already

---

[49] See Map. Ibn Sa'ud's capital, in central Najd.
[50] The well-known Welbeck-Street oculist.

accounted for four of our airmen, besides burying them and reading the funeral service over their graves. No word of my mails.

27 May 1917. Late up with real regrets at the thought of my last day with the kindness, sympathy and appreciation of Cox and Gertrude Bell, which remind me of how I used to feel when working with K. and Colum. To Col. Perry of the Survey, who explained to me how to take bearings and plot out a map to scale. I have a stupid head for these things, and will do my best but with diffidence. Would to God I had learned it all twenty years ago. Fear that bearings will be my limit, and the map far beyond. With Said began packing. Poor devil, he little knows the extent of his trial. Checked with Gertrude Bell the chief points in Syro-Arabo-Mesopotamian liaison scheme: she carries a first-class brain with which it is a pleasure to work. At 5 she and I took Cox out in the motor, almost by force, from his 6 a.m. to midnight seven days a week. Khan Ortma, Marjanía mosque, ancient cannon in citadel, city gate and round the walls far S.E. through the gardens and the dust and back by twilight. He seemed to enjoy it, and I trust Gertrude Bell will continue the treatment. At dinner books and writers, she universal and level in judgment. I begged Cox for some kind of instructions in handling Ibn Sa'ud, and he promised to prepare what his amazing tact calls an *aide mémoire.*

28 May 1917. Late up to a hot oppressive day. Cox read me my letter of introduction to Ibn Sa'ud; as always, a model of clear agreeable writing. Took car to bid farewell to the *Naqíb,* who was more than friendly. Farewell talk with Gertrude Bell, whose frail body must have rest if it is to endure the summer, and discussed *aide mémoire* with Cox. Received from tailor an inferior *zibun* (*quftan*) which will be my desert best, and said goodbye to the lower and coloured staff. Finally, with lively regret and living gratitude to Gertrude Bell and Cox himself: whose kindness I shall never forget. And at 3.30 aboard the *S.I.* We set off down stream at 4, and almost at once I had the advantage of a two hours' compass instruction by Col. Barron. *S.I.* has immense canvas cabins and two long baths (the first I have seen since Karachi) but no berths: so I had to borrow one spare camp-bed from Mac-Munn and to sleep on it without sheets, blankets, pillow or mattress. We went ashore at Ctesiphon, tying up there for the night, and spent an hour about the ruins with MacMunn. The arch, though an architectural achievement, is a thought too pointed to satisfy the eye, and the building has in general that lack of economy in weight and material which characterizes most antique construction. But the real surprise is the façade remote from the river, whose courses of Romanesque blind arcading jump you straight into the Middle Ages. I trust they will make MacMunn G.O.C. after the War. He is the one General Officer I have yet met with the qualifications for a wise political peace commander: and for the rest, it is largely his Lines of Communications that won and hold Baghdad. Dinner comparatively cool. Every one seems to know about my journey, wherever I go, and I detect a *moriturum te salutamus* concern, sometimes a little disconcerting.

29 May 1917. All day in a scorching wind, blowing in upon us earthy dust and sand. I corrected back numbers and pasted photographs, now so dry that they split and chip like toast. Towards evening the General lent me *Blackwood's Centenary,* in which I read twice, with eager disappointment, Charles Whibley's tribute to H.C. ending with four misquotations in two lines. He

labours his charm, but neglects his greatness of being, which Curzon's more kindred essence so loftily indicated in his obituary letter to *The Times*. We anchored in midstream off Shamran, actual railhead in the Kut-Baghdad line, which is to be finished by the beginning of August. Anxious weeks for Transport until that date. Bed 10.30 rather bored by the number of objects one must carry on one's own camel—practically on one's own person: revolver, binoculars, traverse table, compass, aneroid (or it breaks) and water—to say nothing of Kodak, useless if inaccessible. The thought of compass-work in particular fills me with weariness and disgust.

30 MAY 1917. Up 5.30 and ashore with MacMunn at Kut—*"morne plaine"* —of which we walked the streets with Wilson, A.P.O. The Turks on their re-entry hanged about 30 Shia, chiefly to please the Sunni—who wisely followed the Turks at their evacuation, when they removed also a good few Jews, and most of the transportable timber. Almost the only untouched building is the Hammām, a series of cup vaults beautifully resting upon pointed arches. The ruined streets are being repaired as quickly as possible, and the inhabitants are returning from all sides. Townshend's cemetery is in a palm-garden: many filled graves and great pits, and many that still yawn their ponderous jaws for the friendless bodies of the unburied thousands on the opposite bank. Finally to Townshend's house, whose roof, parapeted with bullet-riddled tin, and armed with a small brick dug-out, put me in mind of Gordon's stairs at Khartum. All say he should never have been left there: and having been left, could and should have been relieved. Now, no reforms or prosperity, no victories far or near will ever "wipe out Kut"; and it must remain for ever the site of a Tragedy.

All day long a burning wind, blowing 110° in the shade, and reaching a climax of discomfort when we tied up to leeward of a railway depot. A young Captain came aboard, clean-shaved and faultlessly neat. He lives in a dark brown whirlwind of earth dust, under which all his effects, food included, lie deeply smothered. If he leaves his tent in a gale, the murk is such that he will never find it again. The sand gives him colitis about once a week: and canteen boats sent to relieve him are pillaged by friends, equally necessitous, on the way. He has tea at 5 a.m., no breakfast or luncheon, ("not much tempted to eat") and has to gargle every half-hour at night to clean his throat. "Place is bloody, and could do with some leave"; but far more content than X in Cairo savagely abusing the Cavasses because his paper-knife is the wrong side of his blotter; or a fat Pasha, *se plaignant de sa situation personnelle, sa dignité et son amour propre.* We sat gasping till evening when Macrae told us of Yogis whose nails grow through the back of the clenched fist, fused one flesh in this appetizing penance. Bed 10.30. Cabin temp. 107°, no sheet to lie on, rather a trial.

31 MAY 1917. Furious Simūm still blowing as we reached Amāra at 10. I rested and wrote alternately. Even the woodwork inside the cabin almost too hot to touch. At about 5, feeling that something must be done, I walked across the bridge of boats to look up the local Political, Mackenzie, whom I found absent, his place taken by Taylor, shot through head and ulcer in eye: now recovered and hoping to make career in Mesopotamia. Took me across to Club in Political bălăm, and sent me back to S.I. The bălăm rocked and took in so much water that I turned to abuse the bow gondolier, only to find him

fallen into the Tigris, from which his heels emerged foolishly, to the delight of the ladies washing on the bank. Very late out to dinner with Col. Senior of the Gurkhas, and at 10 across to the Amāra-Qurna train, where Macrae and self made our beds in an open truck, at the end of a truck full of Indians. I slept, under the moon, more comfortably than I have these many days, in spite of the bumping, rumbling and springless jolting.

1 JUNE 1917. Long before 6 the sun seemed to have half-volleyed himself far up the sky; by 6.30 we were at Qurna, where shaved and breakfasted with Mackie, the new, and how fresh, A.P.O.: in appearance the *jeune premier* of a Shaw or Barker play. Left at 8.30 and quickly down the Tigris in his launch, an estimated 4½ hours, but were off Basra in four. Then the shaft broken down, and the last ¼ mile in about an hour. Great heat all the way. Straight to MacMunn's house. Some *Vie Parisiennes* heartened me, and I needed it, for not one line yet to hand from Europe or Cairo—a cruel and needless privation. A. T. Wilson, sublimely and inhumanly efficient, took me in his car, and verified my list of necessities: then round the town to fulfil them. Sometimes I feel the heat and thirst so much that my journey seems a maniac's nightmare: and sometimes all shines smooth and roseate. He pointed out to me returning groups of the Amazon Labour Corps, who work far better than the Arabs, and struck when their British Officer was about to be transferred. Also over the Prison, where murderers economically fold obsolete forms into Government envelopes. Dined with him, and to the Cinema; rough and far more picturesque than the perfected Egyptian *Salle*. Although the (usual N. European) story is illuminated by English descriptions only, the audience seemed to follow the silly melodrama with ease and exactitude. Like all practically temperamental people, their public *pudeur* is in inverse relation to their private *mœurs*, and every time the heroine was kissed, by anybody, the act was received with protesting groans. Similarly French and Italians criticize English and German freedoms and publicities. I sat next to the Persian Consul, who receives his salary (as I begin to believe does all the earth), from Great Britain. After a drink on the old Turkish Serai, to bed, directly under a strong punkah.

2 JUNE 1917. Day in and out of canteens, Fraser, Leach and Weborny, Ordnance Stores. Wilson, everywhere a miracle of willing speed and efficiency. We called on Lady Cox. She gave us a cold ginger-beer, and sewed tapes to my back sun-pad. Dr Borrie to tea: his saintly wife sending, against future replacement, a small tea-basket which should ease my life, and still more Said's, very considerably. He also explained to me at length the uses of the small arsenal of drugs, provided me by the Red Cross, including, I rejoice to note, caster-oil to Win the Hearts of the Froward. A telegram from Kut to say my mails are somehow suspended there: angry relief, and I shall sit at Kuwait until I get them, and read the three months old *Times* in Najd.

MacMunn back to dinner; I sat next to an Australian nurse, who informed me that her family was the only other branch of that of the Earl of Macclesfield.

3 JUNE 1917. At 7 a Syrian member of the Armenian Catholic Church gave me against my journey a right convict cropping. To the unique A. T. Wilson, who in a flash fulfilled my uttermost desire, without in any way retarding his own press of work. Borrie completed my pharmacy, and gave me perman-

ganate instead of the chlorinating powder which is difficult, and long in operation. Next, Howell, I.C.S., about five years my senior, who is journeying with
me to Kuwait. After luncheon to the *Lewis Pelly* (known by local humorists
as the Lousy Polly) in which ignoble little kettle we left Basra at 3.20 and
reached the Shaikh Khazal of Muhámmara's palace a little before 5. A luxurious bálam at once took us to the steps, just beyond the head of which the
Shaikh himself, surrounded by his Persian bodyguard, greeted me, forced me
up the stairs of the Salamlik in front of himself, and led me into one of his
many reception rooms, Bentwood furniture and aniline portrait carpet panels.
He seemed to know about my journey, and wrote me out letters of introduction to the Shaikh of Kuwait and Ibn Sa'ud. Made the suggestion of sending
a sort of Embassy to the Sharíf, but wants encouragement from Cox; who I
doubt not will produce it. Khazal is a soft-featured soft-voiced, soft-mannered
man. So obviously *un des notres* that anything approaching propaganda is
with him ludicrously superfluous. He was inclined to underline this point,
until his reassurances became a tedium to me. We went the round of his
numerous halls of reception, including a fine *Sardab:* but the walls ruined by
Chaldean *alti rilievi* in stucco. His Persian vizier, and creator, who had been
all over Europe, is an interesting figure and, I am told, in his not infrequent
cups a most amusing companion. At about 6 we took leave, descended the
steps, and endured, at the rigid salute, two verses of the National Anthem.
Adagio and *sostenuto* in drums fifes and brass, Khazal bestowing upon me a
life-sized photograph of himself. After arranging with the little gunner captain to go straight through from Fas so as to be in Kuwait by 8, and testing
Marris' verse translation of Horace's *Odes,* a creditable if unlovely performance, I had set, pressed, and appreciated my new camp-bed.

4 JUNE 1917. Waking about 6, found a stiff sea running and great heat.
Howell, overcome by nausea, withdrew below. Discovered that the beastly
little captain had stopped the ship for his swinish slumbers at Fas from 1.30
till 4.30. This gave us the great heat of the day and delayed us until 3.20
p.m. when we anchored at Kuwait off Hamilton's [51] summer residence. He
soon stood by in a sailing-boat and took us off. Bald, good blue eyes. I fear
horribly disappointed at not going with me to Buraida. Less practical than
Wilson, but not less well intentioned. His house about two miles W. of the
town of Kuwait, clean, comfortable and well furnished. A little after 5 the
Shaikh Sālim called in honour of the King's Birthday. A sharply different
type from Muhámmara. Courteous, but with the reserved austerity of a strict
Moslem ruler and saint. His brother paved the way for his accession by dying
of over-eating. Hamilton finds him good in transaction of business, but at
heart fanatical—not in the sense of anti us, but against the education for
which many of his subjects clamour. I liked him, and promised to visit him
next day. His mortifications include the abandonment of electric light, but
stop short of surrendering his interest in the town ice-plant. When he had
gone, Bailey, Hamilton, Howell and self bathed in the sunset, well within
our depths as there are sharks in the channel, and no one seemed to know
exactly where the channel was. At dinner I drank a little glass of old Shiraz
wine, which resembles good sherry, weaker than ginger-beer. We sat out on
the sand under the moon, and to bed about 10.30. About 11.30 I remembered

[51] Political officer and Consul at Kuwait, now Lord Bellhaven and Stenton.

I had left my one indelible pencil outside, so very softly down to rescue it. A little way down the stairs I was startled by being challenged in a loud voice by Hamilton, who sprang from his bed pointing at me and screaming "Who goes there?" I said my name several times before discovering that it conveyed nothing to him as he was only half awake. Suspecting he had a revolver I made no attempt to slip away, and repeated my name until he "took notice". I then found that he held sure enough a loaded Browning in his hand, and was mightily relieved to have escaped. Dreamt for the rest of the night that I was a spy flying for my life.

5 JUNE 1917. The Shaikh Sālim of Kuwait sent his Minerva car for us, and we whizzed through narrow lanes and under covered bazaars at what I thought a hideous velocity, old women and venerable Mullas taking headers into open doorways, to ward off αἰπὺν ὄλεθρον. Sālim's palace is well built, and I remarked the freer disposition of former rulers in the ceilings, which are composed of life-sized chromo-lithographic busts of queens, princesses and artists' models, separated from one another by gold framing. He underwent rather than grasped at being photographed in the midst of his guards, and I promised to see him again before leaving. Gradually collected my trousseau, and round after midday on camels to see the other dhulūls [52] and their equipment. An interminable discussion as to time and routes. As elsewhere I find hustling inevitable, but I like little Abd al-Azīz, and approve of him as my caravan-bashi. [53] My dhulūl's paces inferior to those of best Egyptian Coastguards, so far as I remember them. But I have not ridden since mid-May 1914, so shall suffer a good deal at first. Kuwait is a clean agreeable little town, in climate far superior to Basra. Sea-going vessels on archaic lines and of beautiful finish are produced in great quantities. Market good but dearer than those of Iraq. We returned to the house by car, and took it again to go to tea with Mylrea, [54] the American Missionary and his wife, whom I admired for their holding up of the clean European torch of ordinary decent living in these rebarbative regions. She had been three summers in Kuwait and found it a paradise compared with Bahrein. We bathed again on the muddy low tide.

6 JUNE 1917. We rode round to the Consulate, a journey which, owing to badly packed saddle galled me cruelly, and tore away some skin, an annoyance just before my pilgrimage. I wrestled with Ibn Sa'ud's agent Badalla al Nafīsi, in combination with whom and my little *aphone* caravan-bashi Abd al-Azīz, I evolved a plan of voyage. All, like old Ibn Husain, whom we saw this morning, apprehensive of raiders, and anxious for me to go with the lumping cumbrous Butter Caravan. I finally agreed to go with this caravan (which they call *Hadhra*), as far as Irtwía, whence I must spring on to Buraida. Back about 5, and anointed my wound with whisky. Mylrea, who is a doctor, would have me let the wound heal before starting, but if the camels from Zubair arrive in time I shall go.

7 JUNE 1917. Saw Amir or Chief of the Caravan, and settled to catch them up at Subuhíya on Saturday morning (9th). Every day growing hotter and

[52] Riding-camel mare.
[53] Chief of caravan.
[54] Still there, 1937.

nearer to Ramadan. Bade farewell to Shaikh Sālim, who appears to have but little use for Ibn Sa'ud:

"Blow, blow, thou hot Simūm,
Thou givest not such a gloom
As benefits forgot"

was his refrain. Hamilton says Ibn Sa'ud in his own heart dislikes the Sharīf, but is on excellent terms with him. In any case unlikely to fight—anybody. Thence to Khazal of Muhámmara, who had followed me in his second yacht. He dared not come here in the first, which was, he says, given him by Sālim's late father Mubārak. Sālim challenges him in vain to produce one Kuwait witness to the deed of gift, and the matter has induced a delicacy. After luncheon we returned in the Shaikh's fiacre at such gallant speed that, crashing against a large rock in the middle of a narrow street, we broke the near wheel, and had to walk on through the bazaars, which shut from 10 till 4, until another carriage was procured. There I talked with an Arab sergeant from Laodicea and a private from Emesa who had deserted from the Turkish Army. Told me that six months ago Fakhri Pasha and Haidar [55] were in Medina; no foreigners, plenty of food and 32,000 (*sic*) troops. I have provided Said with a revolver (*Lavolva* he calls it) and 10 rounds, not to be loaded until needed, and he is now reassured against the peril of awaking with his "leg or head between the jaws of a savage *dhobb* or *"utt al imiri"*.[56] Bathed voluptuously alone, wishing it were Abukir and no sharks. Hamilton then took me over our water-skins and general gear, upon which I looked with *désintéressement* only tempered by the knowledge that my life depends upon their quality and resistance. Hamilton, who was at Temple Grove and has a son there now, then gave me an *aperçu* of his life and times. So after talk on the sands and hopes for the camels, to bed, sick and vexed at this waste and delay.

8 JUNE 1917. A fretting fretted day. No sign of the camels all the morning, so we asked the Shaikh, who is "sure all will be well", to send out and look for them, there being some fear of their having been raided on the way. I then wandered about unable to settle to anything, thinking what more I could possibly have done to ensure punctuality. Read some stupid Andrew Lang, the historical "mysteries" of obscure Scottish clans. Who cares who murdered whom? I find my second Max.-Min. Thermometer marks a higher temperature for Min. than for Max. So after 5 walked across the deep hot sand to ask Mylrea's advice; and finding him out conversed with his wife, a good Arabic scholar, with inside knowledge of Kuwait Home Life. Punishment for theft, beating; usually mortal. Mubārak's Circassian widow married by Khazal, but lives at Kuwait. Many women attend mission services, and callers sometimes 200 a month, but town in general fanatical. I played a little Fauré, Wagner and *Herzlich* Bach on their home-tuned-and-repaired piano: found Mylrea as much at sea over my thermometer as myself; met Calverley, author of an article "Whose wife shall she be?" which I remembered having read in *Moslem World*, and walked back in the dark, falling heavily on some rocks and

[55] See p. 179.
[56] Wolf or tiger-cat.

cutting my hand. My gall still unhealed and sometimes painful. Whisky hurts, but ineffective. Hamilton back with news that (*a*) no sign of Zubair camels, (*b*) Sālim's cannot be got in till to-morrow, (*c*) two messages have arrived from Ibn Sa'ud, in six days. He not at Buraida but Zilfi: wishes to make peace with Ibn Rashīd. Of course another night here, and another day sacrificed to the unknown A.P.O. of Zubair. The art of life shines most happily in the mild endurance of unnecessary evils and annoyances. Any fool can put up with an earthquake. Caravan of 600 camels and 300 armed men went on ahead yesterday. And at 10 p.m. two forerunners of my Zubair lot came in; the rest before dawn. They had travelled close to the coast to avoid raiders.

9 JUNE 1917. Rose 5.30 and was almost immediately laid low by a return call by the Shaikh of Muhámmara, who arrived before I had bathed or shaved, and stayed until after 9. Hamilton, who was printing films upstairs, left me to endure the first hour alone. Showed me private letter from Ibn Sa'ud to effect that (*a*) Ibn Rashīd had offered peace but refused the conditions of rupture with Turks and an understanding with Sharīf, (*b*) his monthly £5000 was inadequate to the upkeep of Najd. I refrained from asking M. how Ibn Sa'ud had "managed" when he had nothing from us at all: and told him all he could answer (for he obviously desired to make moral capital with Ibn Sa'ud) was that he had informed H.M.G. Muhámmara had not shown the letter to the Shaikh of Kuwait, whom he fears. We ciphered telegrams to Cox. Hamilton received his mails from England; and our small caravan, the luggage having gone two hours ahead, left Kuwait just before 5 steering due S. for Subuhíya, where I part company with Hamilton. Here I learnt that which, had I known it before, might well have deterred me from the expedition: viz. that these Najd Dhulūls, unlike the Egyptian Coastguard trotting Hagína, do the better part of their journeying at the slow back-breaking walk of the camels that carry earth to Giza across the Kasr al-Nil Bridge. I had been ready for heat, thirst, long hours, but this announcement, added to the pain of my galled skin, came very hard. In about an hour my camel-man, Mirshid, returned with the Khatun [57] whom I mounted and mean to take across if her feet will stand the rougher going.

Wore a black *aba*, which, though apparently not necessary as far as Buraida, is essentially and vitally so in the Hejaz. Just before 7 we stopped for the sunset prayer and did not go on till nearly 8, setting our course with the Jiddi (Pole Star), in line with the saddle pummels, and going first on Corvus, then Scorpio. Later I got down and walked 3 miles, after which we let the *Hamla* go on, and lay down on the sand, neither hot nor cool, but very hard, from 11.30 till 3. Thence with 10 minutes' halt for dawn prayer, we went on fast, the sun rising just before 5, reaching Subuhíya wells and the Buraida caravan well before 6. I am straining to keep at least my times exact, and carry traverse table, set to course, with glasses, water-bottles, rifle and compass on the pummels. Sun spectacles incomparably helpful.

> "The men to whom I owe my life
> Are Davidson and Regenstreif" [58]

---

[57] The "Lady", the best camel procurable.
[58] Cairo opticians.

and I treasure them like the newborn, only wishing they were triplets;

> "Or, if I may not praise a Hun,
> I owe my life to Davidson."

10 JUNE 1917. That is, I begin to hope I shall have it to owe. Nevertheless, a relief in small contretemps, because they are small. The back, of my Rurki chair snapped irreplaceably. Said smashed my only looking-glass. Hamilton and I lay back in the Simūm, drinking water almost continuously. The water is deep brown and got the better of me by continually blocking the filter and covering the tube with a rich green paste; so that I am reduced to boiling, or, when as generally there is no time for that, turning it into blood with a drop of my permanganate *révélateur*. But heat ethics are broad, and I have already reached the stage of not judging by taste, colour, temperature or smell, but by quantity only. Also of shaving, face-sponging and teeth-brushing from the sole contents of my aluminium mug. Also of not wasting sweat of brow by wiping away, but rather of using scientifically to cool eyes. The Simūm is hotter and stronger than a *Khamsīn*, and soon makes all metal, leather and woodwork inside the tent too hot to touch. Even if your drink were cold, the coolest receptacle for it is a cup hotter than the hot plates at the Ritz. Soap has no mystic union with the water, but keeps itself *to* itself as if it were oil: nor can I justly blame it. By 9 the thermometer inside the tent registered 123° and we did not consider it part of our duty to see what it was in the sun. The only hope is to wrap up, especially head, and drink water: which gives one time to think for the next stages, one well in 8 days and every drop carried in the curiously improper water-skins, upon which, as they frisk and heave on the camel's back, I now look with a direct and personal interest. Full's Life; Empty's Death is their motto. It was very much too hot to sleep in the tent, and as travelling is mostly by night. . . ? At noon Hamilton gave a meal to the Amirs of the Caravan, which he says, and I hope, will greatly improve my position with them. Personally I regard that great caravan with little less than sick loathing. They will go at a foot's pace, and foul all wells. But Hamilton, Shaikh Sālim, and all are convinced of the possibility of raids, and these have occurred so lately that I am bound to follow their advice. Hamilton is good with Arabs, sitting on the ground and tearing flesh with his fingers. Deeply as I dislike these *saletés,* I shall force myself to them once we are under way, when occasion requires. We being due to leave at 11 p.m., and H. having told me he was at 10, I was at about 5 composing myself for another attempt to sleep when he said, "Don't go to sleep, old chap, when I'm just going", and explained that he had meant Arab time. We photographed each other, and after giving me final advice about sufficient solid food, and accepting as cogent the Amirs' and Abd al-Azīz's ukases, Hamilton rode off to the N. leaving me with an odd sensation of marooning. An annoyance is that the Khatūn being pronounced definitely unfit to travel, I am left to find out, by painful experiment, which of my 23 dhulūls has the least uncomfortable paces. I have as yet conceived no fierce admiration for Abd al-Azīz, my own caravan-bashi, who stands with a straw between his lips and says "No—*Salámtak*" to every suggestion. Pithy Yorkshire is his form, but a strange novice requires a more helpful attitude, and I long indeed for

the Hunters' Rais Hassan,[59] or even for the grotesque but capable Imbārak Sala,[60] to tell one things and to come forward with definite proposals. However, these difficulties can hardly fail to sharpen one up in the end.

For some reason exhausted. Dressed and, when my tent was removed, sat out for two hours listening to the roarings, protestations, expostulations, eructations and ingurgitations of the 600 camels as they were coaxed to work: and wishing I had a similar wealth of expletive. We did not leave till 11.40 p.m. and travelled without halt into the glare and blaze of 9 a.m. (1½ hours too late I think) before we halted. I recited to myself a good many odes of Horace, themes of Bach fugues, Dante and Keats, but the hours passed so slowly that I dared not look at my watch, and I was very tired. Reason for our delay, Amir's fear of starting until the moon was up.

11 JUNE 1917. Wish I had somebody to help Said, who is harassed with heat and dirt and suffers from the brown drink, without one complaint. Tent temperature 11 a.m. only 121° F. because I suppose we are 400 ft. higher. Wish it was 4000. Mīrshid came for help against his Secular Foe, the Thief of Time and Hostis Humani Generis, and I gave him a good whack of castor-oil. Also boracic for a sore-eyed Shaikh. Again unable sleep. O, so bored with camel cans and cannots. The camel was made for man, and not man for the camel. As I write Abd al-Azīz announces, without warning, that we must go at once. Disquieting, for the sun is like molten glass.

Abd al-Azīz had no explanation for this sudden and unscheduled departure, save that the Amir of the Caravan "was afraid". So on across the sand until began to be pressed down by a sort of progressive and cumulative weakness. And now I knew that in this case, as in all others, Stratford is always right, and that it is, with the best will, not possible to hold a fire in one's hand, still less on one's head, by thinking on the Frosty Caucasus. As my strength ebbed out of me I tried to hold it by the tags appropriate to the situation, *rebus angustis animosus atque fortis appre; contra audentior*, etc., and remember with curious exactness deciding not to use *aequam memento* because that takes me through my morning bath when the water is too cold. Was repeating with less and less coherence *Pero levati su vinci l'ambascia, con l'anima che ogni battaglia, se non col grave corpo* ... when the thing came, and I spent my last sense in getting my camel down before falling off it, which I did as it settled to the ground, tearing my old aba in two, and calling to Mīrshid. He propped me against its E. shady side and sheltered me with the umbrella he and many other Beduin carry during the heat. Looked at my watch, saw it was about 4.30, and I think I went off, for suddenly it was past 5 and Said was sprinkling me with water. I stopped him quickly, knowing better what we had ahead, but poured a very little down the back of my neck because the radiant heat seemed to be shooting up against my spine from the sand. Mirshid then began saying that the caravan was far ahead, and that we must catch it up before sunset or we should be left. Our own 20, with Abd al-Azīz, thinking we had halted for other reasons, had gone on and disappeared over the horizon. I found I could not stand, and dare not take brandy till the sun should be near setting. So lay there and was only

---

[59] Warrant-Officer in the Egyptian Coastguards who accompanied Hunter Pasha's Expeditions.
[60] Dragoman at Pyramids.

too weak not to be amused or angry when Mirshid, in his Beduin bird-voice kept repeating: "I am thirsty, I am thirsty." For peace sake I pointed to my bottle and let him take a swig. I could not make out why Said kept leaving me, until he confessed he had been suffering all day from something near dysentery, which he attributed to the green drinking water. He was looking weak and very sorry for himself, so I told him I intended raising his pay as and from June 1st; also that I would give him a pill at sunset. This put wonderful heart into him: making me wonder whether more pay (after seven years) or the announcement of a K.C.M.G. would have pulled me round. Was quite sure not. Mirshid kept saying, "We must go on, go on, or it is finished with us", but I lay on till 6.15 when gave S. his chlorodyne, and drank from my dirty glowing aluminum mug about a table-spoonful of brandy in same of tea. Mounted after five minutes and, gripping pummels hard all the way, caught up main caravan and our camels shortly after sunset. There lay on ground and heard Mirshid telling Abd al-Aziz how I was dying but that he M. had saved my life. A. had only just begun to dispatch searchers for us, and the Amir of the Caravan, whether he knew or no, had not paid the smallest attention to our party. I then gave Said an opium pill, No. 9, and made him prepare strong Bovril, with rice and pepper, into which I jerked some more cognac, and drank straight from the saucepan. Whereupon conferred with A. who rather reluctantly agreed to letting me have three hours' rest, then riding till 8 and camping till 4, reaching Asāfa by forced marching in about 36 hours. Lay down on his assurance, only to be called by him in about an hour, with the news that the main caravan had gone on, that it would be necessary to ride till 10 next morning, resting thence till 2 only, and finally by all night going to make Asāfa on Wednesday morning. It was not safe to leave the caravan day or night for fear of raiders. We were now nearer Subuhíya and could reach it with the water we had, but if we broke down to-morrow we should be definitely cut off. He did not know why the Amir of the Caravan was going back on arrangements made with Hamilton and self. Anyhow Amir had gone on. From the beginning of the trip Abd al-Azīz had not made for me one single constructive suggestion, but I was now desperate, for I was absolutely certain that one more midday would knock me out altogether. Explaining this to him, adding that I was a stranger and he an expert, and asking him to devise something—anything— I would ride all night—that would keep me in the shade between 8 and 4. He could imagine nothing, and urged me to move somewhere at once, preferably Subuhíya, as every hour we remained increased our chances of dying of thirst. I said "I will ride 16 hours if you will grant me those 8", but he repeated that it was not possible. I knew this was the Verdict, and with a dreadful and bitter disappointment [61] mounted about 11, turned back again to the North and rode away, with a weak anger at every footfall of my camel's pad.

12 JUNE 1917. We rode till 3.20, slept till 4.20, and on till 7.40, when pitched tent and rested till about 5, whence through to Subuhīya, at which Mirshid said we should arrive about an hour after sunset, and which we actually reached at ten minutes to ten. Still exhausted and morale devilish low, but knew life saved by falling back. It had been my ambition to help

---

[61] That I must give up the expedition.

in linking up Central Arabia against the Turks, begin a Najd glossary, describe the Sultāni Road and amplify my personal knowledge of Islamic sovereigns. But I assert that to make the journey at midsummer is to run a losing hazard. Later our *hamla*[62] bumped in, and I arranged with Abd al-Azīz to leave at 2.45 a.m. with Said, Mirshid, and tent for the ten hours' journey back to Kuwait. So arose and off by 3: I made all trot till just after 4 when they got down for the prayer of dawn. On in ten minutes for about an hour, when both A. and M. grew suddenly anxious, crying *"Gōm! Gōm!"* —"Enemies"—and I saw in the distance people advancing upon us. Mirshid was off his camel at once, outed his rifle and across towards them, whilst Abd al-Azīz, Said and self got the camels down and our rifles ready. When I saw Said loading his revolver, most heartily wished I had not given him 10 rounds, and feared I should have to treat him like Mr Winkle. Mirshid had gone about 200 yards when A., perceiving I know not how that the remote black specks were friends, called him back, and we went on our way, still trotting. About 6.30 it came over me that I could endure a little sharp travel and fatigue better than another day in the tent, so kept up the trot in spite of Said's groans and protestations until 8.30 when the Gulf and Hamilton's house came in sight; but we were not there for another hour, completely exhausted but in a vale of rest and clean water into which we sank to sleep for several hours.

Hamilton ready with iced fruit, and told me on my awaking that Ibn Sa'ud had gone to Riyādh, which would have been an immense detour in my Hejaz line, and which I could not have hoped to reach before Ramadan, by which time the discussion of any business is almost impossible. My mails meanwhile, having left Baghdad 31. v. 17 had arrived and been sent on by two swift riders into Central Arabia, whence God knows if or when I can ever recover them. Hamilton wired to Cox recommending I should leave by British India *Palintana;* and I, in cipher, for instructions. A tremendous Shamāl blowing, and may delay her two or three days, but for the moment weakness and disappointment make me utterly indifferent. Bad Reuters— Russia, the London air-raid and, worst of all, the failure of the American loan. I stayed in bed all day, and in the evening received very kind letters of condolence and relief from the Shaikhs of Kuwait and Muhámmara.

14 JUNE 1917. Long night and restful; but still weak. Drove with Hamilton to thank Khazal and Mubarak for their courtesy; the former mournfully furious against the behaviour of the Amirs of the Caravan, which he describes resentfully as typical of the Qasīm.[63] At the Consulate charming and characteristic telegrams from Cox instructing me in the dreaded, but obvious and only possible sense. Returned Hamilton my stores, etc. and note with concern that I have practically none but Arab clothes wherewith to return to Egypt. Shamāl growing steadily stronger. Wrote report to Cox and tired to bed.

15 JUNE 1917. Shamāl blew so strong that the sea, at 200 yards, was hardly visible from the sand in the air and from the South the desert seemed to close up on to and over the house. The wind quite prevented navigation, and as the *Palintana* has 12,000 packages to discharge there seems every prospect of waiting for days. I telegraphed to Basra asking if the *Charles Tellier,* for

---

[62] Baggage-camels.
[63] N. W. Najd.

Aden-Suez, could pick me up here. Weak and tired, and inclined as always when out of action and interest, to go to pieces. Read, after twenty years, Merriman's miserable *Sowers,* Psalms and John iii. in Arabic, some Tennyson and Swinburne, and the *Adventures of Sherlock Holmes.* At dinner Hamilton preached to me unconvincingly on the necessity of "keeping abreast" with second-rate Lockes, Gallons, etc. I daresay he is right, but to me the attempt is like drinking bad tea with three lumps of sugar in it. I gave him a list to read, and he two or three to me. In sad need of the strength that can only come from clean Northern cold. Bed 9.30.

16 JUNE 1917. News that *Palintana* could not leave till Sunday and might not till Monday. The air dark and yellow with sand. Reason preserved by the finding of *Jude the Obscure,* which I drank in, on and off throughout the day. But I fear I should have put Sue across my knee, and have done with her long before the end of the second book. Walked with Hamilton to the unused Admiralty coal pier: he of the opinion that there will be a universal slackening in work and enterprise after the War. I the contrary. Walked through bazaars. Nothing, and that dearer infinitely than Nájaf. Much English gold in evidence, which should surely be bought in.

17 JUNE 1917. Put all luggage into the sailing-boat and away from Shwaikh towards the *Palintana;* as we approached the wind suddenly blew down a tempest, before which we turned and ran for the harbour, considering ourselves lucky to squeeze through without mishap. So another day in that Consulate, much of which I slept, and Hamilton more. So in a tired grey heat till dusk when we walked awhile to the North, marvelling at the wealth and resources of this seeming barren corner, where many return each year from Bahrein worth 40,000 rupees. According to Hamilton Shaikh Sālim's life, from an Assurance aspect, is not good. His stinginess, added to his bigotry in the matter of *wein, weib* and *gesang* will do for him one of these days. We went aboard in the jolly boat at 9, and I found the Mylreas would be travelling with me, for Kashmir. A grateful good-bye to Hamilton, and bed on deck about 10.15. *Palintana* 33 years old, but her hydraulic cranes make sleep possible in all operations.

18 JUNE 1917. A day of exceeding irritation. Waking at 6 I learnt from the Captain that no discharging ships had come off during the night, and that we should be lucky if we left by noon. No one had any suggestions to offer, so I sent a note in Arabic to Shaikh Sālim, begging him to dispatch a flotilla at once, and requested Hamilton to do his best. In about an hour eight good ships came, and we were never short again. If only they had told me the night before we could have left at dawn. But the British India Company have a poor little dago agent, equally afraid of Hamilton and Sālim: and Sālim is losing influence over his labour. I marvel that the Company sits down under this loss of £350–£400 a day. By midday there were of course 600 sacks left, and the Captain told me that if he could get the boats to work on the weather side also, we should halve the time, and leave by 3. So I forced them round, and finally, by interference *en gros* and *en détail* with other people's business, got the ship away by 4.40. Later the Captain thanked me, saying we should otherwise have lost another day. Our departure almost exactly a week after my sun-stroke: yet I am still weak and tired; teased moreover with regrets for my misadventure. *Palintana* has to call at Gwadar and Pasni

before Karachi, where she will stop four days, so I have practically decided to go by Quetta, see Bernard,[64] and so catch P. and O. at Bombay by land. My mails of early March must be by this time well into Central Arabia.

19 JUNE 1917. I learn, needless to say, that the *Palintana's* "real" maximum speed of 12 knots can only be attained when she is clean, and that all we can hope for just now is 10½-11. Read Freeman on race and language, which holds well to date, especially in his negation of Austria and Turkey as possible empires. John v, Arabic, and Homer *Odyssey* xix. Slept a long while in the clinging conservatory atmosphere. Mylrea tells me that no Arab, save for very high pay, would venture across Arabia this time of year, nor even out of his house at Kuwait between 11 and 3 by day.

20 JUNE 1917. Before sunset the steep cliffs of Musandam stood up as out of a boiling lake, and we passed through the straits of Ormuz. At dinner the captain lightly announced that we should reach Karachi on Sunday afternoon instead of on Saturday morning, a heavy blow to me. He had ordered 60 revs. per minute (= 11½ knots), but the horrible old Scottish engineer will not give himself the pains to exceed 56 (= 10 knots), and Captain has apparently no means of compelling him now or bringing him to book afterwards. So I am like, for no reason whatever save a variety of permutations and combinations of inefficiency and futility, to see neither Quetta, Agra nor Delhi, to say nothing of missing the Egyptian mail. Said complains piteously of the heat. Bed 10.15. There is air on the saloon hatches, but they make hard sleeping. John vi. Arabic, *Odyssey* xx.

21 JUNE 1917. In every respect the longest day of the year. An increasing swell as we approach monsoon. Captain said most oppressive day he had known for 18 months, but I note I can bear general, i.e. not direct solar, heat better than most people, that is, if their groans are any index to their misery. John vii. Arabic, and *Odyssey* xxii and xxiii—amazing libretto for a Wagnerian opera Μνηστηροφονία, *The Slaying of the Suitors*. I should by now have left Zilfi and journeyed well on towards Riyadh. Bed 9, heavy sea.

22 JUNE 1917. Made Gwadar, a dependency of Muscat on the coast of Baluchistan, about 10.30. Clock advancing ¼ hour per diem. Very fine roadstead sheltered by great ramps of precipitous rocks. Here we at first hoped that our cargo of coarse matting, sharks' fins and dried fish might be aboard by 1, when we could have pushed for Pasni by 8, and so Karachi evening of 23rd. But there proved to be 2000 packages, and the jabbering coolies were not clear of us before 8.30 p.m. So we lay all day in the rolling swell, fair in the blast of the dried fish; reading John viii, *Odyssey* xxiv, a mutilated copy of *Middlemarch,* and late many pages of the *Oxford Book*. Length and general oppression of this voyage heavy on me, but thought of little cargoes like this being continuously collected throughout the War, while Germany, to whom we had been surrendering all such traffic, sits bound and strangled —some consolation. Mylrea sent ashore for forceps and extracted abscessed molar of 3rd officer, and I was glad to supply opium and phenacetin from my case. Very rough night after 9 when we left, so that I had to cling hard to my skylight.

23 JUNE 1917. So rough all day, and so hot, and so disagreeable that I practically suspended animation for the day. The noise and the smell of loading

[64] My brother, in the Gunners there.

-

continued from 8 till 1.30 and I observed and deplored the complete *désintéressement* of the officers, and even hustled on the workers myself. Monsoon swell worse than ever, so that, though able to retain what I had, I would not increase risks by dining. Bed in tempest at 9.15.

24 JUNE 1917. Shaky but still, in spite of big seas running, self-contained. Into Karachi about 10, but nearly two hours tying up, so did not reach Government House till 1.30: where, soon after arrival, telegram from S.N.O. Bombay, saying I must be there Tuesday night, an impossibility. But I find that the P. and O. may be the dread *Nankin*. Looked through Shorthouse's *Little Schoolmaster Mark*, not without pleasure, and later to the Lawrences' weekly At Home, where was delighted to meet Ted Hoare,[65] out to design at *carte blanche* a palace for Jodhpur, besides a variety of banks and shops. Lawrence thinks we are going to administer, not annex Baluchistan and S. Persia, with Chahbar for port and capital. Recommends Indian Moslem lower officials for Iraq.

Ted Hoare to dinner, and a musical woman staying in the house. Afterwards he *Meisters Vorspiel* III badly and Quintet well; she some Brahms and Bach—all driving my thoughts and desires back to decent peaceful civilization. Bed not till 12. A snake had dropped from the ceiling upon Said's head, and he had rather creditably managed to stamp its head in, at the temporary cost of his nerves.

25 JUNE 1917. Left Karachi station 10.50: broad gauge; not uncomfortable, but very hot. After the Indus is supposed to begin the Desert of Sind, which I was agreeably surprised to find a sort of bush, with very little drift-sand, and studded with trees, gardens and small villages. The worst of the Jodhpur-Bikanir line is the constant and infernal noise, which effectually knocks out conversation—almost thought. Sleep short and difficult. The landscape, with its variety of distant hills, trees, earth, water and grass, is poorer but infinitely more human than the great triangular billiard money machine we call the Delta.

Several great peacocks, from time to time, watched our train pass, turning their heads only for the purpose.

26 JUNE 1917. When we reached Marwar Junction at 12.15—1½ hours late —we were informed that the Ahmadabad-Bombay mail had gone on without us, the station-master being forbidden to delay them more than 15 minutes: and I learnt with dull stupor that this would mean reaching Bombay exactly one day later, and so missing the P. and O. However, wired Jukes and Navy begging them to hold the ship, and reply to me at once, intending, if they could not, to visit Delhi and Agra. The others slept, while I wrote, and read again with pleasure and admiration, *Sinister Street*, II. A glorious promise, if only that youth is not murdered in the Aegean.

No telegrams arriving from Bombay I left reluctantly at 5, and was woken up at midnight by a young captain with the news that we had reached Mount Abu, where he had had dinner ordered in advance. I had no fierce desire to begin eating at that hour, but climbed from my upper berth and wandered up and down the desolate platform. No dinner was ready or procurable, so back in no wonderful humour to a broken sleep, in the dense

[65] E. H. Hoare, F.R.I.B.A.

fanless heat. The Y. C. recounted several instances of filthy work by the Turks, awarding them for only virtue, unique defensive ability.

27 JUNE 1917. All day through almost perfect English country. At Ahmadabad at 11.30. Two hours' wait. I therefore took my two young men in a small covered governess cart, of excruciating unease, to see the town, a most entertaining blare of colour but dirty beyond the dreams of an Egyptian village. When you have the chance of observing these people in the mass it becomes easier to compare their type with Egypt, and in bodily physique the fellah is indescribably superior. But he can never approach the Indian fineness of feature and expression, in which it is not hard to trace a fairer Aryan ancestry, dim now and soiled. We drove past lacquered dog-carts to a very exquisite open loggia mosque, of strangely European flavour with its pointed arch, floriated crenellations and rain gargoyles, counteracted by windows composed of marble-traced trees of life. Thence to another little mosque, also of the local sandstone, all, including the cup-domes of dressed stone without a suspicion of rubble. Friendly custodians wholly ignorant of spoken Arabic but quite able to correct my test mistake in quoting the opening chapter of the Koran. We left for what was to me an afternoon of almost poignant appreciation and delight. Great monkeys were chasing each other round the roof girders of the station as the train drew out, seemingly into the Surrey hills. A land of hedges, natural grass, red-tiled farms and homesteads among the trees, fields of arbitrary different sizes, and stiled gates: over all the limpid mellow orderly domesticity of the English country-side, such as I have not seen now these three years. The continuous green allowed me to gaze from the window, without tinted glasses, and with eyes unstrained. All day so, and especially at and around Baroda, where we had tea at 6. The Y.C. always hungry and inquiring after the next meal. At 10 we dined at Surat and to bed, third night in train.

28 JUNE 1917. We were due at Bombay by 6, but it was no surprise to me to be told at 7 that we had broken an axle and should be 2½ hours late. Not only were we passed by the Mail that had left Marwar a day after ourselves, but were forced to shunt aside in favour of local and suburban traffic. At about 8 I lost my patience and jumped, in my pyjamas, into one of these last, so reaching Church Gate station at 8.30. Jukes had a man to meet me, and we drove in pouring rain to the Secretariat, where Kindersley, Resident Under-Secretary, received me into his gaunt Kensington-Gothic suite of most comfortable rooms. I find I have missed the mail, so round after breakfast to Embarkation, where they offered me a cabin in a very small Indian transport *Purnea*. On the way back bought a few clothes and some books from Thacker, a better *librarie* than you will find in all Africa. The streets and buildings of Bombay good proof of what we can do when unhampered by capitulations. Out again at 5 and discovered Tarapooree Walla, a book-shop recalling in its extent, variety and disorder the best traditions of the Charing Cross Road. Ran amok. Finding a singular number of Chess Books, I bought one for father, and, on T. W.'s recommendation, climbed two flights of stairs to Bombay Chess Club, a plain neat room in which a dozen Parsis and Hindus were contending in grave concentration over Staunton men. They welcomed me friendly, and I engaged and defeated an odd Hindu, who afterwards beat me, with the help of a Superior Friend. The company in general agreeable

with an inclination to familiarity; thus my opponent remarked richly that "Our friend is a tough nut to crack". Early to bed but read till 11.45 when finding myself weak and nervy took my first grain of opium (pill) and to sleep.

29 JUNE 1917. Walked up and down the city with Said, who assumes that all big shops must be branches of similar establishments in Cairo. Alas, bought some more books. Went into Cathedral and attempted to test organ, apparently good, but found bellows switch under lock and key. Very ugly church with interesting *basse époque* monuments of Colonels who braved "inexorable Sultauns" and died young for their pains. Lunched with Jukes, and his pretty Jane-Austen wife in the splendour and opulence of the Yacht Club, to which we have nothing in Egypt *simile aut secundum*. Read papers and walked back, losing my way half intentionally, in torrential rain; which seems hardly any augmentation to the natural dampness of the place. According to Kindersley, Parsi = Copt, and Hindu = Egyptian Moslem. Parsis are progressive, assimilative, rich, as against the slower, more aristocratic Hindus. Like Egyptians their first interest is in Government appointments, and they will neglect all the practical and essential points in, say, the Karachi Port Trust Bill, in their endeavour to drag in the irrelevant political herring. Manners in inverse ratio to demands. But I do not think we mingle enough with the better disposed, any more than we do in Egypt. More Rodds, Gorsts and R. Grahams are required. Kindersley then drove me out in a taxi round the town, Malabar Hill and the Towers of Silence, the rich horrible villas and the splendid luxuriant vegetation. Sat a little in the huge vulgar Taj Hotel, and again to the Yacht Club, where we talked with one Williamson, professor in mathematics at Elphinstone College, who had known and journeyed with Francis.[66] Indian Mathematics' level very high, and, to my surprise, Hindus much superior to Parsis. Has turned out one Senior and several Wranglers. Reason of enthusiasm? Two papers 900 marks each in I.C.S. examination. I gather in general that the Willingdons are popular and successful: he hard-worked and she hard-working.

30 JUNE 1917. In pouring rain at 10 aboard the tiny dirty old *Purnea*, carrying Indian troops direct to Suez. So no mails till then, and therefore not one home letter throughout my travels.

8 JULY 1917. Eight days and eight nights of the Monsoon and we are not yet in sight of Aden. The *Purnea*, well under 2000 tons, is carrying over 800 Pathans to work in France. We left in a torrent of rain and, once outside the harbour went first N. and then S. for three hours to avoid the mines such as sank the *Mongolia* last week. Almost at once a sharp squall sprang up and carried away all our awnings, incidentally driving us into the squalid diningroom. Most took to their berths. I sat up against the talk, trying to read, until, the ship heeling over at a yet fiercer angle, the cast iron fastening my chair snapped and I was thrown ten feet through the air against the cabin walls. Nearly stunned, but lucky not to have broken my head. Doctors and others ran out, and soon after I went to bed, and lay there seven days. Sharp but decreasing pain about base of spine. But the weather was such that very few others appeared; and the monstrous intolerable procession of the grey monsoon rollers, like the German army entering Brussels, I missed without concern.

[66] My second brother. See p. 339.

Said of course knocked up at once, and made *acte de présence* thrice in all the week: after which, having nothing save beef-tea in severe moderation, I find myself tired and without the Will to Power. Unable to eat so ventured upon a glass of British India Sherry (*misericordia*) and a ½ pint of G. Goulet Champagne (*Nunc Dimittis*). But did eat. Read Kipling's *Diversities*, Steevens's *India*, Wells's *War, Dynamiter*, and a little Graham Wallas and Metchnikhoff, but with fatigue and unease.

All his youth R. K. gaped upon high officials from an Indian Grub Street, and now, admitted to share the breezy shop of Colonial Ministers, he records with smug pride their uninteresting indecorums. Yet with a gift of writing, for immediate effect, almost beyond belief. But for stimulus and constructive criticism and suggestion, young Britain should be fed on Wells. Turned over storm names θύελλα, and *procella, tempestas,* hurricane (through the rigging), *ouragan* (against the hull), typhoon and the Arab *tuphān,* tornado, cyclone and anti-cyclone. But nothing stronger than "the locks of the approaching storm". If we had struck a mine outside Bombay, we must have been drowned to a man. Rafts and boats as unmanageable as inadequate.

Played the hymns for matins and heard a creditable sermon from a Hull Methodist. The Mohman Pathan Labourers aboard were quite recently engaged in active hostilities against us: now friendly, willing and good tempered. One nearly died from sea-sickness. After dinner I reduced the Captain at Chess: after losing two pieces to him. Always tired physically, mentally and morally: if only two weeks in England....

12 JULY 1917. Yesterday Pathans forcibly washed, the ordeal being made endurable by allowing them to soap each other, which they did with incredible ferocity, one veteran insisting on a conscientious lathering to the inside of his nephew's throat. Now they are being vaccinated. Said down with fever: and like Egyptians of all classes (and indeed most men) believing himself at death's door. Wireless tells us Greece has come in: so more demands on our Exchequer, and *novae tabulae* for all their perfidies.

14 July 1917. Reached Suez 4 A.M., and at 6.15 left *Purnea* in S.N.O.'s launch, too late for 6.45 train. So to H.M.S. *Humber* where learnt from Snagg, with unutterable disappointment, that no mails had come for me. Walked about till 8.30, when returned to ship and breakfasted with him. Sent wireless to Aden for mails. Left Suez 10 reaching Ismailia 1.0. There telephoned to Wemyss who sent the inevitable naval Rolls Royce and bore me to a swift luncheon. Telephoned to Jimmy Watson:[69] and found all well but Stewart Symes recovering from fever and M. Cheetham down with it and waiting for leave. Hear of Murray's recall and Allenby's arrival. Cairo 4.50. No sign of Ismain, so put in at Turf for night. Saw Clayton, etc. and had him to dinner, where he told me of his refusal of the Deputy High Commissionership of Baghdad, giving his reasons. I think he is really lying low and sitting tight for the Interior. Warned me I might expect to be offered something in Iraq.

15 JULY 1917. Ismain tells me that all the papers have announced my permanent transfer to Baghdad, and that the official *démenti* in the *Mokattam* only confirmed the impression. No one expected me to return. Faris Nimr.[70]

---

[69] Lieut.-Col. J. K. Watson, A.D.C. successsively to Lord Kitchener in the Sudan and S. Africa and to the Khedive. Sir Henry's Military Secretary.

[70] Dr Faris Nimr, editor and chief proprietor of the Arabic daily *al-Mokattam*.

from 2.30 to 3.30, I think glad to see me back, and anxious that I should not leave Egypt. 4.15 train to Alexandria reaching S. Gaber now at 8, in accordance with the universal diminution of speed. Watson met me and took me to the Residency, where I dined alone with the Wingates and told them of my journey. Ramleh cool and peaceful.

16 JULY 1917. They made me have breakfast upstairs. At 9 asked Wingate for leave, when he announced to me "the offer by the Foreign Office of the post of Oriental Secretary at Baghdad at £1000 a year". Observing my lack of enthusiasm, he asked my impression of the proposal. I said unfavourable, and suggested discussion at home. He agreed and drafted a wire to that effect.

CHAPTER ELEVEN

Summer and Autumn 1917

The buffets of circumstances, the caprice of fortune, all the inscrutable vicissitudes of life.
HENRY ASQUITH, Aberdeen, 1910 (*cit*. Earl Baldwin)

IN Cairo and Alexandria civilian life glided tranquilly forward into the making and spending of fortunes. I walked but once into the Bazaars. Stocks had fallen in quality as well as in quantity but not, it seemed, so quickly or so low as the critical faculty of gallant purchasers who in their zeal for Oriental rugs ("we may never get another chance") were competing for mats hardly to be distinguished from Axminster or indeed linoleum. The Revolt in the Desert had turned out to be not bookish theory but a working model, and merchants like Abdalla Kahhāl, trading with Arabs and acquainted with its beginnings, congratulated me and enquired after "al-Urenz", a *Shaitān,* and when would he "honour" with me again and drink with them a cup of Yămǎni coffee or a glass of Persian tea. Lawrence to my knowledge never visited the Bazaars again. But in the spirit of the Army there was a change. Officers I met seemed to have shed Gallipoli and to be advancing almost with exhilaration into a new hope, coupled in their minds with the arrival of a new General who, they said, had left France owing to a row, but who suited them well enough. To be told off by this new General was like being blown from the muzzle of a gun which, however, when you regained the ground, seemed to bear you no malice. Hospital nurses on duty eighteen hours a day were now allowed the reasonable relaxation of an occasional dance; and Lady Allenby was wonderfully kind. People were beginning to say that the Turks might live—some of them—to regret having suggested the possibility of Expeditionary Forces moving across the Sinai.

Egypt is a land with a climate in which it is easy enough to maintain good health but hard, once lost, to regain it. I had not shaken off the sun

of Arabia, and was advised by my doctor to inhale after three years'
absence some of the raw, sharp air of Europe. So I left by the P. and O.
Mooltan from Port Said, finding and reading on the deck from two
hundred-weight sacks an accumulated four months' mail. We were,
though we knew it not, in the peak-period of submarine activity, and in
company with the *Messageries Maritimes Lotus* were escorted by two
Japanese torpedo-destroyers. We followed, and increased our danger by
following, the slower boat; and the little Japanese crossed, dodged, and
encompassed us both.

I had at luncheon and dinner been observing a neighbour who consumed at each meal to his own cheek a bottle of champagne. The night
we left Malta he rather embarrassed me by saying that he noticed I was
looking at him, and might it be because of the wine? I trusted I had not
been rude, but could not deny that the wine had something to do with
my glances. "No offence", he replied, "I'm drinking champagne because
I can't as a rule afford it." I murmured that that was why I was drinking
Vin Ordinaire. "I am convinced", he continued over my interruption,
"that this ship is going to be torpedoed: the bills will go down too, and
I shan't have to pay." At 7.15 next evening, July 26th, about a hundred
miles south of Sardinia, sitting at dinner with our lifebelts behind us,
he heard without warning or explosion the five blasts on the siren—*tuba
mirum spargens sonum*—and the entire company rose; but not before
my friend, draining his glass, had whispered across to me: "What did I
tell you?" As he had embarked at Bombay he had drunk down some fifty
pounds; so that if (as I feel entitled to presume) he had not omitted to
insure his effects, he must have found the experience positively pleasur-
able. I forget his face and never knew his name but I remember my
wave of almost affectionate pride in so sublime a compatriot.

There was no sort of panic, or even hurry. We picked up our belts
and walked upstairs. I went forward and saw one or two officers and
three of the crew gazing intently upon a small white bubble which
seemed to be making steadily rather than swiftly for our starboard beam.
The helm had been put hard over and the *Mooltan* was veering rapidly
out of the tiny thing's course. But not rapidly enough for, at the moment
when it seemed to have passed us, there was a dull detonation with a
quivering shock. A great column of green flame shot into the air, and
the deck about ten yards from the bows burst upwards. Immediately the
engines were reversed, and the ship was brought to a standstill.

Although we could not (as people say for weddings and other festivities) have had better weather; although compared with the horrors of
the *Persia* or the *Aragon* we endured scarce an inconvenience (and some

of the passengers professed afterwards not to have disliked the excitement); the memory of that summer evening, despite comic relief, is to me an evil dream. I looked up to the bridge, and was rewarded by the sight of the Captain taking off his uniform (which rendered him liable to capture) and struggling into a tweed suit. A Royal Naval Reserve Officer rushed along the deck shouting "All official mail bags into the ditch" and thither I duly consigned the two I was carrying home pierced and weighted from the Residency—to find afterwards that others, who had not heard the order had (as might I) saved theirs without difficulty for the boats. *Lotus* was steaming out of sight at full speed. One of the destroyers circled round us, throwing off dense volumes of smoke, whilst the other opened a sharp continuous fire upon the submarine. We gathered, belted into curious contours, at our stations, and I was glad to observe that two young subalterns who had been paying discreet attention to two charming foreign ladies now threw off the mask and openly supported them round what was left of their waists. The attention was appreciated rather than needed, for when an officious chaplain passed one of them with "Be brave, little girl" she, looking after him, muttered to me: "If I 'av not ze corks on, I kig 'im in ze stomag."

In my heart I was calculating how long our great hotel floor would remain under us, and sympathizing with the hero in *Maud* who prayed that the solid earth might not melt beneath his feet; wondering also how I could ever have relished the gurgling line of the *Inferno* when the waters close over the ship of Ulysses—*Infin che il mar fu sopra noi richiuso*.

We took to the boats, although the *Mooltan* had as yet no list, by rope-ladder. The only lady (so far as I heard) who had had the foresight to prepare a little bag of prime necessities for travel gave it to a stranger to hold as she climbed down. We carried no more gallant passenger, but when I reached the boat I found her in tears. He had forgotten it. We were rowed to the stationary destroyer through the excellent practice she was still making above, around—it seemed almost through us; nor did our host interrupt his fire while we struggled on board. Meanwhile, as the Commander of the convoy, he had hoisted signals to abandon ship and the Captain of the *Mooltan* with his officers and engineers left her, reaching the destroyer in the last two boats at 8.15. I had taken two snapshots of the *Mooltan* pitching very slightly forward but, although more than an hour passed before we lost sight of her, she never looked like sinking. I had been the last to play the saloon piano, and had carefully closed it: would the copper wound bass strings resist any longer than the steel the acid salt and rust? Would the chest of "Standard Selections" be floating against the saloon ceiling? How soon would my India-paper *Oxford Book of English Verse* become pulp? Why had we not all drunk champagne?

The destroyers divided our company between them and hastened on to guard *Lotus.* Our crew gave us tea with bread and jam, and we slept close but cold and unbelievingly hard on the steel deck. About twelve next day the Captain came down from the bridge and standing near the gun delivered in perfect English what I am sure he intended as a reassuring address. He said we were passing through the section of his patrol most thickly infested by submarines. There was of course no real danger; only, would passengers keep clear of the gun, because, if wanted at all, it would be wanted quick. Towards dusk we received word that the P. and O. launch and an Hotel awaited us at Marseilles, and well after dark we glided into the harbour, where after a happy dozing delay, we were removed in the launch and finally welcomed into the comparative luxury of the Grand *Hôtel du Louvre et de la Paix.* Nothing could have exceeded the care and courtesies we received from the finest Line in the world—including a free Special Train to London and a generous issue of ready money to those who had lost theirs on the *Mooltan.* I telegraphed to the Embassy the word *sinistré* (which for years I had ached to employ), and in Paris, then a City of the Dead, was gratified by a room at the Ritz for ten francs a night—even more by the placards in my friends' offices *"Soyez bref: vos moments sont aussi précieux que les notres."*

I found myself after three years' exile in an England grey, grim and desolate through the absence of Harry Cust. London, though always less dependent on civic and large scale amenities than Paris, seemed even deeper in the trough of the War, with an atmosphere, compared to that of Egypt or India, like that of a besieged city; with restrictions and scarcities approaching the hardships and sacrifices of Germany itself. And who, under the din and misery raining from the heavens, but must cry *"Timor mortis conturbat me?"* At Rochester the warning of the maroons drove the townspeople for shelter into the great crypt of Gundulf's Cathedral. I stayed at the Deanery and with Mark Sykes and his family at Sledmere, until my strength returned and I worked for a while at his instance in the Secretariat of the War Cabinet. I dealt with papers concerning the Near and Middle East, and scrutinized the drafts for the launching of the Most Excellent Order of the British Empire with the same critical eye as Companions of the Bath must have cast, a hundred years before, upon the creation of (my own) Order of St. Michael and St. George. In the offices and along the passages there were Zionists and rumours of Zionists, and Mark Sykes would burst into my room exultant or despondent according as a draft or an interview with Mr. Balfour had been well or badly designed.[1] There were air raids endured at home and in the Criterion Theatre; or seen one evening at Crowhurst from afar

> "Like trailing angers on the monstrous night
> Magnificently fall."

During other week-ends I resumed at The Wharf the hours of interest passed with the Asquiths in Venice, noting with concern the Prime Minister's decline from chess upon bridge; and learnt there first the full horror of Caporetto, when, as Mark observed, we had to begin the War again.

This September Lord Edward Cecil, Financial Adviser to the Egyptian Government, drew up a memorandum drawing attention to certain defects in the system for dealing with the affairs of Egypt at the Foreign Office.[2] His memorandum, having received the observations of that Department, was submitted to the War Cabinet, who decided that a Committee under the presidency of Mr Balfour, assisted by Lord Curzon and Lord Milner, should go into the question. I had heard nothing of this, though I was aware of Lord Edward's views, when I was invited by Mr Balfour to act as Secretary to the Committee and found myself sitting at a round table with these three great men. I was without training in précis-writing or the taking of minutes but I knew the subject better than the Ministers and as well as any of the witnesses. My draft Minutes were read by Lord Milner with careful attention and returned in reasonable time with a few suggested amendments. From Lord Curzon they came back at once, eviscerated and sometimes almost rewritten. From the Chairman I would receive, in spite of frequent telephone Whips to his secretaries, no communication whatever. When the Committee met he would express his genuine concern not to have had time to glance at the Minutes, but seemed after a few moments to have assimilated the essentials at least as completely as his colleagues, causing me to wonder why he ever read a document at all. Perhaps he never did. Essentials for him did not include knowledge of names or titles, even of the Public Servant for whose actions he was officially responsible. "That's all very well", he would object, examining witnesses, "but where does the Gov-

---

[1] "When the Zionists obtained the sympathy of this Englishman they gained an ally hardly less valuable than Balfour himself, in that stage of their struggle when they were striving to get promises of support from individuals translated into a public statement by the British Government as a whole." Blanche Dugdale, *Arthur James Balfour*. G. P. Putnam's Sons, New York, 1937. Vol. II, p. 156.

[2] See p. 157.

ernor-general come in?" "High Commissioner, sir," I whispered. "Surely a matter of this importance would have to be decided by the Viceroy." ("High Commissioner, Sir.") "Anyhow, we've had no complaints about that from the present Ambassador...." It was not easy for a Secretary unused to the production of departmental matter (and with strong views on the point at issue) to formulate uncontroversially conclusions which were seldom reached.

13. x. 17. I submit my draft Report to the Three to-day. Next week they will be at it, and me.... M. will correct some things, C. will rewrite the whole document, and B. will not read it at all. Lord Curzon's handling of my drafts reminds me of the old Cairo Railwayman's formula for the treatment of Egyptians: "Severity always; justice when possible."

23. x. 17. As I said. Captiousness from C. that I have been too precise and categoric: gentle wisdom from M. that I have not gone far enough, and B. would like to hear what they say before giving tongue himself.

Lord Milner's summing up tempers justice with mercy.

(*Memorandum by Lord Milner*)

I have read the draft Report of this Committee and Lord Curzon's remarks upon it. I agree with Lord Curzon that the conclusions of the draft Report are a good deal more definite than anything that was agreed upon by the Committee. But then, as a matter of fact, the Committee has hitherto only heard witnesses. There has been no formal discussion, and very little discussion of any kind between its members. The Secretary was left to make what he could out of the material provided by the witnesses without any instructions from us. He has done this, as it seems to me, extremely well, and his report, while it necessarily represents only his own impressions, focuses the whole subject in a manner which should render it easier for the Committee to come to conclusions than if it had had to discuss the subject without this preparatory work. I do not think we could in any case have settled our Report without holding another Meeting. But with the Draft Report as a basis the discussion should be greatly simplified.

The issue, in brief, was as follows. The substitution of Protectorate for Occupation had increased (I thought it should have diminished) the degree of our direct administration of Egypt. Was the Foregin Office as then constituted administratively capable of directing this increased control? If not, should the control be removed from the Foreign Office to a professional governing Ministry, the Colonial Office, or should the Foreign Office be strengthened by the addition of a specialized Egyptian Department? I had, as I have explained,[8] no illusions as to the delays and irritations of the Residency system. I was nevertheless convinced that a transfer to the Colonial Office would be disastrous, if only for its effect on

8 See pp. 157-8.

Egyptian opinion, where it must be interpreted as a veiled or incipient Annexation; and that the addition to the Foreign Office of one or two experts in Egyptian affairs, exchanged with Egypt sufficiently often to keep them up to date, was infinitely preferable. This Egyptian Department was duly constituted, and continues now, though on a far smaller scale than would have been necessary had not the granting of Egyptian Independence relieved His Majesty's Government of all responsibility for the administration of Egypt.

But I had to leave the Committee long before the decision was taken, or the Department established. The Government had never abandoned in principle the project (which had sent me the previous midsummer into Arabia) of attempting to reconcile, by a special messenger already intimate with Husain, the rival claims, ambitions and personalities of the Hejaz and of Najd. In the beginning of November it was proposed that I should go again, this time not from the Persian Gulf but from the Red Sea. Relations between Husain and Ibn Sa'ud were becoming more and more strained; but Husain, anxious without doubt not to lose the paramountcy he had achieved, was showing no eagerness to forward this project. In order to ascertain whether the enterprise was possible or where the real difficulties lay it was necessary to return to Cairo, and this I prepared to do; though doubtful at heart, and well aware of Husain's genius for the scientific organization of delay.

Mark Sykes arranged for me to join his French colleague, Monsieur Georges Picot, in Rome, and to travel with him thence under French auspices to Greece and Egypt; and in the Foreign Office it was Harold Nicolson, whose father had chased me back to Egypt at the beginning of the War, who immediately provided me with the necessary gold. The night before my departure I went to say good-bye to a lady who having for years practised divination for pleasure had been induced by financial losses to do so professionally. She offered to read my hand, and immediately remarked that I was depressed. My lack of future at the Cairo Residency must have shone in my face, and I told her that she must do better than this. She continued undaunted that, in spite of my gloom, I should in less than eight weeks be raised to a position which would be known all over the world.

Extracts from the surviving diary of my return to Cairo tell me that

I left Charing Cross on 7 November at 1.20, seen off by Father and Francis. Left Folkstone at 4, zigzagging all the way across. Filthily cold, and I noticed everyone wore their corks all the way and no nonsense. We reached Paris three hours late at 8.30 and I got a taxi fairly easily. Observed large number of private cars: also the unrepaired wood-pavement in the Place Vendôme.

Telephoned to Anna de Noailles. Drove to pick up Boghos Pasha Nubar;[4] with him to the station, where we dined in noisy haste and went over the Armenian question. My travelling companion slept in *tenue de vaudeville pudique* complete with sock suspenders, alighting at Chambéry quite silently and without turning up the light.

9. xi. 17. We reached Modane at 10 a.m. and found it under snow, the first I have seen since the winter of 1903-4. Crowds of Italian troops and a few English, including a practical and obliging set of R.T.O.'s, in whose mess I had a cup of coffee. Exchange 69 l. for 50 fr. Here, though of course not so violently as at Boulogne, our hosts have coined money out of us. At first they were definitely and actively obstructive over Railway Transport, but are now beginning to see that our interest in dispatch is common. Lloyd George had passed through Modane the day before. The organization of the line was terribly bad, and an English or American Railway expert would require only half the number of waggons. Officials were nervous of any responsibility and astonished to see our junior subalterns lightly signing for the advance or holding-up of 10,000 boxes of ammunition. Left at 12.30, and found sun, warmth and air the other end of the Mont Cenis. Turin 5. I walked round its gaunt trees till I found the offices of the *Stampa*, of which, however, my friend Bevione [5] had long since ceased to be the Editor, having become a *Deputato* and migrated to Rome. Dined frugally and expensively at the station buffet, leaving at 8.5 with an agreeable French naval officer, son of Denys Cochin, commanding a 400-ton submarine at Brindisi. Bored with his work, as he is not allowed to patrol the Straits but is kept in the open sea, where he has only discharged two torpedoes in 18 months. With one of them he sank an Austrian destroyer. Has all his nation's contempt for the Italians, though he thinks their naval engineers and architects the best in the world, and the lines of their dreadnoughts superior to all others. The few guns that guarded Ancona had been removed so that the city might not be attacked. Sea-planes were essential to his work, but though he had often applied, and plenty were about, none had ever been sent. He himself had once come up fairly close to two Boche submarines. All three had dived simultaneously. He speaks English very well and has been to England several times, though he found one visit sufficed for the climate of Scotland. Finished *Soul of a Bishop*,[6] containing some good meat as always, and thinnish plot. Bishops do not resign any more than Egyptian Ministers, and for the same reason. Occasional caddisms: my sentiments are yet faintly outraged by seeing Queen Victoria "an old German frau". Shakespeare was a stout respectable middle-aged bourgeois and Paul, as Anatole says somewhere, a hot and goat-rank Jew. But all three are surely inadequate descriptions of Great People. Still, the book would be read with advantage by most laymen and every single priest of our Established Church.

10. xi. 17. Reached Rome about noon, and found a Chancery servant with a note from Eddie Keeling to the effect that there were difficulties in the way of my mission. Drove to the Embassy, and found him quite unchanged. He showed me a cable from W—— saying that the Sharīf was making heavy

---

[4] Head of the World Armenian Community.
[5] He had visited Egypt at the beginning of the War.
[6] By H. G. Wells.

weather of my safe-conduct through the Hejaz, and hinting that I had better go round by the Gulf or Basra—I must judge whether it was worth my while to come on to Cairo, etc. I decided of course to do so: better by Birchington-on-Sea than again to Basra.

Contessa L——— who came to luncheon related how she had seen deserters from the North being led through the insults of the crowd in the station, wearing brassards and collars inscribed *Traditore della Patria* and quite indifferent. Received an excellent report of feeling in Milan. Florence was, as always, utterly disloyal; like Rome, where the princes openly declared their *désintéressement* in the nationality or existence of their Ruler: *io sono Principe Romano.* The Palazzo hotel had just been closed for Bochism, but what good was that when far worse treasons were daily uttered and applauded in the *Circolo della Caccia*? [7] The Italians in authority were reaping their reward for allowing German propaganda to work under their noses. It was a matter of common knowledge that the Turin strikes and riots had been financed from Berlin, and sums up to 300 lire had been found in the pockets of "starving and penniless" workmen. Our own Military Mission should have, but had not, heard of the corruption. After lunch Rodd took me to Trinità dei Monti, the scene of most of the pranks in d'Annunzio's *Piacere,* down to the *Piazza di Spagna* and into the Keats-Shelley Memorial House. [8] The room in which Keats died about 10 feet by 8. A wonderful collection of portraits and about 4000 volumes having to do with Keats, Shelley, Byron and Trelawney. Eddie Keeling picked me up at 4. We walked to the French Embassy but could find no trace of Picot. Thence into one or two churches, as we happened to pass them, amongst others the baroque *Gesù* where, it being the King's birthday, there was a crowd. Since the disasters the priests have been praying for the success of Italy, whether by Papal order is unknown. Ministry of Finance illuminated. The first normally lighted streets I have seen for two years anywhere. We visited a huge and very rococo antika shop: prices about the same as elsewhere. Unusual chessmen, old instruments or anything else one asks for, "yesterday" or "to-morrow". Eddie has an agreeable little apartment in the Embassy, with his old medley of good and of grotesque futurist books, and a fair grand piano, which I played to him after leaving the Rodds about 10.

11. xi. 17. Lay late and breakfasted (by their request) in my room, which I detest. Not enough coal for long baths, so hip-tub. White bread, an intermittent rarity. Read and wrote till Picot came, to tell me that we must leave for Taranto the night of the 12th for Patras, Athens, Egypt. I presented him to Rodd. After lunch walked with Eddie in mild rain through the Villa Borghese to the imposing British School of Archaeology (Lutyens), a series of rather unworthy rooms behind a good classical façade. Cost £30,000, the Italian Government giving the site to develop the neighbourhood, which is of great beauty. Mrs Strong, *genius loci,* remembered our meeting in London, when I took her to vet some sculptures and bronzes at Spero in Brook Street just before the War; and promised in spite of hoarseness to take me next morning round the Vatican. Walked back with Eddie very much under the

---

[7] Sports Club.

[8] For the preservation of which he was largely responsible.

spell of the Roman atmosphere, and to tea with G. Tyrwhitt [9] in his pleasant little flat, furnished however a thought futuristically save for the electric light, which falls softly through glass bunches of purple, red and blue grapes hanging from the ceiling. He played a few pieces of his own, based on the music of his friend and master Stravinsky, and ministering I found more to the intellect than to the emotions. I played Eddie a fugue and to bed at 11.

12. xi. 17. At 9.45 in the car with Lady Rodd, picked up Mrs Strong and across the famous bridge (*Tosca,* Act 3) to view the Vatican Galleries where we spent two hours almost perfect save for the cold. Mrs Strong illuminating: learned without pedantry and taste unmarred by Art in the Home. Judged by my standard (she says not a bad one) of what one would like to carry away, have and keep in one's own house, I put the B. M., Louvre, Athens, and Acropolis museums before this collection. Of course the *Amore,* the Michael-Angelo praised *torso* and Augustus, with perhaps ten others. But the furlongs of cold dignity spell for me royal majesty far more than private pleasure. The animal room perhaps the most original feature. We saw the Sistine Chapel, but the light was too feeble for anything more definite than effects. Noticed how, in the most hasty glance round, the poignant quality of Botticelli's work detaches itself from the general.

A cable from Cairo saying the Sharīf had guaranteed my safe conduct. Geoffrey Scott (Attached to the Embassy) took me round fountains and churches ending with *Maggior Pietro,* to convince me of the superior merits of the Baroque, in praise of which he has written a book (*7s. 6d.* without illustrations). I confessed to preferring the circular to the elliptical, also to being a constructional snob. But he argues his thesis well and I shall certainly read his book. I do not quite understand where Baroque begins or ends, nor what it includes. If it is Palladian or if it includes St Paul's it stands in no need of apology. Anyhow I cannot find St. Peter's either within or without nearly as noble as St Paul's. Saw the lapis altar and Bernini's Teresa (Soul's Awakening?) in the *Gesù,* and back to tea with the R.'s, where Miss Ducane, Lady Layard's niece, fresh from the Ca Cappello at Venice, where the Consuls are leaving and Austrian occupation may be near. The Turkish flag said to be flying over Udine: also a mosque there. Dined 7.15 half alone and half with Eddie, who saw me off by the 8.30 train. I had two berths to myself, had gone luxuriously to bed, and was in process of thinking how many people would have superstitiously dreaded berth No. 13 and a sea voyage beginning on the 13th, when the conductor came to say there had been an accident ahead, 7 persons killed, that we should have to get up, down and out in half an hour, and change into another train probably without sleepers. It was blowing hard and spouting with rain. Dressed and lay down again till 2 when we stopped, and I stumbled along with my rug and three boxes, past men with torches guarding a coach that had been thrown on to its back, wheels in the air like a turtle, through a reek of murky burning, to a little train of two carriages into which I thrust and by force found seats for two plainish V.A.D. Nurses. A Servian officer knowing a little English was active and useful. We went on almost at once, without Picot's heavy luggage, reaching Caserta—where we took on more carriages and no longer had to sit on each other's hips and collar-bones under a light that would not turn down—about 5.30.

[9] Now Lord Berners.

13. xi. 17. As Picot was firmly decided not to go on without his *malle,* it was no good wiring to stop the boat, and I of course refused to go on without him. We were rattled by the good news from Palestine and dreaded lest Jerusalem might be taken before we arrived in Egypt. Slept as much as possible. Foggia 11, Bari a little after 1, where for 3 lire each we got paper bags containing, for a starving country, a surprisingly good meal. Taranto 4.30. Our boat had of course gone. So in military car to A.M.L.O.,[10] one Weyland, obliging enough when quite certain one was All Right. Left my things at the Bologna Hotel, and walked round to the Vice-Consul to seek news of Temple, the Medici copyist, with the idea of asking him to dinner. V. C. Watson took me down to the Y.M.C.A. tent, where I found Temple in a blue apron, serving out Teas, Breads and other attractive technical plurals to a siege of sailors. He promised to show me the old town and cathedral next day, but could leave his work for no meal. Then in my horror of eating alone I made the pyramidal error of asking B. whom I took from his brown wig and Rocksavage whiskers to be possibly a pre-War schoolmaster, to dine with me at the Europa. Alas he had been a remount officer, horses were his thing and his heart was in the Bicester. I attempted to drown my misery in a pleasant flowing *Barbera,* and tackled him with conjectural estimates for the upkeep of hounds (*a*) before, (*b*) during, and (*c*) after the War. So to bed with many mosquitoes and continual noises without, about 11.

14. xi. 17. We found there was no chance of a torpedo-boat until Thursday 15th. At 10 I walked abroad with Temple, throughout the new, dull, common' and vulgar, but clean and well-trammed town, to an old woman from whom' Admiral Mark Kerr had bought (and hideously raised the price of) the Greek vases. For the moment a piteous lot of rubbish, but she never knows when the stuff is coming in. We crossed the iron swing-bridge into the old, most attractive, and rapidly disappearing Taranto; and saw the cathedral, a fine basilica with a noble carved and gilt wooden roof, good ancient monolith columns with Ionic and Corinthian capitals, and, outside a severe and oddly defaced Byzantine campanile. The rest (general interior) is silence, but the silver grey baroque chapel to the Irish saint (complete with life-sized silver statue) Cataldo (?) is harmonious and beautiful to the most rigid purist, save for the melodramatic sculpture, which I find intolerable. Temple tells me prices grotesquely high: £3000 for a wretched little villa and £24 a month for a flat. Lunched alone at the hotel, reading with indecent hilarity O. Henry's *Gentle Grafter,* as good short stories as you want; almost worthy to rank with Maupassant, Kipling and Wells. For a walk to see the old town again, but found the bridge open so stood awhile opposite the Fort watching the ships pass in and out. Next to me was a pretty little blue-eyed golden haired girl with a profile of Magna Graecia, also waiting for the bridge. She was going to the Post Office and I gathered that she was 19, of Naples, orphan, only relation *una Zia,* travelled much, was an artista and sang in the Eden musichall under the name of Lea d'Oro, real name Elena, made all her own clothes which were of real silk to the bone, was paid moderately but *spendeva niente,* and had an *amante,* her first, officer in Italian Navy, soon returning to her. I parted from her with friendly good wishes; back and read till dinner which I had in company with Weyland at the restaurant of Sga Bianchi, an ancient

[10] Assistant Military Landing Officer.

Mrs Quickly in a gigantic scarlet silk jersey, whose fruity remarks I interpreted for his gratification; and to bed at 11.

15. xi. 17. To the Museum, a collection that should be more widely known, and of which I was unable to find one photograph: well and carefully shown. One or two fine Greek heads and torsos, a few pretty terra-cottas and a fine collection of vases, inferior I should think only to B. M., Louvre and Athens. Went aboard cruiser *Queen*, who saddled me with six huge dispatch bags for Egypt. At luncheon Scott's *Architecture of Humanism*, a valuable and permanent contribution to honest thought on the subject, and a book I rejoice to have. But Lord, how circumscribed are one's ideas without an occasional contradiction delivered well and flat between the eyes.

Picot had promised to call for me about 2; as, however, he never came I left alone in heavy rain and joined *Carabine* T.B.D. of 350 tons (commanded by a *Lieutenant de vaisseau* Motet) which, with Picot's T.B.D. *Mamelouke* 800 tons, was convoying the cruiser *Charles Renaudel* returning with *permissionaires* to Itea. I found Motet a charming and (apparently) efficient sailor; anti-Italian, anti-modern and even anti-ancient Greek—*"une bande de farceurs"*—good but discriminating *ententiste*, of strong literary tastes (anti-Noailles, pro-Samain), and adoring Kipling and our philosophy of action. He gave me his berth and I went to bed at 9 hating the journey, the absence of port-holes and rat-feeling of being shut down, airless in such a small steel trap. Just before dawn I had an odd dream. I was talking with loved H. C. to whom I said that some of the passages in Maurice Baring's *Gepäck* [11] were unworthy. He agreed and said he would like to talk about it again to-morrow—by which I saw he did not know, as I did, that he was dead. I tried to keep the knowledge from my expression, when I began to notice that he was talking with a woman who had his own face and features. I saw she knew what I did, and with a terrible straining look she signed to me to keep the knowledge from him, and the face became N.'s and I awoke.

16. xi. 17. We passed Sappho's cliff and Ithaca about 6.30, the barrage of nets and mines 10.30, and made Patras (looking small for its 40,000 inhabitants) at noon. The French Consul had the honour to announce that there was no train to Athens for three days, but promised to try and hitch a car for us on to a goods-train next day. So we repaired to the Grand Hotel de Patras, I leaving my despatches, for safety, on the *Carabine*. Picot's and my arrangements for meeting somehow broke down, so I walked alone all over the town, which looked sullen and gloomy by reason of the cessation of all business. Trams and electric light have ceased for lack of coal and the people are almost

[11] Maurice Baring has made some twelve *Gepäcks*, of which the original was *Das Gepäck*. Others are *Uno Avulso Gepäck*, *Das Grosse Gepäck*, *Das Kleine Gepäck*, *Meine Gepäck*, *Das Feine Gepäck*, *Das Gepäck Sappho*, *Das Unbeschränkte Gepäck*, *Das Grenzenlose Gepäck*, *Das Definitive Gepäck*. They consist of small square volumes, very strongly and neatly bound, of blank pages upon which he has pasted poems and extracts of poems cut by himself from other books and forming unique polyglot anthologies of his own choice, in English, French, German, Italian, Spanish, Latin, Greek and Russian. Of these he had given *Das Definitive* to Harry Cust. It accompanied me everywhere and was burnt with the rest of my library in 1931. Another, mentioned on p. 474, *Das Retrospective*, which he gave to Lawrence, is now in my life possession. Lawrence described it as: "A gorgeous little thing: little? It's as fat as Chesterton and Belloc combined, and ever so much riper inside than the best Stilton...,"

starving. But in the Square by the harbour I found a crowd collected round a man in bowler and tail-coat, decorated with one or two (unidentifiable) foreign Orders, who was standing on the box of a cab haranguing them with a noble eloquence. On the seat were half a dozen framed diplomas, and hanging over the front a monstrous plan in section, of the human head and jaw, from which it was evident that the roots of the teeth went not only, as well we know, down to the roots of one's being, but also up to the roots of one's hair. He punctuated his periods, illustrative of the relief he had been able to afford to the Courts of Rumania and Japan, by calling upon sufferers to come forward, and when they did so, pulled down their chins and with a tragic horror explained by the chart the atrocious or loathsome nature of their complaint, and then, if you were standing at all near you sideslipped smartly to avoid the bloody molar which whizzed past your ear. No charge was made for the actual extraction, but Recovery was effected by the subsequent brisk sale of pink tablets, 1 drachma each, which seemed to be palliatives, if not remedies, against all forms of human misery. I watched this for half an hour, and would gladly have continued, but wanted to see the two churches, which I found new, vulgar, and pointless, before going on to tea with Wood the Consul. Misdirected to his house, I walked for 1½ hours along a lonely road that skirts the bay, getting a lift on a butcher's trolley as far as the Municipal Slaughter-House. Then met the Vice-Consul Crew, who explained the mistake and sent me back in his dog-cart. Wood, whose father was Consul-General at Patras, is a fine type, living in a big Georgian house with heavy classical mahogany sideboards. A good fourth-century Stele of family praying to Asclepius: and two good little terra-cotta Tanagras. Family at school (one at Felsted where they get marks for chess). The Woods had not tasted butter for months, had been 22 days without bread, and had had their potatoes dug up and removed by moonlight raiders. Did not know how people were to live through the winter. Patras thought Athens was holding the food up. Trains driven on wood. I dined with Picot and we went to bed early because

17. xi. 17. our train started at 6 and we were called at 4.45. The coffee we had ordered for 5.15 was not forthcoming but the cab was, and we drove in utter darkness to the station with Picot's two trunks, one very large, my three little ones and six huge and heavy dispatch bags. The hotel charged us well over £1 each for our bed and dinner, and the cab 8s. 6d. We were heartily relieved to fall into our carriage just before 6 and to leave with infinite bumpings and shriekings at 6.30. Dozed, read, and talked with Picot. Very full of the years he spent as *Conseiller* at their Pekin Embassy, and sympathetically interesting about the Chinese—their devoted yet interested and inhuman behaviour as servants and their lightning change from laughter to murder. We reached Corinth at 3, and were attached to another goods-train. Throughout the morning and afternoon a lashing tempest of wind and rain, reminding one of that line of Homer quoted by Plato ἥιαι, ὁπωῦίνῳ, ὅτε λαβῦόταιον χέει ὕδωύ | Ζεύς, and Alcaeus's quatrain beginning ὕει μὲν ὁ Ζεύς. At one station a man in a bowler played admirable dances *in modo dorico* on a clarinet, to which four others revolved in a grave circle. At night the storm ceased and we reached Athens at 8 and drove to the Grande Bretagne Hôtel —pension for smallest room £1 and none but pensioners received. Dined

with Picot and we went forth to search for Tanti Rodocanaki [12] at two clubs, from the last of which I removed the page, who guided me to the house in Plutarch Street. T. R. not at home, but a lady leaning from a window next door recommended me to push a card under his door, which I did and so back, to find Reggie Bridgeman, [13] intelligent and obliging. Bed 12.

18. xi. 17. Rose pleasantly late, and learnt from Picot that our T.B.D. left Piraeus at 4.30 p.m. To the Museum, where in especial admiration of the bronzes and vases painted on a white ground. Thence to the Legation by appointment: an odd ramshackle *pomposo* house. Granville [14] received me kindly, heard my story and bade me to luncheon. At luncheon Cairo reminiscences and food difficulties. Granville lent me his motor, in which I drove (Picot in another) to the Piraeus; where, in a fierce gale, we boarded the French cruiser *Démocratie* whose Commandmant gave us the *triste* news that we were to travel on the Greek s.s. *Chios* convoyed by the Gk. T.B.D. *Nafkratusa*, escorting also the Italian s.s. *Sumatra* (maximum speed 8 knots) as far as Rhodes, whence to Alexandria in a total of 3 days. Slightly encouraged by Lloyd George's announcement of five subs. sunk in one day, and accompanied by the Greek Vice-Consul for Tanta, we boarded *Chios*, a typical Greek passenger-boat of 950 tons. We found a young honeymoon couple Mavrogordato-Delta, who had been aboard 12 days and made five unsuccessful attempts to get to Egypt. Captain a *vieux farceur* with a smattering of English. We crossed the bar at 5 and dined better than we had feared about 5.30 by one candle, which was extinguished immediately afterwards, leaving us to make our way to bed in utter darkness. So on, in a fair sea, until about 10 I felt the engine had stopped, so on to the bridge, where the Captain told me he could not see what the *Nafkratusa* was doing, and had therefore lain to.

19. xi. 17. *Aetatis meae* 36. Hardly any sleep. Awoke about 7 to the sound of bugles, and looking out of my port-hole perceived we were back in Piraeus. *Nafkratusa* had deserted us and *Sumatra*, and we had very wisely returned. As we had no wireless it was not even possible to know where the others had gone. I called Picot, still abed and fondly imagining we were on the high seas; and his surprise and anger were elemental. He went to *Démocratie*, where he apparently received sympathy but neither information nor assistance. I left my official stuff in their strong room and back in the little French Ford to the Grande Bretagne where I had Tanti to luncheon. As always most lucid. Terribly convincing on the sad theme of our blunders in Greece. As an instance of the change of feeling at the beginning of the War, some Boches were fêting a victory in the Military Club, and Tanti rose and knocked over their bottles. He should rightly have been expelled from the Club, but 80 members petitioned strongly on his behalf and he remained. Two years later he joined the Venizelists in Salonika, and 200 members of the Club demanded his instant expulsion. He hoped the honours we were heaping on Venizelos would not turn his head—a strange word from a supporter. Our folly in asking Greece to give up Cavalla, recently conquered, that she *had* got, in exchange for Smyrna which we had not got and which was not ours

---

[12] An Alexandrian Greek I had known well in Egypt.
[13] Then Secretary in H. M. Athens Legation.
[14] Earl Granville, H. B. M.'s Minister in Athens.

to givė, had put all the cards in Tino's hands. Our pride prevented us at the beginning from thinking it possible that any country could doubt our ultimate victory, whereas in truth Greece, always in the presence of our Navy, was almost the only power that believed in us. Schenk [15] had not spent more than 12 million francs, but he had spent it well—viz. in buying up all theatres, music-halls and cinemas. He had never worked through bullies or bandits, but had employed a few on dud missions to occupy the attention of Compton Mackenzie's braves.[16] Later I ascended the divine Acropolis for the first time since July 1906 and wandered carefully in its little perfect museum. The impression of the Pallas room almost frightening. Those broken suggestions of holy dreadful implacable maiden wisdom: and the feeling that the sculptor, for the moment failing of the unattainable, stood on the threshold of the real World Dominion. The sky darkening as in a tragic Titian, with splashes of golden sunlight on the distant cliffs and slopes; against that glaucous background, over a city of faint rose and pale green, watched, like a shrine frozen in honey and amber, the Parthenon. The whole curiously corrected by the brick-dry quality of the husky autumn brown tiles. Down past the choragic Lysicrates and the octagonal Temple of the Winds and, with a hard look at the Byzantine jewel [17] under the monstrous cathedral, to tea with Tanti at the *pâtisserie* of the moment. The electric burning low, and no trams all day for lack of coal. To the Cinema, the largest and finest I have ever seen, as big as an English theatre.

20. xi. 17. Tanti called for me at 9.30 and took me round the Bazaar which, though nothing after Cairo or Stambul, is amusing. Many ikons, mostly bad; myriads of sham Tanagras and a few possible Byzantine embroideries; for all, grotesque prices, almost equal to those of Baghdad. Tanti tells me that shippers have made close on 100 million sterling during the War. Freights to Alexandria 300 dr. = £12 per ton. A profiteering tax of 30 per cent. has just been imposed, retroactively, but as there is no central list of merchants' books (which they are bound by law to keep and show) not much result, beyond the heckling of the more honest, need be anticipated. At 11.30 I called by appointment on Count Bosdari, Italian Minister, a sphynx-like and Mephistophelian creature who received me very well, insisted on speaking English, and proved far more communicative than our Legation had led me to expect. Strongly anti-Venizelist and spoke indeed generally *com se avesse Atene in gran dispetto.* "Up till now", he said, "we have made every mistake humanly possible, and I await the last coping-stone of folly, which will be to give the Greeks arms and ammunition, soon to be discharged in our own bosoms. Venizelos has lost all his popularity, and is indeed wise to get himself fêted in Paris and London, for there is nothing doing for him here. And Tino is more dangerous in Switzerland than ever he was in Athens." Bosdari is a Macchiavellian of the old school, embittered because he has not got, and never will get, London. But strange how agreeable is specific, and how tiresome general scepticism and cynicism: what more diverting than a definite attack on Monsieur Z, or more tedious than vague ranting against the Foreign Office, Women or Life? Bosdari kept me nearly an hour and asked me to

---

[15] Baron Schenk, the German Minister in Athens.
[16] See *Athenian Memories.*
[17] The little Church of Ayios Eleftherios.

luncheon next day, though I feared I should have gone. So to Politis at the F.O. A small clean dark man, ex-Sorbonne, clear, civil and intelligent. Asked me my opinion of *X* which I, emphasizing my unofficial position, and premising my eight months' absence from Egypt, gave him full and free. Politis seemed to realize his horror, but said *X* had been from the first whole-hearted for the Cause, and that he was hard up for diplomats. He commented on the folly of the Allies who still allowed a Bulgarian minister and spy-centre to remain at Washington. After some 40 minutes I returned and lunched at the hotel with Adam, of the Legation. Meanwhile Picot had decided to re-embark upon the *Chios, provisoirement* upon his naval authori-ties doing nothing better for him. He read out his "vair strong" telegrams to Paris and to the Admiral at Corfu: *"par suite de la manque d'égards, et de la mauvaise volonté que j'ai partout rencontrées.... La France risque, tant soit peu de ne pas être représentée à la prise de Jérusalem...."* Superb; his voice vibrated, his nostrils dilated, and it was as if the tribune shook; so much so, that for one half second I had the Vision Beatific of something B E I N G D O N E. But the truth is that every French T.B.D. not employed in convoy duty is now busy up the Adriatic. So at 3.30 we again subsidized and bade farewell to the Grande Bretagne and motored down to the Piraeus reaching *Démocratie* at 4.15; there to be informed by the Commandant that "par suite d'une erreur tout à fait lamentable" the French *attaché naval* had taken it upon himself to postpone the departure of our convoy until next day. We agreed in finding this *raide, insensé, inouï, dégoûtant, indigne,* and telephoned to the local French Admiral begging him, as we were there, to let us go. We ascertained meanwhile that *Chios* and *Nike* were both ready to leave within the hour, and I implored them to add this to our message: but they would not, and sure enough, after two hours' delay, we got our answer that "it was impossible, there being no T.B.D. ready". Our Commandant was genuinely sorry for us, and ashamed at *cet étalage d'impuissance* of his own chief: but could do nothing. So, humbly praying to be allowed to leave in the morning, we again returned to the hotel ready, if this were granted, to come back and sleep in *Chios*. I dined at the Angleterre with V.,[18] bitterly anti-French, and obsessed with vague ideas that they were playing for the fall of the Monarchy, in order to republicanize Greece. Back to the hotel where Picot informed me we had to wait until next night, and to bed.

21. xi. 17. Blazing day. In my overcoat, stupidly by a long detour to the theatre of Dionysus, where I sat for half an hour in the throne of the High Priest, absorbing the enchantment of the spot. Soon came the obvious tryst, she in heavy red silk, trmimed with fur, he older and unworthy; and later a whole school of little girls up to 8, dashing and calling out and picking the dandelions that grow about the marble seats. Both a sure tradition of what always must have been there, and so, agreeable. The little girls clean and neat, but far from pretty, save for one pure Attic type, dark, and dressed with surprising taste in blue inch-edged with red, and a red Lemnian Athena snood. Then up to the Acropolis again, to gain it in the sun, but only 20 minutes, as the gates of the Propylaea shut at noon. A peace that passeth understanding in this beauty that once uplifted the earth, home gone and ta'en its wages. Walked back past the two palaces to Hesiod Street, where is

[18] A very good friend, who had been Italian Military Attaché in Cairo.

the Italian Legation. Also at luncheon Vitale and Nani Mocenigo. Talk in English with lapses into Italian. All fairly confident about Venice, and Bosdari himself amiable—a *grande anima offesa*. We left the hotel for the third time at 3 and joined *Chios,* now escorted by *Nike* and a capable Commander Demestika. Left at 5, and were stopped at the bar, our Captain not having renewed his permit of departure to date. However, after 1½ hours delay they allowed us to leave under a disconcertingly brilliant moon. Bed 8.30.

22. xi. 17. Into the magnificent harbour of Melos next morning: approved Byronic towns in inaccessible coves and on jagged peaks. Took thence with us *Sumatra,* her maximum a bad 8 knots, after an amusing conversation with the local French Commandant—small, bristling, practical, all for knocking down not only the Mosque of Omar at Jerusalem, but also all other similar buildings there. Complained bitterly of the amount of convoying necessitated by the three months' leave system and a post to and from French armies abroad thrice a week—all so much bread kept out of France. Found Greeks intelligent sailors but intolerably lazy. We left at 11. Wrote up, finished O. Henry's *Cabbages and Kings* (an inferior S. American *South Wind* but good) and some more G. Scott. Bed 10.

23. xi. 17. At 4.10 we almost ran upon a very large submarine on the surface. *Nike* fired three shots and dropped a depth charge, with hopes of success, and Picot, being asleep, missed all. We were reduced to offering the stokers a Gratification if they got us in before 1 p.m. on Saturday 24th.

24. xi. 17. Sighted Alexandria about 2, and after incredible windings landed at 5, giving the stokers 50 most undeserved drachmae. Dined with Dr Granville and his sister. As my train did not leave until 11.30 p.m. the Granvilles took me to a Charity Revue, where I found myself in a trice among pleasant friends of a dozen nationalities and religions, listening to a song apparently critical of the balance sheet and the punctuality of some local railway. As for the shareholders

> *"ils rentreront dans leur argent*
> *tout dou-, tout dou-, tout doucement"*

whilst an anxious husband found on his return from what he had hoped would prove a normal journey that during his absence:

> *"sa femm' lui fit quatorze enfants*
> *tout dou-, tout dou-, tout doucement."*

I reached Cairo at 7.30 a.m. and the Residency at 8.

In Cairo I was houseless, for I had surrendered the flat to Hassan Helbawi: and workless, for you could not in the War expect to leave your duties in early April and pick them up where you left them at the end of November. Two names had come to dominate Cairo: Allenby, now striding like a giant up the Holy Land, and Lawrence, no longer a meteor in renown, but a fixed star.

CHAPTER TWELVE

7–28 December 1917

Però gli è concedutoche d'Egitto
Venga in Ierusalemme per vedere
Anzi che il militar gli sia prescritto.

DANTE, *Paradiso*, XXV, 55

...and ere his term
Of warfare, hence permitted he is come,
· From Egypt to Jerusalem, to see.

(Cary's translation.)

THOUGH seconded for service as Political Officer with Mark Sykes, I was still Oriental Secretary to the Residency in Egypt. I had left London for the specific purpose of proceeding to Arabia and attempting to reconcile Ibn Sa'ud the ruler of Najd with Husain King of the Hejaz.

Sitting, on 7 December, in the old Chancery,[1] now abandoned to Symes and myself, I opened a telegram informing the High Commissioner that Jerusalem had surrendered and that General Allenby would make his formal entry on the 9th. I would have given my soul to be there but had neither hope nor reason for going. On the 15th, however, Clayton, now Chief Political Officer to the Palestine Force as well as a Brigadier-General, overwhelmed by a rush of strange work, applied for me to accompany him.

I was not able to be there for the entry into Jerusalem, but am going thither with Clayton in two or three days, for a week or two, to help in restraining the two and seventy jarring sects. The cold is said to be intense, so I am having my old coat lined with local white fleeces.

I informed Mark Sykes, adding:

---

[1] The Chancery Staff occupied Lord Kitchener's ball-room throughout the War

I hope to be able to glean a certain amount of possibly interesting information of which I will send you a copy on my return. Lawrence, who was in at the death, tells me that with the exception of ourselves the only contented people are the Latin-Christians, the Jews [2] being secretly and the Moslems openly hostile. As for Cairo, it has not yet recovered from its jubilation over the Italian disasters and has therefore little enthusiasm to spare. I am seeing a good deal of the Zionists here, and am doing my best to promote a friendly exchange of views between them and the Arabs through the medium of the *Qibla* and other papers.

Since, owing to the Sharīf's attitude, we have given up the idea of my Central Arabian Mission we have had several telegrams from Cox urging that it should not be abandoned. The last, dated the 12th, reads as follows: "Several long cipher messages have just come through from Najd Mission via Bahrain. In course of them Philby strongly urges perseverance with deputation of Storrs, for whose safety Ibn Sa'ud takes all responsibility on his emerging from Sharīf's limits." I am therefore, with the High Commissioner's approval, writing a private letter to Abdallah begging him to get his father's permission to see me through his territory. I expect to have his reply by the time I return from Jerusalem, and if it is favorable propose running across to Ibn Sa'ud as soon as possible, doing what I can to make him fall in with the Sharīf, bringing him up against Ibn Rahīd,[3] and coming back to Cairo without further delay.

On the eve of my departure for Palestine I wrote to Mark again:

Since my last to you I have broached Brancker [4] on the possibility of journeying from Yanbo to Wady Ais, Abdallah's camp, by aeroplane; consulting there with Abdallah and continuing by flight to Boraida. To my great satisfaction B. not only accepts in principle but welcomes the suggestion, and is sending for one of his best pilots to discuss ways and means. Clayton also is favourable. I am therefore adding to the letter I had already (with the High Commissioner's approval) written to Abdallah, a postscript to the effect that I may possibly arrive by aeroplane. I should of course take a second place for Rūhi,[5] who would be invaluable on all accounts. Not the least advantage of the plan will be the wonderful saving of time, enabling me to be at your disposal here or elsewhere certainly two months earlier than any other conceivable method. I therefore leave tomorrow with Clayton for Jerusalem, work with him there for a week or ten days, and so soon as Abdallah replies, as I hope he will favourably, make my arrangements, which include warning Ibn Sa'ud to expect me in Buraida at a given date and getting across to him as soon as I can.

[2] My information never confirmed and indeed contradicted both these statements. Yet it had been reported in December 1914 that when General Kress von Kressenstein arrived in Jerusalem with a large German Staff and a few thousand men they were greeted by the Jews with a triumphal arch inscribed with the text: "Blessed are they that come in the name of the Lord", in Hebrew and Arabic characters at the Jaffa Gate.

[3] Ruler of Hayil, soon to be defeated and deposed by Ibn Sa'ud.

[4] Afterwards Sir Sefton Brancker, who lost his life in R 101.

[5] The Persian Mystic of p. 179.

In the light of later knowledge I cannot think that this Mission, even if successful at the time, could have established relations of permanency between Husain and Ibn Sa'ud.

I kept a full diary of my journey with Clayton, part of which I now print:

18. xii. 17. I left Cairo, taking my servant Said, by the 6.15 p.m. with Clayton and Edward Cadogan (Private Secretary to the Speaker) his Assistant Political Officer. We dined on the train with the Captain of a destroyer in the advanced flotilla in the Jutland action, than which no great feat of arms on land, or sea, has been more stupidly underrated by victors. Three of our cruisers engaged—and held—the whole German Battle Fleet, for 11 hours, and got into port under their own steam. Boche shooting good, until they began to be hit themselves. On the approach of our Battle Fleet, they signalled the *sauve qui peut*—and the mist saved them.

We reached Kantara West at 10.10 to find no car[6] so commandeered one. We reached the train 10.30 and had reserved berths in the General's coach (a 2nd class Egyptian State Railways with four chain-hung flaps to each compartment) before the Railway Transport Officer informed me that Said would not be allowed to leave without being sealed with a leaden seal, to be hung round his neck. This should have been done (and I thought mentioned) at the Western Station on the other side of the Canal: it would have saved a tiresome walk and telephone talk for Clayton and me, sending Said off in a strange motor to an unknown destination, and only getting him back three minutes before the train left at midnight. He had forgotten my sleeping bag and pillow, so I shall be cold throughout the journey. Clayton read, by the feeble flickering gas light, the *Grand Magazine,* as he had from Cairo to Kantara.

19. xii. 17. Woke by Rafa, and reached Gaza at 9. Walked up to the Political Camp, a few bell tents with larger square Cawnpurs for meals. Said told me that the Egyptian cook who failed to find a place at £2 a month in Cairo was receiving £7 and the *marmiton* £4. He heard the cook cursing the *marmiton* in English, and was deeply impressed. We found that Picot, with both the Mission[7] cars, had not yet returned from Jaffa, and were forced to lose a day and wait in Gaza. So Clayton and I took a little Ford car, just arrived, and drove to G.H.Q. at Kǎlǎb, some 15 miles away. Gaza is a ruin, and was so long before we took it, the Turks having stripped all the roofs off the houses to cover their dug-outs. A few poor mosques, with square minarets, and low cement cup domes; the country undulating, the sand at this time of year covered with a faint green growth, and producing later a barley fine enough to be exported to England for distillation into whiskey. Riotous hedges and knots of cactus; sand roads, far better at any rate than those through the Euphrates desert and covered for miles with wire netting, giving a surface and appearance of tarring. General effect curiously un-African; European and, with the sea in the background, Flemish dune or low Sussex.

---

[6] To convoy us across the Canal Bridge to Kantara East Station.
[7] Anglo-French Political Mission attached to the Palestine Force.

Clayton excellently well up in battle details, which even with a map, and *sur place,* I find wonderfully difficult to understand and still more to enjoy. It took us over an hour to reach Kălăb, a large camp with all the apparatus of G.H.Q. including electric light. At the Intelligence missed Philip Graves, away examining Turkish prisoners at Rafa, and found as Lieut. young Ablitt, whom I had last seen as a break-down dancer in the role of *ghaffir* at a Cairo soirée, spring 1914. Sanitary arrangements everywhere rigid, and very perfect; the funnels here and there, imploring the meed of the passer-by, especially meritorious. After luncheon for a 2-hour walk with Clayton and find him still, outside and apart from his work, at which he is first class, a personality rich in common sense. Hopeful but uncertain of his future: would like (and do well in) the Interior,[8] but fears the *concurrence* and canvassing of others on the spot. We passed shell craters, many from 8-inch guns, on all sides as we clambered up to Ali Muntar, which commands the whole district, with the sea to the N.W. and on the other side the tracks leading across the plain to Beer Sheba S. and Hebron E. The hill itself had been almost shelled away, and must have been untenable long before we could occupy it. The magnitude of the operations involved is very great and will, quite apart from the celebrity of the *terrain,* deserve and obtain a conspicuous place in military history. There is something human and winning in the country and, if Jerusalem is as it was 9 years ago when I spent a week there with H. C., I should like to be Commissioner of Palestine. Anecdotish dinner; bed about 10, where read Milton's *P.L.* and Watson's *Jerusalem.* Torrents of rain most of the night.

20. xii. 17. Two Ford cars, a touring and a box, arrived for us at 10, and we left after a terrific rain spout about 10.30, with Said sitting on the luggage in the box, as had been his portion in the Baghdad desert. The roads often 18 inches deep in mud and ploughed by the heavy traffic into chocolate and seccotine in which we stuck, and into which we had the pleasure of descending about once every two miles, with some faint far-off conception of conditions in Flanders. Once the box-car drove by mistake into the middle of a little lake from which we were lucky to drag it by a team of eight mules unyoked for our benefit from a passing convoy. We took the road Bait Hanīn, Dair Sanaid, Bait Jarjas, Ejju. By Dair Sanaid it was so intolerably bad that we each thought but did not say that we could never get through. Panting heat plunging in the mire, and chilly cold in the car. At Julis past the aerodrome the road got better and continued so to "Junction".[9] Lorries and Red Cross cars innumerable and many hundreds of Egyptian Labour Corps repairing the surface. We reached Junction at 3.30 and, the box-car being nowhere in sight, attempted to reach new G.H.Q., and in the effort walked a mile up a steep hill of wet prehensile loam to find ourselves no farther than the Flying Officers Camp; who pointed out to us on the horizon another which might (they could not say) be G.H.Q. We gave it up and tramped down again past a straggling train of Turkish prisoners at the end of a 16-mile march. One had fallen, and the guard who thought he was shamming was inclined to be a little rough with the butt of the rifle. A voice

[8] As Adviser to which Ministry he might have saved Egypt some of the horrors of 1922.

[9] The junction between the French Jerusalem-Jaffa and the Turkish military line to Beersheba.

from the rear: "Try 'im wif the other end, George." We thought he looked famished and he said to me in Turkish: "Let them cut my throat, I can't stand", so got him carried the last two miles. The box-car kept us waiting more than an hour, so that we did not arrive till 4.40 amid growing darkness, clouds and no moon, but a much better road. The last visible land-mark was the Crusader *Garde Blanche*, a great white spur far to the right front. Over one of the passes we ran into a cloud belt, and soon after the water in the engine began to boil from the continual strain of intense first speed. The last hour in an eager air under a clear gentle half moon was beautiful and impressive, if a little dangerous, as the frequent precipices are coped by no sort of parapet, and a skid sent an ambulance waggon with wounded to their account only last week. We drew into Jerusalem, silent, unlighted, and apparently deserted, about 7, and stopped, searching for Fast's Hotel at a street corner. I asked where we were, and somehow I knew it was the door of the British Bible Society to which we had gone with Harry Cust on the morning of our arrival in 1910, yielding to his desire (of course vain) to possess a Bible printed in Jerusalem. (I remember how a few minutes afterwards we twice drove into and sundered Prince Eitel Fritz's State Procession.) The door was shut but the placard still over it. We walked down to the Hotel, which being German had been allowed by the Turks to maintain its electric light engine. Now run by Syrians who take in officers at P.T. 45 (9s.) *pension*, from which I cannot see how they can derive one millième's [10] profit. Notices and maps in German still in heavy evidence. The first person we met was Bill Borton, now a General and Governor of Jerusalem, in a dressing gown, returning from his evening bath. He informed me that the only tolerable places in Jerusalem were bath and bed. We dined with the P.M., Col. Llewellyn, Chief Constable of Wiltshire, once in the Navy with Wemyss and Charles Cust, and retaining, in spite of his gigantic bulk, his original clean-shaven breeziness. Bill joined us later, flooded with office routine and unable to step out and see life. The most urgent problem is of course food. The city has been on starvation rations for three years, and is now cut off, not only—as throughout the War—from the revenues accruing from the pious and the curious and the corn-ships of Odessa, but—since the Turks left—from the vital grain districts of Salt and Kerak beyond the Jordan; nor have other complications been eased by the billeting of two Divisions in the City (though of course outside the walls), a measuring contrary to previous decision, but necessitated by the heavy rain and intense cold. Picot [11] is making a nuisance of himself, but might I am sure be smoothed down by occasional consultations on religious, financial, educational propaganda or archaeological matters. His donations of £100 notes are less enthusiastically received than they might be if it were possible to get change for one sovereign. Though the Turkish 100-piastre note was quoted between 12 and 17 piastres and is now naturally even lower, so many people stand to be ruined that it is vital even at a slight loss to Government to maintain

---

[10] One-tenth of an Egyptian piastre: therefore = 1 farthing.

[11] Letter to Mark Sykes of 15 December: "I gather from Picot that he is greatly dissatisfied with his and the general position in Palestine. Throughout our voyage he was addressed by French, Italians, Greeks and the British Naval Authorities as the French High Commissioner . . ."

some quotation both for it and the *beshlik* (*6d.*). As usual the Jews have cornered the small change, for which they extort a commission of 5 or 6 per cent. Surely here is a chance for Zionists to stop these filthinesses. Town healthy, and only one V.D. case to date. Bed 10.20, cold.

21. xii. 17. Hot bath from a little boiler heated by chips in the passage. Noticed for the first time the continuous firing of heavy guns (somewhere from the neighbourhood, as I learned afterwards, of the Mount of Olives), which seems to go on day and night. Llewellyn gave me some butter and half a ration for breakfast (the difficult meal), but there seems to be plenty of bread, at any rate in the hotel. Then round to Borton's office where were Gabriel Bey Haddad, his confidential secretary, and Albina, Mark's ex-dragoman or what not. Borton was discussing with Clayton the question of provisional Law Courts, which I should have given to an English expert to do, and a French to draft. I proposed seeing the Chief of the Municipality and the Mufti and, neither being in nor to be found, spent a vagrant morning waiting for their arrival. Rain was falling three inches deep. I walked down with Said (who up to that moment imagined we were in Jaffa) to the Jaffa gate, turned to the left and into Morcos' Grand Hotel, quite unchanged since our visit. I found Morcos, asked for the old Visitors' Book, and there turned up our three names on 5 April 1910. Morcos' Hotel had been taken by the Americans for a Hospital, and I visited and talked with a wounded Turkish officer whose shoulder had been shattered. Morcos had had all his electric plant, 30 beds and L.T. 16,000 taken from him by the Turks and was ruined; but will I doubt not after the Peace with new-spangled ore flame in the forehead of the morning sky. To one or two of the miserable antika shops, including Tarazi whose brother's shop is opposite Shepheard's in Cairo: but *ex nihilo nihil*. The contrast between Baghdad, where you would be put to it to find a stone, and Jerusalem, where I defy you to produce a brick, is remarkable and, for permanence, all in favour of Jerusalem. After luncheon to the Armenians in the Harat and Dair al-Arman. Their convent, which I visited in 1910, is a building of great interest and even greater complication. Their Patriarch and Synod were removed by the Turks to Damascus with instructions to carry all precious relics with them "for safety", instructions which were neglected in fact though obeyed in form, by the Illustrious Exile. His viceregent Monseigneur Kud estimated his flock at 800-1000 souls, plus 300 refugees; several hundred of the latter were now at Salt beyond the Jordan *dans la plus grand misère*. The need of food was paramount, more urgent than money. Their council chamber contains large portraits of Victoria and Edward VII when Prince of Wales. Their Church of St James has a charm difficult to define, a sort of mystic Byzantine basilica, square with two aisles, with the piers supporting the central dome covered with blue Kutāhia tiles. They showed me the tomb of St James, is the Church's Patron. On the way back I called again at the Municipality and found the President Hussein Effendi al-Husseini taking the chair at a meeting, which he left to talk with me in the reception room. Middle aged, well bred, speaking, I subsequently discovered, very fair English, having visited England and America; he gave me an impression of honest and obliging weakness. The Turks several times threatened to deport him and he lived (like King Constantine when we saved his throne 10 years ago) with his trunks packed

and strapped. He was unaware of the state of Medina [closely besieged by Lawrence's Arabs] which I gave him with frankness. The Jerusalem Muslims number some 11,000 Sunni (mostly Shafai or Hanafi rite). Several Turkish officials have left their families in the city, confiding in the English name. I arranged to visit the Mufti in his court next day at 9.30. Thence a longish walk to the Armenian Catholics where Monseigneur Joseph Kalebjian the Patriarch Vicar led me up to his bed-sitting room by the feeble gleam of a night-light floating in a tumbler, all he has had in the house for the last three years. His Cathedral is called The Church of the Fourth Station, or of the Spasm, and is supposed to stand upon the spot where Mary suddenly came upon Christ carrying the cross, and swooned. On his appointment as Vicaire in 1915, he found the Convent 15,000 fr. in debt and wholly without revenues; *"par conséquent il menait une vie pénible privée de tout comfortable"*; before the War, *"nos fidèles étaient presque 50 personnes"*; which the deportations from the north *"augmentèrent jusqu'à 130"*. There are also some 400, chiefly women and children, in the parts beyond Jordan, wandering about in the last distress. I promised to do my best for this amiable and courageous man and walked back to the hotel through the moon- (but nothing else) lit bazaars, the most romantic and picturesque I know. Said complaining of the darkness, I borrowed the Arab gendarme's revolver and covered Said with it at each corner till the Arab praised God aloud and begged leave to enter my service. After dinner to visit Picot in the gigantic French Convent, and found him bitter because (*a*) Allenby had not presented the notables at the Entry to him, as well as to the French and Italian Military Representatives, (*b*) because no French guards had been put round the Holy Sepulchre and the Casanova,[12] (*c*) because there appeared to be no progress made in the "Anglo-French civil administration", and, "public opinion in France was growing sensitive". He would never have agreed to come out if he had known. He said we had no idea of the rejoicing there had been in France over the fall of Jerusalem, and I said: "think what it must have been for us who took it." We in England were of course insular and old-fashioned and when we saw the religious orders expelled from France and settling with us, the crucifixes taken down from the Law Courts, and the name of God expunged from masonic rites, rows with the Vatican (where we, though "Protestants", were yet represented), we ignorantly wondered why our gallant allies should so bother themselves (and us) with the joint policy of the Holy Land. (I wrapped all this up a little.) He replied that *"C'était dans leur sang—plus fort qu'eux-mêmes"*—and would have to be reckoned with. Warned Borton, and through him Clayton, of Picot's attitude, and to bed about 11.

22. xii. 17. Brilliant sunshine and pleasant warmth, in which I walked with Said and the Arab policeman right across the town to visit the Grand Mufti, who holds his court in a building the windows of which look into the Harem al-Sharīf. He received me in a square very high barrel-vaulted mediaeval chamber, cleanly whitewashed and with a low divan stretching right along the wall facing the door, and dividing in the midst so as to admit an arm-chair behind a small table with a green baize. The Mufti, Kāmel Effendi, a cousin of Hussein Eff., is Mufti "by right of descent". About 45 years old,

---

12 The vast Franciscan guest-house.

with refined regular features and a pleasant address. Knows Egypt well, having studied four years at the Azhar. Has not seen the *Mokattam* or any allied paper for three years, and gleamed at my promise to provide a month of them. From time to time litigants appeared, singly always, before him, received what I took to be a sentence and noiselessly retired, without very much interrupting the course of our conversation. I stayed with him more than an hour, and gathered amongst other *faits divers* that his Wakf and Orphanage Treasury contained some L.T. 4000 worth of dud Turkish notes, out of which he would have to pay some 70 employees at the end of the month. He offered me the services of a cousin to take me over the Háram, into which we had entered, and were about to go into the Dome of the Rock, when we were stopped (as at the Gīlāni shrine in Baghdad) by Indian soldiers, who brought me the notice to the effect that no office, N.C.O. or man was on any account to enter the building. I had seen it twice seven years ago, and remembered enough to insist on seeing it again before leaving Jerusalem. So distributed alms to some children and withdrew, sending thanks and compliments to the Mufti. Through the Jewish quarter where many were enjoying their Sabbath, sunning themselves on the roofs. Visited the Greek Patriarchate, where I was received by eight bishops and about a dozen canons and minor prelates and led into the Consistory. Their Patriarch and Synod had also been deported to Damascus, and they were mournful at the thought of the first Christmas for many hundred years without him. Talked half French and half Greek and exchanged healths in a liqueur glass of strangely unappetizing wine. It appeared the Turks had grievously robbed them, but they had preserved their library and relics. Pressed me to visit the Holy Sepulchre and saw me off with much circumstance. I then walked out to lunch with Albina at his house in the Jewish quarter next to the Jewish Arts and Crafts School. His mother, out here throughout the War, a fine woman, told me the Turks cut down over 10,000 olive trees (*tarde crescentis olivae*) [13] to drive their trains; a barbarous gelding of this difficult soil. At the hotel picked up Said and the Arab and went for a long walk about the town. Met two officers and helped them to acquire trifling relics at possible prices. Came back outside the walls, visiting the lately finished heavy and painstaken German hostelry [14] for pilgrims, where I found and conversed with a red-headed German priest. Passed, but postponed revisiting, Gethsemane and the Mount of Olives. The city is indeed quick with every time and kind of tragic memory, and has perhaps passed the age of its productivity, though surely not of its interest and attraction. Not the hopeless beauty of the Venice, the embalmed majesty of Thebes, the abandon of Ferrara, or the melancholy of Ravenna; but something past yet unalloyed and throbbing, that seems to confound ancient and modern, and to undate recorded history.

Clayton returned from G.H.Q. and told me of the feat of our troops in the Auja by Jaffa, killing and capturing many Turks; and we talked until at 11 the electric light faded away.

23. xii. 17. A piercing wind added horribly to the daily crisis of getting up, and the bath water almost made me reconsider my whole system of life. Walked out with Said and Salim the Arab, and a Bukhara Jew who prom-

---

[13] Twelve years before they bear.
[14] The Paulus Hospiz outside the Damascus Gate.

ised to show us every kind of miracle. At 11 I went by appointment to the Assembly of the Ashkenazi Jews, some twenty of whom received me with much ceremony in the council chamber, a long commonplace room on the first floor (approached by an outside staircase) and quite unworthy of the Rembrandtesque fur-gowned, fur-hatted, ringletted Rabbis sitting on either side of me down a long deal table. The only tongue they all understood was an ultra-German Yiddish, though individuals spoke Arabic and French, and one self-elected speaker on my right hand very tolerable English. I asked them if they had noticed that the date of Allenby's entry coincided with the Maccabean feast of Hanukah, and received a roar of assent, together with the curious item that the news of the Great War reached Jerusalem on the 9th of Ab, the anniversary of its destruction by Titus. There were some 28,000 Jews in the city, of whom (strangely) 16,000 *"les plus importants en quantité et qualité"*, were Ashkenazim; and 14,000 Sephardim, also a number of unspecified from the Yemen and Bukhara. All had suffered greatly from the Turks, especially after the abolition of the Capitulations, which had taken away the protection afforded them by foreign nationality. Arrest for any reason was followed by a beating before enquiry—*castigatque auditque dolos* —as in Virgil's Hell. The Balfour Declaration had of course been misinterpreted by the Turks, but had nevertheless caused great enthusiasm. I promised to procure them the original text. I taxed them with cornering small change, and was met with mixed defences and denials. "They had not cornered, but if the Muslim wheat and sesame dealers refused to accept even Egyptian paper (now 6 per cent. depreciated), and, while paying in bank-notes, would only accept hard coin, who could blame them if they did corner?" [15] At this juncture, jam, Richon le-Zion brandy, sugar and almonds were brought in for our enlivenment, and I was forced to answer to toasts for the liberating Army to raise my glass to the health and prosperity of the Jewish Community in Jerusalem. When I asked them if there were, as in Europe, any poets, artists, or musicians among them, one replied coldly that their thoughts and energies were chiefly concentrated upon religion, to which I rejoined that the Father of Solomon took a less narrow view of Life. (Murmurs of assent, but they are fanatics.) They rose to Zangwill, the Cattauis, Suares and Mosseri's of Egypt and one Hornstein of Kieff. I left this remarkable and powerful Synod after about an hour, and seemed to breathe an easier atmosphere. The guide took us an interminable walk to the remotest end of a distant Hebrew Colony, studded with Bukharis, male and female, in original Russian Ballet costumes, until, in the last house, we intruded upon a mother, daughter and grandchild all sitting up in one bed, and waited in

[15] Cornering was not the only form of exploitation practised. Our War postal censorship was so successfully operated that months elapsed before correspondence began to reveal that delays in transit and even worse were being ascribed to its malignity. A printed begging letter was shown me, of which one hundred had been posted to various parts of the world. When the sender was summoned it was discovered that he had had them printed twenty years previously, and had thousands of them in his house. The posted letters were destroyed and his stock confiscated, but at his earnest entreaty not destroyed until he had removed from the top of each page the sacred name, printed in Hebrew, of Adonai; a task which kept him fully occupied with the scissors for about ten days. He was by no means poor, and was warned that if he used the Post again thus, worse would befall him.

front of them, whilst their chevalier dug from beneath a distressingly coarse and ugly necklace upon the strength of which he had dragged us these weary miles. In the next house a beldam produced from under her bed with ominous chokings a couple of silk Bokhara petticoats, just not good enough to buy. Said said: "The man has laughed at us, let us beat him", but lulled by hopes for a better future I let him off.

If Borton breaks down I confess I would give a great deal for the chance of succeeding him, and sincerely believe that with his present actual staff of quasi-experts I could do something with the position, which seems to require sympathy, energy, and imagination more than routine administrative experience. Yet I have no chance.

Just before starting out I went into the drawing-room and found a young Captain in shorts, with cigarette dangling from his lips, playing the most difficult Chopin and Liszt with consummate technical skill. Amidst the hotel music a book of "Selections" of which No. 9, "Hurrah! Es kommt der Kaiser. Automobilsmarsch by von Translatene", was a characteristic item. After luncheon drive with Clayton and his intelligent Intelligence, Woods (son of the Admiral), to see if any spots dangerously near the firing line or within signalling distance thereof are still inhabited by Germans. First to their gigantic [16] convent on the Mount of Olives, opened by Prince Eitel Fritz in 1910. The effect evidently desired and certainly achieved is of massive Rhenish mediaevalism. Some Sisters were still, but will not much longer remain, in their rooms within 9000 yards of gun positions. We climbed the great tower, which dominates Jerusalem, with one of the noblest prospects on earth, and found on the top gallery our searchlight, telescope and telephonist. Just below, a fine carillon, the big bell of which bears the legend: *"Spes et salus una Christus"*. Coming down we heard an organ playing an Anglican chant, and pushing through a door found ourselves at early evensong in a Byzantine chapel, I thought very beautifully conceived (even to the olive-grey mosaics, so often fatal) except for the atrocious paintings on the ceiling.[17] Two-manual organ with the Boche system of lever-press stops. Thence to the Russian Monastery, empty and deserted, but too easily accessible to evil-disposed signallers—even assuming that we can still consider the Rusks as our Allies. So round the city by blocked and devious roads to Bethlehem, which I remembered and cherish as of surpassing merit. A British sentry turned us from the yard-square entrance to the Church of the Nativity, where Picot is going to reassert France's protectorate of Latin Christianity by attending the Christmas Eve Mass in state, with a guard of 20 Spahis. Allenby is sending Gen. Bulfin and staff to keep our end up, and I (secretly) made up my mind to be there. We walked round to the street behind, to the shop where in 1910 H.C., N. and I had bought relics and great mother-of-pearl necklaces. The shameless vendor was still as shameless as his stock, and had already unloaded £50 worth of holy fakes upon Gen. Shea's conquering Staff. Round to the convent where Cave, a 2nd Lieut. with a Canadian accent, is, with one subaltern to help him, acting coolly and most efficiently as Military Governor of Bethlehem and district. Back by

[16] Already H.Q. of the 20th Corps.
[17] "Featuring" the Kaiser and Kaiserin.

6.30 and dinner with X and Y, perhaps the greatest living master of the conversational *cliché*. Wrote and bed in dark. 11.

24. xii. 17. I had engaged to take round the town Cadogan and Francis Rodd. Borton was uncertain whether or no he would attend the Nativity Mass, and I walked up to the office to decide him. He said no; and I was about to return and accept Picot's offer of a lift when Borton recalled me, but by the time I had reached his room Piépape the French, and later d'Agostino the Italian, commandant had the advantage of me. As soon as the latter had left, Borton called me in and told me that d'Agostino was furious at the French pretensions in Bethlehem, and was not certain whether he and the Italians would attend the Mass: what was he, Borton, to do? I said that if they were treated on equal terms with the General of the conquering British Army I could not see what they had to complain of, and if it was the Governor's business to make up everybody's mind for them, whether they should go to church or no, well, really, really, etc. Borton agreed to answer in this strain at 2.30 and at the same time asked me to go with him to the service and also out in the afternoon to consult the local Governor as to entries, places, etc. Then showed F. and C. the bazaars, without, however, finding one single desirable object, save a 1*s*. inscribed Armenian plate. The Mufti, Chief of Municipality, and Greek Patriarchate, returned my call, the last with an enormous basket of large uneatable grapes. At 4 drove out with Borton in a pelting rain to Bethlehem, where we had the gratification, only possible under British rule, of seeing French *poilus* going in and out of the Nativity Church and ourselves denied admission by an English sentry. A confusion of orders of course, but I thought odd. Back to Cave, who appears to have received all sorts of contradictory instructions, and then to Jerusalem. There found Brig.-Gen. FitzGerald, Guy Dawnay, Deedes and George Lloyd. We dined at a large table together, and I liked Dawnay exceedingly and admired his youth (he looks about 30) and ability. At 10.30 Borton and I drove off again in a torrent to Bethlehem which we reached about 11, passing straight into the Latin Church, round and behind the Orthodox and Armenian. The building a sharp disappointment: a commonplace eighteenth-century vaulted basilica, the walls distempered duck's egg blue, the organ in the place of the East window, and the altar and reredos gaudily and tawdrily adorned with tin and tinsel vases and images. On the right front of the nave stood a richly gilt throne with a *prie-dieu* in front, and in the aisle beyond, the women; the married ones, in most decorative high mediaeval coifs.[18] In the first row of the other side, armchairs for Bulfin and Staff, Borton and self. The service had been going on for hours before we sat down, and we had forty-five minutes more before at midnight all the bells rang: a deputation of prelates walked down the church and returned with Picot—*tête de circonstance*—his Staff, two Cavasses with great staves of office, and Bulfin with his two A.D.C.'s. The Italians never turned up at all. The Mass then began with two of the Franciscan Friars emerging and ceremonially censing Picot, who bowed gravely in return: not a whiff for Bulfin or the Governor. The Abbot, a gigantic man with a figure like an apse and considerable carriage, knew apparently but little of his part, and the voice of prayer was frequently merged in the hoarse cue of a very able prompter. The

---

[18] Said to date from Crusades.

ritual seemed best performed by eight little scarlet-robed Syrian acolytes. The singing, which proceeded from a choir behind the altar was creditable (canons and simple fugal movements being attempted) rather than agreeable, and could anyhow never have done much good with an organ composed exclusively of the cheapest and tinniest reeds. About forty British officers sitting behind us, and on our left, including eleven up in the pulpit, the crowd. At about 1.30 a.m. an immense candle, 2 inches thick, was lit and presented to Picot: a 1-inch to Bulfin, and small rook-rifle bore to the rest of us. The clergy walked down in procession, followed by Borton, self and the rest round the church, up the beautiful Greek basilica through a narrow door and down steep steps into the Crypt of the Manger, the walls and ceiling of which were hung with heavy satin brocade. After a number of prayers and a really impressive hymn, a doll-baby which had been carried round on a little gilt bed was lowered into the recessed niche of the Manger; and the procession, of glittering vestments, rich armorial copes, uniforms and waning candles, paced back the same way, each step accentuated by the two cavasses driving the iron ferrules of their heavy staves against the stone flagging, with curiously arresting effect. The service continued till about 2.30 a.m. when we made a state exit and subsequently joined Picot upstairs and sat down some twenty strong to a gargantuan supper of turkeys, foie gras, etc. brought by St. Quentin [19] from Cairo. I next to Piépape, *sympathique et bon garçon*. Left after 3 to find the torrent still falling and the roads in rivers. Poor Borton very low again, complaining of grave insomnia and burning pains in the back of his head. I tried to cheer him with "to make the time pass by, droll legends of my infancy", and I hope succeeded a little. Could not find Said, so woke and had my top-boots pulled off by the drowsy Abyssinian porter, and got into bed just before 4, eyes throbbing from the lights.

25. xii. 17. Woke with great pain in eyes about 7.30, but lay on till 9 listening to the rain. Later round to the Armenian convent, most fascinating of places, and examined in greater detail their Church Surp Hagop [20] and its collection of fine but not quite first-class carpets and altar cloths rich with all the tradition of Byzantine broidery and brocade; copes and mitres, each *gemmis crustatus et auro*, and finally the library (which is also a little vaulted church with carved and heavily gilded old wooden screen) containing 3000 manuscripts numbered and catalogued, many unique and some of very great beauty. The librarian is fully alive to their excellence, which is, he told me, only surpassed by the 5000 volumes at Echmiadzin. I think on the whole the atmosphere of a large library is the best I know. Before luncheon Clayton told me that Borton had written his resignation, which Allenby had accepted; and showed me an official paper from Cathcart Garner [21] describing his symptoms as being those of a complete breakdown and necessitating instant cessation of all work. Then out into the downpour with Clayton, George Lloyd, Fitz-Gerald and Cadogan to the Holy Sepulchre, which not opening until 4 we walked down to the Háram al-Sharíf and about the site of the Temple. The tiles were shining deliciously, and the water brought out all the undertones of the marble columns and stone flags, a glorified union of the Piazza San

[19] Then Military Attaché to the French Agency; 1936, French Ambassador to the Quirinal.
[20] St James.
[21] Principal Medical Officer to the Military Administration.

Marco and the Great Court of Trinity. We climbed back by the Via Dolorosa and entered the Great Church a little after 4. Clayton and I kissed the marble slab of the Tomb, and explained the whole place so far as I could remember it to the four soldier servants we were also convoying. So far as I can recall them, my impressions, though aesthetically and architecturally better founded, resume what we felt seven years ago: firstly, that the faking of the sites and the indignity with which even when authentic they are now misrepresented, is an irritation, an imposition, and an affront to the intelligence; secondly, that the pathos, grandeur and nobility of the ancient City of the Heart easily countervails these very real annoyances:

> "How beautiful, if sorrow had not made
> Sorrow more beautiful than beauty's self."

Aesthetic death is swallowed up in spiritual victory.

The weather, which had drenched us as long as we were under it cleared up as we reached the hotel, but George Lloyd, Cadogan and I decided we would not be so easily mocked, and walked down past the Damascus Gate while Lloyd put before me, with his usual and unique objectivity, the alternatives which for the moment distracted him. Austen Chamberlain had wired offering him the Secretaryship of the Allied Finance Committee; Dawnay hinted at odd utilities here; Lawrence and Hejaz called him South; and his Regiment, much praised by FitzGerald, West. I urged 3.

For dinner Dawnay produced four half-bottles (the last) of the Hotel Bubbly and talked afterwards agreeably of porcelains: later of the tragedies of Gallipoli. I am reading nothing but snatches of *Paradise Lost* whilst waiting for the bath to fill. No letters or news since we left Cairo.

26. xii. 17. No news still except George Lloyd's account of the Pope's Commination of whosoever should attempt to retake Jerusalem. Morning wrote and worked. After luncheon, walked with Woods through the Gate of the Column and up the Mount of Olives where we stood by the batteries that were shelling towards Jericho. Entered again the little dome that marks the Ascension where Harry Cust quoted the *In Memoriam*.

Down past Gethsemane to the place where Stephen was stoned καὶ ἐκοιμήθη —and fell asleep. Later dined in the Casa nova with the very agreeable Franciscans and several Italian officers, an hilarious but uninstructive evening from which I returned with Francis in marvellously brilliant moonlight.

27. xii. 17. Wrote and after luncheon took Borton out for a walk round the walls, returning through the Háram, whence the sunset struck the loftier buildings and the distant mountains of Moab with an exquisite burning glow as of pure fire.

28. xii. 17. Rose early to see off Borton and waited from 8.15 till 8.30 in the cold until his two cars appeared, and he drove into space. I was sitting shivering at breakfast before leaving myself for Cairo when Rees Mogg the A.A.G. beckoned me out with a mysterious gesture, and, beginning by saying that I should want another uniform after all, showed me a telegram from G.H.Q. appointing me, with the temporary rank of Lieutenant-Colonel, Military Governor of Jerusalem.

CHAPTER THIRTEEN

1917–1920

"I was glad when they said unto me ..."

Psalm cxxii.

THIS telegram seemed to be not so much an offer as an order of appointment, to be accepted—or obeyed—forthwith. Said unloaded my box from the Ford and carried it, uninstructed, into the best, I think then the only, suite of rooms in Fast's Hotel. I walked round in heavy rain to the Governorate established in a long row of uncomfortable offices on the first floor of Hughes' Hotel, opposite the Municipal Gardens in the Jaffa Road. I possessed no military competence whatever, and very little administrative experience, but I did have an inside knowledge (with examples positive and negative) of the processes of Government and the interactions of Oriental communities; combined with a deep enthusiasm (still with me) for the task, and a wild exhilaration at the chance which had been put into my hand. Above all "the amazing difference between *doing,* and advising suggesting and recommending as has been my business all these years". I made the acquaintance of my Staff; Colonel Rees Mogg, A.A.G., already sickening for a serious illness, with his calm and capable assistant Captain Bristowe; Colonel Garner, an insistent Irishman of the Egyptian Health Department, and Major Bourke, an enterprising, unflurried D.A.Q.M.G.: above all, I renewed my friendship with Gabriel Haddad Bey, a Syrian Christian who had been brought in as Local Adviser by Borton from Alexandria: a man as able as he was loyal and charming, whose services in those first days of general ignorance and suspicion I cannot overrate. I learnt what I could and, returning to Fast's for luncheon, heard in the hall a Major-General, complete with A.D.C., enquiring for the best rooms. Mr. Fast regretted that these had been taken by the Military Governor. "I am the Military Governor", replied General Watson, who in his haste to report for duty from South Palestine had not received the telegram countermanding his appointment. I gave him the "suite" for the night, and took him round the City. Eighteen months later he arrived in Jerusalem once more; this time as Chief Administrator.

The British troops who, through bitter cold and blinding sleet, fought their painful and perilous way foot by foot up and down the stony peaks and valleys of the mountains of Judea, found, when they delivered Jerusalem, glamour and glory such as the Great War seldom gave; but they found little else. They were indeed welcomed by the inhabitants, in something near an ecstasy of hope and joy. For these were the days when the trace of a great fear was yet in men's eyes, and the gulp of relief still at their throats: when for friendship with the Allies, true or suspected, whole families of Christians had been exiled, at an hour's notice, into the interior of Asia Minor, a Moslem Kadi hanged at the Jaffa Gate, and a young Jewish girl tortured to suicide. But the Turk, when he struck his flag and the Camp in which he had bivouacked rather than settled for four hundred years, carried with him in his retreat money, records, registers, drugs and surgical instruments, much furniture, all food—and, generally, everything that could be of the smallest use to the City or to its liberators.

Snow was falling throughout Judea, so that having arrived for a fortnight only, in the thin "near"-uniform which I had ordered for the Fall of Constantinople and worn through the torrid heat of Mesopotamia, I felt the cold, and applied for two days' leave in Egypt to buy a real uniform (with tabs and badges of rank); which being (very properly) refused, I did my first month's office work in a box-cloth overcoat with a paraffin stove between my knees.

Throughout those early days in Jerusalem my chief, my nightmare anxiety, was the scarcity of food amounting almost to famine. One morning early in January I became aware of a crying and a screaming beneath my office window. I looked out on a crowd of veiled Arab women, some of whom tore their garments apart to reveal the bones almost piercing their skin. And the sight in the hospital of the children's limbs swollen with emptiness was not good; nor was the dread lest we should have delivered Jerusalem only to starve her to death. Brief extracts from my detailed appeal to G.H.Q. explain the urgency:

Food Supply of Jerusalem Zone

For the moment, the security of the City against hostile attack being guaranteed by the British Army, the question of food comes first; and I consider that the Authorities and Charitable Organizations interested ought to know how we stand and why.

Until the War Jerusalem drew its supplies from two external sources rather than from the immediately surrounding country. It was dependent for its Grain partly upon the Districts of Salt, Kerak and others East of the Jordan, and partly upon imports of flour by Sea from Jaffa. From the day that Turkey entered the War, the Sea was cut off but the Land remained open. Now that the Trans-Jordan Districts are still in Turkish hands Jerusalem stands, as regards its normal sources, isolated. It is almost impossible to estimate the quantity of Wheat in the City or neighbourhood, but it should be remembered firstly, that the population, divided up into numerous and mutually hostile communities and subjected to centuries of organized pauperization,[1] is both improvident and helpless; secondly, that the Turks have not the reputation (when they do leave a place) of leaving much that is eatable or movable behind them. It is possible that stocks may exist in the City and the country round about, but the opinion prevails that no large quantities are likely to be found in dealers' hands. Since the British Occupation the City has been living mainly upon pre-existing stocks, for the total arrivals during the last month are hardly equivalent to four or five days' consumption. As for the villages, the Fellahīn who may have any reserve stocks have hidden them and absolutely decline to sell except against payment in gold. Any attempt therefore on the part of the Government to purchase locally would have the double result of sending up prices and further depreciating the Egyptian Bank Note. To meet this situation an official Tariff establishing maximum prices for all articles of primary necessity together with a declaration of all stocks, has been promulgated, and been in operation since the morning of the 5th. The results so far are hardly encouraging. Bakeries are closed down, and little bread is on the market to-day. To sum up, Jerusalem is not and cannot at the present moment be considered self-supporting. Something must be done to supplement the cereal deficiency, or at least to keep the poorer classes, which form the majority of the population, provided with cheap grain. A minimum of 200 tons a month imported from Egypt will be required, and steps to supply it should be taken immediately.

I was sitting at my desk the afternoon following the dispatch of the Note when a Staff Captain broke in and announced that the Commander-in-Chief was walking up the stairs. It was my first sight of General Allenby, who had come with characteristically generous encouragement, "to thank me for taking charge". When he had questioned me as to the state of affairs he asked me if there was anything special I wanted, and I answered: "The food." Next morning and regularly henceforth lorry-loads of wheat arrived without fail, and I breathed again. They were not allowed to return empty.

A number of persons here of several Communities, who were originally Jaffa residents, have been asking permission to return thither. This is desir-

[1] "Jerusalem is as perfect a specimen of organized pauperism as you would wish to find. In normal circumstances, when the faithful of the three great religions are willing and able to pour money into the place, this may or may not be a desirable state of things; for the moment it greatly adds to our difficulties."

able in so far as it does not conflict with 'existing Military Regulations, as it tends to a re-establishing of normal conditions; but they have no transport. I have therefore arranged that once they have satisfied us that they are medically fit and economically self-supporting they may be repatriated in the empty wheat lorries.

The A.S.C. lorry drivers were no less discriminating than considerate, for of all the hundreds that drove by, my Staff could not remember seeing one plain or elderly woman on the box seat.

I was now able to write:

have just turned the corner. Three times last week I went round the bakers' shops with two special gendarmes, and forced them to sell at the Tariff price. Women first, next children and men last: otherwise the first two got nothing. At that time there was not enough to go round.... The task is not eased by the entire disappearance of all small change, partly owing to mistrust of the Egyptian bank-note (now fallen to 65 per cent.) and partly because the silver is being cornered. I am therefore increasing the proportion of nickel, and may have to issue 1s. and 2s. notes.[2] But if my sleuths catch one of the hoarders....

None ever did, and before we were able to stabilize the currency, by the obvious but not very easy process of substituting Egyptian for Turkish, Jerusalem was to add to her list of strange sights that of a frantic crowd, provided with money but unable to spend it, prevented by mounted police from rushing the Ottoman Bank for small change. But within a few days a Food Control had been organized for flour, sugar and kerosene, with the necessary staff, sheds, warehouses, and transactions running into scores of thousands of pounds. In my early enthusiasm I even began to prepare an Unemployment List, and only abandoned it when I found that it must comprise some 90 per cent. of the population.

The key position in Jerusalem, internationally speaking, was held by the Spanish Consul, Count Ballobar. This agreeable young diplomat had represented (besides his own country) the Neutral, then the Allied, and now also the Central Powers—almost all the known or civilized Powers of the World. He was responsible for all their Archives, for payments made by or (more rarely) to them, as well as for the checking and answering of innumerable enquiries. He was disillusioned and pleasantly cynical about the majority of the Powers under his protection, and from the beginning was most helpful.

I have just had to dinner the Spanish Consul, who was here throughout the War, and kept a day-to-day diary. Now longing for a few oysters and lobsters at Shepheard's. He tells me the Boches were quite indifferent to the

[2] I never did.

fate of the City, and drank and laughed till the night before Evacuation. Jemal was *sâle type* but *bon garçon*, and Enver *aimait beaucoup la boisson*: Falkenhayn and Kress *sympathiques*.

His diary, judging from other samples with which he occasionally favoured me, is, to my regret, not likely to be published *in extenso* during his lifetime.

When I had visited Jerusalem in 1910, Russian establishments held pride of place outside the walls, with a quarter covering many acres, and a Cathedral and public squares for the accommodation of their great Easter pilgrimages: though Germany seemed to be fast overtaking Russia, with the tremendous Protestant Hospice—the Kaiserin Augusta Victoria *Stiftung*—dominating Jerusalem from the Mount of Olives; the towering Lutheran Church of the Redeemer within the City; and, covering the Damascus Gate and the intersection of the roads to Syria and Trans-Jordan, the crenellated Roman Catholic Hospice of St. Paul. The longer-established French and Italian monasteries and hospitals, though for the most part equally large and even more hideous, seemed to be less conspicuous. Save for Roman Catholic pilgrims, Orthodox activity appeared then more obvious and widespread than Latin.

In 1917 the Russian buildings, deserted and half-ruinous, served to house troops and military services. I soon found Hughes' Hotel small and otherwise unsuitable, so I moved into the *Paulus Hospiz,* paying from the first day a rental (of £1000), all German property of Roman denomination having been hastily declared to belong to the Holy See; whereas the *Stiftung,* a Protestant foundation, had to await the general settlement of German claims in Palestine. I remarked from this and subsequent experience that although our requisitioning authorities were scrupulously courteous in their necessary exactions and evictions, nevertheless with relatively unprotected Protestants, Greeks or Armenians they were not reduced to bargaining; a most-favoured-nation treatment which the Military and for some time the Civil Government reserved for the two universal Powers—Rome and Zion. Similarly for relief of all kinds there were waiting organizations and funds for Christians and Jews, but not for Moslems. For them a free dispensary and soup kitchens were soon established, for which I was able to collect large sums from the generous Egyptian people.

Russian priests and monks had alike disappeared, but I found on my third day, sitting in the road under a heavy rain and breaking stones for a few piastres, a group of some forty white women of various ages, in black conventual robes. They were the Russian nuns, ladies of honoured families who had left their country to serve God in a contemplative Order on the Mount of Olives, and were now absolutely destitute. They were brought immediately within doors, and, through the ubiquitous and eager Syrian Relief Fund, provided with the wool, thread and material for terribly needed warm clothing.

The Ophthalmic Hospital of St. John of Jerusalem is a long picturesque building on the east of the Bethlehem Road, straggling down the slopes of the Valley of Hinnom, and so known by the Arabs as *Abu Salālim,* the Father of Staircases. For many years before the War it had rendered selfless, unpropaganded and deeply appreciated service to patients of all races and creeds ranging from the Sinai to Aleppo. I found it in a pitiful state, as the Turks had used it for an ammunition-dump and blown it up on the eve of their retreat. Nothing seemed to happen as quick as one wanted, for it took the best part of a week to clear it of exploded and unexploded cartridges and to summon the expert advice of MacCallan from Cairo; and some months before the Hospital could be rebuilt by the Order and made ready to receive patients.

G.H.Q. of the Egyptian Expeditionary Force was still in Cairo, but General Allenby's Headquarters, Advanced G.H.Q., formed a large camp pitched at Bir Sālem—then known as "Beer Salaám"—on the sand and among the olive groves of the little Crusaders' town of Ramleh. I was soon invited there; to find myself wondering what sort of a General was this, who had gained a brilliant and decisive victory, who knew all there was to be known about birds, beasts, and fishes, who had read everything and who quoted in full at dinner one of the less-known sonnets of Rupert Brooke. I rode with him out to the orange groves, mounted on his giant charger Hindenburg, and I can feel now my shame and horror when the great beast put his hoof into a small pool of water and splashed my Chief from head to foot. Next week, walking on the walls of Jerusalem he demanded chapter and verse from a companion who pointed out a plant there as "the hyssop that groweth on the wall". He could name the birds of Palestine, though they towered over the Mount of Olives beyond the eyesight of ordinary men. It was impossible to supply him with books fast enough, even during the 1918 campaign. During the War a number of persons became personages, not all of whom achieved personality. Allenby would have had that even if there had been no war. The normal Gordian knots of sophistry and intrigue he cut with the double edge of intuition and honesty. When anything went wrong there was a local and a world-wide distribution of blame, never from Allenby. Those who worked in Palestine for that loyal, great-hearted chief will remember that he never intervened save to support, and will salute with grateful and affectionate admiration the last of the Paladins.

In the *Stiftung* on the Mount of Olives were the Headquarters of the 20th Corps; in the City were those of the 60th Division; commanded respectively by Sir Philip Chetwode and Sir John Shea. Each of these distinguished Generals did everything that could have been done to smooth the military path of a newly created civilian Colonel, and my gratitude to both is profound. The 60th Division provided within three weeks of our occupation an admirable variety entertainment, produced by the *Barnstormers;* to the stalls of which I was kindly permitted to bring a numerous contingent of Moslem, Christian and Jewish dignitaries, religious as well as secular, supplying them *sotto voce* with a decarbonized analysis of the libretto. Hardly any of them knew English: every single one asked, and was allowed, to come again. I found the Staff hardly less resourceful than the Generals themselves. One of the Aides-de-Camp, reading in the Mess an illustrated weekly, seemed unable to drag his eyes beyond a photograph not far from the beginning. It was that of a beautiful actress, hitherto unwilling to accept his adoration at face value. He tore out the page, crumpled it a little, drove a slim cane neatly through the background, and sent it home to the lady with a letter to the effect that while wealthier admirers might lavish upon her costlier gifts he could only send (more precious to him) her portrait, found by him bullet riddled, on one of the battlefields of the Holy Land. During his next leave he languished no more.

The Military Administration I served was called Occupied Enemy Territory Administration (South), and was known and pronounced in three syllables as O.E.T.A.—O-ĒĒTA. After the conquest of Syria there was added O.E.T.A. (East) extending from the borders of Palestine to the extreme of Aleppo, and including Trans-Jordan. The immediate head of O.E.T.A. (S.) was Clayton, under whose unruffled equanimity and sympathy no problem seemed insoluble. As Chief Political Officer to the Force he was far too busy (even if he had desired) to interfere in detail. He expected, but never inflicted, proposals. He was never in the way and never out of the way. The northern boundary of O.E.T.A. (S.) ran from a little north of Jaffa through Ramallah to Jericho, the Turks still holding Samaria. The Governorate comprised at first no more than the Ottoman *Kaz*-District of Jerusalem—including the sub-districts of Bethlehem, Jericho and the occupied portion of Ramallah.

The military regime was for all concerned paternal, whimsical even, rather than stiff and harsh. In the offices, papers were "passed to you", and items of information would have been considered almost improperly exposed if they had not concluded with the invariable enclitic "Please". Yet we were still well within the period of military precautions. On New

Year's eve rumour compelled me to issue notices in English, French, Arabic and Hebrew (printed at the Franciscan Press of *San Salvatore*) warning the public that: "Any persons found stripping or robbing or in possession of the arms or accoutrements or clothing of the dead of any nationality", or "concealing or attempting to conceal any Turkish Officer or Soldier, will render himself liable to be dealt with under Martial Law." Curfew was, I think, at eight; a small loss to the population in such weather, and with a total lack of amenities. The Army maintained all roads of military utility (none other survived), and reserved them for military traffic. (Their cost between the liberation of Jerusalem and Allenby's great advance was £100 per kilometre per month.) Alongside most of them ran tracks, known by the genteel as "Diversions", whose purpose was pleasantly indicated by a notice: "To be used by horses, mules, camels, donkeys and civilians." [3] The Commander-in-Chief and the two Corps Commanders used Rolls-Royce cars: Brigadier-Generals and upwards Vauxhalls: Colonels Sunbeams and the rest Fords. The Governorate had a fleet of fourteen Ford "box-cars" for ration and relief purposes. There was not, when I took over, one single private car or telephone in Jerusalem.

The difficulties of travel to Palestine must have seemed to applicants quite intolerable, and aroused bitter complaints all over the world. But O.E.T.A. had to bear in mind fine gradations between neutral and enemy subjects, even in religious Orders, and the scarcity of food and accommodation; and when these obstacles were overcome it was as often as not weeks and months before a berth could be obtained—an additional delay for which though not responsible we generally received the blame. Every civilian who wished to enter or leave Palestine had to obtain a special permit from the authorities in Cairo, apart from the passport regulations of foreign countries, and every ticket for the trains to and from Egypt had to be officially registered and canvassed before permission was given to buy it. Within Palestine itself travel permits were compulsory for travellers, even on foot, to Jerusalem or any other town or village, and were only abolished when I discovered that they were almost universally disregarded. In respect of internments I made exceptions (as in Egypt) for some German and Austrian Franciscans, and for the German chief representative of the "American" Colony; and never had cause to regret either. Those who could evaded our watchfulness. During one of my absences "the Italians introduced six monks and one lay brother

---

[3] The horses and mules were nearly all military: generally, the local stock of cattle was exhausted.

disguised as soldiers, who demobilized themselves and donned ecclesiastical habits on arrival". [4]

Our finances were a harmless necessary blank. "All my Financial Adviser can tell me of the Budget is that we have no Revenue, and do not yet know the rate of our expenditure." The immediate liabilities of Jerusalem far exceeded the assets and, as always at the overthrow of governments, it was the official classes, hitherto sheltered and privileged, that suffered most acutely. Scores of officers and officials who had served the Sultan for years were utterly without resources. Their claims could not be accepted without verification, a matter of toil and of time (some, with dignified resignation, had not presented any): but once verified, all were honoured. The ultimate generosity of the British Government in the matter of compensation far exceeded that of any other, save perhaps the United States (of which I have no knowledge). One or two landowners might be dissatisfied with their assessments, but as a rule the error was the other way. An Arab Administration officer who had lost an arm "on duty" received a war gratuity before the Department concerned had ascertained that the loss had been caused by a fall from a donkey. I relieved my feelings by quoting to him the Armenian proverb: "He who mounts an ass has one shame; he who falls from it two." [5]

The Turks had removed with them from Jerusalem among other objects of value the chiefs of Communities such as Damianos, the Orthodox, and Ormanian, the Armenian Patriarch and other outstanding personalities. The Qadi had been taken with a view of holding up the religious courts and embarrassing a Christian Administration by forcing upon them a Moslem appointment. I nominated the Mufti acting Qadi, and there was no interruption of work. The excellent Mayor of Jerusalem, Husseini al-Husseini, died early in 1918 and I had to appoint a new Mayor and Council.

Owing to the foul state in which the Turks left the City, we stand in a very fair danger of a typhus epidemic, and cerebro-spinal meningitis is increas-

---

[4] Letter to myself (on inspection) from Asst. Military Governor.

[5] "During the War a large number of British soldiers of all ranks were imprisoned at a town in the interior of Turkey called Afiun Kara Hissar. They often ran short of money, but there was a little Greek trader on the spot who honoured their IOU's and supplied them with the necessities of life. Some time after the War was over, a small dark figure staggered up the steps of the War Office, bearing a sack from which he produced many hundreds of these chits, every single one of which was settled by the debtor if still alive, and by the War Office if he had died. That little man returned to the East wealthy beyond his utmost dreams, and his story lost and continues to lose nothing in the telling. It is not every nation whose chits would thus have been honoured, or who would thus honour their chits, and there are many villages and towns throughout Anatolia where they are now more admiringly remembered than another much more famous Scrap of Paper." Sir Ronald Storrs, *Great Britain in the Near and Middle East* (Cust Foundation Lecture, 1932).

ing very rapidly. The rain has made the roads almost impassable, and until the Railway reaches us again (the Turks rooted up the French Company's Jaffa-Jerusalem line) it is very difficult to bring up sufficient drugs, disinfectants and other vital necessities. If, on the other hand, the rain ceases to fall, (we have only had nine inches out of an average twenty-five), there will be an irreparable drought in the summer.

Colonel Garner would rush into my office asking how he was going to "Shweep ut away" if I did not give him brooms. There were no brooms anywhere. The shops were empty. There was no street and very little private lighting, for few householders could afford lamps, so that the city went to bed at sunset and, outside military formations, there was not one light to be seen in Jerusalem from the Mount of Olives; from which it was still possible to hear and to witness all the phases of the fight for Jericho. As late as 15 March fear of pestilence evoked the necessary (and most unpopular) public order forbidding the sale of old clothing or mattresses until they had been disinfected.

The fellah was a shivering bundle of rags. Beggars swarmed, and the eye, the ear and the nose were violently assaulted at every corner. With the help of the Army seven Sanitary Sections patrolled the streets daily, and it was made the duty of one man to keep the Via Dolorosa, from Pilate's Judgment Hall to the Holy Sepulchre, free from offence. The reek of the prison and the sight of the prisoners—sentenced (if at all) we knew not for what—and their misery froze the soul. In the absence of charge-sheets or even verbal evidence they were released; and with the first aid of Colonel Whittingham, summoned from the Egyptian Prisons Administration, we fortified a new Prison (complete with Regulations, Uniforms and Rations) in the Russian Quarter.

Less serious, but if possible almost more annoying, was the result of unscrupulous Turkish and German distribution of the chairs, tables and beds of the various religious establishments. They would requisition anything and everything for a Moslem Propaganda College, giving a receipt as often as not quite undescriptive. The College, wanting money, would have sold to a third party, with the result that during our first weeks the original owners, imagining they could have their property back at once, would break into the houses of the actual possessors and remove or attempt to remove it by force. The difficulties of deciding between such claimants can easily be imagined. When an excited Friar appeared claiming ten bedsteads, a dozen wardrobes and scores of knives, forks and spoons, scattered all over the City and none of them marked, who could pronounce what was whose?

As if these things were not enough, there were added to our troubles thousands of refugees. Over two thousand desperate Armenians besieged the saintly but incompetent *locum tenens* of the Armenian Patriarchiate. There were the Christian refugees from Salt, a city older than Genesis. When the British troops had first crossed the Jordan they had been welcomed and assisted by the Saltis. These, when the troops withdrew, followed them to Palestine, foreseeing death from the Turks if they remained, and O.E.T.A. had to face the feeding and housing of Saltis as well as Armenians. Later I find:

> 7000 refugees—Armenian, Syrian, Latin, Orthodox, Protestant and Moslem suddenly flung on my hands this week: a good deal of typhus, but malaria not expected till autumn. No easy matter feeding and looking after them and I have had to detail three members of my Staff for the purpose.

But we did not have to face them unaided; and I should like to place on record the debt of gratitude owed by them and by us to the Syria and Palestine Relief Fund, the creation of the late Dr MacInnes, Bishop in Jerusalem. None of my officers will forget what it meant to be able to count upon Stephen Trowbridge, Secretary, Representative, and Director of the Fund in Jerusalem, for the disposal of an apparently unlimited number of tired, harassed refugees. And which of all of us but must remember with affection my Relief Officer, the late Commander Everard Fielding, R.N.V.R.? In control of an official file, the despair of the office: tried sometimes I fear by the impatience of the Military Governor at the woes, untimely presented, of some widow complete with several orphans from Kerak. But of an unfeigned kindness and charm: treating those poor people as individuals and not as cases or numbers, with the same discerning courtesy that had enabled him, as Secretary of the Psychical Research Society, to placate, exorcise or disprove the night-wandering ghost. As a devout Roman Catholic he was in a position to convince the Latin authorities that (contrary to the usual practice in Palestine) there was no thought of national or sectarian propaganda behind our Relief. Some of these local authorities were indeed suspicious. An empty Roman hospice had been commandeered for the temporary accommodation of women and children from Salt. The Rector complained to me that the Syria and Palestine Fund was abusing its position by introducing tendencious and specifically Protestant forms of worship. This sort of behaviour being the opposite to that for which we stood, I paid a surprise visit to the Hospice just before prayer time, as a result of which I was able to inform His Reverence that (without rejecting his designation) the ceremonies were limited to the recital in the refugees' own Arabic language of The Lord's Prayer. Withal I should like to pay my tribute to the helpful kindness and consideration shown to O.E.T.A. in the early days by the three outstanding representatives of the Roman Church, the saintly Cardinal Camassei, Latin Patriarch, the powerful and astute Friar Ferdinando Diotallevi, Superior of the Franciscans (an enthusiastic philatelist), and the scholarly and distinguished Father Paschal Robinson (now Archbishop of Tyana and Papal Nuncio in Ireland), of whom I knew not whether to admire more the austerity of his life—for when was he known to eat, drink or sleep?—or the wisdom of his luminous counsel.

O.E.T.A. could also turn for help to the American Zionist Organization and, in even more ample measure, to the American Red Cross, who soon established their Unit in a great house belonging to the Bute family, later the seat of the French Consulate. Its leader was Colonel John Finley (now editor of the *New York Times*); a scholar, an orator and a walker who made light of the tramp from Jaffa up to Jerusalem and down again to Jericho; and who (assuming I had been there before) blenched not when I conducted him through Hezekiah's Conduit [6]— even when I suddenly disappeared under water with the electric torch— and through whom I was honoured by being chosen a member of the great American brotherhood of the φβκ.

The Administration of Occupied Enemy Territory was of course a temporary measure, and General Allenby's first proclamation, drafted by Mark Sykes and translated into French, Italian, Arabic and Hebrew, had announced that Jerusalem was under Martial Law, and would remain so as long as military considerations made it necessary. Martial Law would be strictly in accord with the Law and Usages of War as laid down in the *Manual of Military Law*. The ultimate fate of Palestine none then knew, though the Balfour Declaration made its incorporation into a presumably French Syria less and less probable, even if Jerusalem were internationalized: Jewish policy dreading the position of a tolerated minority in a great Arab majority. The tripartite Sykes-Picot Agreement, internationalizing the whole of Palestine save a British Haifa and Acre and a French Upper Galilee was speedily nullified by the defection of

---

[6] "Did I tell you that I took Colonel Finley of the American Red Cross right through King Hezekiah's Conduit, rather a drastic experience the first time. You go down a flight of steps in the bowels of Mount Ophel under the S.E. corner of the Temple, plunge up to your waist into flowing water, and grope with an electric torch through the darkness, crouching most of the way owing to the lowness of the rock ceiling, for just over ten minutes until you emerge into the ancient Pool of Siloam. We were so pleased when we did get to the other end to have got there without the tide having risen or the roof fallen in, that we instantly turned and walked back again, and I am now prepared to take select parties up and down the chilly stream."

Russia.[7] We imagined that the new government, whatever it might be, would take over at the end of the War, then vaguely predicted for some time next summer. Nevertheless, the Military Administration—*rien qui dure comme le provisoire*—with military cars, rent-free quarters and Camp Commandants, continued beyond the Armistice in 1918, after the Peace Treaty in 1919 (under the Foreign Office) until 1 July 1920—and even then some of us had still to wear our uniforms until we could procure civilian clothes.

"Furthermore", the proclamation ran, "since your City is regarded with affection by the adherents of three of the great religions of mankind, and its soil has been consecrated by the prayers and pilgrimages of devout people of those three religions for many centuries, therefore do I make known to you that every sacred building, monument, holy spot, shrine, traditional site, endowment, pious bequest or customary place of prayer, of whatsoever form of the three religions, will be maintained and protected according to the existing customs and beliefs of those to whose faiths they are sacred." The now famous doctrine of the *Status Quo* was the bedrock of the General's policy (as it must be of any honest military occupation) in secular as well as in religious matters and, though frequently difficult to interpret and bitterly assailed (as well as invoked) by one or both parties in every subsequent controversy, this same *Status Quo* proved a strong tower of defence against the encroachments from all quarters to which O.E.T.A. was continually subjected.

The Church of the Holy Sepulchre was for some time guarded by British, French and Italian sentries, and was Out of Bounds to the soldiers who had fought to free it from Ottoman rule. This rule, here at least not oppressive, had been represented within by an hereditary Moslem guardian, a dignified figure in turban and *quftan,* whose ancestor had been appointed to the place by Omar, the conqueror of Palestine in the seventh century. Strong suggestions were made to me by undenominational Christians that this Moslem ward over the holiest place in Christendom was an outrage, which no Christian Governor should tolerate. Few of these critics had ever entered the Holy Sepulchre (or indeed any other church): none had paused to consider what manner of Christian would have proved an acceptable candidate for the post. The Orthodox Community would never have tolerated a Roman Catholic; nor a Roman an Orthodox or an Anglican—even if the Anglican Church had possessed, or aspired to "rights" in the Sepulchre. Neither could have endured a Protestant—assuming that any Protestant would have consented to act.

[7] Our ally immediately published all papers relating to these Agreements, with the express intention of embarrassing their late supporters.

The Shaikh did his work well, maintaining the *Status Quo* and public order as long as he could, and on occasion calling in the police. I will go so far as to say that he was the one functionary, military, civil or religious, from High Commissioner to municipal scavenger, against whom throughout my nine years in Jerusalem I never heard a complaint. But neither these considerations nor his merits might have availed against this specious agitation had I not been enabled to reinforce them with the unanswerable order of the *Status Quo*.

France had been recognized ever since the reign of Francis I (some centuries before Monsieur Combes had inaugurated the policy of expelling the Congregations from home, to exploit them politically abroad), as the Protector of Latin Christianity throughout the Ottoman Empire.[8] This Protectorate, interwoven in sentiment with traditions extending from Godefroi de Bouillon to *Partons pour la Syrie,* still meant a great deal to the French; and though its continuance under a Christian allied Government would have constituted an almost insulting anomaly (which every Palestinian assumed we would liquidate forthwith); though the "allied" arms which had liberated Jerusalem were exclusively British (the martial but grizzled French and Italian contingents being avowedly of ceremonial and representative intention), the ritual pre-eminence of Monsieur Georges Picot and his staff was, as I indicated in my journal,[9] loyally and punctiliously observed.

These were not the only arguments urged against our generally strict application of the *Status Quo*. The largest, most powerful and oldest established Roman Order in the Holy Land was the Franciscan. Their *Custodia,* dating back seven hundred years, wielded an influence far beyond that of their hierarchical superior the Latin Patriarchate, a revival (some said a creation) of the nineteenth century. The Custos had in the past the right to fly from the peak of his vessel the flag of the Cross Potent, the Latin or Crusaders' Cross of Godefroi de Bouillon, with the five crosses in one typifying the Five Wounds of Christ. "Their Beatitudes", the Patriarchs were three, Orthodox, Armenian and Latin; only one ecclesiastic, the Custos, was addressed as *"la Vostra Paternità"*. Though Patriarchate and the *Custodia* differed on almost every conceivable question, they had this in common that while international in spiritual dominion they were in sentiment and in policy predominantly Italian. An Austrian Monsignore may be granted the Rectorship of a Hospice erected by Austrian subscriptions; a French Dominican may

---

[8] A French consul said to me once: "It is as much as my post is worth to be seen in a church in France and as much as it is worth not to be seen in a church in Palestine."
[9] P. 297.

preside over the French *École biblique de Saint Étienne;* as an extreme deference to the British Mandatory, an Irishman might (seven years after the Occupation) be created Patriarchal Bishop; but the appointment of a French or a British Patriarch or Custos would offend tradition only less than the transfer to that great dignity of the Grand Rabbi. Now the Italian *Custodia* had long chafed at the French Protectorate, and I was confronted only the day after my appointment by a telegram from Rome which I remember began: "Cessando la dominazione turca cessa ... il protettorato francese"; [10] and could only reply under the *Status Quo* we were in Jerusalem not to abolish, but to maintain. Secular, even military pressure was then applied. I was waited on by Colonel d'Agostino, Commandant of the Italian *Distaccamento* (of the same "representative" character as the French *Détachement*) a *simpatico* but elusive officer occupied mainly in holding Indabas of Italian local subjects, and making a corner in the few carpets left by the retreating Turks and Germans. He repeated (what he appeared to consider) his threat issued to Borton that neither he nor his men would attend any service at which "honours" were offered to France; and seemed surprised at my *désintéressement,* though not indignant, for he invited me on the spot to an admirable dinner at the Casanova.

It was reassuring after these preliminary skirmishes, that the Foreign Office should "convey to the Military Governor an expression of Mr Balfour's high appreciation ..." and gave me confidence for those to follow.

The French Protectorate lasted until the San Remo Conference in April 1920, when it was declared to have lapsed on the allocation of the Mandate. Even then the Latin Patriarch continued to address the Palestine Government through the French Consul-General; to whom Liturgical Honours, the outward symbol of the Protectorate, were (with an un-Latin absence of logic) rendered until formally disallowed by the Vatican in 1921. Both Governments fought a protracted rearguard action for the maintenance of their Holy Sepulchre guards, which were actually not withdrawn before 1922.

There were numerous other attempts by most of the "have-not" communities to profit by the War and alter the *Status Quo* in their favour. In the matter of the Liturgical Honours, and in some others, satisfaction was peaceably obtained by explanation, reason and patience.

The military nature of O.E.T.A. assisted us also in the postponement until after the War of the wearisome, irritating and potentially dangerous

---

[10] "With the cessation of Turkish domination ... there ceases also the French Protectorate."

problem (so enthralling for unborn, new-born or re-born nationalities) of national flags and national anthems. General Allenby saved an infinity of bickering, perhaps some bloodshed, by deciding that no national flag whatever should be flown in Occupied Enemy Territory, save one Union Jack over the residence of the Commander-in-Chief. Orders thus imposed from the beginning soon become usage and tradition; and fifty years' discomfort might have been avoided if this course had been taken on General Wolseley's arrival in 1878 as first British High Commissioner and Commander-in-Chief of Cyprus.

I twice infringed the *Status Quo;* once against my will and to my regret, and again deliberately and to my lasting satisfaction. O.E.T.A. infringed it, in one respect, consistently, seriously, and in the circumstances justifiably.

Of all the places hallowed by the Passion of Christ none is more beautiful, few so authentic, as the Garden of Gethsemane. Times unnumbered have I wandered there, and I can imagine no service more moving than that held on Maundy Thursday (at which I had nine times the privilege of reading the Lesson), in the ancient olive grove under the moon and stars. The upper part of that Garden belongs to the Russian Orthodox Church, who erected there many years ago an all too solid chapel in the approved Muscovite architecture. The lower half is the property of the Franciscans. They discovered in an evil hour traces of the foundations of a basilica, said to date from Justinian. The Custos, while disposed to agree in private conversation (who ever disagreed privately in Palestine?) that Terra Santa was over-doctored, over priested (especially by other denominations) and over-policed, somehow could not perceive that it was also somewhat heavily over-churched. His ambition and his application was to complete (in other words to build anew) the basilica of Justinian, to say nothing of another church upon the summit of Mount Tabor. Over this last, still far the wrong side of the Turkish lines, I felt but a limited competence. The thrice holy site of Gethsemane I longed to save, so temporized and discouraged. Soon, however, questions began to be asked and pressure exerted upon me by higher military coreligionaries of the Custos. They reminded me that the Garden was the absolute property of the applicants, and suggested that not being of their persuasion, it was doubtless difficult for me to appreciate the conception of turning the Garden once more to what it had been in the reign of Justinian. My prayer that it should be allowed to remain as it was in the time of Christ was a final proof of the narrowness of my outlook. Military Commands are not resigned in war-time, and even if they were, I had no particular reason to suppose that my successor would prove more zealous for

Jerusalem or less amenable than myself. It was anyhow improbable that a town-planning ordinance could have resisted the demand. Nevertheless, learning on good authority that there was in Rome itself a strong feeling against the expenditure on bricks and mortar of money so urgently and universally needed by the faithful—going so far as a decree prepared for the Papal signature forbidding any further building in Latin Gethsemane —I limited my approval to the completion of the foundations. But the Custos knew well when to bide his time and when to act. The Papal decree was never signed. The application was duly renewed and the Civil Government were most reluctantly obliged to cede permission for the *Ingeniere Architetto* Signor Barluzzi to hide by masonry from the kneeling pilgrim yet one more of

> those holy fields
> Over whose blessed acres walked those feet
> Which fourteen hundred years ago were nailed
> For our advantage to the bitter cross.

I turn with relief to another basilica, built by Constantine, restored by Justinian, abolishing no garden, and enshrining the Grotto of the Nativity in Bethlehem. Early in the nineteenth century the Orthodox Patriarch had built between the extreme eastern pillars of the nave a hideous rubble wall some fifteen feet high, stuccoed battleship-grey and entirely blocking from view the gleam of the gilded ikonostasis and the dimmer distances of the apse. His object was to prevent desecration by Moslems, though I never heard, nor do I think it likely, that any such had occurred for decades. This ignoble severance of the very life-cord of Constantine's great temple I could not bear. I determined to remove it, and became convinced as I advanced into the complications of its ownership and consequential rights that, if it fell not under the edict of a military despot, it would stand for ever. Both Greek-Orthodox and Gregorian-Armenian authorities were finally prepared to agree to its demolition—though the Greeks hesitated when they learnt that the Latins approved—each on the condition, at first to my surprise, that themselves, and not the others, should be allowed to pay for the work. I found that the reason for this startling offer was that payment for any modification of a site was held to establish ownership thereto. Being admitted by both parties as outside any such claims, I was allowed the honour of effecting the payment myself. Once down, I knew the wall would never be replaced, and truly, as the picture shows and the pilgrim may still see from the white stripes down the two tawny-dark columns, there has been here an unscreening of great beauty.

The Military Administration notably contravened the *Status Quo*, in the matter of Zionism. Palestine had been (and in 1918 half Palestine still

XIXTH CENTURY WALL, BLOCKING BASILICA OF NATIVITY
TILL 1918

EAST END AND IKONOSTASIS REVEALED, 1918

was) a province of the Moslem Ottoman Empire, and the vast majority of its inhabitants were Arabs. Under the *Status Quo* we were entitled (and instructed) to impress upon those desiring immediate reforms that we were here merely as a Military Government and not as Civil Reorganizers. Our logical procedure would therefore have been to administer the territory as if it had been Egypt or any other country with important minorities; making English the official language, and providing Arabic translations and interpreters, and treating the resident Jews, Europeans, Armenians and others as they would have been treated in Egypt.

Far different from this conception was the attitude of O.E.T.A. General Allenby's very first proclamation and all that issued from me were in Hebrew, as well as in English and Arabic.[11] Departmental and public notices were in Hebrew and, as soon as possible, official and Municipal receipts also. We had Jewish officers on our staffs, Jewish clerks and interpreters in our offices. For these deliberate and vital infractions of military practice O.E.T.A. was criticized both within and without Palestine. They were surely justified by the announcement by Great Britain and the almost universal endorsement of the Balfour Declaration on 2 November 1917, which gave any occupying Power the right to assume, though the League of Nations was then unborn and Mandates hardly conceived, that the ultimate Government would have to reckon with Zion.

Pleasant as was the unchartered freedom of a Military Governor, and reluctant as any Governor would be to circumscribe it, I soon began to feel that, unless I speedily obtained good legal advice, no subsequent Act of Indemnity could cover my irregularities. I therefore procured the services of Major Orme Clark, the consequent founder of modern justice in Palestine. He was assisted and shortly succeeded by Norman Bentwich, my old friendship with whom (I am proud to hope) Arab, and sometimes Jewish, criticisms of him, and frequent Jewish criticisms of myself, served only to draw closer. About then Colonel Rees Mogg was replaced by Major Lord William Percy, an organizer to whom the Governorate owed and probably still owes some of its best features.

The first, and for many weeks the only, financial intimation I received relative to my appointment was a Minute to the effect that I had ceased to draw pay from the Foreign Office.

March 10. Am still without any emolument, and often sigh with the Psalmist: "Wherewithal shall a young man pay his way?"

---

[11] Adding yet another to the countries governed in three official languages; the French, German and Italian of Switzerland; the English, Turkish and modern Greek of Cyprus; the Latin, Norman and English in late twelfth-century England. In Palestine, once before, a certain inscription "in Greek, and Latin, and Hebrew."

A month later:

"Now about £400 overdrawn at my bank": "Now been in this place five months without receiving a single penny." "Thank you very much for your *démarche* through Prince Arthur to the War Office. I received my first trickle of pay just six days too soon to allow me to give a dinner to my staff to celebrate half a year's office without emolument of any kind."

This perhaps avoidable delay did not make it any easier for me to welcome to my house all who passed through Jerusalem; for military privileges, even including free postage (all over the world for two months and for some time after to all places in Palestine and Egypt) were more than set off by coal at £14 a ton—when procurable at all—and olive wood, almost the only alternative fuel, proportionately dear—partly because of the British attempt to repair the Turkish ravages of whole groves by forbidding all felling save of dead or dying trees. Prices for everything imported continued for months and years proportionately high. Profits were enormous; yet British Trade showed no more enterprise than it had exhibited in Cairo at the beginning of the War. Even with the thousands of troops passing through Jerusalem and hungry for newspapers and novels, it was impossible to "interest" London or Cairo booksellers. I tried Cook's Representative, but his Principals forbade this departure from tradition.

With a staff now reinforced, I felt justified in going down to Cairo to supplement my Constantinople-Baghdad khaki by a recognizable uniform. Egypt after a 1918-Jerusalem presented its traditional contrast of abounding fleshpots: more acutely to my servant Said than to myself. In vain I would remind him of the sanctity of Jerusalem: *"Al-Quds bálad sharíf"*—"Jerusalem is an honourable City". *"Naam"*, "Yes", *"Sharíf"*, he would admit, but nevertheless the holy place was lacking in *tamaddun,* civilization—by which he meant the tramways, cinemas, and huge cheap emporia of Cairo. Nor was it until we had crossed the Canal, passed Zagazig and reached Benha, fifty minutes from Cairo, that he would detect the *"zau"* and *insāniya,* the politeness and humanity, of the capital of Egypt; and certainly the sun and ease, the great shops, the street lighting, the h. and c. laid on, did transport one in a trice to a peach-fed atmosphere remote indeed from the austerities of Zion.

These occasional renewals of fourteen years' Egyptian contacts were to prove invaluable to me. To pass for a few days from cold to warmth, from grey to blue; an officer without official duties, a tourist with the knowledge of a resident—always to a complete change of surroundings—was a never-failing stimulus. I savoured the strong Arabic of Egypt after the singsong intoned Syrian. Above all, I was happy to have no part, save of sympathetic anxiety, in the estranging bitterness of the early 'twenties. Even the station-masters on the journey, chiefly Copts, were most of them old friends. Once, later on, I had to wait for a couple of late hours at Benha. The first class waiting-room was crowded, and Morcos Effendi led me towards the Ladies' Waiting-room. I protested that all I wanted was a deck-chair on the platform, and he was explaining that the room was seldom used and empty now, when a tall veiled Moslem lady behind us asked in Arabic whether it was the custom here to bring men into the women's quarters. I apologized profusely and withdrew, vexed with my host. On the Lloyd Triestino boat next day I found myself sitting next to a stranger. "You were very courteous to me last night..." began Rosita Forbes....

On my return from Egypt I moved from Fast's Hotel to the old vaulted German Consulate, and remained there with Percy until the autumn, observing with pleasure much of Harry Hotspur in his swift, combative intelligence. When later in the year, we were joined by Ernest Richmond, our table became a miniature law-Court. Richmond could bear no Kipling, whom Percy held infinitely superior to Scott, Richmond's favourite author: both turned to rend my preference for Wells, Richmond more violently, but Percy with a legal method which somehow conveyed a moral censure and under which the cross-examinee found himself insensibly propelled from the witness box into the dock. These "all-in" combats proved a valuable training for subsequent bouts with Muftis, Patriarchs and Zionist Leaders. I was relieved to find that it was not only with me, or on literary topics, that Percy knew no compromise. He was an ornithologist of wide reputation and I therefore asked him to show the Commander-in-Chief, on his first visit to my new Governorate, the Natural History Museum which the Germans had formed in the basement. On the way down I heard the Field-Marshal describe in detail a bird he had seen on the way up to Jerusalem, and ask its name. "There *is* no such bird", said Percy. At the first case they reached I heard again: "Why, here's the very bird", but "No one could have guessed that from *your* description", said Percy.

The Duke of Connaught visited Jerusalem in March 1918, braving the persistent cold of the Judaean hills. When after lunching in the Governorate H.R.H. presented to Count Ballabar his well merited C.M.G., I was able to admire the perfection of his French accent and, when I escorted him round the City, the exactness of his visual memory. The interior of the Dome of the Rock struck him as looking brighter than on his first entry, thirty-three years before. It had in fact been re-gilded by the Sultan Abd al-Hamīd in 1890. He drew my attention to an Austrian Artillery sword, carried by an Arab Police officer, some thirty yards distant. Accustomed though he was to all permutations and combinations of military medals he did nevertheless indicate surprise when confronted with a Jewish policeman of his Guard of Honour who was wearing together (and had honourably won) the French *Croix de Guerre* and the German Iron Cross.

Eastertide, the culmination of the Christian year, is almost throughout the world the season when, if only for three days, the death of strife becomes the victory of peace. Easter in the Holy Land, and most of all in the Holy City, had meant for generations the sharpening of daggers and the trebling of garrisons. Centuries before the first Easter, the Passover—a ritual of romantic beauty second only to our celebration of the Last Supper—had been reverently observed by every Hebrew householder. The conjunction of the two great festivals and the fame they brought aroused the apprehensions of Saladin, who instituted about the year 1200 the Moslem Feast of *Nabi Musa,* the "Prophet" Moses in the same month; building for him a cenotaph on the Palestine side of the Jordan not far from Jericho.. These three preponderating events of the three Religions summon into Jerusalem, together with the genuinely pious, hordes of the politically and the criminally turbulent, in the very crisis of the riotous Eastern Spring.

But the local and indigenous Christian communities needed alas! for their fratricidal tumults no outside provocation. Already during my first fortnight:

The Greeks and Armenians, whose respective Epiphany and Christmas fall on the same day, came to blows in the Grotto of the Nativity at Bethlehem, and had to be parted by the special guard (chosen from experts at these disgraceful brawls) that I had posted there.

The height of exaltation and of possible disaster was the Orthodox ceremony known as the Holy Fire; a brilliant mystery, half political, half pagan; marred sometimes by drunkenness, savagery and murder; whose climax of horrible slaughter is recounted in Curzon's *Monasteries of the Levant.* Neither Orthodox Greeks nor Armenians, the chief (but far from the only) danger points, could in 1918 be controlled by their deported Patriarchs, and those left in charge—as so often—durst not appear conciliatory. Easter was now upon us. The matter could not be left to take its course and I submitted to G.H.Q.:

The Greek Orthodox Easter falls this year on 5 May. During the two preceding weeks there are a number of solemn festivals, culminating in the ceremony of the Holy Fire which takes place on Easter Eve, 4 May.

Throughout Holy Week the religious fervour of the Greek Community in general is at white heat, and the situation has always required firm handling. In this connection I enclose, for your information, a statement showing the number of soldiers found necessary by the Turks to keep order in the Holy Sepulchre. It will be seen that the minimum requirements during Lent have always been 50 men, whilst for the actual celebration of the Holy Fire at 7 a.m. on Easter Eve, no fewer than 600 troops have been employed.

An additional complication exists this year in the absence of the Greek Patriarch or indeed of any high Orthodox prelate to take charge of these services. The Greeks have for the moment no Priest higher than an Archimandrite, whose status is not considered sufficient for the task. If, therefore, the matter is left to take its own course, the ceremonies will either not take place at all, or, if they do, will infallibly be marred by serious and discreditable disturbances.

I presume that it is no part of the Military Administration to decide upon the intrinsic merits of miraculous manifestations, and that, in accordance with the Commander-in-Chief's general instructions re non-interference and the maintenance of the *Status Quo* in such matters, it is not desirable that we should explicitly or implicitly prevent the services being held. The effect, indeed, upon the Christian population in general would be deplorable if we did. If, therefore, they are to be celebrated at all, it should be with a maximum of decorum, and it would be a fitting proof of the spirit of the new, as well as a contrast to that of the old, administration, if they could be conducted with a minimum parade of armed force.

After careful study of this situation, I am of opinion that it will be impossible to guarantee this order without having recourse to Turkish means and methods, unless a Prelate of suitable degree is allowed to proceed to Jerusalem, and to take temporary charge both of the Orthodox Convent and of the Orthodox Ceremonies in the Church of the Holy Sepulchre. He should arrive not later than a fortnight before the Greek Easter on Sunday 22 April, and should remain until the Greek Low Sunday, 29 April. If a suitable choice is made I hope to be in a position to propound a scheme whereby the celebrations may be performed with decency, reverence, and an absolute minimum of armed display.

I have received this week petitions from the Executive Committee of the Greek Orthodox Patriarchate and from the Lay Community, referring me to these considerations and begging that an Archbishop or Bishop be delegated for this purpose. The Patriarchate desire me to convey a request to the Patriarch of Alexandria to send one of his Metropolitans, while the Lay Community mention the Archbishop Porphyrios II of Mount Sinai.

There can be little doubt that, were there no superior objection, His Beatitude Monseigneur Photios, Patriarch of Alexandria, would himself be the most suitable person to undertake the mission, but I am given to understand that his avowed dislike of Damianos, the exiled Patriarch of Jerusalem, would probably cause him to omit his name from the prayers, a slight which could not fail to produce bad feeling here. An alternative would be that Monseigneur Photios should be invited to send a specifically Venizelist Metropolitan, but I understand that a permit of entry thus extended to a high ecclesiastical dignitary of one denomination might involve similar concessions to other churches, which it is for the present undesirable to grant.

The third solution is the despatch of the Archbishop of Mount Sinai. Porphyrios II was consecrated by the Jerusalem Patriarchate and may therefore be said to fall within its jurisdiction. He is expressly named by the Lay Community, and is also acceptable to the Patriarchate. The only query that might be raised to his candidature would be based upon the differences subsisting between him and the Patriarch of Alexandria, but as these are not of a nature to reflect discredit upon the Archbishop, I do not see that they need concern Jerusalem. I have had official and social relations with Porphyrios II for the last ten years; he is equally well known to General Clayton, and has, I believe, had more than one conversation with the Commander-in-Chief. He is a sensible and tactful man of the world, and would be the first to see the advantage to his own prestige if these difficult weeks could pass off under his presidency without disturbances, so that I am convinced that with him a satisfactory arrangement could be concluded.

I would therefore request that Porphyrios II, Archbishop of Mount Sinai, should be permitted to proceed to Jerusalem not later than Sunday 15 April, remaining there until Sunday 29 April, both inclusive; that transport should be found for him both ways, and that I should be advised as soon as possible if and when this is approved in order that I may take the necessary steps to have him invited to Jerusalem in the regular and traditional manner.

R. S.

Military Governor,

March 17, 1918.   Jerusalem.

My proposal was accepted and His Beatitude Porphyrios II, Archbishop of the Autocephalous Orthodox Church of Mount Sinai, was formally invited and installed as τοποτηρητής or *locum tenens* of the Patriarch. He was nervous before the ordeal, and so, in varying degrees, were all concerned. Each Acting Patriarch threatened that unless he were allowed to obtain in the ceremony some advantage intolerable to the other he could not be held responsible for rioting among his congregation on this, the first celebration for many centuries under Christian authority, of the Holy Fire. I had to answer each (as had others after me, two or three times a year to the various communities), that no one had asked either to be responsible, which was the duty of the Government. And now it was Easter Eve. Haddād Bey disposed the Arab police; and I stood with a half-dozen officers in front of the Sepulchre to keep the passage safe for the Archbishop. I was to preside seven times more at the Holy Fire, and would have been glad to continue that part of my duties indefinitely; for there is in it a Dionysiac mysticism, heightened by the memory of

what has happened there in that past, which seems in Jerusalem but a
backward continuum of the throbbing present. On this first occasion our
experiment was entirely justified. The few (but fairly hard) blows aimed
by the Armenians at the Archbishop, as he passed in glittering tiara from
the Tomb to the "Golgotha Chamber", were intercepted by my outstretched arm, and the mediaeval tumult dwindled to boulevard prose
as he gasped into my ear: *"Mon cher, vous m'avez sauvé la vie."*

The ceremony of the Holy Fire has for so long been a standard and
orderly festival with every contingency anticipated, that few even in
Jerusalem will realize the anxious importance we attached to the success
of its first celebration. It brought me "congratulations and thanks" from
my Commander-in-Chief, with kindling references to "tact and skilful
handling of a difficult and delicate situation"; together with a second
message from Lord Balfour, this time a telegram: "It is my wish to
express my satisfaction at successful management of this ceremony."

Water, even in the rainy season, was already an urgent problem, the
troops alone accounting for incredible quantities, and the sudden demand
for bath water contravening all tradition. The nearest rivers or lakes being
two thousand feet below the level of Jerusalem, and many miles distant,
the City had ever since its foundation depended largely upon rain
collected in cisterns constructed as a rule in each cavity formed by the
quarrying of the stone which had built the house. The great cisterns constructed by Solomon under the Temple area and containing some eleven
million gallons, were fed partly by rain and partly by three rock-hewn
open tanks, known as Solomon's Pools, perhaps because of their proximity to Urtas—*Hortus Conclusus*—the Closed Garden, the traditional
setting of his Song of Songs, near Bethlehem. Pending the restoration of
these, I obtained authority for the Royal Engineers to clear and rebuild
the spring reservoirs of Birket Arrūb, said to have been established by
Pontius Pilate, some 22 miles along the road to Hebron. They piped the
entire distance with remarkable dispatch, and the relief was immediate
but alas short-lived. The project was unfortunately based upon the only
statistics and calculations then available, compiled by a French engineer
under the Ottoman Government. The flow from Arrūb proved far less
than we hoped, and even with the assistance of Solomon's Pools the first
rainless year involved Jerusalem in a disastrous drought. Desperately the
Administration turned to Ain Fárah, the "waters of comfort" of the
twenty-third Psalm. Until and sometimes even after this system had been
installed, the Municipality was reduced to the ruinous expedient of water
trains, three, four and five a day, dragging the heavy tanks up the steep

Judaean gradients from Lydda. Stand-pipes were erected at the street corners, and there was seen the pitiful spectacle of long queues, chiefly of little children, waiting in the sun with one, sometimes two, four-gallon petrol tins, each costing a whole piastre, or twopence halfpenny, to fill. As I write, the comprehensive and I trust final project for the Jerusalem Water Supply, its great expense now justified by the accumulated wealth of Palestine, is announced as completed.

During my first few weeks in Palestine nothing impressed me more than the variety of other people's impressions. Apart from intellectuals, who considered that Jerusalem had delivered its message to humanity (and so more or less shot its bolt) and travellers who had actually been there before, I discovered many grades of religious and geographical ignorance. Some of my correspondents "had not heard there was such a place". Others "had always thought it was a place in the Bible". I was occasionally asked whether the Church of the Holy Sepulchre was A.D. or B.C. A baronet begged me to show him the way to the Villa Rose, which he had been told he really ought to see before leaving. It proved to be his "approach" to the *Via Dolorosa*. Most visitors fell into one of two categories, the ecstatic who prostrated themselves at every site, even when two or more were credited with the same event, and the sceptical who explained away evidence and tradition which they would have accepted implicitly for Tiberius or Shakespeare, and who seemed to expect a macadamized Gethsemane and a Temple of Solomon rendered in corrugated iron. Many were "disappointed with Jerusalem" because "it was so different to what they had expected". The roads were even worse than the hotels and in place of the Holy City they found—a smell.

I soon noted a sharp rise in my social and general stock, receiving from England and Egypt congratulations and laudatory forecasts from personages who had but a few weeks before regarded me with entire detachment. Acquaintance was claimed and old friendship recalled. There was even suggested the honour of consanguinity with a Miss Beulah Storrs, of Salt Lake City, Utah. Autographs, "captured" Turkish standards, especially the original flag of truce on the surrender of Jerusalem, were in lively request. So, particularly, were postage stamps, and many were the unused sets demanded of me by "a father" or "a mother" of "a wee tot with all heaven in her blue eyes" from way out in Wisconsin or Oklahoma.

Local petitions were no less ingenuous. I had not been appointed three days before I received from an Orthodox Arab an appeal clearly intended to combine a recognition of British conventions with a delicate personal flattery. It concluded: "I do beseech Your Excellency to grant my bequest, for the sake of J. Christ, Esq.; a gentleman whom Your Honour so closely resembles."

MY HEBREW AND ARABIC SEALS AS MILITARY GOVERNOR

CHAPTER FOURTEEN

The Pro-Jerusalem Society

Urbs beata Jerusalem dicta pacis visio,
Quae construitir in coelis vivis ex lapidibus.

(7th century, A.D.)

I

IN Jerusalem of all places on earth man must not live by bread alone. I had been there but a few weeks when I was aware of a tendency to demolish the interesting and the beautiful and to substitute for them the cheapest and most immediate commonness in design or material that could be procured. The fifty previous years of unchecked religious exploitation had already hidden or thrown out of scale most of the ancient northern and western walls, by the building hard against them of colossal and hideous convents and monasteries. O.E.T.A. could at least protect Jerusalem by an aesthetic, as well as a liturgical and political *Status Quo,* and I found a positive pleasure in replying to a request for a concession to run trams to Bethlehem and the Mount of Olives, that the first rail section would be laid over the dead body of the Military Governor. (This attitude was for years attacked as unprogressive by immigrants unaware that the motor-bus had long superseded trams in most places not committed to their retention by heavy capital outlay.)

The basis of building and town-planning control dates from a Public Notice No. 34 of April 8th, 1918, in which it was forbidden to demolish, erect, alter or repair the structure of any building in or near Jerusalem without my permission in writing, under a maximum penalty of £E. 200. This was shortly followed by another forbidding the use of stucco and corrugated iron within the ancient city. Both these materials were and are inexcusable. Jerusalem is literally a City built upon a rock. From that rock, cutting soft but drying hard, has for three thousand years been quarried the clear white stone, weathering blue-grey or amber-yellow with time, whose solid walls, barrel vaultings and pointed arches have preserved through the centuries a hallowed and immemorial tradition. A third Notice absolutely prohibited advertisements, save on one or two

PUBLIC NOTICE

No person shall demolish, erect, alter, or repair the structure of any building in the City of Jerusalem or its environs within a radius of 2500 metres from the Damascus Gate (Bab-el-Amud) until he has obtained a written permit from the Military Governor.

Any person contravening the orders contained in this proclamation, or any term or terms contained in a license issued to him under this proclamation will be liable upon conviction to a fine not exceeding L. Eg. 200.

R. STORRS
Colonel
Military Governor.

Jerusalem, 8th April 1918.

AVIS

Personne n'est autorisé à démolir, construire, changer ou modifier n'importe quel bâtiment dans sa structure à Jérusalem ou dans ses environs sur un rayon de 2500 mètres partant de la porte de Damas, (Bab-el-Amud) sans avoir obtenu un permis écrit du Gouverneur Militaire.

Toute personne contrevenant, soit aux ordres contenus dans cette proclamation, soit à la teneur du permis octroyé, s'exposera après condamnation, à une amende ne dépassant pas L. Eg. 200.

Le Gouverneur Militaire
R. STORRS
Colonel

Jérusalem, le 8 Avril 1918

اعلان

لا يجوز لاي شخص ان يهدم او يبنا او كان في منطقة القدس او حولها ضمن دائرة نصف قطرها
۲۵۰۰ متر ابتداءً من باب العمود فان يبين انه حصل او غير ذلك البناء قبل ان يحصل
على رخصة خطية من محافظة الحاكم العسكري .

كل شخص يخالف هذه الاوامر واي شرط من الشروط المعطاة في رخصة التي سمح له
اعطائها لها للاعلان يعرض نفسه بعد حكمه والحكم المغرم عليه الى حزة لا يتجاوز المئتين جنيه .

الحاكم العسكري
الكولونل
. . . ا ستورس

القدس الشريف في ۸ نيسان سنة ۱۹۱۸

מודעה רשמית.

אין אדם רשאי להרוס, להקים, לשנות או לתקן מבנה כל בנין בירושלם או בסביבותיה בתוך קצר
של מאנ מאתים מטר אלפים מתוך (באב אל עמוד) עד שיקבל רשיון בכתב מהשר הצבאי
כל אדם אשר יעבר על הפקודה אשר במודעה הזאת, או על איזו תנאים מהתנאים אשר נתן לו
לפי המבאר במודעה ז. אחרי נקום שא יהיה עליו על מכס עד 200 ליט.

ירושלם, 8 אפריל 1918.

השר
ר. שטורס.
(הקולונל)

small authorized hoardings in commercial quarters, and out of sight of the walls of Jerusalem.

Although these three orders were not universally popular and may have occasioned a few temporary hardships, they did at least insure the provisional Military Administration against the charge of encouraging or permitting vandalism. But the inhabitants of a place are not exhibits to be held back in picturesque discomfort in order that the sentimental tourist may enjoy her anticipated thrill. Mere prohibition was of course never intended. It is not enough to stop men doing ill: you must help them to do well. To make these measures constructive two adjuncts seemed essential: that the Heads and representatives of the Communities concerned should be interested and consulted, and that money should be available in order to transmute our deliberations into action. I therefore founded the Pro-Jerusalem Society, which became in effect the Military Governor civically and aesthetically in Council, and so was able to assemble together round one table the Mayor of Jerusalem, the British Director of Antiquities, the Mufti, the Chief Rabbis, the Presidents of the Italian Franciscans and the French Dominicans, the Orthodox, the Armenian and the Latin Patriarchs, the Presidents of the Jewish Community, the Anglican Bishop, the Chairman of the Zionist Commission, the Dominican Fathers Abel and Vincent, *Capitano Paribene* (with the *Distaccamento* and afterwards Italian Minister of Fine Arts), with other leading members of the British, Arab, Jewish and American communities. The official language found to be most convenient was French, in which also the Minutes were kept; but animated asides—sometimes almost broadsides—were discharged in Arabic, Turkish, Hebrew, and even Armenian. These differing and elsewhere discordant elements, bound together by their common love for the Holy City, supported the Society most loyally, and whatever might be the stress of politics without, they consistently refrained from introducing controversial matter within the Council walls. I am truly grateful for all they did for Jerusalem, as well as proud to have been their President for our eight years' existence.

Many of the leading merchants, realizing how greatly the future prosperity of Jerusalem depended upon its preservation as Jerusalem (and not an inferior Kieff, Manchester or Baltimore), subscribed liberally to our funds; and in Egypt, England and America, Moslems, Christians and Jews, suspicious of any creed, culture or policy other than their own, gave gladly to a Jerusalem which represented all three. I realized then the power of the name of Jerusalem; I realized it even more afterwards when appealing for other countries or causes. I became, I am happy to believe, a convincing and successful *Schnorrer*.[1] My subscription list, of cheques ranging from £3 to £600, included from Cairo the names of Smouha and Btesh, the Syrian Community, and the editor of the *Mokattam;* in Jerusalem the Anglo-Egyptian Bank, Sir Abbas Effendi Abd al-Bahá,[2] the Mufti, several Jewish firms, the Imperial Ottoman Bank, the Crédit Lyonnais, the Anglo-Palestine Bank, the Banco di Roma, the 51st Sikh Regiment, the Zionist Commission, the Municipality, and the Administration; in Europe and America, Lord Milner, Sir Basil Zaharoff, Lord Northcliffe, Sir Alfred Mond, Mrs Holman Hunt, Mrs Carnegie, Messrs Pierpont Morgan, and Messrs Kuhn, Loeb. I found institutions more generous than individuals, and (especially in America) men than women.

As the Society was financially, so it remained administratively independent. Early in March I had borrowed the services of W. H. MacLean, the Town Planner of Alexandria and of Khartum, "not to plan so much as to bring out regulations which will at any rate preserve the unique character and tradition of Jerusalem". This plan was further developed by Professor Patrick Geddes, who concentrated upon the attempt, unhappily not successful, to isolate the Holy City in the centre of a park. A final Town Plan was to be adopted and developed with the assistance of a Government Town Planning Ordinance, some years later.

In my search for a Technical Assistant something more than Architect and Town Planner, I remembered that almost the only good "Entertainment" lecture I had heard at Charterhouse had been delivered by one C. R. Ashbee, a disciple of William Morris. Ashbee was now in Egypt. He visited Palestine, prepared me an interesting report upon the civic possibilities of Jerusalem and was appointed Civic Adviser and Secretary of the Pro-Jerusalem Society. Our object was defined as "the preservation and advancement of the interests of Jerusalem, its district and inhabitants"; more especially: "The protection of and the addition to the amenities of Jerusalem, the provision and maintenance of parks, gardens and open spaces, the protection and preservation with the consent of the Government, of the Antiquities, the encouragement of arts, handicrafts, and industries in consonance with the general objects of the Society", and certain other cultural activities. Careful steering was sometimes needed to avoid impinging on the interests of the Municipality, and the Departments of Antiquities and of Public Works. I think all three (and perhaps we also) bore and forebore, and I at least look back upon our mutual relations with gratitude and pleasure.

[1] Yiddish for a professional beggar.
[2] See p. 337.

The Psalms of David and a cloud of unseen witnesses seemed to inspire our work. "Build ye the walls of Jerusalem." We put back the fallen stones, the finials, the pinnacles and the battlements, and we restored and freed from numberless encroachments the mediaeval Ramparts, so that it was possible to "Walk about Zion and go round about the towers thereof: mark well her bulwarks, set up her houses." Of the interest and variety of these three sacred miles I never grew weary. We repaired, cleaned, and cleared of many hundred tons of modern Turkish barrack rubble, the Citadel, generally known as the Tower of David, which crowns the lower courses of Hippicus and Phazael recorded by Josephus. Much desecration we averted, but sometimes we were too late, and could only prosecute. The Roman staircase at Siloam was saved, but already a building contractor had stolen some twenty tons of Roman stonework which he carried off by night on the backs of donkeys. He was fined £50 and had to return the stones, but they could never be put back in the exact positions from which they had been taken.

The severe winter of 1917-18 had a deplorable effect upon the wind-racked north-west façade of that utmost fulfilment of colour, rhythm and geometry, the Dome of the Rock. The brilliant tiles were constantly falling from the walls, and frequently to be found for sale in the City. I was fortunate enough to enlist for a technical Report on the interior as well as the exterior of the Mosque, Ernest Richmond, once architect to the Egyptian Waqfs, then eating out his heart in the Imperial War Graves Commission; and for the carrying out of his recommendations the Mufti launched an appeal for Islam, which may be thus translated:—

Peace be upon you, and the grace of God and His blessings. This sacred Mosque, to which God translated His Prophet one night from the Mosque in Mecca, and in which one prostration before God is counted by Him as five hundred—is it not the Aqsa Mosque which God has blessed? Yet it is neglected, and for several decades was overlooked, until decay has set in in its frame, and its ornamentation has faded, and the whole edifice stands in peril of disruption, which may God avert. Who desires the loss of this precious gem, unique in its grandeur, its form, its architecture, the soundness of its foundation, and the perfection of its structure—this wonderful building, the like of which may not be seen on the face of the earth, which causes the greatest architects to shake their heads in wonder and to confess their incapacity to produce its like even if they were all to put their heads together?

Now, when the men of the Occupying Power, and, in particular, H. E. Colonel Storrs, Governor of the Holy City, saw the ruined state in which stood the Mosque, and learnt that the revenues derived from its private waqfs (without taking into account the difficulty of obtaining rents at all in those days) do not exceed what is required by way of expenditure for the mainte-

nance of religious rites—when Colonel Storrs saw that, it was an eyesore to
him, and he expressed his deep regret, and set about at once—may God
watch over him—and applied for an able engineer of those who have exercised themselves in the repair of ancient places of worship.

His appeal met with prompt answer, for very soon the British Government
sent out from its capital the most celebrated engineer and competent for this
great work. This is Major Richmond, known to the greater part of our
Egyptian brethren for the good work done by him in their own places of
worship. No sooner arrived than he set to work at once, tucking up his shirt-
sleeves of activity, and displaying the utmost interest in minutely examining
and investigating, and then reporting on what ought to be done. Having
examined everything bit by bit, and with the utmost care, he drew up a
report fully explaining what was required for the restoration and preservation
of this noble edifice, and dwelt specially on the necessity of speedily setting
to work. He also showed an estimate for materials, apparatus, and the skilled
labour which is required for such delicate work, which would necessitate
about £80,000, which is not much if the object be to preserve such sacred
precincts to which humanity flocks from all parts of the world; not much—
God willing—for those charitable, good people who wish to lend God a pious
loan which He will repay to them times over, to extend their generous hands
towards Him from all parts of the globe, East and West, and answer His
call, which is His, by saying: "Lo! Our riches we entail unto Thee." For
verily, he erects the Mosques of God who believes in God. Verily, also, God
will not suffer good works to go unrewarded.

In the course of his investigations Richmond had rediscovered over
"King Solomon's Stables" in the Temple area the original furnaces and
kilns in which the Mosque tiles had been fired. I remembered the name
of Mark Sykes' Armenian, David Ohanessian, who had created the
Persian bathroom at Sledmere, and summoned him from Damascus with
another expert from Kutáhia to report upon the possibilities of designing,
painting, glazing and firing the new tiles in the ancient furnaces, instead
of in the European factories from which the Dome had been repaired
for the last fifty years.

How near we were to disaster you will realize when I tell you that the
German architect supplied by the Kaiser four years ago for the same purpose
proposed that the N.W. side of the Octagon, where winter's rains and ruins
have most disordered the porcelain shell, should be re-covered with cast-iron
tiles from the Fatherland.

The Administration found means of sending Ohanessian to Constantinople, whence he returned with his workpeople from Kutáhia and, helped
by a contract for the Mosque tiles with the Waqf authorities and a grant
from Pro-Jerusalem, was established in the "Dome of the Rock Potteries".
Their productions (apart from the Mosque tiles) in the form of tiles,

"DOME OF THE ROCK" TILES

The letters from right to left are: Yod, shīn, vaw and the unpronounceable 'ain—Yashwa' or Yeshu'a. ("Yod", the smallest letter in the Aramaic and Hebrew alphabets, reappears in English as a "jot")

JERUSALEM STREET-NAMING

vases, bowls, ewers, goblets, beakers, and plates [3] have now for years been on sale in Cairo, London (and some other cities of England), Edinburgh, Cape Town, and New York. One of them (of which I think there must be examples in every continent) shows an exact copy of the name of "Jesus" found on a Jerusalem potsherd in the Aramaic writing and of the time of Christ. The Potteries also carried out the tiling with which I was permitted in memory of certain members of my family to cover the interior of the Chapel of St John in St George's Cathedral; in deepest blue relieved in white by the eight-pointed cross of the Order of St John of Jerusalem.

Sympathizing with the Mufti's desire that there should be no commercial enterprise even on the outskirts of the Háram (though it is allowed to be the favourite playground of the little Moslems of Jerusalem), I transferred the Potteries to some old rooms close by under the shadow of the *Turris Antonia,* on the site of the "castle" into which the Roman soldiers carried St Paul.

A discerning conquerer in 1850 could have established the shops, convents and hotels well away from the old City and have left the grey ramparts in a setting of grass, olives and cypresses. By 1918 the time was past for seeing Jerusalem adorned as a bride, but it was not too late to determine that for the dumb soul of the City the names at least of her streets in English, Arabic, and Hebrew, preserved by tradition or reverently bestowed, should be proclaimed in blue or green tiles glittering against the sober texture of her walls like chrysoprase and lapis lazuli.

For the naming of new or unnamed streets, as well as for the renderings from one language into another, a committee with representatives of the three communities was afterwards constituted. In the old walled City such titles as the Spice Market were preserved; *Haret al-Sháraf*—"the Lane of Honour", became Honour Lane, and *Tariq Bab al-Sitti Mariam,* Our Lady's Street: *al-Wad*—the Valley—reverted (in its European version) to the classical Tyropaeum. There was Water Melon Alley, Dancing Dervish Street and Stork Lane, all literal translations. *Bab al-Magharbah* (the Gate of the Moroccans) was linked with London as Moorgate. On the seventh centenary of St. Francis I named and formally unveiled the inscription-tile [4] of St Francis Street, immediately outside the Franciscan Monastery—perhaps a worthier commemoration than the posters' *"Evviva il Serafino d'Assisi"* with which the City walls were being liberally be-plastered. For the new City without the walls we adopted St

---

[3] A faience model of the Dome was the Palestine Moslems' wedding present to our Princess Royal.
[4] See list of illustrations.

Paul's Road, Godfrey de Bouillon Street, Nehemiah Road, Tancred Lane, Allenby Square, Sulaimān Road, Cœur de Lion Street, Saladin's Road, Street of the Maccabees, Queen Melisande's Way, and the Street of the Prophets.

I had met in the Cairo bazaars with occasional specimens of glasswork, coloured red, blue or green from Hebron, and having inspected the Hebron furnaces felt we could not let die the blowing of these vessels in the same shapes, by the same process, in the same place and by men of the same race, as in the days of Abraham. We were able to find the glass-blowers an immediate market and later advised them on questions such as fuel and transport.

Ashbee's energies were also directed to weaving. We subsequently bought the looms which the American Red Cross had set up for the relief of Armenian and Syrian weavers, and installed them in the ancient Cotton Market, the *Sūq al-Qattanīn*. This fine mediaeval bazaar had degenerated through neglect into a public latrine. The shops were filled with ordure, the debris was sometimes lying five feet high and the picturesque doors had been broken up for firewood by the Turks. We restored the vaults, roofing, and walls of the *Sūq,* put in looms, and by the close of the first year were employing, on a self-supporting basis, some seventy people. The apprentices worked on the guild system, and the first task of each was to weave the material for his own dress. Although the Jerusalem looms were killed by foreign competition, they served nevertheless to provide constructive and useful work during a difficult period; besides renovating a beautiful and historic quarter of the City.

Pro-Jerusalem also launched forth upon an annual Salon or Academy of the visual arts; and exhibitions of Town Planning, ancient Moslem Art and modern Palestinian Crafts, were held in the great halls of the Tower of David. Thus then for Pro-Jerusalem.

In times of stress and forced inactivity, interest and information are more than ever necessary for thinking men. Early in 1918 we therefore organized at the little house in the Municipal Gardens a public Reading Room well provided with the latest newspapers and periodicals in English, French, Italian, Arabic, Greek and Armenian, adding a frequent bulletin of war and general news. I founded a Chess Club "with a Christian (myself) President, Jewish Treasurer, Latin Catholic Secretary, and Moslem Members of Committee", and in due course held a tournament, at which the first four prizes were won by Jews, and the fifth by the Military Governor. As a preparation for a School of Music, my first mixed musical parties gave but dubious results.

On Thursday I gave an evening musical party to 30 of the *élite* civil and military, male and female. Two pianists, expressly brought up by car from Jaffa, played classical duets, and the evening between the items was clearly a success, the buffet being applauded and even encored.

Yet there was always hope for music in Jerusalem.

For the Jerusalem School of Music I had to collect the Committee, explain the object, discover the talent, negotiate for a house, bargain for instruments (as you know there's a piano famine both in Egypt and Palestine), borrow the celebrated violinist Tchaikov from the Front (*a*) as inaugurating Professor and (*b*) as fund earner by going to Egypt to give concerts (also to be arranged and advertised) in Cairo and Alexandria.

From the beginning three-quarters at least of the professors and 90 per cent. of the pupils were Jews. I therefore sent for the Christian and Moslem members of the Council and warned them that anxious as I was to keep the management and ownership of the School, as of my other enterprises, international and non-political—nevertheless if their proportion of both were not materially increased in six months' time, I should present the institution to the Jewish Community. After waiting six months without result, I duly handed it over.[5] Some time also in that first year I founded the Jerusalem Chamber of Commerce (still in vigour, and long with the same Hon. Secretary); I prohibited all Bars (though by no means the consumption of liquor at tables) in Judaea; and I had printed in San Salvatore by the kindly Franciscans the *Occasional Poems* of Henry Cust.

The reign of Bertie Clayton was too good to last. Administration was beginning to interfere with his duties as Chief Political Officer, and he was replaced by a Chief Administrator, Major-General Sir Arthur Money, the first (in every respect) of the three Chief Administrators of Occupied Enemy Territory. General Money remained awhile with his Staff at Bir Sālěm. Against their transfer to Jerusalem the argument of "two kings in Brentford" was applied, and the possibility of finding elsewhere a purely administrative and non-political capital for O.E.T.A. The undoubted advantages of this idea—a Delhi versus a Calcutta—particularly for the Governor in Calcutta, are outweighed by the consideration that any other capital of the Holy Land but Jerusalem is inconceivable. O.E.T.A. duly advanced upon Jerusalem and occupied (at great expense of restoring and installing) the Hospital of the London Mission to the

---

[5] " . . . my only conditions for the bequest are:
1. That the School shall continue to be called the Jerusalem School of Music.
2. That it shall be open to all seeking instruction without distinction of race or creed; and
3. That the existing staff . . . shall be treated with all possible consideration." 28. iv. 1920.

Jews, for the three or four months before the departure to the North of the 20th Corps made available the *Stiftung* on the Mount of Olives.

I have nothing but pleasant memories of my relations, personal as well as official, with General Money. He treated me throughout the year in which I served him with the utmost consideration. But although he and, of his successors, Sir Herbert Samuel, spared no pains to preserve the position and authority of the Governor, I shall always look back to the first months in Jerusalem with peculiar affection: and I maintain that, given sympathy with the place and the people, enthusiasm for the work and average strength and resourcefulness, there is no position in the world more satisfying than that of a Military Governor. So long as I enjoyed the friendly understanding of Clayton and the confidence of the Commander-in-Chief, my word was law. As there were no lawyers, judges or courts, it was the only law. Better still for Palestine then, there were no newspapers. Legally and journalistically we lived in a State of Innocence. To be able, by a word written, or even spoken, to relieve distress, to right wrong, to forbid desecration, to promote ability and goodwill is to wield the power of Aristotle's Beneficent Despot. When for instance the Jews wished to rename Fast's Hotel *"King Solomon"* and the Arabs *"Sultan Sulaimān"*, either of which would have excluded half Jerusalem, one could order it, without appeal, to be called the *"Allenby"*. Technical illegalities may have been committed, but the advantage of being able to execute by a stroke of the pen obviously needed reforms which can later be amended or abolished, is very great. The experience has made me wonder whether legislation elsewhere might not be expedited by giving some new laws a temporary or trial run. I may have failed—worse than a thousand irregularities—in making the utmost use of the power I was given: I know I never abused it. Work went on all day and much of the night; physical conditions were grotesque, but that brief period before the arrival of O.E.T.A. in Jerusalem stands out, blockily and stereoscopically detached from the rest of my career, as an image of intense and radiant delight.

"Such", administratively,

> "was that happy Garden State
> When man first walked without a mate.
> But 'twas beyond a mortal's share
> To wander solitary there.
> Two paradises 'twere in one
> To dwell in Paradise alone."

II

I do not propose to treat in detail the development of the Palestine Administration by General Money, its continuation under his successors Generals Watson and Bols, or its final establishment as a Civil Government by Sir Herbert Samuel; assuming, as in the previous chapter, the routine administrative processes save when their difficulty or unusualness seems to justify separate mention. Good accounts dealing with the first seven and a half years of modern Palestine history may be found; unofficial in *Palestine, The Land of Three Faiths,* by P. P. Graves, and in Norman Bentwich's *Palestine;* semi-official in the *Encyclopaedia Britannica* (14th edition) and in the *Handbook of Palestine;* and official in the Reports, annual and quinquennial, of Sir Herbert Samuel. Let it suffice to remind the public that it was Sir Arthur Money who laid the first foundations of the future Palestine Government.

Whilst O.E.T.A. was absorbed in the peaceful problems of administration, there was being elaborated a few miles below us the most brilliant, dramatic and decisive victory gained by either side on any front of the War. No resource of strategy, from ostentatious movements and secret replacements of troops to misinforming Orders allowed to fall into enemy hands, was neglected which might create the impression that the main attack would be made on the Eastern flank and not by the way of the sea. In May I received confidential instructions to inform the Manager of the Allenby Hotel under seal of secrecy that all his accommodation would be urgently required in a few weeks' time. It was enough. The news, as anticipated, leaked through the lines to Turco-German Intelligence, that G.H.Q. was about to go East; and all their defence plans were altered accordingly. In a flash Allenby broke through on the West, captured Damascus, drove what was left of the Turks out of Syria, and but for their immediate capitulation would have been well on his way to Constantinople. Sir Philip Chetwode wrote from Nablus:

22. ix. 18. ... This has been the *most* wonderful show. The Turkish Army West of Jordan destroyed in 36 hours. In one donga leading from Nablus we found 87 guns, 56 motor lorries, 4 motor-cars and 400 transport wagons. The whole country is littered with war material. Prisoners won't be far off 30,000 when all are in.... Our casualties three to four thousand in all.

One of my Staff wrote to me later from Jerusalem (I being then in Haifa):

Prisoners, war material, etc. keep pouring through the City all day long and only yesterday I saw about twenty German lorries coming in driven by their own German drivers with an escort of about six Britishers all told.

It was my first proximity to a great triumph and I celebrated it on return from work that night by playing upon my Steinway a medley of "Vittoria" from *La Tosca,* Handel's Marches from *Jephthah* and *Scipio,* Parry's "Wedding March" from the *Birds* of Aristophanes, the Pilgrims' Chorus and the Entry of the Gods into Valhalla.

Military Governorates and Governors for a suddenly doubled O.E.T.A. had long been arranged, and General Money was eager to give them a swift preliminary inspection.

Haifa. My latest is that I came up from Jerusalem last Friday with General Money, leaving at 7.40, reaching Nablus at 11, Jenin at 2, and Haifa at 6.30. His car was, as generally, out of repair, and we used my humbler but very serviceble Sunbeam. The drive after Jenin is of peculiar interest and beauty; across the Plain of Armageddon, past Megiddo with the Carmel Range gradually asserting itself on the left, until one turns the corner and finds oneself almost in Haifa. We stayed the night at the Carmel Hotel, from which I ran down for a sea bathe before leaving at 8 next morning. On the way back we met the C.-in-C. in his Rolls Royce, which we learnt later he smashed about 10 miles farther on against a great boulder in the road. The coast scenery and the Plain of Sharon are very beautiful, and will one day be immensely rich. Tul Keram about 12.30, Lydda at 4, where we learnt from G.H.Q. that the C.-in-C. had decided that I should be detailed from Jerusalem for three or four weeks to establish the administration in the Northern District. I was in the middle of rather urgent affairs in Jerusalem, and begged for an extra day or two to put them straight, but he frogmarched me out almost at once. The only item in which I may be said to have got back on him was a car, my own having a broken spring. I said I could not go unless one was sent for me, and so had a comfortable journey of six hours in a Vauxhall.

The pressure is naturally high, and hardly any of my Staff have as yet appeared. Those that are here are mostly ill in bed. Am staying for the moment with General Bulfin, Commanding 21st Corps, at the top of Mt. Carmel. He was obliging enough to have the private chapel of the Monastery he occupies converted into my bedroom, a goodish concession for a fervent R. C. The view from the Mount over the Bay of Acre and inland is as good as you could desire, but I have little enough time to enjoy it, for flattering though it is to be chosen for such duties, they are far from being the sinecure we have always dreamt of for each other, and at present my office hours are 8-1 and 2-8.

General Money returned to Jerusalem, and O.E.T.A. abandoned the London Jewish Mission Hospital for the *Stiftung* now vacated by the 20th Corps. Percy was my deputy at the Governorate.

... have now set the H.Q. and Administration of this district upon a fair footing, and impatiently await the arrival of a successor. I took for Residence the Austrian Consulate, a good little house right under Mount Carmel, looking across the Bay of Acre, over the Lebanon to the Great Blue Hermon.

Living there with Ernest Richmond and James de Rothschild, son of Baron Edmond who founded many of the Palestine Colonies. A red-hot chess player, carrying throughout the Flanders campaigns a small steel cylinder containing the men and fold-up board. (His own invention: now patented by Vickery.) E. and I rise at 6: take the car at 6.45 down to the beach: swim for a half-hour and spend the remainder of the day in work.

Of their unsparing help (by handling odd problems on the spot without bothering me for instructions) and comradeship after work I have grateful memories. The difficulties of establishing a government in the Haifa District, though numerous, were in the absence of religious enthusiasm simple and straightforward compared with Jerusalem and, unlike those of Jerusalem, they seemed to decrease as the days passed. Among unexpected incidents one of my Staff found in the drawer of his desk several sheets of unused Turkish stamps, removed from the local Post Office by a Dominion trooper, and forgotten. Next day he brought me rather wistfully a letter from the trooper asking for the parcel to be forwarded: and was greatly relieved when I thought it would be more dignified (as well as kinder) to overlook the irregularity and not even to acknowledge such a communication. Towards the end of my second day an Arab was ushered into the office and handed me, half puzzled and half apprehensive, the following note:

Military Governor,
  Haifa.

I found this man cutting fuel on Mount Carmel without a permit. As a lifelong Friend of the Trees, and realizing the irreparable damage he was doing, I administered to him on the spot a sound thrashing and have sent him to you for necessary action, please.

H. Smith,
Lieut.

There were as yet no regulations promulgated against the cutting of timber other than olive trees; and even if there had been, liberal interpretations such as this of the Laws and Usages of War for the ultimate advantage of the conquered, by youths of the loftiest ideals, did not make the country any easier to govern.

I renewed in Haifa my friendship with Abbas Effendi Abd al-Baha' and his Bahai followers, whom I had last seen imprisoned in Acre on my visit in 1909. I found him sitting in spotless white, noble as a prophet of Michael Angelo. He placed at my disposal the training and talents of his community, one or two of whom I appointed to positions of confidence which they still continue to deserve.

Just before leaving Haifa I had an unforgettable experience.

The C.-in-C. passed through yesterday on his way to Beirut and Damascus. I went for a ride with him along the beach of the Bay of Acre, and a wonderful thing it was to see the E. Anglian regiments tearing out of their camps to see him pass. No cheering, but rigidity and a tense constrained smile of pride. (So, in the same country, might the veterans of Macedon have gazed upon Alexander.) He said: "I suppose it's because they're E. Anglians: no one pays much attention to me as a rule."

I grew more and more homesick for Jerusalem and returned there as always with delight.

To-morrow I go round with General Money about Nazareth and Tiberias and on Friday return to Jerusalem to supervise the concert I have arranged with Tchaikov for my School of Music. Later I propose arranging others at Cairo, Alexandria, Kantara and Ismailia. Enclosed from Mayor of Jerusalem may amuse you.

The Mayor's letter, in Arabic, intimated (with pleasant Oriental exaggeration) that my "absence had proved a source of loneliness"; conveyed "congratulations to the General—that Roaring Lion"; and concluded after a closely written folio sheet with a proverb that the best of speech is that which is brief and to the point—*Khairu 'lkalāmi ma qálla wa dall*—and a prayer that I might "remain protected".

I left the German Consulate in Jerusalem for the quarters vacated by General Money in the house of the German Protestant Pastor (which was to be my home for seven years) having with me Ernest Richmond and Father Waggett of Cowley, then a Political (or perhaps a Politico-Religious) Officer and invaluable in his maintenance of close and sympathetic relationship with the three Patriarchates.

On 11 November the weather broke, and the "former" rains came down in torrents. About three the telephone rang, and Dalmeny [6] announced from G.H.Q. that the Germans had signed the Armistice at six in the morning. After telephoning the event to the Military Units, I went out imparting it to any soldiers I met, to the Patriarchates, the Custodia, the "American" Colony and the Mufti. As I drove up to the Mufti's house some R.A. Unit sent up Verey Lights, which came down so slowly that I thought for an instant they must be stars. The Mufti, rising finely to the moment, dwelt on those who had given their lives to bring about all this glory. I afterwards learnt that O.E.T.A. Staff in the *Stiftung* had rushed into the Chapel, sung three verses of God Save the King, consumed a fair amount of champagne and rung the bells of the Hospice; inaudible to the ears of the City. All civilians were enchanted with the good tidings, none doubting that they meant final peace; and so were most soldiers, though some "wondered what they would do now", and one Mess, determined not to be impressed, informed me—news for news—that "the Cheese Ration began to-day".

---

[6] General Allenby's Military Secretary; afterwards Lord Rosebery.

For most families throughout the world the Armistice meant the end of fear. In Rochester the Cathedral bells were pealing, and my mother was thanking God that all her four sons had come through the War, when the Admiral of the Nore called to tell her that her second, Francis, had died the night before. Next day I heard the perversely impossible sentence. Francis was my nearest in age, and closest in pursuits and outlook on life.

As I walked this evening from Olivet across the Kedron to the North East corner of the Temple, memories of Francis glinted from the golden pinnacles of Gethsemane: earliest in the night-nursery, when I was going to be a Life Guardsman, he a General, and B. a Volunteer; our nurse's occasional injustice to him; cricket against the tree in Grosvenor Gardens on Saturday afternoons, and in the front hall of No. 2; his early skill at swimming under water: the *Post Horn* in E flat that he learnt with Miss Clarke in Miss Grigg's lodgings at Westgate: his nervousness over Touch Last: Temple Grove where I visited him and B. my first term at Charterhouse and tipped them both 4*d.*; football with Holloway at Westgate, and his ecstasy when the Bowler was knocked off; his eagerness to squeeze out of everything he touched something more transcendental than it contained—as in the desperate cut on his tennis service and the heartrending sacrifice of a knight and pawn in his Muzio Gambit; his change from a saintly childhood to a violent youth: his precocious intimacy with Pope and Keats: his amazing appreciation of Shakespere, Thackeray, Swift and Aristophanes: his skill in English Verse and success at the Cambridge Union (B. and I never achieved); his absolute straightness, conscientiousness and unworldliness; his irritability; his round-arm bowling; his boisterous affection for elderly nurses and governesses; his astonishing knowledge of Sherlock Holmes and celebrated crimes; his proper insistence upon seeing morning and evening papers; his love of the grotesque; his reading Law at the dining-room table, rolling a guinea-pig up and down with his left hand; his true religion streaked with classical paganism, and his dread of long and frequent services; his expletive objections but ultimate compliances; his having the Psalter by heart; his ear for an air and absence of it for the harmony: his abiding and never-changing goodness of heart— my conviction that he never did or thought a wrong thing in all his life.

Next day the good Franciscans celebrated Mass for my heretic before the Holy Sepulchre.

18 Dec. General Money is going on leave, and I am appointed Acting Chief Administrator and become a Brigadier-General. Both would have been infinitely enhanced if Francis could have come out and looked at me (a joke of his and mine) as the side figures in a sacred picture look up at the central, which we used to do one to another whenever either had had a piece of more than usually outrageous luck.

I moved up to that gaunt, wind-swept, reverberating prison the *Stiftung,* and enjoyed my first (and longest) period, about a third of a year, as *de facto* Governor of Palestine.

I confess the constant and exacting work of a Tetrarch gives me the greatest pleasure. But unless for a few minutes a day I can devour something general, universal, and wholly unconnected with business, I feel as if I hadn't shaved before breakfast nor cleaned my teeth after.

There was a great deal to be done: all of it interesting, much important, some unpopular. Military Government, comprising military duties in addition to purely civil administration and postulating at first that the new and foreign ruler must in the beginning be largely in evidence, is necessarily an expensive business, which should as time goes on grow "Fine by degrees and beautifully less". After visiting every district I reduced the Military Governorates from twelve to six.[7]

Early projects were beginning to become accomplished facts. Thus in February 1919 General Allenby reopened in formal state before representatives of every language and community, the reconstructed Ophthalmic Hospital of the Order of Saint John of Jerusalem.[8]

Mark Sykes visited Palestine on his way North into Syria and Anatolia, to investigate the condition of the Armenians. ("Mark with me again, giving as always a maximum of trouble and a maximum of delight.") Both there and in Palestine he found affairs politically far more complicated than he had hoped, and I had never known him so uncertain of the practical truth of his dearest convictions.[9] We were at Haifa when he left Palestine. After a long walk, during which he favoured me with inimitable renderings of a French priest pronouncing Latin, an Orthodox bishop taking a service, the Indian Government's spelling of Moslem names, and the sort of "crusted" Service Member who might be expected to be returned at the next Khaki Election, he stepped into a boat and was rowed through the gathering dusk to a French cruiser, continuing the conversation until his voice was lost in the distant knocking of the rowlocks.

I heard once from him—a rebuke, that he had left behind the key of his dispatch-box; and then of him, a telegram that he was dead—at the very moment when his rare union of goodness with brilliance, talent with duty, true religion with wittiest analysis of its exponents, and generous sympathy with widely differing creeds and races, were

[7] On the allocation of the Mandate they were further reduced to three. In 1922 Palestine was divided into two Governorates; South, including Jerusalem with Jericho, Bethlehem and Ramallah; Jaffa, Hebron, Gaza and Beersheba: and North including Haifa, Samaria and Galilee. On my departure in 1926 the Southern District was redivided into Jerusalem and neighbourhood, and the above four divisions.

[8] See p. 305.

[9] "He wore himself to death, interpreting Arab and Zionist aspirations to each other and to the politicians of the West." Blanche Dugdale, *Arthur James Balfour*, vol. II, p. 167.

becoming an Imperial asset of increasing value throughout the Near and Middle East.[10]

Between four and six in the afternoon I used to visit villages and sometimes the Police [11] posts, with three or four footballs—as long as I could afford or the Y.M.C.A. provide them—for the young men and boys, with an Arabic rendering of the rules of Association; convinced, as I am, that even English boys would "go" political without some such outlet for their energies. Sometimes I walked along Olivet to the Russian Convent of the Ascension. I had copied out the four parts of the Meistersingers Opening Chorus and, conducting with a walking stick, did my best to impart its beauties to the elderly Russian nuns. Their voices in all four parts (bass included) were exquisite, and they seemed to enjoy Wagner, but as my knowledge of Russian was limited to the standard English *Dobra, Yudra, Karashov, Okhrana, Bolshevik, Menshevik* and *Preobrajensky,* and they knew not a word of any other language, our rendering, though full and melodious, was not always accurate.

I was granted leave in the summer of 1919 and travelled from Alexandria to Marseilles on a troopship. There had been a small-pox scare, and vaccination was ordered for all when, to our general but helpless indignation, one private soldier by refusing (on the ground of having once seen a man die from the operation) held up the whole ship's company at Malta. There were still R.T.O.'s [12] at Marseilles, and officers returning from duty were still receiving free First Class and Wagon Lit accommodation. London was in the full glare and glitter of Victory. There I had the good fortune of seeing the Peace Procession twice, first in Lower Belgrave Street, and, by cutting through the crowds, again

---

[10] Shane Leslie's *Life of Mark Sykes* quotes my letter to Lady Sykes—"What can I say? Ever since the spring of 1911 when I first met him Mark has been a centre of interest and affection in my life. His amazing range of knowledge, the extent and variety of his gifts, his chivalrous noble nature, and his sunny never-failing kindness are things that make the eyes dim, even at writing them down. Zionists, Arabs, Armenians are in mourning with us. Whatever justice they may receive will be very largely due to him; and they must all feel with me that they have lost a unique friend. How I rejoice that I rose at four and journeyed till eleven to spend a few precious hours with him in Haifa, and was the last to see him into his skiff that was to take him to the *Cosmao.* Even then I thought him thin and worn, and rejoiced at his five days' enforced rest. He was harassed too a little at the growing Arab-Jew tension, and struggled as none else on earth could struggle to allay and avert it."

[11] "I beg to thank you in the name of the District Police Force for your very much appreciated gift of a Foot ball, which you presented on Friday last, at a match which was arranged for the purpose, on the Barracks Square. The Teams were composed of Moslems, Christians and Jews, captained by (*a*) Sgt Shwili (Jew), and (*b*) P. C. Badawi (Moslem), and it is of interest to note that utmost harmony prevailed throughout 50 minutes of play. A knowledge of the rules of the game is not a strong point with the District Force at present, but the spirit of fair play and a keenness to be taught is abounding, and instruction in the art of football is being undertaken."

[12] Railway Transport Officers.

from Carlton House Terrace. Said spent most of his time ascending and descending the moving staircases of the Underground Railway, and never recovered from his surprise at their being *Balash* or gratuitous. Throughout my visits I heard that he enjoyed below stairs universal success as a master humorist.

Boats returning Eastward seemed scarce, and I was warned I might have to wait in Paris. I waited there a week, raising £1000 for Pro-Jerusalem and listening in the afternoons, to Melba rehearsing. She let me choose, and sang very beautifully Duparc's *Phidylé* and Fauré's *Clair de Lune*.

14. ix. 19. Breakfast 9.15 with Mr Lloyd George in the Rue Nitot. Present Paderewski, Bonar Law and Miss B. L., Maurice Hankey, and later Winston Churchill and Seely. Of course Paderewski knocked out any talk of Jerusalem and Palestine by the urgency of the Polish-Bolshevist situation. At first L. G., by talking round and over sooner than at a subject, seemed to me a less practical man than the Slav pianist on his right. At the same time fire, and great good humour. Paderewski's thesis was that instead of arming Letts, Finns and Boches against the Bolshevists the Allies might well help the Poles, who were quite prepared to take it on. All then started against him, but when he had talked for two hours most seemed to think his proposals should be examined—a great feat in my opinion. All agree that Bolshevists, especially Lenin, will remain in power but are modifying their tactics. He considers Lenin an honest idealist, Trotsky a scoundrel, but the more powerful of the two. Agreed that England, France and Italy will not spend another bob in fighting Bolshevism. . . . The party broke up about 11.30, they in Rolls Royces to visit devastations and Chemin des Dames. Then the Paderewskis gave me a lift to where a car had been sent for me, and I was bumped to Balincourt near Pontoise through the Forest of St Germain in 85 minutes. Party *en famille chez* Zaharoff, with Séligmann the *antiquaire* to luncheon. Z. the millionaire of my dreams, lying out with one foot swathed for classic gout, and an electric bell-push in the cedar tree communicating with the secretary. He pushed it when I had shown him my Jerusalem plans and at once wrote me off a cheque for £500.

Unable to find any sailings from Marseilles, I was sent on to Rome, there to hope for something from Taranto.

Embassy, Rome, 20. ix. 19. I left Paris by the *Rapide* on the Tuesday, having to take a Wagon-lit berth for Said to get him on to the train (Ow! Ow!) [13] and reached Rome very tired well after midnight on Wednesday. In the train Mrs Berenson; accompanied by an American Presbyterian chocolate King, from whom I duly lifted, or ever he got away at Pisa, a cheque of £200 for Pro-Jerusalem. I have seen Sforza, the Under-Secretary for Foreign Affairs and a gentleman. And twice Monsignor Ceretti, Under-Secretary at the Vatican, who Gaisford (John de Salis's understudy) thinks will one day be Pope.

[13] Travelling no longer free.

Yesterday nearly an hour with Cardinal Gasparri, Cardinal Secretary of State. I find the Vatican State apartments agreeable. There is, to begin with, a little lift, I suppose the most dangerous in the world, used rather than managed by a holy but absent minded machinist. As the spaces between the walls are neither walled nor wired in, and as the lift door won't or doesn't shut there is nothing whatever to prevent one falling or stepping out into infinite space. So much so, that in conveying a visitor to the fourth floor, the liftman prefers not to stop the machine for, say, the inferior clergy, who have to nip briskly out to their intermediate destinations, judging the exact moment for themselves as best they can. The corridor distances are illimitable and the pomp of the *Stanze* never failing. Silver sand-castors pleasantly supplied in place of new-fangled blotting paper.

Audience with the Pope. I was 5 minutes early: (15 seems cringing, and exact punctuality risky.) I was introduced by the clerical *cameriere*, in purple silk, to the magnificoes, who were pleased to congratulate me upon my Italian (then they must congratulate all foreigners). Exactly at 11.30 a bell rang and I was ushered through five exquisite rooms in marble and damask into a very large and lofty chamber. The Pope met me almost at the door, and conducted me between two rows of gold damask chairs facing each other to a throne, on which he sat, motioning me to a chair quite close on his right. He is small, dark, young in appearance: wears spectacles and seems slightly deaf. Very animated expression and exceedingly quick in seizing the point. He was dressed in a *soutane* and short cape of the richest and heaviest white silk, *moiré,* with a broad waistband of the same, and a little round cap. His shoes were of crimson velvet richly embroidered in gold, and he wore round his neck a heavy gold chain from which hung a cross of large and very fine emeralds. Emerald also, cut oblong and mounted in diamonds, is the ring of Peter. All Prelates and officials drop on their knees as they enter the Presence. Passed to the burning subject of the day. I begged him to believe that the Military Administration had in no instance used its position for Anglican propaganda. He agreed, but said he had good reason for believing that others had done so for theirs. Throughout the audience I was impressed by the frankness and friendliness, no less than by the acute simplicity of His Holiness' manner. And I consider that the state of confidence clearly subsisting between the Vatican and our Mission reflects the greatest credit upon John de Salis and Hugh Gaisford.

The Pope kept me until 12, ten minutes over the regulation full audience, and gave me my sign by saying that the Cardinal Secretary of State would like to see me before I left Rome. I bowed over his hand, and again from the door (seeing out of the tail of my eye that he expected this) and left him. Then half an hour with Gasparri who pumped me about my audience. He read me aloud his reply to the *Custode:* then put it into the envelope, licked it up and gave it to me bidding me to remember that I knew nothing whatever of its contents.

Dined with the Marconis. He told me that all through the War he received hostile, neutral and friendly wireless, through an iron box inside his house. (So we in Egypt, searching for enemy appliances on the roofs of houses, may be said to have wasted our time.) They introduced me to the Neapolitan writer, Mathilde de Serao, whose books I knew—old and immensely fat and voluble. I am told anti-British; but very good company. Had always desired a *marito serio Inglese* for her pretty little daughter (on the right) but had put up in the end with an Italian (left).

I was honoured by an audience with the King of Italy. It was in Bethlehem that he had heard of his father's assassination and so of his own succession to the throne; and his general knowledge of Palestine was very accurate.

I felt before and knew after my return to Jerusalem that the Governor's chair, though not comfortable, was not uncoveted; and that I should be well advised not to leave it empty for long.

That autumn there arrived in Jerusalem a small American group known to us as the "Cementers" for the purpose of encouraging good fellowship and, generally, of bringing people together. Mrs Ulysses Grant McQueen and Mr William McCracken together with their *Jerusalem News* (its motto "Jerusalem news is good news") entertained us charmingly for several months; but the Cementers, like Mr Ford's Peace Mission—and the League of Nations—were appraised with less mercy than humour, presumably for not achieving 100 per cent. success.

III

THE PASSING OF O.E.T.A.

Cedant arma togae

The spring of 1920 opened for me with great happiness, turned in the twinkling of an eye to sorrow and anxiety and ended before the summer in vindication and confidence. In February I enjoyed with my sister Monica and a friend my first holiday within Palestine, contemplating as an appreciative tourist in the North people and problems for which I had been but a year since personally responsible. The Governor of Haifa taught us poker, to which my deanery-bred sister took with surprising interest and success, though as a true Storrs and Cust so lacking in the card instinct as to need (no less than her brother) nightly reminding of the rules of the game.

We stayed in Tiberias and, returning by boat from the synagogue at Capernaum, were reminded of the Gospel story by the startling fierceness of a sudden tempest. Travelling South by Samaria, I found installed as Governor of Nablus Jack Hubbard, whom I remembered as an enthusiastic cockfighter at Westgate-on-Sea, searching continually for promising material in the pages of a weekly called, I think, *The Feathered World*. As we entered Nablus, Palestine was invested by the densest snowstorm

DOME OF THE ROCK UNDER SNOW

(*From a photograph by Professor A. Cresswell*)

known for many years. Telephones broke down and there was no wireless. I was anxious to be in Jerusalem as soon as possible but had no hope of getting the car through the snow. Hubbard therefore contracted with a *Nabulsi* Moslem to drive us to Jerusalem in a wagon and pair. We had not gone more than two or three miles when the horses, slow from the first, refused to move further and we learnt with less surprise than disgust that the owner had omitted to feed them. We were forced to return and Hubbard immediately clapped him into prison, whence he was enlarged (for the afternoon only) as being the only man handy to guide us to the house of the Samaritan High Priest. Glancing round during my first interview with this unique survival of antique and unblended Israel, I noticed the manacled prisoner accommodated, as official guide, beside the rest of the party with a chair and coffee—the best, perhaps the last he was likely to taste for several days. Next day we set forth again, abandoning the car at Sinjil [14] for police horses, on which we rode—one of the most dramatically beautiful journeys imaginable—into Jerusalem. The countryside, solemn and deserted, gleamed under the darkness with its own hidden light, like a Transfiguration of El Greco. Much of the road, especially the last few miles, was so hard to distinguish that leading the way my horse stepped over the edge into a drift which closed well over the top of my head, to the startled gaze of my companions, as though I had suddenly and in silence been swallowed into the earth.

In Jerusalem I found that the Municipal Council and staff had dealt with the situation by taking to their beds, and that the military detachments had come to the assistance of the Governorate by clearing paths for traffic and generally heartening the population. The unfortunate Indian soldiers, almost dying in their tents with cold undreamed of, had taken refuge, finding none other, in the unoccupied wing of an almost empty convent. Complaints exaggerated the admitted mistake into a scandal, and the men had been at once turned out into the snow, without even the few hours' grace necessary to prepare them alternative quarters.[15]

About this time Sir Herbert Samuel [16] paid a visit to Jerusalem; my chief recollection of which is that he was kind enough to attend a full meeting of the Pro-Jerusalem Society and that he was said to have

---

[14] Called after a Crusader Raymond de Saint Gilles, Count of Toulouse. Twenty-four miles from Jerusalem.

[15] By a curious paradox the only occupants of a district that a Military Governor does not govern are the military. He is the Commander-in-Chief's Civil Administrator.

[16] "Herbert Samuel has just arrived, and is about to establish a new constitution. Reasonable, I hear; though that epithet in Judaea has but a relative significance."

dictated a Currency Memorandum, extending to three score pages, of which not one comma had to be corrected.

In March I had the happiness of welcoming to my house my father and mother, and the pride of observing how immediately they gained the affection of the Communities; his interest and willingness to learn from Moslems and Jews as well as from Christians, her resolute sympathy when, for instance, she prescribed and presented a packet of Mothersill to Cardinal Camassei on the eve of a dreaded voyage to Rome. I had need of their loving presence, for in politics Jerusalem was growing more difficult and less agreeable. Arab resentment against the Balfour Declaration was now louder as well as deeper. The growing success of violence in Egypt was an open encouragement to extremists, and plaintive grievances were now becoming truculent demands. Both Arabs and Jews were confronted with an Administration that was less of a happy family than the original O.E.T.A.; the difference perhaps between the beginning of a picnic, and the end. After eighteen months of peace, and still under purely negative instructions from home, the military and civilian elements began to react differently and not always consistently to the exactions and protests with which they were assailed. On the one side were the Jewish and Arab politicians supported respectively in England and in Egypt and expecting immediate yet detailed examination of complaints; on the other side a school of thought condemning as unsoldierly all "politika", which, so far as some of us could gather, seemed to mean dealing with people as reasonable beings. And so the time drew near to the Feast of the Passover and to Easter Day, 1920.

"Moslems are far more orthodox here than in Egypt," I had written after my first few weeks in Jerusalem, "so is everybody, worse luck." Nabi Mūsa, the apex of the Moslem year, was the single occasion on which the Mufti, who rode in the procession, and the Mayor who with the notables received and entertained it in a tent on the crest of the last hill before the Jericho road, were the chief figures in an official ceremony. Both for them and for us the transition between the Ottoman and the British control of this festival was a delicate matter, for it marked too sharply, unless the Administration was prepared for a little give and take, the passing of thirteen hundred years' Islamic theocracy. The Turkish Mutasárref had always received the sacred banners in his Governorate and attended the "Call" in the Háram precincts, where an Imām formally proclaimed the Festival; the Turkish Government had provided for Nabi Mūsa as well as for Ramadan cannons, ammunition and gunners announcing sunset and dawn; and the band of the Turkish garrison had led the pilgrims from the Mosque to the Marquee.

The Mutasárref's duties I fulfilled myself; and the Army, entering into the spirit of the thing, not only produced the gun salutes (some at very trying hours) but paraded a regimental band for the hot, exhausting, and sometimes disorderly ceremony of the march. There are doubtless serious objections to this employment of a British Military Band, but on these early occasions it was more than justified by the intense satisfaction it gave to the population, Christian as well as Moslem; both of whom felt that the British were taking an interest in their traditions and were, generally, trying to do the right thing. Indeed, I am convinced that without this support from the original military authorities the Arab discontent, already beginning to smoulder, would have broken out even earlier than it did. Later local Command was less appreciative of our difficulties. In 1920, when anti-Zionist feeling was already tense, the band, long-promised, was suddenly refused a few days before Nabi Mūsa (though there was none other in Palestine); but finally, on my urgent application, allowed to perform. I had attended the "Call". The procession of the pilgrims was to be shepherded as before by our Police. Blood runs hot in the Palestine spring but apart from occasional scrapping between the Nablus and Hebron pilgrims, Nabi Mūsa was normally a blameless (if rather pointless) event, consisting of a week's hot sticky holiday by the Dead Sea, with mild feasting, booths of fruit and sweets, and shows ranging from an indelicate variant of Punch and Judy to the circumcision of anxious little boys before a gaping assembly of proud relations. No untoward incident had hitherto occurred, but in 1920 the air was full of rumours and of that nervous quality to which the altitude of Jerusalem undoubtedly contributes. We had made what were then considered adequate dispositions, though I had more than once represented that the placing of the Jerusalem police force in charge of a young Lieutenant was hardly fair to the City, to me, or to himself. The pilgrims not being expected to arrive at the Jaffa Gate until after midday, I went with my father and mother to Easter Matins at St George's Cathedral, ordering a member of the staff to warn me there as previously, so soon as the procession was within half an hour of Jerusalem. He forgot. As after the Service I was walking with my parents the three hundred yards to the Governorate, my orderly Khalīl murmured softly behind me in Arabic: "There has been an outbreak at the Jaffa Gate, and a man has been wounded to death." It was as though he had thrust a sword into my heart. Even now the mere memory of those dread words brings back the horror of the shock. The days that followed have been described by most of those concerned with a bitterness which it is no purpose of mine to increase, nor would I renew grief unspeakable.

Enough that for the time all the carefully built relations of mutual understanding between British, Arabs and Jews seemed to flare away in an agony of fear and hatred. Our dispositions might perhaps have been better (though they had been approved by higher authority), but I have often wondered whether those who criticized us in Europe and America could have had the faintest conception of the steep, narrow and winding alleys within the Old City of Jerusalem, the series of steps up or down which no horse or car can ever pass, the deadly dark corners beyond which a whole family can be murdered out of sight or sound of a police post not a hundred yards away. What did they know of the nerves of Jerusalem, where in times of anxiety the sudden clatter on the stones of an empty petrol tin will produce a panic? The Police were but partially trained and wholly without tradition. There was no British Gendarmerie: we had not one single British Constable. A year later, after troubles no nearer than Jaffa, I wrote:

Things are still very anxious down there, and by repercussion here. Last Friday a horse bolted outside the Walls and in five minutes every shop was shut and armoured cars patrolling the streets again.

It is no exoneration of Governorate or Police to remember that O.E.T.A.'s subsequent handling of the situation was not appreciably happier. General Bols [17] called for an enquiry, and a Commission composed of a General, a Colonel and a lawyer from the Egyptian Service was summoned to adjudicate responsibility.

The Commission has so extended its Terms of Reference as to embrace everything bearing upon the intention of the Supreme Being towards this unhappy land: more than Moses wrote or Renan imagined. Some would like to unloose responsibility upon the Local Executive but *"Cet animal est très méchant, quand on l'attaque il se défend"*. So we remain, all of us, in unstable equilibrium until, after two years and a half, somebody can be found to take any decision.

The Commission were the guests of the Chief Administrator, until an English lady had the hardihood to point out to him the impropriety of a judicial body accepting the hospitality of an interested party; upon which they descended to the Allenby Hotel. They sat in the Law Courts and there stood before them for examination not only the heads of Communities, long anxious for such a chance for mutual recrimination before an appreciative crowd, but also Senior British Officers of the Administration, including the Governor. As no action was taken on the Report submitted by these sudden experts in the Public Security of

[17] Third, and last, Chief Administrator, following Generals Money and Watson.

Jerusalem, and as it was never published, the only result of the Investigation was to humiliate and embarrass a number of public servants then standing in peculiar need of all possible support. But there was unhappier even than this. The immediate fomenter of the Arab excesses had been one Haj Amin al-Husseini, the younger brother [18] of Kāmel Effendi, the Mufti. Like most agitators, having incited the man in the street to violence and probable punishment, he fled. The police, eager to retrieve him, visited his brother's house and searched it. Had they consulted me I should not have permitted the visit, but sent a member of my staff to ascertain by enquiry. Nevertheless the Police were strictly within their rights, which the Turks would most certainly have enforced without the slightest hesitation. The Mufti at once proceeded to O.E.T.A., complained that his honour had been insulted, and handed back (as no longer safe from depredation) the C.M.G. he had recently received. This grotesque insolence was actually tolerated and the Mufti, instead of being struck off the Roll of the Order, had his Insignia subsequently reconferred, almost with apologies, as if for a renewed obligation. "There", indeed, "Antony, we all fell down."

When things go politically wrong in Jerusalem all sorts of unconnected issues, normally dormant, are apt to rear their unauspicious heads. Regulations are tightened up by Moslem authority; difficulties increase for visiting the tombs of the Patriarchs in Hebron, and the ownership of Rachel's Tomb,[19] on the Bethlehem Road, is vigorously canvassed. After the Easter troubles the first incident over which both Arabs and Jews were at pains to ruin their respective good causes took place at the Wailing Wall. The first I heard of the matter was the following letter from the Zionist Commission:

We are informed that the Mufti, with your approval, is undertaking repairs on the Wailing Wall. I voice the protest of the Jewish people of Palestine against this action. The Wailing Wall is the western wall of our temple, and has stood since the destruction of the Temple. This Wall is regarded as their holiest possession by fifteen million Jews throughout the world. They have not forgotten it for one moment ever since the Dispersion. Before the stones of the Wailing Wall the Jewish people pour out their heart to God. After the occupation of Jerusalem by the British armies, the Commander-in-Chief promised, in the name of the British Government, to protect the Holy Places, without outside interference. And now the Wailing Wall, the Holy of Holies of the Jewish people, is being repaired without ever the opinion of the local Hebrew community having been asked. A sacrilege has been committed, both in the religious and in the historical sense. If there is any real danger of the falling of the uppermost courses of the Wall, the local

[18] And successor.
[19] An almost certain site.

Hebrew community should have been informed, when the necessary steps to repair the Wall would have been taken. We beg even to doubt the reality of any such danger. Why has this danger become so suddenly apparent—just at a moment when the minds of the inhabitants are disturbed by political events? Was there a need for these repairs to proceed on Saturday—when hundreds of Jews stand in prayer near the Wall? Are the religious feelings of the Jews entitled to no consideration whatsoever?

I most emphatically request that an order be given to stop the repairs. If an architectural survey shows that there is any immediate danger and that it is necessary to repair the upper courses of stones, let the work of reparation be entrusted to the Jewish community of Jerusalem.

The only fact which emerged from this letter (assuming, as I did, its truth) was that the Waqf authorities by their method of exercising a hitherto uncontested right had been guilty of a piece of unwarrantable and calculated bad manners. I therefore dispatched my Civic Adviser, a Fellow of the Royal Institute of British Architects, to report as to whether the repairs were in fact necessary, and if so, what could be done. He replied as follows:

I visited the "Wailing Wall" this morning at 11 a.m., and also saw there Mr Slousch, Mr Meyuhas and Mr Ben Yahuda. I went on to the roof of the Waqf Buildings over the wall that is being repaired, and I saw the architect (Mr Shiber) and the workmen.

I have to report as follows:

1. The repairs to the roof and to several metres below it are imperative for the protection of the Waqf buildings and also for the wall below them. It is, however, unnecessary and undesirable for work to be done during the hours of prayer as fragments must inevitably fall on the heads of the worshippers.

2. I see no evidence of any interference with old masonry. The workmen have been merely raking out plants and cementing stone joints to keep out water in the future. It is, however, less necessary in the large lower stones than in the upper.

I have therefore given orders to Mr Shiber on your authority as follows:

(a) No work of any sort is to be done during the hours of prayer.

(b) The stone cleaning and pointing is not to be carried below a distance of 3 metres from the top of the roof until the matter has been gone into more carefully.

It was finally decided that repairs, if and when necessary, should be executed by the Department of Antiquities on the lower courses of the Wall, and that the upper portion should be repaired by the Waqf, with every regard for the safety and comfort of the worshippers below, no work to be executed on Fridays or Saturdays. This decision limiting Moslem rights of repair to the uppermost courses of masonry evoked a sharp protest from the Mufti.

The first act of the Tragedy, religious hardly even in name, of the

Wailing Wall had been concluded peacefully, and according to tradition. Blood was to flow years afterwards, and an International Commission in 1930 approved by the League of Nations to adjudicate, before the fall of the curtain.

The Easter troubles incidentally brought to a head the question of the Mayoralty of Jerusalem. Mūsa Pasha Kāzem al-Husseini, who as Mayor should have represented impartially all three communities, had recently been impelled as head of one of the chief Arab families to make himself leader and spokesman of the opposition to the Mandate. I had met him one afternoon marching before a rabble to demonstrate against the Zionist Offices, and bade him take them and himself home lest trouble should arise. The same evening I warned him that he must make his choice between politics and the Mayoralty. During the riots he became first intractable and then defiant, and I informed the Administration that I proposed to dismiss and replace him forthwith—to be greeted with the suggestion that an English Mayor should be appointed, thus taking away yet another of the few important positions to which a Palestinian could aspire. It was easier to refute this suggestion than to be certain of finding in an atmosphere so charged a substitute at once capable and willing; and with Lord Kitchener's hunt for a Prime Minister fresh in my memory, I decided that for such crises the proverb of being off with the old love before being on with the new was hardly applicable. I therefore sent for Rāgheb Bey el-Nāshāshībi, an able and determined ex-Deputy of the Ottoman Parliament, offered him the Mayoralty and requested him to confirm his acceptance in writing on the spot. I was glad I had done so when twenty minutes later I intimated to Mūsa Pasha (not without regret, for he had rendered service and proved himself on occasion a courteous Arab gentleman) that the time had come to make a change. The Pasha said: "Your Excellency is free to act, but I would recommend you to wait, for I have certain knowledge that no Arab will dare to take my place." I handed him Rāgheb Bey's letter. When he had read it he rose, thanked me for my past support, assured me of his continued friendship, shook hands and walked erect and slow out of my office.[20]

The passing of O.E.T.A. was tinged with comedy. There seemed to be no suspicion that our regime was not to remain indefinitely, no foreboding of transience, for quite late in May 1920 I was shown at headquarters the elaborate scheme of an apparently permanent Military

---

[20] The Municipal Council was then composed of six members: two Moslems of whom the Mayor was one, two Christians (one Orthodox and one Roman) and two Jews. I added the innovation of Jewish and Christian Vice-Mayors, to act alternately in the Mayor's absence.

Administration, elegantly engrossed, and providing for a Chief-of-Staff, assisted by a galaxy of Colonels and Majors in charge of the familiar A., Q. and M. Departments. The baseless fabric was almost complete when it was shattered for ever by a telegram announcing the appointment of Sir Herbert Samuel as first British High Commissioner of the Civil Government of Palestine. The news was not universally welcome, especially to those not retained in the new Service, and there were gloomy prophecies of impending battle, murder and sudden death. We were enjoined (and could hardly refuse) only to wait and see for ourselves the inevitable result of Mr Lloyd George's madness. Nevertheless O.E.T.A. was able to render one last unacknowledged service to Zionists by suppressing or suspending the provocative interpretations of the mandate contained in some of their extremer Press telegrams from London.

Meanwhile Sir Herbert had telegraphed inviting me to continue in the Civil Service as Governor of Jerusalem and to act as Chief Secretary until the arrival of Colonel Wyndham Deedes.[21] As Senior surviving officer I was therefore sent down to greet him on his arrival in Jaffa. The following fragment of the diary I never found time to continue recaptures to some extent the atmosphere of those uncertain exciting days.

I had intended upon the arrival of the High Commissioner to keep an elaborate diary but find that the pressure of work absolutely prevents me from doing this. I must, therefore, dictate before I forget what happened.

I should begin by saying that in spite of strong representations on my part, Gen. *X,* on the advice of Gen. *Y,* insisted upon the High Commissioner's journey being made by motor though it was patent to everybody else that the railway arrival was not only politically more impressive but also safer from the point of view of public security. I had, with difficulty, obtained permission some ten days before to telegraph to the High Commissioner asking which he would prefer, and the day before his arrival received a reply from Rome in which he elected to travel by rail. In spite of this *X* and *Y* held to their opinion.

I left the house with my policeman Khalīl in Bols's Vauxhall at 5.30 p.m. on 29 June; my mother nervous on account of the rumours prevalent that we were in considerable danger. And indeed I had received the Sunday before an explicit warning through a Moslem lady who knew her not to travel in the High Commissioner's car. After luncheon, on the day of my departure, Mr Cory, the American member of the Nile Projects Commission, in accepting a lift from me, remarked drily that he would flatly have refused it if offered twenty-four hours later. It was a beautiful evening and all went well as we went downhill towards Kolonia when suddenly the steering-gear seemed to give way and the car rushed over the edge into the ditch, luckily on the ascending side of the mountain. I got out to find the right front portion of the chassis snapped in two owing to a flaw in the steel (mother later

---

21 Afterwards Sir Wyndham Deedes, C.M.G., D.S.O.

of opinion this might have been done intentionally by some evil-wisher!) We were not going more than fifteen or twenty miles an hour and there had been no violent bump, so I exonerated the driver, left him to look after the car, and, not daring to count certainly upon a lift, started walking back to Jerusalem. It was exceedingly hot and when I had gone twenty minutes I began to have doubts that I should ever find anything to take me along. I met and stopped a Ford containing Tchaikov and Seal [22] with two ladies going down to give a concert at Jaffa. They had no room, but offered to give me a lift: until they saw my luggage. Continuing, I stopped another Ford which contained my old friend the Rabbi Aminoff of the Bukhara Community. I explained to him my plight, and he welcomed me to a place before him, one of the retainers nursing my suitcase and the other my tin box. At the hair-pin bends we were overtaken by a better, faster, and less occupied Ford which stopped and offered to take me in. I accepted with relief, and found that the driver was a Syrian with the rank of Captain in the British Army whom I had once interviewed with a view to employment in the O.E.T.A., His wife was an entertaining woman, gratified because I knew Zahlé, the place of her birth in the Lebanon, and other villages there; indignant at my asking if they were Maronites, and quoted a saying "his blood is as heavy as that of a Maronite"; but agreed with my resenting their being Protestants and saying that Syrians and Near Easterns should either be Latin or Orthodox.

Reached Bir Sālem at about 8 and dined at 8.30. Hot sticky weather; sat afterwards conversing, when the G.O.C. came up, beckoned me to the balcony, and referring to Sir Herbert's telegram, which I had not failed to send him, gave it as his opinion that if they forced the High Commissioner to go by road when he had expressly preferred rail, and anything happened to him, the Army would be placed in a foolish position. I replied that this had been my opinion for some ten days. Thereupon he recommended that I should ask Sir Herbert next morning which he really preferred, and take him accordingly; as a camouflage train had been provided and would be under steam at Ludd. It was then 10 o'clock and I telephoned to Jerusalem warning O.E.T.A., Governate and Police of this possibility, and went to bed. Next morning by armoured Rolls-Royce to Jaffa (across the fields at some 55 miles per hour oblivious of bumping owing to the marvellous springs) and got to the Jaffa Governate at 9.15 where I found Bramley [23] and Postlethwaite [24] in possession, sending off crowds of applicants for passes to the Grand Stand. Made a variety of arrangements. At a quarter to ten the ship was sighted. She was travelling at great speed and I reached the beach only just in time to be met by the Port Officer with the request to get into the gig at once and go out. This I did under fire from several Kodaks and a cinema. The landing-stage had been pleasantly decorated, and there was a great expectancy in the air. I got out about 10.15 quite close to where *Centaur* came to anchor, flying three Union Jacks, at half-past. I went on board and was delighted to find Sir Herbert in white Diplomatic uniform wearing the Star and purple ribbon of the Empire together with the (far prettier) Star of the Belgian Order of

---

[22] Violinist, Director of the Jewish School of Music and Piano professor at the Jewish School of Music.
[23] Chief of Palestine Police.
[24] Military Governor of Jaffa.

Leopold. He was very cordial and thanked me for coming. I begged him to go back in the Port launch as they had taken great trouble in decorating it for him, and found that he was anyhow obliged to do so as the ship's barge drew too much water to make the landing-stage. We started away under a salute of 17 guns, effectively answered from the shore battery.

Personal participation in various theatres of the War upset for many their comparative historical values. I may have exaggerated the relative interest and importance of the Arab Campaign. If so, I am not alone in my exaggeration. Here, anyhow, as I stepped ashore with the man chosen to execute so tremendous a decision, and presented to him the assembled leaders of a people almost faint with happiness and moving as if in the glory and freshness of a dream come true, I was acutely conscious that I was walking in something stranger than history—the past summoned back and made to live again.

In the argument of train against car we agreed that it was the arrival in Jerusalem rather than the departure from Jaffa that counted, and decided to drive out Ludd,[25] taking the train thence to Jerusalem. The man beside our driver was heavily armed and I concealed from Sir Herbert in my left hand a loaded and cocked Browning pistol (a precaution of which he remained in ignorance for over fifteen years). I remember being surprised at his surprise in finding the officials of O.E.T.A. still wearing military uniform, and his necessary but to me distasteful solution of differentiating us pending the arrival of civilian clothes by the adoption of purple tabs. The Jerusalem reception though marred by certain absences was only less cordial than that of Jaffa, and it is worthy of record that neither before, during or after the journey was there the slightest attempt at outrage or even incivility. Sir Herbert's actual entry into office is recorded in the Orders for the Arrival at Government House (actually the last to be issued by O.E.T.A.):

Arrival of His Majesty's High Commissioner
In Palestine at Government House.
Between 13.00 *and* 14.00
June 30th, 1920.

As the car enters the outer gate a salute of 17 guns will be fired from the grounds of Sir John Gray Hill's house,[26] and Union Jack flown.

His Excellency will alight from the car (while the National Anthem will be played) and inspect the Guard of Honour, which will be drawn up in the open space facing the Hospice.

His Excellency will then proceed on foot to the Porch where he will be

[25] The Military junction: since rightly renamed Lydda.
[26] Now part of the Hebrew University.

received by the Mayor of Jerusalem (introduced by the Acting Military Governor) [27] and the Members of the Municipal Council.

The Mayor will read an address of welcome which he will then present to His Excellency in a casket. His Excellency will reply and will be subsequently received by the Chief Administrator on the steps.

Heads of Departments will be present in the Entrance Hall, and will be introduced to the High Commissioner.

The Company will then adjourn to Lunch.

The Guard of Honour will depart.

[27] Lieut.-Col. Popham.

CHAPTER FIFTEEN

Excursus on Zionism

Vere scire est per causas scire

I

I THINK that more than half my readers, having skimmed through the illustrations of this book, will then turn to the Index and (pausing only to ascertain whether their own names occur there) pass directly to the last letter of the alphabet—to the mystic, the almost frightening, metallic clang of Zion.[1] May I warn those not interested in this question to beware. Though the territory involved is in extent negligible, though the inhabitants have produced nothing that has mattered to humanity, nevertheless, the problem of reconciling their rights and grievances with the promises made to and the aspirations cherished by an Israel that has meant and still means so much to the world, is apt to become an obsession, rarely accompanied by temperance, soberness or justice. So I summon up my heart to write dispassionately of Zionism under the three Military and the first two Civil Administrations, adding perhaps later comment; well aware that I may be risking thereby the toleration of my Jewish, the confidence of my Arab, the respect of my Christian friends. Zionism is viewed from four different aspects. By enthusiastic supporters, minimizing difficulties and impatient of delay: these comprise I suppose a fair

---

[1] The original draft of this chapter was written before the 1936 disturbances in Palestine. Since their suspension, several studies of the situation have appeared of which two are objective and one other important. I allude to the Report of the Royal Commission (not received until *Orientations* was in galley-proof); Hancock's *Medicine of the body politic* in the *Survey of British Commonwealth Affairs* and Mrs Dugdale's *Arthur James Balfour*. All three have enriched my footnotes and reinforced my arguments. I have also read Lord Melchett's sincere and moving *Thy Neighbour;* the frankly Zionist *Palestine at the Crossroads* of Ernest Main; Farago's able and impartial *Palestine on the Eve* (published in the United States under the title of *Palestine at the Crossroads*) and the weekly *Palestine,* of which I am unable to better the *Survey's* description. "This cleverly written paper is printed by the 'British Palestine Committee', a body about which the present writer has failed to get precise information. The phrasing of the paper is that of the British liberal imperialist; the content is exclusively Zionist."

proportion of universal Jewry and many Gentiles outside Palestine. By declared adversaries, including all Palestinians who are not Jews, Roman Catholics (uninterested in the Old Testament) all over the world, and British sympathizers with Moselm or Arab views not concerned with formulation or maintenance of world policy. By persons unconcerned, or suspending or unable to form a judgment (I suppose about one thousand millions). By the official on the spot, loyal to the Mandate his country has accepted, yet wishing to justify his office to his conscience; and by persons connected with the British Government and Legislature, the League of Nations and the Press. I respectfully address myself to all four categories.

What does the average English boy know of Jews? As Jews, nothing. At Fretherne House, between the age of seven and ten, I had met a Ladenburg, and a charmingly mannered Rothschild who seemed to know everything, in the sense that you could tell him nothing new, and who impressed me (as have other Jews later in life) with a sense of unattainable mental correctness. He did not come to school on Saturday (which I envied), and was not allowed to be flogged (which I resented). Of Temple Grove I have no Jewish recollections. At Charterhouse were two pleasant brothers Oppé (very much cleverer than myself), who appeared in chapel at half-past seven every morning with the rest of us. At Cambridge Ralph Straus was one of my best friends. There must have been other Jews in these institutions, but neither I nor my companions knew them as Jews. I never heard my father mention Jews save in connection with the Old Testament, outside of which apart from an occasional Rabbi he had hardly met one. My mother used to recall with relish how she had let our house at Westgate-on-Sea to a well-known Jewish family; excellent tenants, but so orthodox that they had taken down and inadvertently left in the cellar all our "sacred" pictures—including a reproduction of the Infant Son of Charles the First by Van Dyck. In Egypt I soon met and still enjoy the friendship of the leading Jews, a powerful colony of Sephardim originally from Italy, Damascus and Salonika. I was invited to the weddings and other festivals of the Suares, Rolo, Cattaui, Menasce, Mosseri and Harari; their Rabbis occasionally consulted me as Oriental Secretary—so much so that my appointment to Jerusalem was, according to Rabbi della Pergola, fêted in the Synagogue of Alexandria. Like their predecessor Joseph and like Sir Solomon de Medina, knighted by King William III at Hampton Court in 1700, they were loyal to the country of their adoption, and as bankers and Government officials enjoyed and deserved good reputations. As with all Jews, there was usually a crisis of some sort or other in the internal organization of their Kehilla—Jewish Community—of which you could hear widely differing versions in the bazaars and in Kasr al-Dubara. Their leaders were consulted with advantage, alike by Khedivial Princes and by British Representatives.

This then, apart from the Old Testament (Psalms almost by heart) and Renan's *Histoire du Peuple d'Israel*,[2] was the sum of my knowledge of Jewry until the year 1917, an ignorance which Providence was pleased to mitigate for me in middle life. My wife had never met a Jew until she reached Jerusalem after our marriage in 1923. I had much and still have much to learn. Nevertheless, having loved Arabic throughout my career—with the Egyptians, who speak it best, and the Palestinians, whose citadel of identity it is; having played a small part in the Arab National Movement; having studied and admired Jewry, having received much kindness from many Jews (and been pogromed in their Press as have few other Goys [3] or with less cause); above all, having been for the first nine years of the British Administration Governor of Jerusalem, striving according to my lights for the good of all creeds, I should feel it cowardly to omit my experiences of the early and the later working of Zionism. Being neither Jew (British or foreign) nor Arab, but English, I am not wholly for either, but for both. Two hours of Arab grievances drive me into the Synagogue, while after an intensive course of Zionist propaganda I am prepared to embrace Islam.

Europe had learned before, during and particularly after the War, the full significance of Irredentism (invented but unfortunately not copyrighted by Italy): practical Zionism, or Irredentism to the *n*th, was new to most and stood alone. I happened to have learned something of it from the chance of my few weeks in the War Cabinet Secretariat, but with 95 per cent. of my friends in Egypt and Palestine (as in England) the Balfour Declaration, though announcing the only Victory gained by a single people on the World Front, passed without notice; whilst the few who marked it imagined that the extent and method of its application would be laid down when the ultimate fate of Palestine (assuming the conquest of its northern half and final Allied victory) had been decided. Those who had heard of the Sykes-Picot negotiations in 1916 cherished vague hopes of Great Britain being awarded Haifa as a British

---

[2] I read him again in Jerusalem: "a little out of date, but very stimulating: not very popular with the Jews, who dislike (for instance) Abimelech being described (rightly) as a worshipper of Moloch. Renan himself venerates the Patriarchs and the Prophets, but appears to dislike all between them."

[3] Gentile or non-Jew.

Possession. Mandates were unknown, though President Wilson's Fourteen Points seemed to indicate that Palestinians (then generally considered as Southern Syrians) would be allowed some voice in their political destiny. By the early spring of 1918 O.E.T.A. was already beset with, and its seniors working overtime upon, new and strange problems.

When therefore early in March Clayton showed me the telegram informing us of the impending arrival of a Zionist Commission, composed of eminent Jews, to act as liaison between the Jews and the Military Administration, and to control the Jewish population, we could hardly believe our eyes, and even wondered whether it might not be possible for the mission to be postponed until the status of the Administration should be more clearly defined. However, orders were orders; and O.E.T.A. prepared to receive the visitors. Confidential enquiries revealed Arab incredulity of any practical threat. Zionism had frequently been discussed in Syria. Long before the War it had been violently repudiated by the Arab journal *al-Carmel* as well as officially rejected by the Sultan Abd al-Hamīd in deference to strong Moslem feeling; [4] to which it was presumed that a Christian Conqueror who was also the greatest Moslem Power would prove equally sensitive. The religious Jews of Jerusalem and Hebron and the Sephardim were strongly opposed to political Zionism, holding that God would bring Israel back to Zion in His own good time, and that it was impious to anticipate His decree.

The Zionist Commission travelled by train from Egypt, and after some *contretemps* whereby they were marooned awhile on the platform of Lydda Station, arrived by car in Jerusalem. I received in the Governorate Major Ormsby-Gore, and Major James de Rothschild, Political Officers, Lieut. Edwin Samuel, attached, Mr Israel Sieff, Mr Leon Simon, Dr Eder, Mr Joseph Cowen and Dr Chaim [5] Weizmann, President of the World Zionist Organization. Monsieur Sylvain Lévy, an anti-Zionist, was attached to the Commission as representative of the French Government. The party being under the official aegis of the British Government, I assembled in my office the Mayor of Jerusalem and the Heads of Communities in order that they and the visitors should meet, for the first time anyhow, in surroundings at once official and friendly. The Jerusalem faces were unassuming. I find among my letters home the plan of the dinner party with which I followed up this first meeting, annotated for my mother's information:

[4] In 1911 Messrs Nossig, Frumkin and Knesevitch had been discouraged by the British Agency from buying land between Rafa and Arish. The intended introduction of Jews was noticed unfavourably in the Egyptian Press.
[5] Russian spelling: pronounced in English *Háyyim*.

Mr Abu Suan of Latin Patriarchate	Mūsa Kāzem Pasha al Husseini, Mayor of Jerusalem	Mr Silvain Lévy,[6] French Orientalist	The Mufti of Jerusalem	Sa Grandeur Thorgom Kushagian, Armenian Bishop of Cairo (acting Armenian Patriarch)	Arif Pasha Daudi, ex-Ottoman Official of good family
Major Ormsby-Gore					Lt.-Col. Lord Wm. Percy
Mr D. Salameh, Vice-Mayor of Jerusalem (Christian Orthodox)	Major J. de Rothschild	His Eminence Porphyrios, Archbishop of Mount Sinai, Locum Tenens Orthodox Patriarchate	Military Governor	Dr Weizmann	Ismail Bey al Husseini, Director of Education

After proposing "The King" I explained that I had seized the occasion of so many representatives of communities being gathered in Jerusalem to clear away certain misunderstandings aroused by the visit of the Zionist Commission. Dr Weizmann then pronounced an eloquent exposition of the Zionist creed: Jews had never renounced their rights to Palestine; they were brother Semites, not so much "coming" as "returning" to the country; there was room for both to work side by side; let his hearers beware of treacherous insinuations that Zionists were seeking political power—rather let both progress together until they were ready for a joint autonomy. Zionists were following with the deepest sympathy the struggles of Arabs and Armenians for that freedom which all three could mutually assist each other to regain. He concluded: "The hand of God now lies heavy upon the peoples of Europe: let us unite in prayer that it may lighten." To my Arabic rendering of this speech the Mufti replied civilly, thanking Dr Weizmann for allaying apprehensions which, but for his exposition, might have been aroused. He prayed for unity of aim, which alone could bring prosperity to Palestine, and he quoted, generalizing, a *Hadith,* a tradition of the Prophet, "Our rights are your rights and your duties our duties".

It had been from a sense of previousness, of inopportunity, that Clayton and I had regretted the immediate arrival of the Zionist Commission; certainly not from anti-Zionism, still less from anti-Semitism. We believed (and I still believe) that there was in the world no aspiration more nobly idealistic than the return of the Jews to the Land immortalized by the spirit of Israel. Which nation had not wrought them infinite harm? Which had not profited by their genius? Which of all was more steeped in the Book of Books or had pondered more deeply upon the prophecies thereof than England? The Return stood indeed for some-

---

[6] Who withdrew from the Commission and Organization during the Peace Conference.

thing more than a tradition, an ideal or a hope. It was The Hope—
Miqveh Yisroel, the Hope of Israel, which had never deserted the Jews in
their darkest hour—when indeed the Shechinah had shone all the
brighter,

"a jewel hung in ghastly night".

In the triumph of the Peace the wrongs of all the world would be
righted; why not also the ancient of wrongs?

Zionism was created by the Diaspora; throughout the ages it has slept
but never died. A remnant shall return [7], shall return with joy; "next
year in Jerusalem". In Russia, where Jewish suffering if not bitterest
certainly lasted longest, there appeared in the last century the *Hovevéi
Tsiyón*[8], the Lovers of Zion, burning with the love of Zion, *Hibbáth
Tsiyón*—to behold her face before they died. Disraeli, the first imperialist,
wielding an Empire, creating an Empress, still yearned in his heart and
cried in his lyric romance for Zion.[9] Before the end of his century there
arose a giant in Israel, splendid to look upon as the bearded and winged
deities of Assyria. The scandal of Dreyfus convinced Theodor Herzl
that there was no refuge for the soul of Jewry, either from martyrdom
or assimilation into nothing, save an individual land, state, and name:
die letzte Anstrengung der Juden. What other land could there be than
Eretz Yisroel, the Land of Israel? The spirit of world Jewry was moved
by the grand conception, as the spirit of modern Greece used to be
moved by the Μεγάλη Ιδέα—the Great Idea—of Constantinople, only
more profoundly and far more justifiably; for the supreme intellects of
Athens had lived and died five hundred years before the Roman built
Constantinople, whereas the creative spirit of Judaism was of The Land,
and ceased to create when The Land was taken from them. Therefore
this Austrian Jew, Theodor Herzl, was able to stand before the Sultan of
Turkey, empowered to buy back from him Palestine for the Jews. But
that tremendous boon which the Sultan might have granted, the Caliph,
fearing the anger of his Moslem Empire, refused; and once more hope
seemed to die. There were already projects for colonization in South
America when Joseph Chamberlain, the greatest Secretary of State of
the greatest Colonial Empire, had the vision to offer Zion in exile a
healthy, fertile and beautiful territory in East Africa. For many, includ-

---

[7] Some, however, hold that all such prophecies were fulfilled when the Jews returned to
Jerusalem from Babylon.

[8] The conventional spelling "Choveve Zion" gives a false impression to the English reader.

[9] In *Tancred* (1847) a Jerusalem Jew says: "The English will take this city; they will
keep it." It is not unreasonable to assume that in securing Cyprus for Great Britain he felt
that, sooner or later, the step would bring Palestine and Syria within the orbit of British
Control.

ing Herzl himself, the quest seemed to be ended; and the offer would have been accepted but for a small group headed by one strong Russian with the face and the determination of Lenin himself, and with Zionism coursing in his blood.[10] I remember Chaim Weizmann asking me as in a parable whether a band of Englishmen, banished for many years all over the world, would accept as a substitute for home permission to "return" to Calais: so felt he and his for the prospect of Zion in Uganda. Uganda was rejected, and Weizmann became a Lecturer in Chemistry at the University of Manchester, then in the constituency of Arthur James Balfour. The statesman whose heart was in science would take refuge from party routine with a scientist whose soul was in politics, and the first seeds of sympathy were sown. With the War came a demand for high explosives only less imperative than that for human lives, and Acetone, an essential ingredient of Trinitrotoluol—T.N.T.—was found to be unprocurable outside Germany. Its absence appalled the British Admiralty, but not the brain of the Jewish chemist. At his word the school-children of the United Kingdom were seen picking up horse-chestnuts by millions, and the Acetone famine ceased. Weizmann subsequently registered but did not press his claim for the invention, which was, on the skilful pleading of Sir Arthur Colefax, honoured, though none too generously, by the British Government.

But Acetone had registered another claim far more precious to the inventor; and the name and proposals of Weizmann and his colleagues, strongly supported by Arthur Balfour, Herbert Samuel and Mark Sykes, penetrated to the Supreme Council of the Nation and of the Allies.[11] On 2 November 1917, one week before the expected fall of Jerusalem, despite two formidable oppositions—British Jewry, preferring to remain "hundred per cent. Englishmen of 'non-conformist' persuasion", and an India Office ultra-Islamic under a Jewish Secretary of State [12]—there was launched upon the world the momentous and fateful Balfour Declaration. By this instrument Lord Rothschild, bearer of the most famous name in world Jewry, was informed that "His Majesty's Government view with favour the establishment in Palestine of a National Home for the Jewish people and will use their best endeavours to facilitate the achievement of that object, it being understood that nothing shall be

---

[10] "Herzl gratefully accepted the Uganda scheme and submitted it for ratification by Congress in 1903. . . . The Seventh Congress 1904 . . . decided not to embark upon the Uganda adventure. . . . Herzl died of a broken heart in 1904." Lord Melchett, *Thy Neighbour*, 1936.

[11] I am speaking figuratively, and agree that "Mr Lloyd George is not quite accurate in describing British policy in Palestine as a kind of *quid pro quo* for the patriotic action of the Zionist leader. The Balfour Declaration was not part of a bargain, nor a reward for services rendered." Blanche Dugdale, *Arthur James Balfour*, vol. II, p. 165.

[12] Edwin Montagu.

DR CHAIM WEIZMANN
(*Bronze by Jacob Epstein*)

done which may prejudice the civil and religious rights of existing non-Jewish communities in Palestine, or the rights and political status enjoyed by the Jews in other countries". Mere promulgation by the British Cabinet of such a pronouncement would have been useless without the support of the principal Allies. Dr Weizmann was fortunate indeed in his colleague Dr Nahum Sokolow, who obtained the adoption of the Declaration both from the French and Italian Governments, as well as from the Vatican, in letters addressed by those Governments to him personally; thus insuring its acceptance by the Peace Conference at Versailles. And it was Sokolow who as Head of the Zionist Delegation pressed for the British Mandate for Palestine.

The Declaration enjoyed an excellent Press, together with general and generous support from thousands of Anglican priests, Protestant ministers, and other religiously-minded persons throughout the Western Hemisphere; only the Central Powers bewailing their own delay in promulgating a similar document and the Church of Rome indicating early though not immediate reserve. In the numerous British constituencies enjoying a Jewish vote the Declaration was a valuable platform asset, and there was good reciprocal publicity in the almost apocalyptic enthusiasm telegraphed by politicians of standing to the Zionist Organization.

Behind the adoption of so novel a thesis by the most level-headed Cabinet in the world on the recommendation of a Russian Jew, there were alleged to lurk other considerations than mere eagerness for the fulfilment of Old Testament prophecy. British espousal of the Hope of Israel would, it was hinted, serve triply our interest as well as our honour by ensuring the success of the Allied Loan in America, hitherto boycotted by anti-Russian Jewish Finance; by imparting to the Russian Revolution, of which the brains were assumed to be Jewish, a pro-British bias; and by sapping the loyalty of the Jews fighting in scores of thousands on and behind the front for Germany. We may record with relief that even if these material inducements had influenced the decision, the Balfour Declaration was on results utterly clean from such profit.[18] The American Loan went much as had been anyhow expected; no sympathies for Britain accrued from the Soviets (which shortly denounced Zionism as a capitalist contrivance); and the loyalty of German Jewry remained unshaken—with the subsequent reward that the world is now contemplating.

[18] "As late as January 1918, our Ambassador in Washington reported, on the authority of Mr Justice Brandeis himself, that the Zionists 'were violently opposed by the great capitalists, and by the Socialists, for different reasons'. This in itself shows how baseless was the idea, once very prevalent, that the Balfour Declaration was in part a bargain with American financiers." Blanche Dugdale, *Arthur James Balfour*, p. 231.

In spite then of non-Zionist and anti-Zionist Jews, world Jewry was at last within sight of home. No more would an infinitesimal minority out of all her sixteen millions creep to Jerusalem for the privilege of being allowed to die on sufferance as in a foreign country. No longer would the Jews remain a people without a land, in exile everywhere; Consuls of the Spirit, bearing witness among aliens to the invisible glories of a vanished kingdom.[14] Civilization had at last acknowledged the great wrong, had proclaimed the word of salvation. It was for the Jews to approve themselves by action worthy of that confidence: to exercise practically and materially their historic "right". The soil tilled by their fathers had lain for long ages neglected: now, with the modern processes available to Jewish brains, Jewish capital and Jewish enterprise, the wilderness would rejoice and blossom like the rose. Even though the land could not yet absorb sixteen millions, nor even eight, enough could return, if not to form The Jewish State (which a few extremists publicly demanded), at least to prove that the enterprise was one that blessed him that gave as well as him that took by forming for England "a little loyal Jewish Ulster" in a sea of potentially hostile Arabism.

The mainspring of the Zionist ideal being the establishment of a Hebrew nation, speaking Hebrew, upon the soil of the ancient Hebrews, an urgent though unpublished item in the duties of the Commission was to produce certain *faits accomplis* creating an atmosphere favourable to the project (and stimulating to financial supporters) before the assembly of the Peace Conference. Early in 1918 the twelve foundation stones —to every tribe a stone—of the Hebrew University were formally laid in the presence of a distinguished gathering which included the Commander-in-Chief. The intrepid Commissioners soon advanced (to our admiring sympathy) upon the organization of the Jewish Community, not without a measure of success. The exclusive use of the Hebrew language was imposed upon Jews with a severity sometimes irritating to others, sometimes indeed comic, but in my opinion entirely justified in theory and by results. It was perhaps vexing for a tax or rate collector who had heard a Jewish householder conversing with a Moslem friend in good Arabic to be informed that the speaker knew Hebrew only, and could not understand (or accept) a receipt printed and verbally explained in Arabic. But in this and many other matters Zionism was only applying the Turkish proverb *Aghlama'an choju'a sud vermezler*—"To the not-

---

[14] Spiritual Zionism on unterritorial lines had henceforth no more bitter enemy than the practical Zionist. "*Bogéd, bogéd*—Traitor", exclaimed a Rabbi, when I mentioned to him (on a Cunard tender) the name of a famous Hebrew writer; "*Tziyoní ruhní*—spiritual Zionist!"

crying child they give no milk", and thereby accelerating the tentative processes of the Military Administration. Again, a fervent Zionist from Central Europe or America might be daunted if his platform "message" in Yiddish was greeted and drowned by howls of *"Dabér Ivrít"*—"Speak Hebrew!" I myself was puzzled when, inspecting a Zionist Dental Clinic, I asked a man, whose face I thought I knew, what was wrong with him. To my surprise he signified in Hebrew that he could not understand me. The secretary of the Clinic was called from the room, when the patient added in a hurried undertone: "I've a terrible toothache, but if I say so in anything but Hebrew I shan't be treated for it." The anomaly was heightened by the absolute refusal of the orthodox Rabbis to converse in anything but Yiddish, reserving the holy language for sacred purposes. Many Gentile residents and most visitors derided this drastic revival of Hebrew, asking: "How far will Hebrew take a Jew? Not even as far as Beyrut"; and only tolerating it on the explanation that it must entail a rapid diminution of the German language, *Kultur* and influence.[15] But what other language could a Jewish national revival in Palestine have adopted?

Dr Weizmann further attempted an enterprise whose success would have been so dramatic as to exalt the horn of Zionism with joy and honour throughout the world. The Wailing Wall of Jerusalem is geographically the Western Wall—*Ha-Kotél ha-Maáravi*—of the Háram al-Sharīf—The Noble Sanctuary. Structurally and archaeologically the Wall is the Western Wall of the Temple Area, founded on nine courses of massive undressed blocks laid by Herod, some perhaps even by Zerubbabel and Solomon; and four higher courses of Roman or Byzantine masonry completed by eleven of Saracenic, of Turkish, even of nineteenth-century construction. Legally and juridically it is a portion of the surface of the Hărăm and, as such, the absolute property of the Moslem Community. Historically, the most famous wall in the world; spiritually, the heart of Israel. The Wall is subtended to the west by a strip of pavement some six yards deep which, together with some grey stone hovels and paths on a space a little deeper than a square described on the length of the Wall, constitutes the Jerusalem section of the Abu Mádian Waqf, a pious bequest dating from the reign of Nur al-Din, suzerain of Saladin, in favour originally of Moroccan pilgrims now become residents.[16] The Wailing Wall is the one sacred place left to the

---

[15] The battle between German and Hebrew in Palestine was fought out before the War and lost by the *Hilfsverein der Deutschen Juden,* a German Jewish society for the assistance of Jews in the East, which advocated the use of German in the Schools.

[16] The documents proving undisputed ownership are preserved by the Shaikh al-Magharba —Shaikh of the Moroccans, the *Mutawalli* or Guardian of this Waqf and of the "Tomb of Abū Mádian" hard by, and are registered in the books of the Moslem Court in Jerusalem.

Jews from their former glory, and the custom of praying there extends at least back to the Middle Ages. It is to this ancient wall that the hearts of Orthodox and indeed of universal Jewry turn from all over the world, especially upon the even of Sabbath, during Passover, the Jewish New Year, the Day of Atonement, and the 9th of the month of Āb, the traditional date of the destruction of the first and third Temples. Such is the strength and continuity of the tradition that the Jews may be said to have established an absolute and acknowledged right of free access to the Wall for the purposes of devotion at any hour of the day or night throughout the year, for, though it is sometimes asserted by Moslems that they could legally erect a wall debarring public approach, no Mandatory Government could countenance so flagrant an infringement of the *Status Quo*. On the other hand, the Jewish right is no more than a right of way and of station, and involves no title, expressed or implied, of ownership, either of the surface of the Wall or of the pavement in front of it. Dr Weizmann proposed that he should acquire this precious space for Jewish worship; not indeed by purchase (for Waqf property may not be sold), but by the lawful and frequent practice of exchange against some other acreage. He offered to expend £75,000, which sum was to include the rehousing of the occupants, and he was prepared if necessary to raise his offer much higher. I was instructed to examine and report upon this proposal. I attached, and still attach, no more sanctity to the Abu Mádian than to any other Waqf: I was prepared rigorously to control any future building there: it seemed improbable that the Jews would desire to cheapen or to desecrate the surface of their holiest place, and the balance of the money could be devoted to the cause of Moslem Education. I therefore supported the project before Clayton and General Money, both of whom approved it. Haddād Bey was of opinion that the chances of acceptance were anyhow small, and would be infinitesimal if the offer came direct from the Zionists; I therefore consented to open the negotiations myself. I subsequently received a petition of protest from a representative body of leading Arabs, and, towards the end of September, found the general delicacy of the situation so greatly increased by parallel and unauthorized negotiations, which had been simultaneously opened by the Jews without my knowledge (or that of Dr Weizmann), that on the urgent advice of Haddād I was compelled to recommend that the project should be abandoned. There can be no doubt that he was right. Even if the Mufti had been willing himself, he would have had to reckon with the quivering sensitiveness of his own public (quite apart from their growing fear of Zionism) over the slightest rumour of interference even with the ground adjoining the outside of the walls of the

Háram al-Sharíf.[17] The acceptance of the proposals, had it been practicable, would have obviated years of wretched humiliations, including the befouling of the Wall and pavement and the unmannerly braying of the tragi-comic Arab band during Jewish prayer and culminating in the horrible outrages of 1929.

If after waiting for nearly two thousand years an impetuous people are suddenly informed that they may return home, they will arrive pardonably keyed-up to expectation of high immediacies; and it was from the Jewish point of view one of the ironies of the situation that something seemed to prevent the Government from granting them, not only the barren approaches to the Wailing Wall, but apparently anything else picturesque enough to arouse the enthusiasm of universal Jewry. Dr Weizmann offered to procure several hundred mechanical ploughs, and so by the autumn of 1918 to provide wheat and barley for the needs of the British Army: the offer was refused. One of the first outward and visible signs of nationhood is a national flag. Thousands of light blue and white flags and banners mounting the shield of Solomon had been prepared joyfully to float over houses or wave in triumphal processions: almost immediately they provoked such a commotion that their use had to be virtually prohibited. The Zionist National Anthem *ha-Tiqvah* which played before a mixed audience produced awkwardness sometimes resulting in untoward incidents. Everywhere was a sense of frustration, hope deferred, promise cheated of performance.

If this disenchantment had been merely negative, "still we have borne it with a patient shrug". But that within the first decade of their charter Jewish blood should four times have stained their soil and that none of the rulers—so few, it seemed, of the murderers—should be held to account, added fierce anger to the bitterness of death. If their lawful defenders could not or would not defend them from treacherous assault, who could blame them for the secret collecting of arms to defend themselves?

The great adventure of Zionism soon drew upon itself, not necessarily from those most concerned, a withering fire of cheap and ill-informed criticism. At a time when Jews all over the world were pouring their money into Palestine without hope of material return or even of beholding the country, wiseacres knew that "there must be money in it somewhere, or the Jews would not be going there". The Army riddle—"What is a Zionist?" "A Zionist is a Jew who is prepared to pay another Jew to go and live in Palestine"—was based on the supposition that the move-

---

[17] The Parker excavations of 1910-11 *within* the Area (a very different matter) had provoked an explosion of indignation all over Turkey.

ment was financed by millionaires, whereas it was, in truth, mainly dependent upon the yearly shekel of the uncounted poor. Who again had ever heard of those sedentary stockbroking Jews really consenting to the dull physical toil of labouring on the land?—as if a race debarred for two thousand years from holding one acre could be expected without opportunity to give proof of deep love of the soil; as if the thousand deaths by malaria of the pioneers in marshes and dunes had no significance, any more than the young European graduates ploughing the plain of Sharon or breaking stones on the parched high-roads of Galilee.[18] Who that descended with Sir Herbert Samuel for the first Blessing of the New Vintage in *Rishón-le-Tsiyón*—First into Zion—and saw the proud skill of the harvesters and the tears of holy joy in the eyes of the older men when the British High Commissioner read the portion of the Law in Hebrew, could dare to doubt their physical energy or their worship of their land? It was not from lack of bodily prowess but from excess of individual skill that the Maccabean Football teams were defeated, though narrowly, by British Regiments; whilst in the Police Boxing Championships the Jewish Constables inflicted upon their Arab comrades a punishment bravely endured but so severe as to be almost more painful for the spectators. Recruiting for the Jewish Regiments, though good in the Palestine Colonies, had indeed elicited a poor response in the East End of London; but once in the east end of the Mediterranean the 38th, 39th, 40th and 42nd Battalions, Royal Fusiliers—Jordan Highlanders as they were inevitably called—speedily disproved by their fighting qualities the facetiously applied motto of "No advance except on security". A British

[18] "We are too liable to think of the Jews in those times just like the Jews of mediaeval and pre-emancipation times—people addicted peculiarly to finance and usury, with little aptitude, or rather opportunity, for agriculture and war. It was in Christian Europe, after so many walks had been shut to them, that the Jews betook themselves on a large scale to the handling of money, and developed those exceptional capacities which some people suppose to inhere in the Jewish nature as such. In the ancient world the Jews had no special reputation as financiers or usurers. Josephus, at the end of the first century A.D., was able to write—he was speaking of the Jews of Palestine—'We are not a commercial people; we live in a country without a seaboard and have no inclination to trade.' If you put together all the things said against the Jews in the remains of Greek and Latin anti-Semitic literature, you never find that they are attacked as usurers." (*Legacy of Israel*, p. 35.)

For the contrary opinion about Jews and land-tenure:

"It is true that Jewish migrations in historic times have often been provoked by persecutions, but the question remains whether the original nomadism brought about by geographical reasons has not been just as determining a factor as the political-religious factor in shaping the Jew's wandering life. We note large Jewish migrations in the middle of the sixteenth century (the Jewish migration towards eastern Europe), and in the nineteenth century (the Jewish migrations to America).

"The nomadic habits of the Jews have also to do with the fact that the Jewish race has not been able to attach itself to the soil, has not been able to build states of its own. Does it not say in Leviticus: 'And the land shall not be sold in perpetuity; for the land is mine: for ye are strangers and sojourners with me'." Ragnar Numelin, Ph.D., *The Wandering Spirit*, p. 287. (Macmillan and Co., 1937.)

General commanding one of the detachments which took Jerusalem told me at the time that the most reckless bravery he had ever seen was shown by a young Jewish lance-corporal of a London Regiment who, mounting over a ridge into sudden sight of Jerusalem, seemed to be transported and transformed, rushed alone against a Turkish machine gun, killed the entire crew, and captured the gun. Equally unfair, indeed wilfully blind, is the tendency even now of those who concentrate upon Arab grievances or the mistakes of individual Zionists, and ignore the magnificent dedication of heart and brain, of strength and strain, of time and treasure lavished by World Zionism upon the Land of their soul's desire.

Is this, finally, a time for the Mandatory of the Nations to show herself laggard or ungenerous in offering not mere sympathy but their destined and appointed refuge to the helpless victims of that pogrom of Central Europe which is compelling the horror and indignation of the civilized world?

II

> But when the chosen People grew more strong,
> The rightful cause at length became the wrong;
> And every loss the men of Jebus bore,
> They still were thought God's enemies the more.
> Thus, worn and weaken'd, well or ill content,
> Submit they must to David's Government.
>
> JOHN DRYDEN, Absalom and Achitophel.

The thesis of Zionism had been in part upheld by the general ignorance of the nature and conditions of Palestine; which was vaguely imagined as consisting of hills far away but green until the destruction of the Temple by Titus A.D. 70, after which they reverted to Desert, still potentially fertile, though practically uninhabited. It was assumed that the indigenous population of Palestine was small, "backward" [19] and unimportant: that as brother Semites, they would welcome Jews, and as poor men, capitalists: that somehow their interests would not only not suffer but would positively be advanced by an influx of enthusiastic and energetic "kinsmen": that they must realize the Jews were "returning" by the will of the League of Nations. (It was further presumed by average cynical opinion that none of the fifty-two signatories were going to quarrel with their Jews over so remote and objective an issue—to say the least were not going to retain them against their will: "Let My People go?" "Yes verily, and by God's help so I will!") The Palestinian opposition to Zionism therefore came on the whole as a surprise, sometimes

---

[19] As it had been before the intensive arrival of the European Christians towards the end of the nineteenth century.

almost as an outrage, to the world at large. An act of chivalrous generosity (at no expense to the Donors) was being heckled and thwarted by a selfish, petulant and fanatical reaction.

Not all this opposition was unreasonable or reactionary. For four centuries the Arabs, Moslem as well as Christian, of Syria and Palestine (one country though administratively divided into two),[20] had groaned under the heavy empty hand of Ottoman misrule. After the Young Turk Revolution in 1908 the grasp had seemed for a while to lighten, but too soon the Arabs found that though forms might alter, facts remained unchanged—that even now they were denied the official use of the noble Arabic language. For the generation before the War a hope had arisen. The gaze of Syria was bent on the South-west, where across the Sinai, barely one hundred miles away, shone before them another ancient country, restored to prosperity and endowed with the civilization of Europe by the power of Great Britain and the genius of an Englishman. The English yoke in Egypt, compared with that of the neighbouring Powers elsewhere, seemed in Syrian eyes easy and uninterfering. A national Sovereign sat on his throne, assisted by a Council of Egyptian Ministers, against a background of parliamentary institutions. No attempt was being made to impose the English at the expense of the Arabic language or culture, or to manipulate the Customs tariffs for the benefit of British trade.[21] For Syrians the hope had been that after the next war Britain would expel the Turks and do for Syria what she had done for Egypt. Syrian politicians in Cairo had frequently endeavoured to interest the British Representative in their grievances and aspirations, but, in deference to French views about Syria, they had never been received, officially or unofficially (a refusal which did not always prevent some of them from resting awhile in the Residency garden and then reporting to their colleagues outside the gates—and sometimes to the Representative of France—that they had enjoyed a most encouraging interview).

The next War came. The Arabs of the Hejaz received, early and un-

---

[20] Owing to the number and delicacy of international problems in Jerusalem, the Mutasárref, or Governor of Judaea, corresponded directly with Constantinople, and not through the Vali of Syria, though Palestine and Syria were one military command.

[21] This British fairness of outlook in the matter of contracts is well seen in the reply to the protests of the British Boilermakers, Iron and Steel Ship-builders and Gas-holder-makers Society when the contract for a Nile Bridge was adjudicated to the *Fives Lille* Company because of their £18,000 lower tender. "It is impossible for the British Government to do more, in connection with the placing of orders by the Egyptian Government, than to give all the assistance they properly can to the representatives of British Firms who offer tenders, and to see that no unfair preference is given to others." This attitude was appreciated by Egyptians: by foreigners not believed—and understandably, for which of *them* would have acted thus?

asked, assistance, arms, and unconditional independence. Though British forces crossing the Sinai and advancing into Palestine met with no active military co-operation from Arabs (for Lawrence's Arabs were not from Palestine, and the Turks had broken up their Arab Regiments to distant fronts); [22] though the passive resistance of the civil population to the Turks was worth almost nothing to the advancing army: nevertheless, Syrian Arabs of influence had paid with their lives for their Allied sympathies, when a score of them were executed at Beirut, and when the Mufti of Gaza was hanged, together with his son, at the Jaffa Gate of Jerusalem.[23] With the British "Liberation" of their country they found their hopes not accomplished but extinguished. Throughout history the conqueror had kept for himself the territory he conquered (save in those rare instances where he returned it to the inhabitants): and that Britain should take and keep Palestine would have been understood and welcomed. Instead she proposed to hand it, without consulting the occupants, to a third party: and what sort of third party! To the lowest and (in Arab eyes) the least desirable specimens of a people reputed parasitic by nature, heavily subsidized, and supported by the might of the British Empire. If the Jews were "not coming but returning" to Palestine—the distinction sounded verbal [24]—on the strength of a Book written two thousand years ago; if there were no international statute of limitations and the pages of history could be turned back indefinitely, then let the Arabs "return" to Spain,[25] which they had held quite as long and at least as effectively as the Jews had held Palestine. That it was the Book that counted, that Arab Spain meant nothing to the world beyond two or three palaces and a few Spanish derivations, whereas Palestine of the Hebrews meant the Legacy of Israel, could hardly be expected to appeal

---

[22] Except the 2nd Arab Division which distinguished itself in the first successful defence of Gaza 1917, and which was the last recruited largely in Palestine.

[23] My Arab orderly said: "He was a good man, greatly respected; therefore we all assembled to see him hanged."

[24] Even with the authority of Aeschylus:

ΑΙΣ. ἥκω γὰρ ἐς γῆν τήνδε καὶ κατέρχομαι,
ΕΥ. δὶς ταυτὸν ἡμῖν εἶπεν ὁ σοφὸς Αἰσχύλος.
ΑΙΣ. οὐ δῆτα τοῦτό γ' ω κατεστωλμυμένε
ἐλθεῖν μὲν εἰς γῆν ἔσθ' ὅτῳ μετη πάτρας·
χωρὶς γὰρ ἄλλην συμφορᾶς ἐλήλυθεν·
φεύγων δ' ἀνὴρ ἥκει τε καὶ κατέρχεται.

AESCH. For I am come returning to this Land.
EUR. Our clever Aeschylus has said the same thing twice.
AESCH. It's not the same, you babbler.
A Man "comes" to his country when he has never been banished,
For he simply comes without any misfortune implied,
But an exile both "comes" and "returns".
Aristophanes, *Frogs*, ll. 1022—— (405 B.C.), tr. Lucas and Cruso.

[25] Or the Welsh to England.

to Moslem or Christian Arabs of Palestine as a justification for their ultimate subjection or extinction.[26]

The setting-back of the political clock set minds also back into fanati-
cisms, dying and better dead altogether. In the excitement of the Holy
Fire, the Shabāb—the Arab Young Men—would chant (for the Passion
of Christ is still vivid in that heart of Christendom):

"Sabt al-Nur 'ayyídna	"The Sabbath of Fire is our Festival
Wa zurna qabr Sayyídna.	And we have visited the tomb of Our Lord.
Sayyídna Aisa al-Massih;	Our Lord is Jesus the Messiah;
W'al-Massih atāna,	The Messiah has come to us,
B'dammu ishtarāna;	With His blood he bought us;
Nahna al-yom farāha	We are to-day rejoicing
W'al-Yahud Hazzāna."	And the Jews are mourning."

Moslems, though everywhere more tolerant of Jews, not only as Ahl al-
Kitāb, People of the Book, but also as "fellow-monotheists", than of
Christians, nevertheless revered Jesus as *Rūh Allah,* the Spirit of God.
Moslems as well as Christians would protest—"What! hand our country
over to the people who crucified Our Lord Jesus, *illī salabū Sayyídna
Ísa!"*

Arab disappointments over the fact of the National Home were far
from being allayed by the manner of its announcement. The Declaration
which, in addition to its main Jewish message, was at pains to reassure
non-Palestinian Jews on the score of their national status, took no account
whatever of the feelings or desires of the actual inhabitants of Palestine.
In its drafting Arabs observed the main and positive portion to be reserved for the Jewish people, while the other races and creeds already in
Palestine were not so much as named, either as Arabs, Moslems or
Christians, but were lumped together under the negative and humiliating
definition of "Non-Jewish Communities" and relegated to subordinate
provisos.[27] They further remarked a sinister and significant omission.

[26] That the Arabs had "achieved" nothing in Palestine was undeniable—though the new
and interesting doctrine that the inhabitants of a country can only retain it by proof of
"achievement" seems hardly that of self-determination. What was an Arab to think when
his title to the soil was publicly questioned by Jews? As it still is: "It is obvious that the
Arabs have not the slightest historical claims to the possession of Palestine. Their only
claims are the claims of people inhabiting the Land for centuries past...." M. Edelbaum,
3 July 1936 (letter to *Great Britain and the East*).
Palestine, 23 Sept. 1936 thus disposes of the title to the soil based on a mere 1200
years' continuous occupation: "The doctrine, put forward as something like a sacred dogma,
appears to be that any people who at any time happen to find themselves in control of an
area are eternally entitled to its exclusive possession, no matter what contribution they fail
to make and succeed in preventing others making to the cause of humanity and civilization."
[27] "What are the communities of Palestine? The reader of newspapers would answer,
without hesitation, Arabs and Jews. Yet the mandate contains no mention of an Arab
community." *Survey of British Commonwealth Affairs*, 1918-36, p. 434.
I remember the indignation of the Building, Roadmaking and other Departments of the
Public Works Ministry, Cairo, at being budgeted as "Services other than Irrigation".

While their religious and civil rights were specifically to be safeguarded, of their political rights there was no mention whatever. Clearly, they had none.

These and other suspicions and apprehensions were brought to a head and manifested definitely for the first time on the arrival of the Zionist Commission,[28] explanations and justifications for which were received with growing incredulity. The Arabs felt that the Commission was the thin end of the wedge, the beginning of a Government within a Government. They were not alone in this interpretation. In order to keep in close contact with Jewish affairs, I had appointed an able young Jew as Secretary, a position he had also held for Dr Weizmann. During my absence in Haifa I heard from the acting Governor: "Cornfeld informed me that he was instructed to make a report to the Zionist Commission on the work in this office, but I stamped on that heavily and told him to send the report to me. He has done so, and I notice a proposal to establish a 'Jewish Bureau'." Here was no question of the hidden hand, of Secret Protocols of the Elders of Zion [29] or of any other criminal absurdity invented by anti-Semitism, but rather of a genuine misinterpretation of the degree of liaison that should subsist between an official Administration and an officially-recognized Commission. Arab suspicions seemed to become certainties publicly verified by 1921, when the Moslem-Christian Delegation visited London seeking for further light upon the policy of His Majesty's Government, and were repeatedly recommended by the Colonial Office to get into touch with the Zionist Organization.[30]

Again, the pay of a clerk or a policeman sufficient for the Arab standard of living being considered insufficient for the European Jewish standard, Jewish policemen and clerks were being subsidized by the Zionist Commission; so, even in 1921, were railwaymen and telephonists. The Mayor of Jerusalem was assailed by demands to employ Jewish labour for road construction and repair: road labour, not being like Public Security a key position, received no Zionist subvention; if therefore the Mayor was to meet these demands, he must not only throw Arabs out of employment, but by paying their rivals higher wages materially raise his road bill and, in the end, the rates. Leading Jews in England were known to have the immediate ear of more than one Cabinet Minister: no Arab had. Hardly one of the Commission could speak Arabic. On the other hand they and other Jews (far more than Arabs)

[28] Zionists, *"Tsîyŏním"*, so light a Hebrew anapaest, became in Arabic the uncompromising *Sîhŏnîyîn*.

[29] Shortly to be exposed by Philip Graves in *The Times*.

[30] "But there is another aspect of the Jewish community, in which its relationship to the mandatory power might almost be termed that of an *imperium ex imperio*. This aspect is typified by the Jewish Agency." *Survey of British Commonwealth Affairs*, 1918-36, p. 458.

knew English, which was necessarily the test language for service in the Administration.[31] What limit could there be to their influence when (in 1922) the celebration of the King Emperor's Birthday could in Palestine be postponed two days so that it should not fall upon the Jewish Sabbath? And this though it had been duly observed on the Moslem Friday in 1921. Would the date of the least important festival have been altered on account of the Moslem Friday? [32] If, in his indignation at such a change of date, the Arab absented himself from the Birthday celebrations, he would appear to be lacking in respect for a King whom on the contrary he regarded with veneration.

The official adoption in General Allenby's first proclamation of the Hebrew [33] language, with its gradual extension throughout Governmental and Municipal activities, naturally entailed an ever-increasing staff of Hebrew interpreters, translators, stenographers, typists, printers and administrative officers, all supported by the tax-paying majority, which contemplated unedified the refusal of linguistic martyrs to part with cash against receipts in Arabic. For one reason or another every circumstance or step taken to implement the Balfour Declaration [34] evoked a swelling chorus of protest against an admitted departure from the Laws and Usages of War. Between anxieties and suspicions the pitch of good relationship was being irreparably queered. Dr Weizmann suggested to me that as a gesture of sympathy and friendliness he should present the Mufti with a Koran. I procured him a magnificent example from Cairo. The Mufti, preferring a private presentation, elected to accept the great manuscript unattended in his Office at the Moslem Law Courts. By that evening Arab Jerusalem had decided that the box taken into the room had in reality contained money.

The spirit of opposition throve in the unsettlement resulting from the

[31] I found this fear expressed in Rome on my visits of 1919 and 1922, during which last Cardinal X remarked that it was not the mass immigration elements in Zionism which alarmed him so much as the preponderating influence in Palestine which might be acquired by a comparatively small number of Jews occupying high positions. He said that in Hungary the proportion of Jews was only 5 per cent. of the population, but as high as 40 or 50 per cent. in the learned professions. This inclined him and others to be sceptical when they saw high official positions given so soon to Zionist Jews. I was at pains, on both occasions, to correct His Eminence on this point. Very few Jews, or Arabs, then held or now hold senior official positions.

[32] June 1922. It is of course true that rest on the Moslem Friday is permissive but on the Jewish Sabbath obligatory.

[33] Jewish Colonies on earlier Arab sites have naturally given them Hebrew names: the Arab thus sees some score of traditional Arab villages disappear from the map, and from official documents.

[34] And some that had nothing to do with it: "I had arranged for a Military Band to play on Saturdays in the Municipal Gardens, and I have to receive a deputation of leading Moslems who complain that their religion and their prestige are being undermined for the benefit and by the machination of the Zionists (orders given that Band shall play until further notice on Fridays, Saturdays and Sundays)." (Letter to Mark Sykes.)

inordinate delay in the promulgation of the Palestine Mandate, which, though officially awarded to Great Britain in April 1920, was, owing to difficulties with France, Italy and the Vatican, not signed until July 1922. Meanwhile Arab uncertainties had synchronized with those of President Wilson, who early in 1919 proposed to the other Big Three that a Joint Allied Commission should be sent to enquire what would be the unfettered self-determination of the Ottoman Empire. The proposal could only have emanated from or been acceptable to a person without knowledge of or interests in the Near East; but the Three agreed in principle, doubtless hoping to elude practice by subsequent defection. For once the President had thought ahead of his colleagues and had his way: the American members of the Commission started alone. Its Western wing, the King-Crane Commission, composed of two distinguished American statesmen, Dr Henry C. King and Minister Charles R. Crane, forthwith descended upon O.E.T.'s East and West and South and North, and began to enquire from the various and opposed communities what were their political aspirations, thus appearing to reopen to appeal a *chose jugée* and so restarting the general unsettlement. Few that had the privilege of meeting Dr King or of knowing the surviving Commissioner will be disposed to doubt that, though the hands that signed their Report were the hands of King-Crane, the voice was the voice of Crane. It appeared that from Cilicia to the borders of Egypt all tongues, creeds, and nations save the Jews (who were for British Zionism) and the Roman Catholics (who were for France) desired as their first choice an American Mandate: failing which the vast majority favoured Great Britain. When it is remembered that to the anticipating Eastern mind the nationality of the Commission (apart from the known wealth and rumoured Liberalism of America) predetermined that of the Mandatory, it will be understood that these findings were more favourable to Great Britain than would be gathered from a literal reading of their text. The Commissioners recommended a single Mandate for a united Syria, including Palestine (with a retarded Zionism) and the Lebanon; the Mandatory, failing America, to be Great Britain, with the Amir Faisal ibn Husain as Constitutional Monarch. In their dislike of any partition of United Syria they quoted W. M. Ramsay: "The attempt to sort out religions and settle them in different localities is wrong and will prove fatal. The progress of history depends upon diversity of population in each district." [35] The answer of the Immanent Will (returned through the

[35] This Report, which was signed on 28 August 1919 and presented to the American Commissioners in Paris the following day, was, doubtless for the best of reasons, not published until the end of 1922, and even then unofficially in the *New York Times*. In a Confidential Annex "For the American People" the writers dealt with the "interference"

Dynasts of Versailles) to these reasoned recommendations was, that within one year United Syria had been divided into two Mandates and Faisal expelled; and that within three years its Northern portion, the French Mandate, had been redivided into five separate territories, each complete with full machinery of government, under the (sixth) supreme government of a High Commissioner in Beirut.

The eagerness of the Arabs, North and South, for a United Syria (strongly supported by Faisal in Paris) was not merely anti-French or anti-Zionistic. Even had they obtained this, the career previously open to talent in the Ottoman Empire would have been reduced by two-thirds. Kiamil Pasha, a Cypriot villager, had been four times Grand Vizir. Abu l'Huda, an Arab of Aleppo, had as Astrologer to the Sultan wielded for years an even more absolute though far less honourable power. Mahmud Shawkat of Baghdad had become Grand Vizier as recently as 1908. The two Arab Pashas I found in Jerusalem had held positions of administrative responsibility in Arabia and in Mesopotamia. After the partition of Syria the leading Palestine Arabs, conscious if not of "Hands that the rod of Empire might have swayed", at least of some ruling capacity, found their ambitions henceforth confined to subordinate or municipal functions, with preference given to two foreign races, within a territory no larger than Wales. It was therefore no matter for surprise that the representatives of ancient families, whether associated with the Ottoman Government or as great landowners, should wage a consistent and resentful rearguard action against the passing of their ascendency. Is not History a record of the reluctance of aristocracies and oligarchies to relinquish their position or to share it, even with their own people? But to share it with foreigners! For foreigners the Central European Jews were to the Arabs of Palestine, despite the oft-quoted Semitic bond of language—foreigners in all the essentials of civilization, and mainly Western both in their qualities and their defects. *Identity* of language is a bond: a common linguistic origin of several thousand years ago is no more than an academic fact. Linguistic fellow-Semites might possibly be driven into alliance by a Mongol invasion, but when a Shaikh enquired how far Englishmen had acted upon their Indo-Germanic kinships during the past half-century, what was the answer? In default of the Semitic bond there survived, perhaps fortunately, no Canaanite tradition.

and attempted influencing of the populations. While good enough to allow that a comparative minimum of these practices was reported in O.E.T.A. (S.) they nevertheless proceeded to quote rumours and unsubstantiated stories of "pressure" exercised at Jaffa and Gaza. All I can say is that I myself, having been asked by one or two Arabs once or twice what they should say, and having replied that they should tell the truth, refused to receive any more questioners, conveying to them this standard reply through a subordinate: nor do I believe that any officer in General Money's Administration acted otherwise.

The injunction, under Article 6 of the Mandate, that the Administration "shall encourage in co-operation with the Jewish Agency close settlement by Jews on the land, including State lands and waste lands not required for public purposes" in Palestine, sounded with a curious difference in different ears. To the world at large it seemed a reasonable satisfaction by the bestowal of surplus, unused and unwanted areas. To the Zionist, who had hoped that with the prosperity of British rule his rapidly augmented population would need every possible acre of land in the country, it was the obvious initial minimum of concession unwarrantably delayed by the Government. The thinking Arabs regarded Article 6 as Englishmen would regard instructions from a German conqueror for the settlement and development of the Duchy of Cornwall, of our Downs, commons and golf-courses, not by Germans, but by Italians "returning" as Roman legionaries. For such loss of national and political future repeated reassurances of strict and scrupulous maintenance of religious rights and sites (assumed under British rule everywhere) were about as satisfactory compensation as would be German guarantees to Englishmen for the inviolable conservation of the Court of Arches and of Westminster Abbey. Article 6 has not yet been "implemented", owing to the lack of available State property, but it still stands in the Mandate, and is still being vigorously pressed by Zionists. "The Jewish Agency would appreciate an opportunity of examining any Government lands still unallocated, with a view to applying for any areas suitable for Jewish settlement." [36] The resentment of leading Arabs increased when they were pilloried in Zionist reports and the general literature based thereon as *Effendis*.[37] The Fellah, the peasant, was a fine fellah, a stout fellah, with all the bluff and blunt virtues conventionally ascribed to peasantry by those who know it least. He was also unorganized and inarticulate. The *Effendi* on the other hand was a decadent "capitalist" parasite, a selfish obstructive agitator of an Arab Majority not ill disposed if only "left to themselves". His "small clique" of "feudal gentry exploiters" was bound in the end to be "eliminated" and so entitled to no quarter, even if some British officials chose to be taken in by his veneer of "cringing" good manners. *Effendis* in that sense of the word there certainly were and are throughout the Near and Middle

[36] Dr Weizmann's letter to the High Commissioner, covering annual Memorandum to the League of Nations for 1935. 30 April 1936.

[37] Effendi is an early Turkish corruption of the Byzantine αὐθέντης, an authentic, or gentleman. It corresponds to Mr in conversation and to Esquire upon an envelope. Bey may be regarded as the equivalent of a Knight or Baronet, and Pasha of a Peer. None of the three is hereditary, though the son of a Pasha is a Bey by courtesy. The Turks were chary in their creation. I found but two in Palestine after the War, and in Transjordan one. Pashas are addressed as "Excellency"; there are therefore more Excellencies in one province of Egypt than in the whole British Empire.

East; in Palestine the *Effendi* might as a whole be defined as an Arab of the ruling or professional "black-coated" class, debarred from employment for political as well as for economic reasons. The *Effendi's* good will was not perceptibly stimulated by the theory that while the Arabs East of the Jordan were a splendid people and the real thing, those West of the Jordan were not Arabs at all but merely Arabic-speaking Levantines.[38]

Material advantages were admittedly increased for many, though not for all, Arabs, especially near the City and the towns. But at what a price! Was it altogether dishonourable for Arabs to sigh for a less advanced, but a traditional, an Arab civilization? The peasant of Siloam would not have been a peasant if he had not profited by being able to sell his cauliflower for sixpence instead of a halfpenny; the improvident landowner would have been more, or less, than human if he refused tenfold the value of his land. Yet both might mutter, in the words of the Palestine chicken: *At'emni al-yōm: u'ushnuqni bukra*—"Feed me up to-day: wring my neck to-morrow."

In spite—or because—of official glosses on the original text of the Declaration, Arabs seemed to understand less and less what, if any, were its limitations. It was said that though Dr Weizmann's moderated demands at the Peace Conference went beyond what he considered sound, they were the minimum requisites of other prominent Zionists. On the King's Birthday of 1921 Sir Herbert Samuel pronounced a statesmanlike speech which reassured the Arabs, and the world. He defined the Declaration as meaning that "The Jews, a people who are scattered throughout the world, but whose hearts are always turned to Palestine, should be enabled to found here their home, and that some among them, within the limits that are fixed by the numbers and interests of the present population, should come to Palestine in order to help by their resources and efforts to develop the country, to the advantage of all its inhabitants." Within two months the good effect of the speech in Palestine was undone by its violent denunciation at the Carlsbad Zionist Congress. Herzl's original "Judenstadt"[39] was indeed absolutely and permanently excluded by the British Government as well as repudiated by official Zionism; but with the Revisionists, swayed by the versatile and violent Vladimir Jabotinsky,[40] declaiming publicly at the first Zionist Congress at the

---

[38] This ethnologically correct, but nationally misleading thesis, is also embodied in the Foreign Office *Handbook of Syria and Palestine*, pp. 56-7, 1920.

[39] As long ago as 11 February 1899, "Glasgow Zionist" wrote to the *Speaker:* "Zionism does not even dream of founding a state for all Jews"—an equivocal repudiation.

[40] "... in those early years the work of fomenting discord was aided by the extravagant and provocative utterances of a small section of Zionists." Blanche Dugdale, *Arthur James Balfour,* vol. II, p. 161.

Hague that what the Jews really wanted was not a Jewish National
Home, but a Jewish State, which of the three (if any) was an Arab to
believe? All he knew was that in advanced politics the extremists of
the past generation were the Liberals of the second and Conservatives
of the third.[41] Above all, how could he forget that when Dr Weizmann
was asked at the Peace Conference in Paris what he meant by the
Jewish National Home, he had replied that there should ultimately be
such conditions that Palestine should be just as Jewish as America was
American, or England was English.[42]

Zionism is a world movement. Arabism does not exist. Although it is
said that a knowledge of Arabic will take you from India to the Atlantic,
yet Arab merits, defects, rights and grievances are essentially local in
character, even when reinforced by the Vatican and by the relics of
Pan-Islam. The Arab of Palestine therefore feels himself under an overwhelming inferiority in the presentation of his case to the conscience of
the world.[43] He is aware that he has not the ability, the organization, least
of all the material resources or the audience for effective propaganda.
He is well aware that such of his leading Moslems as have toured the
East for support have not succeeded in creating a favourable impression
even upon their co-religionists in Egypt, India or Arabia. Against the
scientifically controlled publicity of the two major continents he has
about as much chance as had the Dervishes before Kitchener's machine
guns at Omdurman. From time to time his cause is "taken up", usually
with more courage than skill, by some English supporter (Thackeray's
"young Mr Bedwin Sands"), too often the travelled *amateur* of picturesque survivals who "defended" the Turk, as the first gentleman in
Europe, against the massacred Armenian. In British politics Conservatives
were at first inclined to be pro-Arab (with notable exceptions in the
Upper House) and Liberals and Labour pro-Zionist. Politically, all the

[41] What, for instance, is the Arab reader to deduce from the following reasoned statement? "It is an important feature of the peculiar character of the Palestine Mandate that
while in all other cases it is the actual inhabitants of the countries in question who are the
beneficiaries of the Mandates, under the terms of the Palestine Mandate, it is *the Jewish
people as a whole* who are the beneficiaries jointly with the existing population of Palestine.
This distinction is one of paramount importance, both in principle and fact. It means that
while the rights of the Arabs are based on their residence in the country, the rights of the
Jews are independent of this qualification, for the Trust being held by Great Britain for
the Jewish National Home to be established in Palestine for the benefit of the Jewish
people, it does not depend on the numerical strength of the present Jewish population of
Palestine. By virtue of this Trust any Jew no matter where he lives is a potential colonist
and beneficiary of the Trust." J. M. Mackover, *Governing Palestine*, 1936.

[42] Israel Cohen, *Jewish Life in Modern Times*, p. 310.

[43] "... one further inequality. This was inequality of access to the ear of the British
democracy. Jewry was represented in every layer of English society—in the Lords and the
Commons, in powerful capitalistic organizations and in the Labour party, in the press
and in the Universities." *Survey of British Commonwealth Affairs*, p. 462, 1918-36.

Arabs in the world would not have turned at the Polls one single vote. On the contrary, I have been asked by a Member as guest at a Party luncheon in the House of Commons, whether the Palestine Government were advancing as swiftly as possible with the National Home, "for", he said "I have in my constituency some thousands of Jews who are continually enquiring, whereas", he added with engaging but unnecessary candour, "I have no Arabs".

All too soon feeling deepened down to primal instinct, which was fired by misguided and irresponsible agitators to outrage. But "have not the Jews been arming from the first, and later has not the Government allowed them, granted them, great cases of rifles? What they have beyond that who can know? But could any man believe that the beehives bursting with revolvers found by the English in the Haifa Customs were not one of a hundred more successful consignments?" [44] And with illicit arming who, the Arab asked, was the proved aggressor?

III

Semper ego auditor tantum! Nunquamne reponam? [45] JUVENAL I.

I have attempted to describe, I hope not without sympathy and justice, the aspirations of Zionism formulated in the Balfour Declaration, endorsed by the League of Nations, and interpreted by the Zionist Commission, together with their repercussion upon the indigenous Arabs of Palestine. Grappling with this situation was a British Military Administration, the third, and ostensibly directing party, confronted with a problem unique in history; by some interpreted as the problem of how *A* should "restore" the property of *B* to *C* without deprivation of *B*. The mistakes and misfortunes in the handling of this experiment were by no means confined to any one, or any two, of these three suddenly assembled and ill-assorted partners; nor can they be dissociated from the Managing Directors in Downing Street or the fifty apathetic shareholders meeting in Geneva. All concerned manifested with a frequency that

---

[44] "In October 1935 a mysterious munitions-transport arrived in Jaffa. The weapons were hidden in cement-sacks, addressed to an unknown Isaac Katan in Tel Aviv. When the cement-sacks were opened, the customs officers found 300 rifles, some 500 bayonets and 400,000 rounds of munitions in 359 of them. The discovery of this unfortunate merchandise led to demonstrations, gave rise to an embittered campaign in the whole Arab Press, and finally, on 26 October, resulted in a strike of protest in Jaffa. On this day the Arabs of Jaffa tried to attack Tel Aviv, but the Government still had the control tightly in its hands and dispersed the crowd.

"It was later revealed that the munitions-transport was not intended for the Jews, but belonged to a large smuggling syndicate which was trying to import weapons into Abyssinia in a roundabout way." Ladislas Farago, *Palestine at the Crossroads.*

[45] "Always the auditor, and nothing more!" Gifford.

seemed not to decrease with years the "blank misgivings of a creature moving about in worlds not realized". Almost from the beginning O.E.T.A. incurred a critical Zionist Press which soon developed into Pan-Jewish hostility. We were inefficient, ill-educated; those with official experience strongly pro-Arab, violently anti-Zionist,[46] even anti-Jewish. Governing and governed had each one clear advantage over the other, for if O.E.T.A. officials could not be removed by Press agitation, they were by a proper British convention precluded from defending themselves in public; with the result that the difficulties [47] they encountered on all sides are even now not generally appreciated.

The truth is that some (though by no means all) of the Zionist criticisms of our inefficiency might have been justifiable if they had been directed against a planned, trained and established Civil Service, But what was O.E.T.A.? It was the remnant of the small staff originally chosen for the purpose, with accretions of the officers placed by the Army in temporary charge of newly conquered areas: without expectation of long continuance, still less of permanency. And who were these officers? What had they been before the War? There were a few professional soldiers. Apart from these our administrative and technical staff, necessarily drawn from military material available on the spot, included a cashier from a Bank in Rangoon, an actor-manager, two assistants from Thos. Cook, a picture-dealer, an Army coach, a clown, a land valuer, a bo'sun from the Niger, a Glasgow distiller, an organist, an Alexandria cotton-broker, an architect (not in the Public Works but in the Secretariat), a Junior Service London Postal Official (not in the Post Office but as Controller of Labour), a taxi-driver from Egypt, two school-masters and a missionary. The frequency and violence of Jerusalem crises were such that "My Staff Capt. told me (of one of Percy's successors) that he punctuated his work with groans, ejaculating 'The place is a nightmare, a *night*mare!' " Our three Chief Administrators were Generals changed (after the first appointment) too quickly to accomplish anything. The War Office and the Foreign Office between them provided neither precise instructions for policy nor trained administrators. Yet it would have been easy to appoint as Chief of Staff or Head of an Executive Secretariat some militarized

---

[46] "I attended an infinitely tedious Arab version of *Hamlet* (title role addressed throughout as Shaikh *Hamlik*) concluding with friendly references to Great Britain for having delivered the Arabs from Turkish domination and total repression of the Arab language, together with hope for the prosperity of the nation and the language. I had naturally to acknowledge these loyal and anti-Ottoman sentiments, and duly received a few days later an official protest from the Zionist Commission for having attended and encouraged anti-Zionist demonstrations (called for copies of speeches: nothing offensive found, discovered that proceedings were reported by a young Jew ignorant of the Arabic language)." (Early 1918 letter to Mark Sykes.)

[47] My recital of these difficulties is not to be taken as a general endorsement of O.E.T.A.

Colonial or Chief Secretary—perhaps from Ceylon—familiar for a quarter of a century with the broad principles and technical minutiae of administration. Here indeed was our weakness, and for lack of this tradition and experience we doubtless expended much unnecessary time, tissue, and, I fear, money. Two sharp notes to Headquarters remind me how poor our liaison sometimes was.

Towards the end of last week a certain number of would-be Palestinian delegates and others interested in the question of a Palestinian Congress and a possible Palestinian Delegation to Europe visited me and informed me that they had had an interview with the Chief Administrator, who had recommended them to elect their delegates, and promised to facilitate their journey. As the only instructions in my hands were to the effect that the Palestinian Congress must not assemble, I was compelled to maintain a noncommittal and even incredulous attitude. I would remark that the already great difficulties of Jerusalem politics are greatly increased for the Military Governor, unless he is kept continually and accurately informed of receptions and negotiations deeply affecting the public interest which are being carried on with the authorities by notables of his District in his District.

Again:

Shortly before noon yesterday I received telephonic information, confirmed later by your letter, to the effect that 300 Arabs of Abu Kish were proceeding by train and horseback to Jerusalem, and instructing me to have them stopped both at the Station and on the road at Kolonia. I therefore cut short an engagement of long standing at Ramallah, got into touch with O.C. Troops, who provided 30 men with lorries, Lewis guns, rations, etc., for two days, and sent them with all possible dispatch to Kolonia. I further arranged with the Police for a representative of the Governorate, with an interpreter, to be present both at the Station and Kolonia. Both trains from Ludd were duly met; the troops remained at Kolonia all night, and a picket was posted on the Nablus Road in case the horsemen should advance by way of Nebi Samwîl. Not a single Arab of Abu Kish arrived by either of the trains or on horseback. It would be interesting to know (a) why, if the rumour was correct, the Arabs could not have been dealt with at Ludd [48] and Ramleh [48] respectively, and (b) if the rumour was false, what steps were taken to verify or confirm it before inflicting upon the Governorate, local Police, and O.C. Troops, Jerusalem, this apparently unnecessary expenditure of valuable time.

On the other hand, there was a high level of zeal, goodwill, ability and interest in the task to hand; the word "overtime" was unknown, and work ceased only when it was finished. We tried by these efforts to atone for admitted deficiencies, and I believe that the first High Commissioner, with eleven years' experience of Whitehall, found that we had not been altogether unsuccessful.

[48] Neither at that time in my district.

The main charge against O.E.T.A., more serious because it implied deliberate bad faith, was that of anti-Zionism. It cannot be denied that there were amongst us two or three officers in high positions overtly against the declared policy of His Majesty's Government. In due course these were eliminated (for one only saw fit to resign). One or two who would gladly have remained in Mandatory Service became extreme Arabists when discharged for reasons of economy. While emphatically repudiating the general accusation that O.E.T.A. was disloyal to its own Government, we may yet allow that the more eager arrivals from Central Europe were not altogether unjustified in arguing from these known examples to the possibility of others unknown. They knew nothing of British Officers, probably conceiving them as a variant of a Prussian Drill Sergeant. They came from a country where the official *Chinovnik* class lay awake at night excogitating pogroms; where Father Gapon, the priest who led hundreds of innocent men to be shot down, was but one of innumerable state-paid *agents provocateurs*. They found that while a good proportion of O.E.T.A. (having come from Egypt) spoke Arabic, none as yet knew Hebrew: hardly one, Russian or German. The British were often seen conversing with Arabs; more seldom with Jews. What more likely then that, so far from calming the Arabs, they were encouraging their opposition to the National Home?

Some of us were very soon on the Black List of Zion, an injustice which though not prejudicing our work did entail some needless irritation, as for instance when I found myself publicly accused of having intentionally caused the Wailing Wall negotiations to break down; verifying, not for the last time, the Arab proverb that "The peacemaker shall not profit, save in the rending of his garments." On my first leave home in 1919 I wrote to General Money; "Saw G. R. at the Foreign Office, where Lord Curzon came in and told me of a fierce attack made on me on the 2nd of the month by the Commission, who stated openly that I ran an anti-Jewish campaign during the three months of your absence." Again, on my way back to Palestine I "lunched with the Berensons (taking £10 off him for Pro-Jerusalem), and with Sokolow at the *Meurice* to meet Ussishkin, the great Russian Zionist. Good massive head, but almost no French. Said he had heard nothing but discouraging reports from Palestine and that the Administration seemed to be *nettement* anti Z.[49] I begged them to come out and see for themselves, and

[49] "In the early spring of 1918, Arab leaders in Palestine and Egypt were eager to come to terms with Zionists on the basis of mutual concessions. The Jews responded with the greatest readiness and cordiality. The Arabs' attitude grew more and more reserved, strictly parallel with the increasing antagonism of the British military administration to Zionism and Jewish claims. There are clear indications that in some cases direct advice was given to the Arab leaders ... to abstain from concessions to the Jews. ..."

told them that the slow movers like myself were not only their best friends, but their only hope." [50]

The ardent Zionist from Pinsk or Przemysl, between the bitterly hostile Arab and the coldly impartial British official, always recalled to me Theocritus' description of Ptolemy, εἰδὼς τὸν φιγέοντα, τὸν οὐ φιγέοντ' ἔτι μᾶγγον—"Recognizing his friend, but his enemy even better"; sometimes indeed confusing the two. Jewish Doctors would alienate the Public Health Department even where their talents were most admired, and they seemed to suffer (if that is the word) from a failure to appreciate the point of view of the other man (Arab or British) only equalled by that of their latest persecutors, the German nation. Few writers have written more beautifully or sympathetically about the Jewish people than the brothers Jacques and Jérôme Tharaud. *L'Ombre de la Croix* is a pathetic revelation which must have immensely increased the volume and quality of interest in Israel. Yet because (apparently) of their description of Bela Kun in *Quand Israel est Roi,* the Editor of the newspaper that had commissioned *Quand Israel n'est plus Roi* was given the brusque alternative of suppressing the later chapters or of losing the Jewish advertisements.[51]

The British officer, work as he might, felt himself surrounded, almost opposed, by an atmosphere always critical, frequently hostile, sometimes

"But notwithstanding this artificially-created antagonism on the spot between the local Arab leaders and the Jews of Palestine, the National Arab leadership, in their desire to foster the Arab national cause, were trying to enlist the help of the Jewish people by expressing their sympathy with the Zionist aims and willingness to collaborate with the Jews in the rebuilding of the Jewish National Home in Palestine."

"... Bitter enmity to Jewish national aspirations ... vigorous, unscrupulous propaganda against the Jews ...; unfortunately it found the sympathetic ear of the British authorities on the spot, who, for quite other reasons and considerations, were opposed to the Jewish aspirations."

From Political Report of the Zionist Organisation, quoted by J. M. Mackover, 1936.

Of these grave allegations some specific proof should be, but never has been, given. Is the world seriously asked to believe that the Palestine Arabs, so soon as they realized its implications, needed prompting and were not spontaneously opposed to political Zionism?

[50] Before leaving for England I had written: "The Christian Communities have no idea of allowing Jerusalem to lose any of its prestige as the centre of the Christian religions, and are far from sympathetic to my efforts to place the Jews in every way upon an equality with the others."

Our intentions were better appreciated by Jews with a knowledge of the Near East. The Special Committee of Egyptian Jews, Jack Mosseri, P. Pascal, Dr Waitz, A. Alexander, for Relief of Jews in Palestine, wrote to me on their return to Cairo: "to convey to you its deepest thanks and gratitude for the reception accorded to its delegates in Jerusalem, for the interest you showed in this work, and for the arrangements made for them. We are deeply sensible of the assistance you have given us, and we express the appreciation not merely of ourselves and our afflicted brethren in Jerusalem but of all Jewry. We should be happy to receive from you any suggestions as to the method and progress of our work."

One such word to any of us from official Zionism would have shown, at the least, a recognition of our difficulties.

[51] *Op. cit.* last chapter.

bitterly vindictive and even menacing. After the Easter riots of 1920 and the November riots of 1921 (before the mutual spheres of responsibility between Governorate and Police [52] had been properly defined), I had to endure such a tempest of vituperation in the Palestine and World Hebrew Press that I am still unable to understand how I did not emerge from it an anti-Semite for life. The clamour indeed subsided so soon as it was clear that the British Government had no intention of yielding to it, and I think Jewry has since drawn its own conclusions from the succeeding five years of undisturbed peace in Jerusalem. After the Jaffa riots of May 1921, and most of all after the outbreak in 1929, the abuse of executive officers became proportionately louder and fiercer,[53] sparing only the thrice-blessed technician—the geologist, the bacteriologist and the veterinary surgeon. The British officer responsible for the Wailing Wall in 1928 received 400 abusive letters, from Jews all over the world. In agonies such as these who would not sympathize, who would expect a philosophic calm? Yet when I revisited Palestine in 1931, and found the British Administration fully convinced that in any future crisis, while the Arabs might be their enemies, the Jews certainly would be, I could not help asking myself how far these wild, derisive indignations could be said to have furthered the cause of Zion. However this may be (for my book is not written to criticize but to record—sometimes to speak for those who cannot speak for themselves) the Jews still detest, while the Arabs regret, though they often abused, the Military Administration.[54]

Visiting America years later, I was struck by the thoroughness with which the caricature of the British officer had been disseminated. Several American Jews expressed surprise that I was "not the same" as they had read in their newspapers. In 1934 a Jewish wheat magnate of Chicago told me that he had been to his amazement and disgust sharply rebuked by a travelling Zionist leader for attributing a measure of Palestinian

[52] During the Easter period of 1920 the Jerusalem Police Force was, as stated in Ch. XIV, under the command of a junior Lieutenant.

[53] "The Jews once more had a feeling that it was inconceivable this could have taken place against the wishes of the British officials." *Thy Neighbour,* p. 176.

Even this remarkable statement is as milk-and-water to the heroic denunciations of the time. Yet all these, and later troubles had been foreseen during the War by Talaat Pasha, himself a Dönmé, or crypto-Jew, who stated, in the interview with Count Bernsdorf (quoted in his *Memoirs*): "I will gladly establish a National Home for the Jews, to please you, but, mark my words, the Arabs will destroy the Jews."

[54] Even in April 1936 the Palestine Officer of the Civil Government had the pleasure of reading that "The British Government in Palestine has great virtues, but sometimes one thinks of its unimaginative officialdom in terms of Bunyan's parable of the man who works, eyes cast down, with the muck-rake, and does not see that someone is standing by and offering him a crown." *Palestine,* vol. XI, no. 10, p. 2.

The respective rôles of Briton and Zionist are no less tactfully than appetizingly contrasted.

progress to the British Administration. Only this year I learnt that a Jewish lady who had left a British Dominion to settle in Tel Aviv was horrified by the stream of abuse poured there upon everything British. Such manifestations are what is called in Arabic *Kufr al-náamah*— "Denial of the Blessing", and certain it is that no blessing can attend them. Whatever our defects, I have yet to hear that the most virulent of these critics is able to suggest an acceptable alternative Mandatory. Still, these attacks had their uses. They taught one to keep one's temper. I find my only comment home on the general atmosphere was: "I do not want to end my career as a Ritual Sacrifice." They also drew British officers closer together. At the Armistice "Reunion Dinner" in 1921, when the speeches were over: "To my surprise I heard my name shouted aloud; and then a clapping, stamping and roaring which continued for two or three minutes. I recognized that this din was a definitely organized ovation of sympathy and protest against the attacks to which I have been subjected by the Jewish Press; and was so affected thereby that I could hardly reply." I believe my colleague Harry Luke was greeted with an even more significant demonstration at the St Andrew's Dinner in 1929. Yet we both had plenty of British critics.

What made some of us think that we might not be wholly and always in the wrong was the relative lack of success then enjoyed by the Zionist Commission with considerable sections of local Jewry. Modern working Zionism had its origin, certainly its mainspring, in Russian Jewry, for which Britain was to provide and America to furnish a National Home. If there was no Herzl but Herzl, yet Weizmann was the prophet of Herzl. The spirit of the living creed, predominantly Russian, was reflected in the personnel, particularly the permanent personnel of the Commission, and in the outlook of the Commission not only upon the Administration but upon all the Sephardim of the Near East, indeed upon all Jews other than the Ashkenazim from the Northern and Central East of Europe. In England we had known of the Sephardic or Spanish as the "Noble" Jew. In the new land of Israel he was if not despised at any rate ignored as a spineless Oriental. Yet it was this same Eastern background that would have rendered the Sephardim, had the Commission deigned to employ their services, ideal agents for dealing or negotiating with the Arabs, with whom they had maintained a close and friendly contact ever since the Expulsion from Spain in 1492.[55] Very soon I found that my old friendship with the Egyptian Sephardi families told, if at all, against me—and true it is that, partly from the delicacy of their

[55] (And from Portugal in 1497.) Sephardi Jews were established in Spain before the Roman Emperors: and had materially assisted the Arab conquest thereof.

position in a Moslem country, partly from lack of Zionist encouragement, Egyptian Jewry had proved lukewarm to the Cause. I found such as I was able to enlist invaluable.[56]

Early in 1918 Sir Victor Harari Pasha, a well known Jewish figure in Cairo, wrote to me suggesting that I should take his son, then serving in the Camel Corps, on my Staff. By a stroke of genius he enclosed an Italian War stamp, bearing a portrait of Dante with the legend

La domanda onesta
Si dee seguir con l'opera, tacendo.
"To fair request
Silent performance maketh best return."

On such an appeal I would have appointed a Crétin. Far from this, Ralph Harari was not only an excellent Finance Officer, but a complete success with Moslem and Christian alike; with all indeed save with an almost ostentatiously-ignoring Zionist Commission. When the Pasha came to visit his son I invited to meet him the leading Moslem dignitaries, and was struck by the immediate cordiality of their relations. They were of the same tradition; they spoke (in every sense) the same language. I am not attempting to praise Harari Pasha at the expense of any member of the Commission when I say that it was the difference between sending the Captain of the Oxford Cricket Eleven to negotiate with a Master of Hounds, and sending Einstein. For weeks after Harari left I was asked by the Mufti and the Mayor what chances there were of the *Basha* revisiting Jerusalem. With all deference to expert opinion, yet speaking as one ceaselessly striving to promote friendships between Arabs and Jews, I cannot but think that more use might and should have been made by the Zionists of the Sephardim.[57]

Some of the Russian leaders seemed rather to glory in having lost that practical and tactful knowledge of men, that imaginative understanding of opponents, which has borne a Disraeli or a Reading so high above the average of humanity. They were in Palestine of right;

[56] "Little more than a generation (after the expulsion) saw a Jewish community in Palestine some ten thousand in number, with the influence and leadership in the hands of the Sephardim." *Handbook of Palestine*, 3rd ed., p. 58.
The Sephardim were first in the field by centuries throughout the Near and Middle East. Dr Weizmann's address before the Basle Congress: unfortunately not of 1918 but of 1931: "One such channel of communication we already possess in our Sephardic communities, with the many ties of language and custom which they have with the Arab peoples among whom they have so long lived."
[57] "The Zionists are completely informed upon every aspect of the problem, save that of Palestine and the Palestinians. They do not know the languages, nor will they employ the Egyptian Jews who do know them: the consequence is that their frank intentions of policy alarm the present aborigines only less than their reassurances." (Letter to Mark Sykes, 1918.)

they were not going to cringe to Sudan-trained officers who treated them like natives (and yet it was as natives that they were returning) and they were inclined to mount "An eye like Mars, to threaten or command"; sometimes both. A Government measure might be Zionistic enough to evoke angry protests from the Arabs: by the other side it was taken as a matter of course. It was a cause of complaint how few of the British knew Hebrew, but when I asked why so few Zionists spoke Arabic the answer was: "We will, when they learn our language."

Dealing with some of these representatives was a sort of intellectual Jiu-Jitsu which I sometimes positively enjoyed, though there were moments when I took secret refuge in Dryden's inspired couplet:

> God's pampered people whom, debauch'd with ease,
> No king could govern and no God could please.

And I can never forget that for the School of Music, for concerts, for opera, as well as for our Exhibitions of painting and sculpture, I depended for existence upon the Jews. Even here, the painters and sculptors once threatened at the last moment to boycott a *Salon* because for some reason or other I was compelled to admit the public through the smaller external door instead of through the great gate of the Citadel.

Their *Kultur* was exclusively and arrogantly Russian. Your smatterings of early Latin and Greek, your little English or other classics that might survive twenty years' marooning out of Europe, were sounding brass and tinkling cymbals if you had not also Turgenieff, Gogol and above all Dostoevsky—of whom you were reminded that no translation conveyed the faintest reflection. Occasional brain-storms seemed to lift the curtain and disclose for a moment that deep-seated intellectual contempt of the Slav for the Briton which, surviving Czardom, continues to complicate Anglo-Russian relations. Lord Cromer once wrote that there was one sort of brain under a hat, quite another sort under a tarbush. In Jerusalem the thoughts that streamed from the Samovar had small resemblance to those that issued from the coffee-pot or the decanter: not worse, not better, but different—as revealed in their terrifying brilliance at chess, their passion for interminable argument. This impression was not merely Gentile or anti-Slav prejudice. In the summer of 1918 Levi Bianchini, the Sephardi Captain of an Italian Dreadnought (and an honour to any navy or nation) was attached to the Zionist Commission. He confided to me, with wistful humour, that in Tel Aviv he was never safe from an unannounced political visitor at three in the morning until he placed a Marine outside his house with orders to admit no one out of hours. He added (and I easily believed) that his action had been strongly resented.[58] A leading Dutch Sephardi once begged me to believe that "what you admire in them is Jewish, and the rest—from beyond!" Hebraists used to complain of the Yiddish and Slavonic "sufferings" of Hebrew pronunciation, causing it to jar in their ears, and sighed for "original" Sephardic. I dare say we were stupid in assuming that these tremendous Russians were like the European Jews we had hitherto known: perhaps they also might have realized sooner that we were not *Chinovniks:* and it took us time to learn one another—time and close association. Meanwhile we regretted that such British, Dutch or (with the exception of the able Dr Ruppin) German Jews as made their way on to the Commission seemed to count less there than their Russian colleagues, and that there was intense and open soreness at the appointment thereto of a distinguished British officer, Colonel Kisch—of whom it was murmured that he could not be a good Zionist because he played hockey.

There were other bewilderments for British officials mainly concerned with "straight" administration. To some of them it seemed that Jewish[59] political aims occupied too large a proportion of the time and the thoughts of the Administration—that the good administration of the country was no longer the primary end, but that the primary end was becoming a political end. These should logically have resigned, yet some of them were our ablest administrators. There was unease, and mutual criticism within our own ranks. To others the constant leakage of information by telephone and otherwise was disconcerting, though a few of us derived a simple pleasure from frustrating these knavish tricks. (I remember snatches of the constantly changing cipher employed between Sir Wyndham Deedes on Mount Scopus and myself by the Damascus Gate. The High Commissioner would be "Queen Elizabeth's husband", the Mufti, "Cantuar", the Latin Patriarch, "He who is above all criticism"; and we doubled in and out of French and Turkish, enriched by tropes and

[58] In August 1920 he was mistaken for a French officer and murdered in a train by Syrian Arabs, a cruel loss to the cause of Anglo-Jewish understanding which I recorded in an obituary letter to the *Palestine Weekly.* "His was the large humanity of a great and general culture. I remember him on more than one occasion, when individuals or classes had been giving what the company in which he found himself considered an unwarrantable degree of annoyance to the community, repeating with that air of noble and gentle excuse which so well became him, 'they are poor people, they are poor people'. I can imagine no anti-Semite, no Italophobe, no hater-on-principle of Classes or of Governments who knew him that will not relax something of the tensity of his feeling in a glow of friendliness whenever he remembers the help and the inspiration that were Levi Bianchini."

[59] Mr Leonard Stein on the other hand in his reasonable if necessarily one-sided *Zionism,* while admitting that "The duty of O.E.T.A. was simply to maintain the Status Quo", adds (on the same page) that "O.E.T.A. only half understood the Balfour Declaration". Presumably that unpopular and unrewarding half which it was nevertheless somebody's business to bear in mind.

metaphors from the cricket and the hunting field, in our endeavours to baffle the Shūlamīt of the Switchboard.)

If the Administration of Palestine was not altogether beer and skittles for the Gentile official, it must have seemed for some of his British Jewish colleagues little better than one long embarrassment.

On the departure of Major Orme Clark as Legal Adviser the post was filled by his junior, Norman Bentwich, who thus became Attorney-General to the Civil Government. I had known him at Cambridge and in Egypt, and cherished an admiring friendship for an Israelite who, with all his talents, was indeed without guile. Unfortunately Bentwich was not only the son of an original *Hovév Tsiyón* but the author of a book on Zionism which, though written before, appeared after his appointment. As Law Officer it was his duty to draft and to advise the Palestine Governments upon Laws, Proclamations and situations frequently of extreme interest to Jews and Arabs alike, and nothing on earth would convince the Arabs of the impartial purity of his conclusions. "It is not possible", they would answer, "the better Zionist he is, the worse Attorney-General." Some of his British colleagues were inclined to agree that his position was delicate, while he was severely criticized by Zionists for excessive moderation. It is not often that too great love of a country proves a bar from dedicating to it the maturity of one's experience and qualifications, but such was the pathetic fate of Bentwich. He refused more than one promotion (including the Chief Justiceship of Cyprus, where he would for good reasons have been welcomed by others besides myself) and finally, bowing to the general opinion, abandoned the Palestine Government (but never the Land of Israel) for the Hebrew University. There his first lecture as Professor in the Chair of International Peace was rendered impossible by the behaviour of young Jewish students, to quell which it was found necessary to call in British Police.

Albert Hyamson was a learned and agreeable North-London Orthodox Jew, author of one or two well-written books on Jewish subjects, a figure esteemed and respected not only by his colleagues, but by the Orthodox Jewry of Jerusalem. He had been a British Civil Servant in the General Post Office, and now found himself (via Jewish interests at the Paris Peace Conference) employed as head of the Immigration Department, applying the necessary but complicated regulations for the admission of Jews under the Mandate. These regulations (like those of the Customs for most people) it was for many a point of honour as well as a pleasure to defeat; and the families of temporary brothers and sisters, the relays of spinster wives and married fiancées all destined for the same husband, the arrivals on a three months' permit who never become departures, severely test the vigilance of the Controller. Hyamson accepted or rejected applications with the conscientiousness traditional in the British Civil Service, and in consequence soon became one of the most unpopular figures in pan-Zionism; which has created of him the brazen image of a Jack-in-office, sadistically thrusting back the persecuted immigrant for the sake of a misprint in his passport—an image that the scores of thousands of Jews admitted through his Department have not yet availed to demolish.

My observations on some of the difficulties of the Administrator, especially with East European Zionists, are written in no less good faith than is the rest of my book, yet I feel that I may not have allowed for the sensitiveness of two thousand years' ill-treatment. I have mentioned the admirable entertainment given by the 60th Division within two months of the taking of Jerusalem. To avoid all risk of offence, I had checked the programme myself. On the second evening a performer was taken ill at the last moment, and a surprise number substituted. He proved (without intentional offence) to be a caricature of the "ol' clo'" music-hall Jew, and I could have wished him anything (and anywhere) else in the world, especially when two or three Jews rose and walked out of the house. At the time I thought their sensibility was exaggerated, and I continued to think so until the autumn of 1995, when after a fortnight in a friendly and courteous Venice, I stayed a few days in Paris, and was taken to the *Théâtre de Dix Heures*. There, mingled with several witty and delightful recitations, I found myself listening consecutively to three scurrilous and ignoble attacks upon the motives and honour of England. In the misery of my impotent indignation I suddenly realized, and knew I could never forget, something of what these Jews had felt.

I have suggested that no monopoly of error can be ascribed to any one of the three interested parties of Palestine, and I have attempted to indicate one or two respects in which the British Government, as well as the Zionist Executive, might conceivably have been better advised.

People who consider themselves martyrs are not on that account necessarily saints. Some of the Arabs in their bewilderment and indignation more than repaid the injustices they felt they were suffering from British as well as Jews. It was not long before Arab Nationalism, despairing of other weapons, had recourse to fanaticism and reaction, notably after the death of the old Mufti, Kāmel al-Husseini; and the Government was (as happens sometimes in private life) most bitterly vilified by those who had best reason to be grateful. I have come upon my Minute on the report of the Chief Secretary's interview with a notorious agitator:

Interesting as showing in a very mild version the lines on which the Shaikh perorates when assured of no cold light of fact upon his invective. Every statement is either an *expressio* or a *suggestio falsi*. No Arab Nationalist is "dogged because of his Nationalism with spies" (? Secret Agents), who are reserved in Palestine, as in other countries under British rule (but in no independent Oriental country), for persons whose actions are likely to bring about a breach of the peace. The Government has dealt with particular leniency with the Shaikh himself, as he is well aware; and has, so far from attempting to work against the Supreme Moslem Council, refused to listen officially to much not unjustified criticism against a worthy if inexperienced body which it has itself created and consistently supported.

The British Administration, Military and Civil, had from the first extended to Arab Moslems a sympathetic encouragement they had never received from the Moslem Turks. The Northern façade of the Dome of the Rock was saved by no Arab initiative, but by British application for a British architect; and when funds were needed to extend the repairs to the Mosque of al-Aqsa (after Mecca and Medina the most sacred shrine in Islam) the leaders of Arab agitation were not only permitted, but encouraged and assisted by the generous liberalism of the High Commissioner to make collections throughout the Moslem world. (His honourable confidence was justified.) Under British rule every piastre of the Moslem religious endowments was now used exclusively for Moslem purposes in Palestine, instead of being largely diverted to Constantinople; and certain wealthy endowments, sequestered by the Turks eighty years before, were returned to the Waqf authority. Apart from other direct benefactions, there can be no doubt whatever that all the material and some of the intellectual amenities of life were multiplied by the stimulus of Jewish resources fostered under a British Administration. It might have been supposed that a Chamber of Commerce would be unobnoxious to religious sectarianism, even in Jerusalem; yet its inception was for a while suspended because Moslems, though constantly proclaiming their identity of interest with their Christian brethren, were holding out for larger representation.

This unhappy attitude was accentuated by a tendency frequently observable in peoples (and in persons) recently liberated from long and tyrannical oppression. Nothing, as the British found in Egypt of the 'eighties, could be more delightful than to succeed an Ottoman Turkish regime. For the first few weeks all is joy, hope and passionate gratitude. But it is not long before the late victims begin to discover that British prosperity is less immediate than they had hoped, and that meanwhile the irksome payment of taxes or compliance with new-fangled sanitary regulations can no longer be evaded by influence or bakshish. "By Allah!"

things were better under the Turks.[60] (Moses himself went through this on the frequent occasions when the whole congregation murmured against him.) They also discover that under the mild impersonal British rule lapses from manners (hitherto ruinous) pass unnoticed, anyhow unpunished: and some will soon venture upon presumptions and rudenesses they would never have attempted under their former masters. As is said in the Egyptian proverb: "They fear, but do not respect." The temptation grows to attitudinize their public, to brave dangers of floggings and hangings which they well know they will never be called upon to endure. Sir Eldon Gorst used to say that his prestige in Egypt would be immeasurably enhanced if only he could commit once a year one act of glaring illegality, the bazaars arguing: "If the Ruler must obey the Law like me, how is he my Superior?" The French Administration in Syria had frequent and double tastes of these impertinences, when Damascus cried: "Give us all the Zionists in the world, if only under British rule", while Jerusalem answered: "Give us even French exploitation, provided it be without Zionism."

In a word, what with the feasts, the fasts, and the anniversaries, the impassioned conferences and congresses with the resulting journalistic diatribes; what with the protests, the boycottings, the shuttings of shops, the stupid provocations and the disgusting retaliations, there were those among us who would cry, with Mercutio, "A plague on both your houses!" and would sigh for the appointment of some "crusted" African or West Indian Colonial Governor, who would "knock their heads together", or "give them something to cry for".

Here then were two parties each with a strong case to plead, yet, each being his own lawyer, having but too often (as the saying is) a fool for his client. The Arab patriot adjuring his hearers not to allow one foot of the sacred soil conquered by their forefathers to pass into the clutch of the obscene invader, might sometimes be himself a land-broker, only too anxious to sell his own and his friends' property to buyers of any land and of all nationalities. Zion could muster many able but some irritatingly disingenuous pens, arguing for instance that the French troubles in Syria proved that ours were not due to Zionism, and would have befallen us under any dispensation.[61]

---

[60] Their extremists now overreach or stultify themselves when, for instance, the Mufti declares to the Royal Commission: "Under the Ottoman Constitution the Arabs enjoyed all rights and privileges, political and otherwise, on an equal basis with the Turks"!

[61] Zionism had at least united (for the first time in history) Arab Moslems and Christians, who now opposed a single front to the Mandatory. During a crisis between the Moslems and Christians of Syria this dialogue appeared in the Damascus newspaper *al-Maarad*:

Christ. "What is the way, O Muhammad, to set our two nations, Syria and Lebanon, in unison?"

The earliest recognition I received in Europe of the realities of the British officer's position in Palestine was from the lips of Mr Lloyd George. I had first met him during the Peace Conference, and he was good enough to invite me to breakfast with him alone at 10 Downing Street. Greeting me sternly, he remarked that complaints of me were reaching him from Jews and Arabs alike. I answered that this was all too probable, imagining for a moment from his tone that he was leading up to my resignation. "Well", he said as we sat down, "if either one side stops complaining, you'll be dismissed." A principle which should hearten All Ranks in the Palestine Service for some decades to come.

IV

Car l'impossible, voilà notre tache. NIETZSCHE

Such then were the phases of the situation and the sentiments of those therewith concerned during the eight years from 1918 to 1925.

After the crowded quinquennium of Sir Herbert Samuel, something of a halt was called in construction. For three years Lord Plumer sat on Mount Scopus. Under the shadow of that great name Palestine knew so perfect a peace that the Government denuded it of all its defences— as the succeeding competent but unfortunate Administration found to their cost in the ghastly summer of 1929. The bitterness surviving that tragedy was still evident in 1931, when I observed an almost complete social cleavage between the British and the Jewish communities. Since then Palestine had gone so rapidly ahead, in wealth as well as in population, that I felt justified in the spring of 1936, despite one or two anxious letters from Arabs and Jews, in writing: "The present High Commissioner has succeeded in winning the confidence of the Jews to a degree unattained by any of his predecessors, and has had the good fortune (and the courage) to have his term extended for a further period of five years. He has under him, permanently stationed, a repressive force such as no other High Commissioner has wielded, so that, whatever other problems may assail him, he is at least free from that haunting obsession —the breakdown of Public Security...." Prophecy is indeed the most gratuitous of human errors.

If this chapter has contained more of British lack of policy and of the difficulties of practical Zionism than of Arab errors and crimes (the word

---

Muhammad. "Ask Moses to send them a party of his men."

It is true that since France assumed the Syrian Mandate in 1920 six High Commissioners have failed to bring peace to Syria, or to prevent the thirteen national revolutions that have taken place.

cannot be avoided), the reason is in part that Zion and England stand responsible as creators of the situation.[62] As wielders of all the resources of modern civilization, it was for them to set a pace which native Palestine could follow. As springing from the New Testament as well as from the Old, and from the gracious humanism of the ancient world, it was theirs to call a tune with which the rhythms of simpler peoples might without violence be moulded into counter-point. The cumulative result of their combined failure in London and in Palestine was an explosion of feeling so momentous that the greatest Power in the world, after near twenty years' experiment and experience, required, in full peace time, an Army Corps and all the panoply of war to control the "liberated" civil population; and the Arabs are able to boast that in calling off a guerrilla warfare maintained for six months, they yielded neither to British arms nor to the economic necessity of salving their orange crop, but to the advice of an Arab Dreikaiserbund, and have thus established an institution and a precedent no less unpalatable to Britain than to Zion.

I suppose it was the mutual reaction of accelerated Jewish immigration and a period of exhilarating prosperity and intensive construction which seemed to justify the argument that, if with 1000 immigrants prosperity appears to increase 100 per cent., then with 10,000 it will increase 1000 per cent., with 100,000, 10,000 per cent.; that if there is at a given moment economic absorptive capacity for greatly increased immigration, the increase should forthwith be authorized; and that as the Arabs complain anyhow, a few score extra thousands make no particular difference. At all events the curve of authorized entry, and with it of unauthorized, grew spectacularly steeper after 1932: the authorized reaching 31,000 and 42,000 for the next two years, and culminating in the record figure of 61,849 for 1935, to say nothing of the ten thousand clandestine but undeniable additions. At this point it was apparently felt that something must be done to placate the "non-Jewish" population;[63] and the establishment of the Legislative Council (promised in the White Paper of 1930) on a basis of numerically proportionate representation was put forward by the High Commissioner in Council; approved by the Secretary of State for the Colonies; announced by the High Commissioner in December 1935; and published to the world. The proposal was welcomed

---

[62] "We insisted upon having the mandate for Palestine assigned to us. We also virtually dictated the terms upon which the Council of the League endorsed the action of the Principal Allied Powers, and made itself responsible for supervising our mandatory administration." *Economist*, March 1936.

[63] This thesis does not commend itself to Lord Melchett. *Thy Neighbour, vide* pp. 226, 227.

by the Arabs as a whole, especially by the more intelligent who stand to gain by an increase of civilization, though a few hesitated lest its acceptance should involve or imply their acceptance of the Mandate. It was immediately boycotted by the Jews. Dr Weizmann hurried back from Palestine, just in time for the Commons Debate. "The heavy brigades of Press, platform and Parliament", I wrote, "are being wheeled into action against the proposal for a Legislative Council, though this is implicit in the Mandate and explicitly promised to the people as well as to the League of Nations, besides being recommended by a High Commissioner whom the Jews have good cause to trust. There is much to be said against the establishment of representative legislatures in unsuitable Mediterranean countries, as successive High Commissioners and Governors of Cyprus and Malta have found to their cost. But this is not the chief or original objection of the Zionists, who attack the project because the Jews are to be allotted seats in proportion to their actual population; going so far as to postulate that there should be no sort of constitution until Jews are in parity or a majority and so able to safeguard the key provisions of the Mandate—and this though all reference to the National Home, Immigration and kindred subjects is already ruled rigorously out of order in the debates of the Council. Yet if ever a people seem to deserve at least the opportunity of official public utterance, it is the Arabs of Palestine. The National Government has, happily for its own good name, resisted this last clamour, whose only effect has been to convince the Arabs, hitherto hesitant for fear of appearing to accept the Mandate, that there must be something to their advantage in a project so bitterly denounced by the Jews. (In March 1923, when the Legislative Council was first proposed and was boycotted by the Arabs, the Jewish Press was indignant at the 'weakness' of the Government and asked: 'Now that elections have been ordered by an Order-in-Council and it was proclaimed that anyone interfering with the elections would be prosecuted, why was this not carried out? Why was not the poisonous agitation stopped?')"

In the subsequent debate in both Houses, the Arab case may be said, without exaggeration, to have gone by default. A Zionist listener in the Gallery of the Commons might have been edified by hearing speech after speech showing intimate knowledge even of the details of the Zionist side, and dismissing, as semi-comic, the *"donums, feddans—* acres or whatever they call them" of the Arabs. One voice interjected: "Are there not Arab capitalists?" Mr Winston Churchill, Public Orator of the British Empire, adroitly shifting his ground to the German treatment of Jews, shouted aloud, "Vile tyranny!" and shook his fist at the ceiling. Not a soul could disagree with him; yet the Germans admitted among the record entry of 61,849 amounted to less than 16 per cent. Mr J. H. Thomas took shelter behind his Geneva obligations and, although the Government escaped defeat by its own supporters, the world knew that the Palestine Legislative Council was adjourned *sine die* before it had ever been opened. No doubt all these speakers were logically right, and perhaps Parliament should have been spontaneously consulted before the taking of so momentous a decision; yet the immediate adoption of the Council might have proved cheaper, and could not have proved dearer, in treasure, prestige and blood—British as well as Jewish and Arab—than its rejection. On the principle of "no hope can have no fear" the Arabs, now desperate, embarked upon a "peaceful strike" which inevitably degenerated into the situation in which Great Britain found herself contemplated by the ironic amusement of the Nations. Moderate Arab leaders, unencouraged by any prospect of association with the Government of their country, and so with no motive for assisting it, were reluctantly compelled to stand in with extremists. Arab violence, resulting largely from the manner of the Commons' and still more of the Lords' rejection of the Legislative Council, was now claimed by the Zionists as the immediate justification thereof. Arms for the insurgents, as well as money, poured in from neighbouring countries, perhaps also from a more distant Power. It was, therefore, still possible though highly disingenuous to argue that the insurrection was not spontaneous, but engineered from abroad. The appointment of a Royal Commission [64] failed to stop what was becoming a small war; though it succeeded in alarming the Zionists, who feared that its recommendations could tend, however slightly, in but one direction.[65] Both they and other thinking people revolted at the suggestion of yielding to violence—a Danegeld to which especially in the East there is no limit; some seeming to forget that this general violence had followed, and was in great part the result of, five peaceful and unsuccessful delegations to Whitehall and six special but often unimplemented Commissions to Palestine. It cannot be questioned that violence on this occasion succeeded to the extent of bringing about the appointment of the Royal Commission and in the increased interest and numbers of the "Arab" committee in the House of Commons. All parties in England were agreed that violence must unquestionably and unconditionally cease or be made to cease: and that the Royal Com-

[64] Advocated by *The Times* in a leading article entitled *Political Zionism* on 11 April 1922.

[65] *Palestine* ingenuously supported Lord Lytton's previous proposal for a Royal Commission to examine (and so modify or prevent) the Legislative Council, as being "intelligible". "But . . . a Commission of this kind . . . alarming. . . ."

mission should then lose no time in proceeding to Palestine. Whatever its conclusions, or whatever the degree of their acceptance by the Government and the Legislature may be, there are meanwhile certain considerations bearing upon both sides of the problem which, judging by recent declarations, appear even now to be but imperfectly appreciated. The Arabs base their opposition to the terms of the Mandate upon the following arguments:

(*a*) It is contrary to their natural right to their country.
(*b*) It is contrary to British and Allied pledges given to the Arabs.
(*c*) It violates the general principles of the "Mandate" as set forth in Article 22 of the Covenant of the League.
(*d*) It is self-contradictory.
(*e*) It menaces and endangers their existence, present and future, and stands as an unsurmountable obstacle in the path of their national aspirations and political goal.

They will be well advised to cut out (*a*) and (*b*), and to concentrate upon the remainder, of which the Royal Commission is empowered to examine the force. With regard to (*b*), Palestine was excluded from the promises made to Arabs before those British operations which gave freedom to so large a proportion of the Arab peoples. The claim, though still credited by many, has been so often disproved that it is no longer a bargaining asset. As for (*a*), I cannot do better than quote the sober words of Lord Milner: "If the Arabs go to the length of claiming Palestine as one of their countries in the same sense as Mesopotamia or Arabia proper is an Arab country, then I think they are flying in the face of facts, of all history, of all traditions, and of associations of the most important character—I had almost said, the most sacred character. Palestine can never be regarded as a country on the same footing as the other Arab countries. You cannot ignore all history and tradition in the matter. You cannot ignore the fact that this is the cradle of two of the great religions of the world. It is a sacred land to the Arabs, but it is also a sacred land to the Jew and to the Christian." The sooner, therefore, that they abandon these two theses, and concentrate upon possibly remediable grievances, the sooner are they likely to obtain a measure of satisfaction. Whatever measure they do obtain they should strive by peaceful and lawful endeavour to maintain or even to improve, remembering that any subsequent resort to violence could not fail to lose them the degree of sympathy they have recently acquired, and so to be more sharply and severely repressed. They must learn, above all, that it is precisely persons sufficiently balanced and humane to realize that there is an Arab side to Zionism who will be most profoundly revolted and alienated by such specimens of Arabian chivalry as the shooting of a Jewish scholar at his desk, of a hospital nurse on the steps of her hospital and the bombing of a baby's perambulator. The Turkish proverb *"Baluq bashdan koḳar"* —"The fish goes rotten from the head"—applies here; and "Leaders" who not only fail to prevent but refuse to denounce this filthiness forfeit all claim to honourable consideration, and might well be made to answer personally for the crimes their attitude has undoubtedly encouraged. Their behaviour and that of their followers loses yet further when contrasted with that of the Jews, whose austere self-discipline under such outrages and the destruction for many of their life-work has won them the admiration of the civilized world. If the Arabs are reasonably successful in removing the "menace to their existence, present and future" cited in (*e*), they might find themselves in a stronger position by accepting the Mandate—perhaps under some further solemn instrument, ratified by the Mandatory and the League, and possibly endorsed by any Powers specially interested. Their acceptance would pave the way to extensions of administrative and legislative autonomy which I shall indicate later, but which could not be contemplated so long as they stood out. The policy I have advocated requires a facing of facts which, as often in life, entails certain undeniable but in my opinion inevitable renunciations, only tolerable upon the receipt of immediate and tangible advantage.

Zionism provides a close parallel to Arab argument (*b*) in the "Agreement" of 3 January 1919 between the Amir Faisal and Dr Weizmann, frequently claimed as "the specific acceptance of the National Home Policy". As the recognized champion of the Arab cause, Faisal was within his rights in excluding [66] from his claims a section of the Arab world for the supposed benefit of the whole; but by so doing he debarred himself from further dealing with that section. Similarly the note by Faisal translated for Dr. Weizmann by Lawrence and reproduced in *The Times* of 10 June 1936 is of interest as evidence of co-operation between two outstanding personalities, and as a holograph specimen of Lawrence's forceful handwriting; but since neither Faisal nor Lawrence was empowered or any longer competent to represent the Arabs of Palestine, it is not relevant. [67]

Zionists high and low in the Press and on the platform still appear bewildered at the continual opposition and "obstinacy" of the Arabs.

[66] "On account of its universal character I shall leave Palestine on one side for the mutual consideration of all parties interested; with this exception, I ask for the independence of the Arabic areas enumerated in the Memorandum."

[67] Yet, late in 1936: "there can be no evasion of the plain terms of the agreement entered into on 3 January 1919 between the Amir Faisal on behalf of the Arab Kingdom of the Hejaz and Dr Weizmann...." *Thy Neighbour,*

"Arab birth-rates have gone up: Arab death and infant mortality rates
have gone down. Out of the quarter of a million Public Health Vote
nine-tenths is devoted to Arabs. The Arab standard of life has risen
beyond all expectation. Arabs are making money....": Yet still...!
Arab objections "therefore cannot be economic: they must be 'political'."
Zionists will not yet admit to themselves, certainly not to the world, that
the Palestine Arab [68] has for hundreds of years considered Palestine, a
country no larger than Wales, as his home; and that he does not consider that there is, within those limits, room for another home, to be
stocked "as of right" from a reserve of sixteen million people. From the
Jewish point of view Zionism, involving many sacrifices, is an idealistic
movement. For the inhabitants of Palestine it is entirely materialistic,
nationalistic, acquisitive, and non-religious. The injunction, oft repeated,
to Arabs "to work with Jews to develop their common country" is a
mere irritation, for it is only their common country by virtue of a bond
which those most affected there have not yet accepted. The Zionist slogan
so reasonable-sounding in England, "neither to dominate nor to be
dominated", has, if it means anything like numerical equality [69]—and
what else can it mean?—a frosty sound in the ears of a poorer, backward
occupant. And when a British journalist of repute writes [70] (in a widely
reproduced article): "Politically I believe it would be wise to build the
National Home as rapidly as possible, even by shock tactics. So long
as the Jewish minority grows slowly, year by year, the Arabs will fight
against destiny. But when instead of the present 28 per cent., the Jewish
population amounts to a clear 50 or 40 per cent., they will bow to accomplished facts. When the Jews are strong enough to defend themselves,
there will be no more talk about driving them into the sea. The German
problem strengthens this argument for haste"—is he not inviting the
Arabs to take a leaf out of his own book? The plain truth which,
twenty years after the Balfour Declaration, must really now be faced is,
that the Arabs of Palestine rejected it from the first and will never
accept it now unless something is done to assure them their economic,

---

[68] The position was ably stated in the above-quoted leading article in *The Times* on 11
April 1922.

[69] "... political majority of the Jews. There is nothing in the Mandate to prevent this....
But we have claimed political parity as a right—let us give it as a right to the Arabs."
Thy Neighbour, p. 251.

"We say to the Arabs, taking full responsibility for our words; today we are in a
minority; tomorrow we may be the majority; today you are the majority, tomorrow you
may be a minority. Whatever may happen in Palestine, we do not want to dominate or be
dominated. We want to be there as equals. We have the greatest respect for your language,
your religion, your holy places. But we, on the other hand, ask you to respect our religion,
language, our labour, and our lives!" Dr Weizmann in an address at Antwerp. *The New
Judaea*, October 1936, p. 5.

[70] H. N. Brailsford in *The Baltimore Sun*.

territorial and national survival. In this they are only ranging themselves with other and far larger countries or nations, including those of the British Empire, which have long since ceased to tolerate foreign large-scale immigration, particularly from eastern Europe. To evoke or account for such universal sentiments neither *"Effendis"* [71] nor "foreign gold" are necessary: though it is not unnatural that Arab leaders should lead, nor that they should clutch at support from whatever quarter. With the dropping of the bogey of the politically as well as economically exploiting *Effendi,* propaganda might be simultaneously lightened by that of the sinister British official, whether hampering the zeal of the High Commissioner in Palestine or in the Colonial Office breathing evil counsels into the ear of the well-disposed but all too dependent Secretary of State.[72] Entrants into the Palestine arena might well bear in mind the placard said to be displayed in Japanese restaurants: "Visitors bring their own manners." Is it not conceivable that officers on the spot, grappling year after year with the difficulties of reconciling both sides of the Mandate, may have as just an appreciation thereof as persons, often in another continent or hemisphere, concerned solely with the advancement of their own cause? [73]

There can be no question of surrendering the Mandate; of stopping immigration; or of continuing it on the recent intensive scale. What the basis of the scale should be, the Royal Commission may possibly indicate. But it can hardly attain for many years the hitherto accepted principle of 100 per cent. entry according to the economic absorptive capacity [74] of Palestine at the moment of authorization. To absorb is not always to digest. There are reasons other than "political" for reduction. Last spring the question of a subsidy to orange-growers was being raised by sections of the citrus industry, which already finds it difficult to market nine and a half million boxes, and trembles at the thought of placing the twenty to twenty-five million boxes anticipated in ten years time. And in general, the aftermath of a construction period, however

---

[71] "Nevertheless the Palestinian Jews ... recognize that the peasant Arabs have been made the tool of Sectional and partizan interests." *Thy Neighbour,* pp. 248-9.

[72] Even in 1937 the legend is kept alive (before the Royal Commission) by Colonel Wedgwood: "The permanent officials regarded Palestine as their enemy", he said. "They had in Palestine an Administration of 'crypto-Fascist officials', whose objections to Parliament had taken the place of objections to the Jews. There is no change except by a complete reform of the Administration in Palestine."

[73] Already in 1922 Philip Graves, Special Correspondent for *The Times,* records the Zionist practice of "ascribing their difficulties to the perversity of the Arabs, the intrigues of the Catholics", above all to the "lack of sympathy" or "hostility" of British officials.

[74] "The economic absorptive capacity of the country" was a partially irrelevant and thoroughly misleading phrase. *Survey of British Commonwealth Affairs,* 1918-36.

brilliant, is a serious problem for the constructing trades and professions.[75] The impartial arbitrator could hardly fail to be interested by Dr Weizmann's estimate [76] that Palestine could within the next fifty years support between fifty and sixty thousand more Jewish families, with an additional 100,000 agricultural Arabs, on the water supply now existing or soon procurable: and considerably more of both if that supply could be increased. It seems further possible that a Legislative Council on something near the lines of that which was frozen out in 1936, might be reintroduced; and that the Zionists and associated forces would not repeat their mistake by opposing it again. As Mr. Amery has written: "To go on refusing representative Government as long as the Jews are in a minority is an almost impossible policy."

The extreme and logical anti-Zionists (or pro-Arabs—they cannot be differentiated, though some would like to have it both ways) are for what they call a "clean sweep", meaning the abolition of the Mandate; apparently imagining that Palestine would nevertheless remain under British control, at all events proposing no alternative solution. Their opinions would command more respect if they organized themselves into some constituted public body prepared to devote time, brains and cash to the cause of an Arab as the Zionist to a Jewish Palestine. Even so, they would shake not the Mandate but the Mandatory, Great Britain, whose place more than one Great Power would be only too happy (though certainly not more competent) to occupy. The Mandate, as I have said, cannot be shaken, for it is the united voice of fifty-two peoples speaking through the League of Nations, which for all its defects is the nearest approach to a world conscience hitherto evolved by humanity. No man, as Aristotle has written, deliberates about that which cannot be otherwise. The Mandate stands; but if the facts I have endeavoured to record have any significance, they may point to the possibility, without heroic measures (which no one has yet been able to suggest), of easing its application.

A solution that has been discussed, and of which the logical reasons and advantages have of late been ingeniously elaborated, is that of Cantonization, Partition or Division, whereby the Jews in the Maritime Plains and the Arabs in the Hill Country would form two more or less

[75] As the Government of Northern Rhodesia found to their cost with hundreds of stranded and unemployable artisans on their hands when the price of copper fell.

[76] Address delivered to the Royal Central Asian Society, 26 May 1936. The above figures are not recorded in the official summary of the proceedings. The census of 1931 estimated that if present trends were continued, the population of Palestine would double itself in twenty years, the Moslem population in twenty-five years and the Jewish population in nine years. The Jewish population in 1931 was 17 per cent. of the total population of Palestine: in 1935 27 per cent.

self-governing communities or cantons, with certain matters reserved, and a general supervision exercised by a High Commissioner in a neutralized and directly administered Jerusalem. The theory, though apparently unassailable when taken point by point, seems unlikely of adoption; as contravening the spirit of the Mandate, as tending to erect two potentially hostile camps within a very small area and—perhaps the strongest objection—as being wholly unacceptable to the feelings and aspirations of the parties concerned. Nevertheless, cantonization shines through the fog of mutual criticism and abuse as an attempt to deal constructively with a rarely difficult problem: and economic or territorial, as apart from political or administrative cantonization may yet have to be considered. I can pretend to no such drastic remedy. Indeed, some of the following observations with the inferences therefrom may be criticized as unimportant or inessential—as very small beer. If so, I would remind these critics of their constant employment of the useful term *iponderabilia*. The smaller and the more obvious, the easier considered; as was proved by Naaman, the Captain of the Host.

One would have supposed for instance that some at least of the Jewish youth of both sexes would be given so intensive a knowledge of the sister language, Arabic, that they might not only converse with Arabs as friends and read the Arab Press of their own and neighbouring countries, but also make some local contribution to the mediaeval and modern history of Palestine (the only period interesting to Arabs), or to comparative Semitics. I remember taking the Chair for a great Jewish orientalist when he lectured on Arabic Literature. The room was crowded with Arab extremists hushed in reverent admiration; and for one hour at least there were three score anti-Zionists the less in Jerusalem. Again, I thought a God-intended opportunity was missed over the Kadoorie Bequest. Kadoorie was a rich Shanghai Jew who left some £100,000 to the cause of Education in Palestine. The Government proposed that there should be a college on public-school lines for both races, with separate provision for each religion and language. The Arabs made no demur, but the Jews were utterly uncompromising for two separate institutions; and they had their way, excluding even the alternative of a joint School of Agriculture, since they insisted on Hebrew as the language of instruction throughout. The Arabs raised no objection to either proposal, even if English were to be used. The Jews refused partly on the ground that they had not waited two thousand years to become standard public-school types. That objection might have been met (though there are worse Englishmen, and Jews, than our Jews from the public schools), and the college modified accordingly; but when some of us reflected upon the generous sympathies and friendships so easy to form at school, so difficult in after-life, we wondered whether the risk of a little British conventionality might not have been worth taking. It is no object of the Mandatory, and far from the spirit of the Mandate, to turn Palestinians of any creed (even if it were possible) into Britons, though all enjoy the coveted privilege of a British passport.

A public service would be rendered to Palestine if one or two well-known Jewish—particularly British Jewish—families of independent means, with no decoration to gain or promotion to miss, would build houses in the neighbourhood of Jerusalem and reside there for some months in the year. Society under Mandated or Crown Colony Government is apt to degenerate into a cross between a Garrison Town and a Cathedral City, and to be overwhelmed by the official element. I know something of the difficulty of entertaining mixed assemblies in Jerusalem, and though I did my best with the means I had, I was conscious that it might have been better done on ground unconnected with politics or administration.

Zionists have repeatedly declared that they do not desire to build up the National Home to the detriment of the Arabs of Palestine. It is therefore all the more unfortunate that the Arabs should have seen almost every step taken by His Majesty's Government to reassure them, vehemently and sometimes successfully assailed. In 1929 an impartial expert in Land Settlement [77] was appointed from the League of Nations in order to ascertain the area available for agriculture and immigration. His report submitted in 1931 let loose a tempest of Zionist indignation, effective, it must be allowed, in that the Government, though apparently accepting his recommendations, has wholly failed to carry them out. The statement of Government policy (based on the above Report and that of the Shaw Commission) embodied in the White Paper of 1930, which served to allay certain Arab apprehensions, was howled down all over the Jewish world. It may have been unfortunately worded. At all events the British Government disavowed its own Department and recanted; with a re-explanation from the Prime Minister. A triumph indeed for Dr Weizmann (and not his first in Downing Street) but, in its result of confirming the worst fears of the Arabs, a Pyrrhic victory. Again, a proposal based on Lord Kitchener's Five Feddan Law in Egypt, to protect the small holder, enjoys a significantly poor Hebrew Press. Even if this law were less of a protection to the *Fellah* than the Administration an-

---

[77] Of such eminence that after a similar mission to Greece he was subsequently sent by the League for the same purpose to China.

ticipates, criticism of its ineffectiveness would have come more convincingly from the Arab side.

The Arabs, though handicapped in many respects, have certain undeniable compensations. They are, the Jews have to become, acclimatized. They still hold a large proportion of the land which, if they will but take advantage of the training available, should provide for their natural and probable increase of population. They must remember that for available world acreage 1936 is, in their own phrase, *Akhr al-Zaman*—"the end of time"; that the day is past for picturesque feudalism, and that if they do not make the best of their own soil, others will. They should look to it—a Legislative Council would help them in this also—that every possible piastre of the Waqf income is spent upon a vocational education based on the best advice they can procure, and they should demand something more than a published accounting audit to make sure their wishes are obeyed. They should endeavour—but this is asking a hard thing—to leave their foolish Husseini-Nashāshībi feuds to join the Montagus and Capulets and the Middle Ages. The Mandate once accepted, there should be no further objection to the scheme wherewith I wearied the Colonial Office from Cyprus and in London for six long years; to wit the higher promotion within the territory,[78] or the transfer to service in other Mandated Territories or suitable Crown Colonies, of exceptionally qualified local public servants, both Arab and Jew. I shall recur to this topic, only remarking now that I know more than one Palestinian who could have served elsewhere with distinction as well as with stimulus and encouragement to the Palestine Service. Some years ago I was asked by a High Commissioner designate whether I had any recommendation to propose. I suggested the nomination of two Arabs and a Jew to the Executive Council. The system worked excellently in Cyprus, with two Greeks and one Turk, who rendered valuable advice, whose sense of responsibility was greatly increased, and who to the best of my knowledge never proved unworthy of the confidence reposed in them. Both of these developments would diminish the temptation of the local authority to support, for the sake of peace and a quiet life, the extremist rather than the potential co-operator in the work of the Government. Such distinguished Palestinians should be personally and worthily received in London by the Secretary of State.

Any finding of the Royal Commission—from the establishment of a Jewish State to the repudiation of the Balfour Declaration—must entail

---

[78] With the object finally of assuring both Maréchal Lyautey's ideal of *"non pas un pouvoir de façade, mais une part effective dans l'Administration et une véritable autorité pour la garantie de leurs coutumes et de leurs libertés"*.

a double disillusion; [79] for the unquestionable maintenance of the Mandate would be the end of any national hope still cherished by the Palestinian Arabs, while the Jews could hardly fail to be mortified by any retarding of Immigration, as well as apprehensive of the effect of any Legislative Council. What is of paramount importance for the future of Palestine is that such recommendations of the Commission as may be adopted by the British Government and approved by the League of Nations should be fully, immediately, and lastingly implemented and, above all, subject to no further exposition or apology. Neither the Jews nor the Arabs conquered Palestine from the Turks, but the British— as may be tragically proved by a visit to any of the great War Cemeteries there. British arms must continue to hold the ring against all local or foreign menace. The "need to rule", so often urged upon the Palestine authorities, exists elsewhere than on the Palestine front. Already in June 1921 I wrote:

> "The King's birthday passed without untoward event save that the High Commissioner's statement created alarm and despondency throughout Zionist camps, and gave, because of its indefiniteness, coldish comfort to the Arabs, who have received far too many reassurances, but expect nothing less than definite Goods of some sort or other."

How many statements have been issued since then, and what have they profited? Such topics can be treated more naturally and less controversially in an Annual Report, prepared like those of Lord Cromer (which used to be an event in London and in Europe as well as in Egypt), and not on the stereotyped Crown Colony model, further neutralized to conform with the *questionnaires* of Geneva. It is by a firm and undeviating practice (the word policy is somewhat blown upon in the promised, half-promised, twice-promised Land), rather than by explanation and counter-explanation, assurance and reassurance, or White Papers however "satisfactorily" drafted, that the Mandatory will maintain confidence—unshaken, unseduced, unterrified. Zionists might also refrain from giving the impression that they are only prepared to sup-

---

[79] The statesmanlike decision of the Secretary of State not to suspend but to limit immigration pending results from the Royal Commission was thus reported in *Palestine*, 11 November 1936: "The Colonial Secretary's statement in the House of Commons concerning the limitation of immigration has made a bad impression on the Arabs. The Arabs hoped and perhaps believed that immigration would be entirely suspended during the sittings of the Royal Commission. This was reported to the leaders in Jerusalem by Mr Emile Ghory, the representative of the Arab Higher Committee in London. The decision not to suspend Jewish immigration, but to grant a labour schedule, however small, has created profound disappointment among the Arab leaders.

"The Executive of the Jewish Agency has issued a statement: 'The Executive of the Jewish Agency cannot but express its regret at the extreme smallness of the present schedule, which it considers inadequate to satisfy even the most urgent requirements of economic development.'"

port the British Representative so long as he conforms exactly with their desires. On the other hand, there is both in official Palestine and at home an unfair tendency to put all the blame upon the Jews for the policy, incidents and situations which have complicated the progress of Mandated Palestine. Though individual Zionists have sometimes shown themselves more provocative to Arabs than appreciative of British endeavour, Zionism is right to put a plenary construction on the Mandate; and it is the British themselves who are exclusively responsible for any original defects of policy, and who have more than once had only themselves to thank for the results of ill-considered yieldings to the various and powerful influences of the Zionist Organization.[80] Whenever, after full consideration, His Majesty's Government has held firm, no party has ultimately been the loser. When for instance the first issue of Palestine stamps was being designed, strong pressure was exerted upon the authorities to render Palestine, in the Hebrew title, by *Eretz Yisroel*, the Land of Israel, the ancient and traditional Jewish name. Jews have never called the country Palestine, which was indeed a Roman name etymologically akin to Philistia. Individual officers might sympathize with this insistence, but the Government was undoubtedly right in resisting a nomenclature intolerable to the vast majority of Palestinians, and in substituting the device, relatively inoffensive to all parties (though giving complete satisfaction to none), of adding to "Palestine" in Hebrew the two Hebrew initials (E.Y.).

We cannot look ahead more than a certain distance; as the Emperor William I answered Benedetti at Ems, no man can guarantee anything *à tout jamais*. It may be that the Arabs, spurred by honourable rivalry, will attain a privileged position and a degree of civilization inconceivable within Zionism.[81] The National Home is beyond question unshakably established. Already its numbers exceed that of the Cypriot nation.[82] If (as many hold for their only belief), religion is dying, or if, with the

[80] "If the British Government appears to show a tendency to wander from the straight path which leads to the establishment of the National Home, or if it seems to be loitering along this path, the Zionist Organization brings into action its extensive resources of propaganda." *Survey of British Commonwealth Affairs*, 1918-36, p. 459.

[81] "Hospitable to various ethnic types and cultures, Palestine has always been a Land of tribes and sects, and very seldom, if ever, the country of one nation and one religion and under one king." Sir G. Adam Smith, *Legacy of Israel*, p. 3.

[82] "There exists in Palestine to-day, as the result of fifty years of Zionist enterprise, a Jewish National Home containing some three hundred and fifty thousand souls, which fulfils the purpose of a spiritual centre for Jewry. It is now possible for a Jew to be born in Palestine and pass through an all-Jewish kindergarten, school and University without ever speaking anything but Hebrew; to work on a Jewish farm or in a Jewish factory, to live in an all-Jewish city of 150,000 inhabitants, to read a Hebrew daily newspaper, to visit a Hebrew theatre and to go for a holiday cruise on a steamer flying the Jewish flag. So far the Zionist aim may be said to be accomplished." Nevill Barbour, *A Plan for lasting Peace in Palestine* (Jerusalem, 1936), p. 15.

same result, some passionless Nordic creed should reduce Holy Places to mere Ancient Monuments, then Palestine would be an easier place to govern. Three great faiths and a dozen denominations would look back with incredulous pride to the battles each fought to maintain its ideal. That time, if ever it come, is many generations distant. But even if Mecca went, and Medina, Jerusalem will bear it out unto the crack of doom; and reasonable tolerance in the visiting and use of the Holy Places—the Dome, the Sepulchre and the Wall—will proceed not from agnostic indifference, but from sympathetic understanding no longer qualified by the fear that concession will merely invite encroachment.

Zionism is admittedly a departure from ordinary colonizing processes; an act of faith. To this extent, therefore, "impartiality" is condemned by Zionists as anti-Zionistic: he that is not for me is against me—a Mr Facing-both-ways, like a neutral in the War. Their attitude may be justified as anyhow constructive: you cannot make omelettes without breaking eggs: "to do a great right, do a little wrong." Will anyone assert that Palestinian Arabs can hope to have the predominance they expected, and but for Zionism would have enjoyed, in Palestine? [83] What is less justifiable (and much less helpful to the cause) is the assumption that the smallest criticism of any Zionist *method* or proposal is equivalent to anti-Zionism, even to anti-Semitism.[84] Such critics must remember that there are many good friends of Zion, there are even many Jews, who hold that the Balfour Declaration cannot be implemented by Great Britain or any other Mandatory because its parts are mutually destructive and incompatible, and that an unwillingness to recognize this can only breed gratuitous and unnecessary additional trouble: in short that unless we are prepared in the final event to see the history of the first return repeated (when the fate of each group of inhabitants was that "they drave them utterly out") we should not have supported Zionism. I cannot agree. The fact remains that we have supported Zionism; and we must continue to support it with undeterred but unhustled moderation and justice.

Nothing great has ever been easy, nor accomplished without deep searchings of spirit. Though I encountered—perhaps not less than others —some of the asperities of Zion, I could never understand the dullness of

[83] The Mufti is on unshakable ground when he declares, to the Royal Commission: "We have not the least power, nothing to do with the administration of the country, and we are completely unrepresented."

[84] "... There is no harm in that [divergences of Zionist opinion]; it only becomes dangerous when these different sections insist not merely that the object shall be carried out, but that it should be carried out precisely in the fashion that commends itself to them. Beware of that danger; I am not sure it is not the greatest danger which may beset you in the future." (From speech by Balfour to Albert Hall Jewish meeting in July 1920.)

soul in Europe which failed to perceive that Zionism, for all its inherent difficulties and gratuitous errors, is one of the most remarkable and original conceptions in history. Concluding a public speech in London during the spring of 1921, after my first but before my second scouring in the Laver of Ablution provided by the Jewish World Press, I proclaimed the faith which after fifteen years, not excluding 1929 and 1936, I see no reason to recant:

"I have mentioned some of the drawbacks of living in Palestine, but you are not to infer that we are not fully aware of the privilege and honour we enjoy in serving there. In Jerusalem there meet, and have met for centuries, the highest interests of the three great religions of the world. From Jerusalem has gone forth at sundry times and in divers tones a God-gifted organ-voice, which has thrilled and dominated mankind. I do not dare to prophesy, for the East is a university in which the scholar never takes his degree; but I do dare to believe that what has happened before may happen again, and that if we can succeed in fulfilling, with justice, the task that has been imposed upon us by the will of the nations, and if we can reconcile or unite at the source the chiefs and the followers of those three mighty religions, there may sound once more for the healing of the nations a voice out of Zion. If that should ever be, not the least of England's achievements will have been her part therein."

POSTSCRIPT

...even now, in this thy day...

This Chapter XV was begun well before the disturbances of 1936 and finished before the Royal Commission had started for Palestine; with an occasional footnote added in 1937. I have made bold to leave it untouched; hoping that its facts, inferences and suggestions, so far as they go, are perhaps less remote from actuality than general opinion, after issue of the Report, would be disposed to allow. The main difference of atmosphere between 1931—my last visit to Palestine—and 1937 seems due less to the disturbances (which could admittedly have been quelled much earlier), or to the appointment, sojourn or historical analysis of the Commission, than to their drastic and startling recommendations. These, though as little expected by the Government as by the public, were accepted by both with a surprising but not unintelligible alacrity. True that, as in Parliamentary Debates during twenty years of incidents and inquiries, the culpable "unreasonableness" of both sides (created by British and League Policy), the "apathy" of the Palestine Authorities (largely due to lack of Home direction), and the admirable diagnosis of the Commission each received an ample acknowledgment from all Parties. The Palestine twins are shown to be temperamentally irreconcileable, and the local practitioners "incompetent"; the general applause being reserved for the brilliant, if ultimately irresponsible, Consulting Specialists. Nevertheless, to a stranger present throughout the Debates in 1936 and 1937 there was one startling change of tone: the proved difficulties of preventing a recurrence of outrage and humiliation had at last established the existence of an Arab cause. There was sparring for position between the Parties (curiously reminiscent of the non-Intervention Committee), as to how, and by whom, the Project accepted with such resolution by the Government, should be sponsored before the League: all three reserving for themselves the maxim, *La recherche de la paternité est interdite.*

There are Jews, Arabs and British who have worked in Palestine more years than the Commission has months, not only in official relations with "maximist" witnesses keyed up, primed and prompted during a period of dreadful tension, but in daily personal contact with Palestinians in their own languages, who are asking themselves—is the Mandate, accepting the first conclusions of the Commission, so utterly unworkable? How far do the premises justify these second-thought recommendations? Would not the sum-total of guards and of safe-guards, of cash and good will required to control these three States, have sufficed to maintain the Palestine Mandate?

The Jews taste the bitterness of progressive disenchantment: the dream of the original Judenstadt; the National Home; lopped by the cutting away of Transjordan, to a Wales, and now, pared down to a Norfolk. And, even so minished, Zionism without Zion; "next year in Jerusalem!" A heavy tribute of gold to a people whose wealth they have already multiplied by ten. Into whatever remnant of Eretz Gisrod can be spared from barracks, Customs Coastguard Passport and Quarantine offices, an ironic—a cynical *carte blanche* for the immigration of world-Jewry. Irresistible overcrowding into necessarily concentrated industrialism; slums. And the Arab answers:—"Norfolk may be cramped quarters for persecuted millions, but it represents a large proportion of my East Anglia. Even assuming that I must cut my losses in order to liquidate the Jewish peril, then at least let it be with less vital sacrifices of my most fertile land, of my entire practicable seaboard. But why should I lose anything?" There might, there should still be, no need. Once secured against the just dread of submergence by a Jewish majority; his grievances now recognized by the Mandatory and proclaimed to the

League and the World, the Palestinian Arab might see fit to reason with his assumed adversary. The natural intelligence of the younger—and perhaps one or two of the older generation might grasp the possibilities of close association with the greatest Empire, assisted by a power that preceded and may survive all the Empires of history. Jewish leaders will realize that, by refusing to concede such an assurance or to content themselves as a slower increasing autonomous Palestine Community, they may indeed secure their majority, but it will be the majority of a pocket borough.

Meanwhile the lover of the Holy Land for its own sake, torn between intellectual assent and instinctive revolt, can only be certain that before any "solution" is super-imposed, far more serious efforts should be made to effect a freely negotiated settlement. Though both sides are for the moment confused by the strong wine offered of sovereign independence, compared with which all other draughts seem but an insipid dilution, they must by now surely have learnt their lesson—the insanity of recent shock tactics, whether by immigration or retaliation. Some have even concluded that the frightfulness of partition was contrived for the specific purpose of terrifying both into reason. But so long as the Arabs, by postulating entire stoppage of immigration, and the Jews, by refusing to renounce an ultimate majority, refuse to take the first steps towards agreement, there can be no hope of an accommodation that could be endorsed by America or approved by the League; and partition, hideous and hateful to all, stares them in the face.

CHAPTER SIXTEEN

July 1st 1920

"And the word of Samuel came to all Israel."

1 Sam. iv. 1

I

EARLY in the afternoon the Chief Administrator formally handed over the Administration to the High Commissioner. He had humorously prepared for Sir Herbert a typewritten receipt for "one Palestine taken over in good condition", which Sir Herbert duly signed, adding "E. and O.E." The Staff lined up for his departure and cheered him farewell as he drove past the gate-house and down the hill for the last time; and O.E.T.A., as O.E.T.A., ceased to exist. Though mostly the same men sat, still in uniform, performing the same tasks at the same desks, we became from 1 July 1920 a Civil Government, which it was my privilege to assist in establishing upon a firm and, we hoped, lasting basis.

Never have I worked harder or with greater satisfaction than as acting Chief Secretary throughout that July, August and September. The Military Administration had indeed been a going concern and might have continued almost indefinitely on the heroic lines of the New Model I have described.[1] But as a Civil Government we lacked (among many things) two prime necessities. There was no security of appointment for Civil Servants and, in the absence of martial authority, there was no legal system. The budget covering the Financial Year from 1 April had been under consideration in Whitehall for months. Civil officials could no longer requisition houses as billets and seemed to be faced with instant eviction. Though we were eager to encourage private enterprise it seemed hardly fair suddenly to abolish Army canteens, and so to deliver households based on canteen prices to the expensive and ill-organized local purveyors.

[1] P. 351.

Not only these but a hundred other problems were handled by Sir Herbert Samuel, though new to the East and accustomed to the clerical and technical perfections of Whitehall, with an ease and rapidity which won our immediate admiration. I was particularly impressed by his resourcefulness; and was not in the least surprised to learn later from Mr Asquith how, in his Cabinet, when some difficulty seemed to defy solution, all eyes (he said) would be found to converge upon Samuel who, drawing from his pocket the small note-block and stub of pencil, that were to become familiar from Dan to Beersheba, would never fail to supply the acceptable formula. His patience and his fair-mindedness were on a par with his resource, nor did I during his five years in Palestine hear of a single instance of his showing lack of consideration or of losing his temper, though for this last there was, Heaven knows, frequent justification. This even calm was by some ascribed to his supposed incapacity for feeling either anger or joy: by those who read him better, to an early acquired philosophic control. As Military Governor, now surviving into a fourth dispensation, I was naturally well known in Palestine and sometimes embarrassingly in the public eye, and I was aware of the anomaly of this position. But Sir Herbert Samuel never made me feel I had grown too big for my boots, and he never failed to support me through good days and through bad in the position, illogically superior to my post, which priority rather than merit had thrust upon me. I had not been in contact with such a capacity for work since the days of Gorst, and sometimes felt the strain of combined routine and construction.

I only hope I am half as useful to him as he is instructive to me. But it is hard work keeping abreast of his creations, and carrying on the current administration: like making a bicycle and riding it at the same time. But the whole rush is definite Fun, and I shall be almost sorry to be my own master again.

In his first letter to me Sir Herbert had written:

You know my policy with regard to the non-Jewish population—not only to treat them with absolute justice and every consideration for their interests in matters relating to the establishment of the Jewish National home, but also to adopt active measures to promote their well-being.

Not once to my knowledge did he fall short of that high principle. Even extremist Arabs resented the religion rather than the person of the High Commissioner: *"Nafsu sharīf"*, they would say, "His self is honourable." In my opinion and, I believe, that of most reasonable men in Palestine, his appointment was a stroke of genius on the part of Mr Lloyd George entirely justified by results. Energy, even with good will, unless accompanied by industry, and the faculty of reading and assimilating Departmental Minutes and replying with clear businesslike instructions, may attract the public but will more often harass the Administration. Sir Herbert possessed all three qualifications, together with an inherited fourth. I cannot conceive that any Gentile High Commissioner could have weathered the storms of Jewish public opinion for five years: perhaps not for two.

The advantages of having as High Commissioner a Minister who had been seven years in the Cabinet and eleven in the Government were immediately and dramatically apparent. Sir Herbert telegraphed to the Treasury requesting that the Budget, which had been in their hands since April, might receive approval, without which it was impossible to make appointments. Obtaining no reply he declared the Budget passed—a defiance of Whitehall before which the boldest Crown Colony Governor would have hesitated. This cutting of the knot was the more urgent because of the dispatches and telegrams from G.H.Q. warning us that we must immediately demobilize all officers whom we did not propose retaining. The feeling of unrest and discomfort in the Administration was increasing daily, for, though at the crisis of his fate, no officer could be certain what it was to be. My position was no less difficult than delicate. Having been neither consulted in the composition of the Budget nor in the later redistribution of the Districts, nor indeed a Headquarters' official since the winter of 1918-19, I was forced suddenly to "get up" these and other problems like a subject for the Tripos. It was a serious thing to recommend for permanent employment officers I had never seen, to a Chief entirely dependent on my knowledge; and a struggle not to retain members of my own Staff who had worked loyally and well, in a greater proportion than the Staffs of other Districts. I know I was fair: I think I was successful. At all events none of my recommendations proved failures. Two of them were Harry Charles Luke (for whom I had been angling since 1918), afterwards Lieutenant-Governor of Malta, and George Stewart Symes, later Governor-General of the Sudan. There was only one resignation, tendered on disapproval of a Zionist Chief before Sir Herbert's arrival, and subsequently withdrawn. I recommended Sir Herbert to accept the resignation and not the withdrawal. Positions were hard to find immediately after the War, and it was frightening to be able by a phrase, a word, a glance, to make or mar a career. One young officer, recently married, came to me in tears, praying that his part against me in a recent controversy might not count against him. It seemed strange that I should be thought capable of this pettiness: his work had been good, and he was confirmed in his post that evening.

Neither Sir Herbert nor I had occasion to blush for what I may term our two mutual nepotisms. One evening he enquired if I saw any objection to the appointment[2] of his son Edwin. "Nebi", as he was called,[3] had made a good impression when attached to the Zionist Commission, and it was in no spirit of complaisance that I declared I should be pleased to take him on the Governorate Staff. The appointment having been decided, I said to Sir Herbert (in perhaps questionable taste): "Sir! I have a cousin." He looked at me, but found no difficulty in consenting; for my cousin, Archer Cust (whom I had borrowed as a Subaltern from his Battery), had, like Nebi, given proof of zeal and capacity; so much so that within a year his services were commandeered as Private Secretary to His Excellency; a riposte

hard, in a way, when I had trained him from the beginning into real utility for the Jerusalem Administration,

but in truth a compliment to both of us. Permanency of employment meant for me that, after sixteen years in the public service without acquiring any rights, I did, on July 1st 1920 in my fortieth year, begin to qualify for pension.

I have said more than once that this book is not an official history, though it may sometimes explain or supplement official history. So I must refer those sufficiently interested to the High Commissioner's Interim Report of his first year in Palestine, for chapter and verse of what was executed or projected during those first three months. He sympathized actively with much that meant a great deal to me and for which, before his arrival, I had fought hard. His first Ordinance (for so we called what Democracy is entitled to call Laws) confirmed my legal control, and extended everywhere my arbitrary restriction, of advertisements throughout that portion of the Holy Land in which I had held sway. He set forth the lines on which towns should be planned. He protected Antiquities and checked dealings in them. My proposal for a Pound Tax on all tourists for the upkeep of Antiquities was found impracticable, mainly owing to the opposition of the shipping companies, who estimated that the amount might "just make the difference" to hesitating pilgrims. But Sir Herbert, who attached as much importance as anybody to the preservation of historic beauty, and always supported Pro-Jerusalem, arranged for a Pound for Pound grant up to two thousand

[2] The suggestion had come from Brigadier-General Deedes, under whom "Nebi" had served.
[3] After the well-known hill of Nebi Samwïl.

pounds annually on all I collected: and entering, as none of his predecessors or successors into the spirit of the thing, tiled the walls of Government House from Pro-Jerusalem kilns, curtained his windows from our looms and ordered his cupboards, tables and chairs from Palestine carpenters. He regulated the entry of immigrants and prohibited the use, in partisan demonstrations, of State Flags.[4] He modernized Ottoman Copyright and Mortgage Law, and provided for Government control of land transactions. He safeguarded the public against the irregular sale of drugs and reorganized the Palestine Police. (But Police organization must always be an affair of "men rather than measures".) He granted amnesties and repatriated Germans. He appointed a Mixed Advisory Council and published simultaneously the date of its first meeting. He inaugurated Co-operative Societies, Commissions for Weights and Measures and Land Credit Banks, and as a good Liberal abolished the censorship of the Arab and the Hebrew Press.

As Military Governor and as Acting Chief Administrator I had from the first forbidden drinking-bars, though with no other restrictions on the sale of liquor, which could be bought for private consumption or consumed at table in hotels and restaurants according to desire. Sir Herbert was good enough to extend my embargo to the whole of Palestine. I also forbade, throughout my nine years of Governorship, Hotel Dances or Cabarets within the old walled City of Jerusalem (the two chief resorts had been within two hundred yards of the Holy Sepulchre), reminding hotel proprietors who protested, of the compensating freedom from taxation traditionally enjoyed by them as dwellers within the Walls. Both these prohibitions, which I still consider were in keeping with the Holy Land and the Holy City, have long since lapsed.

Towards the end of September I was knocked out of work and almost out of life by malignant malaria. On reappearing at the Governorate,

I note that people are consideration itself so long as one is definitely in bed, but that two hours' appearance at the office, however great the effort, is taken as proof of being able to tackle in every variety and profusion the most exacting problems and the longest discussions.

I was ordered to England for treatment, and wrote on the eve of departure:

I have just returned from a *thé d'honneur,* given me at the *Grand New* by Moslem and Christian notables, including the ex-Mayor, the Greek and Armenian Patriarchs, and representatives of most other denominations. Cordial speeches and hopes for recovery and return. I only hope it will not compromise me too much with the Jews.

[4] The Commander-in-Chief's embargo had ceased with the Military Administration.

I sent home and still prize the letter of thanks I received from Deedes "for the manner in which you have ensured continuity in the administration during the passage between the Military and the Civil régime" and the characteristic generosity and humour of Sir Herbert Samuel:

> If the new Administration has achieved some measure of success, it is to you that it is very largely due. I am very glad to know that you "enjoyed" your work here. I should have thought a continuous and excessive pressure of business, with a quite inadequate staff would have come more fittingly within the title of *The Martyrdom of Man* [5]—a copy of which I am sending you with this.

A course of injections and a first Christmas in England since 1903 completed my cure. Years afterwards a Colonial office clerk discovered that though I had been ordered home on medical authority, no certificate to that effect had at the time been forwarded, so that, despite the explanations and protests of the Palestine Government, I was formally docked of the proportionate vacation leave. "When things like that happen", said George Lloyd, "don't worry. It's never the Secretary of State, but a clerk in a garret."

II

"For thither the tribes go up...."

Psalms

1920-1926

What manner of city was the Jerusalem over which this reasonable, resourceful, Jewish, Balliol, Cabinet Minister was in his fiftieth year suddenly summoned to rule: not from the cushioned fortress of Downing Street—where the sharpest inconvenience was the monthly Zionist protest, the triennial Arab delegation, the letter to *The Times* (no action indicated) or the Wednesday question drowned by a huge majority in the House of Commons—but sitting on the Mount of Olives and only less in the maelstrom than the Governor?

Physically, a City of invincible and unutterable attraction, fast emerging from the primitive conditions in which we had found it: but not fast enough, for there were still (and doubtless are yet) tourists whose sensibilities, deserting eyes, heart and brain, appeared to have concentrated in the nose.[6] Officially, inadequate: for we had inherited, save for the

---

[5] Winwood Reade.

[6] Lawrence remarked this same tendency to discount the difficulties of previous conditions in Damascus. *Seven Pillars*, p. 659.

Police Barracks behind the Citadel, almost no Ottoman Government offices, so that we were dependent upon hospices and other religious institutions, Roman, Lutheran and Orthodox, for housing the Departments. These bodies were good enough to accept, often under protest, heavy rentals for establishments they had for the moment no prospect whatever of employing or reopening themselves. In reality the arrangement was a mutual convenience; for the Government could not afford to build. Officials lived mostly in the "German Colony", a series of well-built but stuffy little villas behind the Railway Station, belonging to deported Germans.

The Governorate originally housed also the Officers' Mess and Quarters, and when it shed these, gradually absorbed the Government Departments, until in the autumn of 1925 Lord Plumer left Sir Herbert Samuel's office on the Mount of Olives, and installed his in the room immediately over mine.

I had on my Staff, besides Englishmen, Palestinian Moslems, Christians, and Jews. They worked excellently with each other as with me, and my remembrance of them all is pleasure and gratitude. Beginning, in military days, with Jerusalem, Bethlehem, Ramallah and Jericho (the Ottoman Sub-District of Jerusalem), we soon extended our frontiers up to Samaria; and by including Hebron, Gaza, Beersheba and finally Jaffa found ourselves by 1922 in direct control of the whole of Southern Palestine: an area, I believe, exactly conterminous with that administered by Pontius Pilate. The full Staff met each other only four days in the week, for Friday, Saturday and Sunday were whole holidays for Moslems, Jews and Christians respectively: but the system was in some ways to the public advantage, as it entailed the office being, in effect, open every day of the week.

Chancing upon a "Distribution of Duties" of 1921, I find certain items which do not usually fall to the colonial administrator. The Assistant Governor, besides Office Staff and Organization and Political Affairs, had to deal with "Religions",[7] "Public Meetings" and "Antiquities", while the Inspectors, apart from normal tasks, were confronted with "Food Shops", "Tribal Justice Court", "Military Magistrate", "Civil Marriages and Registration of Divorces", "Repatriation of Refugees", "Special Profiteering Court", "Hebrew Correspondence", "Food Control", "Rent Assessment", "Town Planning" and "Building Permits". The

---

[7] Change of Religion brought far more bitterness and sometimes danger to all concerned than it does in Europe. We applied the Ottoman Law under which "A person under 20 years of age cannot change his religion without the consent of his parent or guardian; and if there is any doubt as to the age of the applicant the matter shall be referred to the decision of the Governor"—a procedure which occasionally entailed most trying interviews.

construction period involved a certain amount of work not all directly connected with my District of Judaea:

We seem to go from Commission to Commission, and committee to committee. I am now sitting on, or presiding over, the Advisory Council, Civil Service Commission, Mines Commission, Nomenclature Commission, Water Supply Committee, Town Planning Commission, Staff Conference, Press Conference, Sporting Club Committee, Transliteration Committee—and others that will doubtless occur to me when this is posted.

Others later were Roads Commission, Local Government Commission and Currency Denomination Committee—which last two shared the fate of their Transliteration [8] predecessor. The Currency Committee's unanimous recommendations for the preservation of the historic Shekel and Dinar were, after my departure, rejected; and the names reduced, as *mils,* to their lowest terms; doubtless to conform with the designs of the coin and stamp issues.

For the seasons of peaceful rejoicing represented by the Christian Easters, the Jewish Passover, and the Festival of the "Prophet" Moses, the Governorate Staff was annually mobilized as for a campaign—almost for a siege. One or more officers were on duty all night: no clerk or typist could leave the office at all without the approval of the Chief Clerk, nor the Chief Clerk without the approval of the Assistant Governor *and* the Governor. Drivers of official cars and external orderlies slept in the Governorate and the Governorate telephone exchange was specially manned, both there and at the General Post Office. We needed all our "masterful administration of the unforeseen" when, in 1921 at the last moment before Nabi Mūsa

the Colonel-Commandant handed me a communication he had just received to the effect that Headquarters had decided "after consideration that permission cannot be given for the attendance of this or any other band"; when the band, which had been promised five weeks before, had already been waiting for some time in the Governorate courtyard. The Colonel-Commandant very properly saved the faces of all concerned by taking upon himself the responsibility for adherence to the programme. The sudden withdrawal of the band would have put us in an awkward predicament, for music is the obvious lead of every crowd, and they will follow it.

It had not however been the custom to employ it at the Jaffa Gate, although it was there as a rule that the danger was greatest. That same year

As the standards reached the Jaffa Gate, which we had barred with Indian Lancers, the bearers suddenly broke to the right and, with the mob thrusting

[8] *Vide* Preface.

behind, burst through the troops into the Old City. Troops then closed up again, and I had to ride into the crowd and tell them not to make asses of themselves. On the whole good humoured, and shook hands with me in such numbers that I am now hardly able to write. Then I turned round and led them, singing and dancing, past the Post Office to the Damascus Gate. One man speared in the backside: crowd pulling up his clothes and showing me the injured portion, which I promised should be taken into the official protection of the Government, and, if necessary, Decorated. This Eastern freedom of speech well received, and a variety of other jokes, which I will spare you, exchanged.

Easter came but twice or (in certain phases of the Armenian Calendar) but thrice a year. The Wailing Wall was a perennial anxiety. After 1919 the action of the Government was limited to maintaining the site of the Wall free from pollution, and upholding the existing law of the land. What this law was it had not been easy to ascertain, particularly with regard to the rights claimed by Jews of bringing with them chairs and benches for the performance of their religious duties. I obtained from the Moslem authorities previous rulings on this subject, from which it resulted that, according to the practice of the Ottoman Government, neither benches nor chairs were permitted. They appeared nevertheless to have been (and folding-chairs still were) occasionally brought by temporary, individual, and unofficial arrangements with the *Maghrábis,* or Moors, in the neighbouring houses: but so far as our legists could discover the Ottoman Government had never receded from the above decision. We therefore informed the Rabbis and instructed the Police accordingly. The Moslem objection to the introduction of benches (which I consistently endeavoured to overcome on grounds of reason and of humanity) was based partly upon the fact that the pavement in front of the Wall was actually the only approach to one or more of the *Maghrábi* houses, and that it was in danger of being blocked if benches or anything of a permanent nature were allowed to obstruct the fairway: but still more upon the theory, unfortunately verified by universal experience in Jerusalem, that any concession or abrogation of existing rights tended to become the thin end of a wedge before which other rights were apt to disintegrate. Chairs, they feared, would become wooden benches, wooden benches iron benches, iron benches fixed stone benches, with the corollary that covering from above against sun and rain and from the side against cold was equally a matter of humanity; so that the Waqf would one day find houses belonging to others erected against their wishes upon their own property. Such exaggerated suspicions had been for centuries at the root of most of the constantly recurring trouble between the various Christian rites at the Holy Sepulchre; where, after all, the conflict was between adherents of one faith, and not complicated by the hopes and apprehensions aroused by the Balfour Declaration.

The bench question came up again in April 1922, evoking another protest from the Director General of Waqfs, together with equally strong protests from the Zionist Commission and the Council of Jerusalem Jews. On 5 May the acting District Governor informed the President of the Council of Jerusalem Jews that, until a settlement should have been reached, no benches should be set up at the Wailing Wall. The Police were again instructed in the same sense. In October of the same year the Chief Rabbi Kuk was similarly notified, nor were any of these notifications subsequently cancelled or modified by the Government. The situation therefore of the *Status Quo* in this matter was well known to all the parties concerned.

The latest occasion on which this vexed question was brought before the public in my time was on the day of Atonement 1925, when, although the Zionist Commission, Chief Rabbinate, and Council of Jerusalem Jews were well aware of the orders, benches and chairs were again brought in such numbers as to evoke protest from the local Moslems to the Police, who referred the matter for specific instructions to the District Commissioner's Office. So soon as I learnt of the occurrence I sent down an officer to the Wall with instructions that worshippers already seated were to be allowed to remain so undisturbed, but that no more chairs should be brought. A protest was received by me next day from the Mufti, and at the same time one from the Zionist Organization. No complaints were brought against the manner in which the Police carried out their duties, but it was urged that previous warning should have been given that the law was going to be maintained, and that worshippers should not have been disturbed in the midst of their devotions. With regard to these contentions I had to remark, firstly that there had been no incident or rumour of incident for two years, and that, had small chairs been introduced in sufficiently moderate numbers, it is more than probable that the question of principle would never have been raised by the *Maghrábis;* and secondly that, in the Holy Sepulchre and other Holy Places, infraction of the *Status Quo,* even in the most sacred services upon the most holy days, had from time immemorial been dealt with immediately and on the spot owing to the strong probability of its being subsequently regarded as a precedent, and being transmuted from an infraction into an integral portion of the very *Status* which it infringed.

In those days there still seemed to exist two possible solutions of the problem: the first and best, that the matter should be mutually arranged

by the Jewish and Moslem religious authorities without intervention
either by the Government or the Zionist Commission: the second, that
the Moslems should themselves erect (at the charge if desired of the
Pro-Jerusalem Society) and maintain as their own property the necessary
stone benches, thereby satisfying the natural and not unreasonable claims
of the Jews and safeguarding in perpetuity their own proprietory rights.

For my endeavours to cope with this and other situations, Sir Herbert
Samuel, like Lord Allenby, was very generous in his acknowledgments.

I am directed by His Excellency the High Commissioner to convey to you
his great satisfaction and appreciation of the fact that during the recent troubles in the country you were able to maintain law and order in your District
without having recourse to the active intervention of His Majesty's Forces.
That you succeeded in so doing bears eloquent testimony to the influence
which you exercise over the population in your District and to the confidence
which the latter repose in you.

W. H. Deedes,
Civil Secretary.

With the removal years ago of Food and Rent Restrictions, the diminution in 1927 of the District to the original area of 1917 and the assumption by the Secretariat of political and other problems previously left to
him, the paternalism of the post of Governor, or Commissioner of Jerusalem has been largely reduced for all concerned, but its interest and
importance are abiding.

Few visitors and not all residents realize that Palestine in general and
Jerusalem above all must be studied and understood through Communities—Moslem, Christian and Hebrew—as well as through individuals.
The system of *millets,* or confessional communities, endemic in the Near
East since the Roman Empire, was fostered by the Ottoman Turks partly
to avoid being bothered with the legalities of brains subtler than their
own, and partly to maintain division. The system has its disadvantages for
Government and governed alike, but despite administrative, industrial
and social blending seems likely to endure, perhaps even reinforced by
the pressure of Zionism. In a London Club you learn by chance, if ever,
what is the religious denomination of a fellow member: you might not
know until the end of a Cairo dinner-party whether a fellow guest was
Protestant or Maronite: in Jerusalem he was introduced, or explained,
according as he was a member "of the Latin" [9] or "of the Greek" Community. Furthermore, the Moslems, Latin Christians and Jews of Jerusalem, are outposts of world communities always on the watch for
injustice against their representatives; so that a decision perfectly fair

[9] Throughout the Near East, Communities are described linguistically: "Latin" rather
than "Roman": "Greek" rather than "Orthodox."

(and accepted as such) for a Protestant or an Armenian, if applied to one of those three may and often does arouse comment and even action in Cairo, Rome, London and New York.

Early in 1918 I wrote to Mark Sykes: "The pettiness, the poignancy, the passion, the mediaeval agony of the atmosphere are exemplified a dozen times in the course of every day's work." Yet I am still of the opinion that "all these sects, creeds, nations and communities, though mutually and reciprocally hating and hated, are in the ordinary relations of life so far as we are concerned, friendly, agreeable, and not unentertaining persons, deserving of the closest attention". Outward solidarity of a Community did not, of course, premise inward harmony. Percy wrote to me during my absence at Haifa the same year:

The Jewish *Vaads* [10] are fighting, and the Arab party in the Greek Church don't go to church for fear they should hear Porph's [11] name mentioned in the prayers. I am contemplating a letter to the Ashkenazi *Vaad* containing my views on the subject of Jewish internecine feuds, but if you propose to resume your position here I think I'd better not send it!

The largest and most important Community in Palestine was that of Islam. Unlike the other two, it was not subdivided into rites, degrees or denominations but into two great partisanships, the Husseinis and the Nashāshībis. The Khaldi family, descended directly from Muhammad's conquering general Khālid al-Wālid, and more ancient than either, was less powerful, though still able to turn the scales of a Municipal Election. The farther you travelled from Jerusalem the less would the other great families, such as the Abd al-Hādis of Samaria or the Baidūns of Acre, admit this supremacy; but in fact they were all working for one side or the other. In the face of Zionism, Husseinis might be said to represent Church and extreme Arab nationalism, Nashāshībis State and making the best of a bad job. The Husseini family was of the two by far the more indebted to the British Authorities; who had confirmed the Ottoman appointment of Kāmel Husseini, the late Mufti, nominated Mūsa Husseini Mayor of Jerusalem (decorating them both), and were directly responsible for the appointment of his successor, Haj Amin. In the O.E.T.A. period I was in close and friendly contact with Kāmel Effendi; until embittered by politics no less reasonable and helpful than charming. He could be capable of courtesies in the grand manner of Islam. Sixteen years after his death Lord William Percy wrote reminding me how

[10] Boards, Committees.
[11] The Archbishop of Sinai, Porphyrios II, was supposed to represent Hellenism to a far greater degree than was the exiled Patriarch Damianos.

As the cavalry returned from Salt some men broke into the Mufti's house, stole two fowls, etc., etc., Allenby was furious and insistent that the Mufti put in a claim against the Corps. My repeated requests to him in that sense were ignored till I sent one as an order from the C.-in-C. The reply in a single paragraph to yourself stated that "the damage was as nothing compared to the kindnesses which I have received from Your Excellency for I regard the acts of the soldiers as those of my children committed in their father's house" —a very notable tribute to that old man.

The Mayor, Mūsa Kāzem Pasha, had all the dignity and some of the good qualities of the traditional Ottoman Governor. The balance was slightly, and for twelve years, redressed by the mayoralty of Rāgheb Bey al-Nashāshībi, unquestionably the ablest Arab in Palestine. He was gifted with an imagination, a swiftness of perception and of action, and an absence of fatalism and *laissez aller* infrequent among his co-religionists; whilst as a planner, not only above ground, he was hardly surpassed by competitors wholly without his other qualifications. His attitude towards his Municipal Councillors was that of a solo instrument towards an entirely muted orchestra. For the public, in matters of House-rating, and of *Sharafīa*—betterment taxes—he was an Oriental incarnation of a Tammany Boss. To watch his expression as he submitted to me some budgetary proposal based upon cogent but quite unacceptable arguments was a satisfaction of which, though often repeated, I never wearied. When, after my departure, the first Municipal Elections were held, Rāgheb Bey was returned; but he failed to survive the second Elections. His chief rival, Haj Amīn al-Husseini, Mufti of Jerusalem and President of Sir Herbert Samuel's Moslem "Supreme" Council, though less in personality and capacity, or in desire to co-operate with the Government, nevertheless created, with his severe yet picturesque turban against the gorgeous setting of the Dome, a more immediate impression, alike upon the local Fellah and upon the politically sympathetic visitor. The pity was that it always seemed, before reaching Westminster, to have faded away.

I am sensible of the honour of nine years' close association with the Latin Catholic Church in Palestine. It brings me memories of noble services rendered to the cause of religion and learning, of the wonderful variety and interest of its Orders, of the architectural tragedy of the Latin church in Bethlehem and the great barrack hospices and convents dwarfing the walls of Jerusalem—and of our occasional small misunderstandings. The later Patriarch, Monsignor Barlassina, was an austere and outspoken Prelate of imposing presence, who had been conspicuously successful in Rome as *Parroco* of St John Lateran. His position as representative of the Holy See was rendered no easier by the immense local prestige of the Franciscans, by the coolly critical and not particularly pro-Italian French congregations, and by one or two minor lapses of his Arab subordinates.[12] The Civil no less than the Military Administration well understood (though some of us regretted) that it was not possible for any Latin ecclesiastic to attend an Anglican service, even on the King's birthday; but they were equally unable to admit the Latin Patriarch's claim of precedence on public occasions, over the Orthodox Patriarch, who represented the church of the country, or over the Armenian Patriarch, even if senior. My official absence from Latin services was at first misinterpreted. Passing through Rome in 1919 I called at our Legation to the Holy See, where

H. G. showed me a letter written by a R.C. of Jerusalem against me, because I attended Orthodox ceremonies. I told him that I considered it my duty to go when asked to Orthodox, Armenian, Moslem and Jew, and would gladly have gone to Latin services if I had ever received one single invitation.

When, as sometimes from the Franciscans, I did receive one, I never refused it.

Of that greatest Order I have indeed so tender a recollection that, seeing the familiar brown habit in any part of the world, I can hardly refrain even now from shaking hands with the wearer. The Franciscans were everywhere. The Palestine prospect was incomplete without a couple of friars somewhere in the middle distance, and, as their headquarters in Rome was the Convent of St Anthony, so in Jerusalem they seemed to enjoy the proverbial *ubiquità di Sant' Antonio.* Very special though not necessarily identical types of character and ability are needed to become *Custode di Terra Santa*: nor could there have been a greater contrast than between the two *Custodi* whose friendship I was privileged to enjoy: Ferdinando Diotallevi, of the Marches, *fine mouche,* philatelist, iron disciplinarian, with an unhappy craze for bricks and mortar; and the solid, good-natured Neapolitan Aurelio Maretta.[13] Who could have been milder than the venerable Irish Father Egan (with whom I used to play chess)? Who fiercer than Father Godfrey Hunt when arraigning the iniquities of the Copts? The brethren as a whole liked the Moslems, as *brava gente,* the Jews they regarded almost as beings from another planet; and they reserved their fire for the Orthodox Patriarchate and Church, which occupied most of the holy places and with which they were consequently involved in frequent and deplorable altercations.

[12] As for instance when the Latin Priest at Ramallah circulated a scurrilous attack on the Government, over a local educational appeal.
[13] In 1934 by an extraordinary chance I met the two together in Palermo.

Dante's "holy athlete" St Dominic was brilliantly represented by the Convent and *École biblique de St Étienne*. The Dominicans indeed constituted the intellectual aristocracy of Christian Palestine. Supreme as classicists, orientalists, Assyriologists; witty as well as profound, and entirely detached from the scrimmage of the communities, these delightful Frenchmen were a spiritual haven of which I must have taken all too frequent advantage. They welcomed to their hall Sir Herbert Samuel's lecture on the Centenary of Lord Byron's death, mine upon the League of Nations, with a humanism we could all appreciate, for, over and above the erudition of Pères Vincent and Savignac, did not Père Abel habitually smoke an English pipe and tobacco, and had not the illustrious Père Lagrange sailed so close to the wind that some of his works had only just escaped the Index? I was in close and admiring contact with the philanthropic work of the other Religious Orders. Hundreds of poor boys must have learnt their skill at the forge or on the land from the good Salesians; and how many orphan girls owe all their light in life to the white-coifed Sisters of St Vincent de Paul under the gracious dignity of La Mère Supérieure Récamier?

Unlike the Latins in Palestine, the Orthodox or (from the language of its liturgy) "Greek" Church enjoyed no world protection or associations. If anything, Palestine Orthodoxy suffered by such external contacts as it possessed; for the attempt to preserve it less as the church of the Palestine Orthodox than as an outpost of Hellenism—almost of the modern Church of Athens—was a source not only of constant intrigue and wire-pulling,[14] of anxious colloquies with the Greek Consul in Jerusalem, and of journeys by the Archbishop of the Jordan to Athens, but also of increasing discouragement and bitterness to the Orthodox Arabs of the country. The only spiritual exhortation received by the unfortunate "Arabophone " from his earliest youth was administered, if at all, in a language which not one in a thousand could understand. Theoretically indeed he might, if he had overcome these initial disadvantages, aspire as a neophyte to preferment in his national Church, but the 'Αδελφότης—the Orthodox Brotherhood—is an absolutely close corporation: there were no Arab Metropolitans, Bishops or even Archimandrites, and a modern Arab Patriarch (though there have been such in the remote past) was about as probable a prelate as an English Pope. No wonder then that the Orthodox Arabs seemed to pass from protest

---

[14] "The defeat of the Venizelist Government in Greece is likely to affect the dispute in the Orthodox Patriarchate here. The Venizelist Metropolitan of Athens, Meletios Metaxachis, who has actively supported the Anti-Patriarch party, has been deposed by the new Greek Government in favour of his Constantinist predecessor (deposed by Venizelist) and the Damianos party is naturally (if discreetly) jubilant."

to protest, from conference to conference; that, to the best of my recollection, the Orthodox Churches, save for baptisms, marriages and deaths and the great (picturesque and exciting) Festivals were oftener empty than full; and that there was a steady leakage into Rome and Protestantism (though not to the Anglican Church, which, as originally instructed by Archbishop Benson, honourably refuses any such "conversions"). Apart from these necessities, I could never see that Orthodoxy rendered to its faithful any services whatever. There was no sort of parochial life; the entire energies of the Synod, as of the Bishops, Priests and Deacons, seemed to be directed to the guardianship of the Orthodox Holy Places from real or imagined encroachment by other Christian denominations. I had not been Military Governor a month before

the Greeks and Armenians whose respective Epiphany and Christmas fall on the same day, came to blows in the Nativity at Bethlehem, and had to be parted by the special guard (chosen from experts at these disgraceful brawls) that I had posted there.

When I decided to preserve from obliteration the only surviving tombstone of a Crusader, the Englishman Philip d'Aubigny, within the precincts of the Holy Sepulchre, patient lobbyings (in spite of my friendship with the Orthodox Patriarch) and representations that the Status Quo would be more gravely infringed by the disappearance of an existing inscription than by its removal a few inches, were necessary before I could obtain consent. Even then, when I met the Director of Antiquities and the Architect of the Pro-Jerusalem Society before the door of the Sepulchre to open the tomb, we were far from astonished to behold the surrounding roofs, terraces and battlements thronged with black-stoled Greek Caloyers, contemplating with mournful anger the preservation in their despite of a Latin monument.

This guardianship (the amiable Patriarch would reply when I argued the Arab position) was the real and original purpose of the Orthodox Church in Palestine, which they had maintained, often with their lives, through many centuries of infidel domination. Their endowments were the result of foreign and not of Arab munificence, and Christian ministrations in the accepted sense, though admittedly important and desirable, were a supererogation beyond their primary scope. The Easter Churches (as is known) concentrated from the beginning upon the formulation rather than the dissemination of dogma, but the Orthodox Church of Jerusalem did maintain until the War a certain number of schools and the theological college of the Holy Cross. The War ruined that Church for many years. From 1914 Russia, her principal supporter, had ceased to exist; there were no pilgrims from anywhere; their tenants were unable to pay rents: while Orthodox Rumania had signalized her extension of territory by an act of spoliation which we were powerless to prevent. ("Damianos", I wrote to my father in 1924, "has just returned from Rumania, whose Sovereign presented him with 500 sacks of flour, in token, His Beatitude presumes, of the £500,000 worth of Patriarchal property confiscated by the Rumanian Government in Bessarabia.") The Patriarch had therefore been compelled to borrow for current expenses large sums at intolerable rates of interest. O.E.T.A. found the Church, Convent and community bankrupt, and saddled with a debt of £600,000, almost all contracted by the Patriarch Damianos. In his financial hand to mouth existence Damianos moved in a mysterious way, and I attribute my uninterrupted happy relations with him to the fact that almost the only Palestine Committee upon which I did not sit was the Orthodox Finance Commission. No confraternity was more loyally pro-British than the Orthodox: not once did they fail to celebrate with a Te Deum the Birthday of King George the Fifth and the anniversary of the Liberation of Jerusalem,[15] or to pray for our King; they even introduced the practice of reading in English as well as Greek the Christmas Gospel in the Grotto of the Nativity at Bethlehem. The Orthodox Church followed (and, in Palestine only, still follows) the Julian Calendar, which keeps the year exactly a fortnight behind our Gregorian. On the night of January 13th 1918 I had my first unforgettable experience of the undisciplined Oriental pageantry of an Orthodox Mass.

I attended the Orthodox New Year's Service in the Holy Sepulchre, or rather the last hour and a half of it. (Total length from 11 P.M. till 3.15 A.M.) The singing if monotonous is impressive, and the final procession, thrice round the Sepulchre itself and the last time round the whole Church as well, halting for half a minute at the four points of the compass, dearly stirs the imagination. Afterwards, in the vault of the Archimandrites we eat breed and oranges, and I found in my slice (by a crude and obvious compliment) the small gold piece which is supposed to bring luck in the coming year; the priests meanwhile simulating astonishment and delight.

Damianos "the most Blessed and Holy Patriarch of the Holy City Jerusalem and of Palestine, Syria, Arabia, beyond Jordan, Cana of Galilee and Holy Zion", 133rd Patriarch in direct line of office, was in every way a remarkable figure. Born in Samos (and accused of flooding the Patriarchate with Samiotes) he rose to become Patriarch of Jerusalem,

[15] "14. xi. 18. During our procession from the Patriarchate to their Te Deum at the Holy Sepulchre, two small boys walked before the Archbishop and myself and scattered rose leaves under our feet. And half-way through the service I was made aware, by repeated staccato blows on the crown of the head, that a basket of roses had been emptied upon me from the clerestory." The Archbishop was Porphyrios of Mount Sinai, the Patriarch not having returned from exile in Damascus. See p. 322.

and to remain so, for no less than twenty-two years. Twice he had been expelled by Greek influence: twice restored by Arab pressure upon the Ottoman Government. Pitched battles were fought in the streets of Jerusalem by supporters who assumed (wrongly) that he must be pro-Arab because the Greeks hated him bitterly. But once Damianos had returned from Damascus in 1919 after his removal there by the retreating Turkish Army, permutations and combinations of his own Synod were powerless to break his authority: to his death he ruled them all with a rod of iron. He was the most splendid prelate I ever saw. Well over six feet in stature, his beard as white as snow and his tiara scintillating with gems, he easily dominated any gathering. Seven Christmases did I walk immediately behind him in the procession round the Basilica of Constantine at Bethlehem. The crowd pressed hard upon us, their eyes flashing against the candles we carried. The great brazen candelabra depending from the roof of the church were set swinging perilously to and fro until the colonnade seemed to sway in the shadows. His Beatitude might have intervened in the Service a moment before to snuff a guttering candle or loudly to rebuke a Metropolitan for some error in his interpretation of the Liturgy; but as he paced along, incredibly majestic, the Arab women of Bethlehem and of the Villages of the Shepherds would lean forward in their tall mediaeval coifs, whispering *"Huwa", Huwa",*—"It is he—he", pluck at the hem of his robe and press it to their children's lips. For in spite of its defects of indifference, supineness and corruption,[16] Orthodoxy was still the national Christianity of Palestine, an Eastern Church in an Oriental country. At the end of my farewell visit to Damianos before leaving Palestine he signed to me with his hand. I bent my head: he blessed me and, as I rose, kissed me on the forehead.

Apart from the outstanding personality of Damianos, his indignations with the Finance Commissioners and his efforts to make the Government exile recalcitrant Metropolitans, Palestine Orthodoxy comes back to me mainly in the engaging smile of the Archimandrite Gerassimos, Treasurer of the Holy Sepulchre, and his courteous habit of providing me on State occasions with a large bouquet, not easy to reconcile with uniform; the subtle charm of Archbishop Timotheos, who succeeded to the Patriarchate in 1935 after a three years' death-grapple with the forces of Hellenism; the admirable luncheons of the Archbishop of Bethlehem, the timidity of the Orthodox Arabs of Jerusalem until reinforced by the intellectual firebrands of Haifa: the heavy incense: the blare and flare of the Holy Fire.

---

[16] It has been well said of the Orthodox Church that the wonder is not that it is faint and wounded and perplexed, ʰⁿt that it exists at all.

Although the Coptic Convent of Jerusalem afforded me the welcome opportunity of exchanging a little Egyptian Arabic, I cannot pretend that the monks were then ideal members of the body politic, or worthy representatives of the Coptic Church. Their Patriarch in Cairo, whose age was estimated at anything over one hundred and ten, needed all that remained of his energies to combat the reforms in his own community, and could spare for the Copts in Jerusalem no more attention than to send them as Metropolitan a Prelate whose position had become impossible in Egypt. In the fifteenth century these pertinacious brethren had by gradual and constant encroachment succeeded in erecting a little chapel adjoining the back of the Edicule of the Holy Sepulchre. So small is this shrine that it can contain but one person, and the priest is obliged to celebrate the Mass with a congregation kneeling in the circular fairway of the Church. The Franciscans would assert and maintain the public right of way by appearing at mid-Mass with the daily supply of bread, meat, vegetables and wine, and perhaps one or two heavy benches, for their comrades lodged in the church, and struggling through the worshippers with a zeal which would hardly have won the approval of St Francis. There was at that time no Egyptian Consul in Jerusalem, and the Copts appealed to me both in writing as Governor and orally as to a fellow-Egyptian.[17] Their letter was a typical unverifiable Jerusalem *Borotésto* or protest, such as was issued by any Community two or three times a year,

...wounding a number of our persons who when examined obtained a report from a Medical Doctor [18] for five and seven days suspension of work.... We, therefore, in the name of religion, moral and every legal law, strongly protest against such hideous behaviour that makes everybody's brow sweat, including the very barbarians of Africa who are in the lowest state of barbarism. We notice that the British Mandatory Government is purposely overlooking this despotic procedure by the Latins....

Yet there was unfortunately no doubt but that the Franciscans were technically in the right, as were the police in assisting them. I therefore reasoned with the Archbishop, so that he undertook to prevent any further resistance; but I was mournfully unsurprised to receive in due course the following straight word from the Latin Patriarch, through whom the Franciscans then had to address their official correspondence.

[17] I found later that we were acting according to British tradition. As early as 1906 the British Embassy in Constantinople was protecting the rights of the "Coptic Priory" in Jerusalem against Turkish encroachments.
[18] Whose names I never succeeded in obtaining, any more than that of the "Medical Doctor".

Excellency,

I have repeatedly called your attention upon the insufferable arrogance of the Copts, but it seems that till now Your Excellency has given no orders on this account, because even this morning they prevented the servant of the Franciscans carrying food, to pass through.

Therefore I declare you that from to-day we will not more allow them to incense in our Chapel, and from to-morrow, if the servant will meet with opposition in passing through we shall force our passage in order to keep the rights which we always enjoyed.

I have the honour to be
Yours respectively,
Louis Patriarch.

I could only inform the Patriarch in reply that on each occasion the Copts had duly promised that they would do nothing to impede such access; and regret that their congregation had failed to obey the injunction not to prevent the Franciscans carrying food, cooking vessels, and wine from passing through and over them whilst they were kneeling at Mass. But I did venture respectfully to suggest to His Beatitude that as the Mass in question was celebrated but four times a week, it might be possible without in any way abrogating or receding from a right which was admitted by all, to instruct the servant responsible to choose some other time, or even to walk the few extra yards which would obviate his disturbing the administration of the Holy Eucharist—a proceeding which, I was convinced, His Beatitude must surely be the first to deplore.

This mild response was apparently without avail, for the next incident I can remember is the hurtling arrival at my office of Father Hunt, his blue eyes blazing with at last justifiable anger. The Copts, whose convent gives on the Ninth Station of the Cross, had retaliated by emptying their slops out of the windows onto the exact spot upon which the Friday procession of Franciscans up the Via Dolorosa was accustomed to kneel.[19] Whatever the previous merits or demerits of either side, this was intolerable: but could anyhow be handled under the Law of the Land. The Coptic Superior was recalled to Cairo: the Franciscans abated their noble rage, and the correspondence with the Latin Patriarchate, on this topic, ceased.

Aloof from these wrangles (save in the annual Procession of the Holy Fire) stood the Syriac Church of St Luke, a small and very ancient community, speaking indeed the oldest language of any—the antique Syriac of the Old and New Testaments. They owned one comparatively minor Holy Place, the grave of Joseph of Arimathea,[20] and their worthy Jerusalem Representative was, unlike most of his colleagues, the recipient rather

[19] At the end of the "Street of Bad Cookery", the Rue Malcuisinat of the Crusaders.
[20] Which would hardly be accepted by Glastonbury historians.

than the occasion of troubles, frequently invoking my protection against his own hierarchical superior in Antioch or Damascus. After my last (and most unwilling) intervention on his behalf, I was happy to be able to report to the High Commissioner that I had interviewed the Syriac Patriarch and that His Beatitude, exercising his prerogative of mercy, had not only permitted Bishop Elias to retain his episcopal vestments and beard, but had appointed him to the spiritual charge of the Syriac Church in Egypt at a stipend of £E.5 per mensem.

In the complicated division of rights and duties among the various churches having to do with the all too numerous Holy Places, there was alas enough pettiness to satisfy those who concentrate upon the weaknesses of human nature; as well as to make some of us rejoice that the Anglican Church was clear of any such "ownerships". Enormous importance was attached to the rigid protocal established for every conceivable incident. When for instance from excessive cleaning one of the nails holding the silver star [21] in the Bethlehem grotto of the Nativity worked loose, the following letter duly arrived from the French Consul-General, in 1920 still the representative of Latin Christianity:

> *Jérusalem le 8 Mai 1920.*
> *Monsieur le Gouverneur,*
>   *Le Rd. Père Président Custodial de Terre Sainte m'informe, d'après un rapport du Père Gardien du Couvent Latin de Bethléem, qu'un clou de l'Étoile d'Argent du lieu de la Nativité est ébranlé et me prie de faire prendre les mesures d'usage en vue de sa consolidation.*
>   *Je vous serais obligé, dans ce but, de vouloir bien envoyer à Bethléem un fonctionnaire du Gouvernement auquel s'adjoindra Mr Jean Rahil, mon premier Drogman, pour assister à cette opération et rédiger le procès verbal conformément aux précédents.*
>   *Veuillez agréer, Monsieur le Gouverneur, les assurances de ma haute considération.*
> *L. Rais.*

What, superficially, could furnish a clearer or sadder negation of the spirit of Christ than was revealed by a report from my Arab Sub-Inspector after an incident in Bethlehem?

Subject: Cleaning of the Basilica of the Nativity.

Mild protests were made but finally given up. It is worthy of mention, however, for record purposes to state:

(1) That the Greek Orthodox Community may open the windows of the Basilica throwing Southward, for the time of cleaning only.
(2) That the Greek Orthodox Community may place a ladder on the floor

---

[21] Marking on the marble slab the actual place of the Nativity.

of the Armenian Chapel for cleaning the upper part of this Chapel above the Cornice.

(3) That the Armenians have the right to clean the North face of the pillar on which the Greek Orthodox pulpit is placed, up to the Cornice only.

(4) That by mutual agreement the following has been arranged.

(*a*) That the Greeks should attach their curtain tight to the lower nail No. 2 at the foot of the pillar which lies South-East of the left hand set of steps leading to the Manger.

(*b*) That the Latins should have their curtain fall naturally down the same pillar leaving a space of 16 cm. between it and that of the Greek Orthodox.

(*c*) That Nail No. 1 be left unused by any of the Communities.

(5) Whenever the Government is to clean any part of the Basilica the necessary implements should be Government's.

(6) The above arrangements, however, are subject to alterations in case of any official documents in favour of any of the above communities being produced before next year's cleaning.

The Anglican Community's "paper" strength (like that of most Conservative majorities) was a good deal superior to that of any but a King's Birthday or an Armistice Day congregation. Many abstained from church attendance on the ground that the Cathedral clergy, few and overdriven, afforded them no personal ministrations. "Like all British communities abroad", I wrote to my father, "we clamour for chaplains and other church amenities, but are seized with a vertigo when asked to pay." We computed in 1922 that the total salaries of Jerusalem Anglicans amounted to £66,000, and that half per cent. of all salaries would yield the £300 annually required. This sum we failed to raise.

The Anglican Cathedral of St George started by being, and might have remained, the annual rallying place of all nations and creeds on 9 December, the anniversary of Allenby's Liberation of Jerusalem. Bishop MacInnes, working hand in hand with the Governorate (then rich in the knowledge and resource of H. C. Luke, the Assistant Governor), organized and conducted a Service of Thanksgiving which was attended not only by the clerics of all denominations save the Latin Catholic (though Latin diplomats and officials were there), but by the Moslem Mufti and the Sephardi Grand Rabbi. The Bishop presided in cope and mitre, the High Commissioner and his Staff, the Governor and the Consuls were in uniform, and the Arab holders of Ottoman *rutbés* in the Turkish full dress. The lessons were read in English, Hebrew and Arabic; and in Greek by the Orthodox Patriarch robed in his vestments. On the departure of Sir Herbert Samuel this unique and deeply appreciated[22] reunion of the Great Faiths in the City revered by all three convened by

22 "It is most encouraging to find the Thanksgiving Service so welcome in all quarters. . . ." Letter from Assistant Governor to myself.

the Mandatory of the Nations appointed for their common welfare, was discontinued against the will and without consultation with the Bishop, on the ground that one or two denominations (who had never protested officially or privately) might prefer to hold isolated services of their own.

For all its rather frigid twentieth-century Gothic, its aisles narrowed by panic on a building overdraft, and its conventional stencillings, St George's Cathedral was to me the most intimately personal church in Palestine. I am no less happy to have read the Lessons there for nine years, than to have persuaded the Bishop to abandon *Hymns Ancient and Modern* for the *English Hymnal*.

Nearly thirty years of the Near and Middle East have inclined me to the opinion of those who would assist the Eastern Churches to grow stronger within by education and training, rather than weaken them by enticing their members into other denominations. Nothing seemed to denationalize an Arab, a Copt or an Armenian like becoming a Protestant, or "Brutestánt"—as he more often pronounced himself. I could never see that his almost unctuous respectability, his open contempt for the venerable institution which he or his father had abandoned, were at all superior to incense and ikons. If he wished you Happy Easter as you left the service, it was with a gentlemanly Nordic restraint, as if sympathizing with a bereavement; whereas his cousin of the old faith shouted aloud "Χρίστος άνέστη," "Christ is risen", and in some places fired his gun against the wall of the Church.

Even our own people were sometimes no more liberal or understanding than those of other communities often supposed to be more uncompromising. I have mentioned the fine work of the Syria and Palestine Relief Society; yet after many weeks

you will hardly believe that I only succeeded last month in making the S. and P. R.S. co-opt to their Committee a Latin Catholic, Greek Orthodox and Muhammadan member; though they purport to assist all these Communities with an equal and impartial hand, and were in fact, with trifling exceptions, already doing so; yet they would not see that they had everything to gain by assuming temporarily the virtue of toleration.

Similarly:

the admirable lady, when presiding over the Talitha Cumi Girls' School, taken over by us from the Germans, and now under control of a small committee of which I am Chairman, fought tooth and nail, and even provoked, faced, and went through an incident in the school before she would allow the few Jewish and Moslem pupils exemption from the daily Christian service. It was only when, as representing the C.-in-C., I absolutely declined to countenance such intolerance, and clearly had the Committee with me, that she receded from this position.

Of minor sects we had a Mormon Missionary who, though he effected no published conversions, played a very sound set of tennis; and there was the "American" Colony.[28] Since the majority of the members were Swedes or Norwegians, the name was not popular with the American Consulate; and it was perhaps inevitable that the German nationality of their chief member rather than their English-speaking affinities should have been emphasized during the German Occupation. The Colony represented a primitive churchless Christianity, whose exact tenets, a species of Latter Day Adventism, I never succeeded in discovering, but which at first caused them to regard the Anglican Cathedral as little better than the House of Rimmon in which, however, an annual knee must be bowed on the King's birthday. They were cynically said to have come to Jerusalem to do good, and stayed to do well. The truth is that they did both. Their shop, "The American Colony Store", besides producing infinitely the best photographic series of Jerusalem and the Holy Land, catered also for the visitor-pilgrim-tourist class with a thoughtfulness, a thoroughness, which defied the competition even of the Jews and Armenians. Their model camels, inkstands and Bible bindings in olivewood, their Masonic gavels carved in the white limestone of King Solomon's Quarries, their sealed phials of guaranteed Jordan water; their copies of the silver Jewel shown by the Franciscans as the Cross of Godefroi de Bouillon, their Bukhara silks, their Bethlehem Women's robes, were better, more knowledgeably described, and more attractively shown, even than the antiquities of the Protestant Armenian Nasri Ohan. But a considerable portion of the wealth thus acquired went back into the country, in the shape of charities and innumerable kindnesses to the Arab population, Moslem as well as Christian. And I sometimes wonder how far the British community remembers all the advice and assistance which we never failed to receive in the early days when we knew nothing and they everything, from Mrs Vester, the great-hearted and charming leader of the "American" Colony.

Time and space forbid me to attempt the description of the best known churches, of the Holy Sepulchre or of the stately Basilica of the Nativity; but I cannot leave Christian Jerusalem without tribute to the less well known but in some respects most perfect of all, *Surp Hagop,* the Armenian Cathedral and Convent of St James. Stretching along Mount Zion from the Citadel to the south-western extremity of the City Wall this is by far the best situated and, from the pious care of its prelates, the best preserved of the ancient convents of Jerusalem. I regarded the

[28] Which, owing to its disruption, has disappeared from the 3rd edition of Sir H. Luke and Mr E. Keith Roach's *Handbook of Palestine.*

Armenian community with mingled sympathy and admiration. Their Patriarch, the celebrated Ormanian Surpazan, had been exiled by the Turks, who had also signified their desire to remove the treasury of St James to Damascus, "where it would be safe from the depredation of the Allies". Such a suggestion could not be disregarded, and several heavy chests, locked, corded and sealed, were duly loaded into the wagons of the retreating army—to the temporary depletion of the Convent coal-supply. Through no fault of its own, the community was bankrupt, and £80,000 in debt. In their communal disputes the Armenians were only less difficult—as also they alone had suffered more—than the Jews:²⁴ their dispositions being as rigid and unyielding as their language.

Since the Russian Revolution, whereby the position of their *Catholicos* in Soviet Etchmiadzm had become one of great difficulty, that of the Patriarch of Jerusalem was considered as the highest in the Armenian Church. The Armenians in Palestine were in general sober, thrifty and industrious—a good element in the population;²⁵ and the standard of cleanliness and morality in their convent was higher than that of any outside the Latin Catholic, Anglican and Protestant institutions. The Cathedral of St James, with its inlaid pavements, its marble traceries, its graven metal screens, its austere high lighting, was as delicately sumptuous as a casket of Tutankhamen. The Treasury behind the heavy curtain, the ponderous door only to be opened by three keys held by three priests, revealed a gleaming wealth of jewelled mitres, tiaras and antique vestments, of brilliantly illuminated manuscripts,²⁶ and silver and ivory croziers; culminating in the sceptre of King Hetūm, a slender tapering rod nearly a yard long, cut from a single block of amber.

In the Cathedral of St James the glory and the misery of an ancient race is transmuted into static mellow beauty. Every year my last visit before a holiday, my first on return, was in the late afternoon to this delightful and beloved shrine; and I had myself locked within its iron portals for an hour on the eve of my final departure from Palestine.

---

²⁴ A Jew should know something of suffering. Israel Zangwill wrote, after the War: "I take from Israel the crown of thorns to place it on the brow of Armenia."

²⁵ "It would be difficult, perhaps, to find the annals of a nation less stained with crime than those of the Armenians, whose virtues have been those of peace, and their vices those of compulsion." From a Letter of Lord Byron.

²⁶ One, the "Gospel of the Birds" holds its own with any manuscript in the world. In the colophons of these MSS. the monkish writer protests his unworthiness: "Least of the clergy, the unprofitable clerk Stephanus, miscalled a priest, which in name alone he is, and not in deed" and "Hardened sinner and foreigner, unfruitful of good and unprofitable in all ways, the unmentionable Aretas."

CHAPTER SEVENTEEN

1917–1926

A man so various that he seemed to be
Not one, but all mankind's epitome.

I

PALESTINE Jewry is a microcosm of world Jewry minus one element: millionaires are represented rather than actually resident. Jews surviving by the end of 1917 had been mainly the Orthodox and the aged, since neither had been worth persecuting and both would be an economic liability rather than an asset to the conquerors. They were a pathetic element; many famous for their learning and piety, all on the verge of starvation. The Jewish community and their liberators owed a deep but sometimes forgotten debt of gratitude to a Dutch Ashkenazi banker who being a neutral had been unmolested by the Turks. Mr Siegfried Hoofien was a tall fair man of non-committal appearance, a good command of deliberate English and great financial and organizing ability. For weeks he stood forth as the leader and interpreter of his people. I saw him almost daily, and it was thanks to him not only that Jewish relief was placed on a practical basis, but that we were reminded (as early as January, when we had one or two other preoccupations) to send him down to Egypt to bring back the *Mazzoth*, the Unleavened Bread,[1] in time for the first Passover of Liberation. For nine years I partook of this solemn and dramatic feast in the houses of Jewish friends, but never with so deep a feeling of significance as in that spring of hope and exultation. So logically perfect a Zionist was Mr. Hoofien that he told me at his Passover table that Zionism would still be a power for good, and that he would still be a Zionist, if there were not a single Jew in Palestine.

[1] Estimating the Jewish Communities of Jerusalem and Jaffa (including Tel Aviv) together at 40,000, 60,000 Rotls or 18,000 kilograms or 180 tons of *Mazzoth* were required. This demanded 200 tons of wheat, 75 per cent. of which was to be distributed among the poor and the rest sold. How many tons would be required to-day? I suppose 2000.

Despite this enthusiasm he was (characteristically) allowed, on the arrival of the Zionist Commission, to lapse from public life into the comparative obscurity of the leading Jewish banker.

No Jew needed his or our help more than Rabbi Aminoff and his unfortunate Bukharans. These had been men of substance, robed on festal days in Bukhara silks which Bakst would have envied. They were now cut off alike from access to their properties and news of their relations (both swallowed up by Bolshevism), and the antika shops of Jerusalem had profited cent. per cent. over the sale of their brilliant *quftans*. The Bukharans were the most demonstratively grateful of all the communities we endeavoured to assist.

The Orthodox Rabbis, remote from politics and administration, moved in a world of their own. Their sunless, sedentary lives, their furry *streimels,* their venerable faded velvets, combined to produce an *ensemble* so repellent to most visitors that they would commiserate with me on having to govern such apparitions. On the contrary, the extreme Orthodox such as Rabbi Sonnenfeld and the followers of *Agudath Yisroel* never occasioned either to me or to the police the faintest trouble whatever. From the Administrator's point of view they were ideal subjects, for all they desired was to be left in peace and the practice of their religion. For a long time they were not only not pro- but violently anti-Zionist, and I think their sympathy for me was sometimes enhanced by the attacks I suffered from their political and unreligious brethren. Having no funds save those derived from the Faithful in Russia and Poland—a source almost dried up—and from their official headquarters in Frankfort, they sometimes found their Orthodoxy to be their only weapon. They would declare that the *Kasruth* or Kosherdom of the less Orthodox was not Kosher at all, and refused to eat the flesh of animals so slaughtered. As the control of slaughter-houses is a matter of public interest, both sides would lay their case before me. I found the controversy, like nearly every Talmudic problem, of enthralling interest, and was at pains to study the whole question of the *Shekhíta* or Ritual Slaughter; with the result that what I did not know of the various officials and operators connected with the slaughter—the requirements of *Menakerim* and the problem of the *Réah*—was after a while hardly worth knowing.

The two official Chief Rabbis, appointed after the first voluntary organization of the Jewish community, was extraordinarily typical of the Ashkenazi and the Sephardi Vaads which they respectively represented. Rabbi Kuk, a dignified figure with the folds of his rich black robe carelessly disguising his cruciform Order of the British Empire, and his ample beaver hat, spoke always at formidable length, and with a confidence (hardly rivalled by the Latin Patriarch himself) that his words must be accepted as *ex cathedra*. His colleague, Rabbi Meyer, late of Salonika, with his command of French and his air of a man of the world who would not be disturbing the Governor but in this particular protest had to associate himself with a more rigorous partner, was as pure Levant as his Egyptian turban of blue satin wound tightly round a soft red fez, and his galaxy of those Balkan decorations which used to reward diplomacy in the Ottoman Empire.

The arrival of the Zionist Commission in the spring of 1918 marked a turning-point in the history of Palestine hardly less important than the British conquest. Henceforward the Palestinian could exclaim, modifying the celebrated dictum of the Khedive Ismail: *"Mon pays n'est plus d'Asie; nous faisons partie de l'Europe."* For what European University, diplomatic chancery, or legislative assembly, would not be the richer by the personality of Dr Chaim Weizmann, during more than twenty years the controller (whether in the chair or not) of universal Zionism? An almost feminine charm combined with a feline deadliness of attack; utter disillusion over both Gentile and Jew, together with burning enthusiasm and prophetic vision of what negotiation may still win from the one for the other. Ruthless and tolerating no rival, yet emotional; contemptuous but (I ultimately found) a fair dealer. He was a brilliant talker with an unrivalled gift for lucid exposition: did he not explain Einstein's Relativity to my sister and myself at luncheon until for a moment I dreamed that even I understood? As a speaker almost frighteningly convincing, even in English; when he sometimes played down to his audience by complaining that a course of action was "not cricket". In Hebrew, and even more in Russian, overwhelming; with all that dynamic persuasiveness which Slavs usually devote to love and Jews to business, nourished, trained, and concentrated upon the accomplishment of Zion.[2]

Chaim Weizmann was always the leader in Palestine (save when he was grappling with the American Zionists, sometimes restive at paying the piper while Russia called the tune), and the Administration saw all too little of Dr Nahum Sokolow, the Nestor of Zionism. Here was deep wisdom, inexhaustible knowledge; and a wealth, a saga of Jewish stories available for the admiring curious in eleven languages. Weizmann was a galvanic battery, not everywhere perfectly insulated: Sokolow a draught of a classic and incomparable vintage. Happy the movement that could combine such vivid and complementary forces.

[2] During his latest address before a learned Society in London I heard one Jewish critic behind me whisper to another: "He dared not have said that before a Zionist audience"; and I wondered that so little allowance should be made for a Prime Minister whose constituency is the entire Jewish world.

The Commission was also fortunate in enlisting the aloof distinction of James de Rothschild. The name of his father, Baron Edmond, was revered even by Moslems and Christians who, with the Jews, had been quick to note that, while the Balfour Declaration had been specifically addressed to Lord Rothschild, neither he, nor any other member of that House, English or Continental, save the Baron, had hitherto shown any practical interest in Palestine. Had James de Rothschild cared to put himself forward, he could easily have captured the popular attention, and I do not believe that his colleagues realize even now the full extent of his loyal self-effacement. Another figure, modest in himself but very scornful of us; then a junior Manchester Zionist, now a master in high finance (yet still a Zionist), was Israel Sieff.

No more gallant officer, no more charming and cultivated companion could have been imagined than Vladimir Jabotinsky. Had he not translated into English verse the poems of Akhad Ha'am, and the Divine Comedy into Hebrew? Was there ever discipline of troops more effective or magnetic than his? Withal I can imagine no one man who, if allowed his extreme logical way, would more certainly than this Arch Revisionist have involved Palestine, and perhaps Syria too, in battle and sudden death. His drastic suggestions at least served the Cause to this extent, that they made the most forward official Zionism seem by comparison to be the essence of practicable moderation. I associate him, because I was once compelled to offer both men the alternative of disarming or being put under arrest, with Pinhas Rutenberg, perhaps the most remarkable Roman of them all. Thick-set, powerful, dressed always in black; a head as strong as granite and an utterance low and menacing through clenched teeth. He is no politician, he explains; all he wants is "wurrk", and such is the grip of his "r's" that your hands seem to close over an imaginary pick—or pen. He is no politician? He was with Kerensky in the last pre-Soviet days; and had his advice, which was to shoot Soviet leaders quick, been taken, something other than Bolshevism might have reigned in Russia now. (Perhaps chaos.) Now he has harnessed the Jordan to light, heat and energize Palestine. His Power Houses are like himself; the rugged Sphinx-like contour of Government House, Jerusalem, is said to be Rutenberg rendered in stone. No politician! If, in a time of trouble for Israel, he were to raise his hand, he would be followed by all the Jews of Palestine, and as an impartial employer of Arabs as well as Jews, possibly by some of the Arabs also. A faithful friend, and I should think a particularly disagreeable enemy.

Adon Menahem Ussishkin stood in a class by himself. He was said to have done wonderful work for Zionism in Russia, and so to have a claim to sit on the Commission in Palestine. Obvious as the day and as open in his opinions and tactics, he was known even among his own people as Menahem Pasha. To us he might well have been Czar Menahem; and when he was announced for an interview I braced myself to take my punishment like a man, praying only that my subordinates might keep an equal control over their tempers.

Who could refrain from admiration of Eliezer Ben Yahuda? A small frail figure with sharp eager features and but one lung, this practical visionary of genius forgave me many shortcomings because I did on the first anniversary of the Balfour Declaration venture to deliver a brief public address in the Hebrew language which he had restored to human speech. I liked Ben Yahuda, and used to visit him and talk with him at length on his immortal and unique achievement. Ireland and Hungary have by means of Movements and Committees rekindled the flames, never dead but till recently flickering, of Erse and of Magyar. Here was a man who by himself had summoned from a sleep of two thousand years—almost from the next world—a mystic antique utterance; breathing into it the breath of new life, so that the word of the Prophets became also the word of the leader writer (their modern counterpart), the man of science and the schoolboy in the football field. Ben Yahuda died at his work of the great Hebrew dictionary, but not before he knew it was accomplished:

> *e sulle eterne pagine*
> *cadde la stanca man.*

One of my earliest Jerusalem memories is of another kindly and learned Jew, who invited me to inspect his library and coin collection. Next day I received this letter:

26 February 1918.

Dear Sir,

To-day being the Jewish Purim a custom to send little gifts, I hope you will not refuse me to accept these two small coins of my collection. One is Pilatus the Roman Governor of Jerusalem and the other one with the palm tree is of Simon Bar Kochba the last Jewish Governor of Jerusalem.

I hope that you will accept them both in token of the pleasure I had of your visit yesterday.

Yours very truly,

I. Raffaelli.

I returned them with an appreciative message that the Governor could accept nothing from any living soul. Three or four years afterwards he died. Next morning his family put into my hands two little envelopes addressed to me in his writing with the hope, which I could not gainsay, that my refusal no longer applied.

When, early in 1918, a lady, unlike the stage Woman of Destiny in that she was neither tall, dark nor thin, was ushered, with an expression of equal good humour and resolution, into my office I immediately realized that a new planet had swum into my ken. Miss Annie Landau had been throughout the War exiled in Alexandria from her beloved Evelina de Rothschild Girls' School, and demanded to return to it immediately. To my miserable pleading that her school was in use as a Military Hospital she opposed a steely insistence: and very few minutes had elapsed before I had leased her the vast empty building known as the Abyssinian Palace. Miss Landau rapidly became very much more than the Headmistress of the best Jewish Girls' School in Palestine. She was more British than the English, flying the Union Jack continually as well as exclusively so soon as that was permitted. She was more Jewish than the Zionists—no answer from her telephone on the Sabbath, even by the servants. She had been friendly with Turks and Arabs before the War; so that her generous hospitality was for many years almost the only neutral ground upon which British officials, ardent Zionists, Moslem Beys and Christian Effendis could meet on terms of mutual conviviality. Only once was her social ascendancy challenged, and then by her own community. The occasion arose from a concert I arranged late in 1918 to provide funds for the Jerusalem School of Music. I had impressed upon its director, the accomplished violinist Tschaikov, that as neither the School nor the audience were exclusively Jewish he should at the conclusion confine himself to the first six bars of God Save the King; a condition he promised to observe. As he advanced to the front of the platform, we rose, when what was my consternation to hear not that confident, basic melody but the Smetanesque melancholy of the Zionist National Anthem. After a bar or so (Tschaikov casting upon me the agonized glance of one succumbing to *force majeure*) the Chief Administrator asked me hoarsely "What's that?" and when I answered *"Ha Tiqveh"*, asked again "What's that?" "Zionist National Anthem". He sat down sharply, and was of course followed by all his officers and, with reckless British courage (but in an evil hour for herself), by Miss Annie Landau. She was forthwith pilloried as a traitress to the Cause, though there was no immediately apparent means of punishing her. The Zealots' opportunity came with her first Ball, which they announced that no self-respecting Jew could possibly attend. All my sympathies were with Miss Landau, as a friend, as a hostess, as public benefactress number one; but I was powerless to lighten her natural despair at being boycotted by her own people. On the evening of the dance three Jewish fathers waited upon me in the Governorate. They had called to enquire whether I wished them to attend the dance, and seemed disappointed at my refusal to give them a direct injunction. The unhappy men had been undermined by treachery in their own homes: their wives and daughters had bought new frocks, and had every intention of using them. When four hours later I contemplated the line of patriots, some resentful, others defiant, all duly following up the staircase in the triumph of the daughters of Israel, my satisfaction was tinged with sympathy for men and brothers, as I realized that in one relation of life there is indeed neither Jew nor Gentile.

Every year I partook of Miss Landau's Feast of Tabernacles—Succoth—usually held in the precincts of the Orthodox Jewish Hospital of Shaare Zédek, whose Director the gentle German-Jewish Dr Wallach was the first in 1918 to send me my portion of *Mazzoth*, and is still my very good friend. Every single door in his hospital, including extra doors giving on to each staircase and landing, was kept locked, and had to be unlocked and relocked from a huge bunch of keys which the Doctor carried as he showed you round. I was never able to understand the reason of this practice, nor to learn whether it was German, Jewish or peculiar to Dr Wallach. At these Succoths you might meet the tragic, haunted figure of Dr Jacob Israel de Haan. He was a Dutch Jew; short, fair and extremely orthodox (else he had not been Miss Landau's guest in the Shaare Zédek); a good poet in the Dutch language and correspondent of, I think, *The Telegraaf*.[3] He had abandoned his career in Holland to serve the cause of Zionism in Palestine, and was bitterly disappointed that official Zionism seemed unable to make any use of his services. I have recorded the initial failure of the Zionist Commission to obtain the best results from local and Sephardi talent, but I will admit that de Haan may have been a difficult subject to place. Indeed, I told him that, much as I enjoyed his conversation in my house, I would not have had him on the Governorate Staff for anything; and I warned him that if he were not more temperate in his language he might get beaten up by his own people. Facially he was an intellectual version of Vincent van Gogh, whose dreadful glare of an unknown terror sometimes blazed in his eyes also. One morning I would see him hurrying past, gripping that comfortless black satchel without a handle, his *serviette d'avocat*. The next day his gold-rimmed spectacles would peer out of a white silk *kuffiya* as he drove across the Jordan in full Beduin costume—now become a Nordic Arab—to visit the Amir Abdallah. His talk on books was superb, causing me to lament the more

---

[3] I had heard of him even before his arrival, for he was interested in Semantics or Significs, and was so known to a connection of mine who had translated Bréal's work into English. I find, in answer to some request for travel facilities: "Nina's Dutch Zionist Significist had better work through the very powerful Zionist Organization in London: if he has not heard of it yet, his own mental significance must be restricted; and if he has, and been rejected by them, it is not for Christians to out-Herod."

that I could not understand the *Niewe Karthago* and his other poems that he gave me. And on a day when my whole official being was dismembered by the Hebrew world, he left at my door a Baudelaire, magnificently printed by some Dutch Press in which he was interested, with the inscription: "When all my people are cursing you, I send you this for a token that I believe in you, and in what you are trying to do." So, until my leave in the summer of 1924, the little Doctor would let off the steam of his angers in my house, and go away, I hoped and believed, happier than he had come. Then, in London, the Press telephoned that a Dr Jacob Israel de Haan had been murdered in the open streets of Jerusalem, not in an Arab Quarter; had I any opinion? I had not; but I still have a deep sympathy and regret for a man desperately alone, and "perplext in the extreme".

I am rendering no injustice but a tribute to the Hebrew Press immediately before and during the 1920's, when I recall that it represented the brass and the percussion rather than the strings or the wood-wind of the journalistic orchestra. The two principal newspapers, both dailies, were the *Doar ha-Yom,* or Daily News, and *ha-Áretz,* The Land.[4] When things went wrong (and there was consequently most need for moderation) these two would rival one another in a blare of hatred and contempt which besides vexing the spirits notably augmented the difficulties of all concerned.[5] The editor and apparent owner of the *Doar ha-Yom* was Itamar ben Avi, the excitable but attractive son of Ben Yahuda, who increased a natural resemblance to Lord Northcliffe by cultivating a Napoleonic shock over the right temple. We were on pleasant personal terms: indeed, after any particularly fierce attack he would call (preferably not by day nor at the Governorate) to explain that he had only averted the stoning of his premises (so furiously were the people raging together against me) by the insertion of this necessary minimum of abuse. He fur-

---

[4] Short for *Eretz Yisroel*, the Land of Israel.

[5] It is fair to record that the Jews were at least as violent in their opinions of each other. On the production of a Kol Yisroel, a newspaper representing extreme Jewish orthodoxy, a suddenly constituted body "Jewish Ultra Orthodox", *Sh'Lume Emune Yisroel,* published the following opinions:

"Brethren sons of Israel and the whole Yeshub!

"Raise your eyes and see the whole shocking and filthy atmosphere created by the Diskins, Zonenfelds, de-Haans and 'Agudath Israel' men.

"Let us all raise our voice powerfully! Let us tell them: 'Remove the old mask and counterfeit Orthodoxy from your faces and let not Jerusalem become destroyed and ruined!'

"Who asked you to invade our property! You have defiled Jerusalem! Do not continue to do wrong by inducing your men to go to jail so they can be sanctified, and by not letting them repent; you stand on your determination to both in the blood of a defiled Jerusalem. Woe, the skies are horrified to see such terrible defiling of the Name.

"Let all of us, old and young, assemble as one man and express our sharp and determined protest against the doers of this great sin—against the defilers of the honour of Jerusalem and her learned men."

nished me with an amusing instance of the *exalté* side of the Jewish genius when I remarked that it was fortunate the Jews of Jerusalem did not resemble the *Doar ha-Yom;* Jewish crime statistics in Palestine were comparatively low. "Low!" he exclaimed indignantly, "They may be low in Jerusalem, but I can assure you that in New York they are tremendous!"

The *ha-Áretz* was for some years more consistent in its hostility, until one day I took my courage in both hands and visited its offices in Tel Aviv. I went prepared to find a second Menahem Pasha arrayed against me, and was agreeably surprised to be greeted by a friendly, reserved and cultivated Dr. Glickson, the only man apart from Rutenberg, Weizmann and Maurice Baring who has made me regret my ignorance of the Russian language. The Hebrew Press in general shared with the Arab the defect of refusing to verify information before casting it into print. Scores of gross and sometimes comic errors [6] could have been avoided if the editor would have telephoned to the Government office concerned; and it was not until my last year that I was able to establish this system with the *ha-Áretz.* This "Dutch Courage" of Press intemperance in times of trouble served mainly to inflame the feelings of Arabs and British, as well as Jews. Some even shook their fists as I drove past (but soon ceased, apparently disconcerted by the receipt in return of a punctilious military salute). Chance favoured me once when I opened as guest of honour an exhibition at Tel Aviv, and two young indignants ostentatiously walked out as I rose to speak and in again (to point their moral) directly I sat down; a miscalculation which forced them, before a delighted audience, to endure the speech repeated word for word in Hebrew.

For daily news in English we were dependent upon *The Palestine Bulletin,* which consisted of two or three sheets of foreign telegrams, local information and official announcements. At first inclined to be tendencious, though milder than the Hebrew Press (or it would not have sold to Gentiles), the *Bulletin* became notably more impartial under Gershon Agronsky, an American trained journalist with something of the clear-cut decisiveness of Lord Lloyd. My colleagues were often bored by the lengthy descriptions of Teas, Luncheons and Dinners given in honour of the seventh, tenth, twenty-fifth or fiftieth anniversary in the career of some "famous" Zionist worker of Cracow or Pittsburgh; I found them no harder to bear than the detailed accounts of golf and football matches in the British Daily Press.

[6] Visiting Syria, my wife and I reached Damascus late at night, went straight to bed, and left at seven o'clock next morning. The Jerusalem Press published a spirited account of a banquet given in our honour by the Arabs of Damascus, in the course of which I had announced that I had been appointed His Majesty's Ambassador at the Court of Pekin.

"Where is God", asks van Gogh in a letter, "if not among the artists?" I cannot think He was invariably to be found with the painters of Palestine. All were zealous; two or three good; most seemed to concentrate upon acquiring the temperament rather than the qualifications of the artist. Nevertheless my feeling, after fourteen years in Egypt, was of enchantment to find any local painters at all. The two outstanding artists of my time were Rubin and Bomberg; Rubin with a whimsically interesting vision, Bomberg seeming to record a powerful cosmic stare. Rubin made friends everywhere; Bomberg passed from incident to incident. "Discovered" by Solomon J. Solomon, assisted by Sargent and Muirhead Bone, he had in 1923 been dispatched to Palestine by the Zionist Organization to paint propaganda. Apart from Bomberg's personal eccentricity, there were inherent possibilities of trouble in that Mrs Bomberg, though a Zionist, was not a Jewess, and that Bomberg, though entirely Jewish, was strongly anti-Zionist. Once in Palestine (fortified by a letter of introduction from Edward Marsh) Bomberg produced some admirable sketches and drawings of camels, mountains, and Arab villages, the last especially lending themselves to strong cubistic treatment. While I could not blame him for finding such subjects more easily convertible into terms of art than the facts of Jewish progress, enterprise and development, I felt that his Zionist sponsors were hardly receiving the sort of value they had reason to expect for their money, though I did consider that his paintings were at least as likely to attract the world to Palestine as the mechanized sower going forth sowing, or groups of merry immigrants dancing round Old Testament maypoles. Having broken with his original backers, Bomberg proceeded to execute some remarkable aspects of Judea in a happy blend of topographical and artistic reality. I arranged his journey and sojourn in Petra, whence returning he arrived in Jerusalem with some excellent canvases (one of which is now in the Birmingham Art Gallery) and a largish donkey standing in the rear half of his Ford car. The two landscapes of and from Jerusalem which he did for me were the best presentments that I have ever seen of those immortal prospects: the light white summer dust parched and blinded: the stones cried out. They were Jerusalem.

I remember Dr Weizmann regretting that the greatest sculptor in Russia, who was a Jew, could choose for his masterpiece nothing more racial than a statue of Peter the Great. In Palestine (perhaps as a result of the Doctor's *Ukase*) the common tendency was dreadfully the reverse. Shutting my eyes after ten years' absence, I can recall little beyond an unending series of Shulamīts, Jeremiahs, Rabbis in Synagogues or refugees in the snow. "Art" rugs were (most un-Mosaically) stencilled with portraits of Herzl or Samuel, brass ash-trays stamped with seven branch candlesticks or Solomon's Seal. This attitude, these exhibits, may have stimulated nationalistic expression but, especially as cultivated at the Bezalel Art Institution, they were the negation of art—often the death of craft.

Music is purer than visual art, and offers less opportunity for the cruder and more obvious 'forms of nationalistic propaganda. The Zionist Anthem *Ha Tiqvah* (after the old Russian and Austrian the finest of National Anthems) is far more Slavonic than Hebrew in feeling. It was unambitiously harmonized, and I always wondered that no musician had been at pains to write Variations and a Fugue on its strong simple melody. Meyerbeer and Mendelssohn are the only two standard composers of unquestionably Jewish extraction. Of these, Meyerbeer was dead beyond even fashionable resurrection at Covent Garden; and the influence of Mendelssohn, if any, was in the direct line of the great classics. Unshackled therefore by the tradition or necessity of producing specifically Jewish music, the natural genius of the Jews immediately attained an astonishingly high level of musical study and performance. The concerts of our Musical Society were an abiding pleasure, both from the quality of the music and from the spirit of the audiences— enthusiastic for Gentile, pardonably delirious over Hebrew virtuosity. On such occasions the hall would be rushed with amusing indiscipline by a few scores of ticketless devotees, passionately convinced that they had as much right to be there as anybody else. And I well remember my wife's amazement, as Chairman of the Committee, at the proportion of reduced or free tickets, or the half-dozen seats to one Press critic, that Mr Horovitz, as Secretary, considered the least the Society could accord. It is my firm belief that with official encouragement as well as private support Palestine may well become a centre of solo, chamber and orchestral music not inferior to Paris, Rome or even Vienna [7]; with the additional and rare advantage that even a mixed Palestine audience could hardly extract political significance from a sonata, a quintet or a symphony.

By 1922 we had begun to think of that less pure if more sumptuous and infinitely more costly form of music, Grand Opera (like tapestry, a criterion of higher civilization); and after one or two unsuccessful tentatives on our part [8] the Jews, under the resourceful Golinkin, succeeded;

---

[7] Some months after this claim was made, Toscanini proved it to the world.

[8] I find a 1922 circular reading: "A group of persons interested in art and music in Palestine met recently under the chairmanship of Mr Ronald Storrs, C.M.G., C.B.E., Governor of Jerusalem, to consider the possibility of starting an Opera Company in Palestine. The programme with facts and figures was discussed; and the conclusion was arrived at that the idea is feasible and can take shape in the near future provided a sufficient number of residents will take a practical interest in it." Nothing came of this.

proving incidentally the merit of Hebrew as a language for singing. The voices and the acting surpassed the orchestra, and the accommodation of the house was primitive. Heavy boots reverberated along the bare-planked corridors, and young men in white trousers and Russian blouses prowled up and down selling chocolate and pistachio nuts. The play was, very much, the thing; with an atmosphere remote as yet from the bourgeois rendezvous of the Paris Opera House, still remoter from the tiaras and unpunctualities of Covent Garden.

The immunity I have suggested for abstract music did not always save the musicians—as a troupe of White Russian Singers discovered on being seriously assaulted by Jerusalem Jews with recent persecutions hot in their memory. And there was the incident occasioned by the performance in Jerusalem of *La Juive*. One of the defects (minor elsewhere than in Jerusalem) of Halévy's opera is that it introduces upon the scene the daughter of a Cardinal. Its announcement therefore evoked a sharp protest from the Latin Patriarch, with the demand that the performance, billed for that night, should be canceled. The Administration sympathized with His Beatitude, but were unwilling to penalize the Company. A "formula" was found whereby the "Cardinal" should become on stage, hoardings and programmes alike, a Judge: and the piece was duly licensed though the Patriarchate stoutly maintained their objections. What then was the astonishment of the Government to receive from His Beatitude that evening a graceful appreciation of their just "firmness", and of the good effect it could not fail to produce in right-thinking circles! On enquiry they found that owing to some internal dispute the cast had struck, and refused to play: thus providing the solitary instance of the Palestine Government—perhaps of any Government—being accorded credit they did not deserve.

Hebrew drama without the help of melody was heavier going for the uninitiated; but even so, could anyone remain unstirred by, or ever forget, the terrifying *Dibbuk*, the tragedy of demoniac possession, startlingly presented by the Eretz-Israel Company?

I talked often with Ákhad ha-Ām ("One of the People") the essayist of spiritual Zionism; shy, courteous and distinguished, but already frail in his last illness; and I have always regretted I did not see more of the blunt simple Háyyim Nahaman Bialik, the Arch-Poet of the Hebrew Renaissance. Bialik's *Hakhnissíni* (Take me in!) has often been translated, but never so well as in the version which Jabotinsky gave me in Jerusalem; and which I now print, opposite the Hebrew original.

Hakhnissini tahat kenafekh	Be my mother, be my sister,
Va-hayi li em va-ahot	Screen my head beneath your wing,
	And my prayers, by God un-
V'ihi hekekh miklat roshi,	answered,
Kan tefillotay ha-niddahot.	To your bosom let me bring.
Bi-sh'at rahamin, ben hashemashot,	And at dusk, the hour of mercy,
Shehi va-agal lakh sod yissuray:	Stoop, I'll whisper you the truth:
Omrim yesh ba-olam neurim-	People talk of you—what is it?
Hekhan neuray?	Where is it, my youth?
Ve-od raz ehad lakh etvadda:	For my soul was burned by fire
Nafshi nisrefa be-lahavah,	From within, or far above;
Omrim ahava yesh ba-olam-	People talk of love—where is it?
Ma zot ahava?	What is it, to love?
Ha-Kokhavim rimmu oti,	Stars were bright, but they deceived me;
Haya halom—gam hu avar.	Gone the dream I dreamed before;
Atta en li kelum ba-olam,	Now my life has run to nothing—
En li davar.	Nothing more.
Hakhnissini tahat kenafekh,	Be my mother, be my sister,
Va-hayi li em va-ahot,	Screen my head beneath your wing,
V'ihi hekekh miklat roshi,	And my prayers, by God un-
	answered,
Kan tefillotay ha-niddahot.	To your bosom let me bring.

Apart from the works of these two fine writers the only Jewish book of outstanding merit produced in or about Palestine was Dr Klauzner's remarkable Hebrew *Life of Christ,* a study not only scholarly but sympathetic [9] and the first to be written on that theme by an orthodox religious Jew.

Two memories very clear in my mind illustrate the sort of unexpected attitudes that were found so disconcerting by officials from well established African or West Indian Colonies. I was walking with my wife on a Friday evening up the long street in the Meo Sheorim—the "Hundred Gates" [10] when we came upon a dense crowd of people. Crowds are not good in Jerusalem, and should never be allowed to gather. Pushing into the middle, I found an Arab taxi-driver earnestly claiming his fare. He had left Jaffa with a Jewish passenger that afternoon. By the time they reached this their destination the sun had set, the Sabbath had begun, and no sort of financial transaction could take place. There was no refusal to pay: "the driver had only to call on Sunday morning" (thus making

[9] Translated into excellent English by Canon Danby of St George's Cathedral, Jerusalem. Afterwards Professor of Hebrew at Oxford.

[10] I know not why so named. The only other use of the epithet I can remember was in ancient Thebes, which was constantly cited as ἑκατόμπυλος, hundred-gated.

two more journeys of forty miles) "and he would receive his money."
The gathering was animated but, as befitted the sacred hour, in excellent
temper. The Arab was a little dazed by the situation, which the Jews
were honestly puzzled by his inability to understand. He had no Hebrew
or Yiddish, without knowledge of which their Arabic seemed unintelligible. An onlooker, neither Arab nor Jew, discharged the debt and was
punctiliously (and I believe gratefully) repaid on Sunday morning.

During my third or fourth attendance at the Holy Fire I suddenly
noticed about ten yards from me that extra furious eddy and surge of a
mob which means killing. The vast and lion-hearted police officer Ibrahim
Stambūli ploughed me a path to the swirl, where I found to my horror
that a Jew had made his way (on this occasion of all) into the Church
of the Holy Sepulchre, and had been discovered. I suppose death was
about one minute away from him. Half a dozen constables, not without difficulty, carried him out of the building into safety. Next morning
he called at the Governorate to complain of police interference in a place
where he had just as much legal right to stand as they or I.

Zionists had reason to be proud of their creations, but their propaganda
was sometimes overwhelming. The unsuspecting tourist would be hustled
round communal settlements, Ost-Frisian Bulls, kosher abattoirs, maternity hospitals, Lodzia Sock Factory, Delphiner Silk Looms, Raanan
Chocolate Ovens and Silicate Brick Kilns, till his brain reeled with the
curves, graphs, diagrams and statistics. Tel Aviv, the Hill of Spring,[11]
excites very different emotions in different breasts, even conflicting emotions in the same breast. There indeed roars the street where rolled the
sand: there if anywhere on earth is the triumph of achievement. In 1909
sixty Jewish families living in Jaffa formed a resolve: *"Evneh venivnet"*—
"I shall build thee and thou shalt be built." Now on the barren dunes
stands a city of 130,000 inhabitants, the quintessential Jewish city, one
of the most significant cities in the world. The lettering which greets
your gaze, naming streets, banks, and shops is Hebrew; generally the
impressive square characters, sometimes alas! the repellent round Art
script, mocking and demeaning the ancient austerity. All over the world
shop-signs and names are of revealing interest. Jerusalem and Tel Aviv
were no exceptions, especially in their renderings of Jewish and Polish,
and even French originals. Several doctors were "Specialists in all diseases". "Diplomatic Midwife" did not necessarily denote a lady of more
tact and patience than the average *Sage Femme Diplomée*. A *Modiste*
proclaimed her skill in "Dresses for Balls and Street Walking". There
was too much building in Tel Aviv for the space, and much of the

11 Ezekiel iii. 15.

architecture had clearly been added after construction. Banks and doctors, lawyers and midwives were almost alternate along some of the crowded thoroughfares, and in the residential quarters the daughter of every house (home from the *Gymnasium*) might be heard tinkling out her daily portion of Grieg.

If you dislike Jews, if you do not actively like them—stand clear of Tel Aviv. They will say the Jews are the salt of the earth; you will reply that you cannot dine off salt. The concentration of Judaism, body, mind and soul can indeed be overpowering. I make bold to confess that I did like Tel Aviv, and that I would not willingly go near Palestine without a glimpse of its pulsating energy. As I write it is as though the Mayor, Mr Dizengoff, *pater patriae,* were conducting me once more round his creation: I listen to the latest prodigy of the Hopenko School of Music: in the hospitable villa of Siegfried Tolkowsky I realize the talismanic significance of the Citrus Industry—and almost acknowledge my guilt for not having refused to shake the hand of the supposed anti-Semite Henry Ford. I did my best when in Cyprus to support Tel Aviv through its Levant Fair; and I shall always wish the place and the people Good Luck—Mazal Tov. Economists may enquire what, apart from oranges, potash and bromine, is the permanent hinterland of this phenomenon, which needs so much more than it can offer in exchange. The answer is that the hinterland of Tel Aviv is the sixteen million Jews of the world.

II

So far as the Consular Corps was concerned, our relations with the Powers continued to be friendly. France, in every way our most important ally, was for some years represented by the *"coup d'épingle aux anglais"* type of pre-Entente days, further stimulated by the rearguard action they thought fit to maintain for the retention of the religious *protectorat français.* Under this spirit accidents easily became incidents, and incidents were magnified into minor crises. They imputed to our officers *l'esprit colon;* we thought them *messieurs les ronds-de-cuir.* A complete change to a relationship of trust was effected by the appointment of the charming and distinguished Gaston Maugras, who was immediately welcomed by the Administration as a colleague rather than a foreigner, and through whom Anglo-French contacts became, what they should always be, a reciprocal pooling of information and of confidence.

The Italian Consuls were friendly from the first, and became intimate in the time of Villarey and Tritoni. Their Government, not content with the far-flung possessions and influence of the Franciscans, manifested for years an extreme eagerness for the ownership (by bargain or purchase) of the *Coenaculum,* the so-called Place of the Last Supper, a fourteenth-century Gothic building owned and venerated as the Tomb of David by the Moslem community.[12] The Mandatory is precluded (and protected from any such concession by the Status Quo, interference with which is dreaded in Palestine hardly less than is in France the reopening of the Treaty of Versailles. Now and again some Palermo professor would publish an article accusing the Mandatory of anti-Latin conduct and partisanship with the Greeks and Jews, but such questions were never raised officially.

The Spanish Consul, a retiring but agreeable man of overwhelming piety, had special relations with the Franciscans, whose Finance Member, the *Procurador,* as well as the friars of Ain Karem, must by statute be of Spanish extraction. No Egyptian Consul was appointed until 1925, nor German until just before my departure in 1926. The pleasant Greek Consul sat watching the Orthodox Patriarchate; Belgium was represented by Mr Tolkowsky of Tel Aviv (until as a Jewish patriot he resigned the post), and Mexico by a Christian Arab who flew his tutelary flag from the most tremendous flagstaff in the Near East.

Although the salaries of officials were (compared for instance with those of Cyprus) relatively high, so was the cost of living; and mutual entertainment, very frequent in Military days of free rations, fuel, and cars, seemed to decrease as the Administration and their families grew larger and older. One or two determind hostesses were still receiving in 1926, but their efforts had begun to resemble a game of tennis in which the service is never returned. My wife and I were At Home every Sunday from four till seven, and seldom had less than thirty visitors in pretty equal proportions of all the communities. A good Sporting Club had early been formed, open (after some of us had refused to support it otherwise) to all races and creeds. A Ladies' Club started, but stopped. A Social Club, in spite of meetings, circulars and projects never came to anything.

I had the honour of founding and of being the first President of the Jerusalem Dramatic Society. Strongly supported by the High Commissioner and illumined by the acting and producing genius of a Treasury official, F. Aylmer Harris, this Society mounted with distinction *Twelfth Night, Macbeth, Patience, Dear Brutus* and *A Midsummer Night's Dream.* The casts were agreeably mixed; King Duncan, the Assistant

---

[12] I learnt on good authority in Rome that the possession of the *Cenacolo* was of no direct interest to the Vatican, by whom, however, it was known to be the strong desire of the Italian Government.

Governor; Snug, a joiner, an Arab, Tewfik Nasr; and among the fairies, some children of Israel Sol Biras, Hannah Yahoudah Carmen Friedlaender. I tried to extract the maximum good from these performances by having the plots translated weeks before into Arabic and Hebrew, circulated round all schools and published in the local Press. For Shakespeare and *Patience* we had at least two matinées for schools; at which also my wife and I arranged that, for the first time in Palestine History, Moslem ladies should be present, chastely concealed in boxes covered with mosquito-curtains dyed brown to intercept the gaze of the curious. *Macbeth* (though many found the plot more congenial) was less successful than *Midsummer Night,* there being only two children's parts to attract relations. For these entertainments, for concerts, and for exhibitions I circularized Government Departments, Hotels, and the Press five weeks, one week, and the day before the event; I informed churches, mosques and synagogues; they were proclaimed by the Town Crier and by streamers across the Jaffa Road (for the benefit of the unrealized illiterate and deaf with whom all communities abound). Hardly ever did I fail to receive when all was over three or four communications from ladies deploring that for "a Show which people say was *so* successful" somebody could not have taken a little trouble to let people know beforehand.

For other entertainment you could shoot partridge and sandgrouse in the Jordan valley, and might even be so fortunate as to kill a descendant of the few wild boars left by the Australians. At Lydda was a pack of hounds which hunted jackals through the olive groves. At the Meet (it was a point of honour to attend) on Boxing Day we sometimes mustered nearly a hundred strong.

Besides the pageantry of the major festivals, residents were occasionally treated to an unexpected amenity. Early in 1922 representatives of the Fox Film Corporation descended upon Jerusalem for the purpose of screening against the sixteenth-century walls the capture of the City by Titus. These realists soon found the Palestine colour to be all too local. The legionaries, borrowed from the British Regiment, and duly accoutred in *palliums* and helmets, had hardly begun the assault when a real (though trifling) alarm elsewhere caused them to hurry into their tunics and trousers and decamp. Nor were the operators more fortunate when they descended to the plains to record a camel charge by Beduin. Two or three hundred of these warriors were expensively collected and furnished for the occasion with gilt "property" javelins. The ground was chosen and measured, and the cameras placed. But the temptation was too strong for the children of Ishmael; and the camels, complete with riders and armament, galloped out of focus into space, to be no more seen.

Would that I could remember more of the remarkable visitors to Palestine. One quality they had in common: the greater the man the deeper his appreciation of Jerusalem. Lord Milner came twice: the first time in the days of O.E.T.A., when I took him down to Hebron to see the great mosque built over the Cave of Machpelah.[18] At tea afterwards with the Military Governor we found tennis, and I was asked to play. An Arab handed me the balls for service and as he turned to pick up more emitted a curious clank. Looking closer I discovered that both he and his colleague at the other end were long term criminals, heavily chained by the ankles, whom the local police officer had sent up from the gaol to act as ball boys. I could not believe that such a practice (convenient though it were) would favourably impress a Cabinet Minister, but Lord Milner seemed to endure it with fortitude. On his second visit in 1922 after the first unsuccessful Egyptian negotiations:

He told me that there was no reason on earth why an Egyptian Agreement infinitely more satisfactory to ourselves should not have been reached in London last summer. Adli was intelligent, sympathetic and willing; and by clinching the matter then M. could have obtained reciprocal guarantees from the Egyptians which the actual Agreement (if so it can be called) has not given us. The Egyptians were prepared to do almost anything so long as they were allowed foreign representatives. They would have declared and acknowledged a military zone, not raised the question of the Sudan, and allowed the Advisers to continue in Office. But the whole thing was upset owing to the opposition of X, acting on Y.

By July 1920, the position of Faisal in Damascus had become impossible. He really believed that Lord Allenby would intervene or even support him against our French Allies, and his disillusion and expulsion in 1920 after so glorious an entry a bare twelvemonth earlier was a pathetic, almost a tragic episode. His decline and fall are dramatically shown by the translations he gave me of the last telegrams exchanged.

21. vii. 20.

Monsieur le Général Gouraud,
Having accepted all the conditions stated in your note of the 14th inst., and finding in spite of that the French troops advancing towards Damascus, and desirous, on the other hand, to avoid till the last moment a useless effusion of blood, I ask for an arrest of operations of the troops which would enable us to discuss affairs as indicated by your telegram received to-day. A member of the Government is proceeding to see you with a commission to discuss affairs in the name of the Government.

Faisal.

18 *Handbook of Palestine*, p. 111, "a-b".

Général Gouraud,   23. vii. 20.
    Beirut.

We refuse war, but the acceptance of your last note will certainly lead us to a civil war and every member of the Government as well as myself will be personally exposed to danger. We are disposed to execute fully your ultimatum of 14 July, four conditions of which have already been carried out and we engage ourselves to execute it loyally if the French army will retreat from the places it has just occupied.

                                             Faisal.

                                               27. vii. 20.

From Colonel Toulat, Chief of the French Mission. To H.R.H. Amir Faisal.

Damascus

I have the honour to communicate to Y.R.H. a decision of the French Government requesting you to leave Damascus as soon as possible by way of the Hejaz Railways, with Y.R.H.'s Family and Suite.

A special train will be at the disposal of Y.R.H. and Suite. This train will leave the Hejaz Station at 5 hours to-morrow the 28 July 1920.

I beg Y.R.H. to accept the expression of my high consideration.

                                             Toulat.

On the 31st French aircraft were dropping proclamations denouncing Faisal and threatening reprisals if he did not leave Syria immediately. By 2 August the lamentable scene had shifted to Haifa, whose Governor had suddenly received and accommodated the Amirs Faisal and Zaid, fourteen other first class passengers, six servants and two cars. Faisal was eager and fretting to reach Alexandria before Lord Allenby left for England. "Faisal and Zaid", wrote the harassed Governor, "and their A.D.C.'s are no trouble, but it is the other notables who are round the place and in and out like a swarm of bees, and one never knows how many meals are required for lunch or dinner." In addition to this party

"The following want to go to Suez

Bodyguard of 17 with rifles	72 followers with
5 motor-cars	25 women
1 carriage	25 horses.

They cannot stay on here indefinitely."

We are all [I wrote home] exceedingly grieved for him, and are far from certain he has been quite fairly treated. . . . Faisal hopes to win through to England by Genoa. As it is, with the murder of my poor friend Bianchini,[14] he has chosen a *brutto tempo per arrivare in Italia.*

I went with Sir Herbert to greet Faisal and Zaid when the train of exile passed through Ludd, where we mounted him a guard of honour

[14] P. 388.

a hundred strong. He carried himself with dignity and the noble resignation of Islam,

> Nor called the gods with angry spite
> To vindicate his helpless right

though the tears stood in his eyes and he was wounded to the soul. The Egyptian Sultanate did not "recognize" him, and at Qantara station he awaited his train sitting on his luggage.

By December he was in London, faithfully attended by Haddād (by that time a Pasha), and I was doing my best by introducing him to publicists and politicians to further his cause. On such occasions I persuaded him to wear his Arab robes; with no little difficulty, for so remote was he from the London atmosphere that he really believed he would create a better impression in faultless evening dress. Not all these great men seemed to realize that it was the politics and not the literature or archaeology of the Arab world that he had come to discuss. After enduring a ten minutes' *questionnaire* from Rudyard Kipling as to the size, number, origin and significance of camel brands in the Hejaz, he asked me in Arabic over the poet's shoulder: "Does this man take me for a camel dealer?"

Mr Winston Churchill's visit to Palestine in 1922 was brief but memorable. By his swift momentous decision to accept and install the Sharīf Abdallah as Amir of Transjordan, he created in a few minutes a new Principality. So appreciative was he of the beauty of the Temple Area by moonlight that he seemed thereafter to grudge every moment spent away from his easel.

In the spring of 1925 preparations were made on an imposing scale for the formal opening by Lord Balfour of the Hebrew University of Jerusalem. The universities of the world sent their delegates, and I had the honour of presenting the Address of the Public Orator of Cambridge. "Next week", I wrote home, "A.J.B.: an event much wished for by the Jews, conspued by the Arabs, dreaded by the Police." It seemed incredible that so distinguished and delightful a person could be for the Arabs Public Enemy Number One, yet the anxiety lest they might somehow succeed in treating him as such was upon me day and night. Neither he nor those with him had the faintest conception of the risk he was running, or of the strain which his presence imposed. What chance indeed had he of being allowed to realize the depth of Arab feeling when the scores of abusive telegrams awaiting him at Government House were destroyed by his secretary without his being informed of their existence? On the other hand, from all accounts few men can ever have received an ovation comparable with that accorded him at his reception in Tel Aviv—the delirious accumulated enthusiasm of two thousand years. At the opening ceremony on Mount Scopus he impressed that critical gathering less by his eloquence, which was easily surpassed by Sir Herbert Samuel's, than by the splendour of his personality.

We have seen a good deal of A. J. B., who, though his visit has put the clock of reconciliation back by at least a year, was, as always, all that is most fascinating as company. He lunched with us thrice, and visited the whole city save only the great Mosque, into which the Police and I agreed that it was highly undesirable for him to penetrate.

During our luncheon before his walk to the Church of the Holy Sepulchre I was called to the telephone by the Police. They warned me that the atmosphere was bad, and begged me to abandon the expedition. I had agreed to omit the visit to the Dome of the Rock, a privilege which no Christian would desire to claim if the Mufti were churlish enough to refuse it. But entry to the Sepulchre was a right which it was intolerable should be denied to Arthur Balfour. I therefore decided to take the risk. The steep narrow streets were packed with sullen, silent onlookers. As they returned my salutations, I hoped that my guest would take their greetings as addressed to himself; and learnt afterwards that he had. About the door of the Church the throng was so dense that we arranged to open another exit through the Coptic Convent. In a trice the crowd had guessed the plan and rushed round to await the party—which therefore departed by the main door and returned home in peace. Lord Balfour left Palestine "without untoward incident, so that high official credit is awarded to the Police: in the event of trouble you might have heard more of the Governor". He found the other side of the Tel Aviv picture at Damascus where, but for the swift diversion of his train to an unexpected station, he must inevitably have been torn in pieces. And the journey that had begun so brilliantly ended (after an agonized prayer for his departure by the French Governor of Damascus) in two days' marooning on a liner in Beirut Harbour, guarded from a hostile shore by the circling of a French torpedo-destroyer.

The relations of the Palestine Government with the Palestine representatives of the Holy See up to 1921 though correct could hardly be called cordial, and bristled with misunderstandings. I would receive, for instance, a letter from a Monsignore accusing the Palestine Postal Administration of having caused the loss of a number of signed photographs of the late Pope which he had sent to Roman Catholic notables of Jerusalem, and threatening to write to the Press to complain "of the manner in which the British Administration in Palestine treats Catholics". We held an enquiry and discovered that the photographs had been lost in Italy. About midsummer of that year I suggested to Sir Herbert Samuel that I should make (at my own charges but not counting it as leave) a visit to Rome, resume the contacts I had started in 1919 and explain directly to as many Prelates as might be found there in the summer the realities of the situation. I was deeply sensible of the courtesy and fairness with which my unofficial mission was welcomed. I was received (for the second time) by the Pope in a private audience lasting half an hour. His Holiness had evidently been receiving alarmist reports as to the "preponderating influence of Jews" and the partiality of the Palestine Government, and I was able to prove to him by facts and figures that these fears were unfounded. Cinema performances, which had apparently been represented as if introduced by the British, were common long before the British Occupation: on the one occasion on which the Latin Patriarch had drawn my attention to an undesirable film, I had had it suppressed, for which I had received the Patriarch's official thanks. No ball, public or private, was now allowed within the Walls of Jerusalem. The Pope seemed mollified, and said that these things proved that *buona volontà* on the part of the authorities was clearly not wanting; but added that he had heard that the Government permitted, without effective opposition, the existence in Jerusalem of many ladies of doubtful reputation. I thanked His Holiness for affording me the opportunity of explaining exactly what had been done to combat these practices. On our entry into Jerusalem, we had found no less than 500 such women living in a special quarter. Of these I had returned as many as possible to their places of origin so soon as possible, and had, more than two years ago, abolished the quarter. There might be still a certain number, but it was in any case infinitesimal when compared with what we had originally found, and I submitted that with the utmost vigilance it was difficult to ensure to any city, however sacred, complete exemption from this particular form of abuse. This was what the British Administration had achieved in two or three years in the Holy City: was the Eternal City, after eighteen centuries, wholly immune? His Holiness agreed that such an ideal was at present unattainable. I derived from this audience the impression that the Pope had been for some time subjected to very great pressure, which had certainly succeeded in prejudicing him against the Palestine Administration. He remarked, for instance, significantly, that "it would be a great disgrace to any mandatory if, after a certain period, the departure of the Turks should be openly regretted".

The Pope was desirous that I should not leave Italy without seeing

Cardinal Gasparri, the Cardinal Secretary of State. I therefore hung about Rome for some days waiting for his return from his holiday, and finally took train and car with Cecil Dormer of the British Legation to the Cardinal's home in the tiny village of Ussita in the Marches. We entered the village church, capable of holding perhaps a score, and found the famous prelate celebrating Mass before a dozen worshippers. After the service he took us to breakfast in his cottage. He was good enough to listen attentively to my explanation of various questions that had been raised by the Patriarch or the Press. I observed throughout these audiences and interviews that Roman dignitaries in Rome were genuinely desirous of arriving at the truth, and open to conviction on matters not only of fact but of policy; and I left them with a respect and admiration which were not diminished by the courtesy of His Holiness in sending a Monsignore to the station to bid me farewell.

Throughout my visit I was impressed (ten years before the Concordat) with

the close relations between the Vatican and the Italian Government, as also the deference paid to the Cardinal Secretary of State by Government officials. The day I visited the Cardinal the Minister of Fine Arts was travelling over 100 miles to see him, and I found that the telephone authorities had instructions to give priority to calls from the Vatican to the Cardinal in his remote mountain village.

The Administration were kind enough to offer me a public banquet at the end of December 1922 on the fifth anniversary of my appointment.[15] By this time the funds of the Pro-Jerusalem Society were beginning to run low, partly owing to the disconcerting practice whereby original contributors announced that their subscriptions had really been donations; and I obtained the willing permission of the High Commissioner to spend my 1923 leave visiting America for the purpose of collecting new members. Crude such a project sounds to-day, and remote indeed from the financial actuality of the late 'thirties. Thanks largely to the wonderful hospitality of Mrs Cornelius Vanderbilt I was enabled to treat the United States in precisely the same manner as we accuse Americans of treating Europe. My three weeks proved a concentration of quintessential experience. Besides the entertainments devised for me by my hosts (I was listening to a *matinée* of *Tannhäuser* within half an hour of landing) I went almost every day to the Metropolitan Museum, heard Jeritza at the Opera, visited the Cabarets with Otto Kahn (a tremendous flask in his

---

[15] I remember attempting a comparison between actual conditions and those of December 1917; the contrast in 1937 would be sharper still, and materially to the good, save perhaps in the supplanting of the grey building-stone of Jerusalem by international reinforced concrete.

pocket), saw the Ziegfeld Follies including the rapturous Messrs Gallagher and Sheean,[16] danced in Greenwich Village, read the lessons in the Cathedral of St John the Divine, addressed United Methodists, Presbyterians and the English Speaking Union, studied Boston and Baltimore, stayed with the Bibescos in Washington and was accorded half an hour's audience by President Harding immediately before hearing him announce in the Capitol his acceptance of the Baldwin Debt Settlement. I visited Chicago as the guest of General Dawes (who was playing *Tristan und Isolde* as I entered his house), delivered addresses on Lincoln's Birthday in Springfield, Illinois, at the Luncheon Club and the Opera House, inspected the Packard Works at Detroit and had an hour's talk with Henry Ford, broadcast on the wireless, and tumbled into the *Berengaria* with several thousand pounds in my pocket,[17] having enjoyed the country and people to the limit of the possible; but more dead than alive. The shameless and dreadful work of asking for money, to be spent (by no means upon charity) thousands of miles away, taught me many things. Men were still more generous than women and required less explaantion before giving. Social anti-Semitism existed to a degree unknown in England. Extreme Zionists were extreme indeed, and actively disliked by non-Zionist Jews. Several Jews refused money for Pro-Jerusalem lest they should thereby further Zionism. I lost donations from non-Jews by refusing to undertake that such funds should not benefit Jews. (The purport and the strength of Pro-Jerusalem had from the first been an utter rejection of religious and racial preferences.) The distinguished lawyer Mr Paul Cravath had been kind enough to ask a score of friends interested in Palestine to meet me at dinner. I gave my exposition under the impression that there were no Jews present. When I had finished, a fellow guest bearing a name honoured throughout American Jewry came up and expressed himself as so well satisfied with my thesis that he hoped I would lunch at his club and meet a Zionist gathering. I expounded my theme there on the same lines. As I was putting on my coat in the hall someone behind me muttered to his companion, "Well, if that's all we're going to get . . ."— and for a moment I felt I was back in Jerusalem.

I had hardly returned from this journey before I was summoned to the deathbed of my mother—I suppose the first overwhelming sorrow in most men's lives. For us it was—illogically perhaps—deepened by the sight of the Cathedral and the streets of Rochester crowded to overflowing as the

---

[16] I observed generally that on the American comic stage the wearing of an Egyptian fez or tarbush was accepted on sight as a standard joke—almost like the red nose or too small a hat on the English boards.

[17] And this though I had crossed and recrossed the Dean of Windsor, then appealing for St George's Chapel.

great horses drew the farm-wains with their pyramids of flowers behind the woman from whom so many had known an individual kindness or encouragement. Happiness came in July when my father celebrated my marriage in St Peter's, Eaton Square, amid all the surroundings and some of the faces of my earliest youth. Jerusalem showed herself very gracious: the communities greeted my wife on the platform, there were festoons of palm and pine branches and kindly welcomings from Moslem, Christian and Jewish Municipalities in Jerusalem and Bethlehem, Ramleh, Jaffa and Tel Aviv. Her influence quickly radiated through and beyond my house, ranging from the management of the Musical Society to insistence that a reluctant Public Health Department should provide in the Government Hospital a Harīm maternity ward for the training of Moslem midwives.

One of the many delights of Palestine is the ease with which places famous in the past and beautiful to-day can be visited within the fortnight's local leave to which officials are entitled. We drove through the orange groves of Nabk in Aleppo; walked the bazaars, climbed the Citadel, and visited the oldest synagogue in the world; we entered the little grotto church, high on Mount Silpius over Antioch, where "the people were first called Christians"; and stooping under Apollo's laurels we drank from the still haunted Fountain "in that sweet grove of Daphne by Orontes"; we wandered in Petra, Palmyra, Baalbek and Jerash,[18] and we travelled in Syria with the brilliant but disenchanted French High Commissioner, Henri de Jouvenel. Sometimes we went down to Egypt, finding it at each descent less dramatic a contrast with that simplicity of Palestine, which in early days had been so sore a trial to my Egyptian servant. We stayed with my great martial chief Lord Allenby, the last military occupant of the Residency, whose renown was only exceeded by his humorous self-deprecation. Who else in that exalted position would have described a Cairo Consul General as "a very good fellow, and we all like him: he was the President's Doctor, so he knows about as much about his job as—I do about mine". We stayed with Lord Lloyd, observing his grip of the situation and the various reactions thereto. On his arrival all Egypt had been clamouring for the removal of Nashaat Pasha, the Palace manipulator of the country's destiny. George Lloyd grasped the nettle: there were tears in Abdīn and Nashaat woke to find himself in Persia. Within a year those at first loudest in praise of Lloyd (in England as well as Egypt) were accusing him of arbitrary intervention. As his Rolls-Royce shot past the white-gloved policemen on point duty, critics, remarking the double escort of motor cyclists, murmured acidly of Indian pomp

---

[18] To me the physical presentment of Fustel de Coulange's *Cité antique*.

and circumstance. Had they been at pains to enquire, they would have learned that the precaution had been imposed by the British General Officer Commanding, not unmindful of a Sirdar recently shot to death in a democratically unprotected car. The critical spirit of Cairo seemed to be still marching on.

About the middle of the 'twenties I declined (though gratefully and regretfully) the offer of a Lieutenant-Governorship. Clayton resigned the Chief Secretaryship, and on being sounded I ventured to impart to the High Commissioner my dread of three or four years' distasteful office routine. When therefore my friend Symes was promoted, I rejoiced doubly: that he had gained the position, and that I had not.

And now ended the term of Sir Herbert Samuel, which I felt, and still feel, to be for many reasons, more memorable for good than any for long years likely to occur. I do not believe that any previous five years in the history of Palestine—certainly none subsequent—can show a legacy of accomplishment comparable with that of his orderly, creative and passionless intelligence. His tenure of office was criticized by Moslems and Christians because he was Jewish, by extreme Zionists because he was not Jewish enough. (So boys in the Headmaster's House are apt to lament that his impartiality loses them their fair share of the School Prizes.) I am (as perhaps this book has shown) a pro-man and not an anti-man. Such ideals as I have in life are positive and constructive. But if I were put up against a wall and ordered on pain of death to be anti-something I should (swiftly) declare myself anti-ingratitude and anti-disloyalty, with special reference to Jewish depreciation of Sir Herbert Samuel's work in Palestine. And I firmly believe, if a Gentile may express an opinion on Jewish affairs (Jews express themselves freely enough on ours) that the names of the Big Four who will go down to history in the rebuilding of Zion will be Theodor Herzl, who saw the vision; Chaim Weizmann, who grasped the occasion; Arthur Balfour, who caused the world to renew the ancient Promise in a modern Covenant; and Herbert Samuel, who turned principle into practice, word into fact. Extreme Zionists will be rendering a poor service to Jewry if they make it impossible for a man to prove himself a good Englishman as well as a good Jew.

Once more I found myself on the Jaffa shore, greeting as Chief my third Field-Marshal.

The Plumers have made a good start, but I, whose frequent vicissitudes have made me share Oxford's love for lost or departed causes, am always irritated by the chorus of adoration projected upon the rising sun. Everything that either of them does is construed to the disadvantage of their predecessors, and that by those who but a few months ago were roaring for a prolongation of the Samuel regime.

Whether there be prophecies, mine or anybody else's, about the East, they shall fail. Writing immediately after (and just before) three years' calm, it appeared to me that

the chief difficulties of the future will be economic rather than political, as the bondholders of the Ottoman Debt have insisted on their pound of flesh for Palestine's share of the interest, not only for the period of civil government but for that of the Military Occupation also; thus condemning us to pay some £400,000 extra in the next two or three years—a sum crippling to a Government whose whole budget is hardly two millions.

Within a very few years my prediction was doubly falsified. Public security had become a more serious preoccupation than ever, and the Treasury stood so full that until the 1936 disturbances the difficulty was how to employ the surplus over the ample Reserve. Amongst other effects of the newly acquired wealth of Palestine was the expensive but necessary provision of the Jerusalem Water Supply, which our early poverty could never contemplate. (During the drought of 1925, after organizing five water trains a day, we even feared for a moment that we might be forced to evacuate sections of the population until the coming of the rain.) This was not my only miscalculation. In retrospect, the obverse of prophecy, my letters home seem to attach an excessive importance to three events which, in fact, touched Palestine hardly at all. The Administration was apprehensive to the point of nervousness over the effect of our first Census, traditionally unpopular in the East, which passed off without hitch in 1922. Similarly, the victories over Greeks (and Allies) gained by Mustafa Kemal were seriously taken:

Many expect (and some would now welcome) M. K. and indeed I do not know what force exists to stop him walking into the Turf Club, Cairo;

and the fall of Mr Lloyd George, refracted through the telegrams, seemed to us dynastic—almost like the passing of the Great Duke of Wellington.

In the summer of 1926 I was offered and accepted the Governorship of Cyprus. During our journey back from England to take leave of Palestine we saw at close range Mussolini, with the strength and heavy-lidded impassivity of a Mongol conqueror, address a Coliseum packed with young Fascists. In Athens some officials and editors of newspapers expressed their gratification at the appointment of a Philhellene to Cyprus. In Egypt King Fuad wished us good luck.

I had always dreaded the day when I should have to leave Jerusalem, but the reality was sharper than I had ever dreamed. I realized with a pang that I must wind up Pro-Jerusalem. Under Clifford Holliday who succeeded Ashbee in 1922, we had completed the restoration of the City Walls, Ramparts, and Citadel; repaired the Damascus Gate, Herod's Gate, and the Zion Gate; and removed the offence of the Turkish "Jubilee" Clock Tower from the Jaffa Gate. Under the provisions of a Town Planning Ordinance, developing and legalizing my first arbitrary Proclamations, we had maintained the architectural style of the Old City by preserving flat roofs, vaults, domes, street arches, abutments and buttresses, and by prohibiting asbestos sheets, Marseilles tiles, and corrugated iron. We had placed the ceramic industry on a sound financial footing, organized six more art exhibitions, and published a portfolio of architectural photogravures (with letterpress in English, Arabic and Hebrew) and the first practical modern map of Jerusalem. We had made a Civic Survey of the City and surrounding district, and enacted a definitive town-planning scheme for the Old and New Cities, comprising the conservation of historic monuments, new roads, zones for industries, shops and housing, and the establishment of a green belt round the City and the natural reservation of the valleys of Hinnom and of Jehoshaphat and the Mount of Olives. And it is owing to Pro-Jerusalem that the only surviving grave-stone of a Crusader, the English Philip d'Aubigny, signatory of Magna Charta, Governor of the Channel Islands and tutor to King Henry the Third, is preserved, safe at last under a wrought iron grille from the trampling of feet, before the Church of the Holy Sepulchre. Meanwhile the Departments concerned had grown in scope as well as efficiency; whilst subscriptions to Pro-Jerusalem steadily decreased. Holliday had obtained an official Municipal appointment, and by his private architectural practice was providing a corrective to the Central European proclivities of some of his colleagues. Pro-Jerusalem had always been a personal, perhaps a too personal, Society. In the absence of any clear perspective

> ...it seemed a greater grief
> To watch it wither, leaf by leaf
> Than swiftly pass away.

There were three very drastic weeks of farewells, receptions, and addresses; tiredness and sadness mingled with speeches abroad and the continual hammering of packing cases at home. The Life Honorary Presidentships of Chamber of Commerce, Musical Society and the other bodies we had founded or helped to found, meant to us very much more than an empty compliment. On the eve of our going we climbed the Russian Tower of the Ascension and drank in for the last time that doubly magnificent view: to the East the scarred wilderness of Zin, for all the world like the dead craters of the moon, the dull strong matrix turquoise of the Dead Sea, the amethystine rampart of Moab and of Edom; to the West the walls and battlements, encircling the domes, towers and pinnacles, which, for all their forty sieges and destructions still present intrinsically the distant Jerusalem contemplated and lamented by Christ. A City set in the midst of mountains gaunt, austere, uncompromising but yet of a perfect distinction and in a supreme style: of an atmosphere at once thrilling and poignant, which from the first had taken me by the throat. I walked round and within the City Walls; up and down the Temple Area; I took my long last leave of the Armenian Cathedral and of the Holy Sepulchre. At midnight I made my final inspection of the Police Posts, checked the registers and verified the attendances. Next morning we ran the kindly gauntlet at the station; and at noon of 29 November, accompanied by the boxes containing everything I had acquired in life since the age of twenty-two, we embarked at Jaffa upon His Majesty's Sloop *Cornflower* and sailed for Cyprus.

I cannot pretend to describe or analyse my love for Jerusalem. It is not wholly sentimental, aesthetic or religious—still less theological or archaeological; though I hope it contains something of all five. A little perhaps also that I had worked and enjoyed and suffered there from the beginning; that I knew the people so well and liked them so much; that after misunderstandings had always followed understanding; that I had shared the delight there of my father and mother; that I had begun there the happiness of my married life. Persons of wider aesthetic experience and more facile emotions have often come there to pray and gone away to mock. For me Jerusalem stood and stands alone among the cities of the world. There are many positions of greater authority and renown within and without the British Empire, but in a sense I cannot explain there is no promotion after Jerusalem.

CHAPTER EIGHTEEN

Lawrence 1917–1935

"A pardlike spirit beautiful and swift."

SHELLEY

My Baghdad journal of 15 July 1917 unsupplemented alas, by memory, tells me: "Lawrence and Fielding to lunch. L.'s performance in Syria little short of miraculous and I hope he will get his V.C. Mentioned to me vague Damascus possibilities."[1]

During my leave in London I heard nothing of him: on my return to Cairo at the end of 1917 he was—elsewhere.

Rūhi, whom I had instructed to watch over him in the beginning, told me that Lawrence came to him in Jeddah for further information about the customs and habits of the Hejaz Arabs. Rūhi compiled for him a vocabulary of vernacular Arabic expressions, accompanied him round the coast to Yanbo, Quaddīma, Umlej and Wajh, and there suggested to him that he should leave his uniform for Arab garments. At that time (according to Rūhi), Lawrence "spoke Arabic with horrible mispronunciation"; and though he greatly improved his accent, he never could have passed as an Arab with an Arab—a defect which renders his achievement the more remarkable.[2] He learnt the prostrations of the Moslem prayer, and for a time called himself the Sharīf Hassan, "born of a Turkish mother in Constantinople".

There are other accounts, besides those in *Seven Pillars,* of the dynamiting of Turkish bridges[3] and culverts: none so far as I know giving the impressions of a dynamitee. This was the unsolicited introduction to Lawrence of Carl Raswan,[4] travelling on a Turkish train to Damascus:

[1] Both he and Haddād had thought of me for Military Governor there.

[2] "I could never pass as an Arab—but easily as some other native speaking Arabic." Liddell Hart, *T. E. Lawrence,* p. 24.

[3] The German General Staff pathetically records that "The destruction of 25 Railway Bridges on the Hejaz Railway line from May 1-19 shows how difficult it was to maintain the Hejaz Railway in operation."

[4] A German-American traveller-photographer of unusual artistry.

Somewhere near Deraa in Transjordan, as we approached a dry river bed, we were stopped, and as we looked out of the windows of our carriage, I suddenly saw and heard a terrible explosion, followed by several smaller ones. A bridge, several yards ahead of us, had been blown up with a train on it. It was ahead of our Military Convoy; our cars were shattered by falling debris, but I remember hardly anything, as we were taken away from the place of disaster and had to stay several days near Amman, until the bridge had been repaired.

Early in January 1918 I was sitting in a snowbound Jerusalem when an orderly announced a Beduin, and Lawrence walked in and sat beside me. He remained for the rest of the day, and left me temporarily the poorer by a Virgil and a Catullus. Later on, when in Jerusalem, he always stayed in my house, an amusing as well as an absorbing if sometimes disconcerting guest. He had Shelley's trick of noiselessly vanishing and reappearing. We would be sitting reading on my only sofa: I would look up, and Lawrence was not only not in the room, he was not in the house, he was not in Jerusalem. He was in the train on his way to Egypt.[5]

In those days and (owing to the withering hand of Monsieur Mavromatis' Ottoman concession) for years after, there was no electric light in Jerusalem, and in my bachelor household the hands of the Arab servants fell heavy upon the incandescent mantles of our paraffin lamps, from which a generous volcano of filthy smuts would nightly stream over the books, the carpets and everything in the room. Lawrence took the lamp situation daily in hand, and so long as he was there all was bright on the Aladdin front. He said he liked the house because it contained the necessities [6] and not the tiresomenesses of life; that is to say there were a few Greek marbles, a good piano and a great many books—but (I fear) not enough towel-horses, no huckabacks, and a very irregular supply of cruets and dinner-napkins. Not all my guests agreed with Lawrence.

He was not (any more than Kitchener) a misogynist, though he would have retained his composure if he had been suddenly informed that he would never see a woman again. He could be charming to people like

---

[5] In England also his best friends often knew least of his whereabouts. Hogarth answered my inquiries after my Sargent drawing, lent for *Seven Pillars* in 1914: "T. E. L. (or T. E. Shaw as he now calls himself) dumps his things all over the place. It is probably either with Griggs and Co., his reproducers, or at Baker's house in Barton Street, where T. E. used to live and still I think goes from time to time. I can't get any replies out of T. E. He sent me some weeks ago eight chapters of his book in paged proof and I returned them with comments, but I have heard no more. Two people, Sir Geoffrey Salmond and Sir M. de Bunsen, who had been in his neighbourhood of late, reported well of T. E. to me. Alan Dawnay tells me T. E. is coming here one day in his normal fashion—without notice and refusing to be put up—but days pass and no news of him so—voilà!"

[6] My servant Said once observed: "When your Excellency has none other than Urenz in the house, the cook prepares *ala kaifu*—without bothering himself."

my wife and sister, whom he considered to be "doing" something, but he regarded (and sometimes treated) with embarrassing horror those who "dressed, and knew people". When at a dinner-party a lady illustrated her anecdotes with the Christian names, nick-names and pet-names of famous (and always titled) personages, Lawrence's dejection became so obvious that the lady, leaning incredulously forward, asked: "I fear my conversation does not interest Colonel Lawrence very much?" Lawrence bowed from the hips—and those were the only muscles that moved: "It does not interest me at all," he answered.

I was standing with him one morning in the Continental Hotel, Cairo, waiting for Rūhi, when an elderly Englishwoman, quite incapable of understanding his talk, but anxious to be seen conversing with the Un-crowned King of Arabia, moved towards him. It was hot, and she was fanning herself with a newspaper as she introduced herself: "Just think, Colonel Lawrence, Ninety-two! Ninety-two." With a tortured smile he replied: "Many happy returns of the day."

In those days he spoke much of the press he would found in Epping Forest for the printing of the classics, where, he said: "I'll pull you the Theocritus [7] of your dreams. I'm longing to get back to my printing-press, but I have two kings to make first." He made the Kings if not the press: Faisal in Iraq, Abdallah in Transjordan stand indeed as in part his creations. But with his (and my) old friend Husain Ibn Ali of Mecca his relations were fated to fall tragically from bad to worse. That monarch was alas becoming less and less a practicable member of the Comity of Kings. Fully supported but wholly uncontrolled in his absolutism by the might of the British Empire, he dropped into the unfortunate habit of regarding the mere suggestion of anything he did not wish to do as an attack on his honour and his sovereign rights. An historian with the knowledge and the patience to go through the complete file of *al-Qibla,* for eight years the official organ of the Hāshimi Government in Mecca, could present to the world a state of mind—and of affairs—closer to the Middle Ages than to the twentieth century. In Jeddah money for the building of a mosque was collected by the simple process of the Qaima-qam sending for persons whom the King wished to subscribe, and pre-senting each with a receipt prepared in Mecca for the amount to be cashed in. As late as 1923 hands were being chopped off for theft in Mecca, as prescribed by the original Shari Law. When the telegraph cable between Jeddah and Suakin broke, His Majesty hoped that the Sudan Government would withdraw their request for the customary cash deposit for its repair. Finding them obdurate, he ordered that no ship in Jeddah

[7] To the best of my knowledge there exists no beautiful Greek text of Theocritus.

harbour should use her wireless under penalty of being cut off from all communication with the shore, making no exception for owners engaged on the most important business, or for time-signals. The Jeddah wireless station was kept on the watch all night in order to jam even the receipt of messages by ships, and by sending out meaningless (and sometimes obscene) signals interfered with the daily time-indication from Massawa and the correction of ships' chronometers up and down the Red Sea.

Such being the royal attitude abroad as well as at home, there was matter less for surprise than for sorrow that Lawrence's last negotiations with the man he had helped to raise so high should have been broken off in anger. Time after time the King would go back on agreements made after hours of discussion the day before. More than once he threatened to abdicate.[8] (Lawrence "wished he would.") I myself incline to doubt whether King Husain ever loved Lawrence. There were moments when he and his sons suspected him of working against them, and more than once let fall hints to confidants that he should not be allowed to mingle too much with the Arab tribesmen. Faisal spoke of him to me with a good-humoured tolerance which I should have resented more if I had ever imagined that kings could like king-makers.

Towards the end of my time in Jerusalem I received the notice inviting subscriptions ("by approved persons") for the original limited edition of *Seven Pillars of Wisdom*. I dispatched my cheque at once, to receive it again in a month neatly torn into four fragments, accompanied by the sharpest words I had ever known from Lawrence, to the effect that "in the circumstances" my letter was an insult, and that he was "naturally" giving me a copy, "your least share of the swag". Later he professed a cynical indifference to his magnificent gift, and, when it became known as the Twenty Thousand Dollar Book, recommended me twice to sell quickly, while the going was good. When, with his (and some joint) notes, it was burnt, he immediately collected and sent me a complete set of the original illustrations.

In the interval between Jerusalem and Cyprus I wrote to learn his plans and to suggest a meeting. He replied:

[8] I wrote to my father during King Husain's visit to Amman in 1924, some time before his final ruin, when Sir Herbert Samuel was straining to promote an understanding between him and Ibn Sa'ud: "We are just back from Amman, where we were caught in a cloudburst, and had to remain an extra day and to return by special train through French Syria past Deraa and Sámakh to Afûleh (near Endor) with eight cars on trucks, to the wonder of the countryside. King Husain embraced me several times. We talked with him for long hours in bitter cold, and he kept turning to Clayton and me, and repeating that we were the authors of all his troubles and difficulties: which consist, as you know, in a Crown for himself, a Crown for Faisal, and a coronet for Abdallah. He gave us a banquet with seventy different kinds of dishes: the waiters, walking up and down the top of the tables *à la Mecque*. Lily, not happening to care about any one of the seventy, had to have a few sandwiches on our return to the house."

338171 A C Shaw,
Hut 105
R.A.F. Cadet College,
Cranwell, Lincs.

1. vi. 26.
Dear R. S.,

Yes: I'm too far from London and from affairs to see many people now-a-days. Yet I hear of you and them, sometimes. If you want to see me you had better stay a week-end at Belton. We are about ten miles from it.

In August I'll be away somewhere (no notion where). Sept.-October in Cranwell, November on leave, December on a troopship for I'm on overseas draft, probably to India for a five-year spell. One of the attractions of the R.A.F. is that you see the world for nothing.

Tonsils: yes, rotten things. I haven't any. Lost them, like you.

The Sargent is reproduced and finished. The Kennington is still on the stones. The complexity and extravagance of my colour reproductions have put the Chiswick Press out of gear. They have been two years over them and are still hard at work. August, they hope to finish them. Till they do my book is held up. Yet it must come out, complete or incomplete, before I go abroad. So live in hope. Though what you will think of my personalities (yours and everybody's!) God only knows.

Au revoir,
T. E. L.

In the autumn he resumed:

2. ix. 26.

Dear Ronald,

I'll come over on Saturday the eleventh, to Belton. When? I can't yet tell you. Just carry on with what programme the overlord of Belton has: and I'll fit myself in. If Saturday is unfit for any reason (service life is highly irregular) I'll come on Sunday, and will hang about till I see you. It might be tea-time on Saturday or late, after dinner, on Sunday: but God knows. Just carry on, and I'll loom up sooner or later. I have a motor-bike, and so am mobile.

Book? November probably. Your copy will probably be posted to Colonial Office, and sent on thence by bag to the Governor and C.-in-C. of Cyprus (His Excellency; hum ha). I was exceedingly glad when I saw that news. The Sargent is at Kennington's house (Morton House, Chiswick Mall), finished with. The Kennington has been the most difficult of all the pastels, and is not yet passed in proof. It keeps on falling to bits: looking butcherly-like, in raw-beef blocks of red. Very difficult. Kennington struggles hard with the colour-printers: and I hope not vainly. All over by 15 September, for that is "binding" day, when sheets are to be issued.

More when we meet,
Yours,
T. E. S.

My uncle forgot to warn the butler, who therefore announced that "an airman"·was at the door. Strapped under the seat of his motor-cycle was the bound manuscript of *Seven Pillars,* one or two passages in which he wanted me to check. When, after tea, we were pacing up and down, round and about the lawns and gardens, I asked him point blank why he was doing what he was doing—and not more. He answered that there was only one thing in the world worth being, and that was a creative artist. He had tried to be this, and had failed. He said: "I know I can write a good sentence, a good paragraph, even a good chapter, but I have proved I cannot write a good book." Not having yet seen *Seven Pillars* I could only quote the praise of Hogarth (which meant much to Lawrence) and agree that, compared with the glory of *Hamlet* or *The Divine Comedy,* career was nothing. Still, admitting these to be unattainable, there were Prime Ministers, Archbishops, Admirals of the Fleet, Press Barons and philanthropic millionaires, some of whom sometimes rendered service surely preferable to this utter renunciation? He allowed the principle, but refused the application. Since he could not be what he would, he would be nothing: the minimum existence, work without thought; and when he left the Royal Air Force it would be as night-watchman in a City warehouse.[9]

For all his puckishness, his love of disconcerting paradox, I believed then and am certain now that Lawrence meant what he said; though I thought there was also the element of dismay at the standard expected of him by the public; and I doubted how far even his nerves could ever be the same after his hideous manhandling in Deraa.[10]

I further believe that, though not given to self-depreciation, he did underrate the superlative excellence of *Seven Pillars,* and, as a most conscious [11] artist in words, ached to go further still.

13. ix. 34.

Dear R. S.,

I have been away for a while, during which your P.C. sat on the edge of Southampton Water, peacefully, in blazing sunshine. If all of the years were like this, no man would need to go abroad....

Here are your K. articles,[12] which I return because I know how rare fugitive writings become in time. Once I did three or four columns in the same paper, but I have never seen them since; they gave me the idea that newsprint is a bad medium for writing. The same stuff that would pass muster between covers looks bloodless between ruled lines on a huge page. Journalistic writing is all blood and bones, not for cheapness' sake, but because unnatural emphasis

[9] This attitude is said psychologically to represent a very rare manifestation of the *Gottmensch Komplex.*

[10] *Seven Pillars,* chap. xxxv. More than one member of his Staff told me that after Deraa, they felt that something had happened to Lawrence which had changed him.

[11] Too conspicuous sometimes, as for instance in the effort to avoid ending *Seven Pillars* with the weak but natural phrase "how sorry I was".

[12] On Lord Kitchener from *The Times.*

is called for. It's like architectural sculpture which has to be louder than indoor works of art.

So I'd say that these articles of yours read too "chosen" for press-work; but that in a book they would be charming. You write with an air...and airs need the confinement of walls or end papers or what-nots to flourish. But do airs flourish? I think they intensify, suffuse, intoxicate. Anyhow they are one of the best modes of writing, and I hope you will try to write, not fugitive pieces, but something sustained or connected by the thread of your life.

· · · · · · · ·

I've often said to you that the best bit of your writing I ever read was your dictated account of the report of an agent's interview, pre-revolt, with the Sharīf of Mecca on his palace roof at night. If you could catch atmosphere and personality, bluntly, like that, it would be a very good book. These K. articles might be blunted. You'll have to use the word "I" instead of the bland "Secretary"...[18] Forget the despatch and the F.O. and try for the indiscreet Pro-consul!

Yours,
T. E. S.

He loved discussing his own prose and, if convinced, was humble under criticism, whether of style or of fact. When I told him that he had been too generous to me in the beginning of his book but not quite just in the middle,[14] where, if I was "parading", it was in order to teach him a business at which he was new and I was old, he exclaimed that he would have altered the passage had he known in time.

My wife and I came upon him early in 1929 returning from India by the *Rajputana*, where he spent his time, flat in his berth, translating Homer. He did not dissent when I thought that his *Odyssey* sacrificed overmuch to the desire of differing from predecessors: for instance in rendering ῥοδοδάκτυλος ἠώς—rosy fingered dawn—in nineteen different ways. It is therefore an arresting rather than a satisfying version. Lawrence, though respectful almost to deference of expert living authority, lacked the surrender of soul to submit himself lowly and reverently, even to the first poet. Of Matthew Arnold's three requisites for translating Homer —simplicity, speed and nobility, all dominating qualities of Lawrence's being, he failed somehow in presenting the third, substituting as often as not some defiant and most un-Homeric puckishness of his own, so that Dr Johnson's criticism of Pope's *Iliad* would be no less applicable to Lawrence's Revised Version. The classical Arab could become in a trice a street Arab. Nevertheless Lawrence's *Odyssey* possesses two outstanding merits. It represents Lawrence as well as Homer, and it has by hero-

---

[18] Necessary because the articles were anonymous and therefore in the third person.
[14] *Seven Pillars*, p. 98.

worship or the silken thread of snobbishness led to Homer thousands
that could never have faced the original, or even the renderings of Pope,
Chapman, or Butcher and Lang; just as for countless Londoners the
"approach" to the Portland Vase, visible but neglected for a century in
the British Museum, was induced through its auctioning at Christie's
in the presence of the Prince of Wales.

Lawrence sent me in Cyprus, inviting comment, the typescript of *The
Mint,* a remarkable and sometimes poignant picture of his early days
in the Air Force. The narration was no less fine than the description, but
the contrast between the lives and the language of all ranks was startling
indeed. It seemed that they could only find relief from the cloistered
rigour of their existence by expressing their emotions with an almost epi-
leptic obscenity.[15] I offered, by a necessary minimum of blue pencil to a total
of some thirty pages, to enable the book to emerge from the steel safe in
which I had to guard it when not in use, into general reading: but Lawrence said the language was the life, sooner than falsify which he would
rather not publish at all. Part having appeared during his lifetime in an
English newspaper, under a misapprehension that he had approved, a
copyrighting publication of ten copies prohibitively priced was arranged in
America; none other to appear until his earliest authorized date of 1950.
In the Spring of 1937 the Press stated that an enterprising journalist,
catching the staff of the Library of Congress off their guard, had printed
or described lengthy passages in a public sheet, and so caused a flutter in
the heart of more than one far from imaginary portrait.

He hated public attention save when impersonal enough for him to
appear not to notice it, but was not disappointed when, as nearly always,
his incognito broke down. One day he offered to take my wife and me
to the Imperial War Museum "to see the Orpens". When we came to his
portrait by James McBey, I asked him to stand in front so that we might
for a minute see him against McBey's vision. In a flash the word went
round the Staff that Lawrence was here, and for the rest of our visit we
were accompanied by the rhythmic beat of a dozen martial heels. Lawrence was clearly not displeased, yet when on our departure I remarked
upon the number of our escort, "Really?" he said. "I didn't notice any
one." He was indeed a mass of contradictions: shy and retiring, yet he
positively enjoyed sitting for, and criticizing, his portrait. No one could
have been more remote from the standard of the public school, and I
can as easily picture him in a frock-coat or in hunting pink as in an old

15 Perhaps on the precept of Catullus:
          "Nam castum esse decet pium poetam
          Ipsum, versiculis nihil necesse est."

school tie. In action likewise he was an individual force of driving intelligence, yet with nothing of the administrator; having about as much of the team spirit as Alexander the Great or Mr Lloyd George.

In England we met (as might have been expected) more often unexpectedly than by appointment—in the street, on a bus, or at a railway station. Once, when I was choosing gramophone records, a hand from behind descended firmly upon my shoulder. I had only just arrived in England, and supposed for a moment that this must be an attempt on the part of an assistant at Brighter British Salesmanship. It was Lawrence, replenishing the immense collection of records arranged in volumes round a square of deep shelves in the upper room of his cottage. On another occasion he led me to his publishers where, walking round the room, he picked out half a dozen expensive books, and, as though he were the head of the firm, made me a present of them.[16] He was a loyal, unchanging and affectionate friend, and would charge down from London on the iron steed from which he met his death to visit me in a nursing home, or run up 200 miles from the West of England to say good-bye before I returned to Cyprus. After a convalescence voyage he wrote:

> 338171 A/c Shaw,
> R.A.F. Cattewater,
> Plymouth.
> 5. v. 29.

Dear R. S.,
    Maurice Baring told me you were back. Did it do good? Are you fit, or fitter even?
    I'm down here, too far off to reach London even for a week-end: but the place is good, and the company. So all's well with me.
    Please give my regards to Lady Storrs. I hope she is contented with your improvement.
    M. B. has given me a huge *Gepäck:*[17] five times as fat as yours, and stuffed full of glory. I did not know there were so many good poems, in it, and outside it. Half of it is strange to me.

> Yours,
> T. E. S.

Leaving Southampton for Canada in 1934 we were

greeted[18] by C.P.R. officials and by T. E. Shaw. Him I found, healthier in appearance than ever before, capless in brown overalls and blue jersey. He came aboard and talked awhile of his retirement next March to a small cottage on a maximum of £100 per annum. He would provide bread, honey and

---

[16] They included that deservedly successful War book *The Enormous Room* which the firm had only published on his strong recommendation.
[17] See footnote, page 281.
[18] Canadian Diary.

Bridlington
25. 2. 35

NO : I won't ; Forewords are 'septic things, and I hope never to do another. Bertram Thomas was like the unfortunate woman ; but to strangers it is easy to say " NO " : he must understand that he has no claim on me : nor do I even know what he has written, or why, or whether. No, most certainly No.

Yours
TES

I leave him knows a.m. ... and the RAF that same moment

FACSIMILE OF LETTER FROM T. E. LAWRENCE

cheese for visitors, but could not put them up otherwise than in a sleeping-bag (marked Tuum—his own Meum) on the floor. In order to side-slip the photographers he took me in his Power-boat *Joker* (£180, 25 knots, unupset-able) and allowed me to zigzag it about for 15 minutes. A permanent friend I shall always rejoice to see, with generosities of feeling for person as well as for books.

I never saw him again alive.

Nine-tenths of his letters to me have perished, and only a half-dozen, which never left England, remain. Even these few reveal his power and variety in that rarely mastered art. I had in a moment of weakness consented to ask him to write an introduction to a book on Beduin Life by an artist whose exhibition I had opened. I knew the quest was hopeless, and had only written *par acquit de conscience* begging him at least to let me have an answer I could pass on. His reply, though admirable and richly deserved, hardly fell within this category.

> Bridlington,
> 25. ii. 35.
>
> No: I won't; Forewords are septic things, and I hope never to do another. Bertram Thomas was like the importunate woman; but to strangers it is easy to say "No": he must understand that he has no claim on me: nor do I even know what he has written, or why, or who he is. No, most certainly No.
>
> Yours,
> T. E. S.

I leave here to-morrow a.m.... and the R.A.F. that same moment εἴθε δὲ μηδ'...[19]

Lawrence hated Society, but loved company. He refused the post of Director of Archaeology in Cyprus because of what he chose to imagine the social obligations of an official there. Those who knew him could have predicted the comparative failure of his Fellowship of All Souls, where it is reasonably expected of members to mingle with their fellows and—if not indeed to roll the ghost of an Olympian (a Cambridge accomplishment)—at least to present to the Common Room on occasion a polished spook of Horace. "Conversation", says Gibbon, of the most famous Arab, "enriches and enlivens the mind, but solitude is the school of genius."

Nevertheless, Lawrence liked sometimes to walk and talk with friends. The simplicity of his life was extreme. He smoked no tobacco, he drank no alcohol; but alas, he used a drug. His drug was speed, and speed was

---

[19] From the Greek Epitaph of despair

> ἐνθάδε κεῖμαι
> Ταρσεύς · μὴ γήμας · εἴθε δὲ μηδ' ὁ πάτηρ.

"Here lie I of Tarsus
Never having married, and I would that my father had not."

Mackail, *Select Epigrams*, p. 172, 1911.

the dope which cost him his life. He once raced along the open road against an aeroplane, and led it for nearly a quarter of an hour.

Consider the variety of elements in his composition. It has been given to few to achieve greatness and to enshrine that greatness in splendid prose: to which other of these few has been added the fastidious artistry to plan every detail of the setting up, the illustration, the printing and the binding of the material presentation of his genius? On any topic he was one of those who let fall, whether in speech or writing, the creative and illuminating idea or phrase—unmistakably his, signed all over—which held your memory and recharged your intellectual and spiritual batteries.

Lawrence suffered acutely from public exaggeration in all directions. Like Bassanio he had chosen the leaden casket—"Who chooseth me must give and hazard all he hath." And his reputation when alive, and even after, has been subjected by some to a steady dribble of depreciation. We are told that his military operations were on a small scale. So were those of Thermopylae and of Agincourt. We are told that anybody could have done what he did, with Allenby behind him, backed by the golden sovereigns of the British Treasury. But Paladins of the stamp and stature of an Allenby do not accord themselves, nor resources of the British Treasury to an "anybody". He was accused of a publicity engineered by intentional mystification; and indeed it must have irritated some other public servants to find a man without a handle before his name or letters after it, without a dress suit and with an income of under a hundred a year, nevertheless pursued and chronicled by an eager limelight which seemed in comparison to black out their particular merits. I have even heard his strong columns of English belittled as having been built, as he said himself, upon the foundation of Doughty; and true it is, that Doughty was no less his literary ancestor, than Gibbon Macaulay's. Dante gloried in "taking his fine style from his master", Virgil. If Lawrence lit his candle from Doughty's flame, was the candle any less his own? There are two classes of public servant. Of one it is said: "What is he doing now?" Of the other: "who is Minister of this or Governor of that." The first category will interest and arrest and fascinate the world. Lawrence was one of those first. Mr Winston Churchill is one of them, and so is Mr Lloyd George. The second, a far more numerous category—will be identified as occupying most of the best places.

Lawrence was throughout the last months of his life oppressed by gloomy forebodings. In one of his later letters he spoke of "an utterly blank wall" after leaving his beloved R.A.F.; one of his latest to me [20] ends with three hopeless words of the man of Tarsus.

[20] P. 475.

Ozone Hotel,
Bridlington,
Yorks.

31. i. 35.

Dear R. S.,

No; alas, Hythe will know me no more. I have only a month to do in the R.A.F. and will spend it up here, overseeing the refit of ten R.A.F. boats in a local garage. The name of the Hotel is real. So, I think, is the ozone, or is it the fishmarket that smells. It is empty, cold, and rather nice.

He's a confident personage, your Ptolemaean (?) I have not before seen him.

. . . .

Alas, I have nothing to say at the moment. After my discharge I have somehow to pick up a new life and occupy myself—but beforehand it looks and feels like an utterly blank wall. Old age coming, I suppose; at any rate I can admit to being quite a bit afraid for myself, which is a new feeling. Up till now I've never come to the end of anything.

Ah well. We shall see after the Kalends of March. Indeed, I venture to hope we shall see each other, but I don't know where I shall live, or what do, or how call myself.

. . . . . .

Please regard me to Lady Storrs: and please make yourself again into fighting trim: or perhaps you are, now. Good.

Yours,
T. E. S.

Here is the second half of what was probably his very last letter, written on Jubilee Day to Eric Kennington:

You wonder what I am doing? Well, so do I, in truth. Days seem to dawn, suns to shine, evenings to follow, and then to sleep. What I have done, what I am doing, what I am going to do puzzle and bewilder me. Have you ever seen a leaf fallen from your tree in autumn and been really puzzled about it? That's the feeling. The cottage is all right for me ... but how on earth I'll be able to put any one up baffles me. There cannot ever be a bed, a cooking vessel, or a drain in it—and I ask you ... Are not such things essential to life ... necessities? Peace to everybody.

Lawrence items carried a news value of hard cash, so that when at the end of his Air service he returned to the cottage at Clouds Hill, his welcome home was a row of strange faces blinking and dodging behind a battery of cameras. He fled the place awhile, then crept in, he hoped secretly, by night. They stoned his roof to make him appear. One forced his way in. Lawrence went for him, knocked him down and threw him out. His friend found him trembling—"so many years since I've struck a man". There is no close season for heroes.

Every day, for the last three weeks of his life, a bird would flutter to his

window, tapping incessantly with its beak upon the pane. If he moved
to another window, the bird followed and tapped again. The strange insistence was so visibly fraying his nerves that one morning, when he had
gone out, his friend shot the bird.[21] In that same hour, wrenching his
handle-bars for the last time, Lawrence was flung over them sixty feet
head first on to the granite-hard tarmac.

I stood beside him lying swathed in fleecy wool; stayed until the plain
oak coffin was screwed down. There was nothing else in the mortuary
chamber but a little altar behind his head with some lilies of the valley
and red roses. I had come prepared to be greatly shocked by what I saw,
but his injuries had been at the back of his head, and beyond some
scarring and discoloration over the left eye, his countenance was not marred.
His nose was sharper and delicately curved, and his chin less square. Seen
thus, his face was the face of Dante with perhaps the more relentless
mouth of Savonarola; incredibly calm, with the faintest flicker of disdain.
The rhythmic planes of his features gradually became the symbolized
impression of all mankind, moulded by an inexorable destiny. Nothing of
his hair, nor of his hands was showing; only a powerful cowled mask,
dark-stained ivory alive against the dead chemical sterility of the wrap-
pings. It was somehow unreal to be watching beside him in these cere-
ments, so strangely resembling the *aba*, the *kuffiya* and the *agāl* of an
Arab Chief, as he lay in his last littlest room, very grave and strong and

[21] Virgilians will be reminded of the *Diva* which Jupiter sent in the shape of a
little bird to dash herself against the shield of Turnus in his last fight with Aeneas
(*Aeneid* xii, 861. . . .):

> "Alitis in parvae subitam collecta figuram,
> quae quondam in bustis aut culminibus desertis
> nocte sedens serum canit importuna per umbras—
> hanc versa in faciem Turni se pestis ob ora
> fertque refertque sonans clipeumque everberat alis,
> illi membra novus solvit formidine torpor. . . ."

> Een thus the deadly child of night
> Shot from the sky with earthward flight.
> Soon as the armies and the town
>   Descending, she descries,
> She dwarfs her huge proportion down
>   To bird of puny size,
> Which perched on tombs or desert towers
> Hoots long and lone through darkling hours:
> In such disguise the monster wheeled
> Round Turnus' head and 'gainst his shield
>   Unceasing flapped her wings:
> Strange chilly dread his limbs unstrung:
> Upstands his hair: his voiceless tongue
>   To his parched palate clings.

(Conington's translation.)

Turnus was of the clan *Laurens*:

> "non fuit excepto Laurentis corpore Turni."

(*Aen.* vii, 650.)

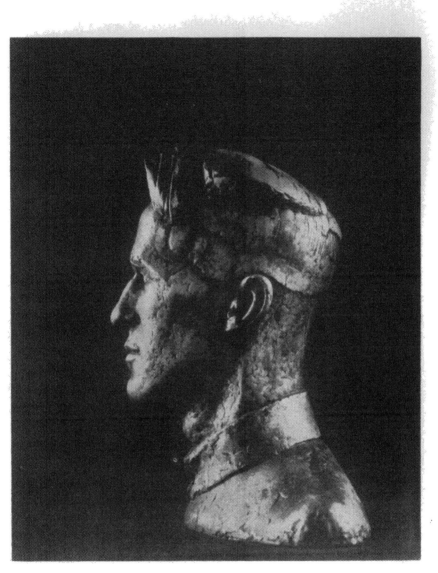

LAWRENCE OF ARABIA

(*Bronze by Eric Kennington in the crypt of St Paul's Cathedral*)

noble. Selfish, to be alone with this splendour; I was sorry, too late, that neither Augustus John nor Eric Kennington, though both within a few hundred yards, should have had the chance to preserve it for the world. As I looked I remembered that my first sight of death had been my beloved Arabic tutor at Cambridge, thirty-one years before, Hassan Tewfik ibn Abd al-Rahman Bey al-Adli—may God be well pleased with them both. As we carried the coffin into and out of the little church the clicking Kodaks and the whirring reels extracted from the dead body their last "personal" publicity.[22]

Some knew one side of Lawrence, some another. I wondered then if any knew him at all, or could imagine what had been his purpose, what the frontiers of his being. Could he have grown old? Had he ever been young? Some think he intended to resume action, for his country. Others that he would have created at least one more great work, for like Plato he felt deeply that what gives life its value is the sight, however revealed, of Eternal Beauty. In this he is with the great Elizabethans—Sir Philip Sidney, with the great Victorians—Charles Gordon—whose whole lives, free from fear and gain (those old perverters of mankind) are a protest against the guaranteed, the pensioned, the standardized and the safety-first existence. Like them Lawrence, even without his work, without his book, was and will remain a standard and a touchstone of reality in life. That vast convulsion of human nature, the War, may have thrown up greater figures; none more gallantly yet practically romantic than the shy, slight, unaccountable emanation of genius who will live in history as Lawrence of Arabia.

[22] Immediately after his death a perverse cult was started, mainly by owners of the privately printed *Seven Pillars* and other monopolists in *Lawrenciana,* of horror at the desecration whereby that masterpiece was made available for the outside world; bringing back to me the protests of the Wagnerian fervent, when others beside the Bayreuth pilgrims were at last privileged to enjoy *Parsifal.*

CHAPTER NINETEEN

November 30th 1926–June 9th 1932

Prima et maxima Orientis Cyprus insula.
AVON. 2nd or 3rd Century, A.D.

THE retina of memory, sometimes dull as bottle-glass for objects of real importance, focuses and records trifles with the accuracy and illumination of a fine lens. Standing in uniform on the deck of the *Cornflower* as she steamed cautiously through the narrow pass into Famagusta, I remembered that this was the second place to which I had gone as a tourist and returned as a Governor; I wondered whether, as at most changes of regime, here also there would be some officers specially in the confidence of the late ruler and therefore now regarded by their colleagues as the Old Gang: and I hoped that my two joint-successors to Judaea would be merciful to my Old Gang—if I could be said to have had one. I knew something of the beauty and interest of the country, and had heard much, and evil, of the prelates and politicians of the towns.

The anchor had hardly dropped before politics began with the Commissioner of the District informing me, not without agitation, that the Mayor of Famagusta's Address of Welcome would be tied up in the white and blue ribbons[1] of Greece. This he said had been the practice for many years: after all the Mayor was not bound to offer any Address: it would be a pity to begin with an incident bound to offend four-fifths of the population. I therefore accepted the scroll of friendly greeting read by the Mayor before the gathering on the quay, and stepped into the little train. There, as we puffed past Othello's Tower, in sight of the great French Gothic Cathedral, through the mediaeval fortifications and into the central plain of the Mesaoria—"between the mountains"—politics continued, as the Colonial Secretary told me how the Legislative Council

---

[1] Exactly the colours of a Cambridge Half-Blue.

had the day before rejected the Budget, because it contained (as it had for many years) a provision of £92,800 [2] under the heading of "Cyprus Contribution to the Ottoman Public Debt Charge"; generally known as *The Turkish Tribute*. Politics intruded for a third time (before I even reached my office) when, at my swearing-in by the Chief Justice in the Antechamber of the Legislative Council, His Beatitude Kyrillos, the Orthodox Archbishop of the Autocephalous Church of Cyprus, was absent by reason of a cold—brought on by the Government maintaining the traditional precedence over him of the Turkish Mufti.

Our car took us slowly past gay-scarfed crowds, under balconies decked with Greek flags, up a long drive through plantations that seemed after Palestine almost like an English park, until a long low barnlike building came in sight. "Anyhow, the stables are good", said my wife. It was Government House.

Forty-eight years earlier the first British High Commissioner of Cyprus was casting about for a suitable Residency. At the same time the British War Office were dispatching a wooden huntment for the officer commanding the troops in Ceylon. Before the ship had reached Port Said the G.O.C. had prudently discovered a stone palace; the precious freight must clearly not be wasted: it was therefore deflected some 250 miles to the north-east, and Ceylon's gain became Cyprus's loss. The fabric was carried up to Nicosia from the beach, section by section on the backs of camels, and put together like a child's box of bricks by a local contractor named Mr Z. Williamson—known later to the world as Sir Basil Zaharoff. The house was bitterly cold in winter (the climates of the two Islands being dissimilar), and we had not been in it two hours before the "first rain", auspiciously coinciding with the arrival of the new Governor, was pouring in cascades through the roof and flooding out the long gallery and the offices of the bewildered Aide-de-Camp. Nevertheless, the little Government House for all its white painted plank walls and ceilings and rotting floors was not without charm, and we grew very fond of it. My predecessors had enhanced its appearance and amenities by enclosing the verandah giving onto the garden with the yellow-stone Gothic arcading traditional in Cyprus, thus forming a low, narrow gallery 120 feet long; and the drawing-room and dining-room were lofty and well proportioned. The gardens would have been possible if the soil had been richer and if the water had been adequate. As the smiling servants unpacked my Byzantine ikons, I heard one (with the pleasant bigotry of the Orthodox

[2] The actual charge on Cyprus was diminished by an annual Imperial grant-in-aid to £42,800.

Greeks) exclaim in surprise as he kissed each: ἀλλὰ ὁ κυβερνήτης χριστανὸς—"But the Governor's a Christian!" [3]

The official *Handbook* [4] will tell you that Cyprus, a British Crown Colony, is an island situated in the Eastern Mediterranean, distant about 40 miles from the coast of Asia Minor to the North and about 60 miles from Syria in the East. The name of the Island, Κύπρος, has nothing to do with the Cypress-tree, κυπάρισσος, though I frequently received letters addressed as if it had. [5] It is the third largest island in the Mediterranean; smaller than Sicily or Sardinia, but larger than Corsica or Crete: nearly half the size of Palestine (or Wales) and a little larger than the countries of Norfolk and Suffolk combined. Its shape was compared in antiquity to an outspread deer-skin, of which the tail pointed East into Asia. The population is some 350,000, of whom four-fifths are members of the Orthodox Church and one-fifth Ottoman Turks. The educated Christians speak a correct, the peasants a corrupt though not uninteresting form of Romaic, or modern Greek: the Turks a purer Turkish, freer from Arabic and Persian words, than that of Constantinople.

Cyprus has every climatic and, save water, every physical advantage, with even more than the variety of Palestine. Nicosia, the capital, and the great central plain may by July be hotter than Cairo, by August as hot as Khartūm, while 6000 feet up on Mount Troödos you are grateful for blankets and fires. In the winter these same mountains will be un-approachable, and so deep under snow that Government Cottage disappears and needs no caretaker; far below, the fields, towns and little seaports are bathed in the sunny radiance of the Italian Riviera.

William Mallock journeyed to Cyprus in the 'eighties, and called his resulting book *In an Enchanted Island*. Enchanted indeed, and enchanting; to-day no less than in the dawn of history. Never, like Egypt, Palestine and Assyria, original or originating, Cyprus has from the first endured, received, transmitted; she has been the meeting-place of contending empires and religions, the clearing-house of Mediterranean civilizations. The altars of Baal and of Zeus, Astarte and Aphrodite, Tammuz and Adonis were similar, sometimes the same and shared. The Chittim of *Genesis* from which King Solomon procured the acacia wood for his Temple is the Kition [6] of the Greeks, of the modern Larnaca. The first known mining for copper was in Cyprus, which continues to be mined to-day

---

[3] Similarly you will hear it said, by and of an Orthodox Greek: "No, he is not an Armenian: he's a Christian." Thou shalt have none other gods but mine.

[4] Ninth edition, 1929, Storrs and O'Brien (who derive no profit from the sale).

[5] The Greek κύπρος and the Latin Cyprus were used in the Septuagint and the Vulgate to translate the Hebrew *Kopher* (the "henna"-plant).

[6] Kition was said to have been founded by Kittim, great grandson of Noah who colonized it after the Deluge.

between Phoenician and Roman workings at Skouriotissa, "Our Lady of the Slag". *Aes Cyprium* stood for copper as distinguished from bronze: every time therefore that you say "copper" you name Cyprus. Thothmes III of Egypt conquered Cyprus 1500 years before Christ; Sargon of Assyria 700 years later. Unmentioned in Homer's Catalogue of the Ships [7] or in the Epinician Odes of Pindar, she fails alike of the Valhalla and of the *Almanach de Gotha* of Ancient Greece. In the Persian Wars the Greek cities of Cyprus fought for Greece, the Phoenician for Persia; but only a few score years later all declared for Alexander, and sent him a fleet of 120 sail. After his death 323 B.C. Cyprus became an apanage of Egypt, governed for 250 years by a viceroy of the Ptolemies until an "incident" occurred, and the island passed under the universal domination of Rome, with Cicero as its third Roman governor. Antony presented Cyprus (as he had Jericho) to Cleopatra. She did not exaggerate when she cried:

> "His bounty was an autumn
> Which grew by reaping: in his livery
> Walked crowns and crownets: kingdoms and islands were
> As plates dropt from his pocket."

But after Actium the crownet reverted to Rome, in whose Empire, Western or Eastern, it remained until 1191. In A.D. 46 Paul and Barnabas (a Jew of Cyprus), accompanied by John Mark, landed at Salamis and crossed the Island to Paphos, where they converted the Roman proconsul Sergius Paulus, so rendering Cyprus the first country to be governed by a Christian ruler. Barnabas returned later to Salamis, his native town, where he suffered martyrdom. (Until Barnabas, the only Cypriot to achieve world-fame had been another Semite, Zeno of Kition, the founder of the Stoic philosophy.) The next event of note was a pogrom (I believe unique in history) carried out by Jews, who in A.D. 117 were said to have massacred some 200,000 Greeks. Throughout the second and third centuries the Byzantine Church of Antioch claimed that the Church of Cyprus came under its rule. The claim was rejected by the Council of Ephesus and not again raised until the reign of the Emperor Zeno. The attack would have succeeded, but for the opportune Ἕυρεσις, the *Évresis* or Discovery of the body of St Barnabas, buried beneath a carob tree near Salamis, with a copy in his own handwriting of St Matthew's Gospel on his breast, where it had been placed by John Mark. There could be no further doubt, and the Emperor conferred upon the Arch-

---

[7] The name Cinyras is mentioned in *Iliad* xi, 19-23, as that of a Cypriot donor of a breastplate to Agamemnon.

bishops of the Autocephalous Church of Cyprus the imperial privileges of signing in red ink, of wearing a purple cloak at Church festivals, and of carrying a sceptre in place of a pastoral staff. Under the Byzantine governors (pleasantly entitled *Katapans*) Cyprus underwent a score or more of Arab invasions, one led by Harūn al-Rashīd. In 1184 a certain Isaac Comnēnus proclaimed himself Emperor or "Despot". He soon proved himself a violent and ruffianly tyrant, and might have continued such until his death if he had not been so foolish as to insult the bride-elect of Cœur-de-Lion, Berengaria of Navarre, when she was storm-driven upon Cyprus during her voyage from Sicily to Acre. Richard landed at Limassol, married Berengaria,[8] chased Comnēnus from Nicosia to Famagusta, and sent him loaded with silver chains to the Castle of Margat near Tripoli in Syria. Cyprus thus became English for the first time, but did not remain so long; for Richard, finding that the Crusade demanded all his men and money, sold the island to the Knights Templar for 100,000 bezants, of which 40,000 were to be paid at once and the remainder by instalments. The Templars soon found that Cyprus was costing them also more soldiers than they could afford, and begged Richard to resume it. He, unwilling to restore the 40,000 bezants, induced Guy de Lusignan to acquire it as some compensation for his shadowy rights to the titular kingship of Jerusalem; and the Lusignan Dynasty—which though foreign gave Cyprus her only period of independence from external control, and of historic brilliance—was established for three hundred years.

In painting and in letters, in the cognate arts of music and architecture, in wealth and splendour, Cyprus under the Lusignans represented the apex of mediaeval civilization. To Kings of Cyprus such widely different authors as St Thomas Aquinas and Boccaccio dedicated works. The rich merchants of Famagusta could give their daughters as dowry jewels more precious *"que toutes les parures de la reine de France".*[9] But the Lusignans went the way of other feudal rulers in the East. Luxury encouraged intrigue, and decadence followed. James, the illegitimate brother of the Queen (Charlotte, wife of Louis of Savoy), and Archbishop-elect of Nicosia, called in the Sultan of Egypt to oust the rightful monarch. He drove his sister from the throne, but committed the double imprudence of accepting a wife, Caterina Cornaro, from the Signory of Venice, and of dying, probably by poison, before the birth of his son James III, who soon followed him to the grave. His widow was permitted for fifteen years to enjoy nominal sovereignty. But Cyprus was (even then) of high value as a naval and military base: Caterina was eventually forced to renounce

---

[8] In a chapel long since destroyed but still punctiliously shown to visitors.

[9] Quoted in de Mas Latrie's three-volume History of Cyprus from Ludolf von Suchen's *De Terra Sancta*, published about 1468.

her rights,[10] and for 82 years the island was occupied (rather than administered or developed) by the *Luogotenenti,* the *Rettori,* and the *Provveditori* of the Venetian Republic. All that the neglect of Venice left to Cyprus was economic ruin and a palace by Sammichele of Verona; but the world is in her debt, though indirectly, for the Tragedy of *Othello.*

In 1570 the Turkish Sultan Selim II, Selim the Sot, dispatched an expedition which took Nicosia, and the following year, after a magnificent resistance of nearly four months, Famagusta. Its heroic defender, Marcantonio Bragadino, was insulted, mutilated, and finally "brutally flayed alive by a Jewish hangman—a spectacle of hideous and unparalleled barbarity. In the sight of the whole city, amidst the sharpest torments, his courage and constancy, and the calmness of his bearing and look, shone so fairly forth that he seemed rather to rejoice than suffer." [11] His skin was stuffed with straw and sent at the yard-arm to Constantinople, where it remained until, some years after, his brother and sons bought it for a great price, carried it to Venice, and laid it in the church of SS. Giovanni e Paolo, its present resting-place.

Throughout the seventeenth and eighteenth centuries a variety of plots, schemes and half-hearted attempts were made to recapture Cyprus for Christendom, but without effect. The island became an ottoman, upon which governing and governed reposed in picturesque somnolence until far into the nineteenth century. The Turkish regime was indeed in one sense a welcome contrast to the harsh tyranny of Venice. To a Moslem conqueror forms of Christianity were indifferent, and the Orthodox Archbishopric found itself restored after three centuries of abeyance. Before long the Porte transferred the administration of Cyprus [12] from the Grand Vizier to the *Capitan Pasha* (Admiralissimo of Turkey and Governor of the Archipelago, having his headquarters at Rhodes), with the curious result that the effective authority in Cyprus passed into the hands of the Cypriot Archbishop,[13] always regarded as the Ethnarch, or leader of the Orthodox-Greek Christians under a Moslem domination. But the Archbishopric presumed too far, and in 1804 had to face a rising of the

---

[10] She retired to Asolo in the Veneto, where she died in 1510, a patron of art and of the scholars of the Renaissance; leaving a tradition maintained by Robert and by Pen Browning, by the grave of Eleonora Duse, and by the music of Malipiero. Her portrait, a masterpiece of Giorgione or Titian, is in the collection of Sir Herbert Cook, Doughty House, Richmond.

[11] Bishop Grazvani's account.

[12] See Sir H. Luke's *Cyprus under the Turks,* Oxford, 1920.

[13] "The Greek Primates are described by Finlay (*History of Greece,* vol. VI, p. 11) as 'a kind of Christian Turks'. They were the official aristocracy under Ottoman rule, Greeks who had rented the taxes of the district from the Voivode or Bey. They in turn sublet the taxes to local magistrates, so that taxpayers, besides their taxes, maintained three classes of fiscal officers." Note to *Byron's Letters* (1901 edit.), vol. VI, p. 248.

populace. In 1821 occurred a more serious disturbance, this time connected with the Insurrection in Greece. The *Capitan* turned in his sleep, hanged the Archbishop, and beheaded the bishops and some two hundred leading personages of the Orthodox communion. Before executing the ecclesiastics, the Turks saddled them like horses, breaking their teeth by thrusting bits into their mouths, and goading them with spurs.

In 1878 Disraeli returned in triumph from the Berlin Congress. My grandfather took my mother to join in the general welcome. Over the crowd she gazed at an old man in a shabby travelling ulster, tired but with shining eyes; who, standing at a window [14] in Downing Street, stretched forth his arms and cried: "I bring you peace—Peace with Honour." The Peace was the Treaty of Berlin. The Honour was Cyprus. Disraeli had spent a day in Cyprus as a young man of six and twenty during that Eastern journey which culminated in Jerusalem and which so deeply influenced his life. The Jerusalem Jew in *Tancred* is made to say: "The British want Cyprus, and they will take it. They will not do the business of the Turk again for nothing." Its occupation had been debated in the British Press of the 'forties.[15] In 1878 the Russian army was at the gates of Constantinople, with no earthly force available to keep her out other than Great Britain. The Sultan's necessity was Tancred's

---

[14] I learn on good authority that Mr. Lloyd George, being urged on his return from the Treaty of Versailles to show himself at the door of No. 10, very properly maintained tradition by asking for "Disraeli's Window."

[15] The following letter from the British Consul to the Ottoman Governor of Cyprus affords a glimpse into the position of Ottoman Christians in the 'forties—and of Canning, the great Elchi:

"British Consulate of Cyprus,
Larnaca, 20 March 1845.

Excellency,

Your Excellency will no doubt long ago have received from the Sublime Ottoman Porte the necessary instructions relative to the formal engagement received from the Turkish Ministers by His Excellency Sir Stratford Canning, Her Britannic Majesty's Ambassador Extraordinary and Plenipotentiary at Constantinople, that no Christian shall henceforward be executed or otherwise put to death in this country for having apostatized from Islamism, and also the most gracious assurance of His Majesty the Sultan, well worthy of so just and benevolent a Prince, that throughout the dominions of His Majesty, neither shall Christianity be insulted, nor Christians in any way persecuted on account of their Religion.

A Greek woman named Maria, daughter of Thomas, who seventeen years ago embraced Islamism, having presented herself to me to express her desire to avail herself of the privilege accorded to her by these engagements by returning to her former Faith, I beg to request that you will give the necessary orders to the Turkish authorities at Limassol for their being put into execution, and also in a friendly manner to remind your Excellency, and the other Ottoman Authorities, of your, and their responsibility should you not suppress any disposition to revive the abolished practice, or any other deviation from the declared intentions of your Sovereign.

I should feel obliged by your Excellency's favouring me with your reply to this dispatch at your earliest convenience, which I am convinced will be of such a nature as to meet the exigencies of the present case, as I am well aware of your Excellency's zeal to act in Conformity to the known pleasure of your August Sultan, and the engagements contracted by your Government.

opportunity, and on 4 June the "Convention of Defensive Alliance" between His Imperial Majesty and Her Majesty's Government was concluded in the following terms:

Article 1

If Batoum, Ardahan, Kars, or any of them shall be retained by Russia, and if any attempt shall be made at any further time by Russia to take possession of any further territories of his Imperial Majesty the Sultan in Asia, as fixed by the Definitive Treaty of Peace, England engages to join His Imperial Majesty the Sultan in defending them by force of Arms.

In return His Imperial Majesty the Sultan promises to England to introduce necessary reforms, to be agreed upon later between the two Powers, into the Government, and for the protection of the Christian and other subjects of the Porte in these territories; and in order to enable England to make necessary provision for executing her engagement, His Imperial Majesty the Sultan further consents to assign the Island of Cyprus to be occupied and administered by England.

In other words Great Britain entered into a formal engagement to maintain the integrity of the Turkish dominions in Asia against Russia; and secured Cyprus. Instead of Turkish reforms there were Armenian massacres, some of the proofs of which, in the shape of decapitated heads and mutilated trunks, floated across the forty miles of sea separating Northern Cyprus from Southern Anatolia; but Great Britain kept her side of the bargain (Turkey not being attacked by Russia) and duly continued to occupy Cyprus until in 1914 Turkey declared war. Cyprus then became Turkish territory in British occupation, until some further step should be taken by Great Britain. It was not possible to declare a Protectorate, because that would imply the existence of a State to be protected: Cyprus was not a State, thereby differing from Egypt, which was a vassal State under Turkish suzerainty. Cyprus was merely a bit of Turkey in British occupation and under British administration. Great Britain therefore annexed Cyprus as a Crown Colony on 5 November, at the same time that the Protectorate of Egypt was announced. But the end was not yet.

In October 1915 a critical situation had arisen in the Balkans, and the Asquith Government were endeavoring to persuade Greece (then under King Constantine) to come to the rescue of Serbia, at that time threatened

I have the honour to be, with high respect, Your Excellency's Most Obedient, Humble Servant,

(Signed) Niven Kerr,
(Seal of Consulate) Consul.
His Excellency Ettem Pasha, Governor of the Island of Cyprus, Nicosia."

with an Austrian invasion. Great Britain was to send 200,000 troops to Salonica and, jointly with Russia and France, to secure for Greece the North coast of the Aegean and Eastern as well as Western Thrace. At this juncture a very curious suggestion was made by Mr. Ronald Burrows, Principal of King's College, an ardent Philhellene and an intimate friend of Venizelos, for the rousing of public opinion in Greece. The High Commissioner was to be instructed to inform the Archbishop and the Greek members of the Legislative Council that England was ready to give Cyprus to Greece at once, on the one condition that Greece should enter the war immediately on our side. The Archbishop with some other prominent Cypriot should then be put on a British destroyer, be sent straight off to Athens, land there and himself make for the first time the announcement in Athens. Supported by a wave of enthusiasm, he should then make his way to the Chamber and there evoke an expression of feeling so effective as to carry away the Government, or drive them out of office and bring in Venizelos. The Foreign Office adopted the matter but not the *opéra bouffe* (and therefore possibly successful) manner of this proposal. The British Minister in Athens, Sir Francis Elliot, was instructed to make a formal offer to the Greek Government; which was inevitably declined by M. Zaimis, headstrong in his confidence in the promises or threats of the Kaiser. The offer therefore lapsed and has never been renewed. In 1924 the Prime Minister, Mr Ramsay MacDonald, replying to a question in the House of Commons, said: "His Majesty's Government are not contemplating any change in the political status of Cyprus." If anything it was the other way, for next year Cyprus was formally recognized as a Crown Colony, with the provisional title of High Commissioner replaced by that of Governor.

We have seen (though many have forgotten) that England occupied Cyprus for strategic and imperial purposes, and not as rescuing or pretending to rescue Cypriots from Turkish misrule. It is unfortunately true that the progress of the Island, though swifter than would have been possible under Ottoman or even Greek administration, has nevertheless been slower than might have been expected under British. For this there have been three main reasons: initial uncertainty of permanence, the Tribute, and Hellenic nationalism. The second at least of these reasons has from the beginning constituted a genuine, a bitter and an always remediable grievance. The first is obvious, and can be briefly stated. Cyprus had been "assigned for occupation", not ceded, and therefore remained an integral part of the Turkish Empire until annexation in 1914. In 1915, but for German influence in Athens, she would have been joined to the Kingdom of Greece. Moreover the occupation of Egypt in

1882, coming only four years after that of Cyprus, secured an unchallenged military and naval base, with control of the Suez Canal. Cyprus became less important than had been foreseen, and was therefore neglected. Governments, like individuals, may be excused for not investing their capital in an undertaking which is not vital to their interests, and which may at any moment pass out of their control without hope of reimbursement. Until well after the War then—after more than forty years of British rule —the economic development of Cyprus had been maintained rather than accelerated by a necessary minimum of British expenditure.

One of the chief differences between the British Empire and all other Empires has been that these have always regarded their imperial provinces as sources of direct revenue to the central Government.[16] Cyprus, though perhaps "of all Turkish provinces the best administered",[17] had been no exception to this rule. The 1878 Convention therefore provided for payment to the Porte of any excess of revenue over expenditure, the excess to be calculated on the average of the five years preceding 1878. The Sultan, in surrendering yet another portion of his inheritance, felt himself justified in demanding that he should not suffer "Not only the disgrace and dishonour, but an infinite loss". Disraeli, eager to clinch his bargain, was from his point of view no less justified in throwing in what must have appeared a trifling and reasonable makeweight. What was entirely unjustifiable was that this sum, which was evaluated with the scrupulous exactitude characteristic of faked accounts of £92,799. 11s. 3d., should have been made a yearly charge, not upon the British Exchequer, but upon the revenues of Cyprus. The basis of calculation was no less iniquitous, for the Porte had followed their usual practice of extracting the maximum of taxation and according in exchange the minimum of service. Their total expenditure on Justice had been £250; the integrity of their judges had been remunerated at the rate of about fourteen shillings a month. No money at all had been spent upon roads, harbours, agriculture, forestry or education, and there was not one hospital in the Island. The first British estimates of 1879 showed a revenue of £172,000 and an expenditure of £52,800, providing an ample surplus for the Tribute, but leaving for Cyprus barely enough to pay for policemen and tax-collectors. Even so, it was found that revenue had been overestimated and expenditure grossly underestimated, so that it became necessary for the Imperial Parliament to vote each year Grants-in-aid to meet the deficit

[16] One of the highest Ottoman officers was always the Muhássil or Gatherer. Before India was added to the British Empire the style of Mr Jos. Sedley was "Collector" (of Boggley Wallah).

[17] R. Hamilton Lang (ex-British Consul in Cyprus), *Cyprus*, etc., 1878.

which occurred when the Tribute had been paid.[18] Not one piastre of this Tribute ever reached Constantinople, for it was from the first devoted to the bondholders of the Ottoman Loan of 1855, which is guaranteed by England and France; for which reason it continued after Annexation by Great Britain in 1914. In 1907 the Grant-in-Aid was fixed at £50,000 a year, after which the nett amount payable by Cyprus became £42,800, and it was because of the inclusion of this balance that the Budget had been thrown out immediately before my arrival. The injustice of the Tribute had not only united Greeks and Turks; it had ranged successive High Commissioners and Governors of Cyprus and their Administrations without exception whole-heartedly on the side of the Cypriots.

These two grievances, negative and positive, absence of interest in development, and infliction of an annual heavy fine, might have alienated (had they been endured even for a year) a community of British blood, traditions and aspirations. Cypriots had none of these. It is commonly stated, though historically more than doubtful, that when Sir Garnet Wolseley[19] landed at Larnaca in 1878 he was waited upon by a deputation headed by the Archbishop who, in his address, used the following words: "We accept the change of government, inasmuch as we trust that Great Britain will help Cyprus, as it did the Ionian Islands,[20] to be united with Mother Greece, with which it is nationally connected." This attitude a large proportion of Greek-speaking Cypriots have never abandoned. Far from being rebuked or deprecated, save by decennial utterances of Colonial Secretaries, the demand for Ἕνωσις, *Enosis* or Union with Greece, has met with open encouragement from eminent statesmen (to say nothing of the 1915 offer), and a generous but sometimes misplaced toleration from successive rulers of Cyprus.

In 1897 Mr Gladstone wrote to the Duke of Westminster: "I subjoin the satisfaction I should feel were it granted me before the close of my long life to see the population of that Hellenic Island placed by a friendly arrangement in organic union with their brethren of the kingdom of Greece." Ten years later Mr. Winston Churchill, as Liberal Under-Secretary of State for the Colonies, heartens the Greek members of the Legislative Council with this swelling period: "I think it is only natural that the Cypriot people, who are of Greek descent, should regard their incorporation with what may be called their mother country, as an ideal

---

[18] "How could administrators do anything when every economy meant more Tribute, when any wise expenditure meant a larger grant-in-aid from the British Taxpayer?" The Right Hon. Josiah Wedgwood, D.S.O., M.P., *The Seventh Dominion.*

[19] Afterwards Field-Marshal Viscount Wolseley; first High Commissioner of Cyprus and last Commander-in-Chief of the British Army.

[20] Whose voluntary cession to Greece by Gladstone in 1863 was regarded by Bismarck as a clear indication of political decay.

to be earnestly, devoutly and fervently cherished. Such a feeling is an example of the patriotic devotion which is nobly characteristic of the Greek nation." Twelve years more, and in the expansive atmosphere of a Socialist Conference at Berne, a future Prime Minister, Mr Ramsay Mac-Donald, invokes a principle now hardly mentionable in polite society when he declares that "The British Labour Party would apply the principle of self-determination to Cyprus". A variety of classically educated Bishops, publicists and Members of Parliament had from time to time supported the Hellenic thesis.

I found the Greek flag abundantly in evidence in Cyprus, especially on the occasion of holidays or festivals, and particularly conspicuous in any town or village which the Governor might visit officially. It was the usual custom on the occasion of such visits for one or two Union Jacks to be flown in deference to the presence of His Majesty's representative, but for one Jack there were scores of Greek flags. It should not, however, be supposed that visits of a Governor were received by the villages with hostility, indifference, or even lack of enthusiasm: I was on the contrary assured by those best qualified to pronounce, and am personally convinced, that few manifestations of his activity gave more widespread satisfaction. He was everywhere welcomed with demonstrative and, I believe, sincere friendliness. The streets were strewn with myrtle, and our car loaded with flowers. The entire village or quarter of the town to be visited would be drawn up on either side of the road, and the pupils of the school paraded. Chairs were provided, and the headmaster of the principal school stepped forward and pronounced an harangue (generally written) describing in exaggerated language the hopes inspired by the visit, reciting the local grievances, and ending by calling for three Ζήτω's [21]—cheers—for His Majesty King George the Fifth, for the Liberal English Nation, for the Governor, and finally, with somewhat disconcerting inconsequence, for Union with Greece or the Fulfilment of the National Aspirations. With such words ringing in my ears, and with the nearer prospect almost entirely occluded by foreign flags, I was forcibly reminded of the position of *Don Juan aux Enfers* where, it will be remembered:

> *"Le calme héros, courbé sur sa rapière,*
> *Regardait le sillage, et ne daignait rien voir."*

After two months' experience of these methods, I adopted and successfully maintained the practice of rising with brusque gratitude after the third *Zeto* and grasping the speaker's hand, so that the undesirable

[21] Long live!

conclusion of his remarks was either curtailed or, if uttered, drowned in the applause of the bystanders.

I should have hesitated to countenance the conditions revealed by these irregular manifestations, which indeed made calls upon any capacity for surprise left to me after twenty-four years' service in Egypt and Palestine, but for my profound conviction that the duty and mutual advantage of establishing and maintaining personal contact with all sections of the population, especially in the rural districts, outweighed the objections. I gathered that in this attitude I had been following the policy of my predecessors, or at least that to which they had eventually resorted, namely to ignore the Greek flag, and not to interfere either by word or act with any outward symbols of attachment to a foreign Power. Indeed, in the absence of special legislation, it was difficult to see what preventive action would be possible: and it had been repeatedly proved by experience that expression of official warning, displeasure or regret served merely to encourage the abuse.

The Union Jack was flown at Government House when the Governor was in residence; over the Court and over the Commissioners' offices and houses in the Districts. Apart from that, a British flag was rarely visible, save periodically outside cafés and restaurants, which suffered this ingenuous sea-change during the visits of the British Fleet. The position was far from satisfactory, but seemed likely to be aggravated by efforts to alter it, unless supported by legislation; nor was legislation imported from other Colonies necessarily applicable in Cyprus.

There had been three occasions upon which measures might possibly have been adopted for the removal or abatement of the flag nuisance in Cyprus: on the original occupation in 1878, on annexation in 1914, and on formal recognition of Crown Colony status in 1925. I could only suppose that my predecessors in their consideration of the problem were confronted by the selfsame difficulties with which I found myself beset, and which the flight of time had progressively intensified. Nor had a High Commissioner's or Governor's disposition to a strong attitude or drastic regulation been appreciably fortified by the public declarations I have quoted.

I further found that a few months before my arrival the Holy Synod of Cyprus had organized a collection of subscriptions towards the Greek Air Force, for which an aeroplane was in fact purchased by the contributions of the Diocese of Kyrenia. My predecessors had been advised that, as the purpose for which the money was collected was legal, the Government had no power to interfere; and official action had therefore been confined to scrutiny by the Police for record purposes of the collections made. I noted that, so far from this easy-going attitude of the Government being appreciated, the police scrutiny (according to custom) of the subscriptions called forth bitter comments from the Press and probably assisted the task of collection; and this at a moment when local politicians were continually harping upon the destitution of the people and the oppressive taxation in Cyprus.

Other manifestations of the Flag spirit, involving constantly increasing mutual reaction and stimulus, were the Educational and Boy-Scout systems prevailing in the Island.

There was no definite anti-British curriculum in the Schools, but they were all actively Hellenizing. All Greek Elementary Schools used the "Analytical Programme" as published in Greece, and adopted by the Cyprus Board of Education. No reading books were allowed in these schools except those that were approved by the "Critical Committee" in Athens. The *Gymnasium* of each town and the Teachers Training College were recognized by the Greek Ministry of Education, and worked under Regulations issued therefrom. Portraits of King Constantine and Queen Sophie, of Venizelos and other worthies, but of no English Sovereign, adorned the walls of the classrooms, together with elaborate maps of modern Greece; while that of Cyprus, if to be found at all, was as a rule small, out of date, worn out, and frequently thrust behind the blackboard. I made a practice of asking one or two questions in each form of the schools in the towns and villages I visited, and discovered during my first few weeks (until my methods became known through the Press) a ludicrous difference between the home and the foreign knowledge even of the best pupils who, though always exactly informed as to the distance between Athens and Thebes (and usually as to the capital of Norway or Japan), would hazard guesses varying from 20 to 1500 miles as to the length or breadth of their own country.

I had received from General Baden-Powell upon my appointment to Cyprus what I believe to be the customary invitation to be Chief Scout of the Island, which, after due inquiry, suggested by Palestine [22] experience, I had the honour of accepting. But I soon found that, with the exception of an Armenian Troop, with whom through my Aide-de-Camp I established friendly relations, there was little scope for British activity. There were, it is true, various troops which dwindled or flourished with the personal interest of the schoolmaster who happened to be in charge. That of Paphos was the only one which appeared to me to do any real Scout work. The others merely paraded, chiefly on special occasions such

[22] Where Jewish Scouts refused to swear loyality to King George V.

as Athletic Sports; or went round the country collecting subscriptions for the Greek Red Cross and Air Force.

According to an official publication of the "Organization of Greek Scouts", all Greek Cypriot Troops were under the Greek Constitution (from which Scoutmasters received their warrants and instructions) and made annual returns to the Greek Ministry of Education. The second article of their Scout Law was "To be faithful to the Fatherland and the Laws of the State". Their flag was the Greek St George's flag, i.e. a broad white cross on a blue ground, with the Scout Fleur-de-Lys in the centre. Each section (or year) received graduated instruction in Patriotism, beginning with the respect due to the Greek flag, the "history of the Greek flag from the most ancient times", "the constitution of the Greek Nation", and leading up to "an extended knowledge concerning the political and military organization of the State and the duty of a citizen". The Greek National hymn had to be learnt by heart.

Although I was advised that 90 per cent. of the population would, if a fair plebiscite were taken with secret ballot, vote for the closest union with Great Britain, I could not help doubting how far the young generation brought up under this Pan-Hellenic curriculum would continue so to vote. At any rate, individuals or groups holding British opinions would never have dared to express them publicly, for to be branded as traitor by a majority, however composed, is not agreeable.

The doctrine of *Enosis,* not being contrary to the law of the land, could be condemned neither as criminal nor lawless, but, since Cypriots were British and not Greek subjects, as "disloyal". Critics of *Enosis* would argue that the original Islanders had been Asiatic, that there had been Phœnician as well as Greek settlers, that Cyprus had never belonged to any ancient Greek Kingdom, that whatever strain had survived from antiquity had been mingled with Lusignan and Venetian blood, that the language spoken was a corrupt form of Greek: in a word that Cypriots were not Greeks, and had no right to call themselves Greeks. And certainly I found that, constantly as Homer, Aeschylus and Sophocles were on the lips of local orators, it was their names rather than their verses which were cited, and then mainly as a proof of Cypriot *Kultur* at a time when the ancestors of their present "enslavers" wore wolf-skins and woad.[23] The only Greek scholar I ever found was the Archbishop, and even His Beatitude would have been defeated by an average Sixth Form boy in a competition in classical Greek prose or iambics. Neither pupils

---

[23] I imagine that the reason why the Greeks and Italians make so much more political play of Homer and Dante than we of Shakespeare is that Shakespeare does not typify a national revival; of which indeed England has not yet felt the need.

nor masters in the schools pretended to read their classics in the original, but studied them through modern renderings in the vulgar and monotonous "Political" [24] rhymes. I once presented a Euclid in his own Greek to the Central Training College for Boys. Observing a glazed bookcase containing the Greek classics presented some years before by a benefactor, I asked leave to examine them. For some minutes the key could not be found. When at length the doors were flung back it became clear that the volumes had never been cut nor apparently opened.

Nevertheless, though the arguments of the critics and my experiences were the truth, they were not the whole truth. For the Greek colonists Hellenized Cyprus as early as the fourteenth century B.C.: the Phœnicians did not arrive until the eleventh century, and then only to occupy two coast stations, Kition and Lapithos, for trading with the indigenous population. Thirty-three centuries of occupation constitute a claim much longer and far more continuous than the claim of Israel to Palestine. But even if Greek origin could not be proved for three thousand years, and had to be post-dated to the comparative modernity of Alexander the Great or to the Byzantine Empire; even if the Athenian of to-day is apt to distinguish Cypriots from other Greeks by the opprobrious epithet of Βους κύηριος—the equivalent of the German *Ochsenkopf* [25]—the Greekness of Cypriots is in my opinion indisputable. Nationalism is more, is other, is greater than pigmentations or cephalic indices. A man is of the race of which he passionately feels himself to be. No sensible person will deny that the Cypriot is Greek-speaking, Greek-thinking, Greek-feeling, Greek, just as much as the French Canadian is French-speaking, French-thinking, French-feeling and French. Both are equally sensitive upon this matter of race. One of my first duties after assuming the Government was to study the Nicosia Museum. In its catalogue I found quoted several Phœnician remains bearing inscriptions. Thinking that these might interest the Hebrew University, I expressed a desire to examine them myself. Not one could be produced. There have been many such all over the Island: none has survived the determination of the Greek majority that Cyprus shall possess proofs of none but Hellenic origin.

[24] "Thè *versus politici*, those common prostitutes, as, from their easiness, they are styled by Leo Allatius, usually consist of fifteen syllables. They are used by Constantine Manasses, John Tzetzes, etc. The name 'political' was probably applied because accentual verses were chanted by the citizens and the factions of the circus on public occasions to express pleasure or disapproval." Gibbon. The sing-song quality is represented by the couplet:

"If that is what you mean to say I can no more behold you.
I told you so, I told you so, I told you so, I told you."

[25] In moments of depression I, too, sometimes wondered whether the Homeric Βόες 'Ηλίου—the Oxen of the Sun—might not have been akin to the early inhabitants of the Island.

Indeed, the race-consciousness of the Greeks is only less persistent than that of the Jews themselves.

It was then a frequent reproach to the Enosist politicians of Cyprus that they were "disloyal"—a tendencious use of the adjective as a synonym for "hostile" or "discontented". Loyalty implies an accepted or anyhow acknowledged relationship, sometimes not unmingled with the sentiment of gratitude, which treacherously broken becomes disloyalty. That hideous thing I saw once or twice during the War, and I felt then, as I know now, that disloyalty, or base ingratitude towards a chief, a kinsman, or a benefactor are injuries which, though ruinous, it is better to endure than to inflict. Not for nothing has Dante reserved the traffickers in this cold meanness for the final depths of his Hell, below the thick blue ice that freezes the traitors, to be brayed in the jaws of Satan.

But Cypriots had not been consulted when they found themselves suddenly transferred—as part of a bargain—from one alien ruler to another, any more than had the Arabs of Palestine when placed under the Zionist Mandate. Cypriot Turks indeed had frequently proffered and shown—as indeed they owed—loyalty to the Power that protected their Minority rights. After their experience of easy-going British institutions, they dreaded conscription, whether under Abd al-Hamīd or Mustafa Kemal, only less than they dreaded Union with Greece. But the political Greeks, though they might admit, grudgingly, that they had gained by exchanging Turkey for Great Britain, considered that this same Great Britain was standing between them and their hopes, that they therefore owed her no loyalty, and that they were justified in taking the utmost advantage of her liberal and generous toleration. Hence the majority of Greek Elected Members had no scruple in breaking the oath they swore on introduction to the Chamber, of loyalty to the British Crown. Once, however, a Greek Cypriot had been admitted to the Civil Service, it became a point of honour, which so far as I know was never transgressed, to support the Government loyally through thick and thin. It is noteworthy that no exact rendering for the word "loyal" exists in ancient Greek; εὔνους—well-minded or well-disposed—being the nearest equivalent. That epithet, with the above qualifications, was perhaps the best that one could hope to apply to the majority of Greek Cypriots, and there had been times, as I have suggested, when Great Britain might have deserved it more thoroughly. Mockers might ascribe Greek patriotism to the desire to evict British officials and enjoy their salaries; and why not? For who but the most helpless savage ever wants (even when he may need) foreign officials? Sceptics, remembering the example of "redeemed" Crete, 40 per cent. of whose revenues went to Athens, wondered how many of the British vacancies would be filled by Cypriots. Nevertheless, agitation for union with another State was in many ways less easy to meet than agitation for independence. Outside observers of the Cyprus situation who recommended that Cypriots should be granted a flag of their own, instead of the Union Jack displaying the badge of the Colony, failed to see that this expedient left matters as they were; it was not so much that Enosists did not want the British flag, as that they did want the Greek flag. On the other hand their grievances were not so immediate as those of the Palestine Arabs, for the British officials and settlers combined affected the balance of population in Cyprus as little as they have in Malta and, at the present rate, would take two centuries to increase at the ratio which takes the Jews in Palestine two years. Was it, after all, so dishonourable not to desire membership of the greatest Empire in history, and to prefer instead the call of the blood and Greece?

As if the handicaps of Turkish Tribute and Greek nationalism were insufficient for a small, impoverished, and highly-strung population, the Liberal Government had decided in 1882 to establish a Constitution on a basis of communal representation, whereby the Cypriots should take a part in the conduct of their affairs. The news was hailed with delight by the Greek Christian majority, and the Archbishop telegraphed to the Colonial office: *"Au nom population Grecque Chypriote je prie votre Excellence soumettre aux pieds du trône de sa Majesté sa profonde reconnaissance pour réalisation réformes sollicitées justifiant notre confiance sans bornes aux sentiments justes et libéraux du Gouvernement anglais."* Moslems received the announcement with the same indignation, though without the same influences to make it effective, as the Zionists did that of a Legislative Council for Palestine in 1936. Their telegrams ran: "... we absolutely object to same, and beg to inform your Lordship that under the circumstances we shall not depute representatives to said Council...." The Moslem community contended, like the Zionists to-day, that their members in the Council should be equal in number to the Christian members. Whilst the Turks had proved themselves entirely loyal to the Crown, they were horrified that "the Greek community (with their constant complaints) whose endless cries of 'We want the Hellenic Government for our rulers' are still echoing from the heights of heaven, are all at once to be granted a privilege which they have never possessed in the past, and which they can claim on no grounds of present grievance".

The Cypriot Turk saw further than the British Government; which forthwith proceeded to promulgate a Legislative Council, composed on the principle that the official members plus the Turkish exactly equalled the number of the Greek members. The Council was enlarged on the same basis in 1925, so that with nine officials and three Turks the Governor's casting-vote could carry any measure against the united opposition of the twelve Greeks representing 80 per cent. of the total population of Cyprus. Normally Turks voted for and with the Government as a matter of course. One issue only, the Tribute drove them to join the opposition, as I discovered on the day of my arrival—an issue in which all Cypriots enjoyed the deep if unavowable sympathy of the whole Administration.

This Legislative Council presumably appeared to the brains which evolved and approved it in Whitehall in the 'eighties to be an ingenious and statesmanlike device. To all concerned with its working in Cyprus, the Governor, his officers, the Greek members, the Turkish members and the inhabitants in general it proved an exasperating and humiliating nuisance. The President (as in most Crown Colonies) was the Governor, who was thus forced to combine in his person the aloofness of the King's Representative, the impartiality of the Speaker, and the partiality of the Prime Minister driving a Bill through the House by means of a minimum but perpetual majority. He was for most business entirely dependent upon the loyalty and the assiduity of the three Turks, and during a crucial clause of the Budget would cast anxious glances upon their third empty chair, whose occupant sometimes found it difficult to be present after dinner. Different Governors might handle the twelve Greek members with varying degrees of consideration but when it came to Supply the screw must be put on or Government would cease; and the Greeks, confronted by the unanimous officials and the three almost mechanical Turkish voters, could not but feel with irritation that they were little better than a debating society. Such authority as they had [26] being entirely divorced from responsibility, the politicans directed their efforts to strengthening their position by rousing popular prejudice; and the Chamber and the Island, especially at Election time, were regaled with floods of wonderfully irresponsible and often anti-British eloquence. Nor could the Turks find their position particularly dignified. Their assistance, based on community of interest with the Government, was assumed without much gratitude even when, under the stern eye of their leader (or after a hurried consultation with him in the Antechamber) they voted against their own convictions.

Cyprus is a purely agricultural country, and three quarters of the population is engaged in agriculture. Most of these were illiterate. 70 per cent. were chronically indebted to usurers and merchants whose

---

[26] *E. g.*, in the important Greek Board of Education to be mentioned later.

actions for recovery (more than half the cases in the District Courts), afforded employment to the numerous advocates, who derived the major part of their professional income from that source. I found on the Council eight advocates, three of whom were money-lenders; one land-owner who was also a money-lender; one bishop of the Greek Church; one merchant and one farmer. Thus though the real interests of the Colony were those of the peasant producer, the interests represented in the Legislature were exclusively those of the numerically insignificant class of parasites who made a living out of him. Between the Tribute and the Constitution, I found the Cyprus which I had been appointed to govern financially spoiled, politically spoilt.

This was enough, but not all. The National Greek-Orthodox Church of Cyprus is national in the extreme and richest interpretation of that obliging and overworked adjective. From 1192 onwards, alike under Lusignan and Venetian rulers, the hand of Latin Christianity had lain heavy on the Church, as on the inhabitants, of the Island; the Orthodox Bishops became vassals of the Latin Bishops, and were obliged to take an oath of allegiance to them and to the Holy See. The Turks, dreading the universal pretensions and connections of Rome, revived and sup-ported the local and relatively isolated Orthodox Church. Infidel rule showed itself in Cyprus (as sometimes elsewhere) more tolerant than Christian rule, but it was still infidel, as the Church had found to its cost in 1821. For nearly six centuries then the only continuous Byzantine and Hellenic tradition had been preserved by the Orthodox Church, the Archbishop of which was therefore accepted by Greek Cypriots and (under the Ottoman *millet* or national unit system)[27] by the Turks also as the Ethnarch or national representative of his co-religionists. It might have been thought that after 1878, under the milder control of a Christian Power with even less of a religious axe to grind than (for example) agnostic, Roman Catholic France, the post of Ethnarch might have been allowed to lapse. He had said his say when the British arrived. No British ruler had since interfered with the Orthodox religion, the Greek language, or the freedom of speech and Press which the British introduced into Cyprus. The national status of the Island might possibly be a matter for discussion in Athens or London, but not for the Governor or the Archbishop. For His Beatitude Kyrillos III I cherished a sympathetic admiration. He was the only spiritually-minded Orthodox prelate—or indeed priest, whom I discovered during my six years' Governorship. He would take tea with me at Government House, I with him in his Palace. We exchanged books. He attended King George's

[27] See p. 422.

Birthday Service in the Anglican Church, I his *Te Deum* [28] the same day in the Orthodox Cathedral. He agreed that logically the Ethnarch was an obsolete survival, but argued, no less logically, that unless Cypriots agitated there would never be *Enosis*—and who else should lead them but their Ethnarch? In truth the good man was often forced by politicians, lay as well as clerical, to say and do things repugnant to his natural delicacy; more than one Archbishop was rumoured to have been poisoned for refusing the behests of extremist or rival factions. For these reasons, the Orthodox Church of Cyprus as a whole—from Archbishop to village priest—was a political rather than a religious institution, and unlike all other branches of the Orthodox Church known to me, strongly anti-British in sentiment; though not in personal relations, for the older generation of Cypriot was essentially courteous, nor did I ever receive from one of them anything but civility and friendliness. Church influence was great, but being based on threats rather than upon spiritual or material services tended to wane with the spread of education. The British Government right refused in Cyprus as elsewhere to admit any authority or intermediary unless constituted by the law of the land. The attitude of the Church towards the State was often resented by outside observers as "not playing the game". These forgot that Cyprus, like much of the Near East, is not yet of our epoch; and expected people all over the world to conform to a sort of English political cricket, the rules of which are not always observed, even in England, where our clergy by no means confine their political activities to the acceptance or rejection of the deposited Prayer-Book. (Throughout the East there is a class of official addicted to foolish carping at the peoples he is set to serve: so that I was sometimes fain to enquire where, if the inhabitants were all virtuous and efficient Nordics, would the complainant, as Great White Raj, be earning his bread and butter. As André Gide has said: *"Moins le blanc est intelligent, plus il méprise les noires."*)

The Administration of Cyprus was one of the lowest-paid of all the British Colonial Services. This was owing partly to the poverty of the Island, partly to the relatively low cost of living (which was automatically raised by every improvement introduced), and partly by the extreme susceptibility of the elected Members of Council on the question of British emoluments. In Palestine, where salaries had been calculated after the War on the basis of a high living index, and of the original rations, lighting and fuel of the Military Administration, local rents and high prices were the chief difficulty, and apart from the expenses of the

[28] I tried my first year to attend as well as these two the Latin and American Services, but found the effort in a Nicosia June physically impossible.

voyage, vacations in England or in Europe cost if anything less than similar periods in Jerusalem. For the Cyprus official on the other hand, life was easier so long as he remained in Cyprus; but the problem of holidays and still more of education often imposed an almost intolerable strain. The result of this short-sighted and uneconomic cheese-paring was that some of the Departments fell from time to time into the hands of misfits and incompetents, who remained untransferred for twenty or twenty-five years, while the good men were soon drawn off elsewhere. Some were pensioned invalids from tropical Colonies, and this practice of treating Cyprus as a sanatorium continued until well after my appointment. Technical and scientific appointments were sometimes vacant for two years because Cyprus could not pay the standard market price which they commanded.

Nevertheless, small as might be the remuneration of the higher British official in Cyprus, it was far larger than the incomes of all but the richest Cypriots or (as the local Press—the *eleftheria* or the *Phoni tis Kyprou*—reminded us about once a week) than the salaries of Cabinet Ministers in Greece and in other Balkan States; while that of the Governor almost equalled the allowance of the President of the Greek Republic. Furthermore, the benefits of extended Government activities take time to prove; whereas the liabilities, in the shape of fresh appointments for expensively-trained Englishmen, are immediate. A zealous Director of Agriculture presses the Governor for a Mycologist to supplement the necessary investigations of his Entomologist into the origins and prevention of crop diseases. In an Island preeminently agricultural it seems reasonable to support the Director and, with the aid of the Turks, the appointment is more or less forced through Council. The young Mycologist duly arrives, disappears into a Laboratory, and may or may not produce tangible results for two, five or ten years. But his initial salary—the minimum for such qualifications in England—and scale of pension, with which the little Colony is debited, are superior to those of all but three or four of the most senior Cypriot officials. Again, the long list of compulsory subscriptions to establishments remote from, though admirable and sometimes demonstrably beneficial to Cyprus, such as the Imperial Institute, the Imperial Mycological Institute, the Imperial Institute of Entomology, the London School of Tropical Medicine, the National Institute of Agricultural Botany, the Colonial Agricultural Service Fund, is not easy to justify or even to explain to villagers clamouring for a road, a visiting doctor, or a water supply. Nor did these officers' salaries represent anything like their total cost to the Island revenues. When Elected Members spoke darkly of "hidden emoluments", the impression they created upon an ignorant electorate was not altogether false; for, though the House, Car, Travelling or Vacation Passage allowances were certainly not hidden, but shown *en bloc* under their respective headings in the Estimates, it was no less difficult in Cyprus than elsewhere to disentangle the amount actually received *per annum* by any individual officer. For these and other reasons the privileged class of British officials were lumped together by the Greeks under the title (which no less flattered than it wronged some of them) of Κυανόαιμοι—"Blue-bloodeds".[29]

It is my earnest belief that, as towards the end of the British Occupation of Egypt, there would have been less resentment shown, and genuinely felt, by the inhabitants, if the Colonial Office had realized that Cyprus (with Mandated Palestine and perhaps Ceylon) possesses characteristics not found elsewhere in the British Crown Colonies. The qualities which are desirable for an official in East Africa may be the same as those desirable for West Africa, or Malaya, or Fiji. Different qualities are required for Cyprus. Officials, more particularly executive officials (Governors included), cannot be considered as interchangeable parts in a standardized automobile. Some with African experience were unable to mix on friendly terms with educated Cypriots without seeming to themselves to sacrifice something of their position as members of the governing race. The wife of an officer, excellent at his work, told me with pride on the eve of his transfer that they had been in Cyprus fourteen years, and never had a "native" inside their house; and was genuinely shocked when I reminded her that she owed to the Cypriots the food she was at that moment consuming (at Government House) and the clothes on her back. A high legal luminary from East Africa was horrified to learn that he would be expected to shake hands with "the natives". "I understand a white gentleman", he perorated, "and a black gentlemen, though I don't let him touch me; but these betwixts and betweens I don't want to understand." [30] These "betwixts" were frequently barristers-at-law, speaking two or three languages, besides a far from Babu English, playing sometimes, like their wives, a good game of tennis and of bridge, and sending their children, when they could afford it, to school in England. Yet the discussion and exposition of the law drew the Bench and the legal officers closer to their Cypriot

[29] See the recommendations of the Royal Commission for Palestine officials.

[30] I sympathized with these late uprooted officials when, after twenty-eight years' service in the Near and Middle East, I found myself promoted to the rule of a million and a half blacks, of whom one only, the Paramount Chief of Barotseland, could have his hand shaken by a white. I did not dispute that protocol, but found the contrast, after lands where you gave your hand to and shared the food of the poorest Bedu camel-driver (or his eyes wondered where you had been bred) almost overwhelmingly disagreeable.

colleagues than any other Department. An Englishman's house is his castle: in Cyprus it was apt to become his social fortress. Into the charming little Nicosia Club one or two Cypriots—Greek, Turk and Armenian—had been elected in earlier and happier days (for the reciprocal bitterness engendered by social slighting is progressive and cumulative); but there had been latterly more than one instance of a young Greek of good family returning after an education in England full of enthusiasm for everything English, to find himself excluded from the Club and from most English society, and so driven into the Cyprus political atmosphere of sullen suspicion and misunderstanding.[31] By a natural paradox, the ultra-local British resident wielded the black ball even more drastically than the English official.

On the other hand, it should be recorded that these same officers showed the utmost kindness and consideration for their Cypriot subordinates, by whom they were for the most part well liked; and that there was something to be said for the reluctance of wives to receiving the relations and friends of Elected Members who seasoned debate with abuse of their husbands, calumniated them before strangers, and openly rejected the British Empire.

It is by many assumed that for all countries coming into the British Empire there has necessarily been an advantage for persons of emergent abilities: but some countries have lost as well as gained by the process. I have shown how the "careers open to talents" were reduced for Mandated Palestine by its excision from the Ottoman Empire. For Cyprus also the British occupation had in this respect acted as a positive disadvantage. There could be no more Grand Viziers from the little village of Piröi, nor from all the 670 villages of Cyprus. For men of capacity, unable to aspire beyond a judgeship or a subordinate legal post, it was cold comfort to be told that there were preferential duties some 6000 miles away for commodities which Cyprus might, and might not, produce. The appeal to Empire sentiment is a mockery worse than useless unless accompanied by the offer of Imperial opportunities.[32] I could cite two or three Cypriot officers who were pronounced by successive Chief Justices (by no means prone to exaggerate the merits of Cypriots) to be worthy by their character and attainments of a place upon almost any Bench in the Empire. The encouragement to such as these, if they could be promoted to some other Colony, perhaps even

---

[31] Almost exactly on the lines of Mr A. E. W. Mason's *Broken Road*.

[32] "The grandsons of the Gauls who besieged Julius Caesar in Alesia commanded legions, governed provinces, and were admitted into the Senate of Rome. Their ambition, instead of disturbing the tranquillity of the State, was intimately connected with its safety and greatness." Gibbon.

more appropriately than within their own (where local connections might make their position delicate) would be very great. Other Colonies might benefit by their objectivity and freshness of attitude, as would their own by their broadened views and deparochialized outlook on return, to say nothing of the stimulus afforded by the study of the English language and of British Institutions. Must all the Crown Colonies be branded with eternal provincialism?

Alien rule is not easy to bear, save by the lowest savages. Without a modicum of human intercourse or the incentive of legitimate ambition, it may become intolerable.

CHAPTER TWENTY

*We are enjoined to labour, but it is not granted
to us to complete our labours.*—Talmud.

ALTHOUGH the art of governing has been said to consist largely in
the skilful evasion of issues, the anomalies and inhibitions I have
attempted to describe seemed hardly easier for the Governor of Cyprus
to bear, than for the governed. But I had no intention of making or
recommending to the Colonial Office any changes without careful
examination and consultation with those who had been longer in the
Island. Even the political extremists must, I thought, realize that a
British Governor, however Philhellene, was not appointed to give away
portions of the Empire, and would be ready to co-operate with me for
the good of their country, whatever might be its ultimate destiny. But
there was one grievance that needed no further study. Before leaving
England I had urged the Colonial Office and, with their approval, the
Treasury, that it was high time to abolish the iniquity of the Turkish
Tribute. Finding that there were still difficulties I suggested that if
His Majesty's Government would remit the annual charge, the Colony
might undertake to contribute £10,000 per annum towards Imperial
Defence. The rejection of the Budget was a challenge, involving stoppage
of Supply, which had forced me to begin my administration by invoking
an Order in Council (hardly less unpopular in Downing Street, for the
trouble it causes, than in Cyprus). It had also, since no Government
can yield to menace, prejudiced the case of those I was doing my utmost
to help. Nevertheless Mr. Amery piloted my Dispatch through the
Cabinet and, after ten months' anxious waiting, I was able to inform
the Legislative Council that the Tribute was abolished. The announcement, which I made immediately before a visit to Rhodes, was received
with joy, and on my return I was welcomed on the quay of Limassol
by the Members of Council who, in the presence of an enthusiastic
assembly, handed me the following document:

5 September 1927.

May it Please Your Excellency,

We, the Elected Members of the Legislative Council of Cyprus, have heard with extreme satisfaction the sympathetic speech which Your Excellency was pleased to make to us on the 31st of August.

We are most grateful to Your Excellency for the great care and consideration which prompted your appeal to relieve Cyprus from the heavy burden of the Turkish Debt Charge. The happy answer of the Imperial Government has fulfilled all Cypriot aspirations concerning this burden, and in the apt words of Your Excellency, spring has indeed been restored to the year.

We earnestly desire that Your Excellency will be pleased to convey our loyal gratitude to His Majesty's Government and to the Right Honourable the Secretary of State for the Colonies for their reconsideration of the situation and for the memorable decision which has now been taken.

We most willingly concur in the conditions set forth in the communication from the Right Honourable the Secretary of State, and we are ready to co-operate in the early enactment of the Legislation necessary to ratify the decision.

In conclusion, we take leave to reassure Your Excellency of our readiness at all times to co-operate in those measures which will serve the true prosperity and welfare of our Colony.

We have the honour to be,

Sir,

Your Excellency's Most obedient Servants,

(Signed)

Nicodemos of Kition	P. L. Cacoyiannis
Luke Zeno Pierides	S. G. Stavrinakis
Stelios Pavlides	Mahmoud Djelaleddin
Dr Eyioub	Kyriakos Pavlou Rossides
G. Hadjipavlou	G. S. Emphiedjis
Haji Eftychios Haji Procopi	Chr. Fieros
Mich. Her. Michaelides	Ph. Ioannides
M. Munir	

When, next Christmas, I visited Egypt, I was to my astonishment greeted with cheers by a crowd of eight or nine hundred Cypriots gathered in the Cairo Railway Station. The Greek weekly published in Heliopolis (like the famous *Roméos* of Athens) in verse, was moved to ecstasy in a poem beginning

ὁ Στὸρρς φιλέλλην Βρέττανος...[1]

—memories over which I was in later years often to muse. Such was the smallness of scale of Cyprus finance that this release of £32,000

---

[1] "Storrs the Philhellene Briton."

"*Grâce aux efforts de Sir Ronald Storrs, ce chapitre à base injustifiée fut rayé du budget de l'île.*" Michel Dendias, *La question Cypriote*, 1934.

Photo: Russell

THE AUTHOR

annually enabled me within two years to reorganize the Departments of Agriculture and of Public Health.

Soon after my arrival a circular was issued to all Departments forbidding (as I had in Judaea) the use of the word "native", and enjoining that of Cypriot; and increasing office hours from 30 to 35 a week. The second of these was easier said than done. To any specific placing of the additional five hours the objections were no less ingenious than varied. An hour extra in the early morning was impossible because in Cyprus delicately nurtured women could not be expected to do their own marketing—and so the husbands must. An hour at the end of the morning would be in the heat of the day. The early afternoon would be too soon after luncheon; mid-afternoon would prevent necessary recreation; late afternoon was the one opportunity for the domestic tea when the little ones could

"Climb his knee, the envied kiss to share".

By early evening the sun had set, and you could not expect the lady clerks to be bicycling home after dark. After listening to disparagements of several alternative schemes, I had to confess that I was indifferent to the exact schedule so long as it amounted to 35 hours; which it accordingly did.

Further, I felt strongly that where an able and loyal Cypriot could be employed in the public service of his country he should be so employed. Before the end of my first year there were appointed two Cypriot puisne Judges, one Greek and one Turk; and a Cypriot Solicitor-General, Crown Counsel and Assistant Auditor. For these two Law appointments British candidates were already being considered, and it was mainly owing to the personal interest of Mr Amery that my proposals were accepted in the face of some criticism. There was to come a day when the critics were not sorry to find the best Cypriot abilities working for and not against the Government. The immediate extension of this principle was unfortunately checked by the absence of technical training available to the Cypriot who, conceiving that the upper grades of the Government were permanently barred to him, had tended to concentrate exclusively upon medicine and law. Soon afterwards scholarships were established for Cypriots in Engineering, Architecture, Forestry, Book-keeping and other subjects, the benefits of which I did not survive to experience.

In 1927 the G.O.C. Troops in Egypt visited Cyprus. I represented to him that Limassol, the seat of the British Garrison, was 2½ hours distant from the Government and from the nearest Railway Station, besides being without telephonic communication, and for tactical and political reasons about as badly placed as it could be; the garrison should therefore be transferred to Nicosia. The General supported me, but the Cyprus Government could not and the Home Government would not afford the cost of the necessary barracks. The troops therefore remained at Limassol during the winter, leaving annually for Mount Troödes when their quarters, from May to mid-November, became through malaria unfit for occupation.

No disciple of Gorst, Kitchener, Allenby or Samuel would have the faintest objection to being reputed "weak" if "weakness" were the policy of the Home Government; but I was anxious to be certain that the Secretary of State for the Colonies realized and (though he could hardly approve) accepted the long-established toleration of foreign national propaganda by speech, by flag and by education in a British Colony. I therefore prepared for him an accurate presentment of the situation, as I had previously of the alternative method of dealing with a similar situation practised less than 300 miles away. Italy occupied the Greek-speaking Ottoman Islands of the Dodecanese [2] during the war in which she annexed Tripoli in 1911, and after that war retained the Islands also. In 1919 Italy almost ceded the Dodecanese to Greece; the draft treaty was in fact ready for signature when Signor Tittoni changed his mind and the Islands remained Italian. Under Fascist Italy Hellenism was being systematically and scientifically extinguished. The very name of Dodecanese, being Greek, had been suppressed and supplanted by *Le Isole Egee,*[3] the Aegean Islands. Nationalities had similarly become religions; you spoke not of Greeks, but of *Ortodossi,* not of Turks, but of *Mussulmani.* One Greek flag only floated throughout the Islands —upon the Greek Consulate in Rhodes. The only Greek newspaper was a translation printed on the back of an Italian original. Most of the houses bore on their walls the stencilled head of a prognathous Duce, and as the Italian flag was lowered at sunset all passers-by were compelled to salute it, stepping from their cabs or cars if necessary for the purpose. There were no "liberal institutions" whatever. I did not propose adopting this policy, though some of it was afterwards to be forced on me, and it would have been well if the portion relating to flags had been adopted on the first British occupation of Cyprus. On the other hand the energy of development shown by the Italians, particularly under that remarkable administrator (and my excellent friend) Senatore Mario Lago,

[2] Thirteen, including their Capital, Rhodes.
[3] Similarly, though not with the same intention, the seven Ionian Islands, the Heptanese, ceded to Great Britain in 1815, were styled in the 1817 Constitution "The Septinsular Republic". The Islands were handed to Greece by Gladstone in the 1860's.

Governor-General of the Aegean Islands, was worthy of the highest commendation. The Islands abounded with every sort of improvement; in Rhodes the visitor was even conscious that the clearing, cleaning and repairing had been almost overdone. Superficial observers have from this lavishness deduced comparisons with the British frugality which will bear impartial examination. British Crown Colonies pay their own way, otherwise neither they nor their central Government could continue to exist. Their extent and prestige render alike impossible and unnecessary the propagandist expenditure which has been devoted to the production, as in Libya and Rhodes, a *suggestiva romanità* Italian rule in the Dodecanese was not, save nationalistically, a grinding tyranny. Still less was it a philanthropic disbursement of Italian revenue superior to the Crown Colony system. Judged by what Greek Cypriots and Greek Dodecanesians would prefer now, there could be no doubt which was the better of the two regimes. Judged by the ultimate advantage to each in a couple of generations, assuming the British Government means business, I am not quite so certain. However this may be, the Colonial Office after due consultation with the Foreign Office commended existing British policy in Cyprus as "statesmanlike", and the only policy to adopt. They also suggested that I should investigate the educational system, with special reference to foreign political propaganda.

I had never before nor have ever since known a satisfaction equal to the gradual erasure of items from the *Agenda* list of the projects I hoped to complete within my term, and their transfer to the list of *Acta*. The process interested me so vitally that I shall beg to be forgiven if I describe it now in what may be thought excessive detail: for five years it was my life.

Fortified by the above-cited instructions I proceeded to visit as many villages as possible in order to find out for myself the real needs of the country. Cyprus wanted many things, but direly needed three, to wit capital, communications (a form and result of capital) and, above all, water. Capital was raised from two sources: the flotation of a Cyprus loan of £600,000 and Mr Amery's far-sighted Imperial measure, the Colonial Development Fund, which granted or lent among approved Crown Colonies a million pounds a year for remunerative or beneficial enterprises. Two hundred thousand pounds went to the doubling of Famagusta Harbour, of which the entrance was so narrow and the quay space so small that many vessels, foreign as well as British, had been debarred from using it; and had lain up waiting for cargoes in other parts of the Levant, using foreign ports owing to the uncertainty of obtaining and keeping a berth in the only British port of the Eastern

Mediterranean. Again, automobilists were unlikely to bring their cars into a country possessing no more than 20 miles of tarred road. Three hundred thousand pounds very soon produced several hundred miles of tarred main roads, with three or four hundred more macadamized and water-bound. Soon the costs and delays of transport went down, while the revenue mounted. The British Mail Service had been calculated on a maddening schedule whereby the outward mail was dispatched some 24 hours before the receipt of the inward, with a consequent loss of some five days a week and great extra expenditure upon telegrams. Having failed with the Alexandria agents of the Khedivial Mail Line, I invited Lord Inchcape to Cyprus, and within a month the merchants were accorded at least a day and night to consider and answer their correspondence.

There was no wireless, the Military installation having been removed after the War: and when, during the laying of the new cable from Larnaca to Haifa, the Alexandria cable was inadvertently put out of action, Cyprus was for two days entirely cut off from the outer world and could have been occupied by a hostile force—and no one else any the wiser. There were no public telephones; only a small Government exchange in Nicosia,[4] connecting with Famagusta and Larnaca for official communication only; so that, as the telegraph service was operated by the Eastern Telegraph Company, working only commercial hours on a commercial basis,[5] the Government (including the Police) was throughout the night, on Sundays and other holidays, without means of communication, save by runner, with more than half the Island. Wireless and telephones proved a weary business for, though I lost no time in making a start and received every encouragement from successive Secretaries of State, my first three years coincided with the long-drawn-out merging of the Eastern Telegraph Company and its allied firms with Marconi's Wireless Company into the single Imperial Communications. Here was no Inchcape to take and carry out a decision, and it was not until 1930 that an agent was empowered by the Merger to sign a preliminary agreement for the erection of a wireless station and the establishment of a telephone service connecting all the principal towns of the Island. It was disappointing to leave the Colony three years later, despite my many and urgent reminders and interviews in London, well before the arrival of one instrument, one pole, one single wire.

Cable and wireless communications were not less but more important than ever now that we had reached the Air Age. Partly because of

[4] There was also a small private exchange with about 100 subscribers in the town of Limassol and a forest telephone service for fire protection.

[5] Thus the Government had no means of keeping check of seditious messages.

the lack of these, no aeroplane or seaplane had to the best of my knowledge arrived in Cyprus since the end of the War. If you lay a ruler on the map from Brindisi to Athens and prolong the line eastward, it will pass directly through Cyprus, whence it continues almost straight to Damascus, Rutba Wells and Baghdad, a total distance of 730 miles; thus cutting off the other two sides of the present triangle, Athens—Crete—Egypt and Egypt—Gaza—Rutba, saving 150 miles, and operating upon one British instead of two foreign territories. In 1927 I proposed to Imperial Airways that, for their India Service at least, Cyprus should

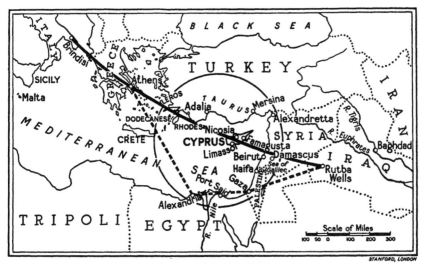

CYPRUS, THE AIR LINK

be substituted for Egypt. I rapidly became the Air bore to the Colonial Office, the Cyprus bore to the Air Ministry and to Imperial Airways. We established an emergency landing ground outside Nicosia, but had to wait until the spring of 1930 before the first two machines actually did land there from Palestine (and created a furore of interest). Lord Thomson and Sir Sefton Brancker promised to bring the ill-fated R 101 over Cyprus.

In September 1930 Imperial Airways, assisted by a grant from the Treasury, introduced an experimental air service between Cyprus, Palestine, and Egypt for the summer months, and in April 1932 began to make Cyprus a permanent link in the Near and Middle Eastern system with weekly calls both ways at Limassol. For the great air-boats of Imperial Airways we could not at first guarantee sufficiently smooth water in winter. The solution to this problem lay in the Akrotiri Salt Lake immediately to the West of Limassol. The surface was ample; the depth, four feet, could be increased to the necessary eight by admitting the sea through an ancient Venetian dyke, at the cost of some £4000 compensation to peasants affected. In addition to this safe, landlocked thalassodrome, the great central plain of the Mesaoria is in itself one vast aerodrome. (The lake has not yet been deepened, and the Eastern service through Cyprus has been discontinued because, I gather, of the roughness of the descent into the Sea of Galilee, their next stop, and the danger owing to the wind for aeroplanes moored on the adjacent aerodrome of Semakh.)

Throughout the Near and Middle East the traveller is apt to wonder how the mighty civilizations of antiquity could have arisen and flourished in regions which seem to have been for centuries past doomed to perpetual drought. Nowhere does this astonishment recur more often than in Cyprus where, until the end of the Lusignan Dynasty in 1489, there had existed for three hundred years a degree of prosperity inconceivable (even allowing for the entrepôt Eastern traffic) without large and constant supplies of water. "Give me water", said a Cyprus farmer, "and I will turn it into money fast enough." But long before the British Occupation Venetian neglect and Ottoman deforestation had so defaced nature and the work of ages that a traveller in the 'seventies can record of the great and once fertile plain of the Mesaoria: "We have travelled in this region for whole days without seeing anything but a dry wild vegetation. . . . I have walked and ridden over the greater portion of the forests but have been overcome with anger and dismay at the terrible exhibition of wanton desolation." [6] Forests may not attract moisture: they certainly preserve it, and a melancholy sight it was after heavy rainfall to behold the precious flood that should have been retained for Cyprus by the resistance of trees, bearing away the life-giving humus in a dull yellow streak miles long into the Kyrenian sea. Rains were violent but capricious. No expert could be sure where, or indeed whether at all, artesian water was to be found. No water-finder known to me would ply his skill—even with his return fare to Cyprus granted and allowances during sojourn—on a basis of payment by results. Scientific water engineers from Europe were expensive, and could guarantee finds no more than their humbler brethren of the hazel-rod. There were grave disappointments, as when I was officially informed of the discovery of a volume of water sufficient to irrigate the Mesaoria, only to discover (after public announcement) that the total quantity available was far less, and the necessary lift far greater, than had been calculated. The best that could be done was to appoint as good a permanent water

---

[6] *Cit.* B. J. O'Brien, *Cyprus*, 1878-1928. Feb. 1928.

engineer, as many drillers with as many boring-plants as Cyprus could afford, and vigorously to follow up every indication. Two hundred new wells and some seven million gallons of irrigation water every twenty-four hours is not an inspiriting statistic for five years' work; yet even that was not easy to attain. One other scheme (of epicurean interest) was completed, whereby some half-million gallons a day were conveyed by pipe-line from an adjoining valley into the district of Lefka, which produces oranges pronounced by an eminent Citrus authority to be superior to those of Jaffa itself.[7]

The forests were once the glory of Cyprus, but the Phœnician copper mines and the fleets of Alexander and Venice began their destruction, which Ottoman felling, fire, and the grazing of boats completed, until it became like the Cyclops' Island in the *Odyssey*:

> ἀλλ' ἥ γ' ἄσπαρτος καὶ ἀνήροτος ἥματα πάντα
> ἀνδρῶν χηρεύει, βόσκει δέ τε μηάαδας αἶγας.[8]

> *Od.* ix, 123–4.

The intelligent conservation and development of the last thirty years have arrested this advancing ruin, as the slopes of Olympus and Troödos, the forests of Paphos, Adelphi and Machaerá, of Lapithos and Stavro-vouni, with their Aleppo pines, Cyprus cedars and oaks now attest. Their worst enemy by far is the goat. In Cyprus one realizes, perhaps for the first time, why the Parable contrasts him so unfavourably with the sheep. His lascive petulance of poisonous cropping burns [9] beyond recovery the young green shoots. Yet the Forest Officer, with the Government behind him, is almost powerless before these three hundred thousand public enemies. The benefits everywhere, and especially in a country like Cyprus, of afforestation on a large scale are incontrovertible: yet there was no more controversial topic in the Island than the extent to which forests should be allowed to grow. Forestry in Cyprus conserves rainfall, clothes ground unfit for agriculture, moderates extremes of climate, improves agricultural lands by stream-shifted deposits, provides in timber one of the staples of civilization, creates regular employment and small holdings for foresters, adds health to the air and beauty to the landscape, and represents at a modest estimate a cash value of nearly three million pounds. But though the forest and the goat cannot live together, the goat is for Cyprus what the pig is for Ireland or the camel for Arabia, the irreplaceable means of subsistence for the very

---

[7] These oranges were duly placed upon the London market.

[8] "Rather the spot continues in solitude, wholly uncultivated, a paradise for the bleating she-goats. . . ." T. E. Lawrence.

[9] Horace calls them "burning" goats—*urentes haedi.*

poor.[10] Moreover, in the democratic days of the Legislative Council, goatherds had to be placated, and goats meant votes.

The principal Forest Officer loved his trees like human beings, only a good deal more. His soul was in his work, and his indignation against such as thwarted it escaped from his Reports in physiological (and sometimes obstetrical) tropes and similes which I had to bowdlerize severely before submission to Downing Street. We grappled with this problem, appointing a Forest Commission with Cypriot members, whose report of sixteen months' work was critically examined by Professor Troup of Oxford and, when I left, was still being considered by the Secretary of State. We added hundreds of miles of forest telephones. We sent Greeks and Turks to study Forestry in England, held forest-produce exhibitions, started Arbor Day, and by employing goatherds on forest work or offering them plots of land in exchange for goats hoped we might be educating them into the "advantages of a more settled life". Nevertheless Forestry and the Forestry Department were unpopular with the Cypriots: to the peasant because he could not live off forests, to the politician because they vexed his constituents; and it is my opinion that, do what we may, generations will have passed before Cyprus can be forced off the Goat Standard.

The lives of the very poor are in all countries the problem of the statesman and the opportunity of the demagogue. In order to put some check upon the ceaseless flow of uninformed comment upon the state of the Cyprus peasantry, I caused to be prepared a *Survey of Rural Life in Cyprus*. The Survey which was made, and still is, available to the public, revealed conditions of living preserved through the Ottoman Empire from a dim past and roughly equivalent to those of Tudor England. Though sad reading, it was to be the basis of much social legislation—as in the treatment of domestic servants—for many years.

Hardly one of the thousand annual "discoverers" of Cyprus fails on his return home to inveigh, sometimes in the public Press, against the Government's "neglect", especially in the matter of hotels—though these are nowhere else assumed to be a function of Government. In 1927 this defect was even more conspicuous than it is now; and if the improvement hitherto has been but slow and slight, it is for the following reasons. The Cyprus Government had not the money to build, nor at first to guarantee the building of hotels. The few Cypriot capitalists had for

[10] "It has been computed that the scrawny nomadic goats are worth, with their dirty milk, poor cheese, tough meat and inferior leather, at most 10s. per head per annum to the island, while the damage done by 'the poisonous tooth of the accursed goat' is at least 20s. per head per annum, apart from the injury due to the shortsightedness, malice, or carelessness of the goatherds in burning forest-pasture and starting forest fires." *The Times*, "Jubilee in Cyprus", 12 July 1928.

generations been accustomed to put their money out to usury and to no other purpose: they mistrusted each other and would not combine, especially in a hitherto untried venture. (Nor did the critical tourist ever dream of interesting himself or his friends in the Cyprus hotel business.) Most British officials and residents dreaded popularization as tending infallibly to raise the cost of living. Starting in this auspicious atmosphere, I proceeded to get into touch with the Egyptian and Palestine English and Scottish Hotel Companies, and later with the Central and Near Eastern representatives of Thomas Cook, who had no agent in Cyprus. My Hotel and Tourism file swelled to portentous dimensions, but, both sides refusing to take any risks and being hot for certainty of profit, I received from both a dusty (and identical) answer. Emissaries of Cook and of several hotel companies accepted my invitation to visit the Island yet, despite the passing of a Law guaranteeing 5 per cent. on approved enterprises, all I could secure were promises that the tourist agencies would concentrate on Cyprus so soon as two or three first-class hotels were built, and that first-class hotels would be built so soon as the agencies could guarantee ten thousand tourists per annum. I never considered that "luxury" class hotels were necessary or desirable in Cyprus, which does not (and should not) attract the peach-fed and jazzing Riviera tourist so much as the visitor in search of beauty, tradition, antiquity and, above all, quiet. Still, something was done by private enterprise in the Island. A large hotel was built on the western spurs of Olympus: a small but clean and adequate hotel and a Garden Club at Kyrenia; and one more hotel apiece in Nicosia and Famagusta. To my lively regret I failed entirely in recalling to these or the other hotels the delicious *pilafs* and other Oriental dishes of the Ottoman Empire and of modern Greece—all long since assimilated into standard Crown Colony cooking.

I founded a Cyprus Chamber of Commerce which might (like the League of Nations) have been more successful if the members had cared to use it. They seemed rather to concentrate upon evading subscriptions, securing free premises, and combining, if at all, in jealousy of Nicosia. τοπικίομος—local *chauvinisme,* runs so strong in Cyprus, that a τοπικίοτης of Limassol or Larnaca would not hesitate to vote against the extension of Famagusta Harbour which would obviously benefit the whole Island, because it might not directly benefit Larnaca and Limassol.

The School of Music and the Musical Society resembled the Chamber of Commerce in that they were established to create, rather than (as in Jerusalem) to supply a demand. The Jewish element (indispensable in the production of music in the Near East) was provided by Kalmano-vitch, a fine musician but a desperate accountant, never quite certain which of the pupils had paid what proportion of their long overdue fees. Interest and standard were maintained by affiliation to Trinity College of Music, London, which conducted annual examinations in Nicosia. On the other hand the Public Library, opened in 1927, was in continual demand (especially, owing to its warmth, in winter). We collected some four thousand volumes in seven or eight languages, and were no less encouraged than honoured by a gracious donation of fifty good books personally chosen from her own library by Her Majesty Queen Mary. The only newspaper taken in was *The Times,* all local sheets being excluded by unanimous request of the mixed official, Greek, and Turkish Committee. The building also housed the Medical Society [11] and the Chess Club, both important in that they provided common ground upon which (in default of mixed clubs) British and Cypriots could meet on equal and non-political terms. I was informed that the Medical Society soon degenerated from science into commerce and politics; but the Chess Club, attended once a week by two or three senior British officials besides myself, proved to the end so constant to our ideal that no acrimony in the Legislative Council was sufficient to deter Cypriot members from their game, even though it had to be played against a "Blue-blooded" immediately after an embittered debate. During my first session there was passed a Placards and Advertisements Law on the lines of the Palestine Ordinance. My wife, in addition to her normal duties, founded St Barnabas' School for blind children, and was almost the only woman, British or Cypriot, to take an interest in the Lepers' Colony, visiting them constantly, and causing me to build for them there a special hospital, clinic and nurses' home.

The year 1928 saw the fiftieth anniversary of the British Occupation of Cyprus, and I determined, after consultation with the Colonial Office, to extract from this Jubilee something of that publicity which the Colony so sorely needed. A Jubilee silver Crown Piece [12] was struck and a set of Jubilee stamps was issued (for twelve months only) which brought to the exchequer a net and direct philatelic profit, over and above normal postage requirements, of twenty thousand pounds. The sporting events included a "Near East" Golf Tournament, and a Cyprus-Palestine Sports Week, when a number of Palestine officials visited the Island, were hospitably entertained by officers of the Government, attended the Races

[11] I presented the Chair with a small marble votive hand from the Temple of Asklepios in Cos, given me during my visit there.

[12] "The only such coin ever struck by a British Sovereign for special circulation outside the United Kingdom." *The Times,* 12 July 1928.

6th Cent.
Cypriot Coin

Founder of the
Stoic School

Finding of body
of St. Barnabus

Mediaeval Map

Arms of Governor

Early Moslem
Shrine

14th Cent.
Monastery
Premonstratensian
Order

Bronze Statue
outside
House of Lords

Lusignan Gothic

CYPRUS JUBILEE 1878-1928

and played tennis and cricket matches, the week's festivities concluding with a Ball in their honour at the Nicosia Club. H.M.S. *Chrysanthemum* visited the Colony, and the Officer Commanding Troops moved up half the Detachment to Nicosia, where both took part in the Police Sports, played cricket and football matches, and held under the auspices of the Chief Commandant of Police in the Magic Palace Theatre the first Boxing Tournament ever seen in Cyprus. Meanwhile rumour had magnified the suggested programme into an imposing political event, to be signalized by the visit to Famagusta of the entire Mediterranean Fleet, an issue of one day's extra pay to all ranks of the Police Force, and a variety of other solemn but unspecified ceremonies, the whole at the expense of the Cyprus taxpayer; in anticipation of which a certain number of agitators began to open a campaign of protest and even of counter-demonstration. I therefore took early occasion to let it be known that the commemoration had no political significance, that no part of the expenditure entailed would be borne by the taxpayer, that the sports programme, which I published forthwith, was not exclusive, and that Cypriot participation would be welcomed. The politicians, thus disappointed of their major grievance, concentrated their offensive upon the sports programme. The Church Synod with the Greek Elected Members of the Legislative Council and the most extreme of the Mayors (moderates not being invited) held, with a stupendous misapplication of sadly needed economic energy and interest, frequent secret meetings during the busiest season of the year to debate at length whether or not Cypriots should participate in the sports. They even went so far as to consult secretly Mr Venizelos and the Synod at Athens as to what course they should adopt. These independently advised participation as in no wise implying a renunciation of the "National Hope"; but by the time their replies had been received absurder counsels had already prevailed, the unreasoning minority had imposed upon their better balanced but more timid colleagues a slogan boycotting the Celebration of fifty years' Enslavement, and had sent a circular to that effect to every village in the Island. At the same time a Press Campaign (opening with a sufficiently impudent anonymous cable to *The Times* from an imaginary Press Bureau) was started, enjoining abstention from even the annual sporting events, including the Police Sports and the Spring Races, at which no "Hellenic horse" was to be run. No single Greek owner withheld his horses from the Races, which were on the contrary the best attended since my arrival in the Island. The Turks compensated, especially at the last meeting, for the relative absence of Greek spectators by running a special train of Moslem sportsmen from Famagusta.

For two reasons the politicians were beginning to be a little less certain of their ground. The "direct action" of the Government in constant visits to the Districts and immediate contact with the villagers, and especially the wide dissemination of a constructive policy, were showing the rural population where their true interests lay; and consequently diminishing the prestige of the Honourable Member *qua* Member, no less than the rapid growth of Co-operative Credit Societies were loosening his grip *qua* Usurer. Again, the absence hitherto of British capital for the development of Cyprus, a long-standing and recurring grievance, had now to be written down as a general and especially as an electioneering asset; and an impartial observer in Athens wrote: "Their leaders watch with anxiety the efforts of Sir R. Storrs to attract British capital and create economic ties between Cyprus and London. Prosperity would prejudice their propaganda in favour of union with Greece." An Athenian Daily hoped that Cypriots would not be seduced by material advantage from loyalty to their Greek Mother.

Throughout these manifestations a pleasant feature was the maintenance of friendly and even cordial relations with Government House by all the members of the "Unionist" opposition. They continued individually to request interviews to serve on Social Hygiene,[18] Museum, Library and other Committees and, under my wife's presidency, did their best from the Archbishop downwards to collect from their compatriots for her Blind School [14] any moneys that might have escaped subscription for the aeroplanes and earthquakes of the "Mother country".

Nevertheless, such grossly exaggerated play was made out of the supposed neglect of Cyprus by His Majesty's Government, my predecessors and their officers during the past fifty years, that I had prepared from official and other incontrovertible documents a contrasting summary of the conditions prevailing in the Island in 1878 and 1928, a copy of which, with illustrative map, together with the completed Bibliography and my attempt at a Chronology of the Island, were published before the end of the Jubilee year.[15]

Cyprus has been so widely presented as the brightest archaeological jewel of the Crown Colonies, in the handling of which the general

---

[18] The Social Hygiene Council was established in 1927 as a result of a visit by members of the British Social Hygiene Council the previous year.

[14] St Barnabas School for the Blind has been generously supported by public bodies in Cyprus as well as by private endeavour.

[15] Lord Gifford, who was Wolseley's Aide-de-Camp in 1878 told me that his riding camel, tethered at one of the gates of Nicosia, was devoured by pariah dogs; also that malaria in Cyprus was so bad that one in ten of the troops there died of it, and more than half of them were always ill.

inefficiency of successive Governors has reached its climax, that I am tempted to set down, for those interested, the facts.

Until about 1865 hardly any attention had been paid to the objects dating from 3000 B.C. to Roman times which were to be found buried with the dead in the rock and earth cave tombs of Cyprus. The history of these antiquities up to the time of the British Occupation is more or less the same as in other Eastern and most European countries—a record of the unscientific removal from the soil of valuable objects for valuable consideration. Archaeological conscience, like some other consciences, is of recent growth; and the American Consul, "General" Louis Palma di Cesnola, F.S.A., assisted by Alexander Cesnola, was no more behind than before his time when he organized a drastic combing out of Cyprus for jewels of gold and of silver, ivories, potteries and statues, which he shipped in remunerative bulk to the American market and which now form an important section of the New York Metropolitan Museum. There was nothing underhand in the General's methods. "My own position", he states in *Salaminia*, "is that of an enthusiastic digger-up of antiquities. I always worked with the countenance and indulgence of the authorities and public officers. I had, indeed, made application in Constantinople for a firman, but never received a positive answer, so I continued digging without it. It is on this account that the reader will not find in the Lawrence-Cesnola collection many large monuments of the statuary class, such as my predecessors had been able to obtain. It was not because I did not find any, or made no researches for them; but I was unable to treat them like small articles which are easily removed." [16] (Presumably because they enjoyed, like grand pianos and refectory tables, that immunity which books and umbrellas have never attained.) He adds: "At the moment of expectation, the excitement of a digger can only be compared with that of a gambler."

So notorious was this exportation (no longer tolerated after 1878) of national and irreplaceable wealth, that Cypriot public opinion, reflected by the Cyprus Legislature, restricted the maximum allowed to discoverers at one-third of their finds, and laid an embargo admitting no exception, upon the export of antiquities from the Island. The gesture was intelligible, but unfortunate in two ways: it encouraged illicit digging and smuggling, and it discouraged legitimate excavation by learned institutions, whose subscribers are after all human, and demand for their glass cases something from the past more vivid and original than maps, plans or even photographs. In 1926 a state of things existed in which the Cyprus

[16] The frontispiece of *Salaminia* gives a pleasant picture of a "removal". Candour like this provides an immediate explanation of the slang use of the verb "to lift".

Government was too poor to excavate its own wealth and was prevented by law from allowing anybody else to do so on acceptable conditions. In 1927, therefore, the old Antiquities Law was modified so as to permit the export of antiques with the permission of the Governor in consultation with his Museum Authorities and Council. The immediate result of this modification was the introduction of Archaeological Societies, such as those of the H.R.H. the Crown Prince of Sweden, and the consequent discovery of important sites such as the late-Homeric Palace of Vouni and the Greco-Roman theatre of Soli, together with immense accessions of specimens for the Museum, and the release of many others as saleable and revenue-producing duplicates.

Cyprus is in truth deadly poor. The Museum grant, "derisory" in the opinion of experts and others, was now as in Egypt and Palestine beginning to be supplemented by the sale of duplicates when, whimsically enough, the same authorities who criticized the crowding of the Museum shelves and were loudest over the smallness of the Vote, deprecated as "undignified" those sales by which alone the Museum was able to purchase cupboards and shelves and to carry on the long-deferred cataloguing and labelling of exhibits. Yet the good work went on. Peasants and owners of antiquities now brought in their finds to the Department, who were better able to offer a fair price. One morning a farmer arrived at Government House bearing a finely modelled bronze hand of heroic size. I dispatched a fatigue party, composed of the A.D.C., my guest Sir Stephen Gaselee, and Sergeant Alexis with the owner to his farm. Within two hours they had returned with a magnificent bronze torso in large and easily restorable fragments. The finder was well rewarded and others soon followed his example.[17] The figure was immediately acclaimed by patriots as a national sovereign, possibly of the Ptolemaic epoch; and great was their disappointment when he proved to be Septimius Severus, a Roman Emperor of African extraction who, worse still, died in York.

And here I must record the debt owed by Cyprus archaeology to Rupert Gunnis, for six years my loyal Aide-de-Camp and Private Secretary. Every moment of his leisure—and much of his other time—was dedicated to the service of the Museum. He discovered in the cellars vast crates of forgotten objects, their labels, when they bore any, faded with

[17] Not much help is given to the cause of Cyprus archaeology when a correspondent of the greatest Daily informs the world in mid-1934 that "bad administration is likewise responsible for the situation which has arisen with regard to archaeological finds. It is the most ordinary thing for the peasant's plough to turn up potsherds, clay figurines or bronze implements. The Nicosia Museum has a magnificent collection of them. The Museum is, however, practically the only buyer and it is now only attracted by the exceptional. *The law forbids the export of antiquities from the Island*"; a statement that had been untrue for at least seven years and was calculated to prejudice the would-be subscriber against what he might well consider an indifference not far short of barbarism.

time. He sorted them, washed them, repaired them, labelled them, and placed them on the shelves, many of which he also provided. He dealt with foreign professors who attempted to browbeat Messrs Markídes and Dikaeos, the Museum Conservators. He followed up in his car forlorn hopes of fantastic finds. He unearthed a large prehistoric grave in the garden of Government House itself. He noted the dates of the luxury cruises months before they arrived, and organized a team of willing ladies, drawn up in the Museum with boxes, paper, string and small change, for the sale of duplicates. At breakfast on the day he would fret about the weather; for in some winds steamers would be deflected to Famagusta—or even be unable to land their passengers at all. No official work would hold him in Government House that morning. When he came back to luncheon I could infer from his expression almost the exact extent to which the Museum had profited. What if he were called swindler or liar by tourists unaccustomed to explore behind the twentieth century, so long as he could report a good day?

I arranged a separate Byzantine section in the Museum, to balance a small mediaeval collection in an old Venetian *fondaco*. Cyprus possessed no portrait of her most famous Queen, Caterina Cornaro. Hearing that one, from the studio of Bellini, would be offered at the Holford Sale, I boldly requested Joseph Duveen to present it. Almost it seemed before he could have received my letter there arrived a cable from New York "Picture cleaned framed on way to Cyprus—Joe"; an imperial munificence the more honourable for its application to a small Crown Colony which the donor was most likely even to behold.

The Museum Council provided a good example (like that of the Pro-Jerusalem Society in Palestine) of what can be done by a few intelligent representatives of communities when not subjected to the third-degree methods of local politics and publicity. The Archbishop Kyrillos attended regularly, with Munir Bey (the indispensable and permanent Ataturk of Cyprus), and three or four other Cypriots elected by the Museum subscribers; happy in the fruitful co-operation possible in the absence of a gallery. Gunnis was soon elected a Member of the Museum Council, and shortly before my departure I appointed him Travelling Member, which, having settled in the Island, he still is. Governors may come and Governors may go, but Gunnis remains; the uncrowned king of Cyprus.

Antiquities underground are far more easily protected (especially since the institution of that *deus ex machina,* the motor-mounted policeman) than the rain-swept and wind-eroded pinnacles of Gothic cathedrals and mountain citadels. The difficulties and the expense of preserving these are far greater than the indignant visitor is apt to imagine. The late Mr

Jeffery, Curator of Ancient Monuments, about to retire when I visited Cyprus in 1913, resuscitated at the age of sixty as Aide-de-Camp during the War, and still Curator until his death in 1935, disposed of a total vote of £600, which included his salary. Owing to his own disposition (and that of some of his critics) less than justice has been done to his painfully acquired habit of making one pound serve where others would have expended ten; to the numerous preservations which he did effect, and to his years of work devoted to the excavating and revealing of the noble Basilica and Forum of Salamis. But much had admittedly to be left undone in years when every surplus piastre was thrice bespoken for hospitals, roads, and water supplies. No assistance could be expected from a Legislative Council where the Greek majority, though not unsympathetic to a Museum whose exhibits might be used to reinforce political theories, had no use whatever for the Gothic remains of Latin Catholicism. To collect entrance fees at the castle of Kyrenia costs nothing, for it contains the police barracks. But there were not enough tourists to pay the wages of guards for remote and inaccessible monuments. Cyprus monuments would cost at least as much to maintain properly as do the mediaeval monuments of Egypt; far more than do those of Palestine. Her total revenue is not one-fifth that of Palestine, not one-twentieth that of Egypt; nor is her number of tourists. For this same reason loss rather than profit is to be anticipated from the sale of photographs and guide-books, and there is no brilliant future for the Corps of Guides, both suggested by the above-quoted journalist-expert. I found very little response in England to my appeal for the only English School in Cyprus; even less for the preservation of ruined masonry, 2000 miles away.[18]

My proposals, early in my term, for a ten-shilling landing-tax on tourists, eliminating petty payments, and enabling the Administration to establish guardians for sites irrespective of the number of visitors to each, shared the fate of those made in Jerusalem, because of the objections raised at the Colonial Office by the shipping companies, that the extra ten shillings on a £40 or £50 return ticket might deflect the traveller from Cyprus to Peking or the Andes. Jeffery did his best with the means at his disposal and carried out valuable but now unremembered work

[18] The archaeological and administrative correspondent quoted on p. 520: "Money is being offered in England now for their preservation. Is it possible that it could not have been found before if a proper appeal had been made? No attempt has been made until recently to make use of the antiquities themselves as a means of raising revenue. Only in two places, the castle of Kyrenia and the Abbey of Bella Paise, is a fee charged for admission. A far greater sum might be raised in this way if the ancient building and sites were better tended and made more attractive to the visitor. There is money to be raised by the sale of photographs and guide-books, and by the licensing of authorized guides. This has never been attempted, and the failure to do so must be classed as bad administration."

for a quarter of a century. The young architect-archaeologist, replete with every modern convenience, appointed in 1934 at a much higher salary and with a far larger grant to succeed where Jeffery had failed, lasted exactly on year.

The first person to perceive that, for a poor country whose needs are well known, what is wanted is not destructive criticism and obvious suggestion but a supply of hard cash, was Lord Mersey. He visited and studied Cyprus in 1934, and returning to England formed a committee honoured by the support of the Archbishop of Canterbury and assisted by a public meeting at the Mansion House. How far he is satisfied with the response to his appeal I do not know. Money is not so easily collected now as when in 1930 it was possible during a week's leave in Egypt to raise over the telephone £2000 for the English School and the Turkish Victoria College for girls in Nicosia. At any rate his committee has saved and is saving from decay monuments of superlative beauty, which is more than all the other critics united have managed to achieve.

With a few exceptions, chiefly of Government property, the historic and ancient buildings of Cyprus belong to the Turkish Evkaf,[19] consequent upon their confiscation from the Latins in 1570. The present Turkish Director, Munir Bey, has always shown a liberal and unfanatical spirit in their custody and conservation. In Famagusta the removal with his assistance of some unsightly modern shops revealed the Palace of the Venetian *Provveditore,* with its imposing sixteenth-century façade by Sammichele. The Banqueting Chamber of "Othello's Tower" over the harbour of Famagusta was converted from a Public Works dump into a hall of reception for distinguished visitors, the first three so entertained being the Queen of Rumania, the Crown Prince of Sweden and the Governor-General of the Dodecanese. The great Cathedral-Mosque of St Nicholas, a triumph of early fourteenth-century Gothic, was thoroughly repaired, and the west end reopened in a manner which disclosed the beauty of the ancient lines.[20] The centre of Nicosia was more or less transformed by the cleansing and proper laying-out of the surroundings of the great Cathedral-Mosque of Ayia Sophia; throwing into new prominence this masterpiece of the thirteenth-century Archbishop Eustorge de Montaign, and of Saint Louis.

These are but a few of the works executed under the close association of the Turkish Moslem Authorities with the Government, by the late G. F. Jeffery, F.S.A.

---

[19] From the Arabic word Waqf, Moslem Pious Foundation; plural Awkaf. "W", becomes "V" in Turkish and here produces Vekuf with plural Evkaf.
[20] The 45 Piastre stamp of the Cyprus Jubilee Issue.

The two Cathedral-Mosques are maintained with the scrupulous cleanliness of all mosques (though not all churches) that I have visited. But there is desolation in their perverted magnificence. The slender Turkish minarets with the *Muezzin* calling to prayer beside the bell-less towers are an architectural as well as a religious outrage. There is mockery within, felt though unintended, in the gaunt white-washed walls, piers and arcades; the benches, carpets and wooden *Mimbars* re-oriented from the Christian aspect, south-east towards the *Mihrab* of Muhammad and Mecca. Whenever I gazed down from the lofty triforium upon the light flickering above the worshippers, bowing and prostrating themselves far below in some great Islamic festival, it was not their murmurs that I seemed to hear, nor the imagined chanting of the choirs of St Louis, but the ebb and flow of the salt waves through the clere-story windows of Debussy's *Cathédrale Engloutie*. On the other hand, there is ruin, but no feeling of desolation, in that "haunt of ancient peace" the Premonstratensian Abbey of Bella Paise. Through the tall windows of the still perfect refectory are framed the cherry blossoms and the olive trees of Kazáphane, the blue Caramanian strait and, delicately violet in the extreme distance, the Taurus Mountains. The Gothic arcading of the cloister frames and detaches stereoscopically from its background of heaven the inconceivable crag castle of Saint Hilarion. In truth other Eastern islands also abound in beauty and tradition. In Cos you may sit under the self-perpetuated plane tree of Hippocrates. High on a steep hill in Patmos is shown the spot where St John saw his Revelation, in a panorama truly apocalyptic, of islets in a leaden sea against a menacing cloud-wrack of Titian. But as mere names they cannot compare with the names of Cyprus: Cape Kormakíti; Mount Pentedáktylon with its five crests, and the wind-beaten slopes of Buffavénto; the little villages of Athalassa, Astromeríti and Peristeróna. The Churches no less: Christ Pantocrator, Lord of All; Zoödotospygi, the Life-giving Fountain; and those recalling the Blessed Virgin—Agniótisa, pure; Pháneroméne, made manifest; Hodegétria, leading on the way; Chrýseleúsa and Chrýsopantánasa, Golden-pitiful and Golden-universal-Queen; Pántiglýkofilúa, All-tenderly-embracing.

In Cyprus the past and the present are illuminated by a various but unbroken chain of association. The Governor's summer cottage on Mount Olympus was built by Arthur Rimbaud,[21] whom I had ample opportunity of proving to be a better poet than *architecte-entrepreneur*. Still sail the archaic feluccas

[21] Rimbaud: born 1854: the friend of Verlaine, who wrote his brief brilliant poems, of which the best known is the *Bateau Ivre,* before he was twenty, abandoned writing for commerce in Abyssinia and died 1891.

> dipping deep
> For Famagusta and the hidden sun
> That rings black Cyprus with a lake of fire

from Damietta, Joppa, Tyre and Sidon to sell hides or to buy barley[22] and pomegranates: their sun-darkened masters knowing no word of Turkish or Greek, and happy to exchange a few in Arabic. The women of Lefkara are still weaving the lace of which Leonardo da Vinci, in 1481, bought panels for the altar of Milan Cathedral. Yeroskípos is beyond doubt ῾Ιερος κηπος—the Sacred Garden of the foam-born Goddess, the shore of Botticelli's many twinkling ocean; and still, after nineteen hundred years of Christianity there are found in the dawn little offerings of fruit or flowers laid by some unknown suppliant of Paphos overnight upon a ruined altar of Aphrodite.

Two memories of departed greatness greeted me in Cyprus, and one old friend whose greatness was now but memory. Kitchener had spoken but seldom of his period in the early 'eighties as Surveyor of Cyprus,[23] and had left there curiously little definite tradition. He was said to have raced, and to have contributed a silver challenge cup to the Cyprus Racing Association. When I had visited Cyprus in 1913 I had made the acquaintance of one Artin, an Armenian, the only important dealer in antiquities. Artin revealed his slender stock, and having done so advanced mysteriously through a series of rooms in his rambling house until he reached an innermost chamber. This he carefully unlocked, and pointed to a small heap in the middle of the floor. Slowly he stripped from it rug after rug, sheet after sheet, finally disclosing a black wooden box bearing the legend "Lieutenant H. H. Kitchener, Royal Engineers". It would have been pleasant to take the box back with me to its original owner, but Artin, who apparently regarded it as a talisman, refused to sell it on any terms. When I returned as Governor in 1926, Artin was dead, and no one had heard of the box. Four years later an old English resident of the name of Peace, dying in the Nicosia Hospital, began to talk of Kitchener and, painfully sifting his memory, recalled that he had possessed the gift of water divining. "He would walk along a road or country path and point to one side or the other, saying, 'You will find water there': and we did." I revisited the Hospital next day to confirm and supplement these

---

[22] Not inferior to that of Gaza of the Philistines which up to the War supplied Glasgow distilleries with whisky for universal Philistia.

[23] "I left Alexandria for Cyprus on the evening of the 28th of September, 1878, in one of the 'Asia Minor' line of steamers. My only fellow-travellers—if a few French and Greek merchants visiting Larnaca in hope of doing business be excepted—were Mr Hepworth Dixon and two officers of the Royal Engineers, Mr Kitchener and Mr Hippisley, sent out to survey the island by the Foreign Office." Mrs Scott-Stevenson, *Our Home in Cyprus.* (Chapman and Hall, 1880.)

recollections, but Peace had died in the night. Kitchener's real memorial in Cyprus is his Map, which his successors through fifty years modified and improved in detail, but did not supersede. I counted it my privilege as well as my duty to place on the wall of the old house in the Nicosia Bazaar a small marble commemoration of the sojourn there of "Capt. H. H. Kitchener, R.E. Director of Survey and Land Registry Office 1880–1883".

The Cypriot Kiamil Pasha,[24] when the Young Turks came into power, had decided to end his days in the place of his birth. His family were of all ages, and Sir Harry Luke has recorded that it was a sight of considerable piquancy to watch his eldest son, a decrepit invalid of sixty or thereabouts, being wheeled up and down the ramparts for his early morning airing in a bath-chair side by side with the perambulator containing His Highness's youngest son, aged about six. An unusual pair of brothers.[25] I found his grave in the cemetery by the little Arab Ahmad Mosque unmarked and, though he had not been dead twelve years, almost unknown: [26] so I set up an ancient column, graving thereon his epitaph in Turkish, of which the English rendering beneath runs:

His Highness Kiamil Pasha
Son of Captain Salih Agha of Pyroi
Born in Nicosia 1833 and in Nicosia died 1913.
Treasury Clerk, Commissioner Larnaca,
Director of Evcaf,
Four times Grand Vizier of the Ottoman Empire.
A Great Turk and a Great Man.

Kiamil had at least been exiled home. But Husain ibn Ali, King "of the Arabs", self-proclaimed Caliph of Islam, father of the King of Iraq and of the Amir of Transjordan, had lived to be driven from his kingdom of the Hejaz; had been rescued by a British ship of war from the beach of Aqaba, and granted sanctuary in an Island where he neither knew nor was known by a single soul. To senior officials he was a commitment, a problem: juniors had never heard of him. I found him in a small villa, tended with filial devotion by his youngest son Zaid; and a touching sight it was to watch this young Prince, who had led regiments in the War and had then passed a year at Balliol College, reading aloud to his

---

[24] See p. 64.

[25] Sir H. Luke, *More Moves on an Eastern Chequer-board*, p. 185.

[26] "The funeral ceremony was in dire contrast to the illustrious rank and station of the deceased. Nothing could have been less impressive. The coffin was borne to the Sofia Mosque, where a few prayers were said outside the building, the body not being allowed inside. Thence it was carried through the principal streets of the town to the burial ground attached to the small mosque in Victoria Street. The procession was little more than a rabble, largely composed of town loafers. The actual interment was brief and altogether lacking in solemnity or dignity." From an eye-witness's account in the *Near East*.

father the dreary commentary of Sālih al-Bokkári [27] on the Koran, and waiting on him day and night. King Husain was popularly supposed to have brought with him (in petrol tins) some of the hundreds of thousands of sovereigns wherewith Great Britain had subsidized the Revolt in the Desert. I believe the hoard to have been infinitely less than credited by rumour, which always magnifies wickedness or wealth: and that it had been scientifically diminished by Palestinian propagandists and petitioners, past-masters in these arts. At all events the old King had the wit, whenever his sons visited him in search of revenue, to forestall their demands by appealing for a loan for himself—as King Faisal complained once during a round of golf-croquet on Mount Troödos. In Cyprus he had been sadly defrauded by unscrupulous merchants, and was constantly begging me to intervene (on Mecca lines) in the procedure of the courts. We exchanged frequent visits with King Husain, and I found him, though familiar with the Turkish language, always pleased by opportunities of speaking Arabic. Almost the only remaining joy of his life was in his two or three beautiful Arab mares. Zahra, the gentlest and most graceful, would step delicately up the flight of marble stairs from the garden and walk without any shyness into the Salamlik,[28] to be greeted by cries of *"Ahlan"*, *"Ma Sha Alláh"*, *"Alláhu Akbar"* or *"Qurrúbi, ya bint ammi"*.[29] The king would call her *"Qurrat al-Ain"*—"Cooling of the eyelids"—and offer her dates which she would eat slowly, never failing to eject the stones on to a plate. One morning he appeared at Government House, begged to see me at once, flung himself into my arms and burst into tears. He had reason, for a dastardly dismissed groom had ripped Zahra and her sisters in the night to discredit his successor, and their master had found them dying in agony.

There had been conferred upon King Husain, whilst still the independent ally of Great Britain, the Grand Cross and Ribbon of the Order of the Bath. Before the honour could reach him, he had lost his country, his crown and his home. I have seen (as well as known) reversals of fortune, but never with such a sense of the irony of fate as when, at the opening of the Cyprus Public Library, I handed the Insignia coveted by Ambassadors, Field Marshals and reigning European Sovereigns, to that dispossessed but still dignified old man.

In the summer of 1928 I took my first home leave. It was the beginning of an epoch in which Diplomats, Ministers of the Crown, even Princes of the Blood were expected to perform the duties of a patriotic com-

---

[27] "Who discriminated 4000 out of the 600,000 traditions of the Prophet Muhammad." Gibbon.
[28] Man's reception room: the woman's is Haremlik.
[29] "Welcome!" ... "God is most great!", "Draw nigh, O daughter of my paternal uncle".

mercial traveller. My ambition was to do the like for Cyprus. I interviewed officials and capitalists, lectured, spoke at public luncheons and dinners, broadcast on the wireless and, by a wearisome persistence, caused Cyprus Cigarettes to appear on the lists of the House of Commons and of several of the larger clubs. Cyprus lemon squash, marmalade, honey, lace and embroidery made their appearance in retail shops in London. In all these importunities I was fortunate in the sympathetic and alert resourcefulness of my Chief and friend, Leopold Amery. (And I would inform his successors that few sights are more stimulating to a Governor than that of the cigarettes, fruits and wines of his Colony conspicuous and acknowledged upon the table of his Secretary of State.)

I soon found that work during holidays is far more exhausting than work during work time, and sometimes feared I had better have gone straight into the country. A Governor in his Colony is spared all thought of engagements or the means of keeping them. His Aide-de-Camp produces and releases Treasurers, Chief Justices or Attorneys General. His Car is waiting at the door five minutes before the hour required. But neither car nor Secretary follow him to London; and if they did he could hardly summon Secretaries or Under-Secretaries of State to attend his pleasure. Muhammad must go to the mountain, as often as not by tube or bus. He must write his own letters, telephone his own messages and run his own errands. A further difficulty on leave is to compress into a few weeks the friendships and interests of a lifetime. Visits and meetings, the viewing of a picture, the sound of a fugue, are marred by the face of the calendar and the tick of the clock, for

> At my back I always hear
> Time's winged chariot hurrying near.

The effort to do these things simultaneously proved too much for me. I had hardly returned to Cyprus before I became aware that I was breaking down. The climax came after an interview with a Turkish Judge when, according to custom, I prepared to dictate a summary of the discussion; to find that I could not remember the subject, the name of the Judge or—in the end—the name of my own stenographer: with the result that I was sent to bed for six or seven weeks, feeding nauseously upon the purple and trembling flesh of raw liver and only finding recovery after a three months' voyage to South Africa and a total absence from work of nearly eight months. (On my return to Cyprus I found in the files a cable that had been dispatched to the Military Authorities in Egypt, enquiring the correct procedure for a Governor's funeral.)

The Legislative Council, of which I have described the composition, met in a small ugly Chamber reached by a narrow stone staircase. The President (usually the Governor), sat at a raised desk upon a large uncomfortable throne immediately under the Royal Arms. On his right were the Colonial Secretary and the Treasurer, on his left the Attorney-General; beyond them the other British members of Council. After a *bloc* of three Turks on the right came the angular horse-shoe of twelve Greek members. At the remote end of the Chamber were three long pews for the public and the Press.

The debates were trilingual, in English, Turkish and Greek, just as those of Sir Herbert Samuel's Advisory Council in Palestine had been in English, Arabic and Hebrew; sentence by sentence an English speech would be translated into Turkish and Greek, a Greek speech into English and Turkish, a Turkish speech into English and Greek. These enforced punctuations damped down oratory, and the proceedings proved for the most part a narcotic rather than an exhilarating experience. The strain on the interpreters was severe and I so sympathized with Messrs Stylianakis, Indianos and Utijian, the harassed Greeks and Armenian grappling with the sudden translation of such phrases as "travelling allowances of Mycologists", "radio-sensitiveness", or "the forest ravages of the processional caterpillar" that, by an innovation, I caused them to sit to their work. It was pleasant to find a certain amount of old Greek surviving in the parliamentary language of the Chamber, such as κονδύλιον "an item" (of the Budget), ἐνίσταμαι "I oppose" and (even more frequently) ἐκτὸς τάξεως,[80] "out of order". The professions and interests of Honourable Members (ἔντιμα μέλη) and their sense of futility and irresponsibility before the permanent Anglo-Turkish majority, their natural desire to preserve their prestige before their more "political" constituents, rendered the Legislative Council, though led on how light a rein soever, a continually less practicable body.[81] It is true that the atmosphere during the discussion of formal legislation was easy and sometimes amusing (for the Cypriots are a humorous race) and that I never met with the slightest personal incivility; but during my illness in 1928 the Greek members tramped out of the Chamber in front of my Deputy sooner than vote the Estimates, and, as in the past, recourse had to be taken to Orders in Council. It became sadly clear that from a certain class of Cyprus politician we could expect no gratitude for complacency. His former masters had never made concessions because they were just or right, but only because they could not be avoided. Every concession Great Britain made

[80] "Dog"-Greek: a literal rendering of the English phrase.
[81] With major or minor crises recorded every few years in the English Press. "The attitude of the Elected Members has of late been such as to inspire misgiving." *The Times,* 1904.

was interpreted as proceeding from motives of weakness or surrender. Owing to the obstinacy of the British Treasury it had not been possible to abolish the Turkish Tribute until the Elected Members had refused supply. Justice was thus taken for expediency, and the trick of refusal seemed worth trying again. In 1929 I therefore informed the Secretary of State that in my opinion there must be a change in the Constitution and urged that it should be amended forthwith. I submitted concrete proposals for the alternative of a larger Council on the lines of the traditional *Mejlis Idaré* or Council of Administration composed of officials, nominated members, and elected members, three-quarters of whom must be bona fide agriculturists actively engaged in practical agriculture. Money-lenders would be ineligible. The unofficial majority would be preserved, though official plus nominated members would exceed elected members. My proposals were well received; but Constitution-changing is a Cabinet matter and I had to wait for my answer until after the impending General Election. This swept the Conservative Government from office, so that I had to begin again with their successors. The conclusion finally adopted by Lord Passfield, the new Secretary of State, was, that in the circumstances there did not appear to be a sufficient case for them to take action, and that things must therefore be allowed to go on as they were. Nothing then, was done to amend the Constitution. A year later, it had to be entirely abolished.

Mention has been made of the extent to which Education in Cyprus was dominated by political considerations. Being (as I hope previous chapters may have shown) a lifelong opponent of anglicization or denationalization I was strongly averse to diminishing the study of the Greek language and classical traditions. But the method of appointing, transferring and dismissing teachers, male and female, by the Greek Members of the Council was open to grave objections. The politicians too often exercised their power for political or petty personal aims. The teacher was usually the only educated man in the village; as a political agent he was therefore almost indispensable to the politicians, who were exclusively town-dwellers. Being dependent upon the politicians for advancement in his profession he had to serve the political purposes of his masters. The system was bad, but had been tolerated, partly because the Government had lacked the financial means to pay the teachers itself. Shortly after my return in 1929 I received numerous petitions from teachers which showed that, bad as the system was in principle, in practice it was even worse. In order that a member of the Board might promote a friend, or vex an enemy, some unfortunate schoolmaster of Paphos would find himself transferred more than a hundred miles to the Karpass

BIRTH OF THE SAVIOUR OF EDUCATION

Blasphemous Greek cartoon. The Governor, with Canon Newham, Director of
Education, as St Joseph, adores the Education Bill: the kneeling
magi are Greek members who voted for it

(This disagreeable illustration is included to show students of Near Eastern
Politics something of the tone of the unlicensed local press. It can be torn
off without injuring the book, in whose text it is not mentioned.)

Peninsula; there were ugly stories of unsavoury inducements pressed upon reluctant schoolmistresses. These complaints proved on examination to be in the main true, and were said to represent but a fraction of the abuses perpetrated. The abolition of the Tribute and a good year enabling me to assume financial control of the machine, I introduced a Bill whereby the elementary teachers of all communities passed from the political committees to the Government, for appointment, promotion, transfer, dismissal and discipline, whilst the salaries of all were raised by a considerable percentage. The measure was greeted with a howl of discerning rage from the politicians, but three independent minded Greek Members, convinced of the rottenness of the existing system and the necessity of Government intervention, voted for and so passed the Bill. Not one of these three was able to present himself at the 1930 elections. In the Athenian Press the "distinguished Philhellene who had abolished the Tribute" [32] became in a trice "the Imperialistic Dictator": in the local Press I was lampooned (in blasphemous caricatures) as the man who had "assassinated Hellenic education". From the teachers, now secure so long as they did their duty, I received verbal and written expressions of deep gratitude.

Even now it was possible, with patience and sympathy, to carry on so long as the three Turkish Moslem members could be trusted to vote with the Government. Unfortunately the Turkish Consul, Assaf Bey, a strong Nationalist and Kemalist, had succeeded in creating a small but active element of opposition to the loyal Turkish majority. I discovered his intrigues and reported them to the Government, who procured his recall, but not before he had so influenced the Turkish electorate that the Greeks were able to secure the election of a Turk who could no longer be counted upon to support the Government. Though a man of straw, he nevertheless possessed in effect the casting vote of the Legislative Council. This completely upset the balance of power. The Greek Orthodox members were quick to perceive their advantage and to follow it up. The Government was thus placed in a position of absolute dependence upon an obstructive, unreasonable and determinedly hostile majority, counting upon and assisted by the dead weight of opposition and detraction continuously (and as a rule not illegally) applied by the schools, Press, pulpit and platform of *Enosis* propaganda. The criticism followed familiar lines, and was consistent only in being always destructive. If the policy was conservative, "nothing was being done": if forward, it became "squan-

---

[32] *La question Cypriote*, written by a Greek about 1930, though not published until 1934: "*...un homme de valeur.......il aime Chypre et nourrit l'ambition de contribuer au développement de ce peuple. C'est donc à bon droit qu'il est devenu l'objet des sympathies des Cypriotes...*", and so on for three pages. Michel Dendias, *op. cit.* p. 157.

der-mania". If limited to physical or practical development, it was derided as "materialistic": if cultural—by lectures, Museum or a Public Library— it was stigmatized as the "imposition of unwanted luxuries to the exclusion of vital necessities". Any course of action adopted *proprio motu* by the local Government was "ill-considered", but any previous consultation of specialist advice in order to ensure the best results was invariably saluted as "the plague of the experts". Such congenial arguments against the attitude of "the foreign ruler" were indeed annually for a few weeks discredited by my speech delivered at the opening of the Legislative Council, when past progress and future programme were surveyed in some detail and placed in the hands of every Mukhtar and Policeman in the language of his village for broadcasting on the following day. Efforts were also made through periodical announcements and such organs as the *Agricultural and Forest Journal* to bring home the truth to those most concerned in learning it, but in the absence of special Press regulations or the dubious and costly expedient of an organ subsidized by the Government it was not possible to insure that the public should be adequately protected from the constant pressure of calumny and abuse.[33]

The years 1928 and 1929 were the most prosperous in the recorded history of Cyprus, but 1930 brought upon us, slower indeed than upon highly organized countries, yet sure and severe, the economic world-blizzard. In order to balance the 1931 Budget without encroaching upon our modest Reserve Fund, the Government was compelled in spite of drastic economies to provide additional revenue. I appointed a mixed committee of British officials, three Greeks and a Turk to make recommendations for meeting the deficit. They recommended a levy on official salaries and the substitution of specific for *ad valorem* customs duties. I accepted these unanimous recommendations, and introduced a bill for effecting the Tariff change into the Legislative Council. The bill was unanimously opposed by the Greek members, including one who had signed the Committee's report—another had been unseated meanwhile for corruption on an election petition—on the ground that it involved an increase of taxation. When the vote for the revised Tariff was taken there was a solid phalanx of ἐνίσταμαιλ's, and the little Turk,—the Thirteenth Greek"—in whose hands the Liberalism of the 'eighties had placed the casting vote of the Colony, voted with the traditional enemies of his race. The bill was thrown out, and once again the Governor was compelled in order to carry on the Government to invoke most reluctantly the assistance of an Order in Council. The levy on salaries was an administrative matter. It

[33] "Freedom of the Press, as often in the East, was the enemy of freedom of speech; and the newspapers prevent the moderate party from being heard." Norman Bentwich.

seemed unfair that amid the general distress the Civil Service alone should remain an oasis of prosperity. Tampering with official salaries is delicate and ungrateful work. Some officers have family commitments which they cannot suddenly cut down. Most feel strongly that, as they are debarred from the benefits of a boom, so they should at least remain immune from the consequences of a slump.[34] Nevertheless the salary cut, renewable annually until better times, was duly imposed. The measure was most unpopular, and most certainly right.

Economic duress is the agitator's meat, though it is the peasant's poison. Up to this time the Hellenic Government, recognizing the essentially liberal character of the British administration of Cyprus, had maintained a discreet and correct attitude towards the Cypriot politicians in Athens as well as in Cyprus. Their Consul in Larnaca, Mr Inglessis, had confined himself strictly to his consular duties. But he was now transferred and succeeded by a very different figure. Mr Alexander Kyrou was a dapper, civil-spoken young man, son of a clerk in the District Court of Nicosia, whose family owned the Athenian journal 'Εστία—*The Hearth*. He had for a while been private secretary to the Greek Minister for Foreign Affairs, who, to avoid offending the *Hestia,* found it expedient to appoint him to the vacancy which he desired. He was constitutionally incapable of abstention from political activity. His first act on arrival was to transfer his Consulate from Larnaca, where like all other Consulates it had been established and where his shipping and general commercial duties were concentrated, to the political Capital, on the grounds that this would "facilitate negotiations with Government Departments". There he soon established close relations with every brand of the Ecclesiastical, Legislative and National agitation. At a Masonic Ball held in Nicosia British participants noted with surprise and disgust an innovation whereby the Greek National Anthem was at a pre-arranged signal rendered, and most of those present rose to their feet whilst the Greek Consul entered and, before taking his seat, bowed his acknowledgments from the central box. As soon as I heard of this outward and visible climax to the intrigues of which I had become increasingly aware, I sent a detailed report to the Colonial Office requesting that the Greek Government should be informed that Mr Kyrou was no longer *persona grata.* Lord Passfield strongly supported my view; the Foreign Office sympathized with it, but required more detailed and concrete evidence before taking action. I wrote again, urging that it was most undesirable that any person appointed as

[34] One or two would speak wistfully of the fortunes they might have made if they had entered commerce, and it was sad to think how many mute inglorious Woolworths and Selfridges were sacrificing themselves as Deputy Assistants of Minor Departments all over the Empire.

Greek Consul to Cyprus should be connected by ties of kinship and interest with local Cypriots. I reminded the Government that they had acted
with exemplary vigour on my representations about the activities of the
Turkish Consul, no better proved and far less dangerous because affecting
a small and loyal community; and I warned them that every day Mr
Kyrou remained in the Island strengthened the anti-British agitation. I
returned to the charge for the third time, with the result that a protest
was made in Athens; when Mr Venizelos agreed that the appointment
was unwise, and said that Mr Kyrou, "who was of a rather irredentist
mentality", ought not to have been allowed to go to Cyprus: in due
course a transfer could be arranged in such a way as not to attract attention.

Before the end of the spring, and long before the promulgation of the
Customs Duties Order in Council, propaganda had produced a tension
hardly less than that of 1922, and supporters of Britain excused themselves from accepting invitations or revealing their real opinions "lest
they should be thought pro-Government". At our last Ball in Government
House the daughter of a Member was severely criticized for dancing in a
Reel with English partners—and her parents for attending at all. By June,
when I had gone on leave, Mr Kyrou was frequently received by a band
playing the Greek National Anthem and cheers for Union with Greece,
so that Greek Cypriots were no less astonished at the immunity with
which he pursued his way than were the British officials and residents.
Some of these not unnaturally ascribed the state of affairs to the lax
Philhellenism of the Governor. Mr Venizelos visited England that summer for the Byron celebrations at Newstead Abbey, and I obtained permission from the Colonial and Foreign Offices to interview him at the
Greek Legation. I had known him both in Alexandria and during the
Peace Congress and found him frank as well as friendly. He insisted
upon his own entire correctness and neutrality and that of his Government, admitted that he could not always rely upon his agents, and promised that Mr Kyrou should be withdrawn from Cyprus "soon". I asked
how soon, and he replied by the end of August. He kept me nearly an
hour, and when I left said he was well aware how hard I was trying
to serve Cyprus. I did not doubt Mr Venizelos' promise but (apparently
without his knowledge) Mr Kyrou was allowed to return to Nicosia
from leave pending withdrawal.

I had now spent five years in Cyprus, and had transferred from the
Agenda to the *Acta* sheet almost every item I had originally set down.
Though I loved the Island, I felt I had been there long enough, and
was anxious to begin again somewhere else. The financial stringency
was such that I had to abandon both the projected Agricultural College

(which Loan money could have built but not maintained) and the Cyprus and Near East Agricultural Exhibition, which would materially have assisted the development of trade. The Colonial Office was sympathetic, but had no vacancy. I returned to Cyprus in August, leaving my wife by the bedside of my stepdaughter, who was gravely ill; seeing no future and full of gloomy forebodings.

"Tu ne me trompes jamais, O mon inquiétude."

The Colonial Office, as "strong" under a Labour as under any other Government, had approved the Customs Order in Council, and as soon as I reached Cyprus I issued it, together with a memorandum explaining, in terms conciliatory to the Legislature, the reasons for recourse to legislation by Order-in-Council. The necessity for the new tariff was recognized among leading merchants, and this was far from being the first Order in Council which I or my predecessors had been compelled to invoke. But for the campaign of misrepresentation, it would doubtless have remained a public matter of ordinary indifference to the community. This is not to say that some of the Members were not genuinely reluctant to accept responsibility for additional taxes in the trade depression or, when the responsibility had been accepted by Government for them, not genuinely conscious of lost prestige. It is nevertheless the opinion of those best qualified to pronounce that, but for the influence of one man upon the action of another, there would have been no disturbances in Cyprus.

The leader of the Greek opposition in the Legislative Council, and by far its most intelligent and impressive member, was Monseigneur Nicódhimos Mylonâs, Metropolitan of the ancient See of Kition. He was a nephew of the Archbishop Kyrillos, the ambition to succeed whom in the Archiepiscopal elections was said to account for the popular violence of his utterances. He was by temperament a reasonable man, who took the trouble to examine draft Laws and Estimates, and presented his arguments and suggestions in a form that was sometimes of positive assistance to the Government. His black-browed, black-bearded, black-stoled figure did not lose its dignity even when he uncoiled his long hair, combed it out and replaited it under his Orthodox headdress in the Chamber itself. He was supposed to resemble Rasputin, notably in his power of contracting the pupils of his eyes to fascinate or overawe an opponent. When he opened his neat attaché-case and rose to speak, he was heard by all with attention and interest. I liked the Bishop, and on one of his visits to me, taking him and his colleagues at their word in the complaints against the existing Constitution, asked him to suggest a better. He had promised me more than once to submit a scheme, but had never done so, doubtless calculating that any extension of self-government under the British Crown would weaken the popular feeling for union with Greece. He was now becoming more and more distant as he daily saw more of the Greek Consul. The same influence was before long to detach him from his own colleagues, with whom in September 1931 he had been in whole-hearted agreement.

On October 1st Mr Kyrou returned from Greece. About the middle of September the Bishop had summoned the Greek members to a secret meeting to decide what course they should follow in consequence of a statement made in Parliament in July,[35] and also to define their attitude to the latest Order-in-Council. It was generally known, and had been mentioned in the Press, that the Members had formally resolved to address a manifesto, subject to the approval of the National Organization, calling upon the people to refuse to pay taxes and to boycott British goods by way of protest. This organization was a nationalist body supported by subscriptions and by the Orthodox Church of Cyprus. A fortnight later Members of Council and of the Organization met at the Archbishopric in Nicosia to discuss the above resolution. Dissension at once ensued; principally because the Greek Members, though pressed, were unwilling to resign the seats in the Legislative Council which only a year before they had bought so dearly.[36] The meeting dissolved in uproar. Three more meetings were held, without result. Resignation apart, no agreement had been possible on the terms of the draft manifesto, which were reluctantly but progressively modified to meet the general opinion (openly admitted by the Press) that an appeal to the people to resist the payment of taxes was doomed to failure. This inability of the National leaders to come to conclusions, the futility of their suggested boycott of British goods, and the fact that they had already paid their own taxes for the year, exposed them to ridicule. There was no ladder for them to climb down. Foreseeing retreat, and determined not to be involved in it, the extremists of the National Organization (who had paid nothing for their seats) resigned.[37]

At a meeting of the Greek Members on 17 October (which proved to be their last) the Bishop of Kition had read out to them and sought their approval of a fresh manifesto he had himself drafted. To this the Members agreed generally, but stipulated that the draft should be considered again in a week's time. The next day they learnt with astonishment that a manifesto in precisely the same terms had been published by

[35] The Chancellor of the Exchequer had announced that the accumulated surplus from the payments made from Cyprus revenue as Tribute to Turkey had been disposed of by Great Britain for the sinking fund of the Turkish loan guaranteed by Great Britain in 1855.

[36] Election expenses sometimes exceeded (illegally) £4000.

[37] Measures prepared by Government to counter non-payment to taxes therefore remained in abeyance.

the Bishop independently under the previous day's date, and had been widely circulated together with a letter tendering his resignation from the Legislative Council. The manifesto included such phrases as "What even if the foreign tyrants rely upon colossal columns of beastly force and power? ... this abomination which is called English Occupation and Administration of Cyprus...." Eight of the Members thereupon abandoned all their previously proposed intentions and concentrated upon denunciation of the Bishop's treachery.

It was remarked that the strongest passages in the manifesto were not in the Bishop's style. Members who had not resigned indignantly ascribed his *volte-face* to a mysterious influence. At five o'clock on October 21st I telegraphed that I had no doubt Kyrou was involved, and that his instant removal would relieve the situation.

On the 18th the Bishop descended upon Larnaca, where he made a speech which though disloyal and inflammatory would, I was advised, by no means certainly support a prosecution for sedition under the criminal code (especially after one or two recent decisions of the courts, notably in Kyrenia). The Bishop was hourly awaiting apprehension by the Police; arrest, martyrdom and widespread demonstrations at his trial and on his release being his plan of campaign. As it was, no consequences of any sort ensued. On the 20th he visited Limassol, to explain his reasons for resigning from the Council. Church bells were rung to summon the people and a cortège headed by a slowly-moving motor car draped with a large Greek flag went out to meet him. He was thus escorted to the stadium, where a crowd of some three thousand people including schoolboys had assembled. To them, to another audience in the town, and next day to the congregation of a village church, he addressed violent harangues enjoining "disobedience and insubordination towards the illegal laws of the immoral, vile and reproachful regime which is called 'English regime' " ... "Down with the vile and reproachful regime!" All three speeches fell completely flat. The crowds dispersed quietly, and there was no sign whatever of impending trouble.

But the Member for Limassol, who had invited the Bishop, was not prepared to admit that his demonstrations had proved failures. On the afternoon of the 21st he therefore telegraphed a highly exaggerated account of the meeting in the Stadium to the Secretary of the National Organization in Nicosia. As a conversation gains in apparent importance when repeated to a third party, so even an accurate account of an event is sometimes more impressive than the event itself. The effects of this telegram were instantaneous. In Nicosia the campaign against the Bishop's independent action had failed because it was generally felt that his policy had been forced on him by the procrastination and half-hearted counsel of his colleagues. The younger men now saw their opportunity to discredit and perhaps displace the leaders. They were out to precipitate the crisis and also to exploit it. The remaining Greek Members quickly decided to resign and from that moment moderation became treachery and violence the only virtue. Government had no knowledge of this telegram or their decisions, and up to the evening of the 21st all the information available in Nicosia was that the agitators were turning against each other, and that one more move in the game of make believe had been played.[38]

On October 14th I had been summoned to London in connection, I afterwards discovered, with a higher appointment shortly to become vacant; and I was to sail on the morning of the 22nd. Somewhat eased in mind by the turn events (as then known by me) had taken, I had spent the evening of the 21st preparing the Christmas presents for the Staff. I remember writing Gunnis's name in Enlart's *Art gothique en Chypre,* which Enlart himself had given me and which Gunnis had long coveted; tying up the parcel and leaving it on the cupboard shelf. I finished my volume of Gibbon and walked round my books, choosing and rejecting for the journey. I was dressing for dinner when the Maltese stenographer announced that a disorderly demonstration was proceeding towards Government House. I telephoned to the Acting Colonial Secretary and to the Commissioner, and in ten minutes they reported to me. We held a brief consultation. The Regulations were quite clear, and the Commissioner of the District took charge. By this time a rapidly swelling crowd of several thousands had arrived at the gateway (there were no gates) to the drive of Government House. Not having heard of the Limassol speeches or telegram, we had no knowledge of the reason of the procession. Night had fallen.

The two officers went down to the gateway. Soon the eight mounted police and bâton party of twelve foot police—all the Commandant could then spare—were assailed with sticks and stones until the horses stampeded and the crowd poured up the drive, sweeping the officers before them. The leaders then struggled through the mass, and appeared in front of the officers and the Police before the porch of Government House. There were cheers, clapping, and continuous shouts of *Enosis.* I informed the Commissioner that when the crowd, which was surging noisily round the door with a trumpet and a Greek flag, had withdrawn to a respectful distance, I would see their leaders. He and they calling

[38] The sequence of events described above was compiled from subsequent enquiry, and was at the time largely unknown to Government. It is drastically reduced from Cmd. 4045, *Disturbances in Cyprus in October 1931.*

from the step of the porch attempted to tell the crowd to withdraw, but without avail. Their words were drowned in shouting. Over the uproar those nearest heard Theophánis Theodótou, one of the better class extreme politicians, who now began to see what he had done, cry: "The Governor justly (δικωίας) refuses to hear us." Shortly after this the leaders, realizing they had no control, and fearing the consequences of their action, sent messages of apology to me and decamped.

The noise grew louder, violent stone-throwing began, and soon all the windows in the front of the house had been smashed, a number of police injured, many of the electric lights broken, and the telephone wrecked. Meanwhile an armed reserve of forty men had arrived. The Turkish Senior Police Inspector asked for permission to fire, but the Commissioner refused because the crowd appeared to be composed mainly of young students, and because he considered further efforts should be made to disperse the rioters by unarmed police. About this time the crowd set fire to the cars in which the police reinforcements had arrived, and proceeded to throw burning sticks and blazing material through the broken windows. As soon as the Commissioner was satisfied that definite attempts to set the house on fire had been made, he decided that rifle fire must be employed. A bâton charge was first launched according to King's Regulations, but broke under a hail of stones from the darkness into the light of the burning cars. The bugle sounded. The Riot Act was read and shouted in Greek. The bugle sounded again, and the police firing party of twelve men discharged a volley. The crowd dispersed, was pursued, and fled.

But already the curtains were ablaze. The fire spread to the roof and took hold of Lord Wolseley's old tinder barrack. In ten minutes Government House, and all that it held, had gone up in flames.

Both during and after the disturbances I was strongly supported by the Colonial Office. The Department refrained from imposing on me doctrinaire or conventional instructions, and accepted and adopted the majority of my suggestions for specific action as well as for general policy. Mr. Kyrou's Consular *exequatur* was immediately withdrawn, and he left, never to return to Cyprus or officially to any part of His Majesty's Dominions. The Legislative Council was abolished. I had immediately summoned the troops from their quarters 5000 feet up on Mount Troödos, 50 miles away—a force parading three officers and less than a hundred men; I cabled for Military and Air reinforcements; and applied the Internal Security Scheme. For three days the situation was critical. Popular leaders were truculent, and τοπικίσμος competed in outrage with Nicosia; when the mob of Limassol invaded the house of the Commissioner, and set fire to it with petrol, well knowing that he, with his wife, his twelve-year-old daughter and two servants, were caught powerless within. With the arrival of H.M.S. *London* and *Shropshire* and three Destroyers, the safety of the ports was assured, and the reinforcement of one company by Air enabled the Officer Commanding the troops to decline the further contingent that had been offered. I am still under my first grateful amazement at the patience and forbearance of both forces in the face of every kind of provocation.

But so long as the Bishop of Kition and his fellow ringleaders remained at large, there seemed to be every prospect of more and worse trouble. There could be no serious question of their guilt, but it was more than doubtful whether sufficient evidence would be forthcoming to secure their conviction: none anyhow could be collected or weighed now. If they were arrested, their followers had threatened to attack the prison in Nicosia, when there could hardly fail to be bloodshed. I therefore determined to deport them under the Defence Order in Council, removing them to the warships until their destination should have been decided. They were allowed to spend their afternoon and evening unmolested, and no doubt went to bed in full expectation of resuming their seditious activities next day. A careful plan was then worked out by the Police and troops combined. Parties of Police proceeded one by one and isolated the houses of Bishop and politicians alike, so that they found themselves in the small hours of the morning removed from their beds and conveyed into custody in H.M.S. *London* and *Shropshire* off Larnaca and Limassol. Two incidents enlivened the process. The loudest and most brazen speaker of the lot barred his front door, rushed through the house and jumped out of his scullery window, to find himself neatly fielded by two delighted Cypriot constables: The Bishop of Kition aroused the sympathy of his gallant hosts in *Shropshire* by removing his priestly hat, around the inside of which he had taken the precaution of fastening the episcopal jewels; and by calling for a stiff whisky and soda. It was generally believed, and I agree, that it was this sudden and unexpected deportation of the leaders, known only when they had disappeared, that cracked the insurrection. It had been assumed, not without justification after our fifty-two years of easy-going tolerance, that the Government would not dare to arrest them for fear of exciting their followers to massacres, and so producing general havoc. The shock of surprise enabled me to take the initiative decisively at a very critical moment. Order had to be restored, and quickly; but the necessary process of arrests, trials, imprisonments, curfews and censorships I found bitterly distasteful. There was consolation in the absolute loyalty of the Cypriot Civil Servants, from the highest to the lowest; manifested no less in the brilliant advice of Neoptolemos Paschalis, the Cypriot Solicitor-General, than in the steadfast courage of scores of constables, Greek as well as Turk, risking their lives day and night against mobs of exultant hooligans. There were indeed more policemen injured than civilians, for the total casualties among the rioters who had destroyed Government House and deliberately burned down that of the Commissioner of Limassol, had stoned the police, set fire to the forests, and destroyed property in nearly seventy villages, was six killed and thirty wounded, whereas the Police had thirty-eight wounded. By the end of the month the Government was in complete command of the situation; and by the end of the year the garrison had been reduced to what should have (but never had) been its normal strength of four officers and 175 men. It was allowed that the insurrection had been put down with a minimum expenditure of time, of force, of money and, above all, of human life.

This did not prevent the tempest of denunciation of the brutal savagery of British troops and Cypriot Police from breaking out in the Athenian, Greek Alexandrian, and Salonika Press. The Balkans and the Levant are past-masters in the craft of manufacturing atrocities, and of smuggling them through any Censorship or Customs control. The editors accepted uncritically, augmented and published every fabrication they received, and indeed the Levantine Press throughout those days makes sorry reading, though less lamentable than the memorandum forwarded to the Houses of Parliament over the honoured name of Admiral Counduriotis. This circular, which proved to be "utterly false, malicious and baseless" I had the gloomy satisfaction of publicly refuting in every detail.[39]   The campaign honoured me by including Σὲρ Ρόναλντ Στόρρς ὁ τύραννος Κυβερνήτης τῆς μαρτυρικῆς Κύπρου ("Sir Ronald Storrs—the tyrant Governor of martyred Cyprus") with the troops, and one of my few sources of merriment after the first dark days was to return from a village inspection or afternoon walk and read in the Athenian Press how the furious petty Satrap, now Governor only in name, his hands dripping with innocent blood, dared no longer show his face outside the walls of his house. Truly the spirit of Greece holds for the Hellenist, as the vibrations of the atmosphere for the musician, infinite possibilities not only of pleasure but of pain.

[39] My telegram to the Secretary of State, published in Cmd. 4045, 1932: "It is a matter of no less regret than surprise that so distinguished a name should have lent itself to utterance of such calumnies against officers and men of Civil and Military Services of a friendly Government."

These regrettable, and I think now regretted, attacks evoked among my friends and other thinking people an indignation which seemed to ignore four general principles. Firstly, the measure of their virulence was the measure of their defeat. Secondly, it is natural to support people of one's own race and language: were all supporters of the Boer War quite sure it was justified? Thirdly, when a position is not particularly strong attack is often the best defence. It would have been fatal in 1935 for the Duce to have allowed his Press to publish the then demoralizing truth that the whole world knew and proclaimed that he was doing wrong; and he logically singled out for counter-attack one Power as responsible for misleading all the rest. Lastly, the calumnies launched against the troops, the police and the Governor were milk and water compared with the heroic abuse habitually exchanged between Royalists and Venizelists; the Athenian maintaining in this respect at least a more exalted standard than the European Press.

As if to balance these atrocity charges by foreign nationalists, some of our own people soon began to criticize the Police for not having warned the Government; the Commissioners and the Governor for undue lenity in dealing with the rioters.

Now there are 598 Greek Orthodox and Mixed Orthodox [40] villages in Cyprus, of which 389 took no part whatever in the disturbance; nor was any evidence ever discovered that the outbreak was premeditated or prearranged. As I have explained, the first demonstration at Limassol fell flat; nor was it the business of the Eastern Telegraph Company to communicate to the Police the contents of the telegram that set Cyprus ablaze. The truth is that the insurgents were no less surprised by their own sudden violence than were the Police. The Commissioner of Nicosia was blamed for not firing sooner, by persons apparently unaware that, apart from his proper reluctance to shoot down school-boys, he could not have played better into the politicians' hands than by creating a score of youthful martyrs to the cause. Between the two extremes of General Dyer and of the Palestine Police on one or two occasions, one clear fact stands out: there is no "right time" to fire. I am aware that I also had been blamed for not intervening and taking the command out of the responsible Commissioner's hands. I will answer, with Montaigne, that "I had rather repent me of my fortune than be ashamed of my victory!" and will content myself without illusion to other documents, with quoting from the telegram which I received from the Secretary of State and which was published in the London Press. "I take this opportunity to convey to you, and to all who are working with you my appreciation of

[40] Out of the 670, the remainder being chiefly Turkish.

the way in which a very difficult situation has been handled." Five years later in Palestine the comparative strength of the forces employed, permanent as well as temporary, the damage and loss of life and the number of months elapsing before the spontaneous cessation of the troubles, were to remind critics of the difficulties inherent in such situations.

It is not easy to write of my last months in the Island. After five years' endeavour to put Cyprus on the map, no man in the world could have felt less satisfaction than I in having to put her on the mat. During the suppression of rioting there is little time to think about personal losses. When the stress is over, it gradually becomes apparent that the background of life has gone; the atmosphere, the past. The merits of the things I had were, so soon as they had disappeared, elevated by rumour to the dignity of a "collection"; and it was to the "collector" that much of the sympathy I received was addressed. As I have said, I was no collector. I bought for the pride of the eye, and some of the things I had were interesting as well as beautiful. Such "collections" as I had were made during many years by an experiencing curiosity and a fair knowledge of Arabic, assisted by the cigars I never smoked, the drinks I never drank, and the cabs I never took. They were a mixed lot. One or two marble Greek torsos, a fine Roman head—with the remembrance of getting into a warm bath with each and attacking it with soap and nailbrush until the original Pentelic or Parian shone honey-cream under the suds. The Byzantine Ikons, dull gold and, however small, majestic: a few Rhodian plates: a Sienese primitive: some Bukhara embroideries and a few rugs, none too good to be kept on the floor.[41] Great brass jugs and broad copper trays with Hebrew and Armenian inscriptions, after the fashion of Jerusalem: two tall wooden hawks of ancient Egypt, and Bomberg's masterly views of Jerusalem. Some 1500 books (two long shelves on the Near East), my heavily-annotated Oxford Homer won as a *bene-* book at Charterhouse, and the first edition of *Candide* bought from David in the market-place at Cambridge. The Steinway, and about a cubic yard of Bach. Sixty or seventy letters (I never counted them) from T. E. Lawrence: many from Anna de Noailles: some from Cromer, Kitchener, Allenby, Milner, Curzon, Amery—reminders that my work had sometimes pleased them—and some from Raymond Asquith, Maurice Baring and George Moore. My mother's letters filed in order from 1904 to 1923, and my wife's grand Maggini violin.

I thanked our friends at the time for their telegrams and letters of sympathy from all over the world, and I thank them again now. A cable "Congratulations on handling" from a man like George Lloyd meant

---

[41] I was curiously reminded of some of them by the *décor* of Morand's *Lewis and Irène*.

something: so did a paragraph in the same sense in Lord Inchcape's annual address to the P. and O. As often in the crises of joy or sorrow, marriage or death, the surprise of unexpected remembrances effectively cancelled out that of an occasional strange silence: but such trifling omissions were more than outweighed by one or two acts of startling kindness. Lord Duveen telegraphed characteristically that a panel of Enghien tapestry was on its way. There came a cable which read: "Sending library *Uno Avulso Maurice.*" [42] Remembering Maurice Baring's sham telegrams from Francis Joseph at the beginning of the War, and from Bola Pasha and Lenin at the end, I answered nothing until a small but heavy chest arrived, containing his own travelling library of little classics in seven languages. *Aureus* indeed the sender! To a little party trying to make the best of that Christmas, the weekly Colonial Office Bag brought a carefully packed square parcel. Inside was an exquisite specimen of antique Chinese jade, and on a scarlet-crowned card greeting from a Lady of Sovereign Grace, "To commence your new collection with, Mary R."

After the suppression of the riots there remained four aspects of the situation which cried for immediate remedy. Grave destruction of property had occurred throughout the Island, and it was obviously unfair that this should be made good out of general revenue, which had been in part collected from Britons and Turks. Events had proved that the Mukhtars, or village headmen, had allowed politics to interfere with their duties of law and order, registration and tax collection; that the use of the Greek flag had led to breaches of the peace; and that the unwarrantable sounding of church bells as tocsins had repeatedly summoned the mob to violence and outrage. Laws were therefore passed providing that the Mukhtars should be appointed by the Government instead of by Election; that no flag should be flown without Government license; and that no church bells should be rung without the permission of the District Commissioner. And the Reparation Impost Law implemented the decision that destroyed property estimated at £34,345 should be replaced and repaired at the cost of the responsible villages and towns. Apart from the deportees and certain agitators relegated to villages, all offenders were dealt with by the constituted assize and magisterial courts for specific offences connected with the disturbance. These measures were inevitably stigmatized as "punitive" by some who have nevertheless failed to show what milder action in face of the acknowledged facts Government could

---

[42] From Virgil *Aen.* VI of the Golden Bough:

> "*Uno avulso non deficit alter*
> *Aureus.*"

> "Though one be torn away there fails not another, golden."

possibly have taken. It is true that the bell ringing Law did prevent the churches from being used to summon crowds to seditious meetings. But permission was not withheld for ringing before and during the usual services, for time signals or for calling the children to school. For some months, however, in five of the six towns and in twenty per cent. of the villages bells remained unrung. This abstention was (as those who ordered it intended) ascribed by sympathizers to the Cyprus "historical background" against which "the silencing of the Christian church bells had been one of the symbols of subjection [43] of the Christian *Rayah* to their Moslem masters..." [44]

The truth, in the historical (and actual) foreground, was that the Archbishop sent emissaries to all Church Communities and village priests forbidding them to ring their bells; in order to create the impression, not so much in Cyprus where the facts were too well known, but in Orthodox countries and perhaps in London, that the Church was in a state of θλίψις, or persecution. The Exarch of Limassol, a sensible man, had filed his request forthwith. A few days later he reported that the Archbishop had instructed him to stop the ringing of all church bells as a protest against the Law. He added he had written to the Archbishop pleading that it would be most undesirable to carry out this order, and that the Law was not regarded unfavourably in Limassol, where the people realized it was much needed.

What after all were the consequences of this clever unwisdom of the Greeks? A smart young diplomat debarred from service over one-fifth of the globe. Two Bishops, exiles for a term to which prudence can hardly put a period. In Cyprus both in and out of the pulpit they had habitually alluded to Government officers as "these vile English": now they were reduced to proclaiming for the benefit of the British Liberal and Church Press their devotion to a Byron-Gladstone abstraction of England. The Legislative Councillors, and all their followers, debarred by a few hours' madness from honourable (though admittedly partial) association in the government of their country. [45] The citizens and villagers saddled with a heavy [46] indemnity bill for their folly—some for the folly of others—in destroying the possessions of their own land. The sorrowful sighing of the prisoner, justly condemned on account of out-

[43] *Survey of International Affairs*, 1931, p. 387.

[44] Islam had for some reason a peculiar horror of church bells: "Every bell is a demon, and its clapper an iron tongue."

[45] Is not the Greek as of old πολιτικὸν ζῷον—a political animal? And is not his conception of Paradise said to be a place where there are elections every day of the year?

[46] With retarded and cumulated interest: The plans for the new Government House, which I approved at a total charge of £25,000, were subsequently rejected, and those substituted have already cost more than £50,000.

rage for which others who had spurred him on should even more justly have suffered. And after all the very question of *Enosis,* of which so many Greeks professed and called themselves the champions, now relegated, with grim logic, to their own Kalends.

The rain, on which the life of Cyprus depends, was inordinately delayed in 1931, and soon a strange story began to be told throughout the Island. A peasant was walking across the Mesaoria to pray for the restoration of his failing eyesight at the Shrine of Apostolos Andreas. Before long he was aware of an old man of venerable aspect to whom he spoke sadly of the drought. "They burned My Ikon in Government House", answered Saint Andrew and, even as the peasant recovered his sight, vanished.

Kullu haraka fí-ha baraka, says the Egyptian proverb; "all agitation has some compensation". The *baraka* for the future Government of Cyprus was clear enough. Had it been possible—and I fully appreciate the difficulties—to grant any one of my three main requests: the transfer of the troops to Nicosia, submitted in 1927: the modification of the Constitution, proposed in 1929 and 1930, or the removal of the Greek Consul, it is morally certain that there would have been no troubles. As it is, future Governors will benefit, solely because of the disturbances, by all— and more than all—the safeguards for which I through five years of peaceful development had vainly petitioned. The Greek Consul was expelled. The Legislative Council was abolished. The troops were brought to Nicosia. The doctrine of *Enosis* was proclaimed illegal. The Union Jack is no longer obscured by foreign flags, and church bells ring for their lawful purposes.

In some ways *plus ça change, plus c'est la même chose.* I read the other day a letter in *The Times* from Mr Athelstan Riley, in which he described a mixed tea-party at Government House. The British sat rigidly at one end of the room: the Greeks and Turks at the other. I was reminded of my own attempts to induce friendly relations, and of the well-meant warning of the gallant Officer Commanding the reinforced Detachment during the troubles: "If I might suggest, Sir, no more mixed tea-parties."

In the spring of 1932 I was offered, and accepted the Governorship of Northern Rhodesia: we left Cyprus in June. In spite of the tension many Greeks asked leave to bid me farewell: some openly, others after dark for fear of being compromised as traitors to the cause. The day before my departure the Archbishop, sadly I think, and now not far from death, came to bid me good-bye. He was good enough to say that I had taken great interest in the Colony, and had translated that interest into deeds. That night an ex-agitator came to shake the hand of "the

Governor who had suffered more and done—perhaps not less—for Cyprus than any of his predecessors". The genial Mayor of Nicosia (in some ways closely resembling his colleague in Jerusalem) telegraphed to Larnaca wishing us "good luck and trusting that your kind and sincere interest for Cyprus and Cypriots which we gratefully appreciate will continue". Indeed, it always will. Who after giving a good deal of himself to a place for five and a half years could, whatever had happened, cherish for the vast majority, with whom he had never ceased to be on excellent terms, feelings other than of friendliness and a desire to serve them still? I came eagerly Philokyprios and Philhellene:

> πολλὰ δ' ἀέλπτως κραίνουσι θεοί.
> καί τά δ οκηθέντ' οὐκ ἐτελέσθη,
> τῶν δ'ἀδοκητῶν, πόρον εὖρε θεός.
> τοῖον δ' ἀπέβη τόδε πρᾶγμα.[47]

And, as I told the Archbishop, I left, and shall always remain, Philhellene and Philokyprios, loving the merry patient people no less than their infinitely romantic Island.

Though I would not have chosen the later process of events, which indeed resulted in some inconvenience to myself, yet as a British Governor and in the interests of Cyprus as a British Colony I would not have had the results otherwise. I believe that for the reasons I have attempted to set forth the crisis in some form or other had to come some time: it seemed odd, and

> curséd spite
> That ever I was born to set it right.

I think I devoted to Cyprus not less of sympathy and zeal than my predecessors, and I know that to my successors I bequeathed a clearer and more regular situation than I inherited. To persons interested in the intricacies of Crown Colony Government, these samples of the development and special difficulties of Cyprus between 1926 and 1931 may prove not unacceptable; for though the scale of enterprise—as of the disturbances—was relatively small, the issues were as great and as universal as any which can arise in far larger territories.

---

[47] "What the gods ordain, no man foresaw, what we looked for is not fulfilled: the gods bring unlooked-for things to pass. Thus befell this strange event." (Last lines of the last chorus of *Medea*, translated by Maurice Baring.)

TROILUS. *What is aught but as 't is valued?*
HECTOR. *But value dwells not in particular will;*
It holds his estimate and dignity
As well wherein 't is precious in itself
As in the prizer.
SHAKESPEARE, *Troilus and Cressida.*

FOR one who has passed thirty years—much more than half of his life—out of England, the changes of thought and habit that have occurred there during that period stand out perhaps more sharply detached than for others, who have been in close and daily contact with ceaseless but infinitesimal modification. Monsieur Paul Cambon, the French Ambassador, contemplating these islands as a foreigner, declared—as his most remarkable impression—that he had lived to witness the complete transfer of political power from one class to another without the shedding of one single drop of blood. To myself, returning home with the curious attention of a tourist, the emergent feature of our modern life is the universal process of levelling—an upward mass-levelling of wonderful rapidity; largely by adapting and recently surpassing the material civilization imposed during the post-War supremacy of the United States. No country that I have visited or studied presents any exception to the general truth that the standard of British living is the highest and its cost relatively the lowest in the world. As a result of this distribution I believe there is in 1937 less disparity in the essentials of life between a working-man and a Prince of the Blood than there was in 1900 between the village schoolmaster and the local squire. For this increasing standardization induced by mass production, and War, and social taxation, an immediate but probably decreasing toll is at present being levied: the toll of spiritual uneventfulness. The general mind is for the moment outstripped by its own physical inventions. Duplication whether of sight or sound exceeds creation. Resulting mass suggestion promises relative safety and ensures positive sameness.

Young applicants to the various Appointment Boards enquire first, of

a post offered them, whether it is pensionable and when it will allow
them to marry: a prudent and domestic attitude fitter for the upkeep of a
lesser republic than for the preservation of the greatest Empire. Beauty-
culture has established universal prettiness and all but abolished individual beauty. The force of advertisement is so strong that the sight of a
clergyman filling his pipe suggests to the beholder even more vividly a
conventual smoking-mixture or a genially democratic Premier; whilst
the passing of a plain van conjures up immediate visions of bevelled
mirrors and dining-room suites in fumed oak.

And as the wind of the War and of war-taxation has eroded the peaks
and is filling up the valleys of different fortunes, so from our happy
tableland of extended advantage do there seem to rise fewer eminences
and landmarks of personality. What public figure (among so many admirable) will command attention with the bearing or the glance of a
Kitchener? Or like Rosebery dazzle by variety—a Prime Minister with
the four folios of Shakespeare and the incunabula of Homer on the
bookshelves of the Durdans and, buried beneath in the garden, his three
Derby Winners? Mercifully there persists unchanged the unassertive
good temper and balance, the traditional abhorrence of extremes—whether
of logic or of temperament—still exhibited to the alternate admiration
and exasperation of the world by the people of England. No other soil
offers so poor a nutriment either to Communism, the child of despair
begotten by War misery upon Czarist corruption, or to its pathological
but inevitable offspring, the totalitarian fascist state. Where does there
survive a nicer hereditary punctilio, from the Earl Marshal's Court of
Coronation Claims, to the instinctively ordered exit of the ladies, from
the smallest dinner party? Where has there arisen less class bitterness?
What hope has the Soviet ideologist in a capital where the Sovereign is
confronted, every time he drives out of his Palace, by a colossal Hammer
and Sickle, poised on a Victorian survival erected years before these
symbols were even imagined in Moscow? The rumoured influx, with
subversive intention, of foreign gold into England is indeed a matter
for moral regret; which may perhaps be tempered by the reflexion that
such bribery achieves almost no political result, that its recipients would
otherwise be a charge on the rates, and that it constitutes the only
reimbursement our Exchequer is ever likely to encash on its loans or
other advances to the three Great Powers involved. Though never a
forcing-house of intelligentsia, and of late unduly neglectful both of
armament and of propaganda, England remains nevertheless in political
sanity the Warden of the Brain, contemplating with steady gaze the
features of a Europe twitching and grimacing under a crown of nerves.

Looking backward with a mind unclouded by official ambitions I must confess myself to have been, until the age of fifty, fortunate beyond my deserts both in the great men I served and in the tasks they set me. Most of them are dead: the rest no longer in power. I can see now that the lack of continuity in any one organized Government Office created in me an overpersonal and un-departmental outlook, whereby the quality as well as the quantity of my work has varied, far more than would have that of a trained civil servant, according as I admired, trusted, and was understood by my chief. Fortunate indeed to have been thrown into close contact with such; and no grudge against others (or destiny) if I sometimes enjoyed less consideration from lesser men. Duty under Cromer, Gorst, Kitchener, Allenby—and one or two statesmen yet living; communion with Henry Cust and with T. E. Lawrence, provide a crystal screen of deep radiance through which I can contemplate with undazzled eyes mere success, if achieved at the expense of spiritual or intellectual diminution. As Cleopatro allows of the humble messenger, "The man hath seen some majesty, and should know": and should discern objectively those many who by long and fruitful attrition with regulations or superiors, the right people, or the party machine, have so rubbed away all angles that they have no original outline left: they started as persons; they may have become personages—at a cost of ceasing to be personalities.

Lucky until fifty? In some ways lucky still. Though I lost my first health, it has in part come back: if my hair has thinned away, then the decks are cleared for further action. As for the things that went in Cyprus, perhaps they were taken because I cared for them too much: more probably to show that even objects commonly called inanimate, over which one has mused often and long, may become almost like those beloved beings, that no seeming death can ever take. I can still shut my eyes and feel each book standing in its place, or mark how the light falls upon the marble Greek athlete, the noble head of Germanicus and the little Aphrodite; and start once more as I catch the wistful eyes of the Ptolemaic boy gazing from the panel of his sepulture. So that I surely keep most that mattered somehow still within me:

> outliving outward with a mind
> That doth renew swifter than blood decays.

The passing of the visible precious and the closing in of the years are a reminder of the various items of existence from which the rest of my life is freely and eagerly disencumbered; of which random samples would include all books about books, save about the four greatest; first editions, water colours, miniatures, Victorian Art revivals, *netuskés*

—with all very small objects (and very large objects)—Verdi, César Franck and Sibelius; cards, golf, shooting and racing; tobacco, spirits, cocktails and liqueurs; restaurants with bands; long and fast motor-car journeys; fervent converts to any religion or cause.

Still unfulfilled is the dream of some little, old house with its garden and tennis court in the quiet English country, which now recedes before me like the mirages among which I used to picture it for so many years. So much the more must I cling to that highest which need not and must not be resigned while strength is left to perceive it—to that particular manifestation of immortal power by which each individual spirit is most deeply moved. I believe, and proclaim my faith, that this solace will proceed increasingly from the great classics of the world; both from their own splendour and from their contrast with the limitations of modern life. True, we may rise from Mr Wells's enchanting *Autobiography* convinced for the moment that the paramount of life is physical science. Yet throughout the War, and after, I never saw one tired man refreshing his soul with a scientific treatise or a mathematical problem; whereas there were many besides Lawrence transported far from their fatigues and anxieties by following those of Patroclus or Odysseus. But these enhancements of delight are strong not only in the stress of a campaign. There are troubles deeper than those of the War; reversals of fortune perhaps no better deserved than previous unexpected felicities; tragic personal surprises from which, as we have recently seen, nations and Empires are no more immune than individuals; "situations and events so monstrously unjust that the mind can hardly register a protest— no man can complain when he is struck by lightning". These are indefinable periods of time when a blind-working universe lies cold beneath the grin of a skull hung in an astral vacuum: *hypochondrie, maladie qui consiste à voir les choses telles quelles sont*. Some happy there are, for whose vision in such dread hours Faith shines through the darkness with the steady radiance of an altar lamp. For others, it flares and flickers fitfully as a torch in the wind and the rain. Yet even for these less happy, consolations are near; and, to such as worship them from the heart, in spirit and in truth, easier of access and more prodigal of their effulgence with the gradually unveiling years. For me they have been and will always be (with ascending climax) Homer, Dante, Shakespeare and the English Bible; together with one tremendous organ-voice that could also converse in some eight and forty well-tempered Preludes and Fugues; and, their counterparts in another dimension, resuming the past, anticipating the future—the great primitives of Flanders. Before such Epiphanies of the God in Man I can but repeat the prayer of a

Moslem, uttered in Basra more than a thousand years ago: "O my Lord! If I worship Thee from fear of Hell, burn me in Hell; and if I worship Thee from hope of Paradise, exclude me thence; but if I worship Thee for Thine own sake, then withhold not from me Thine Eternal Beauty." Even so, Lord. I breathe it in the remembrance of much joy, some sorrow, no resentments; and with deep gratitude for the abiding happiness of my home.

CPSIA information can be obtained
at www.ICGtesting.com
Printed in the USA
BVHW090848030322
630461BV00008B/229